# THE MANAGERIAL MIND
## Science and Theory in
## Policy Decisions

# THE MANAGERIAL MIND
## Science and Theory in
## Policy Decisions

**CHARLES E. SUMMER**
*Graduate School of Business Administration*
*University of Washington*

**JEREMIAH J. O'CONNELL**
*Centre d'Études Industrielles (C.E.I.)*
*Geneva, Switzerland*

**NEWMAN S. PEERY, JR.**
*College of Business Administration*
*Utah State University*

With the collaboration of

## Carol Carlisle Summer

## David A. Heenan
*Dean, College of Business Administration*
*University of Hawaii*

## Boris Yavitz
*Dean, Graduate School of Business*
*Columbia University*

1977

Fourth Edition
RICHARD D. IRWIN, INC. Homewood, Illinois 60430
Irwin-Dorsey Limited Georgetown, Ontario L7G 4B3

658.082
S 955-1

Fourth Edition

*First Printing, January 1977*

ISBN 0-256-01922-3
Library of Congress Catalog Card No. 76–24275
*Printed in the United States of America*

To our parents
*Edgar and Emily Summer*
*Jerry and Mary O'Connell*
*Newman and Grace Peery*

# PREFACE

This book encourages the professional management student to analyze case situations with equal depth in both the technical/economic sphere *and* the *human process* sphere. Whether one is studying strategic planning in Part II, leadership in Part V, or management science in Part IV, the cases and readings present data on both of these important dimensions of organizational life.

Balance between these dimensions is the hallmark of training for policy makers or general managers. The division of labor in a business school requires that some courses concentrate on the technical and economic dimension. Courses in finance, accounting, operations research, market research, or production scheduling should stick to their knitting. If they deviate, it must be in a way secondary to their main goals. Likewise, courses in organizational behavior, organization theory, social psychology, or leadership could never teach techniques of accounting along with their primary goals.

Somewhere in the curriculum, the student should engage in a kind of decision-making practice that develops ability to reconcile diverse insights from different disciplines. Though the curriculum comes bundled into compartments such as "finance" and "organizational psychology," the real world does not come in bundles. Rather, the cases in this book show that it comes to the manager in buzzing confusion. The confusion contains "apples and oranges," or economics and psychology simultaneously. Moreover, advocates from different disciplines of learning may imply to the manager *differing,* or even *conflicting* ideas. The economist may say to the president of Western Office Equipment Company, "Your problem is in the wrong allocation of salesmen to territories." The psychologist may say to this same president, "Your problem is in communication of decisions to the salesmen." Both may be citing "partial truths," but it is the manager who must judge the relative importance of these two factors in action decisions.

This, then, is the primary goal of this book: to provide practice in analyzing real life situations from the two viewpoints mentioned, and practice in forming solutions to problems which take into account both technical factors and human factors.

The authors express a very special appreciation to Carol C. Summer for a kind of work not often found in the preparation of textbooks. This book, like others, requires a large amount of work in the preparation of the manuscript. Carol did the typing, cutting, and pasting for all three of us. She obtained clearances from publishers of the many readings. Unlike most books, this one requires a very intricate cross-referencing scheme to relate many cases to one reading, or one reading to a network of cases. In successive revisions, change in one case question, or in one reading, may result in changes in five or six other parts of the book! It is Carol's meticulous file system, and her patient attention to time consuming detail, which contributed to the success of the manuscript. Without her this book literally could not have been produced.

We also wish to thank Scott Hickey for data collection in the University of Washington Law School case and Peter T. Smith for a comprehensive research case on the High Ross Dam. Jerome Schnee of Rutgers University and Benjamin Tregoe of Kepner Tregoe, Inc., generously provided case materials for this edition. For help in gathering case files we are indebted to Thomas Gladwin (New York University and the Centre d'Études Industrielles, [C.E.I.]), Sven Kihl, and Jean Daniel Poncet. Dougal Mitchell's encyclopedic mind and fertile imagination was of great help in framing some of the questions and readings. Suzanne Gall and Maidy Alwen provided valuable secretarial assistance. We owe thanks to the Centre d'Études Industrielles for its support of our efforts.

*December 1976*                           CHARLES E. SUMMER
                                          JEREMIAH J. O'CONNELL
                                          NEWMAN S. PEERY, JR.

# CONTENTS

**PART III.** Financial Control, Organization Structure, and Human Behavior

**Introduction** . . . . . . . . . . . . . . . . . . . . . . **201**

Allocation of Resources: An Important Social Obligation of Managers. Financial Management as a Technique for Allocating Resources. Financial Information and Human Perception. Use of Management Information Systems.

**PART IV.** Decision Making, Management Science, and Human Behavior

**Introduction** . . . . . . . . . . . . . . . . . . . . . . **331**

Origins of Management Science. Power and Limitations of Science in Management. The Philosophical Importance of Management Science. Examples of Quantitative Techniques and Managerial Problems. Managerial (Policy) Decision Making. Management Information Systems.

**PART V.** Leadership and Organization Development

**Introduction** . . . . . . . . . . . . . . . . . . . . . . **425**

Leadership as an Important Function of Management. Expedient Obligations and Social Responsibilities of Leaders. Concepts and Theories of Human Behavior. Practices and Technologies of Leadership. Training (or) Learning as a Leadership Style.

**PART VI.** Reconciling the Responsibility to Produce with Other Social Responsibilities

**Introduction** . . . . . . . . . . . . . . . . . . . . . . **551**

The Social Responsibility Dilemma: Productivity versus Other Values. Organizational Goals as Social Responsibilities. The Need for Reconciling: The Need for

Judgment and Wisdom. Who Should Make Decisions That Are "Socially Responsible"?

# PART 1 Philosophy of Science and Philosophy of General Management

# Chapter 1. THEORY AND PRACTICE IN GENERAL MANAGEMENT

## THE RELATION BETWEEN THEORY AND POLICY DECISIONS

It is one of the central theses of this book that *theories* are powerful aids to decision making by general managers in policy systems of today —in large complex institutions of the second half of the 20th century. They are powerful in that they help in diagnosis and identification of managerial (action and policy) problems, in the clarification of goals which managers are attempting to reach, and in the prevention of harmful unintended consequences which managers might overlook without the use of theory. They are powerful, also, because they call attention to a wide variety of forces at work in the managerial system—technological forces, economic forces, sociological forces, political forces, and psychological forces. They prevent executives from unknowingly making decisions which satisfy one goal while seriously compromising another, and from concentrating on good technological and economic subsystems (within the larger policy system) while doing damage to the human subsystems.[1] Conversely, they prevent the executives from concentrating on satisfying and harmonious human subsystems while doing damage to efficient technological and economic subsystems.[2] Finally, theories are valuable to the general manager in assembling, organizing, and allocating physical resources in the policy system, and in organizing and influencing the behavior of human beings in that system.

The second central thesis of this book is that theories have serious,

---

[1] The term "human system," as we use it, refers to any frame of reference which describes or predicts how human beings will act or behave. Thus political science and legal philosophy undertake this kind of explanation as well as sociology, psychology, and small group theory. The term "technological and economic system," as we use it, refers to the sum total of all structures and dynamic events that are of a nonhuman nature. Plants, machines, flow of goods in process, inventories of goods, money inventories, cash flows, accounting systems, formal organization structures, job descriptions, and the like, fall within the meaning of this concept.

[2] This is not meant to imply that technological systems are, or are not, ends in themselves. They satisfy human needs through production of goods and services, through provision of employment, and in some cases through provision of a psychologically secure place to "belong" in a large-scale society.

3

sometimes even dangerous, limitations for managers who must make decisions in large complex policy systems of today. Stated in a reciprocal way, *judgment* or *intuition* (often referred to as "art," as opposed to "science" of management) has a powerful place in decision making by general managers.

Any one theory, or any group of theories in a discipline, does not represent reality in the *total* policy system, and may lead the manager to suboptimize, or overemphasize, one part of the system to the exclusion of another. For example, political forces may be overlooked while economic forces are stressed or political forces may be stressed and psychological forces minimized.

It may seem a paradox that theories seemingly have contradictory effects on the decision-making mind at the same time: they prevent unintended consequences on the one hand, but they encourage such consequences on the other. The answer to this, to be more fully explained later, hinges on how theories are used—in the degree of comprehensiveness in their use, in the open-minded entertainment of diverse views, and in the judgmental courage to pick, choose, test, and modify theory in action situations. Another limitation in the use of theories is that they often do not suggest alternatives in terms of things that are operational for the executive—in terms of things he or she can take hold of and change in the world of action. Though theories may be operational for the scientist in terms of his or her controlled and measured experiments, practicing managers react to this limitation by calling them "longhair" ideas, "up in the clouds."

A third and final thesis held by the authors is that there is such a concept as "the managerial mind," or "the policy orientation," which bridges the gap between the power of science and theory on the one hand and the limitations of theory in practice on the other. This particular orientation is characterized by—

**Managerial or Policy Attitudes and Methodology.** These consist of a cluster of attitudes about the nature of policy systems and policy makers, and a philosophy of general management as an endeavor in life, as contrasted with scholarship (science or philosophy) or applied science.

**Substantive Theory of Policy Decision and Management.** This theory is of two kinds: first, recognition of the major policy issues faced by leaders in policy systems which are enduring through changing times and which are faced by leaders in all types of institutions (government, business, medical, voluntary associations), and at varying levels of hierarchy (divisions, departments, whole industries); and second, selected key disciplines and key concepts within these disciplines which are of high relevance to the major policy issues.

A tentative formulation of the first of these ideas (managerial attitudes and methodology) is presented in Chapters 1 through 3 of this book. Evidence for this concept as well as practice in its application is provided in the cases, the theoretical readings, and the case introductions. Regarding the attitudinal-methodological aspects of the managerial mind, the authors make no claim that the statements on these pages are the last word, or even that the attitudes and methodologies are in final, systematic form. Our only claim is that this is the first time these two attributes have been presented from the viewpoint of the general manager or the policy-making executive, *his or her problems,* and the *goals of a policy system* instead of from the viewpoint of a scholar, his problems, and the goals of scholarly schemes of thought.

## THE MANAGERIAL MIND, THE SCHOLARLY MIND, AND THE APPLIED SCHOLARLY MIND

While the following ideas will be made more explicit throughout the introductory chapters, some notion of what we mean when we say "the managerial mind" or "the policy orientation" is necessary at the very outset.

These terms should not be confused with "the scientific mind" or "the philosophical mind." In briefest terms, the scientist and philosopher are engaged in thought rather than action; in understanding the environment rather than controlling it;[3] in selecting out facts for study which meet *their* problems rather than those which meet someone else's (e.g., the general manager's). They are not as much concerned with the *time* or *costs* involved in their decision-making process. Scientists and philosophers thus share common attributes on the basis of which both can be termed, on a higher level of abstraction, *scholars.*

Neither should the terms "managerial mind" and "policy orientation," as used in this book, be confused with the ideas of "the policy orientation" as used by some authors. A "general manager" or "policy maker" is not the same as a "technologist" or "practitioner." Technologists are people who are interested first and foremost in applying concepts from some particular nonhuman-oriented disciplines (physics, engineering, certain branches of economics such as material-goods-machine structures and dynamics) to the action problems of the world.

"Practitioners," on the other hand, are interested first and foremost in applying a discipline, or group of disciplines, from "human sciences" and "human philosophy" to the action problems of the world.[4]

Applied scholars (technologists and practitioners) share one common attribute with scholars (scientists and philosophers). Their life endeavor gives them a high interest value in one body of knowledge, in some branch of theory, in a limited network of conceptual schemes. Thus they pick and choose problems, pick and choose facts to study, and bring a bias to their final conclusions based upon the knowledge in their area of study.

But technologists and practitioners have another characteristic while distinguishes them from scientists and philosophers and which they

---

[3] With the exception of some scholars in moral and ethical philosophy.

[4] For an idea of the orientation of applied social scientists, see Daniel Lerner and Harold D. Lasswell, *The Policy Sciences* (Stanford, Calif.: Stanford University Press, 1951); Warren G. Bennis, Kenneth D. Benne, and Robert Chin, *The Planning of Change* (New York: Holt, Rinehart & Winston, Inc., 1961); and Ronald Lippitt, Jean Watson, and Bruce Westley, *Planned Change* (New York: Harcourt, Brace & Co., 1958). For an excellent example of the clinical method of a practitioner, see Paul R. Lawrence, *The Changing of Organizational Behavior Patterns* (Boston: Harvard University, Graduate School of Business Administration, 1958).

hold in common with general managers or policy makers—they have an interest in the problems of the world. They have an interest in choosing problems for study and selecting facts for observation which leads them to *prescriptions* for action rather than, as in the case of the scientist, description and understanding of nature.

Finally, technologists and practitioners have one other attribute which separates them from policy system and general managers. The latter begin with (1) the policy system in its totality as it exists in the buzzing confusion of the world—in an "open system," and (2) the goals of the organization. In the sense that policy makers choose problems to study which are relevant to the goals of policy systems, they close their system of thought. But in the sense that they pick and choose facts and theories, regardless from which discipline of scholarship they originate, they deal with an "open system." Technologists and practitioners start first with theories from some discipline or group of disciplines and move in the other direction. They pick problems in the total policy system which can be attacked by their disciplines and look for and deal with facts which can be fitted into theories in their area of study. In this sense, the applied scholars have a primary interest in *some* of the problems of the world. It is in this sense, too, that they deal with a system which is more "open" than the scientist's system but is more "closed" or "biased" than that of the policy maker or general executive.

## UNINTENDED CONSEQUENCES IN MANAGERIAL DECISIONS

In making decisions, managers must listen to the advice of many specialists inside and outside the company. Unless the manager[5] has certain attitudes about, and skill in, the difficult task of *applying* these theories it is likely that he or she will face unintended consequences after the decision is made.

The theory of unanticipated consequences arose in the behavioral sciences. It implies that the executives who look only (or more closely) at technological, political, and economic goals of their organization are likely to find that there are some human forces at work which they overlooked and which have consequences such that their original goals are, in effect, not reached. Their goals may be sabotaged, for example, by a hostile group or a labor union. Decisions made and passed on may cause human beings to do something that the executives want, but also to do something that they don't want. In many of the cases in this book this will be seen to be true.

There is, however, another side to the theory of unintended conse-

---

[5] This book is addressed to general managers who perform decision functions. Some may be heavily involved in gathering facts and reasoning; some may be involved only in putting the stamp of approval on decisions made by teamwork of a number of specialists. In either of these two cases, our conclusion is the same. This book is also addressed to a third kind of manager—the specialist who forms part of the influential leadership group. In short, at any given organizational level, there is a group of decision makers (the relatively few) whose mental efforts influence the relatively many. Political science has referred to such a system as an oligarchy. Sociology refers to the smaller group as the influentials or simply as the leaders. Management theory refers to them as executives or managers.

quences which has received little attention. If a manager studies theories from the behavioral sciences and then tries to relate them to case situations he or she will find that many of the things which behavioral scientists imply strongly to executives, *in themselves* would result in unanticipated harmful consequences in terms of economic and technological goals. Any one conceptual scheme from social psychology (including, for example, democratic leadership as implied executive behavior), might have serious unanticipated technological or economic consequences for the survival and growth of the organization, depending on the individual departmental, company, or national situation. That is, various aspects of technological and economic efficiency may be adversely affected to a serious degree if one attempts to operate *solely* on such theories in large complex organizations. In this sense, the behavioral scientist is as apt to be a victim of unanticipated consequences as is the executive, the engineer, or the economist.

## THE LAW OF SUBDISCIPLINIZATION

When writing articles or books for the business leader market, it is highly probable that technologists and social scientists will imply certain courses of action which should be taken in view of the types of more basic phenomena they study. The psychologist will imply that, though there are other important factors, human needs and motivations are most important, and therefore that such alternative decisions as participative leadership or job enlargement are the things that any intelligent business executive will seek. The political theorist will imply that, though there are other factors involved, law and order, based on what the "reasonable man" will see, obviously means that intelligent business executives will seek a workable authority delegation system. The operations researcher, while including other important factors as assumptions or constraints on their models, may give the impression that intelligent business executives will optimize the technological flows in their plant location or inventory system.

This kind of impression, conveyed by so-called "pure" scientists, and to a lesser but nevertheless important extent by technologists in the physical realm and practitioners in the social realm, is a phenomenon that can be called "subdisciplinization." These individuals need not necessarily become company employees, or do consulting work, or even leave the university, though each of these degrees of involvement determines how conscious and explicit they will be about the "other things" in a policy decision-making situation. In the social sciences, where values are more likely to enter scientific theory and where social science frequently merges into social philosophy, scholars frequently develop highly complex and "factual" theories, where subdisciplinization is likely to be hidden in assumptions. This will be more clearly understood and illustrated in Chapter 3."

We are not saying that this is right or wrong, good or bad. It simply exists. It is a natural thing for people who become highly interested in one view of part of the world to exaggerate the influence of this view in the total scheme of things. Read, for example, the introductions to books explaining such divergent theories as those dealing with human groups, industrial dynamics and cybernetics, capital budgeting, or management principles.

This is simply one of the outcomes of the phenomena of specialization. It is more particular than the generic term "trained incapacity" in that we are relating it to (1) the failure of scholars to be fully aware of, or clearly explicit about, the unintended consequences if executives follow their implications; and (2) those specialists in science, technology, or practice who imply to the leadership group in companies, either explicitly or implicitly, that one set of forces in the company is so important that the executive's time, attention, or analytical power should be devoted to these in greater detail than other relevant factors when making managerial decisions.

## REACTIONS OF EXECUTIVES AND THEORISTS

Managers often express feelings ranging from admiration for the application of science, to suspicion of the actual results, a feeling of threat that the "theory boys will take over." This is also expressed in the feelings of some company executives toward business school graduates when they enter employment; or, when we read in the newspapers that officials in the Defense Department have these same feelings about the greatly accelerated rate with which planners, systems men, and a wide variety of specialists, using techniques of powerful analysis, are being given decision-making responsibility.

On the other side of the fence, it is not uncommon to find people from various disciplines in science—technologists who engineer physical science or practitioners who apply social science—who are ambiguous in their feelings toward policy systems and executives who manage them. These range from the feeling that, somehow, executives can't understand the truth and importance attached to their theories, to a feeling of admiration for an executive who has the personality and physical stamina to make complex and definite decisions in the face of ambiguity. There is sometimes the feeling that "uninformed people will take over" (the reverse of the feeling that theory boys will take over).

In both cases, there is the implicit threat to the individual that the other person has something which will depreciate the life work and product of his endeavors. Consciously or unconsciously, the specialist in theory knows that there is no policy system, no real world problem or situation, in which a given theory will work. To that extent, a policy decision is threatening. Consciously or unconsciously, the executive knows that there are many things in the complex problem he[6] faces that he may not see or understand, and that the theories may point up something that he is not knowledgeable about. To this extent, a conceptual scheme is threatening.

---

[6] The common pronoun "he" is used for succinctness and is understood to refer to persons of either sex.

It has become a cliché to say that much of science has grown out of technology, and that it is in trying to solve the problems of the world that some of our most important discoveries (theories) are made, and further, that scholars can therefore reap benefit by studying policy problems and communicating with policy makers. It is also a cliché to say that many of our machines and social systems of today could never have been constructed if some scholar had not generated some theory which allowed such structures. The power of science in shaping nations and companies, is great.

In view of the need for interchange between theory and practice, and in view of the feelings on both sides which inhibit interchange, something should be done to adjust the latter. In Chapters 1–3, we put into words some of the causes of such feelings. In the remainder of the book, we provide practice in the difficult task of using theory in the light of both its advantages and disadvantages.

# Chapter 2. CONCEPTUAL SCHEMES AND SCIENCE

In this chapter we will examine the nature of concepts, of scientific conceptual schemes or theories, and something of the nature of how these are generated by the minds of scientists. By doing this, we set the stage for understanding their power as an aid to people of action—policy makers and general executives—and for understanding their limitations in the control of policy systems.

## CONCEPTS AND ABSTRACTION

A concept is an invention of the mind, a product of the imagination, which enables human beings to make sense out of the world about them. Around us at all times, in our environment, are thousands of objects and dynamic events which give stimulus to the sense organs—eyes, ears, nose, touch—in profusion. After infancy, the human being would be helpless to cope with these unless he or she has some means of cataloging them into terms that have meaning in dealing with day-to-day problems.

Some of these are cataloged as "good" or "bad," as to whether they satisfy or penalize a person's basic desires. These are normative or value concepts, and we label them "attitudes" or "values." Others are relatively neutral in emotional value; they simply *are*. These are descriptive concepts.

As I sit in my office, I see an object with four legs, two arms, and an upright back and I catalogue this as a "chair." The semantic symbol "chair" does not need to be spoken, since I cannot think without conceptualizing and without the power of word symbols. Somewhere along the line in our cultural development, the symbol "chair" was *conceptualized* to denote the particular constellation of characteristics of legs, back, and arms. The process which the human mind uses to conceptualize the enormous complexity of the world into ideas is known as the process of abstraction.

But the chair in my office is really a particular object—it is not exactly like any other chair in the world. It may have a solid back or a cane back. It may have a round seat or square seat. It may have round legs or square legs, or it may even have a big scratch on the back whereas the chair

10

across the hall is new and unblemished. These are particular character-istics, rather than general characteristics, similar to what scientists refer to as divergent phenomena. The point to be made here is that, in the process of abstraction, we select certain abstract characteristics, di-vorced from the total reality of hard cold facts in the world. Only in this way can we make sense out of the buzzing confusion around us. Thus, legs plus arms plus back equals chair—three abstract characteristics are cataloged into a larger concept or idea. The pigeon-hole system in the mind eliminates irrelevant details if we simply want something to sit upon and do not want other attributes. Notice that the concepts we select for thinking depend on what our problem is.

This process of abstraction can proceed to higher and higher levels of abstract concepts. I have another concept in my mind labeled "table," another labeled "bookcase," another labeled "file cabinet." If my purpose is to construct a new "building" for the business school, I know that one of the things I will have to direct my attention to is "furniture," a concept which abstracts on another characteristic or dimension. This concept eliminates, for purposes of this specific decision, the difference between divergent furniture objects (bookcases don't have arms) because the myr-iad of details are not relevant to certain decisions, and because one would literally go crazy if every detail in the environment were to be enter-tained in the mind in every thought or decision.

When we face problems of achieving our goals and subgoals in life, of building buildings, going to work in public transportation, furnishing houses, managing business corporations, deciding on what to have for dinner, getting tired of standing upright, we pick and choose concepts which are useful in understanding the world (analysis), in predicting what will happen "out there" (prediction), and what we might do to get what we want (control). Concepts are therefore powerful mechanisms for thought and action.

Value (attitudinal) abstraction is even more powerful to us in these three respects. We learn that "fire" is "bad" for sticking hands in, but "good" for cooking. We do not have to make decisions over and over about what to do around, or with, fire because we have built-in policies (values and attitudes) in the mind which enable us to react (1) in quick time, and (2) without cluttering our minds with new decisions and facts every time we face similar situations.

Finally, concepts have one other very powerful use to society and to individuals. Semantic symbols or concepts not only aid the individual person to think, predict, and in some measure control things around him; they also enable one human being to pass on *experience, learned* from prior actions, to other human beings. You may have never been bitten by a "snake," but somewhere along the line someone either told you what a snake is (described it in terms of abstract characteristics such as "long" and "round"), pointed one out to you, or showed you a picture. They then gave you a predictive statement: snakes bite; their bites cause sickness or death.

In the conceptual or semantic sense, then, concepts enable cultures to develop. They enable people to control others' behavior; they enable one person to learn and get help from the distilled experience of someone else.

Value (attitudinal) concepts, in fact, are one of the primary ways in which societies control the behavior of divergent individuals and groups. In certain societies, for example, alcoholic beverages are "bad," and this is conveyed through families to children. This is a form of "conscience control." Social pressures, and social penalties, or even the formal codification of value concepts into prohibition laws, are added means of control. But even these could not exist without the existence of concepts and the power of abstraction.

## THEORY AND CONCEPTUAL SCHEMES

So far, we have used the term "concept" to denote any meaningful idea which exists in the mind and which *partially* (in the sense of selecting certain abstract characteristics) describes reality—what is "out there" in the world.

A theory is a form of conceptualization in that it (1) is more precise than the garden variety of ideas generated by common sense, (2) was arrived at by a process of thought which is more rigorous than common sense and day-to-day action, and (3) therefore is more likely to describe what is reality and what will happen "out there."

Let us look for a moment at the second of these. For our purposes, theories can be classified in two ways, depending on (*a*) whether they were developed for the purpose of understanding nature versus controlling nature, or (*b*) whether they were arrived at with the aid of observation or experiment[1] or with the aid of logic and reason alone. The first of these dimensions separates scientific and philosophical theories on the one hand from technological theories on the other. The second dimension separates scientific theories from philosophical theories.

## PHYSICAL SCIENCE AND PHYSICAL SCIENTISTS

Scientific theory is one form of conceptualization which is aimed primarily at understanding the operation of nature, not in controlling nature. This has very important implications for policy makers because many of the ideas generated by scientists either seemingly are beyond the control of the policy maker at the time of his decision, or because they actually are beyond his control (regardless of timing), or because they are irrelevant to his problems and goals.

Additionally, scientific theories are arrived at in a very special way: through observation (or experiment), by the imagination of a hypothesis which explains why things happen, and then by a testing of that hypothesis.

---

[1] The phrase "with the aid of" is very important. Later discussion will show that in many scientific theories, particularly in the social sciences, the theories are not generated *by* observation and experiment alone. The scientist's values, needs, and subjective preconditioning leads him or her to "speculate" or to "imagine" an hypothesis, the hypothesis being a concept which exists in the mind, not solely in the facts.

In the science of astronomy, many years of patient observation of "planets" (note that someone distinguished these from "stars") enabled astronomers to speculate that a planet's orbit was determined by several forces, one of which is the "gravitational force" of other planets (in addition to the gravitational force of the sun). Another factor is the size and mass of both the planet under study and the size and mass of the other heavenly bodies within the field of influence or force of the planet under study.

The following record of the observations and hypotheses that led to the discovery of Neptune serves as an example to show (1) how the scientist, with great concentration of time and effort, is able to come up with understandings of nature which laymen could not attain through common sense; (2) how *measurement* enables the scientist to prove the truth of his hypotheses; and (3) how great amounts of creative imagination, as well as brute facts and observations, are involved in the development of a theory.[2]

> *1820* The first attempt to chart and predict the motions of the three outer planets (Uranus, Saturn, Jupiter) was developed by the French mathematician Laplace in the *Mechanique Celeste.* This theory, based on the mutual perturbations of these planets, was used by Bovard of Paris to construct highly accurate tables of their past and predicted future positions. Jupiter and Saturn moved very satisfactorily according to prediction, but the observations of Uranus showed it to move well outside the tolerable limits of error of the predictions. The outstanding difference noted between the prediction and the observation was one minute of arc (one minute equals one sixtieth of a degree which equals about one one-hundred-eightieth of the sky).
>
> In the light of these circumstances, mathematicians and astronomers of the time approached the problem in two different ways. First they tried to make a generality of all observations of Uranus and thus render the tables of prediction clearly erroneous. Secondly, they tried discarding all older observations, using only the most recent ones. A few years of observation showed that both these methods were inadequate to describe the deviations of Uranus from any predicted path. Past history and fact was of no avail. The question was put forth that perhaps the mass of Saturn had been miscalculated: a rapid calculation showed that the mass necessary to create the noted deviations of Uranus would have to be so enormous as to be impossible.
>
> *1834* An English amateur astronomer offered the solution to the problem of an ultra-Uranian planet beyond the orbit of Uranus. He offered to search for it in a general sort of way if the Royal Academy would supply estimates of its position. Sir George Airy, the respondent to this letter, doubted that the deviations were caused by such

---

[2] From B. A. Gould, *Report to the Smithsonian Institution on the History of the Discovery of Neptune* (Washington, D.C.: Smithsonian Institution, 1850), *passim.*

a planet, believing firmly that the deviations were caused by mis-calculation of Uranus' orbit. His main support of this thesis was a calculation he presented showing the size of Uranus to be in error as well as its heliocentric longitude. Nothing was done.

*1843*   The Royal Society of Science in Göttingen (Germany) of-fered a prize of fifty ducats to whomever would offer the best solu-tion to the problem of Uranus' orbit.

The question having now exhausted all known proofs, combined with the incentives of the prize money, it remained for an astute mathematician to work upon the only remaining hypothesis: that of the ultra-Uranian planet. In England, J. C. Adams undertook such work, and within several years was able to prove that the deviations could be fairly well represented by the gravitational ef-fects of an unknown planet of which he then calculated the motion and orbital elements. The planet he described from his derivations is only one and a half degrees in error from the actual position of the heliocentric longitude as it is now known, and only one-half degree in error from the position along the ecliptic.

But Airy, in replying to all this information presented to him by Adams, merely inquired if the assumed perturbation would also explain the error of the radius vector of Uranus. Adams, incensed, made no reply.

Meanwhile, in France, the mathematician Leverrier had drawn the same conclusion as Adams. His investigations were more thor-ough, though, in that he proved by scientific demonstration and logical deduction that there was no known admissible solution to the problem except that of an ultra-Uranian planet.

*1846*   At this point, both groups began searching the skies for the new planet. Airy, being convinced that it might be possible, set an assistant to sweeping the sky in the neighborhood of the area pre-dicted by Adams. The plan required the comparison of two sweeps, of all stars noted down to the sixth magnitude, in order that the new planet might be detected by its motion. Nothing was found, after this had been carried out.

On August 31, 1846, Leverrier wrote to the Berlin Observatory that now-famous letter stating that if they would but train their telescopes on a certain point in the sky, comparing their results over several nights, they would discover the presence of a new planet. By chance the proper chart for comparison had just been com-pleted; the new planet was discovered two evenings later as an eight-magnitude body whose movements could be shown. The ex-istence of the new planet was thus established.

In the above example, note how the scientists involved could not possi-bly have imagined the hypothesis that Neptune was out there without the concepts of "size," "mass," "heliocentric longitude," and "gravita-tional effects." These concepts of the mind had already been arrived at through generations of other scientists devoting all of their time, all of their energies, and all of their intellectual and creative power to the understanding of celestial movements. This was an example of deductive thinking, or reasoning from certain concepts (force, mass), to prove facts that were not known. It is the opposite of inductive thinking, or the mental process that produced the original theory of force and mass as determinants of planets' orbits. This theory, and these concepts, were formulated from observation of the facts. It is in this sense that science, being the result of efforts of many people, with different mental powers[3] than laymen, have much to offer to the latter in the solution of everyday problems.

Notice also that to the policy maker in the mid-20th century, there is not much usefulness in knowing that Neptune is there. Neither the president of the United States nor the chairman of the Communist Central Committee of the U.S.S.R. is going to change its orbit. But the conceptual scheme of "mass," "size," "heliocentric longitude," and "gravitational effect"—the theory of cause and effect—is very much a policy matter. Laplace, charting Jupiter in 1820, probably did not think that President James Monroe would put a man on Jupiter, or the moon. In our century, until recently, a man on the moon was a matter for comic books and science fiction writers. Today, however, any intelligent citizen, or any president of a corporation which makes rockets, metals, or electronic equipment for the space industry, or who sells food supplies or builds houses for personnel at the missile base in Cape Kennedy, might well recognize that part Laplace had in shaping their lives, determining the products they sell, or, in the case of the space industry, determining the processes and operations which must take place in their companies.

## REPETITIVE VERSUS DIVERGENT PHENOMENA

In a powerful chapter on "The Origins of Modern Science,"[4] Alfred North Whitehead, the eminent mathematician-philosopher, points out that "there can be no living science unless there is a widespread instinctive conviction in the existence of an *order of things*"—that is, scientists believe instinctively that events will repeat themselves, and that the events can be observed (in the skies, in the laboratory) as forming a repetitive pattern. This pattern is described in terms of lower order facts, and then general laws or principles are stated at higher levels of abstraction. For example, repeated observations are made and recorded, and then conceptualized into concepts such as "force," "mass," and "orbit."

Orbit is a pattern, and the forces producing it continue to operate, year in and year out. There are no "divergent" phenomena, no outside disturbances or forces which interrupt the pattern.

Yet there is a paradox here. Whitehead goes on to point out that even

---

[3] The word "different" is used here rather than "superior." Viewed in one way, scientists are specialists who devote their lives to a certain pursuit. Whether this is "superior power" depends upon what one's criteria for "superior" is. For instance, if we measure superiority by the degree of complexity of problems on which a human mind works, policy decisions in policy systems can be distinctly more complex than scientific systems.

[4] Alfred North Whitehead, *Science and the Modern World,* Lowell Lectures, February 1925 (New York: The Macmillan Co., 1925), chap. i.

in the physical sciences, "nothing ever really occurs in exact detail. No two days are identical, no two winters. What has gone, has gone forever. Accordingly, the practical philosophy of mankind has been to expect broad recurrences, and to accept the details as emanating from the inscrutable womb of things beyond the ken of rationality."

In sciences such as astronomy, in which the systems are in reality (as well as the mind) relatively simple, with no disturbing forces, the assumption of repeated patterns seems to yield theories which are true, from year to year and century to century.

Today in the physical sciences, when we get away from astronomy, scientists are discovering that their laws are quite tentative, and that the study of change, differences in detail, and disruptions to the system or pattern are as important as recurring patterns. These divergent phenomena, as opposed to convergent phenomena (patterns), in the modern world of intellectual and cultural complexity are extremely important in the social sciences, and they are even more important in the world of policy making and managerial action. Why? Because, as we shall see later, there are many disturbances in an action system or policy system.

For the present, the following statement by the retiring president of the American Association for the Advancement of Science should help to understand the paradox to which Whitehead refers.[5] In one way, this paradox is caused by the fact that scientists, in their process of abstraction, leave out important details which, as Langmuir points out, "are important in altering the course of human history" and "profoundly affect human lives."

> Up to the beginning of the present century one of the main goals of science was to discover natural laws. This was usually accomplished by making experiments under carefully controlled conditions and observing the results. Most experiments when repeated under identical conditions gave the same results.
>
> The scientist, through his own experiments or from previous knowledge based on the work of others, usually developed some theory or explanation of the results of his experiments. In the beginning this might be a mere guess or hypothesis which he would proceed to test by new types of experiments. . . .
>
> . . . The usefulness of the theory lies just in its ability to predict the results of future experiments. The extraordinary accomplishments of the great mathematical physicists in applying Newton's Laws to the motions of the heavenly bodies gave scientists of more than a century ago the conviction that all natural phenomena were determined by accurate relations between cause and effect. If the positions, the velocities and the masses of the heavenly bodies were given it was possible to predict with nearly unlimited accuracy the position of the bodies at any future time. The idea of causation, or

---

[5] Irving Langmuir, "Science, Common Sense and Decency," *Science,* vol. 97, no. 2505 (January 1943), pp. 1–7, reprinted from *Science* by permission. The authors are indebted to Professor Joseph Bailey of the Harvard Business School for calling attention to the importance of Langmuir's ideas in the practice of administration.

a necessary relation of cause and effect, has long been embedded in the minds of men. The recognized responsibility of the criminal for his acts, the belief of the value of education and thousands of words in our language all show how implicitly we believe in cause and effect. The teachings of classical science, that is, the science up to 1900, all seem to reinforce this idea of causation for all phenomena.

*   *   *   *   *

The theories or explanations which were developed in connection with the natural laws usually involved a description in terms of some kind of a model. In general, instead of thinking of the whole complex world we select only a few elements which we think to be important and concentrate our minds on these. Thus, the chemist developed the atomic theory according to which matter was made up of atoms of as many different kinds as there are chemical elements. These were thought of as small spheres, but no thought was given as to the material of which they were made. When later theories indicated that these atoms were built up of electrons and positive nuclei this made very little difference to the chemist, for he had not needed previously to consider that aspect of the model.

*   *   *   *   *

The essential characteristic of a model is that it shall resemble in certain desired features the situation that we are considering. On this basis we should recognize that practically any theory has many arbitrary features and has limitations and restrictions imposed by the simplifications that we have made in the development of the theory or the construction of our model.

Beginning with Einstein's relativity theory and Planck's quantum theory a revolution in physical thought has swept through science. Perhaps the most important aspect of this is that the scientist has ceased to believe that words or concepts can have any absolute meaning. He is not often concerned with questions of existence; he does not know what is the meaning of the question, "Does an atom really exist?" The definition of "atom" is only partly given in the dictionary. Its real meaning lies in the sum total of knowledge on this subject among scientists who have specialized in this field. No one has been authorized to make an exact definition. Furthermore, we can not be sure just what we mean even by the word "exist." Such questions are largely metaphysical and in general do not interest the modern scientist. Bridgman has pointed out that all concepts in science have value only in so far as they can be described in terms of operations or specifications. Thus it doesn't mean much to talk about length or time unless we agree upon the methods by which we are to measure length and time.

For many years, up to about 1930, the new physics based on the quantum theory seemed to be fundamentally irreconcilable with the classical physics of the previous century. Through the more recent development of the uncertainty principle, developed by Bohr and Heisenberg, this conflict has now disappeared. According to this principle it is fundamentally impossible to measure accurately both the velocity and the position of any single elementary particle. It would be possible to measure one or the other accurately but not both simultaneously. Thus it becomes impossible to predict with certainty the movement of a single particle. Therefore, Ampere's estimate of the scope of science has lost its basis.

According to the uncertainty principle, which is now thoroughly well established, the most that can be said about the future motion of any single atom or electron is that it has a definite probability of acting in any given way. Probability thus becomes a fundamental factor in every elementary process. By changing the conditions of the environment of a given atom, as, for example, by changing the force acting on it, we can change these probabilities. In many cases the probability can be made so great that a given result will be almost certain. But in many important cases the uncertainty becomes the dominating feature just as it is in the tossing of a coin.

The net result of the modern principles of physics has been to wipe out almost completely the dogma of causation.

How is it, then, that classical physics has led to such definite clean-cut laws? The simplest answer is that the classical physicist naturally chose as the subjects for his studies those fields which promised greatest success. The aim of the scientist in general was to discover natural laws. He therefore carried on his experiments in such a way as to find the natural laws, for that is what he was looking for. He was best able to accomplish this by working with phenomena which depended upon the behavior of enormous numbers of atoms rather than upon individual atoms. In this way the effects produced by individual atoms averaged out and become imperceptible. We have many familiar examples of this effect of averaging—the deaths of individual human beings can not usually be predicted but the average death rate in any age group is found to come close to expectation.

Since the discovery of the electron and the quantum and methods of detecting or even counting individual atoms, it has been possible for scientists to undertake investigations of the behavior of single atoms. Here they have found unmistakable experimental evidence that these phenomena depend upon the laws of probability and that they are just as unpredictable in detail as the next throw of the coin. If, however, we were dealing with large numbers of such atoms the behavior of the whole group would be definitely determined by the probability of the individual occurrence and therefore would appear to be governed by laws of cause and effect.

Just as there are two types of physics, classical physics and quantum physics, which have for nearly twenty-five years seemed irreconcilable, just so must we recognize two types of natural phenomena. First, those in which the behavior of the system can be determined from the average behavior of its component parts and second, those in which a single discontinuous event (which may depend upon a single quantum change) becomes magnified in its effect so that the behavior of the whole aggregate does depend upon something that started from a small beginning. The first class of phenomena I want to call *convergent phenomena,* because all the fluctuating details of the individual atoms average out giving a result that converges to a definite state. The second class we may call *divergent phenomena,* where from a small beginning increasingly large effects are produced. In general then we may say that classical physics applies satisfactorily to convergent phenomena and that they conform well to the older ideas of cause and effect. The divergent phenomena on the other hand can best be understood on the basis of quantum theory of modern physics.

*    *    *    *    *

The formation of crystals on cooling a liquid involves the formation of nuclei or crystallization centers that must originate from discrete, atomic phenomena. The spontaneous formation of these nuclei often depends upon chance.

At a camp at Lake George, in winter, I have often found that a pail of water is unfrozen in the morning after being in a room far below freezing, but it suddenly turns to slush upon being lifted from the floor.

Glycerine is commonly known as a viscous liquid, even at low temperatures. Yet if crystals are once formed they melt only at 64°F. If a minute crystal of this kind is introduced into pure glycerine at temperatures below 64° the entire liquid gradually solidifies.

During a whole winter in Schenectady I left several small bottles of glycerine outdoors and I kept the lower ends of test-tubes containing glycerine in liquid air for days, but in no case did crystals form.

My brother, A. C. Langmuir, visited a glycerine refinery in Canada which had operated for many years without ever having any experience with crystalline glycerine. But suddenly one winter, without exceptionally low temperatures, the pipes carrying the glycerine from one piece of apparatus to another froze up. The whole plant and even the dust on the ground became contaminated with nuclei and although any part of the plant could be temporarily freed from crystals by heating above 64° it was found that whenever the temperature anywhere fell below 64° crystals would begin forming. The whole plant had to be shut down for months until outdoor temperatures rose above 64°.

Here we have an example of an inherently unpredictable divergent phenomenon that profoundly affected human lives.

Every thunderstorm or tornado must start from a small beginning and at least the details of the irregular courses of such storms across the country would be modified by single quantum phenomena that acted during the initial stages. Yet small details such as the place where lightning strikes or damage occurs from a tornado may be important to a human being.

*    *    *    *    *

As the implications of the uncertainty principle, especially as applied to divergent phenomena, are more generally recognized the limitations of the idea of causality should have profound effects on our habits of thought. The science of logic itself is involved in these changes. Two of the fundamental postulates of logic are known as the law of uniformity of nature and the law of the excluded middle. The first of these laws is equivalent of the postulate of causality in nature. The second law is simply the familiar postulate that a given proposition must be either true or false. In the past these so-called laws have formed the basis of much of our reasoning. It seems to me, however, that they play no important part in the progress of modern science. The cause and effect postulate is only applicable to convergent phenomena. The second postulate in assuming that any proposition must be true or false implies that we attach absolute meanings to words or concepts. If concepts have meanings only in terms of the operations used to define them we can see that they are necessarily fuzzy. Take, for example, this statement, "Atoms are indestructible." Is this true or false? The answer depends upon what aspect of atoms is considered. To the chemist the statement is as true as it ever was. But a physicist, studying radioactive changes, recognized that some atoms undergo spontaneous disintegration or destruction. The fact is that the chemist and the physicist have no exact definition of the word "atom" and they also do not know in any absolute sense what they mean by "indestructible."

Fortunately such questions no longer occupy much of the time of scientists, who are usually concerned with more concrete problems which they endeavor to treat in common-sense ways.

It is often thought by the layman, and many of those who are working in so-called social sciences, that the field of science should be unlimited, that reason should take the place of intuition, that realism should replace emotions and that morality is of value only so far as it can be justified by analytical reasoning.

Human affairs are characterized by a complexity of a far higher order than that encountered ordinarily in the field of science.

To avoid alternating periods of depression and prosperity economists propose to change our laws. They reason that such a change would eliminate the cause of the depressions. They endeavor to develop a science of economics by which sound solutions to such problems can be reached.

I believe the field of application of science in such problems is extremely limited. A scientist has to define his problem and usually has to bring about simplified conditions for his experiments which exclude undesired factors. So the economist has to invent an "economic man" who always does the thing expected of him. No two economists would agree exactly upon the characteristics of this hypothetical man and any conclusions drawn as to his behavior are of doubtful application to actual cases involving human beings. There is no logical scientific method for determining just how one can formulate such a problem or what factors one must exclude. It really comes down to a matter of common sense or good judgment. All too often wishful thinking determines the formulation of the problem. Thus, even if scientifically logical processes are applied to the problem, the results may have no greater validity than that of the good or bad judgment involved in the original assumptions.

Some of the difficulties involved in a scientific approach to economic problems is illustrated by the following: If we wish to analyze the cause of a depression (or for example, a war) we should ask ourselves what we mean by the word "cause" in this connection. In terms of operations the usual meaning of the word cause is something as follows: It is a common experience, in a study of convergent phenomena, that if a given set of physical conditions are brought about repeatedly at different times, the same result occurs in each case. Except in so far as it is possible to repeat the experiment and get the same result it is impossible to give a definite meaning to the word cause.

In the case of a depression or a war, we logically need to produce, or at least to observe, a given set of possible antecedent conditions and to see whether they are always followed by depressions. Since we can not produce experimental depressions, nor have we sufficient observational data to enable us by statistical means to unravel the enormous number of factors involved, we must conclude that the word "cause" as applied to a depression has an extremely fuzzy meaning.

When we consider the nature of human affairs it is to me obvious that divergent phenomena frequently play a role of vital importance. It is true that some of our historians cynically taught most of our college students from 1925 to 1938 that wars, the rise and fall of a nation, etc., were determined by nearly cosmic causes. They tried to show that economic pressure, and power politics on the part of England or France, etc., would have brought the same result whether or not Kaiser Wilhelm or Hitler or any other individual or group of individuals had or had not acted the way they did. Germany, facing the world in a realistic way, was proved, almost scientifically, to be justified in using ruthless methods—because of the energy and other characteristics of the German people they would necessarily acquire and should acquire a place in the sun greater than that of England, which was already inevitably on the downward path.

I can see no justification whatever for such teaching that science proves that general causes (convergent phenomena) dominate in human affairs over the results of individual action (divergent phenomena). It is true that it is not possible to prove one way or the other that human affairs are determined primarily by convergent phenomena. The very existence of divergent phenomena almost precludes the possibility of such proof.

## OPERATIONALISM IN SCIENCE

In Dr. Langmuir's article, he asks why it was that classical physicists could find such clean-cut laws. The answer is that "the classical physicist naturally chose as the subjects for his studies those fields which promised greatest success" (that is, chose subjects and imagined concepts of a kind that did show recurring patterns).

Today, even with quantum thinking in the natural sciences and emphasis on probability in social sciences such as economics and sociology, we must note one more characteristic of science which bears on its usefulness in the formulation of policy problems and the analysis and solution of policy decisions.

The individual scientist will not select problems to work on nor will he select concepts to investigate unless they are operational to him—unless they fit his method. The two things which determine this are (1) the concepts and events must be repetitive in observation, or reproducible in the laboratory; and (2) they must be things that can be quantified. Only in this way can the scientist test the reality of his "imagined" concepts and hypotheses. Numbers and mathematics are the one thing on which different human minds can agree. If phenomena are not repetitive in an absolute sense, they must be in the statistical sense, so that probability figures can be attached.

For example, chemists have discovered through patient experiment that "hydrogen" (note the concept) has an "atomic weight" of 1, and that oxygen has an atomic weight of 16, and that the "valence" (combining power) of hydrogen is 1 while the valence of oxygen is 2. From these, they can predict that of any amount of water ($H_2O$), say 200 pounds, 11 percent will be made up of hydrogen and 89 percent of oxygen. They do this by dividing the total of the molecular weight $[(2 \times) + (1 \times 16)]$ into the atomic weights of the individual elements ($1 \div 18$). If you do not "believe" this, they can take you into the laboratory, weigh the water sample, reduce it to hydrogen and oxygen, and then weigh them under repetitive, experimental conditions.

J. W. N. Sullivan, one important philosopher of science, states that this predisposition to select out of the universe only those things that could be *measured* experimentally or observationally was due simply to a *faith* on the part of Copernicus, Kepler, and Galileo "that mathematics is the key to the universe . . . a belief which was very proper to born mathematicians . . . [which] gave the mathematical aspects of the universe a much more exalted position than they occupied in the current Aristotelian outlook. . . ."

"[Kepler's] deepest conviction was that nature is essentially mathematical, and all his scientific life was an endeavor to discover nature's hidden mathematical harmonies. Galileo, also, had no doubt that mathematics is the one true key to the universe. It was this persuasion that gave these men their criterion for selection amongst the total elements of the universe."[6]

Whitehead, on the other hand, gives a slightly different reason for the scientist's willingness to deal only with problems which can be reproduced, quantitatively, in experiment or by observation. To him it was a

---

[6] J. W. N. Sullivan, *The Limitations of Science* (New York: New American Library Edition), pp. 128–29. Copyright, 1933, Viking Press, Inc., reprinted by permission.

loss in faith, by scholars, in the dogmatic speculation of the Middle Ages, when philosophy and truth were laid down, speculatively, without reference to facts in the world. Copernicus, for example, felt a great anxiety because he knew that the Ptolemaic theory of the universe was not true. That theory, with the earth as the center, and stationary at that, was a current conceptual scheme of the mind, which explained how the stars rotated around the earth. Copernicus had "heard" that some of the great Greek philosophers had put forward the hypothesis that the earth was in motion. Copernicus then took the sun as his center of reference (he imagined a new theory or conceptual scheme) and proceeded to collect data.

It is significant that in 1973 the concept of operationalism (experiment-quantification) is important in physical science, in some social science, and in the current application of mathematics in business administration, that is, in the field of operations research. One of the better recent textbooks on operations research states:

> The goals of individuals have been the subject of discussion and debate for many centuries. To say that happiness is the goal of the individual . . . does not solve any problem. We cannot define happiness in operational terms. Operationalism is an important concept for understanding operations research. It implies concreteness, the ability to observe, measure, and analyze. . . . We cannot treat happiness as an operational term.[7]

Facts which are operational to the scientist and statistician in the laboratory, quantified and under controlled experimental (repetitive and abstract) conditions, are not always operational to the policy maker; or they may be relevant to his problems, but not of high relevance in terms of his goals; or they may be relevant, but uncontrollable in terms of executive action. Finally, they may be highly relevant, and controllable by the executive, but subject to overriding importance of *other* forces than explained by any one theory.[8]

## THE LESSON OF PHYSICAL SCIENCE FOR POLICY MAKERS

Why have we spent time discussing the nature of science, the idea of divergent phenomena, and the idea of operationalism in science? First, because it helps the policy maker, the person of action, to recognize that the great power of creativity and the enormous amounts of time and energy expended add to the value of many scientific concepts. It also helps to see that the very bias of scientists—their preconditioning and their attitudes—is one of the factors that enable them to see things that

---

[7] David Miller and Martin Starr, *Executive Decisions and Operations Research* (Englewood Cliffs, N.Y.; Prentice-Hall, Inc., 1960).

[8] In many of the cases in the latter part of the book, one of these three limitations can be seen. For example, see the following cases: Midwest Hardware Manufacturing Company and Continental Electric Company.

laymen may overlook. Second, some of the characteristics of science, divergent phenomena, and operationalism have contradictory implications in policy systems—they put a limitation on the degree to which science can be used in policy formation. They indicate that the practicing executive must pick and choose his or her theories, must test them, modify them, use them, or discard them, depending on how they operate in the world of action, where experimental conditions cannot be met, where divergent phenomena are many times as important as convergent phenomena, and where everything cannot be measured by mathematics.

Finally, many social scientists, whether rightly or wrongly, try, with varying degrees of success, to adopt the methods of the physical sciences. To the extent that they do, this chapter has set the state for understanding the nature and methods of social sciences discussed in the next chapter.

# Chapter 3. SOCIAL SCIENCE AND APPLIED SOCIAL SCIENCE

## THEORY FORMULATION IN THE SOCIAL SCIENCES: AN EXAMPLE FROM SOCIOLOGY

In the last chapter, we looked at the nature of conceptual schemes, as formulated by those scientists whose main interest is understanding non-human objects in the environment, for the purpose of explaining how one object or event causes another.

The social sciences occupy a special place in policy making by general executives. In fact, "management" has been defined by some as "getting results through human organizations."[1] Such a definition implies that the proper study of decisions by people of action—military, governmental, legal—should be based on political philosophy, or political science, or one of the so-called behavioral sciences—psychology and certain branches of sociology and anthropology.

In this chapter, we will be looking at the nature of social science, its concepts, and the way they are derived (its methods), in the hope that the reader, in both reading these words and working with the cases, will gain an appreciation for the value of social science, and its limitations, in the world of policy-making action.

We will begin by using an explanation of "The Theory Construction Function of Science" put forth by Ernest Greenwood.[2] The example he cites, that of Durkheim's theory of suicide, is a classic one, often used by social scientists to illustrate their methods:

---

[1] This, of course, is a conceptual idea which puts the relationships between people, and their governance or management, in the center of analysis, rather than the relationships between machines, goods, money flows, and the like. Neither is true: the policy system, as we shall see, is a very complex conglomerate of human structures and dynamics, and technological-economic structures and dynamics.

[2] From Ernest Greenwood, "The Practice of Science and the Science of Practice" presented as a University Lecture at Brandeis University, October 1959, and published as one of the Brandeis University Papers in Social Welfare by the Florence Heller Graduate School for Advanced Studies in Social Welfare, 1960. This Lecture is also abridged in *The Planning of Change,* edited by Warren Bennis, Kenneth D. Benne, and Robert Chin (New York: Holt, Rinehart & Winston, 1962). The latter is considered an excellent collection of writings from the viewpoint of the practitioner—the applied social scientist who is interested in planned change (control) in the environment rather than simply in understanding the operation of nature.

[L]et me describe in more specific language the nature of the scientific activity. The end product of the collective efforts of scientists within a given discipline is a system of internally consistent propositions which describe and explain the phenomena that constitute the subject matter of that discipline. This system is called a body of theory. The function of all science is to construct theories about the what, the how, and the why of the natural world. There is some current misunderstanding regarding this function of science, many laymen believing that only philosophers theorize and that scientists "stick close to facts." I wish to dwell a bit on the theory-construction focus of science. In this connection it will prove clarifying if I were to distinguish between two levels of knowledge with which scientists are concerned. On the first level are first-order facts called *empirical generalizations;* on the second and higher level are the explanations or interpretations of these facts called *theory.* These constitute two orders of abstraction.

### Nature of Empirical Generalizations

To make clear the distinction between these two orders of abstraction, let me present you with a few examples of an empirical generalization. Thus:

a. In Western societies, Jews commit fewer suicides than Gentiles, and Catholics commit fewer suicides than Protestants.

b. American middle-class wives participate in communal health and welfare activities more than their husbands.

c. In cities key commercial facilities concentrate at point of convergence of transportation lines.

d. Juvenile delinquency rates are higher in urban census tracts with lower median monthly rentals.

An empirical generalization may be defined as a proposition about a class of units which describes the uniform recurrence of two or more factors among them. As the term empirical implies, such generalizations are derived inductively by actual observation of the class members. The procedures pursued in their derivation can be operationalized and textbooks on research methods are written to describe them; these involve scaling, sampling, controlled observation, data manipulation, application of statistical tests, et cetera. Given time and patience, there is no limit to the number of hitherto unsuspected empirical generalizations, or first-order facts, that one could discover about the social world. The body of knowledge of a science, however, consists of more than empirical generalizations.

### Description versus Explanation

That shrewd critic of the sociological scene, Robert Bierstedt, in a brilliant article, entitled "A Critique of Empiricism in Sociology," puts the matter in the following form.[3] Surveys, he states, have amassed an assortment of facts about bread consumption in the United States. Thus: Americans are consuming decreasing amounts of home-made and increasing amounts of factory-made bread. Most Americans prefer white to dark bread. Men consume more bread than women. Adolescents consume more bread than other age groups. Negroes consume more bread than Whites. Rural dwellers consume more bread than urban dwellers. Low income families consume more bread than high income families. This factual list might be extended without adding significantly to our comprehension of the American bread consumption phenomenon. To achieve the latter requires a formulation that will tie together these discrete generalizations and will explain their interrelationships. Such a formulation would constitute a theory of American bread consumption.

The function of social scientists is to develop theories which will explain such social phenomena as bread consumption, alcoholism, class conflict, crime, drug addiction, juvenile delinquency, marital discord, population migration, suicide, technological change, urban growth, et cetera. In constructing theory, the scientist uses empirical generalizations as building blocks.

### An Example of Theory Building

I would like to present an idealized description of theory construction taken from Durkheim's work on the social aetiology of suicide. Although now over a half century old, it still remains an impeccable model of theory construction.[4] I have deliberately selected an example at a relatively simple level of theory, thereby ignoring so-called grand and all-embracing theories.

Durkheim begins his search for the societal cause of suicide by casting his net far and wide, garnering all the available facts about the problem. The data yield him a series of empirical generalizations. Careful scrutiny of Durkheim's volume reveals over three dozen such generalizations which assume a wide variety. Let me present some of them.

    *a.* Countries predominantly Protestant in population have higher suicide rates than countries predominantly Catholic.
    *b.* Christians have higher suicide rates than Jews.
    *c.* Countries with high literacy rates have higher suicide rates than countries with low literacy.

---

[3] Robert Bierstedt, "A Critique of Empiricism in Sociology," *American Sociological Review,* vol. 14 (October 1949), pp. 584–92.

[4] Emile Durkheim, *Suicide: A Study in Sociology* (New York: The Free Press of Glencoe, 1951). Translation by John A. Spaulding and George Simpson. Durkheim's theory of suicide presented in this paper is a highly abstracted version of the original, necessitated by space requirements. Any distortions in the theory are the responsibility of this writer.

    *d.*  The liberal professions as a group have a higher suicide rate than the manual occupations.

    *e.*  The unmarried have a higher suicide rate than the married.

    *f.*  The divorced have a higher suicide rate than the married.

    *g.*  The childless married have a higher suicide rate than the married with children.

    *h.*  Average size of family is inversely related to the suicide rate.

Having extracted these empirical generalizations from the data, Durkheim next, in essence, asks the question: What common thread runs through these generalizations? What do Protestants, high literacy countries, liberal professions, the unmarried, the divorced, the childless, have in common that should make for higher suicide rates among them than in their opposite classes? At this point Durkheim begins to speculate, and his speculation bears recapitulation.

If Protestants are more prone to suicides than Catholics, religious differences must be held accountable. Protestantism permits individualism and free inquiry, while Catholicism brooks no scrutiny by the faithful. The more binding the creed, the more unified the religious group and the more attached is the individual to the group. The atmosphere permitted by Protestantism weakens the traditional beliefs that solidify the religious group. That group discipline exerts a preservative influence is borne out by the case of the Jews, a cohesive minority living in compact communities, with a low suicide rate. Attachment to a group must be a potent factor in the suicide phenomenon as indicated by the marital correlates of suicide. Note how the unmarried state encourages suicide and how the disruption of marriage by divorce and death increases its chances. Close examination of the facts reveals that even more preservative than the conjugal relationship between the spouses is the familial relationship between parents and children. In fact, the more children the better. The common thread that runs through these empirical generalizations is clear. A well-integrated group holds its members by strong bonds, preventing them from evading their social obligations by self-elimination, at the same time providing them the support to enable them to perform their obligations in the face of otherwise disabling personal stress. Where group solidarity is weak, the individual feels detached from the group and is thrown on his own feeble resources to sustain him in his personal frustrations.

This, highly condensed, is Durkheim's theory of the social cause of suicide. The theory may now be summarized into a single proposition, *i.e.,* a law of suicide: *Suicide is a function of the degree of group integration which provides the psychic support to group members for handling acute stress.*

## Nature of Theory Building

Durkheim's method epitomizes the scientific process. From a host of apparently disconnected first-order facts he theorizes to a law.

He moves from the facts to an abstract proposition which interprets the interrelationship among them. Note the difference in levels of abstraction between the law and the empirical generalizations. Note how much more abstract is the proposition with which he terminates the theorizing process from the propositions with which he initiates it. Theory may thus be defined as a systematic interpretation in abstract terms of a generalizable trend that prevails within a set of varied facts, explaining the interrelationship among them. Law is the summarization of the theory in causal terms.

As indicated earlier, the derivation of empirical generalizations can be operationalized, but I have yet to find a textbook that will operationalize the theorizing process. The interpretive process, the development of a formulation which will account for a series of facts, is essentially a free-wheeling, speculative one. It is an inferential process whereby the inquiring mind churns the available information over and over, employing all the logical devices and bringing to bear upon it any and all kinds of relevant knowledge. The process allows for a considerable play of the imagination, and the final formulation bears the personal imprint of its formulator.

In this example of fact gathering and speculation-theory construction in the social sciences, the policy maker might well take note of some of the characteristics of the theory itself and of its formulator, Durkheim.

First, the final law of suicide contains two concepts or variables which Durkheim "saw." By the process of abstraction, he simplified the world: "suicide," as an event or occurrence, and "group integration," which determines the suicide rate. These two concepts are, at one and the same time, products of his imagination, and representative of the underlying facts. The intermediate variables with which he reasoned (the other concepts he imagined and formulated) are "psychic support" for handling "acute stress." Thus, we get these cause-and-effect relationships: low degrees of group participation cause a feeling of lack of psychic support in the individual which cause him to be unable to handle problems of acute stress, which in turn cause him to commit suicide.

Second, to test the theory, one can reason deductively from the theory to other facts, just as in the case of the prediction that Neptune was "out there" (Chapter 2). One can look for groups with low degrees of "group integration," and without experiment, deductively predict that members of that group would have a high suicide rate; further, one can then test to see if the members of that group *in fact* have a higher suicide rate.

Third, Durkheim's central theory does not refer to any other causes of suicide. He assumes that group integration is the uniformly constant and most important cause, and that other causes are either less important, or are simply deviant, random events, not relevant to scientific study and rational explanation. He treats suicide as a repetitive, convergent phenomena (in Langmuir's term), a pattern which varies with one central cause—group integration.

Fourth, Durkheim had an interest in studying suicide. He was not interested in making automobiles, wining a war, setting the discount rate of the federal reserve banks, influencing the behavior of subordinate personnel in a factory, or explaining the rise and fall of governments.

If he were interested in a very broad range of problems and events and variables in a policy system, he could not have conceptualized in precise enough terms to produce the power of thought and the understanding of nature, which he did.

Finally, the principle itself (any principle is a statement of explanation—of cause and effect) is not "engineered"—it does not prescribe to a government official *how* to provide group integration. Only by restudying the underlying facts, as to how the various groups provided (or did not provide) integration, can the policy maker infer what they did in a practical sense to influence the suicide rate. This is an important difference in science, technology, and practice.

## THEORY CONSTRUCTION: AN EXAMPLE FROM SOCIAL PSYCHOLOGY

In order to understand the use of theories in policy formulation more deeply, we need another example—one from a practitioner whose interests are nearer to the business organization. This time, we will look at a theory which explains the ways in which "organizations" have certain effects on "individual behavior" and "group behavior" and how the latter two variables reciprocally affect "organizations." This theory, that explained by Chris Argyris in *Personality and Organization*,[5] has received wide attention.

In formulating this conceptual scheme, Argyris utilizes 640 footnotes, many of which draw on empirical research in the social sciences. He draws on a breadth of experimental and observed situations—from studies of motivation in children, of personality tests in business, and of rational behavior in large bureaucracies to studies of why people join trade unions. Argyris is *primarily interested* in how large organizations affect human personality and how they affect informal group behavior. At the highest level, he is interested in what causes conflict between organizations, on the one hand, and the rank-and-file members of organizations, on the other.

With these interests, he proceeds to conceptualize meaning from a wealth of diverse facts which have "come to his attention." The overall theory and its intermediate concepts can be stated in briefest terms as follows:

1.  All human beings have a capacity for "self-actualization" (growth), for developing from infancy in terms of interests, abilities, and activities. Such development satisfies needs, and it is the continuing striving for such development which gives us energy.

2.  The formal organization has four characteristics: jobs are split up

---

[5] Chris Argyris, *Personality and Organization* (New York: Harper & Bros., 1957). The presentation of the theory here is a highly abstracted version of Professor Argyris' book. Responsibility for abstraction is assumed by the authors. The theory is also highly controversial—see the review of Argyris' later work by Mason Haire, *Management Science*, April 1963, p. 505.

and specialized, there is a chain of command, everyone has only one boss, and there is a long hierarchy or pyramid of command.

3. These characteristics of formal organization severely limit the self-actualization, development, and growth of the human being.

4. Rank-and-file members of the organization, thus confronted with a block to their growth and development, either quit, become apathetic (lose their energy), or become aggressive against the organization.

5. The leaders of organizations see the rank and file behaving this way, develop beliefs that they are lazy or hostile, and tighten up on the characteristics of formal organization (step [2]). They define jobs more minutely, stress the chain of command, and rigidify the hierarchical pyramid.

6. This causes the apathy and aggression of employees who remain in the organization to intensify: they become lethargic and devote less energy to their work; or they increase their aggression in the form of cliques to "get around" the rules; or they even form formal labor unions to fight back.

7. The vicious circle continues, with steps (5) and (6) reinforcing the conflict.

Argyris' interest in organization-personality conflict led him to conceptualize a series of cause-and-effect relationships between two highly abstract concepts: "the organization" and "personality." In order to think about these, however, his original interest dictated that he had to formulate some lower order concepts about what a "human being" is and about what an "organization" is. What did he do about these two variables? What did he see? In effect, he said, "A personality (human being) is first and foremost an organism which has an almost unlimited capacity for self-actualization and growth"; and "an organization is a construct with specialized jobs, chain of command, and a hierarchical pyramid."

The choice of these two larger abstractions, "personality" and "organization" with their lower order abstractions, "growth," "chain of command," and so on, enabled him to reason the further cause-and-effect relationships pointed out above.

## THEORY CONSTRUCTION: AN EXAMPLE FROM ECONOMICS AND INDUSTRIAL ENGINEERING

The founder of the discipline of economics, Adam Smith, had as his main interest exactly what the title of his famous book implies: *An Inquiry into the Nature and Causes of the Wealth of Nations.* He was interested in the national balance sheet, the assets and liabilities of a nation, and the national income and gross national product which produces the national wealth. Thus motivated in terms of interest, Smith conceptualized the first and most important cause of the productivity of a nation as the "principle of specialization"—the division of work into smaller parts which produced efficiency of the whole.[6]

---

[6] The relevant argument is presented in this volume as pages 4–15 of *The Wealth of Nations.*

This is the same "specialization" which Argyris refers to as one of the characteristics of organizations, in step (2) in the preceding section, except that the two scholars derived different meanings from it. To Adam Smith, it is the foremost cause of the productivity of an industrial system, yet to Argyris it is one of the causes of apathy or aggression in organizations. Even today, in modern economics, the principle of specialization has important implications for creating larger organizations, for creating staff departments for central planning in organizations, and for realizing "increasing returns to scale."[7]

In the field of industrial engineering and in operations research models, there is implied a certain physical division of labor between parts of the system (including locations, such as jobs, factories, and warehouses). If this division of labor produces the greatest job output in the case of industrial engineering or the optimum balance between the inputs and outputs of an inventory system (in operations research), then the engineers or researchers tend either to ignore the motivational effects of specialization,[8] or to assume that they have less importance than the rational planning of jobs and the flow of material. In this sense, the *interests* of industrial engineers, or operations researchers, simply cause them to select certain variables which are more important in their view of the world.[9] This, incidentally, does not mean that all industrial engineers, operations researchers, and economists ignore the meaning of "specialization" as it occurs to Argyris. It simply means that they must, if they are to accomplish their principal objectives of inquiry, devote their greatest attention to their own expertise and logic, as based on what they are trying to accomplish.[10] In the process of building their models or conceptual schemes, they are exercising the prerogative of a scholar or technologist: to derive meaning from facts *as they see them*.

### CETERIS PARIBUS IN SOCIAL SCIENCE

Even in the pure version of social science, such as in directed toward the understanding of nature rather than the controlling of nature through technology, and as exemplified in the Durkheim theory, the scientist sees certain important, central meanings to a wide variety of facts. Though Durkheim's theory seems the "very model of theoretic and methodologic sophistication . . . [indicating his stature] as a pure social

---

[7] Study particularly the California Federal Savings and Loan Association case, plus the readings, for insight into the meaning of the term "specialization" in relation to internal organization planning.

[8] That is, in their formal models. They cover such divergent phenomena in their assumptions when they study a technological system, but these generally receive less rigorous analysis and proof than the phenomena of primary focus.

[9] For more detailed examples of these views of the world, see the following cases and their collateral readings: Midwest Hardware Manufacturing Company, Western Office Equipment Company, and Sea Breeze Motel.

[10] Many students of Adam Smith, being interested in his major thesis, will not have been "interested" enough to remember his later passages which state, in a powerful way, the harmful effects of specialization on human beings. Smith did not consider these as important as the opposite principle when he formulated economic theory. See Adam Smith *The Wealth of Nations* (New York: Random House, Inc., 1937), pp. 423, 508.

scientist,"[11] there is no assurance that another social scientist will not one day set out to derive different meanings from different orders of facts, thus showing another important cause of suicide, and a different conceptual scheme. In this sense, even in pure varieties of social science, the social scientist assumes *ceteris paribus,* or "other things being equal." Operations researchers and Chris Argyris, because of their choice of when to close the system—of what other things would be assumed to be equal—arrive at totally different meanings of the same phenomenon, specialization.

As one moves nearer and nearer to the control of the environment—when one becomes a technologist, or even more a policy maker—he or she must realize that "other things" are present in the policy system: that divergent or assumed phenomena can be of lesser importance, equal importance, or greater importance than the convergent phenomena presented by the scientist.

Economics has traditionally been concerned, in part, with control of the environment. As scholars who reason, a priori, from "supply" and "demand," economists assume, for example, that all people are motivated by "competition," and they are very careful to state their principles in terms of *other things being equal.* This is a signal to people of action that they are studying only parts of a policy system at any one time.

What we are saying here is that in a policy decision made by a general executive in a policy system, each theory (from each discipline) may predict a certain outcome, in absolute terms, if a given course of action (policy, decision, and strategy) is decided upon. But when many theories, from many disciplines, predict different outcomes, the *absolute* result predicted by each theory must be given a *weight* by the general executive. From the standpoint of any one individual theory, other outcomes from other theories may be weighted lower, the same, or higher, depending on the goals of the policy system as interpreted by the manager. These weights based on goals which the executive is trying to accomplish *are not necessarily the same* as the weight that a psychologist would assign to psychological outcomes based on the goals of psychologists. They are not necessarily the same as the weights an applied mathematician would assign to technological performance, such as the quantities in an inventory control and product planning system, when he or she expresses this system in a mathematical, operations research model.

## WHO HAS THE FINAL ANSWER FOR POLICY DETERMINATION?

In philosophy of knowledge, the term "validity" means that a conceptual scheme of concepts linked together in an explanation of cause and effect is internally consistent. That is, terms are defined precisely and reasoning proceeds according to rules, either the older Aristotelian syllogistic rules or the newer rules of general semantics.

There is no such thing as this kind of "validity" in a policy decision.

---

[11] Alvin W. Gouldner, "Theoretical Requirements of the Applied Social Sciences," *American Sociological Review,* vol. 22, no. 1 (February 1957), p. 98.

There may be validity in each of the separate theories, but that is because scholars used methods to simplify the world which yielded this kind of validity.

In the world of theory, "truth" (reliability) means that the conceptual schemes generated by the human mind through scientific method have been (and can be) verified by repeating the observation or by reproducing an experiment. Thus, Leverrier verified the scheme of "force, mass, heliocentric longitude, orbit" when he predicted that Neptune was there, looked through his telescope, and saw it.

One might also verify the scheme of "suicide-group integration" by observing groups in the real world. The scientist would then go out and look for groups with high or low integration and, using statistical probability, prove that the higher suicide rate could not have been caused by random factors. It therefore must have been caused by the variable or concept of group integration. In this case, the theory of group integration caused the researcher to measure group characteristics only on this scale. He closed out the rest of the world, so to speak.

In the other means of verification (experimentation), were it not for our social mores regarding experimenting with human beings, one might set up two experimental groups, controlled in the sense that (1) the two groups have different degrees of the independent variable, group integration, and (2) in all other respects, the groups are alike. By changing the degree of group integration in one group, one then would measure the difference in the suicide rates which result and subject them to tests of statistical probability. The scientist has deliberately created a factual situation "out there" which eliminates the world in its confusion and simplifies it into a controlled experiment, abstracted from the world. In one sense, then, he is creating a situation, by controlling reality, which produces the very phenomena which his imagination created in the first place. In Langmuir's sense, he is setting up a factual situation in which divergent phenomena are deliberately kept out.

Thus in both the observations and in the reproducible experiments of social science, *ceteris paribus,* other things being equal, presents a special problem. In astronomy, an observational science where the phenomena under study are literally "in a vacuum" and where other things are equal in the reality of day-to-day dynamics, conceptual schemes and reality approximate the same thing. In social science, where controlled conditions create artificial vacuums or where choosing of facts to study "closes the system" and where other things in the complexity of day-to-day events are such that other things are *not* equal, theory and total reality are not necessarily the same thing. Such theories are creations of the human mind.

In answer to our question, who has the final answer for policy determination, the answer is: probably nobody. An executive may seem to question the validity and truth of theories as he or she evaluates them for his or her policy making. Not so! Because the executive has moved away from the closed system of the scholar to the open policy system, he or she must apply another criterion: does the theory work? No one theory fits the policy system with its multitude of interacting variables. As we have said, theories come to grips with a slice of reality, burying the remainder of reality in the *ceteris paribus* assumption. The executive recognizes that a theory may have validity and truth within the closed system of the scholar's purpose. If Durkheim's purpose is to understand suicide, there may well be validity and truth in his statement of its cause. If Argyris' purpose is to understand conflict in organizations, there may well be validity and truth in his more elaborate scheme. If the applied mathematician's purpose is to minimize the cost of holding inventory, there may also be validity and truth in his or her mathematical formula for the optimum lot size, based on a number of technological and economic variables. But when the executives come to policy determination, they must eclectically draw from valid and true theories, those aspects which are relevant to *their* problems, and which aid in their analyses and decisions.

Roethlisberger, in a book reporting on one of the most significant research projects undertaken in social science, points out that there is within sociology and anthropology today a controversy over the "historical" versus the "functional" conceptual schemes. He clearly points out that neither is true nor false, but "more or less convenient or useful for certain purposes . . . [and] its usefulness can only be decided after it has been used."[12] He then cites a rather powerful passage from a book by Thurman Arnold:

> The eye of the artist or poet looking at the human body is different from the eye of the physician looking for pathological symptoms. Neither one has the "true" nor the "false" view of the body. The physician, however, is the better person when therapy rather than decoration is demanded.[13]

## SOCIAL SCIENCE AND SOCIAL PHILOSOPHY

The social scientists' studies of *certain problems* in the environment are complicated by the fact that they cannot isolate their own emotional needs from the hypothesis they generate. In the physical sciences, astronomers are not necessarily mad or happy when they find Neptune in a certain orbit. They do not think this is good or bad.

In the social sciences this is not necessarily true, particularly in the study of organizations. Every social scientist has been living in organizations from birth (the family), and shall be in organizations until death (government, universities, business). As he or she performs the scientific operations noted in the preceding section, selection of facts to observe, interpretation of meanings, setting up of experiments, these value predispositions (positive-negative) influence the total intellectual process in each of its stages.

---

[12] F. J. Roethlisberger, *Management and Morale* (Cambridge, Mass.: Harvard University Press, 1941), p. 69.

[13] Thurman Arnold, *The Symbols of Government* (New Haven, Conn.: Yale University Press, 1935), p. 30.

In this sense, social "science" has something in common with social "philosophy." Faced with limitations on the methods the astronomers use to leave their emotions out of their observations in a pure, simplified system, the social scientist in one sense reasons a priori, i.e., from a combination of assumptions and facts, rather than from facts alone. They are denied the very conditions (a simple, closed system) which would have been a check on their deeper, unconscious assumptions.

Still other scholars, social philosophers, attack large social issues where measurement, observation, reproducible experiment, and validation are not possible. These people reason from assumptions freely and employ logic (philosophy) rather than a combination of fact and logic (science) to explain their concepts. The individual scholar's values are even more likely to influence such theories in these cases. A good example of how different values create different conceptual schemes is to be found in the apparent contradiction between traditional management theory based on economics and political science and certain forms of management theory based on psychology.

Management theory, based primarily on economic principles such as specialization, and interested primarily in the necessity of technological coordination of the inputs and outputs between operating and staff functions, proceeds to reason out such concepts as "division of work," "delegation of authority," and "unity of command (power)." In this sense, management theory is quite akin to political philosophy. It starts with assumptions similar to John Locke's[14]—that "all men are biased" (note that it does not start with "growth") and that people need and want an "indifferent judge," with "authority," so that chaos and anarchy will not prevail (note that there is no reference to the fact that the "indifferent judge" will stifle the "growth" of humans). Management theory also has some unconscious assumptions similar to engineering and operations research. That is, the importance of technological coordination in the production of goods—between the timing, quality, and quantity of work flow, with the aid of central, rational planning—is of paramount concern.

On the other hand, theories based on psychology and small group dynamics imply that, in order to liberate the largest amount of human energy and creativity in the organization, a maximum amount of participation, by group members, is a desirable type of managerial and subordinate behavior. Most of these theories do not refer to the increment of efficiency due to technological coordination by central planners, or expert staff personnel such as engineers and operations researchers, or to the time consumed in patient, "two-way communication" (one of their central concepts). Rather, such theories highlight the fact that such communication arrives at the best decisions on how to structure the business, and at the same time produce the most harmonious human system. (Note that these theories do not deliberately reason with Locke that all people need authority, or with the economists, that all people are competitive.[15]

---

[14] Reproduced herein as pages 53–54 of John Locke, *Concerning Civil Government.*

[15] Note, also, that the assumptions of scholars vary according to the nature of the institution they are studying. Classical economists were "in favor of" freedom of the firm's manage-

Nor do they say that anarchy would prevail without some legalized authority.)

Obviously, we could go on and on in giving examples of differences in conceptual schemes, due to differences in the deeper values of the scholars who formulate them. The point to be made is that in the study of humans as opposed to the study of nonhuman objects and phenomena, values do get into the picture in more than one way. For philosophers, who use assumptions and reasoning, the values can clearly influence what they see, both in terms of selecting assumptions from which to reason and in showing relationships. For applied social scientists, the practitioners who study large complex organizations, and particularly those who study matters of human individuality and organizational attributes, these values influence the choice of facts to observe, the way experiments are set up, and derivation of meaning from those facts.

## THE VALUE OF SOCIAL SCIENCE IN POLICY DECISIONS

In this chapter we have seen some of the methods used by social scientists and social philosophers to arrive at their theories and conceptual schemes.

If there is anything which should stand out to the policy maker, to the person of action, it is the fact that social science provides an enormous pool of experience from a wide variety of people who spend their lives looking for meaning of events within their field. The very bias with which they approach their subjects, occasioned by different viewpoints or preconceptions, or, as in the Durkheim case, occasioned by their interest in a certain problem, means that they see people, organizations, and events in a light not available to laymen. To the policy maker these theories are valuable in determining managerial goals, in creatively formulating alternative courses of action, and in predicting what will happen if policy makers make decisions one way or another. Most important, *in all three* of these steps, they help to prevent a decision being made which later is discovered to have adverse unintended consequences.

For further insight into how the executive uses theory in his or her policy decisions, one might refer to an article by one of the authors which served as a precursor to the present volume.[16]

---

ment to do as it wished, but they never implied that *within* the firm there should be "free enterprise." They imply quite the contrary: that the executive, either as an expert computer of economic data, or as a deterministic agent, should determine jobs and specializations, and allocate resources up to the margin. The applied economists, such as budget analysts, financial planners, and the like, imply even more explicitly that people and other resources should be managed on the basis of expert calculation of marginal revenues, cash flows, break-even charts, and the like.

[16] Charles E. Summer, "The Managerial Mind," *Harvard Business Review,* January–February 1959.

# NOTES ON THE STUDY OF CASES

1. The diagnostic and predictive questions framed in each case introduction will help you apply theories and concepts from a certain discipline of thought (e.g., economics, psychology, political science) to the facts of the particular case situation. These concepts are valuable to help *understand* basic forces at work in the policy system (diagnosis of what is going on), and to *predict* what will happen in the system in the future. Each reading or theory abstracts from the real world certain factors into the closed system view of one discipline. No one of these disciplines can have the final truth or answer to a real world situation in its buzzing confusion. As one writer has put it, the medical doctor and the artist may both look at the human body and "see" different things. Which is *true?* The answer is that neither has the truth of the world in its entirety. Therefore, the diagnostic question helps one see reality, but only parts of reality.

2. The policy questions require the manager to deal with the whole situation—he or she cannot become solely an economist, a political scientist or a psychologist. The result of diagnosis and prediction, which actually reduces the amount of judgment necessary, does not eliminate the need for judgment and intuition. Since certain parts of the world cannot be reduced to science, and since "other things are not equal," judgment must still be used to fill in the factors not accounted for by readings. One must also use a second kind of judgment to put value weights on different scientific predictions because different theories might indeed predict conflicting ideal solutions.

3. In summary, the diagnostic (scientific) understanding of cases demonstrates the power of theory and concepts, if used by practicing managers. The policy-making action questions demonstrate the limitations of science and the need for judgment in the world of action. This dual need for *both* science *and* judgment has been more fully explained in the introductory chapters.

# PART II Strategic Planning and Organization Design

Part II of this book is addressed to four of the most important functions of managers: (1) formulating a strategy for success of the organization in the outside world; (2) designing an organization structure which will accomplish the technical strategy of the enterprise; (3) adjusting this structure to eliminate conflict between human beings who must cooperate if the organization's strategy is to be achieved; and (4) adapting the structure so that the individuals who fill the boxes on the organization chart will feel like contributing their efforts to excellence in their jobs.

## STRATEGIC PLANNING: AN IMPORTANT WAY OF RELATING THE ORGANIZATION TO ITS EXTERNAL ENVIRONMENT

Every organization must achieve some primary goals, otherwise society "out there" will not in the long run continue to support the organization. This is true of a hospital which must render quality patient care at a level of efficiency satisfactory to patients and governing boards. It is true of a public school which must render quality education at a cost that is not unduly high in the minds of the board of education or parents. It is true of a business corporation which must make certain kinds of products of a quality desired by the customer at an efficiency cost that is not unreasonable.

Each of these organizations is chartered by society to perform an economic mission: to produce some good or service which is wanted by people *outside*, and to produce at a level of efficiency that is acceptable externally. Internal efficiency, as important as it may seem, is simply a means to the larger end—social productivity.

The primary purpose of any organization, then, is to serve certain segments of society out there beyond the organization. In an age when social responsibility of the firm (and the managers in it) is coming to be recognized as a question of vital importance, it is well to recognize at the outset that organizations *must* produce what they are chartered for, and what society wants. This is the primary goal of organizations that survive. The primary goal of a hospital is quality patient care produced efficiently. If pollution materials are a byproduct of the hospital, then the

39

managers of the institution may have a responsibility to comply with the health standards of environmental pollution control. But the economic function of producing patient care is still the primary goal. If the primary goal of an airline is to transport passengers and freight and if society indeed wants this kind of transportation, the airline must observe noise limitation requirements, but it cannot deny as its primary specialization the transporting of passengers. Nobody wants to go to an airline pilot for treatment of the liver, and nobody wants a heart specialist piloting his airplane to Chicago.

## THE PRACTICE OF STRATEGIC PLANNING

The cases in Part II all describe real-life managers who are facing the difficult task of trying to keep their organizations up to date by formulating product (output) goals which meet the needs of outside customers, or by adjusting major policies inside the company so that these goals are met. In Vertex Company, Inc., the management has been successful in the past at producing various health care products: shampoos, hair sprays, hair colorings, shaving creams, and lotions. Yet there are developments in society "out there" which mean that the product goals themselves, or the major internal policies that govern operations, may have remained constant while society outside is changing.

A similar situation faces Yarway Corporation managers. The company has been pursuing a product strategy aimed at chemical processes and power industry customers. This has been coupled with a certain geographic strategy involving both domestic and international markets. Faced with growth in the number of product lines carried and in markets served, the management devises an annual planning cycle that will keep both its product lines and its internal resources (people and money) adjusted to changing affairs in society.

With these cases are a number of readings which should help one become a more informed and skillful strategic planner. Drucker makes a powerful case for the need to keep the customer (rather than existing ways of doing things) in mind. Two flow diagrams by Gilmore aid the student in seeing the steps one should go through in strategic planning decisions. Tilles provides a set of criteria which one may use to judge if a company's strategy is a viable one.

Though the General Machinery Corporation, Shoe Corporation of Illinois, and California Federal Savings and Loan Association cases tend to focus on organization design (see below), they show that managers can hardly attack the problem of design without first having a fairly clear idea of the organization's strategy. In this sense, the cases show managers facing the same kind of problem as the one faced in the Vertex Company, Inc. and the Yarway Corporation.

One aspect of strategic planning appears prominently in the cases in Part VI. In all organizations, managers must take into account certain collateral or noneconomic goals, in addition to the goal of social productivity. Racial equality becomes important to the Polaroid Corporation *in addition to* productivity of photographic equipment. Managements of

Firestone, Goodrich, and Tenneco Corporation are seen to take into account occupational health of employees in their strategy *in addition to* society's need for plastic water pipes, flooring, and paint for America's homes.

The fact that strategic planning questions crop up in other sections of the book shows that regardless of the particular managerial function being studied, a company's strategy influences that function. The strategy of Harrogate Asphalt Products, Ltd. (AR) (Part V) influences the leadership style of its president, Mr. Lampton. The strategy of Western Office Equipment Company (Part IV) influences how the managers inside the company can (or cannot) apply management science to the allocation of sales representatives to San Francisco and Salt Lake City.

## ORGANIZATION DESIGN AS A FUNCTION AND RESPONSIBILITY OF MANAGERS

Regardless of whether one thinks that organizations in general are "good" or "bad" (there are both kinds in the world), they are a fact of life. They exist in primitive societies when a group of men fish together and sell their fish to others. They exist in developing countries such as Iran and Ethiopia, where society needs goods and services at an economical cost. They exist in societies such as Russia, the United States, and Denmark with highly developed exchange economies, in which almost nobody can do without the goods and services produced by organized corporations, firms hospitals, government offices, and airlines.

The first step in organization is clearly to assess the environment outside the organization and set goals that are in tune with the demands of society. Goals in turn determine what work, tasks, and technology are necessary to produce the goal. Given air transportation, some manager or group of managers must think out the various tasks and specializations, and the various coordinating procedures or positions which connect these positions (the interrelationships between tasks and specializations). The ticket seller must be related to the baggage handler, the pilot to the scheduling manager, the food service producers to the stewardesses, and so on.

## THE PRACTICE OF ORGANIZATION DESIGN

Three of the cases in Part II show how practicing managers must translate the goals of the company into an organization structure that will accomplish these goals.

In California Federal Savings and Loan Association, there are two primary output goals: a service to savings customers who put their money in the association, and a service to homeowners who borrow money from the association. The association has been designed so that these two jobs are performed in positions (or roles) scattered throughout the branch offices in different parts of California.

At the headquarters' office, there are a series of headquarters staff positions, each of which has the duty of proposing strategies which will satisfy the customer, and designing a network of roles which, if performed, will produce the service. The vice president for savings is supposed to find out what savings customers really want and design jobs to produce savings services. The vice president for loans is supposed to find out what homeowners want and design jobs that will produce appropriate loan services.

The job of headquarters staff vice Presidents is thus (1) strategic planning and (2) organization design.

In addition to specifying the *work* to be done in a given position, the organization design problem always involves designing a second kind of specification. Designers must specify the *relationships* which must exist *between* different positions to produce the final service for the customer. Some of these relationships are for technical coordination. They may be called workflow design, or procedural design. Others are for human cooperation. They often specify whether relationships are to be one of authority, one of advice, or one of informal influence.

The case demonstrates how the savings vice president went about designing services that met customer needs (strategic planning) and splitting up the work to be done between different operating positions in the branches (organization design). It also presents the president with the problem of the *relationship* between the headquarters staff person and the branch managers.

The problem of defining relationships is also facing managers in Shoe Corporation of Illinois. In an industry dominated by large successful companies, here is a smaller company which has gained a niche that others cannot duplicate. It has achieved a quickness of style change, which fulfills an important demand by women who buy shoes. This quickness is achieved by assigning jobs to sales representatives, plant employees, and designers and then specifying certain relationships between them. The key to success has been quick coordination and cooperation. However, as the case unfolds we see that the formal organization design (the job descriptions and specified relationships) simply is not working in practice. To maintain its strategy in the outside world, Shoe Corporation managers must now redesign the organization. Failure to do so may well jeopardize their ability to continue satisfying customers.

Finally, General Machinery Corporation produces an entirely different set of products from California Federal Savings and Loan Association and Shoe Corporation of Illinois. It is a successful producer of automotive parts—ignitions, carburetors, and electrical equipment. But its strategy problem and organizational problem is exactly the same in certain important respects. It has achieved success by supplying customers with something inherently useful and wanted. This "something" turns out to be a combination of (1) high-quality parts invented through its own research laboratories, and (2) a lower price to the consumer through mass-production methods. The *operating* departments are designed to specialize in products that perform different needs for the customer. One division specializes in electronic parts, another in marine parts instead of automotive. At the same time, the Central Research Laboratory contains scientists who are supposed to invent new products for the operating departments to manufacture and sell. As in the other cases, the management of General Machinery Corporation faces the problem not only of designing position descriptions which specify what operators and researchers *do* but other specifications which describe *how they are related to* each other. Unless management can design a workable structure, the whole strategy of supplying customers with high-quality new technology at a low price may be in jeopardy.

# 1. YARWAY CORPORATION

---

## Case Introduction

---

**SYNOPSIS**

For its first 50 years, the Yarway Corporation remained a small private firm serving the domestic power industry with a narrow range of highly engineered products. The firm entered its second half century with an old plant, old products, and aging top management. A new management team took over and launched a far-reaching renewal program. New products were developed. Penetration was achieved in new domestic and foreign markets. Through a licensee, a joint venture partner, and three foreign wholly owned subsidiaries, Yarway initiated international operations in the Far East, Latin America, Canada, and Europe. At home, Yarway spanned the North American continent with a wholly owned subsidiary on the West Coast and a new headquarters/plant complex on the East Coast. Organization building, domestically and internationally, occupied Yarway management in the first half of the 1970s. Despite deep recession, Yarway performed well, entering the second half of the 70s with confidence in their four closely related businesses serving the power and process industries.

**WHY THIS CASE IS INCLUDED**

The Yarway case is an excellent vehicle for practicing a strategic review. The student can explore the determinants of strategy—both those outside and inside the firm. Opportunity-seeking is more the mood of this undisguised case, rather than problem solving in one more pathological case. After a strategy review, students can test their understanding of the strategy/structure linkage by examining the adequacy of Yarway's organization structure in supporting the implementation of Yarway's strategy.

**DIAGNOSTIC AND PREDICTIVE QUESTIONS**

The readings included with this case are marked (*). The author index at the end of this book locates the other readings.

1. What specific threats and opportunities in the external environment (beyond those listed by Yarway executives in the force field analysis at the end of the case) do you find relevant for a review of Yarway strategy?

Read: Gilmore, "Formulating Strategy in Smaller Companies."

2. What specific Yarway strengths and weaknesses (beyond those in the executives' force field analysis) do you find relevant for a review of Yarway strategy?

3. What evidence do you find that values have influenced strategy formulation in Yarway? What values?

Read: Andrews, *The Concept of Corporate Strategy.*

4. Do you find evidence that Yarway management has carefully asked itself the question: What is our business?

Read: Drucker, *Management—Tasks—Responsibilities—Practices.* Webster, *Marketing for Managers.*

5. By reference only to traditional organization theory evaluate the adequacy of Yarway's present organization structure. What is the primary basis for departmentation in Yarway? Are any of the traditional "principles" violated in Yarway's current structure?

Read: *Carzo and Yanouzas, *Formal Organization: A Systems Approach.*

6. As Yarway has become international, has it followed the historical patterns of other U.S. firms? Are there any predictions you would make from the experiences of others for Yarway as it goes further in its internationalization?

Read: Kolde, *International Business Enterprise.* Those who wish an additional analysis of the evolving organization of multinational enterprises, consult in the library John Stoppford and Louis T. Wells, *Managing the International Enterprise* (Basic Books, 1972), Chapter 2.

7. What are the key issues in Yarway strategy that might prompt a restructuring of the firm? Is the present structure adequate to support Yarway's strategy for the 70s?

Read: *Chandler, Strategy and Structure.* Or see Stoppford and Wells, *Managing the Multinational Enterprise,* Chapter 2, as cited above.

8. Examine the role of the executive vice president vis-à-vis the president in light of the conceptual schemes provided by Katz and Kahn, Levinson, and McGrath. Under what conditions would this be a viable role?

Read: Katz and Kahn, *The Social Psychology of Organizations.* Levinson, "Role, Personality, and Social Structure in the Organizational Setting." McGrath, *Social Psychology.*

**POLICY QUESTIONS**

9. Do you think Yarway's strategy for the 70s is realistic in light of market forces and Yarway's capacities? (Review your answers to Questions 2 to 5.)

Read:   Tilles, "How to Evaluate Corporate Strategy."

10. Can you recommend any strategic changes for Yarway for the next five years? Be specific in the following areas: (*a*) product development, (*b*) market development, (*c*) financial.

Review your responses to Questions 1–4.

11. In what way would you propose modifying the Yarway organization structure? Don't forget to take account of the people currently in top management positions. Give reasons for both the changes and the timing of the reorganization.

Review your responses to Questions 5–7.

Read:   Leavitt, *Managerial Psychology,* pp. 317–25.

12. How would you allocate roles to the president and executive vice president within your proposed structure?

Review your responses to Question 8.

---

# Case Text*

---

In the year 1975, Yarway continued its success pattern of the 70s. Despite the recession, the record of achievement showed that Yarway was in the right markets, with the right products, at the right time. Maintaining such a posture worldwide seemed a manageable task for 1976. The longer term challenge was one of sustained balance and performance in the portfolio of business units, in products, in industries served, and in geographical markets covered.

Can Yarway, a moderate-sized, independent company, survive and prosper in the emerging world of supergiant, multinational firms? What would be the future mix among: the historical business, the new field represented by the efforts to develop products and markets in the chemical process industries, and the still newer pollution control service business launched in Connecticut in 1975? Would profitable growth be achieved and maintained in these new businesses without neglecting the traditional one? Would the product mix still serve the basic industrial functions of process measurement and control, heat transfer, liquid storage, and distribution? Would there be more demand for functioning systems rather than products as components? Would the product technology move further along the scale from mechanical to electromechanical, to

---

electronic and then to such technologies as ultrasonics? Would the basic industrial functions continue to be served mainly in the process and power generation (nuclear and fossil-fueled) industries? What changes lay ahead in the pattern of geographic markets, until recently concentrated in the United States and growing in Canada, Europe, and Japan?

## EARLY HISTORY OF THE YARWAY CORPORATION

Three enterprising men—an engineer, a salesman, and a financial backer—founded the firm in 1908 in Philadelphia, Pennsylvania, to serve particularly the power industry with high-quality, proprietary, power plant equipment like valves and pipe couplings. The firm enjoyed steady and profitable growth until the early 50s. At that stage, sales volume had reached $4 million and the products were well established in the domestic market. Exports from the one plant in Philadelphia represented a small percentage of the total volume. The management, still with one of the founders at the top, concentrated on more in-company issues than on the market or competitive environment. Personnel administration consumed much time—job evaluation, wage and salary administration, in-plant communications, establishement of wage incentives, and negotiation of the first union contract. The late 50s were marked by progress in sales forecasting, budgeting, market research, cost control, and the establishment of a merit rating system.

As a new management team took over from the last of the founders in 1962, sales volume stood at $5.8 million but profitability had slipped. The percentage of exports had increased somewhat and some products—notably steam traps—were being manufactured and sold under license in Canada, United Kingdom, France, and Japan. Some important product lines were growing obsolete and had entered the mature phase of the product life cycle. The single plant was now old and crowded.

The new president, D. Robert Yarnall, Jr., had been with the firm since 1949 in the successive positions of personnel director, works manager, and manufacturing vice president. He began the renewal of the company by building a new management team and collaborating with them in formulating basic policies, corporate objectives, strategic guidelines for product, market, acquisitions, and financial management. Under his leadership, the new seven-man team concentrated on a two-pronged effort of running the current operations more effectively and building for the future. They inaugurated an annual planning cycle in which targets were set in five areas (profitability, sales volume, market standing, products, and corporate capability) and reviewed at the end of the year. As first priority, Yarway began renovating existing product lines and searching for new products. During the first half of the 60s, Yarway invested in an expanded training effort and started a stock option plan for executives. By 1965, the company was issuing an annual report, though it was still a private company, and could boast of a 60 percent increase in sales and a 100 percent increast in return on net worth since the succession of the new management team.

## DECADE OF RENEWAL: 1961–1971

After the first decade under the new management, the company had taken on a new look. Financially (see Appendixes A to D), the company had weathered a relatively bad year in 1968 (soft market and heavy expenditures on new headquarters and plants in the United States and Europe and on product development) to show more than a 300 percent sales growth and over a 410 percent profit growth in the decade.

**EXHIBIT 1**
**Financial Comparison (1961–1971)**

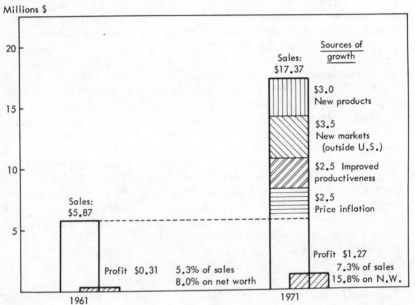

Millions $

Sales: $17.37

Sources of growth

$3.0
New products

$3.5
New markets (outside U.S.)

$2.5 Improved productiveness

$2.5
Price inflation

Sales: $5.87

Profit $1.27
7.3% of sales
15.8% on N.W.

Profit $0.31    5.3% of sales
8.0% on net worth

1961                                 1971

As is clear from Exhibit 1, penetration of new markets abroad, particularly by the replacement of European licensees with wholly owned subsidiaries, and commercialization of new products contributed heavily to the company's growth. In facilities, replacing the one old plant in Philadelphia, Yarway in 1971 had new headquarters and plant (180,000 square feet—one third, offices, two thirds, plant) in suburban Philadelphia, as well as new plants in its wholly owned subsidiaries in Canada (15,000 square feet), Great Britain (5,600 square feet), and the Netherlands (19,500 square feet). Yarway was effectively represented in Japan by Gadelius, K.K., and high priority was being given to building even stronger relationships with this exclusive agent and manufacturing licensee (steam traps). A joint venture company in Brazil had begun to make deliveries of locally manufactured Yarway steam traps in Latin America. As of 1970, Yarway acquired Kingman-White, Inc., of California to obtain a unique new product, the solids flow transmitter. The decade of renewal ended with virtually worldwide market coverage and with new and better products.

Internally, the decade of renewal witnessed the introduction of a management by objectives system for all "exempt" employees, which was tied directly to a bonus system offering significant payoff for high-quality performance on agreed targets. Those eligible for bonus in the United States shared, according to their performance rating and job grade, in a "pot" determined as 20 percent of pretax profits in the United States. The bonus for someone eligible in a wholly owned subsidiary was based on the profitability of his subsidiary in a similar manner.

Another step forward within Yarway was the introduction of an integrated, computer-based, management information system. For this purpose and others, the company followed the practice of using cross-functional project teams.

In the period of growth, 232 new jobs were created, bringing the total employment in 1971 to 540. Of this number, 140 were "exempt" (professional, administrative, and sales engineers) and 400 office and plant staff (180 clerical, technicians, etc., and 220 direct and indirect labor). Average yearly pay had moved from $8,100 in 1961 to $12,400 in 1971.

### Organization Building: 1971–1975

Measured against its own explicit objectives, Yarway did very well under difficult market conditions in the first half of the 70s. Quantitative profit and growth targets were met or exceeded each year. The company reported on-target performance each year on its other three objectives: market standing, product innovation, and upgrading of internal resources. In phases, and without the use of consultants, Yarway developed and introduced during this period an organization form appropriate to the conduct of current business as well as to the building of tomorrow's business. Up to September 1969 Yarway had a functional organization (see Exhibit 2).

Until mid-1972, the Yarway structure was essentially as shown in Exhibit 3.

As the business grew more complex with new typesofproducts,new types of customers, and new geographic markets, strain began to show

**EXHIBIT 2**
**Yarway Organization Chart (up to September 1969)**

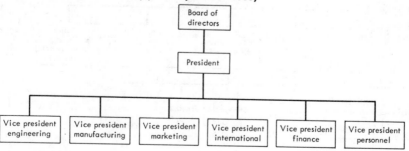

**EXHIBIT 3**
**Yarway Organization Chart (mid-1972)**

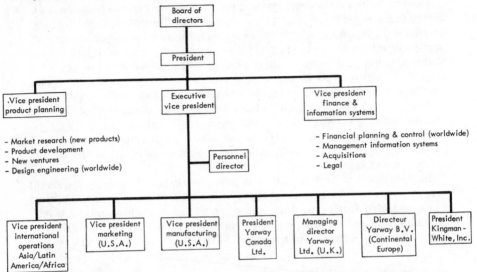

in the structure. Symptomatically, the span of control for the executive vice president became extremely demanding. Concern grew over the slow pace of commercialization of new products. Starting in 1972, the structure in Exhibit 4 gradually emerged so that, as of early 1976, all units are in place and staffed except that the executive vice president temporarily doubles as president, Yarway North America.

**EXHIBIT 4**

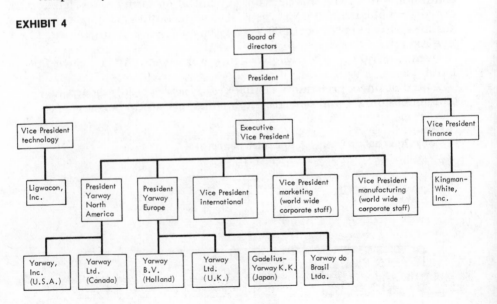

The president is the chief executive officer and as such is accountable to the board of directors for overall company performance. The president and his three immediate colleagues work as a team in strategic matters. The president delegates day-to-day supervision of the established business to the executive vice president and manages by exception but for his involvement in overall policy, planning, and control. The executive vice president chairs the operations team composed of his five or six immediate subordinates. The vice president, technology, is responsible for worldwide product planning and development as well as new ventures. The vice president, finance, currently has responsibility for overseeing Kingman-White, Inc., in addition to his regular job of financial planning and control and management information systems.

(See Appendix E for profiles of the top executives.)

During this period of organization building, each geographical area underwent significant change. The two European operating companies were drawn together administratively under the Netherlands-based Yarway Europe flag. A similar "regional" structure emerged in North America. Equally important in North America was the new structure of marketing specialization introduced in 1973. Three main product groups (see Appendix F) were singled out and distinct marketing teams were formed for each, including customer service, and product application competence. Each team served four market zones across North America. In 1974 Yarway increased its participation in its Brazilian joint venture, Yarway do Brasil Ltda., to 45 percent.

As of July 1975, the long-standing licensee and representative in Japan joined Yarway in a 50/50 joint venture, Gadelius-Yarway K.K. This joint venture manufactures steam traps and other products in Japan and markets throughout East Asia.

In a number of products, Yarway competes with firms of about its own size (as in steam traps) and has the competitive advantage of better worldwide coverage. In the early stage products Yarway simultaneously encounters some larger competitors as well as a host of small, specialized producers.

The purchasing decisions on virtually all the products involve multiple parties—consulting engineers, engineering contractors, original equipment manufacturers, and end users. To sell its engineered products, Yarway employs some 80 sales engineers, in the United States, Canada, United Kingdom, Germany, and the Netherlands. It has a network of sales agents in Japan, France, Italy, Australia, Mexico, and Western Canada, as well as an exclusive distributor organization in North America for the steam trap line. Backing up the sales effort are applications engineers in the United States, Canada, United Kingdom, and the Netherlands.

Yarway products can be roughly classed in the three stages of the product life cycle: (*a*) mature, (*b*) growth, (*c*) early. Among the mature stage products are the valves, gauges, and expansion joints used primarily in power plants and the impulse steam traps. Leading items among the growth stage products are the metering pumps and specialty

**EXHIBIT 5**
**YARWAY CORPORATION 1975—WORLDWIDE MARKET POSITION**

| Markets / Products | United States and Canada | | | | EEC and EFTA | | Japan and Far East | | Other Areas | | Sales Totals by Product Class |
|---|---|---|---|---|---|---|---|---|---|---|---|
| | Estimated Total Market (millions) | Annual Market Growth (percentage) | Yarway Sales (millions) | Yarway Market Share (percentage) | Yarway Sales (millions) | Yarway Market Share (percentage) | Yarway Sales (millions) | Yarway Market Share (percentage) | Yarway Sales (millions) | Yarway Market Share (percentage) | (millions) |
| Mature stage | $ 70 | 2% | $18.9 | 27% | $3.5 | 4% | $2.6 | 15% | $1.3 | 6% | $26.3 |
| Growth stage | 128 | 10 | 3.9 | 3 | 0.7 | — | 0.1 | — | 1.1 | — | 5.6 |
| Early stage | 150 | 10 | 0.5 | — | — | — | — | — | — | — | 0.5 |
| Area sales totals | | | $23.3 | | $4.2 | | $2.7 | | $2.4 | | $32.4* |

* The total is larger than that reported in the annual report because it includes sales of nonconsolidated subsidiaries.

control valves. Representative of the early stage products in the field of specialty instrumentation is the solids flow transmitter. The technology of the mature products is essentially mechanical engineering in the context of thermodynamics. The growth and early stage products bring the company into control technology.

Financially, signs of progress are evident during the 1971–75 period (see Exhibit 6).

**EXHIBIT 6**

|  | 1971 (*in millions*) | 1975 (*in millions*) |
| --- | --- | --- |
| Sales | $17,370 | $30,530 |
| Profit | 1,270 | 2,380 |
| Percent profit on sales | 7.3% | 7.8% |
| Percent profit on net worth | 15.8% | 19.0% |

## YARWAY LOOKS AHEAD

The Yarway management team continues to refine and elaborate the strategy for the 70s. As many as 30 of the top executives contribute to the strategic review led by the president and his immediate associates who are actively involved. The statement below outlines the most recent thinking captured in the "Planning Guide" revised in April 1974. Any such review is done in the spirit of the "Basic Policies" (see Appendix G) as reviewed and approved periodically by the board of directors.

### Corporate Purpose

Yarway Corporation exists to serve people throughout the world by supplying excellent products and services to those basic industries which meet human needs for electricity, fuel, paper, food, fiber, chemicals, and transportation.

### Values/Beliefs

1. Excellence and integrity in all that we do.
2. Worthwhile social contributions.
3. Worldwide scope of activities and attitudes.
4. Self-determination with appropriate accountability.

### Accountability of Yarway Management

1. We are accountable to our *Customers* for satisfying their needs with products and services that give them optimum value in terms of performance and reliability.
2. We are accountable to our *Employees* for providing opportunity, compensation, and supervision, in accordance with the Basic Policies in an environment where each person can find meaning and satisfaction

in his work and where all employees recognize their common interest in continuing achievement of Corporate Objectives.

3. We are accountable to our *Stockholders* for achieving Corporate Objectives and for operating the company in accordance with the Basic Policies for Yarway Corporation.

4. We are accountable to our *Suppliers* for representing our needs honestly, dealing with them ethically, and paying them promptly.

5. We are accountable to the *Community* for operating a company that obeys the law, is a good neighbor, and supports worthwhile community undertakings.

## Corporate Objectives

1. *Profitability*
   For the corporation as a whole, earnings per share should average at least 12 to 15 percent of shareholders' equity (net worth) to accomplish the following:
   a.  *Earn and retain stockholders' confidence.*
   b.  Generate new capital to finance growth.
   c.  Provide for employee profit sharing.
   In this type of business it appears that a net profit rate of at least 7 percent of sales is required to achieve a 12 percent return on shareholders' equity.
   Profit goals and performance of individual operating divisions will be evaluated on the basis of return on assets employed (R.O.A.) and net profit margin as a percent of sales.

2. *Growth*
   The corporation as a whole should grow fast enough to accomplish the following:
   a.  Make profitable use of available resources, including reinvested cash flow and borrowing power.
   b.  Provide purpose and opportunity for present and prospective employees.
   Growth is a result of doing the right things, and not an end in itself. The growth of individual operating divisions will be evaluated in terms of available opportunities and the maturity of the particular business.

3. *Market Standing*
   We aspire to become the highly regarded primary supplier for each business we undertake and seek to do so on a worldwide basis. Overdependence on any single customer, industry, market or product line should be avoided.

4. *Products*
   Products and/or services should be added, extended, or improved as required to satisfy the business plans of the Yarway divisions and/or companies.

Products and/or services should be added to take advantage of unusual opportunities to utilize more effectively the resources of the corporation.

5. *Capability and Productiveness*
   Demonstrable improvements should be made each year in the capability and productiveness of the company's human resources, physical resources, and systems, procedures and controls.

## Overall Corporate Strategies

Products/Services

1. Sell products and/or services which:
   a. Build on strengths and capitalize on resources.
   b. Serve worthwhile purposes.
   c. Meet customers' needs or solve a customer's problem.
   d. Offer excellence and dependable value.
   e. Imply reasonable risk/reward ratio.
   f. Are proprietary if possible.
2. Sell products and/or services which can be differentiated from those of competitors by criteria that matter to customers (by benefits rather than price).
3. Specific Product/Market Strategies have been developed for the following Yarway businesses:
   a. Power plant business.
   b. Steam trap business.
   c. Chemical process industries business.
   d. Pollution control business.

Markets Served

1. Sell to industries which grow because they serve basic human needs (such as electricity, fuel, paper, food, fiber, chemicals, and transportation).
2. Worldwide scope, with particular emphasis on the highly industrialized regions—North America, Latin America, Europe, and Japan.
3. Aim at market segments which are specialized enough to provide opportunity for a moderate-sized company to gain substantial market share.

Technology

1. Geared to identifying and serving present and future customers' needs.
2. Seek inventions, concepts, and know-how, in-house as well as throughout the world—avoid "NIH" (not-invented-here) bias.
3. Emphasis on the "D" of R&D, aimed at achieving and maintaining product leadership.

Manufacturing

1. Maintain "in-house" the capabilities that are required to preserve proprietary values and know-how, assure that customers are satisfied with quality and deliveries and which make sense in terms of ROI.
2. Beyond that, utilize the capabilities of others in order to maximize flexibility and minimize investment intensity—avoid "NMH" bias.
3. Seek rational balance of manufacturing capability in North America, Latin America, Europe, and Japan.

Methods of Sale

1. Sell customer benefits at prices which reflect their value.
2. Avoid overdependence on a single customer or industry.
3. Concentrate marketing expenditures on those businesses which offer good potential to build market share.
4. In mature business, invest enough in marketing to hold market share and concentrate on profitability.
5. Understand the relative inelasticity of demand in industrial equipment markets.
6. Capitalize on, preserve, and promote the name "YARWAY."

Methods of Distribution

1. Flexible approach in the selection of distribution channels.

Organization/Skills

1. Organization structure, staffing, and development to facilitate:
   *a.* Planning and managing today's business successfully.
   *b.* Identifying and building tomorrow's new businesses.
   *c.* Worldwide control of product and financial commitments.
2. Integrated system for goal setting, planning, accountability for results, performance appraisal, and reward sharing.
3. Above-average people, performance, and compensation.

Methods of Financing

1. Maintain sufficient financial assets (including equity, cash flow, and borrowing power) to meet the capital needs of present businesses and make it possible to move quickly when new opportunities are presented.

Size

1. We aspire to build the best company we are capable of building rather than the biggest."

When asked to assess Yarway's strengths and weaknesses for surviving and prospering through the 70s, a small group of top executives produced the following assessment under four headings: (1) external driving forces, (2) external restraining forces, (3) internal driving forces, and (4) internal restraining forces.

## FORCE FIELD ANALYSIS—YARWAY CORPORATION

### External Driving Forces

1. Our markets are the world's basic industries which must meet the steadily growing human needs for power fuels, paper, food, textiles, and shipping.
2. Worldwide demand for higher quality and more sophisticated industrial equipment favors our type of new and better products.
3. Our customers (and the engineering-contractor firms serving them) are becoming increasingly internationalized in their specification and purchase of equipment.
4. Competitors in most lines do not have worldwide market coverage.
5. Growing concern for environment provides good opportunities for pollution control products.

### External Restraining Forces

1. The type of customers we serve are conservative by nature in their purchase of equipment. They are slow to adopt *any* new product or supplier and the process of convincing them to do is slow and costly. (It's nice when you are accepted, however!)
2. Engineers and buyers sometimes have nationalistic feelings which are reflected in codes, purchasing preferences, and so on.
3. The growing concern for environment may slow up the rate of construction of new plants in the power and process industries in the 70s.
4. Local competitive products are increasingly likely to appear in the market as industrialization progresses around the world.
5. The growing tendency to contract for complete systems tends to favor captive equipment suppliers under some circumstances.

### Internal Driving Forces

1. Top management:
   a. Ability and willingness to manage.
   b. Commitment to achievement of excellent results and aspiration to operate effectively on a world scale.
   c. Global viewpoint and growing international experience.
   d. Understand importance of both current operations and building tomorrow's business.
2. Common purpose and mutual trust among major stockholders, board of directors, management, and employees:
   a. Basic policies.
   b. Planning guide.
   c. Management by objectives and appraisal by results with strong rewards system.
   d. Team building—task forces.

3. Continuous product innovation:
    *a.* Defined objectives and strategies.
    *b.* Search, screening, appraisal, and trial venture techniques.
    *c.* Patents and other proprietary values.
    *d.* Pipeline is filled and flowing.
4. International network established:
    *a.* Wholly owned marketing and manufacturing companies in United States, Canada, EEC, and United Kingdom.
    *b.* Jointly owned marketing and manufacturing companies in Japan and Brazil.
    *c.* Sales agents in most countries of the world.
5. Good well-established reputation:
    *a.* Founded in 1908.
    *b.* Well known (at least in Anglo-Saxon markets).
    *c.* Strong customer loyalty.

## Internal Restraining Forces

1. Top management:
    *a.* The fact that ability and vision are limited.
    *b.* Some success already achieved may diminish willingness to take risks.
    *c.* Good international managers willing to go anywhere are hard to find.
2. Stock not publicly traded:
    *a.* Limits its attractiveness as currency for acquisitions.
    *b.* Limits visibility of the company in financial circles.
3. Polycentric rewards system:
    *a.* Bonuses of subsidiary managers now based on profitability of the subsidiary rather than the consolidated corporation.
4. Strategies intended to put primary emphasis on survival and profitability rather than growth of sales, for example:
    *a.* Commitment to be the *best,* not the *biggest.*
    *b.* Concentrate on products of a *specialty* nature.
    *c.* Centralize control of *products* and *finances.*
5. Marketing:
    *a.* Sales capacity may not be strong enough to penetrate the new customers in the worldwide process industries with the emerging control and instrumentation products."

# APPENDIX A

### YARWAY CORPORATION
Consolidated Balance Sheet
December 27, 1975 and December 28, 1974

*Assets*

| | December 27, 1975 | December 28, 1974 |
|---|---|---|
| Current assets: | | |
| Cash | $ 1,074,250 | $ 787,163 |
| Accounts receivable | 8,676,805 | 6,499,798 |
| Inventories, at lower of cost or market | 9,466,051 | 7,098,846 |
| Other current assets | 241,354 | 260,288 |
| Total current assets | $19,458,460 | $14,646,095 |
| Investments in affiliates | 361,134 | 192,062 |
| Property, plant and equipment, at cost: | | |
| Land | 413,033 | 327,151 |
| Buildings and improvements | 4,122,621 | 3,785,287 |
| Machinery and equipment | 6,177,525 | 4,462,447 |
| | 10,713,179 | 8,574,885 |
| Less accumulated depreciation | 4,323,521 | 3,737,154 |
| Net property, plant and equipment | $ 6,389,658 | $ 4,837,731 |
| Intangible assets, at cost, less amortizator | 748,084 | 207,838 |
| Other assets | 42,576 | 59,888 |
| | $26,999,912 | $19,943,614 |

*Liabilities and Shareholders' Equity*

| | December 27, 1975 | December 28, 1974 |
|---|---|---|
| Current liabilities: | | |
| Notes payable to banks | $ 1,480,700 | $ 3,058,636 |
| Accounts payable | 914,838 | 1,497,231 |
| Taxes on income | 1,088,971 | 615,467 |
| Accrued salaries, wages and bonus | 1,733,062 | 1,339,683 |
| Other accrued liabilities | 924,345 | 625,264 |
| Long-term debt due within one year | 167,683 | 72,000 |
| Total current liabilities | $ 6,309,599 | $ 7,208,281 |
| Long-term debt | 6,305,887 | 200,673 |
| Shareholders' equity | | |
| Common stock, $1 par value; 2,000,000 shares authorized; 681,490 issued (681,325 in 1974) | 681,490 | 681,325 |
| Capital in excess of par value | 1,032,210 | 1,029,355 |
| Retained earnings | 12,732,896 | 10,886,150 |
| | 14,446,596 | 12,596,830 |
| Less 3,212 shares of common stock held in treasury, at cost | 62,170 | 62,170 |
| Total shareholders' equity | $14,384,426 | $12,534,660 |
| | $26,999,912 | $19,943,614 |

# APPENDIX B

YARWAY CORPORATION
Consolidated Statement of Income
Years Ended December 27, 1975 and December 28, 1974

|  | December 27, 1975 | December 28, 1974 |
|---|---|---|
| Net sales | $30,525,033 | $23,601,697 |
| Operating costs and expenses: |  |  |
| Cost of sales | 15,041,836 | 11,912,959 |
| Selling, administrative and general expenses | 10,514,828 | 8,477,878 |
|  | $25,556,664 | $20,390,837 |
| Operating profit | 4,968,369 | 3,210,860 |
| Interest expense | 480,739 | 210,554 |
|  | $ 4,487,630 | $ 3,000,306 |
| Other income | $ 22,955 | 34,133 |
| Income before income taxes and other items listed below | $ 4,510,585 | $ 3,034,439 |
| Provision for income taxes: |  |  |
| Federal | 1,400,700 | 993,000 |
| State | 221,300 | 149,000 |
| Foreign | 491,000 | 304,000 |
|  | $ 2,113,000 | $ 1,446,000 |
|  | 2,397,585 | 1,588,439 |
| Equity in net loss of affiliate | 61,788 | 68,788 |
| Income before extraordinary item | $ 2,335,797 | $ 1,519,651 |
| Extraordinary item |  |  |
| Tax benefit of net operating loss carryovers of subsidiaries: |  |  |
| Federal |  | 45,000 |
| Foreign | 40,000 | 75,000 |
|  | $ 40,000 | $ 120,000 |
| Net income | $ 2,375,797 | $ 1,639,651 |
| Earnings per average common share: |  |  |
| Income before extraordinary item | $3.44 | $2.24 |
| Extraordinary item | .06 | .18 |
| Net income | $3.50 | $2.42 |

# APPENDIX C

### YARWAY CORPORATION
Consolidated Statement of Changes in Financial Position
Years Ended December 27, 1975 and December 28, 1974

|  | 1975 | 1974 |
|---|---|---|
| **Source:** | | |
| Income before extraordinary item | $2,335,797 | $1,519,651 |
| Items not affecting working capital in the current period: | | |
| Depreciation and amortization | 750,648 | 547,040 |
| Equity in net loss of affiliate | 61,788 | 68,788 |
| Working capital provided from operations exclusive of extraordinary item | $3,148,233 | $2,135,479 |
| Extraordinary item | | |
| Tax benefit of net operating loss carryovers of subsidiaries | 40,000 | 120,000 |
| Proceeds from issuance of common stock | 3,020 | 88,930 |
| Proceeds from long-term debt | 6,255,454 | |
| Decrease in other assets | 17,312 | |
| | $9,464,019 | $2,344,409 |
| **Disposition:** | | |
| Additions to property, plant and equipment | 2,287,771 | 871,686 |
| Dividends paid | 529,051 | 475,819 |
| Investments in affiliates | 230,860 | 260,850 |
| Reduction of long-term debt | 150,240 | 59,580 |
| Purchases of treasury stock | | 55,000 |
| Additions to intangible assets | 555,050 | 70,950 |
| Increase in other assets | | 46,083 |
| | $3,752,972 | $1,839,968 |
| Increase in working capital | $5,711,047 | $ 504,441 |
| **Changes in components of working capital:** | | |
| Increase (decrease) in current assets: | | |
| Cash | $ 287,087 | $ 188,160 |
| Accounts receivable | 2,177,007 | 1,711,199 |
| Inventories | 2,367,205 | 1,885,285 |
| Other current assets | (18,934) | 55,323 |
| | $4,812,365 | $3,839,967 |
| Increase (decrease) in current liabilities: | | |
| Notes payable to banks | (1,577,936) | 2,408,636 |
| Accounts payable | (582,393) | 916,634 |
| Taxes on income | 473,504 | 232,722 |
| Accrued salaries, wages and bonus | 393,379 | 69,216 |
| Other accrued liabilities | 299,081 | 320,213 |
| Long-term debt due within one year | 95,683 | (611,895) |
| | (898,682) | 3,335,526 |
| Increase in working capital | $5,711,047 | $ 504,441 |

# APPENDIX D

## YARWAY CORPORATION AND SUBSIDIARIES
### Ten-Year Financial Report

| | 1975 | 1974 | 1973 | 1972 | 1971 | 1970 | 1969 | 1968 | 1967 | 1966 |
|---|---|---|---|---|---|---|---|---|---|---|
| **Operations (thousands of dollars):** | | | | | | | | | | |
| Net sales | $30,525 | $23,602 | $20,260 | $17,765 | $17,378 | $16,108 | $14,318 | $12,829 | $11,947 | $11,150 |
| Income before taxes | 4,511 | 3,034 | 3,047 | 2,415 | 2,504 | 1,811 | 1,203 | 721 | 1,308 | 1,885 |
| Net income‡ | 2,376 | 1,640 | 1,654 | 1,308 | 1,277 | 808 | 492 | 165 | 675 | 984 |
| Dividends paid | 529 | 476 | 417 | 349 | 331 | 295 | 252 | 200 | 260 | 239 |
| **Financial (thousands of dollars):** | | | | | | | | | | |
| Current assets | 19,458 | 14,646 | 10,806 | 9,883 | 8,576 | 8,501 | 8,257 | 8,201 | 6,611 | 6,287 |
| Current liabilities | 6,310 | 7,208 | 3,873 | 3,920 | 3,277 | 3,909 | 3,616 | 3,738 | 2,325 | 1,750 |
| Working capital | 13,148 | 7,438 | 6,933 | 5,963 | 5,299 | 4,592 | 4,641 | 4,463 | 4,286 | 4,537 |
| Fixed, intangible and other assets | 7,542 | 5,298 | 4,664 | 4,928 | 5,080 | 5,349 | 5,597 | 5,897 | 6,063 | 2,423 |
| Long-term debt | 6,306 | 201 | 260 | 804 | 1,347 | 1,881 | 2,688 | 3,077 | 3,472 | 539 |
| Shareholders' equity (net worth) | 14,384 | 12,535 | 11,337 | 10,086 | 9,031 | 8,060 | 7,551 | 7,283 | 6,877 | 6,421 |
| **General:** | | | | | | | | | | |
| Common shares outstanding*† | 678,278 | 678,113 | 672,463 | 671,108 | 661,640 | 659,100 | 659,400 | 654,650 | 647,900 | 639,340 |
| **Per share of stock:** | | | | | | | | | | |
| Net worth*† | 21.21 | 18.48 | 16.86 | 15.03 | 13.65 | 12.23 | 11.45 | 11.13 | 10.61 | 10.04 |
| Earnings (based on average shares)*†‡ | 3.50 | 2.42 | 2.46 | 1.95 | 1.93 | 1.23 | .75 | .25 | 1.04 | 1.54 |
| Dividends | | | | | | | | | | |
| Common shares† (formerly B shares) | .78 | .70 | .62 | .52 | .50 | .46 | .40 | .32 | .41 | .35 |
| A shares† | — | — | — | — | — | — | — | — | 3.50 | 7.00 |
| **Ratios and percentages:** | | | | | | | | | | |
| Current ratio | 3.08 | 2.03 | 2.79 | 2.52 | 2.62 | 2.17 | 2.28 | 2.19 | 2.84 | 3.59 |
| Net income to net worth (beginning of year) | 19.0% | 14.5% | 16.4% | 14.5% | 15.8% | 10.7% | 6.8% | 2.4% | 10.5% | 17.4% |
| Net income to net sales | 7.8% | 6.9% | 8.2% | 7.4% | 7.3% | 5.0% | 3.4% | 1.3% | 5.6% | 8.8% |

* Restated to combine A and B common shares in prior years. A shares were exchanged for B shares in 1967 and are designated above as "common shares."

† Restated to reflect 10 for 1 stock distribution in 1970.

‡ 1975, 1974, 1973 and 1972 include extraordinary items representing the tax benefits of operating loss carryovers of subsidiaries.

‡ Changed to Lifo method of accounting for inventories in 1974.

Yarway Corporation / Case

# APPENDIX E

## PROFILES OF YARWAY TOP EXECUTIVES

*D. Robert Yarnall, Jr.* President, chairman of the board and chief executive officer . . . 51 years old . . . graduated as mechanical engineer from Cornell University . . . previous employment with Westinghouse Electric and Leeds and Northrup Co., director of five other companies, and numerous professional and community organizations.

*Theodore B. Palmer, 3d.* Executive vice president . . . 51 years old . . . majored in economics at Princeton University . . . joined the company in 1959 in the personnel function from the Atlantic Refining Company . . . served as vice president, personnel, prior to assuming his current position in 1969.

*George I. Tyndall.* Vice president, finance . . . 56 years of age . . . business administration major at the Wharton School, University of Pennsylvania . . . joined the company as assistant accounting manager in 1959 from Collins and Aikman . . . became treasurer and secretary in 1960, then vice president, finance, in 1964.

*Frank Boni.* Vice president, technology, responsible for product planning, building tomorrow's businesses, and the maintaining of proprietary values . . . 49 years of age . . . mechanical engineer from University of Michigan . . . joined the company in 1962 from Griscom-Russell as director of engineering . . . served as vice president, engineering, prior to assuming his current position in 1970.

*William T. Griffiths.* Vice president, marketing (worldwide corporate staff) . . . 58 years of age . . . chemical engineer from the Penn State University . . . joined the company in 1969 after serving as vice president, marketing, and director of Milton Roy.

*Stanley F. Myers.* Vice president, manufacturing (worldwide corporate staff) . . . 48 years of age . . . majored in industrial management at Antioch College . . . joined the company in 1954 after working with the American Friends Service in India . . . performed a number of functions in manufacturing prior to assuming responsibility for U.S. manufacturing, then to the corporate level.

*R. Henry Seelaus.* Vice president, Yarway International . . . 55 years of age . . . business administration major at the Wharton School, University of Pennsylvania . . . joined the company in 1952 from Fischer and Porter where he had been vice president, finance . . . originally supervised all export activity and business outside the United States including creation and start up of subsidiaries in EEC, United Kingdom, and Canada . . . more recently concentrating on administration of international development activity in the Far East and Latin America.

*Anthony Vervoorn.* President, Yarway Europa B. V. . . . 47 years of age . . . Dutch . . . degree in mechanical engineering and masters degree in economics . . . joined the company in 1964 as managing director and first employee of Yarway's newly formed subsidiary in the Netherlands.

*Chiaki Uno.* President, Gadelius-Yarway, K. K. (Japan) . . . 50 years of age . . . mechanical engineer . . . 15 years of experience with the

Swedish trading and manufacturing company in Kobe, Japan, that recently formed the joint venture with Yarway.

## BOARD OF DIRECTORS

The board of directors is composed of two external directors: C. Graham Berwind, Jr., and Paul F. Miller, Jr.; representatives of two of the founders' families: David C. McClelland and John S. Stoker, Jr.; two operating executives: Theodore B. Palmer, 3d, and George I. Tyndall; and the president: D. Robert Yarnall, Jr., who also represents the third founder's family.

# *APPENDIX F*

## THE FOUR BUSINESSES OF YARWAY

1. Power plant products.
2. Steam trap products.
3. Process products.
4. Pollution control services.

**EXHIBIT F–1**
**1. Power Plant Products**

1. ARC® Values protect centrifugal pumps against overheating. An innovative, self-contained system. 2. Expansion Joints absorb contraction and expansion in steam and hot water lines. Simple, rugged construction. 3. Steam Conditioning Equipment simplifies system design. Includes compact desuperheaters (bottom) for temperature control; steam conditioning valves (top) for both pressure and temperature control. 4. Turbo Cascade® Valves employ unique cascade concept. Control pressure letdown and fluid flow with minimum wear. 5. Unit-Tandem® Valves feature two valves with common body to remove impurities from boilers. Heavy duty, compact design. 6. Indicator Systems provide continuous indication of liquid level in pressure vessels. Remote readout featured. 7. Gages provide visual readout of boiler water levels. Simply maintained. 8. Welbond® Valves feature unique in-line reseating capability. Performance proven in high pressure service.

**EXHIBIT F–2**
**Steam Trap Products**

1. and 2. Industry's largest line of thermodynamic traps efficiently removes condensafe from steam lines. Key to steam and energy conservation. 3. Integral Strainer Traps are used in high pressure marine and utility systems. Compact, easily maintained. 4. Strainers remove solids and impurities from steam lines. 5. Thermostatic Traps feature unique dual range design for faster response to a range of condensate levels.

**EXHIBIT F–3**
**Process Products**

1. Cyclo-Phram® Pumps precisely meter process fluids. Feature low maintenance, rotating plunger design. 2. Solids Flow Transmitters accurately measure mass flow of solids. Simply maintained. 3. Instrument Marking Systems record process data. Includes K-W pens, inks and chart drives. 4. Tank Valves drain process vessels. No seat to clog or leak.

**EXHIBIT F–4**
**Pollution Control Services**

Liqwacon offers liquid waste treatment services to small and medium-sized metal finishing plants within a limited geographical area.

## *APPENDIX G*

## BASIC POLICIES OF THE YARWAY CORPORATION

### Preamble

Yarway Corporation recognizes the mutual opportunities and responsibilities that characterize its relationships with its customers, employees, stockholders, suppliers, and surrounding communities. This recognition leads the board of directors and management to believe that it is desirable to publish the company's basic policies. They have been developed in the light of past history and of present circumstances. As new situations and changed circumstances develop, the board will review the basic policies and make appropriate additions or changes.

### 1. Human Values

The company should be operated to enrich the lives of all people affected by it. Every effort should be made to respect the dignity and worth of all persons. Distinctions will not be made between people because of race, religion, or national origin.

### 2. Integrity

All personnel should maintain at all times the company's tradition of integrity and high ethical and moral standards.

### 3. Opportunity

The company should provide real opportunity for each employee to develop his highest potential, and to know the satisfaction of worthwhile accomplishment in a common undertaking. All employees should be encouraged to give responsible expression to their ideas, beliefs, and convictions with the objective of advancing knowledge and understanding.

### 4. Performance and Rewards

All positions in the company should be staffed by employees who possess the personal qualities and the professional or trade qualifications required to achieve a high standard of performance in their work. The company will expect better-than-average performance of its employees and will reward such performance with better-than-average compensation compared with other companies in the same labor market and industry. A suitable bonus plan or plans, based on profits, sales, production or other measures of performance should be maintained to recognize and reward contributions to the company's success made by employees individually and collectively.

### 5. Teamwork

Management should encourage cooperation and mutual assistance between individuals and groups throughout the company. Problems should be faced promptly and squarely with emphasis on remedial and preventative action, rather than emphasis on past errors and omissions.

### 6. Supervision

Every employee who has responsibility for supervising the work of others should make sure that each of his subordinates understands clearly the results for which he is accountable. Furthermore, every supervisor should clearly establish each subordinate's freedom to act in achieving those results. Individuals and groups in the company should participate whenever practical in making decisions which affect them or about which they have useful knowledge or competence. It is recognized that such participation does not alter the accountability for results of the responsible supervisor, although it can often improve the quality of his decisions, gain better acceptance of them, and provide growth opportunities for his subordinates.

### 7. Growth

The company should grow according to plan. Growth should be in human relationships, creativeness, capability, and productiveness, as well as in sales volume and profitability. Growth should be achieved primarily by means of internal development of products and markets and secondarily by acquisition of companies or products. The rate of growth should be no faster than can be staffed by well-qualified, properly oriented, employees.

## 8. Company Objectives

Specific long-range company objectives should be recommended by management and approved by the board of directors in the following areas:

*a.* Sales volume.
*b.* Profitability.
*c.* Market standing.
*d.* Products.
*e.* Capability and productiveness.

These company objectives, along with appropriate guidelines, should be incorporated in a planning guide for use by all members of management. They should be reviewed annually by management and the board of directors to keep them relevant to changing conditions.

## 9. Planning

Management is expected to take a long-range point of view in all of its planning. Each year management should prepare detailed budgets for the next two years and a forecast of orders by product line for each of the next five years. The budgets should include shipments and gross profit for each product line, profit and loss statements, balance sheets, and major capital expenditures. Budget preparation should be intimately related to development of marketing plans, product plans, organization development plans, and financial plans.

## 10. Military Business

Planned company growth should not be made dependent upon military markets.

## 11. Products

There should be continued development of new and improved products which meet the following conditions:

*a.* New products should fulfill customer needs in a new and better way and serve worthwhile purposes.
*b.* New products should be selected to capitalize on the knowledge and resources of the company.
*c.* New product development should be directed solely toward industrial and commercial rather than military markets.
*d.* New product development should be undertaken only when sound market research promises steady, profitable sales volume.

## 12. Product Quality

Yarway products should be designed, manufactured and sold to the high standards that will provide the user with dependable value in terms of performance and reliability.

### 13. Accounting Practices

Conservative accounting practices should be followed. The maximum allowable write-off should be taken as a charge against current operations for obsolete or slow-moving inventory, depreciation, development expense, maintenance expense, and other such items. Adequate provision should be made for funding pension commitments. All accounts will be audited regularly by a certified public accountant selected by the board of directors.

### 14. Contributions

Contributions in the maximum amount allowable as tax deductions should be made each year to support charitable, educational, and religious activities, either directly or through the medium of the Yarway Foundation.

### 15. Dividend Policy

Total dividends on all classes of stock should total 4 percent of net worth at the beginning of the year.

### 16. Source of New Capital

Modernization and growth should be financed primarily from undistributed profits. When debt financing is required, total debt (including current liabilities) should not exceed 75 percent of net worth.

### 17. Profit Goals

In order to achieve the objectives and policies outlined above, the company should have earnings per share (per year) of at least 12 percent of stockholders' equity.

# Selected Readings

*From*

## FORMAL ORGANIZATION: A SYSTEMS APPROACH*

*By Rocco Carzo, Jr. and John N. Yanouzas*

### TRADITIONAL THEORY

It may be misleading and, according to some, unfair to label a theory "traditional," but we do it only in the sense that the ideas classified as traditional are the ones that prevailed in the early development of organizational theory and practice. Traditional organizational theory can be traced historically, for instance, to 19th-century prototype industrial, military, and ecclesiastic organizations.[1] In this section we lump the ideas of several contributors.

\* \* \* \* \*

### THE THEORY, IN BRIEF

As expected from the emphasis on efficiency, traditional theory prescribes an organizing process that begins with objectives. The objectives are the values that the organization seeks to achieve. Once the objectives have been determined, the next step is to determine the work necessary to achieve those objectives. For maximum efficiency, the theory specifies that the work be divided into simple tasks. Tasks are then allocated to jobs or positions, each of which requires routine and repetitive movements of a single worker. These jobs are grouped into administrative units to meet the need for coordination. There is only one boss at the head of each unit. Furthermore, each supervisor has a span of supervision, that is, each supervisor has limitations and therefore should have only a few subordinates reporting directly to him. Administrative units are then grouped into higher level administrative units. This grouping continues until the organization takes the shape of a pyramid with one supreme official at its apex. Authority to discharge the duties of each job is distributed to each jobholder. The means employed to discharge duties and the jurisdictional area of each official is delimited by laws or administrative regulations. Personnel assignments are made on the basis of the requirements of the job and each individual's ability to perform the tasks. Finally, the rewards given to organization members are based on job performance.

It is apparent from the above that the *work* required to achieve objectives and *efficiency* are the basis for the organizing process. The central problem, according to traditional theory,

---

\* Reprinted with permission from *Formal Organization: A Systems Approach,* Richard D. Irwin and the Dorsey Press, 1967. Excerpts from pp. 24, 28–34, 48–49, 54–57, 65–68.

[1] For a philosophical speculation concerning the origin of the term "traditional organizational theory," see John M. Pfiffner and Frank P. Sherwood, *Administrative Organization* (Englewood Cliffs, N.J.: Prentice-Hall, Inc., 1960), pp. 53–54.

is to make sure that work gets done efficiently through a careful definition of tasks into specialized jobs and then by coordination of the jobs through a hierarchy of administrative units. Gulick emphasizes this breakdown of work as the basis for organization in the following statement:

> . . . . Wherever many men are . . . working together the best results are secured when there is a division of work among these men. The theory of organization, therefore, has to do with the structure of co-ordination imposed upon the work-division units of enterprise. Hence, it is not possible to determine how an activity is to be organized without, at the same time, considering how the work in question is to be divided. Work division is the foundation of organization; indeed, the reason for organizing.[2]

The concepts of traditional theory that we examine in detail in this chapter and the next are: (1) departmentation; (2) unity of command; (3) size of the supervisory unit; and (4) type and amount of authority assigned and delegated to subunits of the organization.

## DEPARTMENTATION

In traditional theory, especially in the writings of Luther Gulick, four bases for grouping specialized jobs into larger specialized units or departments are provided. They are: (1) *purpose,* that is, according to an output, such as a product or service; (2) *function,* that is, according to the kind of work that must be performed; (3) *place,* that is, according to the geographical location served by the organization and/or where the work is to be done; and (4) *clientele,* that is, according to the type of persons for whom the work is done.[3] Before illustrating each of these bases for grouping specialized jobs, let us first portray specialization as the division of a large rectangle into smaller units, shown in Figure 1. This breakdown is important for the following illustrations.

**FIGURE 1**
**Breakdown of a Whole Task**

| $A_1$ | $B_1$ | $C_1$ | $D_1$ |
|---|---|---|---|
| $A_2$ | $B_2$ | $C_2$ | $D_2$ |
| $A_3$ | $B_3$ | $C_3$ | $D_3$ |
| $A_4$ | $B_4$ | $C_4$ | $D_4$ |

## Purpose Departmentation

Organization on the basis of purpose involves differentiating and grouping activities according to an output of the organization, such as a service or product. This means that all of the functions required to supply a service or product, even if the activities are dissimilar, are placed in the same group or department. For instance, if the purpose of an organization

---

[2] Gulick, "Notes on the Theory of Organization," *op. cit.,* p. 3.

[3] Gulick, *op. cit.,* pp. 15–30. These four bases of departmentation may be used simultaneously in one organization. Multiple departmentation is illustrated in subsequent sections.

**FIGURE 2**
**Departmentation on the Bases of Purpose or Function**

|  | Purposes (products) | | | |
| --- | --- | --- | --- | --- |
|  | No. 1 | No. 2 | No. 3 | No. 4 |
| Functions (activities) | $A_1$ | $A_2$ | $A_3$ | $A_4$ |
|  | $B_1$ | $B_2$ | $B_3$ | $B_4$ |
|  | $C_1$ | $C_2$ | $C_3$ | $C_4$ |
|  | $D_1$ | $D_2$ | $D_3$ | $D_4$ |

**FIGURE 3**
**Purpose Organization**

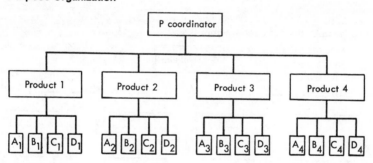

is to create four products, the functions, A, B, C, and D, required for each product would be grouped in each product department. Figure 2 depicts a case in which each of four purposes (products) require four functions. Figure 3 illustrates a grouping in terms of a traditional organizational structure.

## Functional Departmentation

Organization on the basis of functions requires the differentiation and grouping of similar work activities. All of the similar activities are grouped together and identified by some functional classification, such as manufacturing, engineering, marketing, teaching, financing, building, and transporting. In creating some values, an organization may be required, for instance, to perform 16 activities: 4 similar activities under function A, 4 under function B, 4 under function C, and 4 under function D. This type of breakdown is shown in Figure 2 by reading it horizontally. In this case, the dominant type of departmentation is based on the functions that need to be performed. Figure 4 illustrates how activities would be grouped in traditional organizational structure based on functions.

\*    \*    \*    \*    \*

**FIGURE 4**
**Functional Organization**

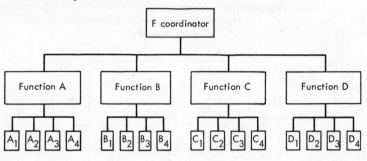

## Place Departmentation

Organization on the basis of place requires differentiation and grouping of activities according to the location where work is to be performed or an area to be served by the organization. Thus, regardless of the similarity or dissimilarity of functions and purposes, grouping is based on geographical considerations.

**FIGURE 5**
**Purpose Departmentation within Place**

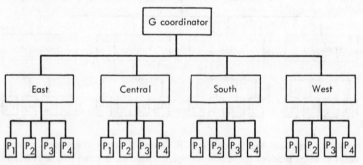

**FIGURE 6**
**Functional Departmentation within Place**

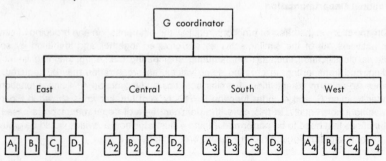

Place departmentation may occur in the same organization where there is purpose and functional departmentation. . . .

Figures 5 and 6 show purpose ($P_1$, $P_2$, $P_3$, $P_4$) and functional (A, B, C, D) departmentation within place organization. These illustrations do not, of course, exhaust all of the possible combinations of purpose, functional, and place departmentation.

### Clientele Departmentation

Organization on the basis of client involves the differentiation and grouping of activities according to the type of person or persons for whom the work is done. Client characteristics—for example, age, sex, income level, type of consumer—are the basis of departmentation. For instance, universities frequently maintain separate departments for the educational services they offer to adults and resident students. Loan departments in large banks may organize on the basis of consumer or commercial services offered to its clients. Department stores often group work on the basis of the client's sex, for instance, men's apparel versus women's apparel; or on the basis of income level, for example, bargain basements for lower income customers; or on the basis of age, for example, children's, women's, and men's clothing.

*      *      *      *      *

### ADMINISTRATION IN TRADITIONAL THEORY

In this chapter, we continue the review of traditional theory, especially as it pertains to administration. Traditional theory is very specific about the administrative structure of formal organization. Its prescriptions about the chain of command, size of supervisory unit, and the dispersion of authority, seemingly leave little doubt about administration in formal organization (in Chapter 4, we indicate that there are some doubts). The underlying premise of the traditional structure is that specialized jobs can be coordinated best by one head, or one boss, that is, there shall be unity of command. This requirement that everybody in the organization reports to only one boss gives traditional structure the appearance of a pyramid with one supreme coordinating boss at the top. We will see this structure develop as the administrative concepts of traditional theory are examined in this chapter.

### UNITY OF COMMAND

According to traditional theory, unity of command facilitates order because it charges one official with an area of responsibility and establishes a chain of command whereby every organization member knows to whom he reports and who reports to him. There is no confusion over who is responsible for organizational activities and over who gives orders and who carries them out. Unity of command forms the basis, therefore, for the hierarchy of authority because it defines the path of authority which extends from the top to the bottom of the formal organization. Fayol explained the importance of the unit of command in the following manner: "Should it be violated, authority is undermined, discipline is in jeopardy, order disturbed and stability threatened. . . . A body with two heads is in the social as in the animal sphere a monster, and has difficulty surviving."[4]

### SPAN OF SUPERVISION

*Size of Supervisory Unit.* A supervisory unit is composed of a supervisor and his immediate subordinates. The size of a supervisory unit is determined by the number of subordinates reporting to the supervisor. In traditional literature, the terms "span of control,"

---

[4] Henri Fayol, *General and Industrial Management,* trans. Constance Storrs (London: Sir Isaac Pitman & Sons, Ltd., 1963), pp. 24–25.

"span of management," and "span of supervision" have been used to denote size of the supervisory unit.

＊    ＊    ＊    ＊    ＊

Each supervisor according to traditional theory must manage not only individual subordinates but also the interactions among individuals and groups. Therefore, according to the theory, the number of subordinates reporting to any one supervisor should be limited to a very few. Traditional organization literature suggests that there exists an ideal number of subordinates that can be managed effectively by one superior.[5] This ideal ratio of subordinates to superior has been called the principle of "span of control" or "span of supervision" and is stated as follows:

> *Principle of Span of Supervision.* The number of subordinates supervised directly by a single executive should be limited to a small number. No executive should supervise directly the work of more than four or, at the most, six subordinates—especially when their work is interrelated.

## ORGANIZATIONAL AUTHORITY

When anyone, say a worker, is assigned to a work activity, he has an obligation to perform successfully—he has responsibility. Coincident with this responsibility, implicitly or explicitly, each worker has the authority to act or the authority to perform the activities required by the assigned work. Although we assume that authority and responsibility occur coincidently, it should be emphasized that the literature of organization theory usually treats them as if they are assigned separately. Writers on the subject stipulate that the assignment of authority should be equal to responsibility.[6] Urwick states, for example, the need for this balance as follows: "To hold a group or individual accountable for activities of any kind without assigning to him the necessary authority to discharge that responsibility is manifestly both unsatisfactory and inequitable."[7]

This same coincidence of authority and responsibility extends to the administrative levels of organization. In a superior-subordinate relationship, for example, the supervisor's authority is derived from his responsibility to coordinate the work of subordinates.

In this context, *authority* constitutes official permission to use the resources of the organization. Thus, an individual worker needs authority to use equipment or to withdraw materials from storage, the industrial foreman needs authority to command his men to do a given job, a hospital nurse needs authority to issue medicine to a patient, the surgeon needs to command the actions of an entire operating team, a baseball coach must have authority to call for the execution of a particular play, and a general manager of a baseball team needs authority to consummate a player deal.

There is another aspect to authority at the administrative level. In order to coordinate the efforts of subordinates, a superior needs to obtain their compliance to orders and commands. For this reason, administrative authority also includes official permission to use some of the possessions of the organization as inducements. Thus, a supervisor is permitted to offer rewards or to impose penalties for the purpose of gaining compliance. Included in the definition of authority, then, is the understanding that in superior-subordinate relationships, the superior has permission to invoke sanctions in order to obtain compliance from subordinates.

In the traditional literature, this authority is called "legal" or "official authority."[8] The

---

[5] Hamilton, *op. cit.;* Graicunas, *op. cit.;* and Fayol, *op. cit.*

[6] For instance, see James D. Mooney, *The Principles of Organization* (rev. ed.; New York: Harper & Row, 1939), pp. 17–23; Lyndall Urwick, *The Elements of Administration* (New York: Harper & Row, 1939), pp. 45–46; Fayol, *op. cit.;* pp. 21–22; and Taylor, *op. cit.*

[7] Urwick, *op. cit.,* p. 46.

[8] Fayol, *op. cit.,* p. 21.

source of this authority is not to be found in the individual, but rather it is derived from the organization.[9] It is an attribute of office or formal position. An organization member has authority because he occupies a certain position and not because of personal characteristics. In this regard, Weber states: "In the case of legal authority, obedience is owed to the legally established impersonal order. It extends to the persons exercising authority of office under it only by virtue of the formal legality of the commands and only within the scope of authority of the office."[10]

James D. Mooney identified authority as the foundation of the first principle of organization—the coordinative principle. He labeled authority as the "supreme coordinative power" and stated that "in every form of organization, this authority must rest somewhere, else there would be no directive for any coordinated effort."[11] Locating its "resting" place in the formal organization involves defining authority according to type and amounts. Two types of authority distinguished in traditional theory are line and staff authority.

## Line and Staff Authority

A relationship in which the occupant of one position can exercise direct command over the occupant of another position is called *line authority*. A superior who exercises direct command over a subordinate has line authority.

A relationship in which the occupant of one position can advise or counsel but not command the occupant of another position is called *staff authority*. A person occupying a position with staff authority does not command others, but rather his responsibility is discharged by providing information, advice, and recommendations. The principal value of staff authority is that specialized knowledge and technology can be injected into the organization to aid the incumbents of positions which have line authority.

\*      \*      \*      \*      \*

## Staff Concept in Business Organization

While the application of the staff concepts has a long history in military and religious organizations, not until recently has it appeared in business organizations. One of the first applications of this concept to a business organization was reported by Harrington Emerson, who applied it to the organization of the Santa Fe Railroad during the first decade of the 20th century.[12] Du Pont used the concept of general staff as early as 1908.[13]

The functional differentiation of advisory and service activities found in the military staff organization, for instance, the general staff and special staff, also exists in the organization of business staffs. On the basis of a survey study of 31 business organizations, Paul Holden, Lounsbury Fish, and Hubert Smith categorized the functions of staffs as: control, service, coordinating, and advisory.[14] The business version of staff organization appears to elaborate the task of staff units, because the control, service, and coordinative activities imply that staff

---

[9] For a discussion summarizing the issues concerning official versus personal authority, see Harold Koontz and Cyril O'Donnell, *Principles of Management* (New York: McGraw-Hill Book Co., 1955), pp. 48–54.

[10] A. M. Henderson and Talcott Parsons, *Max Weber: The Theory of Social and Economic Organization* (New York: Oxford University Press, Inc., 1947), p. 328.

[11] Mooney, *op. cit.,* p. 6.

[12] Harrington Emerson, *The Twelve Principles of Efficiency* (New York: Engineering Magazine Co., 1924), especially chap. ii.

[13] Ernest Dale, *Staff in Organization* (New York: McGraw-Hill Book Co., 1960), pp. 186–87. A survey of 300 business firms reported that approximately 70 percent employ staff assistance for the president. See: "Handy Men with Growing Power," *Business Week,* October 19, 1957, pp. 193–97.

[14] Paul E. Holden, Lounsbury S. Fish, and Hubert L. Smith, *Top-Management Organization and Control* (New York: McGraw-Hill Book Co., 1951), pp. 36–58.

units exercise some degree of authority over the line organization. Frederick Taylor's "functional management" played an important part in the development of staff specialization. Even though Taylor did not use the line-staff classification, he suggested that staff work or as he called it, "brain work" should be differentiated: "All possible brain work should be removed from the shop and centered in the planning or laying out department, leaving for the foreman and gang bosses work strictly executive in its nature."[15] Taylor's classification roughly resembles the line-staff classification. In fact, many of the activities that he removed from the "shop" and placed in the "planning department" are staff activities in modern business organizations.

The modification of the line-staff concept to serve as a basis not only for the differentiation of authority but also for the differentiation of activities, for example, control activities, service activities, and so on, complicates this seemingly simple concept.[16] The inclusion of control and service activities in the staff organization frequently requires line authority. For instance, control activities such as accounting, product inspection, and fire protection are meaningless unless some command authority is vested in them. Service activities such as purchasing and maintenance frequently are given authority that overrides the line organization. This hybrid type of authority, which has been labeled *functional authority*,[17] is really line authority limited to a specified function that can be assigned to a specialized department. This command authority is limited to the specialized function. For instance, an inspection department of a manufacturing firm may have the authority to command the production department concerning the quality characteristics of a product.

The introduction of functional authority in organization, and the tendency to perceive line and staff as types of departments, creates certain dysfunctions in organization.

## AMOUNT OF ORGANIZATIONAL AUTHORITY

Another aspect of traditional theory which has received considerable attention is the delegation of authority, or as Mooney defined it "the conferring of a specified authority by a higher authority."[18] Essentially this means, even in the simplest organization, that authority must be delegated in order to get work done.

The principal issue in the delegation of authority involves the amount of authority to delegate, that is, the centralization of authority in one or a few organization positions as opposed to the dispersion of authority throughout most or all of the levels of the organizational hierarchy.

The early contributors to organizational theory, such as Max Weber and Frederick W. Taylor, were not unique in their concern over the issue of the dispersion of authority. The designers of the Constitution of the United States, for example, were also concerned with the problem of centralization versus decentralization. In the tableau of history this issue has acquired many different labels, for instance, autocracy versus democracy, monism versus pluralism, totalitarianism versus freedom, sectarianism versus ecumenism, federalism versus confederation, social mold versus social contract, organizationalism versus anarchy. Once the political and emotional overtones, shibboleths and labels are removed, the basic issue

[15] Frederick W. Taylor, "Shop Management," in *Scientific Management* (New York: Harper & Row, 1947), pp. 98–99.

[16] Not only does the line-staff classification result in specialization with respect to type of authority, but it also provides a rough guide for the separation of activities into those which are directly (line) and indirectly (staff) related to the attainment of organizational goals. Ralph C. Davis argues that the department concerned with activities which are "organic" to the accomplishment are line departments, while those departments which contribute to the "secondary" and "collateral" organization goals are staff departments. See his *The Fundamentals of Top Management* (New York: Harper & Row, 1951), pp. 205–11, 337–38.

[17] See Koontz and O'Donnell, *op. cit.,* chap. viii; William H. Newman, *Administrative Action* (Englewood Cliffs, N.J.: Prentice-Hall, Inc., 1950), chap. ix; and Holden, Fish, and Smith, *op. cit.,* sec. 3.

[18] Mooney, *op. cit.,* p. 17.

involves the question of how much authority to delegate, regardless of whether the institution is business, education, military, church, or government.

## Centralization and Decentralization

Traditional theory prescribes that authority be equal to responsibility, that is, if a person is assigned certain duties, he *should* also have the permission to commit the resources of the organization necessary to perform the job. The authority to commit resources may range from permission to perform a simple act like drawing necessary tools from a toolroom to permission to perform a major act like an expenditure of $500,000. Thus, if authority is directly related to responsibility, the dispersion of authority throughout the organization depends upon the definition of the jobs and positions.

The dispersion of authority occurs only in terms of degree. Henri Fayol referred to the relativity of the dispersion of authority in terms of centralization and decentralization,[19] or as he suggested, "centralization . . . is always present to a greater or less extent . . . it is a matter of finding the optimum degree for the particular concern."[20] Especially in large organizations, some amount of authority must be delegated, because it may be impossible for one person to coordinate all of the organizational activities. Yet, this does not mean that authority must be delegated completely to the managers of the lower subunits. To the extent that some authority is retained by central management, there exists a degree of centralization in every organization. At a minimum, according to traditional theory, central management always retains *residual authority,* which is the authority to recall from subordinates that authority which had been previously delegated to them. Thus, the dispersion of authority among the levels of an organization cannot be dichotomized into a pattern which is entirely centralized or completely decentralized. In effect, some degree of each pattern of authority dispersion is likely to be found in every organization.

Practitioners have found convenient ways to withhold some authority and yet permit decentralization. This is done usually by delegating operating authority and retaining policy-making authority. A rough definition of *operating authority* is the authority needed to make detailed, specific and repetitive decisions. *Policymaking authority* is confined roughly to formulating basic long-term objectives and adopting courses of action that provide general guides to operating decisions and practices. Let us turn to several examples of this practice.

## Departmentation, Authority, and Size of Administrative Unit

Departmentation refers to the grouping of specialized activities into departments or subunits of an organization. The dispersion of authority and the size of the administrative unit are related to departmentation to the extent that some patterns for grouping activities facilitate decentralization and small administrative units, while others lend themselves to centralization and large administrative units. However, before we pursue these relationships, the term "administrative unit" must be defined. An *administrative unit* is an organizational unit which contains the sufficient component parts to operate autonomously. An administrative unit characteristically resembles a total organization. In other words, it is a unit which can make virtually all of the decisions and take virtually all of the actions necessary to achieve a general purpose. In a business organization, for example, this means that an administrative

---

[19] The terms "centralization" and "decentralization" have been used to describe the geographic dispersion of organizational units, for instance, the decentralization of warehouses in Chicago, New York, and Atlanta as opposed to one central warehouse in Chicago, or the location of sales offices in London, Tokyo, and San Francisco. The use of these terms in this section of the book is limited to the dispersion of authority in the organization, for example, the decentralization of authority to several levels of an organization as opposed to the centralization of authority to one level.

[20] Fayol, *op. cit.,* p. 33. For a critical appraisal of decentralization of authority, see: John Dearden, "Mirage of Profit Decentralization," *Harvard Business Review,* Vol. 40. No. 6 (November–December, 1961), pp. 140–48.

unit is capable of making the necessary decisions and performing the activities needed to finance, manufacture, and distribute a given product. In a military organization an administrative unit is a task force capable of making the decisions and performing all of the duties necessary in achieving a given military mission. In a hospital organization this means that an administrative unit can perform the full line of medical services needed to accomplish its goals.

*Departmentation and Size of Administrative Unit.* Grouping organizational components according to purpose permits smaller administrative units than departmentation on the basis of function. This result can be illustrated with a hypothetical example. Suppose that four functions, A, B, C, and D must be performed on each of four products of a business organization. Departmentation on the basis of function is shown in Figure 7. In the diagram, S represents supervision, M indicates general management, and the solid-line box encloses the administrative unit or the total organization in this case. Since the functions A, B, C, and D require coordination for each product, the coordinating authority for each product must be placed at the level of general management, M.

**FIGURE 7**
**Functional Departmentation and Administrative Unit**

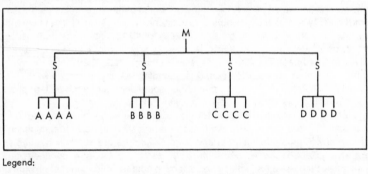

Legend:

☐    Total organization and administrative unit

**FIGURE 8**
**Purpose Departmentation and Administrative Unit**

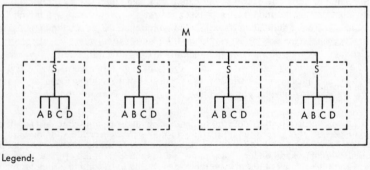

Legend:

☐    Total organization

⌐ ─ ┐
└ ─ ┘    Administrative unit

If the organizational components are grouped according to purpose (or product), the organization would be designed according to Figure 8. The administrative units indicated by broken-line boxes include all of the functions necessary to produce one product. In comparison to the functional departmentation of Figure 7, the purpose departmentation of Figure 8, requires more administrative units but each of the four units is smaller. In addition, the coordinating authority for each product is placed at a lower level of the organization, that is, at level S and there are fewer hierarchical levels involved in the administrative unit.

**Departmentation and Dispersion of Authority.** As we indicated above, departmentation by purpose or product permits the establishment of administrative units at lower levels in the organization than does departmentation by function. It was also possible to place the coordinating authority for each product at lower levels. In terms of the dispersion of authority, then, organization by product allows a greater degree of decentralization than the functional-type organization. This result may be illustrated further with more specific examples of business firms, shown in Figures 9 and 10.

**FIGURE 9**
**Functional-Type Organization**

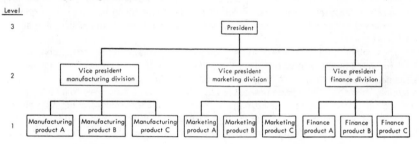

**FIGURE 10**
**Purpose-Type Organization**

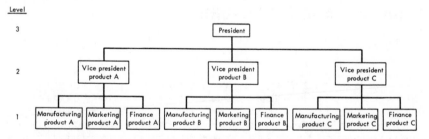

In these illustrations, it is assumed that manufacturing, marketing, and finance are all the functions necessary (of course, there are others, such as personnel, engineering, and purchasing functions) to complete a product. In the purpose-type organization (Figure 10), each of the products divisions can be managed as an autonomous unit. The coordinating authority for each product can be assigned to vice presidents at level 2. The delegation of coordinating authority for each product in the functional-type organization, Figure 9, cannot be delegated below the president, level 3.

### Authority and Service Activities

The delegation of authority and the arrangement of service activities are related since the assignment of work creates a responsibility which in turn, according to traditional theory, must be accompanied by authority. Service activities which may be demanded by several departments can be centralized under one service department or decentralized in each department that needs the service. For instance, if several departments within an organization have a demand for the services of an electronic computer, these services may be centralized in one department and made available to all the users, or an electronic computer installation can be placed in each of the departments. The solution to this organizational problem may be based on what is economically or technologically feasible. From the economic point of view, if each of the departments does not have a sufficient demand for the full use of a computer, this service may be centralized, because it would be uneconomical to employ a computer in each department. . . .

### Authority and Span of Supervision

The dispersion of authority in any particular case is affected by the span of supervision policy adopted in an organization. The number of subordinates assigned to a superior determines, in part, the work load of the superior. In other words, if a superior has a narrow span of supervision, he can devote a considerable amount of time to each subordinate. He can supervise "closely," and retain much of the decision-making authority. Though close supervision is not a necessary consequence of a narrow span of supervision, it is at least possible to occur.

On the other hand, if a superior has a large number of subordinates, the supervisory work load may force him to delegate much of the decision-making authority and to supervise each subordinate less frequently. With a large number of subordinates, the amount of time that a superior can spend with each one of his subordinates may be severely limited. By decentralizing authority, the superior shifts some work and/or decision making to his subordinates, and thus his work load can be reduced. Worthy argues that increasing the ratio of subordinates to superior represents a method of forcing the downward delegation of authority.[21]

*From*

# STRATEGY AND STRUCTURE*

*By Alfred D. Chandler, Jr.*

. . . The following set of general or theoretical propositions attempts to provide some sort of conceptual precision. Without reference to historical reality, they try to explain in fairly clear-cut, oversimplified terms how the modern, "decentralized" structure came into being.

Before developing these propositions, the term *industrial enterprise* needs to be defined. Used in a broad sense, it means here a large private, profit-oriented business firm involved in the handling of goods in some or all of the successive industrial processes from the procurement of the raw material to the sale to the ultimate customer. Transportation enterprises, utilities, or purely financial companies are not then included in this study, while those firms concerned with marketing and with the extraction of raw materials as well as those dealing with processing or manufacturing do fall within this definition. An industrial enterprise is thus a subspecies of what Werner Sombart has described as the capitalistic enterprise,

---

[21] James C. Worthy, "Organizational Structure and Employee Morale," *American Sociological Review,* Vol. 15 (April 1950), pp. 109–79.

which as "an independent economic organism is created over and above the individuals who constitute it. This entity appears then as the agent in each of these transactions and leads, as it were, a life of its own, which often exceeds in length that of its human members."

While the enterprise may have a life of its own, its present health and future growth surely depend on the individuals who guide its activities. Just what, then, are the functions of the executives responsible for the fortunes of the enterprise? They coordinate, appraise, and plan. They may, at the same time, do the actual buying, selling, advertising, accounting, manufacturing, engineering, or research but in the modern enterprise the execution or carrying out of these functions is usually left to such employees as salesmen, buyers, production supervisors and foremen, technicians, and designers. In many cases, the executive does not even personally supervise the working force but rather administers the duties of other executives. In planning and coordinating the work of subordinate managers or supervisors, he allocates tasks and makes available the necessary equipment, materials, and other physical resources necessary to carry out the various jobs. In appraising their activities, he must decide whether the employees or subordinate managers are handling their tasks satisfactorily. If not, he can take action by changing or bringing in new physical equipment and supplies, by transferring or shifting the personnel, or by expanding or cutting down available funds. Thus, the term, *administration,* as used here, includes executive action and orders as well as the decisions taken in coordinating, appraising, and planning the work of the enterprise and in allocating its resources.

The initial proposition is, then, that administration is an identifiable activity, that it differs from the actual buying, selling, processing, or transporting of the goods, and that in the large industrial enterprise the concern of the executives is more with administration than with the performance of functional work. In a small firm, the same man or group of men buy materials, sell finished goods, and supervise manufacturing as well as coordinate, plan, and appraise these different functions. In a large company, however, administration usually becomes a specialized, fulltime job. A second proposition is that the administrator must handle two types of administrative tasks when he is coordinating, appraising, and planning the activities of the enterprise. At times he must be concerned with the long-run health of his company, at other times with its smooth and efficient day-to-day operation. The first type of activity calls for concentration on long-term planning and appraisal, the second for meeting immediate problems and needs and for handling unexpected contingencies or crises. To be sure, in real life the distinction between these two types of activities or decisions is often not clear cut. Yet some decisions clearly deal very largely with defining basic goals and the course of action and procedures necessary to achieve these goals, while other decisions have more to do with the day-to-day operations carried out within the broader framework of goals, policies, and procedures.

The next few propositions deal with the content of administrative activities handled through the different types of posts or positions in the most complex administrative structures. The executives in a modern "decentralized" company carry out their administrative activities from four different types of positions. . . . Each of these types within the enterprise has a different range of administrative activities. Normally, each is on a different level of authority. At the top is a *general office.* There, general executives and staff specialists coordinate, appraise, and plan goals and policies and allocate resources for a number of quasi-autonomous, fairly self-contained divisions. Each division handles a major product line or carries on the firm's activities in one large geographical area. Each division's *central office,* in turn, administers a number of departments. Each of these departments is responsible for administration of a major function—manufacturing, selling, purchasing or producing of raw materials, engineering, research, finance, and the like. The *departmental headquarters* in its turn coordinates, appraises, and plans for a number of field units. At the lowest level, each *field unit* runs a plant or works, a branch or district sales office, a purchasing office, an engineering or research laboratory, an accounting or other financial office, and the like. The four types of administrative positions in a large multidivisional enterprise are thus: the field unit, the departmental headquarters, the division's central office, and the general office.

These terms are used throughout this study to designate a specific set of administrative activities. They do not, it should be stressed, refer to an enterprise's office buildings or rooms. One office building could house executives responsible for any one of the positions or conceivably those responsible for all four. Conversely, the executives in any one of the posts could be housed in different rooms or buildings.

Only in the first, the field unit, are the managers primarily involved in carrying on or personally supervising day-to-day activities. Even here, if the volume of activity is large, they spend much of their time on administrative duties. But such duties are largely operational, carried out within the framework of policies and procedures set by departmental headquarters and the higher offices. The departmental and divisional offices may make some long-term decisions, but because their executives work within a comparable framework determined by the general office, their primary administrative activities also tend to be tactical or operational. The general office makes the broad strategic or entrepreneurial decisions as to policy and procedures and can do so largely because it has the final say in the allocation of the firm's resources—men, money, and materials—necessary to carry out these administrative decisions and actions and others made with its approval at any level.

It seems wise here to emphasize the distinction between the formulation of policies and procedures and their implementation. The formulation of policies and procedures can be defined as either strategic or tactical. *Strategic* decisions are concerned with the long-term health of the enterprise. *Tactical* decisions deal more with the day-to-day activities necessary for efficient and smooth operations. But decisions, either tactical or strategic, usually require *implementation* by an allocation or reallocation of resources—funds, equipment, or personnel. Strategic plans can be formulated from below, but normally the implementation of such proposals requires the resources which only the general office can provide. Within the broad policy lines laid down by that office and with the resources it allocates, the executives at the lower levels carry out tactical decisions.

The executives who actually allocate available resources are then the key men in any enterprise. Because of their critical role in the modern economy, they will be defined in this study as entrepreneurs. In contrast, those who coordinate, appraise, and plan within the means allocated to them will be termed managers. So *entrepreneurial* decisions and actions will refer to those which affect the allocation or reallocation of resources for the enterprise as a whole, and *operating* decisions and actions will refer to those which are carried out by using the resources already allocated.

Just because the entrepreneurs make some of the most significant decisions in the American economy, they are not all necessarily imbued with a long-term strategic outlook. In many enterprises the executives responsible for resource allocation may very well concentrate on day-to-day operational affairs, giving little or no attention to changing markets, technology, sources of supply, and other factors affecting the long-term health of their company. Their decisions may be made without forward planning or analysis but rather by meeting in an *ad hoc* way every new situation, problem, or crisis as it arises. They accept the goals of their enterprise as given or inherited. Clearly wherever entrepreneurs act like managers, wherever they concentrate on short-term activities to the exclusion or to the detriment of long-range planning, appraisal, and coordination, they have failed to carry out effectively their role in the economy as well as in their enterprise. This effectiveness should provide a useful criterion for evaluating the performance of an executive in American industry.

As already pointed out, executives in the large enterprise work in four types of offices, each with his own administrative duties, problems, and needs. The four types operate on different scales, and their officers have different business horizons. The managers in the field unit are concerned with one function—marketing, manufacturing, engineering, and so forth—in one local area. The executives in the departmental headquarters plan, administer, and coordinate the activities of one function on a broad regional and often national scale rather than just locally. Their professional activities and their outside sources of information concern men and institutions operating in the same specialized function. The divisional executives, on the other hand, deal with an industry rather than a function. They are concerned with all the functions involved in the overall process of handling a line of products or services. Their professional horizons and contacts are determined by industry rather than functional interests. Finally, executives in the general office have to deal with several industries or one industry in several broad and different geographical regions. They set policies and procedures and allocate resources for divisions carrying out all types of functions, either in different geographical areas or in quite different product lines. Their business horizons and interests are broadened to range over national and even international economies.

While all four types of offices exist in the most complex of industrial enterprises, each can of course exist separately. An industrial enterprise can include one, two, three, or all four of these offices. Many small firms today have only a single office managing a single plant, store, laboratory, financial operation, or sales activity. Larger companies with a number of operating units carry out a single function—such as sales (wholesale or retail), manufacturing, purchasing, or engineering. Their overall administrative structure comprises a headquarters and field offices. So also today there are integrated industrial enterprises that handle several economic functions rather than just one. Finally, there are the great diversified industrial empires, carrying on different functions and producing a variety of goods and services in all parts of the globe.

Since each type of position handles a different range of administrative activities, each must have resulted from a different type of growth. Until the volume or technological complexity of an enterprise's economic activities had so grown as to demand an increasing division of labor within the firm, little time needed to be spent on administrative work. Then the resulting specialization required one or more of the firm's executives to concentrate on coordinating, appraising, and planning these specialized activities. When the enterprise expanded geographically by setting up or acquiring facilities and personnel distant from its original location, it had to create an organization at a central headquarters to administer the units in the field. When it grew by moving into new functions, a central office came to administer the departments carrying on the different functions. Such a central administrative unit proved necessary, for example, when in following the policy of vertical integration a manufacturing firm began to do its own wholesaling, procuring of supplies, and even producing raw materials. Finally, when an integrated enterprise became diversified through purchasing or creating new facilities and entered new lines of business, or when it expanded its several functional departments over a still larger geographical area, it fashioned a number of integrated divisional units administered by a general office.

The thesis that different organizational forms result from different types of growth can be stated more precisely if the planning and carrying out of such growth is considered a *strategy,* and the organization devised to administer these enlarged activities and resources, a *structure. Strategy* can be defined as the determination of the basic long-term goals and objectives of an enterprise, and the adoption of courses of action and the allocation of resources necessary for carrying out these goals. Decisions to expand the volume of activities, to set up distant plants and offices, to move into new economic functions, or become diversified along many lines of business involve the defining of new basic goals. New courses of action must be devised and resources allocated and reallocated in order to achieve these goals and to maintain and expand the firm's activities in the new areas in response to shifting demands, changing sources of supply, fluctuating economic conditions, new technological developments, and the actions of competitors. As the adoption of a new strategy may add new types of personnel and facilities, and alter the business horizons of the men responsible for the enterprise, it can have a profound effect on the form of its organization.

*Structure* can be defined as the design of organization through which the enterprise is administered. This design, whether formally or informally defined, has two aspects. It includes, first, the lines of authority and communication between the different administrative offices and officers and, second, the information and data that flow through these lines of communication and authority. Such lines and such data are essential to assure the effective coordination, appraisal, and planning so necessary in carrying out the basic goals and policies and in knitting together the total resources of the enterprise. These resources include financial capital; physical equipment such as plants, machinery, offices, warehouses, and other marketing and purchasing facilities, sources of raw materials, research and engineering laboratories; and, most important of all, the technical, marketing, and administrative skills of its personnel.

The thesis deduced from these several propositions is then that structure follows strategy and that the most complex type of structure is the result of the concatenation of several basic strategies. *Expansion of volume* led to the creation of an administrative office to handle one function in one local area. Growth through *geographical dispersion* brought the need for a departmental structure and headquarters to administer several local field units. The decision to expand into new types of functions called for the building of a central office and a multidepartmental structure, while the developing of new lines of products or continued growth on a national or international scale brought the formation of the multidivisional structure with a general office to administer the different divisions. For the purposes of this study, the move into new functions will be referred to as a strategy of *vertical integration* and that of the development of new products as a strategy of *diversification.*

This theoretical discussion can be carried a step further by asking two questions: (1) If structure does follow strategy, why should there be delay in developing the new organization needed to meet the administrative demands of the new strategy? (2) Why did the new strategy, which called for a change in structure, come in the first place?

There are at least two plausible answers to the first query. Either the administrative needs created by the new strategy were not positive or strong enough to require structural change, or the executives involved were unaware of the new needs. There seems to be no question that a new strategy created new administrative needs, for expansion through geographical dispersion, vertical integration, and product diversification added new resources, new activities, and an increasing number of entrepreneurial and operational actions and decisions. Nevertheless, executives could still continue to administer both the old and new activities with the same personnel, using the same channels of communication and authority and the same types of information. Such administration, however, must become increasingly inefficient. This proposition should be true for a relatively small firm whose structure consists of informal arrangements between a few executives as well as for a large one whose size and numerous administrative personnel require a more formal definition of relations between offices and officers. Since expansion created the need for new administrative offices and structures, the reasons for delays in developing the new organization rested with the executives responsible for the enterprise's long-range growth and health. Either these administrators were too involved in day-to-day tactical activities to appreciate or understand the longer-range organizational needs of their enterprises, or else their training and education failed to sharpen their perception of organizational problems or failed to develop their ability to handle them. They may also have resisted administratively desirable changes because they felt structural reorganization threatened their own personal position, their power, or most important of all, their psychological security.

In answer to the second question, changes in strategy which called for changes in structure appear to have been in response to the opportunities and needs created by changing population and changing national income and by technological innovation. Population growth, the shift from the country to the city and then to the suburb, depressions and prosperity, and the increasing pace of technological change, all created new demands or curtailed existing ones for a firm's goods or services. The prospect of a new market or the threatened loss of a current one stimulated geographical expansion, vertical integration, and product diversification. Moreover, once a firm had accumulated large resources, the need to keep its men, money, and materials steadily employed provided a constant stimulus to look for new markets by moving into new areas, by taking on new functions, or by developing new product lines. Again the awareness of the needs and opportunities created by the changing environment seems to have depended on the training and personality of individual executives and on their ability to keep their eyes on the more important entrepreneurial problems even in the midst of pressing operational needs.

The answers to the two questions can be briefly summarized by restating the general thesis. Strategic growth resulted from an awareness of the opportunities and needs—created by changing population, income, and technology—to employ existing or expanding resources more profitably. A new strategy required a new or at least refashioned structure if the enlarged enterprise was to be operated efficiently. The failure to develop a new internal structure, like the failure to respond to new external opportunities and needs, was a consequence of overconcentration on operational activities by the executives responsible for the destiny of their enterprises, or from their inability, because of past training and education and present position, to develop an entrepreneurial outlook.

One important corollary to this proposition is that growth without structural adjustment can lead only to economic inefficiency. Unless new structures are developed to meet new administrative needs which result from an expansion of a firm's activities into new areas, functions, or product lines, the technological, financial, and personnel economies of growth and size cannot be realized. Nor can the enlarged resources be employed as profitably as they otherwise might be. Without administrative offices and structure, the individual units within the enterprise (the field units, the departments, and the divisions) could undoubtedly operate as efficiently or even more so (in terms of cost per unit and volume of output per worker) as independent units than if they were part of a larger enterprise. Whenever the executives responsible for the firm fail to create the offices and structure necessary to bring together effectively the several administrative offices into a unified whole, they fail to carry out one of their basic economic roles.

The actual historical patterns of growth and organization building in the large industrial enterprise were not, of course, as clear-cut as they have been theoretically defined here. One strategy of expansion could be carried out in many ways, and often, two or three basic ways of expansion were undertaken at one and the same time. Growth might come through simultaneous building or buying of new facilities, and through purchasing or merging with other enterprises. Occasionally a firm simultaneously expanded its volume, built new facilities in geographically distant areas, moved into new functions, and developed a different type of product line. Structure, as the case studies indicate, was often slow to follow strategy, particularly in periods of rapid expansion. As a result, the distinctions between the duties of the different offices long remained confused and only vaguely defined. One executive or a small group of executives might carry out at one and the same time the functions of a general office, a central office, and a departmental headquarters. Eventually, however, most large corporations came to devise the specific units to handle a field unit, a functional department, an integrated division, or a diversified industrial empire. For this very reason, a clear-cut definition of structure and strategy and a simplified explanation or theory of the relation of one to the other should make it easier to comprehend the complex realities involved in the expansion and management of the great industrial enterprises. . . .

\* \* \* \* \*

## The Creative Innovation

. . . The inherent weakness in the centralized, functionally departmentalized operating company and in the loosely held, decentralized holding company became critical only when the administrative load on the senior executive officers increased to such an extent that they were unable to handle their entrepreneurial responsibilities efficiently. This situation arose when the operations of the enterprise became too complex and the problems of coordination, appraisal, and policy formulation too intricate for a small number of top officers to handle both long run, entrepreneurial, and short-run, operational administrative activities. To meet these new needs, the innovators built the multidivisional structure with a general office whose executives would concentrate on entrepreneurial activities and with autonomous, fairly self-contained operating divisions whose managers would handle operational ones.

Complexity in itself, it should be emphasized, did not assure innovation or change; some responsible administrator had to become aware of the new conditions. Furthermore, awareness had to be translated into a plan for meeting the new conditions, and then the plan had to be accepted by most of the senior executives. Since such a program dealt with the relations between persons rather than with technological or mechanical developments, the working out of the plan was more complicated than merely bringing a new product or process into effective use.

\*    \*    \*    \*    \*

*The Conditions for Innovation.*  Size, measured by volume of output, capital invested, and men employed, was clearly only one aspect of the new complexity. Growth by diversification into new lines of business and continued vertical integration in widely separated geographical areas proved more significant. . . .

\*    \*    \*    \*    \*

## ORGANIZATIONAL INNOVATORS

Unless structure follows strategy, inefficiency results. . . . Volume expansion, geographical dispersion, vertical integration, product diversification, and continued growth by any of these basic strategies laid an increasingly heavy load of entrepreneurial decision making on the senior executives. If they failed to re-form the lines of authority and communication and to develop information necessary for administration, the executives throughout the organization were drawn deeper and deeper into operational activities and often were working at cross purposes to and in conflict with one another.

Yet structure often failed to follow strategy. . . . A primary reason for delay was the very fact that responsible executives had become too enmeshed in operational activities. . . .

# 2. VERTEX COMPANY, INC.

---

## Case Introduction

---

### SYNOPSIS

Vertex, after some 30 years in the toilet preparations business, has carved out a market niche of products each serving a specific health care purpose. Shifting competitive patterns, market trends, and increased government regulations prompt a fresh look at Vertex strategy. Of late, growth in sales revenue has slowed and there has been a slight downward drift in profit margin and return on equity. Some key managers are beginning to question the conservative approach of Vertex under the leadership of its 60ish founder and largest stockholder.

### WHY THIS CASE IS INCLUDED

Vertex management is living through one of those crucial moments in a company's history when it's time to ask: What business are we in? What business will we be in if we continue as we are now doing? What business should we be in? The student has the data to tackle these questions in a systematic way by applying what we have learned in the past 25 years about strategy formulation.

### DIAGNOSTIC AND PREDICTIVE QUESTIONS

The readings included with this case are marked (*). The author index at the end of this book locates the other readings.

1. What business is Vertex in? What is the functional definition of its product line?

Read: *Drucker, *Management—Tasks-Responsibilities-Practices.*
*Webster, *Marketing for Managers.*

2. Why is Vertex in business? What values are reflected in what Vertex does or how Vertex does what it does?

Read: *Andrews, *The Concept of Corporate Strategy.*

3. Taking into account product, market, and distribution channels, describe Vertex's present strategy.

Read:   *Cannon, *Business Strategy and Policy.*

4. List major trends or changes in Vertex's external (including competitive) environment. Which ones represent threats to the successful implementation of its current strategy? Which ones represent opportunities which might reinforce or modify existing strategy?

Read:   *Gilmore, "Formulating Strategy in Smaller Companies."

5. What are Vertex's internal strong points and reasons for relative success? What are Vertex's internal weak points or factors which jeopardize future success? (You may organize your analysis around functions such as marketing, R&D, and production.)

6. Putting together the threats and opportunities from the external environment and Vertex's comparative advantages and disadvantages, what options should it consider in terms of mission? The business(es) it choses to be in or competitive strategies.

Read:   *Gilmore and Brandenberg, "Anatomy of Corporate Planning." Pessemier, *New Product Decisions.* Review the Cannon reading from Question 3.

7. Using the Tilles criteria, which are the strategic options which best fit Vertex in its competitive situation?

Read:   Tilles, "How to Evaluate Corporate Strategy."

### POLICY QUESTIONS

8. What strategic changes would you suggest to Dr. Alcott? Any sequence or priority for implementation? (Review your answer to Question 7.)

9. What other management priorities would you suggest to Dr. Alcott in order to assure success with your revised strategy for Vertex? (Think carefully about your answer to Question 5.)

10. What process (activities, sequences, roles, people to be involved) would you suggest to Dr. Alcott for accomplishing his own strategy review at Vertex?

11. As a security analyst for an investment service, evaluate Vertex versus its major competitors. Do you have any reservations about Vertex? Why?

# Case Text*

Vertex was founded in 1947 in Chicago, Illinois, by Dr. Charles B. Alcott. At that time, Dr. Alcott was 30 years old and had been a highly successful research chemist. He left the large pharmaceutical company, for which he had worked since getting his Ph.D. in chemical engineering from M.I.T., to establish Vertex. He had been doing some work on the effects of various oils on the skin and this led to a new and effective formulation for shampoo. Dr. Alcott invested his limited savings, mortgaged everything he had, set up a small production process, hired a salesman, and Vertex was born.

Over the years, other functional products were slowly, but consistently developed under Dr. Alcott's personal direction. Currently, Vertex produces and markets two limited lines of toilet preparations (Standard Industrial Classification 2844):

*Women's Toiletries.*  BEAUTISHEEN Brand.
  Hair spray, hair coloring, shampoo.
*Men's Toiletries.*  NORTHWOODS Brand.
  Hair tonic, shaving cream, preshave lotion, after-shave lotion.

Exhibit 1 provides additional product information.

Vertex has grown to sales last year of $125,646,000. It has corporate headquarters and main production facilities in Chicago, Illinois. Vertex employs 2,800 people, of which 450 are in sales. All products are distributed and sold nationally. The current organization for the company is shown in Exhibit 2.

All products are manufactured in the Chicago plant. Certain steady, high-volume products such as shaving cream and after-shave lotion are

**EXHIBIT 1**
**Product Lines and Products**

| | |
|---|---|
| Women's Toiletries: | |
| Hair spray | Brand name: Beautisheen |
| | 3 oz. aerosol can, 24 pack case |
| Hair coloring | Brand name: Beautisheen |
| | 2 oz. glass bottle, |
| | 48 pack case assortment, or |
| | 12 pack case single color |
| Shampoo | Brand name: Beautisheen |
| | 5 oz. glass bottle, 48 pack case |
| | 10 oz. glass bottle, 24 pack case |
| Men's Toiletries: | |
| Hair tonic | Brand name: Northwoods |
| | 3 oz. glass bottle, 24 pack case |
| | 6 oz. glass bottle, 24 pack case |
| Shaving cream | Brand name: Northwoods (regular) |
| | 8 oz. aerosol can, 48 pack case |
| | Brand name: Northwoods Breeze |
| | (mentholated and mint) |
| | 8 oz. aerosol can, 24 pack case |
| Preshave lotion | Brand name: Northwoods |
| | 5 oz. glass bottle, 24 pack case |
| After-shave lotion | Brand name: Northwoods |
| | 4 oz. glass bottle, 48 pack case |
| | 8 oz. glass bottle, 24 pack case |

**EXHIBIT 2**
**Organizational Chart**

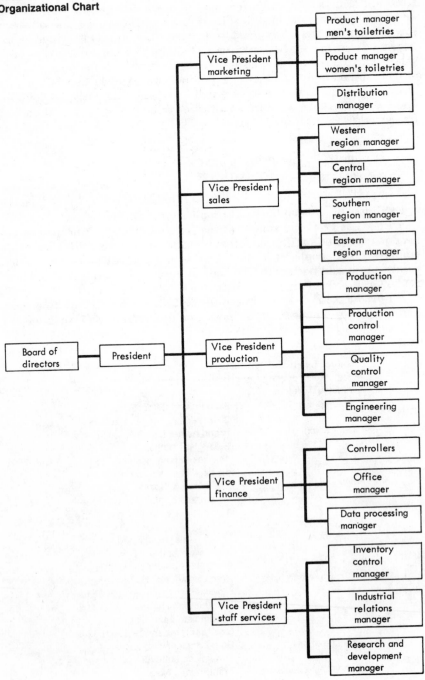

also produced in smaller plants located in Philadelphia, Pennsylvania, and Los Angeles, California. The plants have several production lines equipped to perform various combinations of liquid blending, dry blending, emulsifying, aerosol pressure packing, etc. They are designed for optimum flexibility and the various types of mixtures can be easily routed to different filler-cappers for glass bottle, plastic bottle, metal can, or pressure-pack filling.

Stemming from Dr. Alcott's strong interests in manufacturing processes, Vertex engineering has produced several advanced and proprietary blending and packaging processes. This process technology has given Vertex manufacturing operations very efficient and flexible product changeover capability.

Next to advertising, distribution is a most critical function for Vertex and for this industry. Each product line usually has six promotional campaigns per year. Many of these involve special packaging, display inserts, etc. These are timed to coincide with national advertising. Getting the right product to the dealer or distributor at the right time while maintaining good inventory control, is critical to both dealer goodwill and to Vertex profits. Management is justly proud of its highly effective computer-based inventory system. While no specific data is available, the Vertex system has to be about the best in the industry.

All products in the Vertex line are of very high quality and command premium prices in their markets. Vertex has never marketed on price, though they have reacted to severe competitive price cutting when necessary. Each of the products in the women's and men's lines has been designed to fill a specific health care purpose within the general need that product satisfies. For example: hair products feature the "natural look" and include protein, nondrying agents, and natural oils; shampoo includes a dandruff control agent; shaving cream includes a natural moistener, etc.

A few years ago, Vertex attempted to broaden its after-shave market. They introduced various scented lotions designed to appeal to different images men might have or want to create for themselves. This venture was very unsuccessful.

Sales projections for the current year, which has just begun, call for a 9 percent increase over last year. Generally the product lines are subject to only minor seasonal sales fluctuations. For a few products, peak sales might reach a high or low of plus or minus 8 percent of the norm. The 450-man sales force is distributed nationally among four regions and 17 districts. The salesmen contact distributors (wholesalers) and the large direct-sale retail accounts in their territories. The merchandising men, who are usually the newer salesmen, sell by contacting retailers directly with special promotions. The orders they receive they "turn over" to the wholesaler for that area. According to the importance of the customer and his volume of purchases, he is either rated Class A, B, or C, and is called on every 30, 60, or 90 days, respectively. All national accounts are handled by the district manager for the area where the account's offices are located.

The Vertex sales force has a reputation for being among the best in its industry. All new Vertex merchandising men are well trained in the detail and service work to be performed in any account outlet. Along with this basic in-store work, they have traditionally stressed the personal health care features of the Vertex product lines. This approach has been particularly effective in those outlets, such as drug stores, where there is a more personal and professional relationship between store personnel and the customer. Consequently, Vertex has been able to maintain a higher proportion of sales to drug stores (45 percent) and to department, variety and specialty stores (40 percent), than its competition. The remaining 15 percent of sales are through supermarket outlets.

All promotion is the direct responsibility of the marketing manager. Each product line has a product manager who reports to the marketing manager. His responsibilities include packaging, advertising, pricing, displays, selling materials, forecasts, etc. The advertising media used vary with the product and include newspapers, magazines, theater programs, radio, television, dealer helps, window displays, and counter displays. Trade journals are also used to acquaint retailers with special deals and promotions. Cooperative advertising is used to some extent. Although the toiletries industry generally gives rebates to dealers or their clerks for selling a new product, Vertex corporate management does not approve of this, and thus has greatly restricted its use.

Over the years, Vertex has been about at industry average in allocating 17 percent of its revenue for advertising and promotion. With ever increasing competition, Vertex has increased this to about 20 percent of revenue. The thrust of Vertex advertising and promotion has been directed toward middle and upper income adults. With advertising expenditures being so critical, marketing must be aware of consumer and environmental trends and adjust expenditures accordingly. For example: management anticipated the trend in men's dress toward multicolored and styled shirts, leather and jewelry accessories, etc. They recognized that this would add many new gift alternatives to the traditional white shirt as competition for men's toiletries. They quickly shifted expenditures to another theme.

Exhibit 3 shows selected years of sales and market share for Vertex.

For its size, Vertex operates with a relatively simple functional organization. Key positions are noted in Exhibit 2. All officers and key managers are well experienced and have proven records in their specialty in this industry. These top vice presidents work closely together with Dr. Alcott, who is currently president and chairman of the board. This team approach has always given Vertex a time edge on competition as far as recognizing apparent product improvement possibilities within their product lines. This early recognition provides for the careful and thorough product research and testing which has been so important to Vertex.

Vertex allocates about 1 percent of revenue for research and development. This is about double industry average. They have a very small and proficient staff including Dr. James Shields, who is nationally known in cosmetic research. The research function relies on sales and marketing

**EXHIBIT 3**
**Sales and Market Share History**

| Product | Last Year | | Three Years Ago | | Five Years Ago | |
|---|---|---|---|---|---|---|
| | Sales (*in millions*) | Market Share (*percent*) | Sales (*in millions*) | Market Share (*percent*) | Sales (*in millions*) | Market Share (*percent*) |
| Women's Products: | | | | | | |
| Hair spray ......... | $ 24,180 | 8.6% | $ 22,780 | 6.7% | $15,241 | 6.3% |
| Hair coloring ....... | 15,420 | 6.2 | 14,031 | 4.9 | 9,972 | 4.7 |
| Shampoo.......... | 24,378 | 6.0 | 22,908 | 4.7 | 15,601 | 4.4 |
| | $ 63,978 | | $ 59,719 | | $40,814 | |
| Men's Products: | | | | | | |
| Hair tonic.......... | $ 17,460 | 17.6* | $ 13,610 | 16.4% | $11,250 | 15.9 |
| Shaving creme ..... | 17,250 | 15.4 | 13,211 | 15.6 | 10,097 | 16.0 |
| Preshave lotion .... | 4,794 | 28.2* | 3,721 | 27.0 | 3,068 | 25.9 |
| After-shave lotion... | 22,164 | 18.6 | 17,100 | 17.9 | 14,181 | 17.4 |
| | $ 61,668 | | $ 47,642 | | $38,596 | |
| Total......... | $125,646 | | $107,361 | | $79,410 | |

\* Indicates dominant market share in the industry.

to provide information on new or modified consumer needs. Research, then, determines which of these needs Vertex can fill in unique or novel ways so as to maintain the Vertex health care identity. Thorough and complete development and testing in selective product areas has been the Vertex way. President Alcott has built his products and marketing around his strong belief in research which he expresses as: "While it's best to be best and first, it's better to be best than first." As an example, while several competitors have introduced combined shampoo-hair coloring products, Vertex is not as yet satisfied with its own formulation.

Product improvement and new products are the way of life in this industry. Trends in personal grooming attitudes and practices, as well as changes in technology, governmental regulations, and competitive directions are under constant surveillance. Vertex has used this kind of information primarily to spot new or changing needs within its present product lines. For example, menthol and mint shaving creams were added to the Northwood line four years ago while a new rinsing agent for removing hair spray was added to Beautisheen shampoo two years ago. While Vertex has made sound product improvements over the years, its rate of change would be fairly conservative by industry practices.

The stock of the company is publicly traded, though the Alcott family is the largest single stockholder and controls the board of directors. President Alcott feels this control, and the ability to set direction it provides, has been a significant factor in the company's growth to date.

Over the last several years, Vertex has maintained a stable, if not outstanding, profit picture. As in other ways, President Alcott's philosophy and viewpoint influences how the company looks at profit and return. He feels that no company deserves a just return unless its products serve very real needs and are of unquestionable quality. He has been critical of those companies that have entered the industry with inadequately developed and tested products. Dr. Alcott feels this has been true not only in the United States, but in international markets as well. In several cases, U.S. firms have entered international markets with products not adequately researched and adapted to local needs and requirements.

Though Vertex has stressed a plan of conservative growth in revenue and profit, growth has primarily been a result of concentrating on products and markets. Vertex has never based its profit potential on a high-risk, high-return venture. Although the Vertex management team works very well together, an increasing number of key managers have begun to question this philosophy.

Corporate return on sales has stayed about even as a percent of revenue. This has varied some by product line. Return on stockholder's equity has slightly decreased. Exhibit 4 shows selected years of profit and return for Vertex.

**EXHIBIT 4**
**Profit Return Performance**

|  | Last Year | Three Years Ago | Five Years Ago |
|---|---|---|---|
| Company: |  |  |  |
| Revenue.................... | $125,646,000 | $107,361,000 | $79,410,000 |
| Return on sales |  |  |  |
| (pretax).................. | 12.3% | 12.7% | 12.9% |
| Return on stockholder's |  |  |  |
| equity (aftertax)............ | 14.8% | 14.7% | 15.0% |
| Women's Toiletries: |  |  |  |
| Revenue.................... | $ 63,978,000 | $ 59,719,000 | $40,814,000 |
| Return on sales ............. | 14.4% | 13.8% | 13.4% |
| Men's Toiletries: |  |  |  |
| Revenue.................... | $ 61,668,000 | $ 47,642,000 | $38,596,000 |
| Return on sales ............. | 10.2% | 11.4% | 12.4% |

Even in periods of economic slowdown, Vertex has generally maintained its sales growth and profit stability. This has been done through increases in advertising, even stronger sales support to each account, and well-executed price increases.

Current plans call for maintaining the across the board budgetary constraints set last year. This tight cost control program, in conjunction with projected sales increases of 9 percent each year, produced a profit plan of 13 percent pretax this year, 13.6 percent next year, and 14.2 percent the year after.

*Please Note*

Exhibit 5 provides background and data on the toilet preparations industry in the United States. This industry statement also includes brief write-ups of six typical major firms which compete with Vertex in this industry.

### EXHIBIT 5
### Industry Statement—Toilet Preparations, United States

Over the past two decades, the toilet preparations industry in the United States has been growing twice as fast as the national economy. At the manufacturers' level, sales are close to the $5 billion mark. This exceptional and continuing growth is generally attributed to increasing emphasis on good grooming and youthful appearance, and on the ever increasing standard of living. The industry (Standard Industrial Classification 2844) includes shaving preparations, perfumes, toilet water, colognes, hair preparations, dentifrices, and miscellaneous cosmetics and toilet preparations.

While there are over 300 firms in the industry, the majority of the business is held by less than 15 of them. Recently expanded federal regulations relative to product testing are resulting in increased costs. This will probably result in many small firms being acquired or pushed out of the market by rising costs.

Channels of distribution include supermarket and drug store chains, which buy through their headquarters' purchasing offices. The independent supermarkets, grocery stores, and discount houses are usually serviced by "rack jobbers." A rack jobber is an individual or firm with delivery trucks which go around to the stores that are its customers and fill these display racks to a preagreed upon level with the products they distribute. Drug wholesalers distribute the products to independent stores. A few companies utilize the direct, house-to-house selling approach. Where this is done, the company usually has a completely separate field sales organization which buys its merchandise from the parent company.

Over the past 10 to 15 years, there has been a marked shift in sales patterns through different types of outlets. Drug store sales have declined by one-third and now account for 26 percent of toilet industry sales. Sales through large food stores (supermarket) quadrupled to the point where they now account for 24 percent of the market. House-to-house selling has increased by one-half and provides 21 percent of the market. Sales through all other outlets (department, variety, and specialty stores) have declined by one-third and now account for 29 percent of the market.

In recent years, packaging innovation has become an increasingly important promotional factor. Elegance, boldness, and sophistication are a few of the adjectives that might describe the more unique and distinctive packages. The ordinary glass bottle and jar were followed by the plastic squeeze bottle, the "roll-on" container, the metal squeeze tube, etc. Fancy plastic bottles and

**EXHIBIT 5 (continued)**

aerosol cans followed in turn. Special holiday packaging and gift sets are also being tried by many companies.

Opinions on package size proliferation vary widely in the industry. Some companies feel that it is necessary to have a size for every type of customer or market segment. Others feel that this presents unnecessary manufacturing and inventory costs. Usually one size packaging tends toward the larger size packages for two reasons. First, the customer perceives more value for the money. Second, it assures that the first-time customer will give the product an adequate test.

Advertising is a major expense in selling toiletries. Budgets for this generally run between 15 percent and 20 percent of sales. However, some firms have been successful with an ad budget of only 3 percent.

Cooperative advertising, network and local television, and magazine ads are the main alternatives used. Cooperative advertising involves a store running an ad in a local newspaper which stresses buying a particular manufacturer's products at that store. The manufacturer then reimburses the store for part of the ad cost. It may take up to half a year or more for a new advertising program to have a noticeable effect on sales. New programs may take as much as a year to pay for themselves.

While some of the needs that products in this industry fill are relatively stable, health care needs for example, others are quite changeable. For instance, there has been a rapid increase in products which serve personal appearance needs over the past few years. Also, there has been increased stress on products that serve various male and female youth needs. The trend toward longer hair has created needs for new products for men, such as hair spray, hair driers, and tangle remover rinses. Needless to say, product life cycles in this industry are often subject to relatively rapid change. Also, manufacturers are finding new needs for existing products. For example, the use of various baby products for adult purposes.

As of three years ago, it was expected that the *rate of growth* of men's toiletries would exceed that of women's toiletries. This did not materialize in the United States, however, due to changing hair styles and the popularity of beards. The growth rate of men's toiletries has continued to be less than in women's toiletries. Changing hair and beard styles, however, would suggest that the growth rate of men's toiletries should accelerate over the next few years and could equal that of women's toiletries.

Launching a new product involves a process that varies widely in the industry. Some firms, notably the larger ones, will go through elaborate test marketing lasting a year or more. Successful results usually lead to an intensive manufacturing effort and inventory building, followed by a product launch across the entire country. At the other extreme is the practice often followed by smaller firms,

**EXHIBIT 5 (*continued*)**

as well as by some large firms. This starts out with a strong intuitive feeling by competent and experienced top management that a product will succeed. This may be followed by quick secretive testing of the product with consumer panels followed, rapidly by regional product launch which is then expanded across the country. There are many variations within and between these approaches.

**TABLE 1**
**Industry Sales (United States)**

| Major Product Lines | Selected Product Sales (*in millions*) | Total Industry Sales (*in millions*) |
|---|---|---|
| Men's toiletries | | $ 553 |
| Hair tonics............................ | $ 99 | |
| Shaving creams....................... | 112 | |
| After-shave lotions.................... | 119 | |
| Preshave lotions...................... | 17 | |
| Men's colognes ...................... | 104 | |
| Other ............................... | 102 | |
| Women's toiletries | | 2,469 |
| Hair colorings........................ | $250 | |
| Hair sprays .......................... | 283 | |
| Hand creams ........................ | 185 | |
| Face creams.......................... | 228 | |
| Makeup .............................. | 873 | |
| Fragrances .......................... | 409 | |
| Other ............................... | 241 | |
| Miscellaneous toiletries | | 1,821 |
| Dentifrices........................... | $391 | |
| Shampoos............................ | 406 | |
| Soaps and detergents................. | 348 | |
| Deodorants........................... | 450 | |
| Other ............................... | 226 | |
| Baby toiletries | | 88 |
| Total industry sales | | $4,931 |

Table 1 shows a summary of recent government figures for *selected* product sales in each major product line, as well as total industry sales by major product line for the United States.

This industry is a profitable one. Return on stockholders' equity averages 15 percent to 16 percent for toiletries, whereas, the average for all industries ranges between 9 percent and 10 percent. Pretax profits average about 15 percent in the toiletries industry and 7 percent to 8 percent for all other industries.

Table 2 summarizes sales by men's and women's toiletries for six

**EXHIBIT 5** (*continued*)

**TABLE 2**
**Current Sales per Year of Typical Firms in Men's and Women's Toiletries (in millions)**

| Firm | Men's Toiletries | Women's Toiletries | Total Toiletries Sales |
|------|------------------|--------------------|------------------------|
| A............. | $57.8 | $439.0 | $496.8 |
| B............. | 23.8 | 120.5 | 144.3 |
| C............. | — | 83.1 | 83.1 |
| D............. | 67.3 | 86.0 | 153.3 |
| E............. | — | 250.7 | 250.7 |
| F............. | 40.4 | 435.5 | 475.9 |
| Vertex........ | 61.7 | 64.0 | 125.7 |

typical larger firms in the industry. A comparison with Vertex is given.

Following Table 2 is a brief description of each of these six firms.

## FIRM A

Firm A has grown steadily through the use of house-to-house selling. The sales people are usually women working part-time.

Over the past few years, there has been an increasing tendency for housewives to be away from home during the day. With increasing leisure time, they are either taking jobs or becoming involved

**Firm A—Sales and Market Share**

| | Sales (in millions) | Market Share (percent) |
|------|---------------------|------------------------|
| Women's Toiletries: | | |
| Hair sprays................... | $ 67,000 | 23.3%* |
| Hair colorings................. | — | — |
| Shampoos..................... | 78,000 | 19.2* |
| Face creams .................. | 45,100 | 19.8* |
| Makeup....................... | 185,000 | 21.2 |
| Fragrances................... | 32,300 | 7.9 |
| Hand creams ................. | 31,600 | 17.1 |
| Men's Toiletries: | | |
| Hair tonics ................... | 14,800 | 14.9 |
| Shaving creams............... | 22,200 | 19.8 |
| Preshave lotions ............. | 2,400 | 14.4 |
| After-shave lotions ........... | 18,400 | 15.5 |

* Indicates dominant market share in the industry.

**EXHIBIT 5 (*continued*)**

in community activities. This is beginning to slow down sales growth and to increase the turnover of saleswomen. Consequently, Firm A is known to be considering setting up some kind of mail-order operation.

With the house-to-house selling approach, the customer is confronted only with Firm A's package at the time of the sale. Thus, there is no opportunity for the customer to compare it with competitors' packages. This has resulted in Firm A's packaging not having been as lavish and expensive as the rest of the industry's. With its below-average pricing structure, it would be very difficult for them to get into elaborate packaging.

Advertising is minimal and concentrated in women's magazines. It is aimed at keeping Firm A's name in front of the consumer so she is aware of it when the saleswoman calls.

**FIRM B**

Firm B started out merchandising housewares by the "party-selling" approach where a woman invites her friends and neighbors to her home for an evening at which time the Firm B representative demonstrates the products and takes orders. About 15 years ago, they set up the field sales organization as a separate group and began looking for other products which could be merchandised in the same way. Toiletries were chosen and the results have exceeded expectations. With a full line of products, toiletries have now become the dominant part of their business.

The orders are taken by the saleswoman at the time of the

**Firm B—Sales and Market Share**

|  | Sales (*in millions*) | Market Share (*percent*) |
|---|---|---|
| **Women's Toiletries:** | | |
| Hair sprays | $17,800 | 6.3% |
| Hair colorings | — | — |
| Shampoos | 24,000 | 5.9 |
| Face creams | 20,700 | 9.1 |
| Makeup | 45,400 | 5.2 |
| Fragrances | — | — |
| Hand creams | 12,600 | 6.8 |
| **Men's Toiletries:** | | |
| Hair tonics | 7,100 | 7.2 |
| Shaving creams | 8,800 | 7.9 |
| Preshave lotions | — | — |
| After-shave lotions | 7,900 | 6.6 |

**EXHIBIT 5 (*continued*)**

demonstration and then are mailed to the customer. This is followed by periodic direct mail pieces which have a high return. The hostess is compensated for her effort by being given free merchandise in proportion to the amount of orders placed by her guests. This approach keeps selling costs at a minimum and has enabled Firm B to keep its prices down. However, increasing postal rates are starting to have an effect on profitability.

**FIRM C**

Firm C is a stable company that has been in the professional end of the business for about 20 years. They sell high-quality, specialty products to beauty shops for use in the shop. Their distribution is handled by the regular beauty shop wholesalers. Over the past five years, customers have increasingly been buying these products from their beauty shop operators so they could get the same quality at home.

This has opened up a whole new business for Firm C, which has tripled its volume in five years. Their advertising is still limited to beauty trade magazines. However, they have developed small point-of-purchase displays for the beauty shops. Thus, Firm C volume should continue to expand very rapidly.

Hand cream is the only new product that has been added to their line. As a result of hearing many beauty operators complain about not being able to find a hand cream that was adequate, Firm C decided to develop one. This product is also enjoying an excellent "take-home" business.

Rumors in the trade suggest that they will add a line of a smaller consumer package size for all products in the near future. This will probably expand their volume even more.

**Firm C—Sales and Market Share**

|  | Sales (in millions) | Market Share (percent) |
|---|---|---|
| Women's Toiletries: |  |  |
| Hair sprays | $23,200 | 8.2% |
| Hair colorings | 24,200 | 9.7 |
| Shampoos | 30,000 | 7.4 |
| Face creams | — | — |
| Makeup | — | — |
| Fragrances | — | — |
| Hand creams | 5,700 | 3.1 |
| Men's Toiletries: None |  |  |

**EXHIBIT 5 (*continued*)**

**FIRM D**

Firm D is an old-line company. For almost 50 years they have been a dominant factor in men's toiletries. The recent emergence of "high fashion" and changing styles in men's clothing and appearance has resulted in corresponding changes in men's toiletries. They have been a slow follower rather than a leader in this change. Nevertheless, they have managed to hold onto the number one market position in shaving creams and after-shave lotions. This is probably because of their established following among older men.

### Firm D—Sales and Market Share

|  | Sales (in millions) | Market Share (percent) |
|---|---|---|
| Women's Toiletries: |  |  |
| Hair sprays | $13,000 | 4.6% |
| Hair colorings | — | — |
| Shampoos | 29,700 | 7.3 |
| Face creams | 7,300 | 3.2 |
| Makeup | — | — |
| Fragrances | 36,000 | 8.8 |
| Hand creams | — | — |
| Men's Toiletries: |  |  |
| Hair tonics | 13,700 | 13.8 |
| Shaving creams | 25,900 | 23.1* |
| Preshave lotions | 2,800 | 16.7 |
| After-shave lotions | 24,900 | 20.9* |

\* Indicates dominant market share in the industry.

In general, it has been difficult to learn about pending product and marketing changes by Firm D. Their moves tend to be slow and deliberate and are made without the use of test markets. Instead, top management seems to rely on their experience and instinct in making these changes. Package proliferation has not been characteristic of Firm D, as most of their products come only in one size.

They market through the normal industry distribution channels. Their advertising support has been at the low end of the industry range at about 4 percent of sales. It consists mainly of magazine advertising and point-of-purchase displays.

Generally, Firm D's pricing structure has been slightly above the industry average. Here again, in pricing, they have also been a follower.

**EXHIBIT 5 (*continued*)**

**FIRM E**

Firm E was launched only eight years ago by merging two small companies, one primarily in women's hair preparations and the other primarily in facial preparations. Together these companies produced about $40 million in sales at the start.

Innovative packaging and creative advertising were two key factors which spurred the company's exceptional growth. Although it utilizes normal industry distribution channels, it was the first to recognize that supermarkets could become an increasingly important distribution channel. As a result, it put heavy emphasis in this area and benefited accordingly.

**Firm E—Sales and Market Share**

|  | Sales (*in millions*) | Market Share (*percent*) |
| --- | --- | --- |
| Women's Toiletries: |  |  |
| Hair sprays | $11,600 | 4.1% |
| Hair colorings | 44,800 | 17.9 |
| Shampoos | 32,100 | 7.9 |
| Face creams | 10,000 | 4.4 |
| Makeup | 79,500 | 9.1 |
| Fragrances | 72,700 | 17.8 |
| Hand creams | — | — |
| Men's Toiletries: |  |  |
| None |  |  |

It relies heavily on television advertising. Its ad budget has recently been increased and now amounts to 26 percent of sales. It also relies heavily on special promotion where the customer gets something free with a purchase. Often this free item is a small package of another Firm E product.

Its managing style could be called bold, and sometimes brash. To support this aggressive posture and style, it has always put premium prices on its products.

This dynamic management team is continually looking for new growth opportunities. It is known that it has been considering expansion into international markets as well as launching a brand line of cosmetics directed at the black ethnic market. Getting into this market involves mainly new packaging and advertising. The international market would require new channels of distribution which would take longer and require an investment.

**EXHIBIT 5 (*concluded*)**

**FIRM F**

Firm F is a progressive marketer and product innovator that started in business in the late 1940s. They have a continuing record of steady growth in the United States. About three years ago, they started to move into international markets. This business is now very profitable, although it was a disaster at the start. For example, their venture into Latin America got into serious trouble because they did not adequately take into consideration cultural differences in the design of their products and packaging. Overseas business, principally Europe and selected parts of Latin America, now accounts for almost 10 percent of their sales. It is expected that they will continue to push for more growth in these areas.

Their broad product line has evolved as a result of selected acquisitions over the years. However, with their present breadth, it is expected that this expansion route is no longer as useful to them. Their tendency to put products out in many package sizes has generally been resisted by the competition. Undoubtedly, their large market makes it easier for them to follow this route.

Firm F was first in the industry to go to television advertising. Television and magazine ads continue to be the mainstay of their advertising program. From time to time, they also make use of cooperative advertising and special promotions, particularly to launch new products.

**Firm F—Sales and Market Share**

|  | Sales (*in millions*) | Market Share (*percent*) |
|---|---|---|
| Women's Toiletries: |  |  |
| Hair sprays..................... | $16,400 | 5.8% |
| Hair colorings.................. | 59,000 | 23.6* |
| Shampoos...................... | 35,800 | 8.8 |
| Face creams .................. | 33,500 | 14.7 |
| Makeup........................ | 204,000 | 23.3* |
| Fragrances.................... | 63,700 | 15.6 |
| Hand creams.................. | 23,100 | 12.5 |
| Men's Toiletries: |  |  |
| Hair tonics .................... | 9,800 | 9.9 |
| Shaving creams................ | 12,400 | 11.1 |
| Preshave lotions .............. | 3,100 | 18.2 |
| After-shave lotions ............ | 15,100 | 12.7 |

\* Indicates dominant market share in the industry.

# Selected Readings

*From*

## MANAGEMENT—TASKS-RESPONSIBILITIES-PRACTICES*

*By Peter F. Drucker*

### The Purpose of a Business

To know what a business is we have to start with its *purpose*. Its purpose must lie outside of the business itself. In fact, it must lie in society since business enterprise is an organ of society. There is only one valid definition of business purpose: *to create a customer*.

Markets are not created by God, nature, or economic forces but by businessmen. The want a business satisfies many have been felt by the customer before he was offered the means of satisfying it. Like food in a famine, it may have dominated the customer's life and filled all his waking moments, but it remained a potential want until the action of businessmen converted it into effective demand. Only then is there a customer and a market. The want may have been unfelt by the potential customer; no one knew that he wanted a Xerox machine or a computer until these became available. There may have been no want at all until business action created it—by innovation, by credit, by advertising, or by salesmanship. In every case, it is business action that creates the customer.

It is the customer who determines what a business is. It is the customer alone whose willingness to pay for a good or for a service converts economic resources into wealth, things into goods. What the business thinks it produces is not of first importance—especially not to the future of the business and to its success. The typical engineering definition of quality is something that is hard to do, is complicated, and costs a lot of money! But that isn't quality; it's incompetence. What the customer thinks he is buying, what he considers value, is decisive—it determines what a business is, what it produces, and whether it will prosper. And what the customer buys and considers value is never a product. It is always utility, that is, what a product or service does for him. And what is value for the customer is . . . anything but obvious.

The customer is the foundation of a business and keeps it in existence. He alone gives employment. To supply the wants and needs of a consumer, society entrusts wealth-producing resources to the business enterprise.

### The Two Entrepreneurial Functions

Because its purpose is to create a customer, the business enterprise has two—and only these two—basic functions: marketing and innovation. Marketing and innovation produce results; all the rest are "costs."

---

* From pp. 61, 77, 80–81, 83–89, 90–93 in *Management—Tasks-Responsibilities-Practices*, by Peter F. Drucker. Copyright © 1973, 1974 by Peter F. Drucker. Reprinted by permission of Harper & Row, Publishers, Inc.

\*   \*   \*   \*   \*

. . . Every one, in other words, has his answer to the question "What is our business and what should it be?" Unless, therefore, the business itself—and that means its top management—has thought through the question and formulated the answer—or answers—to it, the decision-makers in the business, all the way up and down, will decide and act on the basis of different, incompatible, and conflicting theories of the business. They will pull in different directions without even being aware of their divergences. But they will also decide and act on the basis of wrong and misdirecting theories of the business.

Common vision, common understanding, and unity of direction and effort of the entire organization require definition of "what our business is and what it should be."

### "What Is Our Business?"—Never Obvious

Nothing may seem simpler or more obvious than to know what a company's business is. A steel mill makes steel, a railroad runs trains to carry freight and passengers, an insurance company underwrites fire risks, a bank lends money. Actually, "What is our business?" is almost always a difficult question and the right answer is usually anything but obvious.

One of the earliest and most successful answers was worked out by Theodore N. Vail (1845–1920) for the American Telephone and Telegraph Company (also known as the Bell System) almost seventy years ago: "Our business is service." This sounds obvious once it has been said. But first there had to be the realization that a telephone system, being a natural monopoly, was susceptible to nationalization and that a privately owned telephone service in a developed and industrialized country was exceptional and needed community support for its survival. Second, there had to be the realization that community support could not be obtained by propaganda campaigns or by attacking critics as "un-American" or "socialistic." It could be obtained only by creating customer satisfaction. This realization meant radical innovations in business policy. It meant constant indoctrination in dedication to service for all employees, and public relations which stressed service. It meant emphasis on research and technological leadership, and it required financial policy which assumed that the company had to give service wherever there was a demand, and that it was management's job to find the necessary capital and to earn a return on it. The United States would hardly have gone through the New Deal period without a serious attempt at telephone nationalization but for the careful analysis of its own business that the Telephone Company made between 1905 and 1915.

\*   \*   \*   \*   \*

### Who Is the Customer?

"Who is the customer?" is the first and the crucial question in defining business purpose and business mission. It is not an easy, let alone an obvious question. How it is being answered determines, in large measure, how the business defines itself.

The consumer, that is, the ultimate user of a product or a service, is always a customer. But he is never *the* customer; there are usually at least two—sometimes more. Each customer defines a different business, has different expectations and values, buys something different. Yet, all customers have to be satisfied in the answer to the question "What is our business?"

\*   \*   \*   \*   \*

It is also important to ask "Where is the customer?" One of the secrets of Sears's success in the 1920s was the discovery that its old customer was now in a different place: the farmer had become mobile and was beginning to buy in town. This made Sears realize early—almost two decades before most other American retailers—that store location is a major business decision and a major element in answering the question "What is our business?"

American leadership in international banking in the last twenty years is not primarily the result of superior resources. It is largely the result of asking, "Where is the customer?" As soon as the question was asked, it became clear that the old customers, the American corporations, were going multinational and had to be served from a multitude of locations all over the world rather than from New York or San Francisco headquarters. The resources for serving the new multinational customers did not come from the United States but from the international market itself, and, above all, from Europe and the Eurodollar market.

The next question is, "What does the customer buy?"

The Cadillac people say that they make an automobile, and their business is called the Cadillac Motor Division of General Motors. But does the man who spends $7,000 on a new Cadillac buy transportation, or does he buy primarily prestige? Does the Cadillac compete with Chevrolet, Ford, and Volkswagen? Nicholas Dreystadt, the German-born service mechanic who took over Cadillac in the Depression years of the thirties, answered: "Cadillac competes with diamonds and mink coats. The Cadillac customer does not buy 'transportation' but 'status.' " This answer saved Cadillac, which was about to go under. Within two years or so, it made it into a major growth business despite the Depression.

### What Is Value to the Customer?

The final question needed to come to grips with business purpose and business mission is: "What is value to the customer?" It may be the most important question. Yet it is the one least often asked.

One reason is that managers are quite sure that they know the answer. Value is what they, in their business, define as quality. But this is almost always the wrong definition.

For the teenage girl, for instance, value in a shoe is high fashion. It has to be "in." Price is a secondary consideration and durability is not value at all. For the same girl as a young mother, a few years later, high fashion becomes a restraint. She will not buy something that is quite unfashionable. But what she looks for is durability, price, comfort and fit, and so on. The same shoe that represents the best buy for the teenager is a very poor value for her slightly older sister.

Manufacturers tend to consider this as irrational behavior. But the first rule is that there are no irrational customers. Customers almost without exception behave rationally in terms of their own realities and their own situation. High fashion is rationality for the teenage girl; her other needs—food and housing—are, after all, still taken care of by her parents, as a rule. High fashion is a restraint for the young housewife who has to budget, who is on her feet a great deal, who has "her man," and who no longer goes out every weekend.

The customer never buys a product. By definition the customer buys the satisfaction of a want. He buys value. Yet the manufacturer, by definition, cannot produce a value. He can only make and sell a product. What the manufacturer considers quality may, therefore, be irrelevant and nothing but waste and useless expense.

Another reason why the question "What is value to the customer?" is rarely asked is that the economists think they know the answer: value is price. This is misleading, if not actually the wrong answer.

Price is anything but a simple concept, to begin with. Then there are other value concepts which may determine what price really means. In many cases, finally, price is secondary and a limiting factor rather than the essence of value.

\*    \*    \*    \*    \*

Xerox owes its success, to a large extent, to defining price as what the customer pays for a copy rather than what he pays for the machine. Xerox, accordingly, has priced its machines in terms of the copies used. In other words, the customer pays for the copy rather than for the machine—and, of course, what the customer wants are copies rather than a machine.

\*    \*    \*    \*    \*

But price is also only a part of value. There is a whole range of quality considerations which are not expressed in price: durability, freedom from breakdown, the maker's standing, service, etc. High price itself may actually be value—as in expensive perfumes, expensive furs, or exclusive gowns.

\* \* \* \* \*

What a company's different customers consider value is so complicated that it can be answered only by the customers themselves. Management should not even try to guess at the answers—it should always go to the customers in a systematic quest for them.

\* \* \* \* \*

Yet even such businesses should start their attempt to ask "What is our business?" by first asking, "Who are our customers? Where are they? What do they consider value?" A business—and for that matter, any institution—is determined by its contribution; everything else is effort rather than result. What the customer pays is revenue; everything else is cost. The approach from the outside, that is, from the market, is only one step. But it is the step that comes before all others. It alone can give understanding and thereby replace opinions as the foundation for the most fundamental decision that faces every management.

## When to Ask "What Is Our Business?"

Most managements, if they ask the question at all, ask "What is our business?" when the company is in trouble. Of course, then it *must* be asked. And then asking the question may, indeed, have spectacular results and may even reverse what appears irreversible decline—as shown by the example of Vail's work at Bell Telephone and of the reversal of the carpet industry's long-term downward trend.

The success of General Motors also resulted from asking "What is our business?" when the company was floundering. When Alfred P. Sloan, Jr., became president in 1920, GM was in deep trouble and barely viable. Sloan's definition of the purpose and mission of GM, and his development of both strategy and structure from this definition, gave GM leadership and outstanding profitability within three years or less.

\* \* \* \* \*

The most important time to ask seriously "What is our business?" is when a company has been successful. To understand this has been the great strength of Sears, Roebuck. It is also one of the secrets of the success of Marks & Spencer in Great Britain. . . . And not to have understood this is a major reason for the present crisis of American schools and American universities.

Success always obsoletes the very behavior that achieved it. It always creates new realities. It always creates, above all, its own and different problems. Only the fairy story ends "They lived happily ever after."

It is not easy for the management of a successful company to ask, "What is our business?" Everybody in the company then thinks that the answer is so obvious as not to deserve discussion. It is never popular to argue with success, never popular to rock the boat.

The ancient Greeks knew that the penalty for the hubris of success is severe. The management that does not ask "What is our business?" when the company is successful is, in effect, smug, lazy, and arrogant. It will not be long before success will turn into failure.

The two most successful American industries of the 1920s were anthracite coal mines and railroads. Both believed that God had given them an unshakable monopoly forever. Both believed that the definition of their business was so obvious as to eliminate all need for thought, let alone for action. Neither need have tumbled from its leadership position—the anthracite industry into total oblivion—had their managements not taken success for granted.

Above all: when a management attains the company's objectives, it should always ask seriously, "What is our business?" This requires self-discipline and responsibility. The alternative is decline.

**"What Will Our Business Be?"**

Sooner or later even the most successful answer to the question "What is our business?" becomes obsolete.

Theodore Vail's answer was good for almost two-thirds of a century. But by the late 1960s it became apparent that it was no longer adequate; the telephone system was no longer, as in Vail's days, a natural monopoly. Alternative ways of telecommunication were rapidly becoming possible. By the late sixties it had also become apparent that the traditional definition of the telephone as an instrument to transmit voice messages had become inadequate, both because of the rapid growth in data transmission over telephone wires and because of the increasing possibility of transmitting visual images together with the voice. Vail's simple and elegant definition of the business of the Bell Telephone System was in need of reexamination.

The brilliant answer which Alfred P. Sloan, as the new president of General Motors, gave in the early 1920s to the question "What is GM's business?" also held good for an amazingly long time, right through World War II and the postwar recovery. But by 1960 or so, while Sloan, though retired, was himself still alive, the answer had become inadequate and inappropriate. That GM has not raised the question again and apparently has not seen the need to think it through again surely has a lot to do with the evident vulnerability of the company to consumer dissatisfaction, public pressures, and political attack, and with its inability to attain leadership position in the world automobile market.

Very few definitions of the purpose and mission of a business have anything like a life expectancy of thirty let alone fifty, years. To be good for ten years is probably all one can normally expect.

In asking "What is our business?" management therefore also needs to add, "And what *will* it be? What changes in the environment are already discernible that are likely to have high impact on the characteristics, mission, and purpose of our business?" and "How do we *now* build these anticipations into our theory of the business, into its objectives, strategies, and work assignments?"

\*    \*    \*    \*    \*

Management needs to anticipate changes in market structure resulting from changes in the economy; from changes in fashion or taste; from moves by competition. And competition must always be defined according to the customer's concept of what product or service he buys and thus must include indirect as well as direct competition.

**The Unsatisfied Wants of the Customer**

Finally, management has to ask which of the consumer's wants are not adequately satisfied by the products or services offered him today. The ability to ask this question and to answer it correctly usually makes the difference between a growth company and one that depends for its development on the rising tide of the economy or of the industry. But whoever contents himself to rise with the tide will also fall with it.

One example of a successful analysis of the customer's unsatisfied wants is Sears, Roebuck, of course. But the topic is so important as to warrant further illustration.

Sony asked the question "What are the customer's unsatisfied wants?" when it first decided to move into the American consumer market in the mid-fifties. Sony had been founded right after the end of World War II as a manufacturer of tape recorders and had achieved modest success with its products in its own domestic market. It had entered the U.S. as a small but reliable supplier of high-priced professional tape-recording equipment for broadcasting studios. Yet the product with which it first established itself in the American mass-consumer market was a product it had never made before—portable transistor radios. Young people, Sony's analysis of the market showed, were taking the existing heavy, clumsy, and expensive equipment—phonographs weighing many pounds, or battery-powered radios with audio tubes—on picnics, camping trips, and other excursions. Surely here was an unsatisfied want for a light, cheap, and yet dependable instrument. Sony did not develop the transistor—Bell Laboratories had done that, in America. The Bell Laboratories people, however, as well as all the electronic manufacturers in America, had decided that the customer was not yet ready for transistorized equipment. They looked at the wants of the customer that were satisfied by the existing equipment, wants for equipment that was meant to be kept in one place. Sony, by asking "What are the *un*satisfied wants?" identified a new growth market—and within an incredibly short period established itself worldwide as the leader and the pacesetter.

\* \* \* \* \*

### "What Should Our Business Be?"

"What *will* our business be?" aims at adaptation to anticipated changes. It aims at modifying, extending, developing the existing, ongoing business.

But there is need also to ask "What *should* our business be?" What opportunities are opening up or can be created to fulfill the purpose and mission of the business by making it into a *different* business?

IBM had long defined its business as data processing. Prior to 1950, this meant punch cards and equipment for sorting them. When the computer came, and with it a new technology in which IBM had not the slightest expertise, IBM, asking, "What *should* our business be?," realized that data processing henceforth would have to mean computers rather than punch cards.

Businesses that fail to ask this question are likely to miss their major opportunity.

\* \* \* \* \*

*From*

# MARKETING FOR MANAGERS\*

*By Frederick E. Webster, Jr.*

[Editor's note: Professor Webster uses the expression "generic product concept" where other authors use "functional definition of product."]

### Generic Product Concept

One last characteristic of the marketing concept central to understanding its usefulness in strategic planning is its focus on the benefits delivered by a product rather than its physical characteristics. A diamond drill tip is not a hard hunk of carbon but a durable and precise cutting tool that offers the user higher reliability and lower cost in use than alternative drills. Air freight is not an airplane but a high-speed, highly reliable transportation service offering benefits in the form of reduced breakage, loss, and handling expense; lower inventories; and more efficient customer service. As Professor E. Raymond Corey of the Harvard Business School has succinctly put it, "A product is what it does." Industrial buyers are buying profit-creating and cost-reducing products and services on the basis of estimates of supplier reliability, service, technical assistance, and so on as well as on the basis of personal satisfactions in terms of status, security, ego enhancement, and job satisfaction for the buyer. Housewives in a supermarket are buying not just nutrition but also convenience, affection, creativity, and social approval.

---

Definition of the generic product values to be offered in the market is a key step in strategic planning, one requiring a high degree of creativity and sophistication. The nature of the generic product concept defines competition. For example, what is the generic product concept defines in a video tape recorder? Is it an entertainment device competing with stereo radios and tape recorders, regular television sets, movies, and other forms of entertainment? Is it an educational device competing with books, correspondence courses, and formal education? Or is it a communication device competing with telephone, airline travel, sales conferences, and other means of bringing people together? From which areas will major competitive innovations come to eventually destroy the profitability of the video tape recorder? Obviously, different companies will answer this question differently—but not all answers will be equally useful to guide the company in its strategic planning.

A tendency to define the generic product concept—and thus the nature of the business—too narrowly is one of the major sources of weakness in strategic planning. This makes the firm blind not only to opportunities for product and market innovation but also to threats from unanticipated sources of competition. Theodore Levitt labeled this tendency "marketing myopia" and became famous for his observations about the railroads who defined their business as railroading rather than transportation and thus failed to anticipate and respond to increased truck and airline competition. He had similar observations about petroleum companies defining their business as discovering and refining oil rather than providing energy, only to be repeatedly saved from the consequences of their narrow-mindedness by developments occurring outside of their industry such as the internal-combustion engine, plastics, and petrochemicals. No doubt Levitt's point is valid: A major strategic weakness is to define the business in terms of today's narrow products and technology rather than in terms of enduring and basic customer need satisfactions. The question, "What business are we in?" is central to all strategic thinking and can only be answered meaningfully by reference to the basic human satisfactions the firm ultimately provides in the marketplace.

\*    \*    \*    \*    \*

*From*

# THE CONCEPT OF CORPORATE STRATEGY\*

*By Kenneth Andrews*

### Strategy as Projection of Preference

We must acknowledge at this point that there is no way to divorce the decision that names the most sensible economic strategy for a company from the personal values of those who make the choice. Executives in charge of company destinies do not look exclusively at what a company might do and can do. In apparent disregard of the second of these considerations, they sometimes seem heavily influenced by what they personally *want* to do.

\*    \*    \*    \*    \*

We will be able to understand the strategic decision better if we admit rather than resist the dimension of preference. The professional manager in a large company, drilled in analytical technique and the use of staff trained to subordinate value-laden assumptions to tables of numbers, may often prefer the optimal economic strategy because of its very suitability. Certain entrepreneurs, whose energy and personal drives far outweigh their formal training and self-awareness, set their course in directions not necessarily supported by logical appraisal. Such disparity appears most frequently in small privately held concerns, or in compa-

---

\* Reprinted with permission from *The Concept of Corporate Strategy,* Dow Jones-Irwin, 1971, Excerpt from pp. 104–6, 108–9, 112–13.

nies built by successful and self-confident owner-managers. The phenomenon we are discussing, however, may appear in any company.

Our problem now can be very simply stated. In examining the alternatives available to a company, we must henceforth take into consideration the preferences of the chief executive. Furthermore, we must also be concerned with the values of other key managers who must either contribute to or assent to the strategy if it is to be effective. We therefore have two kinds of reconciliation to consider—first, the divergence between the chief executive's preference and the strategic choice which seems most defensible and, second, the conflict among several sets of managerial personal values which must be reconciled not only with an economic strategy but with each other.

      *    *    *    *    *

We should in all realism admit that the personal desires, aspirations, and needs of the senior managers of a company actually *do* play an influential role in the determination of strategy. Against those who are offended by this idea either for its departure from the stereotype of single-minded economic man or for its implicit violation of responsibilities to the shareholder, I would argue that we must accept not only the inevitability but the desirability of this intervention. If we begin by saying that all strategic decisions must fall within the very broad limits of the manager's fiduciary responsibility to the owners of the business and perhaps to others in the management group, then we may proceed legitimately to the idea that what a manager wants to do is not out of order. The conflict which often arises between what general managers want to do and what the dictates of economic strategy suggest they ought to do is best not denied or condemned. It should be accepted as a matter of course. In the study of organization behavior, we have long since concluded that the personal needs of the hourly worker must be taken seriously and at least partially satisfied as a means of securing the productive effort for which wages are paid. It should, then, come as no surprise to us that the president of the corporation also arrives at his work with his own needs and values, to say nothing of his relatively greater power to see that they are taken into account.

If we accept the inevitability of personal values in the strategic decision that determines the character and the course of a corporation, then we must turn to the skills required to reconcile the optimal economic strategy with the personal preferences of the executives of the company. . . .

      *    *    *    *    *

To many caught up in the unresolved strategic questions in their own organizations, it seems futile even to attempt to reconcile a strategic alternative dictated by personal preference with other alternatives oriented toward capitalizing on opportunity to the greatest possible extent. In actuality, however, this additional complication poses fewer difficulties than at first appear. The analysis of opportunity and the appraisal of resources themselves often lead in different directions. To compose three, rather than two, divergent sets of considerations into a single pattern may increase the complexity of the task, but the integrating process is still the same. We can look for the dominant consideration and treat the others as constraints; we can probe the elements in conflict for the possibilities of reinterpretation or adjustment. We are not building a wall of irregular stone so much as balancing a mobile of elements, the motion of which is adjustable to the motion of the entire mobile.

As we have seen, external developments can be affected by company action and company resources, and internal competence can be developed. If worse comes to worst, it is better for a man to detach himself from a management whose values he does not share than to pretend he shares them or to wonder why they think as they do.

      *    *    *    *    *

. . . It is not necessary, however, for all members of a management to think alike or to have the same personal values, so long as strategic decision is not delayed or rendered ineffective by these known and accepted differences. Large gains are possible simply by raising the strategic issues for discussion by top management, and by admitting the legitimacy of different preferences, and by explaining how superficial or fundamental the differences are.

      *    *    *    *    *

*From*

# BUSINESS STRATEGY AND POLICY*

*By J. Thomas Cannon*

[Editor's note: Accompanying text omitted.]

**Selected "What" Action-Strategy Areas**

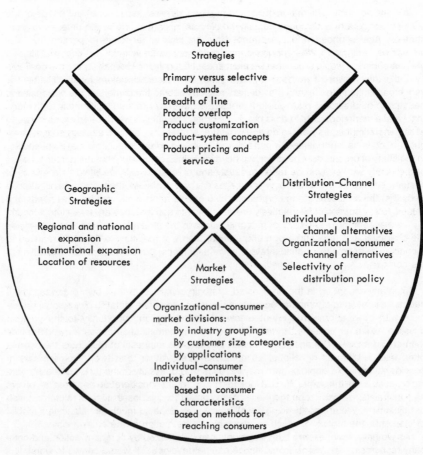

Product
Strategies

Primary versus selective
demands
Breadth of line
Product overlap
Product customization
Product–system concepts
Product pricing and
service

Distribution–Channel
Strategies

Individual–consumer
channel alternatives
Organizational–consumer
channel alternatives
Selectivity of
distribution policy

Geographic
Strategies

Regional and national
expansion
International expansion
Location of resources

Market
Strategies

Organizational–consumer
market divisions:
By industry groupings
By customer size categories
By applications
Individual–consumer
market determinants:
Based on consumer
characteristics
Based on methods for
reaching consumers

**Selected "How" Action-Strategy Areas***

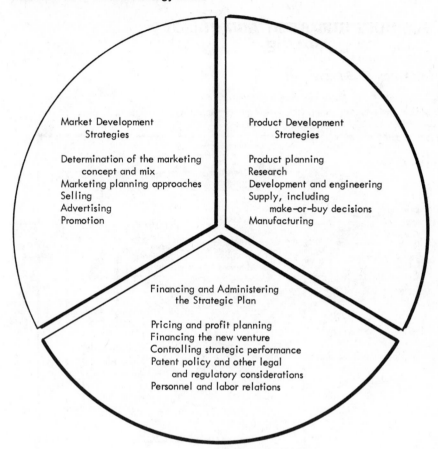

Market Development
    Strategies

Determination of the marketing
    concept and mix
Marketing planning approaches
Selling
Advertising
Promotion

Product Development
    Strategies

Product planning
Research
Development and engineering
Supply, including
        make–or–buy decisions
Manufacturing

Financing and Administering
    the Strategic Plan

Pricing and profit planning
Financing the new venture
Controlling strategic performance
Patent policy and other legal
    and regulatory considerations
Personnel and labor relations

---

*From*

# FORMULATING STRATEGY IN SMALLER COMPANIES*

*By Frank F. Gilmore*

**Model of New Approach (for strategy formulation)**

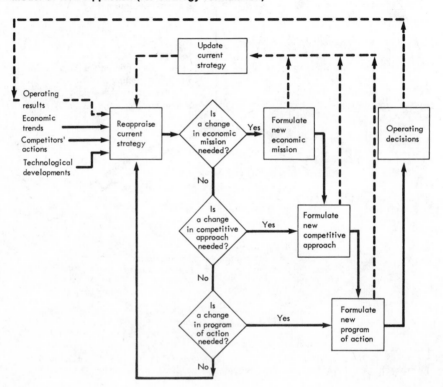

**1. *Economic Mission.*** This is concerned with the kind of business the company should be in, and what its performance objectives should be.

**2. *Competitive Approach.*** This is concerned with finding the product-market-sales approach that will accomplish the economic mission, and with deriving pertinent goals in the various areas of the business.

**3. *Program of Action.*** This involves a search for efficient means of implementing the competitive approach.

---

* From "Formulating Strategy in Smaller Companies," *Howard Business Review,* vol. 49, no. 3 (May–June 1971), p. 172 (excerpts). Reprinted by permission. © 1971 by The President and Fellows of Harvard College; all rights reserved.

*From*

# ANATOMY OF CORPORATE PLANNING*

*By Frank F. Gilmore and R. G. Brandenberg*

**FIGURE 1**
**Formulation of Economic Mission**

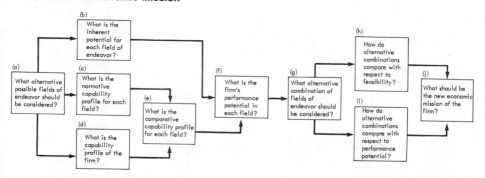

Problem: What kind of business should the company be in and what should the performance objectives be?

*a.* A field of endeavor is a sphere of business activity within which a firm operates. It may be characterized by a common thread such as technology or product-market orientation. For a small company, a segment of an industry may constitute its field of endeavor, and it may be thought of as specialized. A larger firm may be active in several related fields of endeavor within an industry and be considered integrated. Or a company may be acting in several unrelated fields of endeavor and be thought of as diversified.

*b.* Inherent potential defines the extent to which a field of endeavor offers the possibility of achieving objectives in four critical areas of performance: (1) growth—both rate of growth and outlook for continuance of growth; (2) flexibility in relation to the uncertainties of technological change; (3) stability in resisting major declines in the business cycle; and (4) return on investment. The performance of leading firms in the field offers some indication of the potential inherent in the field.

*c.* A normative capability profile is a composite statement in quantitative and/or qualitative terms of what it takes to be successful in a field of endeavor. Measures are needed in such functional areas as research and development, marketing, production, finance, and management. A study of the capabilities and sources of synergistic strength of the leading firms in each field can provide a point of departure in estimating requirements for success.

*d.* The firm's capability profile is a statement in quantitative and/or qualitative terms of the firm's capabilities in the functional areas defined in the normative capability profile.

*e.* Relating the firm's capability profile to the normative capability profile for each endeavor will serve to develop comparative profiles while indicate how well the firm's capabilities match the requirements for success in each field.

*f.* The firm's performance potential in each field may be derived by matching the comparative capability profiles with inherent potential in each field with respect to growth, flexibility, stability, and return on investment.

*g.* It may be desirable for the firm to be active in more than one field of endeavor. If integration or diversification appears attractive, possible combinations of the more promising fields should be formulated at this point.

*h.* Alternative combinations of several fields of endeavor may be evaluated with respect to feasibility by comparing resource requirements. Resource requirements will reflect the degree to which synergy is realized under each alternative.

*i.* Also, alternative combinations of fields of endeavor may be evaluated with respect to growth, flexibility, stability, and return on investment. Particular note should be paid to the degree to which synergy is realized under each alternative.

*j.* The final decision with respect to the combinations of fields of endeavor (together with associated performance goals) defines the economic mission of the enterprise. The foregoing analyses are concerned with the problem of choosing a combination of fields of endeavor and objectives from an economic point of view. To this information base top management must add noneconomic considerations and business judgement in order to arrive at a final decision.

---

* From "Anatomy of Corporate Planning," *Harvard Business Review,* vol. 40, no. 6 (November–December 1962), pp. 63–64. Reprinted by permission. (excerpts). © 1962 by The President and Fellows of Harvard College; all rights reserved.

# FIGURE 2. Formulation of Competitive Strategy

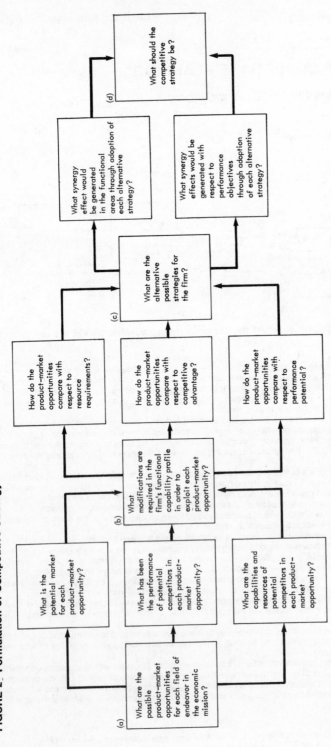

**Problem.** How should the firm pursue its objectives in each field of endeavor specified in the economic mission?

*a.* Product-market opportunities (characterized by the significant features that are expected to influence their outcome) are specific combinations of product-market-sales approaches which define possible ways of exploiting a field of endeavor.

*b.* Based on the information developed in the preceding three steps, an analysis may be made of the firm's functional capabilities with respect to research and development. Marketing, production, finance, and management. Changes required for successful implementation of each alternative product-market opportunity may be defined as product-market plans.

*c.* Combining plans for the more attractive product-market opportunities with one another, or with existing plans in fields of endeavor in which the company is already operating, will serve to develop alternative strategies for the firm as a whole.

*d.* The decision as to the competitive strategy of the firm defines the directions in which the company will move toward its objectives in each environment included in the economic mission. The particular ways in which performance objectives will be pursued in each field of endeavor, together with the functional goals necessary for their accomplishment, are specified, thus providing the framework for development of a program of action.

# 3.  SHOE CORPORATION OF ILLINOIS

---

## Case Introduction

---

### SYNOPSIS

The Shoe Corporation of Illinois (S.C.I.) is a small shoe manufacturing firm which specializes in low-priced shoes that are copied from leading fashion designers of New York and Europe. Its flexibility gives it a competitive advantage over larger producers in the shoe industry and enables S.C.I. to fill a niche in the industry. However, its flexibility also gives rise to problems of integration between production sales, and design. The introduction of new models requires special handling and is disruptive for production. This results in some problems between the styling manager and production. New styles also require special practies on the part of salesman who have established informal integrative practices with Freeman, the statistician, to process new orders. These informal arrangements deviate from formal company procedures. Flynn, the S.C.I. designer, recommended that S.C.I. introduce original designs but this recommendation was disapproved by the president. Flynn persisted in his idea and has worked secretly with Freeman to introduce two original models which yielded very different results.

### WHY THIS CASE IS INCLUDED

This case provides an opportunity to analyze two problems frequently facing organizations: the problem of integration and the problem of motivation as it relates to broader questions of corporate policy. Firms operating in a turbulent environment must be highly flexible if they are to survive. Such flexibility presents problems of integration which are manifested in numerous technical problems as well as the human problems of organizational conflict. The latter type of problems bring into focus a number of structural alternatives which an organizational policy maker can consider.

It is often recognized that an organization needs to provide an opportunity for individual growth if individuals are to remain highly motivated. This case can be used to illustrate that questions of individual growth can have far-reaching implications for corporate policy and especially for marketing policy as is the case here. A change in marketing policy can involve a requirement for changes in organizational structure, investments, long-range commitments, and ultimate questions of corporate identity. These issues get to the heart of corporate policy and must be carefully considered before a change is entertained.

## DIAGNOSTIC AND PREDICTIVE QUESTIONS

The readings included with this case are marked (*). The author index at the end of this book locates the other readings.

1. Why are larger competitors able to undercut the prices of the Shoe Corporation of Illinois (S.C.I.) on "stable" shoes? What would S.C.I. probably have to do to become competitive on these product lines?

Note: This question may be approached by common sense. Imagine that Shoe Corporation of Illinois has $625,000 invested in certain shoe machinery which produces 12,000 pairs of shoes a year. This machinery depreciates $62,500 per year until it wears out in ten years. What is the fixed cost per unit of shoes? Now suppose that a much larger company sells 500,000 pairs and invests $15,000,000 in machines which will wear out in ten years. The depreciation per year is $1,500,000. What is the fixed unit cost per pair of shoes?

Another approach to this question might be more technical and precise application of microeconomic theory. Study the long-run price curves in any economics text.

2. Corporate strategy is often based upon some advantages a particular corporation has relative to other firms in the industry. Sometimes a firm seeks to identify itself in a niche based upon some unique advantage which can serve as a basis of specialization that a firm enjoys more than its competitors. Alternatively, a firm can develop competitive strength which is more broadly based due to economies of scale or diversification schemes. What approaches seem to be used by Brown Shoe and by S.C.I.? Evaluate the corporate strategy of S.C.I. based upon its compatibility with the structure of the industry and upon the criteria offered by Tilles.

Read: Tilles, "How to Evaluate Corporate Strategy." Drucker, *Management—Tasks-Responsibilities-Practices.*

3. Marketing strategy is an important policy area for many business organizations. What is the basis of the marketing strategy used by S.C.I.? Does the introduction of original designs by Mr. Flynn suggest any major changes in that market policy?

Read: Pessemier, *New Product Decisions.* *Beckman and Davidson, *Marketing.*

4. Total production costs can be decreased up to a point by increasing the quantity of a product produced per production run. Such a procedure

reduces the scheduling changes and influences the costs of the inventory system because lot size is directly related to setup costs per unit produced. What would be the likely effect on total inventory costs of minimizing production costs through using "optimum" production quantities?

Note: Optimum production quantities means roughly "just the right quantity of output," taking into account various factors which cause the cost of a pair of shoes to increase. There are many such factors, such as handling and storage costs, capital cost of shoes standing in inventory, and costs that depend on the lot size of an item produced— the setup costs. These include clerical cost of preparing these customer orders and converting them to production schedules, down time of machines while changing from one style to another, and so on. For some aid in answering this question, see Elwood Buffa, *Modern Production Management.*

5. In addition to inventory costs being inversely related to total setup costs of production, sales revenue might be similarly related to production costs. What is the likely effect of the speical treatment afforded "pilot runs" on production costs? What is the likely effect of this special handling on sales revenue?

Read: *Rapoport and Drews, "Mathematical Approach to Long-Range Planning."

6. Bureaucracies are often characterized by a high reliance on rules, written procedures, precise job descriptions, and an organizational hierarchy. It is sometimes argued that these characteristics encourage efficiency at the expense of innovation and flexibility. Would you classify S.C.I. as a bureaucracy? Why do you think Ferguson is insisting that salesmen send new orders to him instead of to Freeman?

Read: Merton, "Bureaucratic Structure and Personality."

7. What are the possible explanations for Flynn's recommendation and subsequent action to promote shoes designed by S.C.I.? What might explain Freeman's cooperation with Flynn and Freeman's special interest in new designs? Is there any conflict between the motivational factors influencing these two men and the broader interests of S.C.I.?

Read: Maslow, *Motivation and Personality.* Gellerman, *Motivation and Productivity.*

8. What do you think is the cause of the problems between Lawson and Robbins? Are the causes of these problems different from those which resulted in problems among Ferguson, Freeman, and the salesmen?

Read: Litterer, "Conflict in Organization: A Re-Examination." *Seiler, "Diagnosing Interdepartmental Conflict." *Lawrence and Lorsch, "New Management Job: The Integrator."

## POLICY QUESTIONS

9. Assume that you are a consultant hired by Allison to review and evaluate S.C.I. corporate policy. You are asked to specifically look at

marketing policy. Write a letter to the president summarizing the advantages and disadvantages of introducing original designs and recommend the marketing policy you feel is most appropriate.

Read:   See readings for Questions 1 through 3 above.

10. One approach to avoid some of the adverse effects of a bureaucratic organization is through the use of participative management. To what extent does S.C.I. use participative management? What are the effects of the use of participative management on the authority structure of S.C.I.? Is this causing other problems?

Read:   McGregor, *The Human Side of Enterprise.*

11. What should Allison do to ensure that his managers remain highly motivated? In order to answer this question, see if you can use path goal analysis to outline the action to motivate Flynn, Ferguson, Freeman, and Robbins.

Read:   Readings for Question 7 above. *Evans, "Leadership and Motivation: A Core Concept."

12. How would the establishment of an "integrator" position in the organization structure of S.C.I. help solve the various technical problems? How might it solve the various human problems?

Read:   See readings for Question 8 above.

# Case Text*

Shoe Corporation of Illinois produces a line of women's shoes that sell in the lower price market, for $11.95 to $13.95 per pair. Profits averaged 25 cents to 30 cents per pair ten years ago, but, according to the president and the controller, labor and materials costs have risen so much in the intervening period that profits today average only 15 cents to 20 cents per pair.

Production at both of the company's plants totals 12,500 pairs per day. The two factories are located within a radius of 60 miles of Chicago: one at Centerville, which produces 4,500 pairs per day, and the other at Meadowvale, which produces 8,000 pairs per day. Company headquarters is located in a building adjacent to the Centerville plant.

It is difficult to give an accurate picture of the number of items in the company's product line. Shoes change in style perhaps more rapidly than any other style product, including garments. This is so chiefly because it is possible to change production processes quickly, and because historically, each company, in attempting to get ahead of competitors, gradually made style changes ever more frequently. At present, including both major and minor style changes, S.C.I. offers between 100 and 120 different products to customers each year.

---

* Copyright 1977 by Charles E. Summer. Names and places have been disguised.

**EXHIBIT 1**
**Partial Organization Chart of Shoe Corporation of Illinois**

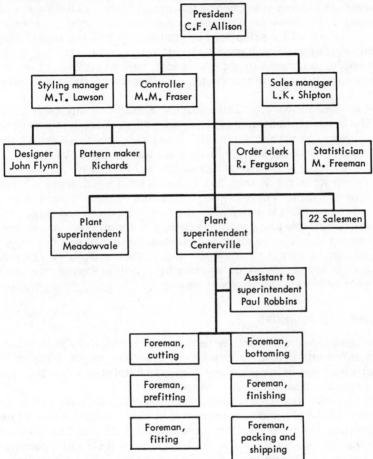

A partial organization chart, showing the departments involved in this case, appears in Exhibit 1.

## COMPETITIVE STRUCTURE OF THE INDUSTRY

Very large general shoe houses, such as International and Brown, carry a line of ladies shoes and are able to undercut prices charged by Shoe Corporation of Illinois, principally because of the policy in the big companies of producing large numbers of "stable" shoes, such as the plain pump and the loafer. They do not attempt to change styles as rapidly as their smaller competitors. Thus, without constant changes in production processes and sales presentations, they are able to keep costs substantially lower.

Charles F. Allison, the president of Shoe Corporation of Illinois, feels that the only way for a small independent company to be competitive is to change styles frequently, taking advantage of the flexibility of a small organization to create designs that appeal to customers. Thus, demand can be created, and a price set high enough, to make a profit. Allison, incidentally, appears to have an artistic talent in styling, and a record of successful judgments in approving high-volume styles over the years.

Regarding Illinois' differences from its large competitors, Allison says:

> You see, Brown and International Shoe Company both produce hundreds of thousands of the same pair of shoes. They store them in inventory at their factories. Their customers, the large wholesalers and retailers, simply know their line and send in orders. They do not have to change styles nearly as often as we do. Sometimes I wish we could do that, too. It makes for a much more stable and orderly system. There is also less friction between people inside the company. The salesmen always know what they're selling, the production people know what is expected of them. The plant personnel are not shook up so often by someone coming in one morning and tampering with their machine lines or their schedules. The styling people are not shook up so often by the plant saying "we can't do your new style the way you want it.

## MAJOR STYLE CHANGES

The decision about whether to put certain style into production requires information from a number of different people. Here is what typically happens in the company. It may be helpful to follow the organization chart in tracing the procedure.

M. T. Lawson, the style manager, and his designer, John Flynn, originate most of the ideas about shape, size of heel, use of flat sole or heels, and findings (the term used for ornaments attached to, but not part of, the shoes—bows, straps, and so forth). They get their ideas principally from reading style and trade magazines or by copying a top-flight designer. Lawson corresponds with publications and friends in large stores in New York, Rome, and Paris in order to obtain by air mail pictures and samples of up-to-the-minute style innovations.

When Lawson decides on a design, he takes a sketch to Allison, who either approves or disapproves it. If Allison approves, he (Allison) then passes the sketch on to Shipton, the sales manager, to find out what lasts (widths) should be chosen. Shipton, in turn, simply forwards the design to Martin Freeman, a statistician in the sales department, who maintains summary information on customer demand for colors and lasts.

To compile this information, Freeman visits salesmen twice a year to get their opinions on the colors and lasts that are selling best, and he keeps records of shipments by color and by last. For these needs, he simply totals data that is sent to him by the shipping foreman in each of the two plants.

When Freeman has decided on the lasts and colors, he sends Allison a form that lists the colors and lasts in which the shoe should be produced. Allison, if he approves this list, forwards the information to Lawson, who passes it on to Richards, an expert pattern maker. Richards makes a paper pattern and constructs a prototype in leather and paper, sends this to Lawson, who in turn approves or disapproves it. He forwards any approved prototype to Allison. Allison, if he too approves, notifies Lawson, who takes the prototype to Paul Robbins, assistant to the superintendent of the Centerville plant. Only this plant produces small quantities of new or experimental shoe styles. Such production is referred to as a "pilot run" by executives at the plant.

Robbins then literally carries the prototype through the six production departments of the plant—from cutting to finish—discussing it with each foreman, who in turn works with men on the machines in having a sample lot of several thousand pairs made.

When the finished lot is delivered by the finishing foreman to the shipping foreman (because of the importance of styling, Allison has directed that each foreman personally deliver styling, Allison has directed that each foreman personally deliver styling goods in process to the foreman of the next department), the latter holds the inventory in storage and sends one pair each to Allison and Lawson. If they approve of the finished product, Allison instructs the shipping foreman to mail samples to each of the company's 22 salesmen throughout the country. Salesmen have instructions to take the samples immediately (within one week) to at least ten customers. Orders for already established shoes are normally sent to Ralph Ferguson, a clerk in Shipton's office, who records them and forwards them to the plant superintendents for production. In the case of first orders on new styles, however, salesmen have found by experience that Martin Freeman has a greater interest in the success of new "trials," so they rush orders to him, air mail, and he in turn places the first orders for a new style in the interoffice mail to plant superintendents. He then sends a duplicate of the order, mailed in by the salesmen, to Ferguson for entering in his statistical record of all orders received by the company.

Three weeks after the salesmen receive samples, Allison requires Ralph Ferguson to give him a tabulation of orders. At that time, he decides whether the salesmen should push the item and the superintendents should produce large quantities, or whether he will tell them that although existing orders will be produced, the item will be discontinued in a short time.

The procedures outlined here have, according to Allison:

> . . . worked reasonably well. The average time from when Lawson decides on a design until we notify the Centerville plant to produce the pilot run is two weeks to a month. Of course, if we could speed that up, it would make the company just that much more secure in staying in the game against the big companies, and in taking sales away from our competitors. There seems to be endless bickering among people around here involved in the styling phase of the business. That's to be expected when you have to move fast—there

isn't much time to stop and observe all of the social amenities. I have never thought that a formal organization chart would be good in this company—we've worked out a customary system here that functions well.

M. T. Lawson, manager of styling, says that within his department all work seems to get out in minimum time, he also states that both Flynn and Richards are good employees, and skilled in their work. He mentioned that Flynn had been in to see him twice in the last year:

> . . . to inquire about his [Flynn's] future in the company. He is 33 years old, and has three children. I know that he is eager to make money, and I assured him that over the years we can raise him right along from the $15,000 we are now paying. Actually, he has learned a lot about shoe styles since we hired him from the design department of a fabric company six years ago.

John Flynn revealed that:

> I was actually becoming dissatisfied with this job. All shoe companies copy styles—it's generally accepted practice within the industry. But I've picked up a real feel for designs, and several times I've suggested that the company make all its own original styles. We could make S.C.I. a style leader and also increase our volume. When I ask Lawson about this, he says it takes too much time for the designer to create originals—that we have all we can handle to do research in trade magazines and maintain contracts feeding us the results of experts. Besides, he says, our styles are standing the test of the market place.

## "PROJECTS X AND Y"

Flynn also said that he and Martin Freeman had frequently talked about the styling problem. They felt that:

> Allison is really a great president, and the company surely would be lost without him. However, we've seen times when he lost a lot of money on bad judgments in styles. Not many times—perhaps six or seven times in the last 18 months. Also, he is, of course, extremely busy as president of the corporation. He must look after everything from financing from the banks to bargaining with the union. The result is that he is sometimes unavailable to do his styling approvals for several days, or even two weeks. In a business like this, that kind of delay can cost money. It also makes him slightly edgy. It tends, at times when he has many other things to do, to make him look quickly at the styles we submit, or the prototypes Richards makes, or even the finished shoes that are sent for approval by the shipping foreman. Sometimes I worry that he makes two kinds of

errors. He simply rubber stamps what we've done, in which sending them to him is simply a waste of time. At other times he makes snap judgments of his own, overruling those of us who have spent so much time and expertise on the shoe. We do think he has good judgment, but he himself has said at times that he wishes he had more time to concentrate on styling and approval of prototypes and final products.

Flynn further explained (and this was corroborated by Freeman) that the two had worked out two plans, which they referred to as "project X" and "project Y." In the first, Flynn created an original design that was not copied from existing styles. Freeman then gave special attention to color and last research for the shoe and recommended a color line that didn't exactly fit past records on consumer purchases—but one he and Flynn thought would provide "great consumer appeal." This design and color recommendation were accepted by Lawson and Allison; the shoe went into production and was one of the three top sellers during the calendar year. The latter two men did not know that the shoe was styled in a different way from the usual procedure.

The result of a second, similar project (Y) was put into production the next year, but this time sales were discontinued after three weeks.

## PROBLEM BETWEEN LAWSON AND ROBBINS

Frequently, perhaps 10 to 12 times a year, disagreement arises between Mel Lawson, manager of styling, and Paul Robbins, assistant to the superintendent of the Centerville plant. Robbins says that:

> The styling people don't understand what it means to produce a shoe in the quantities that we do, and to make the changes in production that we have to. They dream up a style quickly, out of thin air. They do not realize that we have a lot of machines that have to be adjusted, and that some things they dream up take much longer on certain machines than others, thus creating a bottleneck in the production line. If they put a bow or strap in one position rather than others, it may mean we have to keep people idle on later machines while there is a pile-up on the sewing machines on which this complicated little operation is performed. This costs the plant money. Furthermore, there are times when they get the prototype here late, and the foremen and I either have to work overtime or the trial run won't get through in time to have new production runs on new styles, to take the plant capacity liberated by our stopping production on old styles. Lawson doesn't know much about production and sales and the whole company. I think all he does is to bring shoes down here to the plant sort of like a messenger boy. Why should he be so hard to get along with? He isn't getting paid any more than I am, and my position in the plant is just as important as his.

Lawson, in turn says that he has a difficult time getting along with Robbins:

> There are many times when Robbins is just unreasonable. I take prototypes to him five or six times a month, and other minor style changes to him six or eight times. I tell him every time that we have problems in getting these ready, but he knows only about the plant, and telling him doesn't seem to do any good. When we first joined the company, we got along all right, but he has gotten harder and harder to get along with.

## CERTAIN OTHER PROBLEMS THAT HAVE ARISEN

Ralph Ferguson, the clerk in the sales department who receives orders from salesmen and forwards totals for production schedules to the two plant superintendents, has complained that the salesmen and Freeman are bypassing him in their practice of sending experimental shoe orders to Freeman. He insists that his job description (one of only two written descriptions in the company) gives him responsibility for receiving *all* orders throughout the company and for maintaining historical statistics on shipments.

Both the salesmen and Freeman, on the other hand, say that before they started the new practice (that is, when Ferguson still received the experimental shoe orders), there were at least eight or ten instances a year when these were delayed from one to three days on Ferguson's desk. They report that Ferguson just wasn't interested in new styles, so the salesmen "just started sending them to Freeman." Ferguson acknowledged that there were times of short delay, but there were good reasons for them:

> They [salesmen and Freeman] are so interested in new designs, colors, and lasts, that they can't understand the importance of a systematic handling of the whole order procedure, including both old and new shoe styles. There must be accuracy. Sure, I give some priority to experimental orders, but sometimes when rush orders for existing company products are piling up, and when there's a lot of planning I have to do to allocate production between Centerville and Meadowvale, I decide which comes first—processing of these, or processing the experimental shoe orders. Shipton is my boss, not the salesmen or Freeman. I'm going to insist that these orders come to me.

# Selected Readings

*From*

# MARKETING*

*By Theodore N. Beckman and William R. Davidson*

**Low-Price Policies.** Some vendors follow a policy of underselling competitors. A notable historical example is the famous R. H. Macy & Company department store in New York. Over a number of generations, its policy has been to sell at less than the shopped price for comparable items. More recently, this policy has been used by various discount houses, especially Masters, Inc., and E. J. Korvette, Inc., both of which operate a number of establishments in eastern markets, and Polk Bros. of Chicago. This price policy is by no means confined to the field of retailing. In the wholesaling of goods, arrangements are frequently made whereby the vendor agrees to supply his customers with merchandise at or below the lowest price quoted by competitors, thus following the policy of "meet or beat" competitors' prices.

There are some manufacturers who believe in and follow a low or lowest price policy. In some cases a low-price policy may be relatively temporary expedient to meet conditions in an unsettled market. For example, the St. Joseph Lead Co. attracted considerable attention in 1960 with a policy announcement that it would discount any competitive posted price for zinc by one-half cent per pound.[1] This policy was adopted when prices for the commodity were very unsettled, and all suppliers were making special concessions of one form or another to customers. Buyers were uncertain about alternative costs available to them. Hence the policy announcement of this major supplier was a means of communicating to the trade that a customer could not likely do better by buying elsewhere. When market conditions become more settled in early 1961, and discounting of base selling prices diminished, St. Joseph rescinded its lowest price policy and reverted to its previous policy of selling at the market level.

A low-price policy, pursued on a continuing basis, is likely to succeed in markets in which there are considerable latent demands at lower prices, and the manufacturers most likely to do so are those with a relatively high physical efficiency. Such a policy tends to widen the market and to give the seller the opportunity of utilizing his facilities to best advantage. A bold and imaginative policy of low or greatly reduced prices can sometimes reach such broader bases of potential demand involving new applications that the low price becomes in itself a product innovation. This has been aptly illustrated as follows:[2]

"A new synthetic fiber, for example, may be so costly and high priced that it is used only for surgical and other very limited purposes. By dropping the price in anticipation of reduced costs, the hosiery and fine apparel markets may be reached; still further down the price scale, the rug, carpet, and industrial markets may be tapped."

---

* Theodore N. Beckman and William R. Davidson, *Marketing,* Seventh Edition. Copyright © 1962, The Ronald Press Company. (Excerpts from pp. 689–91.)

[1] "Zinc Breathes Easier—and Hopes," *Business Week,* January 28, 1961, p. 103.

[2] Clare E. Griffin, "When Is Price Reduction Profitable?" *Harvard Business Review,* September-October 1960, p. 129.

There are definite limits, however, to what may be deemed desirably low prices for any period of time. Unless the reduction is a matter of competitive necessity, no businessman can be expected to reduce his prices materially in the face of a belief that he would not be compensated by sufficient increases in sales volume and satisfactory profitability on the basis of cost and revenue factors applying to the larger volume marketed. Assuming a homogeneous product, the price of the product may be constant at a given time and no firm may be able to sell above the ruling price. No lower price, therefore, need be quoted in order to get the business. In fact, a further lowering of price may bring retaliatory action from competitors or at best may result in a permanent lowering of prices by all of them. In any event, when the basic policy is to sell at relatively low prices this is assigning to pricing a major and an offensive role in the marketing mix.

\* \* \* \* \*

*Selling at Relatively High Prices.*    Some firms find it possible to market products at a relatively high price. This is not ordinarily practical on a sustained basis unless there is a strong degree of market control. Such control may be achieved by significant differentiation in the physical attributes or the functioning of products which are protected by patents or which are manufactured according to complex or secret processes that are difficult to duplicate. In some cases significant differentiation may exist as a result of unusually successful promotional effort which has created an exceptional favorable enterprise or brand image. If the product is a complicated durable good, either consumer or business equipment, differentiation may exist in the form of an outstanding reputation for installation or maintenance service, which may be more important to the user than initial cost.

Selling at a relatively high price level may also be a temporary expedient under certain conditions. For example, a firm brings out a product which is entirely new in its class in some distinctive way, but feels that competitors will follow with similar product modifications after some period of time. The decision may be to price at a relatively high level initially, to recover product research, developmental, and promotional costs as quickly as possible, before it becomes necessary to meet intensive competition. As another example, relatively high price levels are sometimes established on new products or substantial product modifications in order "to try the market." The firm may be totally lacking in information about the nature of elasticity of demand. If it must actually experiment, it is much easier to start with a price that is too high and lower it later, if necessary, than to do the opposite.

When a firm decides to sell at relatively high prices, the assumption is that price is not a very important factor in getting or retaining business. The role of price in the marketing mix is nearly a negative one, having been subordinated almost completely to product development, advertising, or other ingredients. There remains, nevertheless the major management problem about deciding just what specific price to establish.

*From*

# MATHEMATICAL APPROACH TO LONG-RANGE PLANNING*

*By Leo A. Rapoport and William P. Drews*

Almost everybody will agree that over-all optimization is desirable. At the same time, however, there still is a widespread belief that the best plan for an integrated business will be obtained by letting each of the component activities improve its own efficiency as much as possible. Another common view is that for purposes of optimal planning it suffices to

\* Reprinted by permission of the *Harvard Business Review*, May–June 1962, pp. 77–78.

evaluate and screen projects or budget proposals on the basis of their individual profitability. These are serious misconceptions.

Mathematically it can be demonstrated that the maximum of a composite function generally does not correspond to the values of variables which maximize the individual components of that function. A simple graphical illustration of this situation in the context of economics appeared in a recent article by Edward G. Bennion.[1] The optimization principle has also been stated in clear terms by Peter F. Drucker:

". . . If there is one fundamental insight underlying all management science, it is that the business enterprise is a *system* of the highest order. . . .

"The whole of [such] a system is not necessarily improved if one particular function or part is improved or made more efficient. In fact, the system may well be damaged thereby, or even destroyed. In some cases the best way to strengthen the system may be to *weaken* a part—to make it less precise or *less* efficient. For what matters in any system is the performance of the whole. . . .

"Primary emphasis on the efficiency of parts in management science is therefore bound to do damage. It is bound to optimize precision of the tool at the expense of the health and performance of the whole.

"This is hardly a hypothetical danger. The literature abounds in actual examples—inventory controls that improve production runs and cut down working capital but fail to consider the delivery expectations of the customer and the market risks of the business; machine-loading schedules that overlook the impact of the operations of one department on the rest of the plant; forecasts that assume the company's competitors will just stand still; and so on."[2]

Admittedly, the above statements are somewhat general and, therefore, might appear as unfounded abstractions to the hardened skeptic. A simple example, however, might help to illustrate their practical importance:

In the case of our hypothetical oil company in Exhibit I, suppose that one of the refineries should find it most profitable to install a particular processing unit of Type T in order to utilize a certain low-price crude, $C_t$. The installation of this unit would be justified *from the refiner's viewpoint* by showing an attractive return on incremental investment. This "conventional" approach, however, may overlook the aspects of functional interdependence.

Bear in mind that the installation and efficient utilization of a processing unit of Type T would commit the producing function to a continued supply of crude, $C_t$. This crude, although low priced (on the outside market), may not, in fact, be the least costly to produce, nor would it necessarily remain the least costly as greater amounts of it become required in the future. Accordingly, from an over-all viewpoint, it could prove more desirable to install a different processing unit of Type S. This other unit might be more expensive to install or to operate than Type T. In compensation, however, it would permit utilization of some other crude, $C_s$, which in the long run might be less costly to produce than crude, $C_t$.

Under such conditions, it is apparent that over-all company economics could actually be improved by weakening the economics of one of the refineries.

### Danger of Suboptimization

The preceding example, oversimplified as it is, highlights one of the basic shortcomings of the conventional methods of economic analysis. This shortcoming amounts to excessive "suboptimization" from the viewpoint of investment planning. . . .

---

[1] "Econometrics for Management," *Harvard Business Review*, March–April 1961, p. 100.

[2] "Thinking Ahead: Potentials of Management Science," *Harvard Business Review*, January–February 1959, p. 26.

*From*

# DIAGNOSING INTERDEPARTMENTAL CONFLICT*

*By John A. Seiler*

"Purchasing and production are always at each other's throats. I don't know why they can't get along better."

"If the way research and engineering work together were typical for all departments in our company, our executive vice president would be out of a job. Somehow those guys are able to work out their disagreements."

"Sales and production just refuse to deal with each other. Every time a decision is needed, someone higher up has to do a lot of handholding or head-knocking. Why won't they bargain?"

## TRADITIONAL EXPLANATIONS

Why are some interdepartmental relationships successful and others not? Managers typically find themselves advancing one or the other of these explanations:

One popular opinion is the "personality clash" theory, which holds that stubborn prejudices and differences in ingrained personal styles (none of which are actuated by organizational influences) are behind nonproductive relations. As compelling as this explanation often seems to be, it fails to account for the fact that we seldom, if ever, encounter a group composed of people with identical or even closely similar personalities. . . .

Another view holds that failure in interdepartmental relations is the result of "conflicting ideas." This theory asserts that nonproductive relations occur between groups whose respective memberships are so different in terms of skills, training, job activities, personal aspirations, and so on that they cannot possibly find a common area in which to communicate. While this explanation seems to apply to some nonproductive relations, it is not unheard of to find an advanced research group which works quite effectively with a nontechnical, highly consumer-oriented sales group. Seemingly, at least, groups can differ on many counts without a breakdown occurring in their relations. Furthermore, it is not unusual to find groups with remarkably similar points of view which seem to go out of their way to make trouble for each other. Something in addition to different points of view must be playing a part in forming the character of these relationships.

A third popular explanation for nonproductivity puts the blame on competition between groups for authority, power, and influence. Breakdowns occur because each department operates from an entrenched position which, if compromised, will bring the group nothing but defeat and loss of influence. Many nonproductive relationships seem to display characteristics of this kind. But if this theory is to be sufficient unto itself, the only productive relationship would be one in which either or both of the groups had no desire or opportunity for influence over the other. Under these conditions, passivity would seem to be a requirement for productivity. Yet the most highly productive relations appear to take place between aggressive, confident, and high-achievement departments. Apparently other determinants, in addition to competition for prestige and power, must be operating to make interdepartmental relations successful or unsuccessful.

*    *    *    *    *

---

* From "Diagnosing Interdepartmental Conflict," *Harvard Business Review,* vol. 41, no. 5 (September–October 1963), excerpts from pp. 121–25, 128–32. Reprinted by permission. © 1963 by the President and Fellows of Harvard College; all rights reserved.

## BALANCE OF ENERGY

Fundamental to understanding why some relationships are productive and others less so is a recognition that people have limited energies. When a multitude of demands are made on us, we naturally assign priorities to them. If the demands for organizationally productive work take second place to other demands, then the organization loses out. Demands on departments can also be viewed in this way. If a department's energies are consumed by plottings of defense and attack, little time will be left for devotion to more fruitful business. Consequently, departments, too, must assign priorities to demands on their energy.

\*     \*     \*     \*     \*

### Group Control

The setting of priorities by groups is not much different. Groups are, after all, only interdependent individuals who keep their group membership because it is valuable to them. The uniqueness of a group, that which makes it more than the simple addition of its members' wishes and actions, lies in its ability to motivate member behavior toward goals which are attractive to the entire group but which are not attainable by any member alone. Primary among these goals, of course, and basic to group life in general, is the satisfaction of a person's need to belong to something. But groups provide more than simple social satisfaction to their members. They also provide protection from other groups and individuals. They contain power which can be used to gain liberties, self-respect, and prestige for their members. In return for these benefits, the member submits to group discipline.

When a group's existence is threatened by such changes as a formal reorganization which will disperse its members, by rumors of layoff or firing, or by technical change disrupting the relationships among members, the full energy of the group is mobilized. There is a tightening of member discipline, particularly centering on the activities most likely to thwart any alarming changes. On such occasions, the only "work" done is that which protects the group from jeopardy. On the other hand, when groups do not fear for their survival, but see before them a challenging opportunity to work together toward an end of positive value to the group, all their energies become absorbed by the project they are working on.

Energies freed from defense will seek outlets in activities which strengthen the group's ability to survive in the long run and which add zest to the life of its members. If the work formally available to the group is dull and lacking in challenge (or if other obstacles such as restrictive supervisory actions or lack of member skills get in the way), activity is likely to be predominantly social in character. If the work is challenging, and obstacles are not present to hinder its meeting the challenge, the group is likely to find its formal assignment a satisfying outlet for the application of its energy.[1]

### Productive Focus on Task

Company A developed and manufactured ethical pharmaceuticals. The activities required to transform a product idea into a marketable item were performed in sequence by subunits of the research, engineering, and production departments. An idea would first take form in a research department test tube. It would then be evaluated by research chemists and chemical engineers in the pilot plant. Next, new process equipment would be designed by mechanical engineers and job designs laid out around the equipment by industrial engineers. Actual plant construction and placement of equipment were accomplished by construction engineers, and, finally, production responsibility was assumed by production chemists. The members of these formal units agreed that research had the highest prestige of all the work

---

[1] The cases cited in this article have been taken from the case and project research files of the Harvard Business School and are reproduced by permission of the President and Fellows of Harvard College.

groups and that the relative prestige of the other units declined in the order in which each became actively involved in the new product sequence.

\* \* \* \* \*

Company A had an outstanding reputation for important production innovations and rapid development of ideas into mass-production items. Nevertheless, there was frequent argument among research, engineering, and production as to who should take responsibility for the product at what point in the development sequence. Engineering wanted control at the pilot plant. Production wanted control from the time the product entered its physical domain. Research wanted control, as one of its members put it, "until the actual factory yield reaches the theoretical yield."

\* \* \* \* \*

The physical, mental, and emotional energies of these departments appeared to be devoted to the work at hand to a very high degree. While not absent from their relationships, conflicts took the form of tension between the inherently opposing values of quality and economy. The result was a competitive balance between the extremes of both. Why was conflict not destructive in this situation? There are basically three reasons:

1. Each of the three departments represented a social unit in which members could find not only satisfaction for their needs to belong, but also job interest, promotion opportunity, and so on. No one of these departments suffered from internal fragmentation.
2. At each point of significant interdepartmental contact, the members of the interacting groups agreed on certain important ideas as to how work should be accomplished. Wherever technical interdependence required intergroup contact, the groups tended to view each other and their common work with a markedly similar appreciation.
3. The hierarchy of authority among the departments was identical to the informally agreed-upon prestige hierarchy among these departments. This hierarchy was determined by technical work limits set by one department for another, and by the initiation of activity by one department for another. The work done by research, for example, limited what the chemical engineers could work on but, at the same time, was the impetus which set the chemical engineers to work on each new product. The same was true of relationships down through the development sequence.

Very simply, then, a man (or a group) told another what to do and when to do it, he did so as a member of a group of superior prestige, as agreed on by both groups. We might say that the orders which passed from one group to another were "legitimate," since most workers feel that it is legitimate in our society for a person of higher prestige to direct the activities of someone with less prestige, while it is illegitimate for the opposite to occur.

\* \* \* \* \*

The three elements—*internal social stability, external value sharing* and *legitimate authority hierarchy*—comprise a triumvirate of measures which indicate the extent to which departmental energy will tend to be freed for productive work. These factors can be thought of as minimum requirements for interdepartmental effectiveness. For, in their absence, it is highly unlikely that either intrinsically interesting work or encouragement from supervision will achieve much in the way of productivity increases.

\* \* \* \* \*

## VARYING VIEWPOINTS

In each of these four cases, the forces siphoning energy away from productive work have been of a particular kind. In each instance, relationships within groups were at least socially satisfactory. . . . The work of the various groups was intrinsically interesting to group members. Supervision was relatively permissive in allowing group members to "complicate" their lives about the work itself. Obviously, these elements are not always present in organized situations. Equally obvious from our cases is the fact that these elements, by themselves, do not result in effective interdepartmental relations, though they may be considered to contribute to such relations if other conditions are also met.

## Focal Points

What the above cases focus on are the troubles caused by differences in point of view and legitimacy of authority. What these cases teach about group conflicts arising from these two trouble sources is just as true for our understanding of the interrelationships of individuals, for intergroup problems are only special cases of interpersonal issues. The only difference between them is the complexity of dealing with the problem, since the individual persons in our cases are representatives of social groups. Thus, their behavior cannot be modified by actions which are based on the assumption that groups respond exactly as do individuals. In short, the causes of conflict are similar, but the remedies are different.

What happens when groups suffer from authority and viewpoint conflicts is summarized in Exhibit 1. Like any diagram dealing with a limited number of factors, Exhibit 1 runs the danger of implying that these cause-and-effect tendencies represent all that need be known about interdepartmental relations. Such as implication, were it intended, would, of course, be fatuous. Research in the area of interdepartmental problems has scarcely begun. Furthermore, we have already noted that other factors can be expected to intervene and render the exhibit's hypotheses, as they should be called, inoperative. Three of these factors have been emphasized—group cohesion, job interest, and supervisory practices.

## EXHIBIT 1
**Dominant Influences in Interdepartmental Relations**

| | Where points of view are closely allied | Where points of view are in conflict |
|---|---|---|
| Where authority* is consistent with prestige differences | We will tend to find... | We will tend to find... |
| | ...Collaboration and productive conflict | ...Energies absorbed by efforts to force points of view on other groups. Relations will be formal and often arbitrated by outsiders. |
| Where authority is inconsistent with prestige differences | We will tend to find... | We will tend to find... |
| | ...Energies devoted to regaining a "proper" authority relationship. Relations will usually be distant and between low hierarchical levels of the two groups (e.g., messenger). | ...Energies initially expended on forcing points of view and righting authority relations, but the task will be so patently fruitless that the groups will break off contact rather than expose themselves to further threat. |

\* As indicated by work flow.

Once we allow for these mitigating factors, however, we will find it useful to conceive of interdepartmental relations as though they were subject to the dominant influences cited in the diagram. The manager can make this concept more relevant personally if he reviews his own observations of interdepartmental conflict to see how they compare with the kind of analysis described here.

## PLAN FOR ACTION

While the primary purpose of this article has been to explain certain types of interdepartmental problems, the question inevitably arises, "Suppose some sense can be made of interdepartmental difficulties by this kind of thinking; what then do we do with this understanding, even if it does prove to be accurate? How would we go about applying it to lessen interdepartmental conflicts in our company?" Let's look at some action ideas which stem from what has already been said.

### Stop, Look, and Listen

As frustrating as it might seem, the first suggestion is to stop to see if action is required and, if it is, whether it is feasible. It often may be wise to heed the admonishment (in reverse of the usual form), "Don't just do something, stand there!" The basis for this wisdom lies in the fact that formal organizations often display some of the characteristics of a biological organism, particularly insofar as the latter has some capacity to heal itself. The administrator, if this contention be true, may find the role of the modern physician attractive. He attempts to control the environment so that natural healing processes can take place unhindered within the human body. . . .

\*    \*    \*    \*    \*

### Types of Resolution

Our cases (and there are unlimited examples like them) have shown that some interdepartmental difficulties go beyond the capacity of the groups to resolve them at anything but a survival level, if that. That level may well be, and often is, intolerable for the organization as a whole. Let us look at the two alternative types of resolution.

First are the resolutions which arise in response to conflicts of authority. In such cases the work flow designed into the organization (e.g., the passage of blueprints from production engineering to production) violates the notions of the organization's members as to who legitimately should, by right of superior prestige, tell whom what to do. Although such problems are not restricted to particular hierarchical levels of the organization, they do tend to become more intense wherever prestige relations are ambiguous or under threat. The higher one goes in many organizations, the more these conditions tend to apply. There are several ways of resolving such problems:

1. An obvious solution is to take whatever steps are available to reduce prestige ambiguity and threat. For example if . . . management has realized how pertinent production's resentment at being rated "second class" was to the interdepartmental problems in which it was involved, investigation might have produced ways of clarifying production's status and of enriching its participation in important decisions. . . .

2. Another step in reducing the amount of nonproductivity in illegitimate authority relations is to reorganize subunits of the organization in such a way that authority and prestige become consistent. . . .

\*    \*    \*    \*    \*

This crucial aspect of conflict resolution—receptivity to change—brings us to the second major strategy for helping departmental energies engage in constructive action instead of working against members of another department. This strategy involves what might be called intergroup counseling, therapy, or training. Conflicts in points of view are susceptible only to this strategy, short of complete personnel turnover in one or the other of the warring departments. And, because authority illegitimacy must inevitably engender conflict of viewpoint, it too can be mitigated, if only partially, by intergroup training. Several aspects of this strategy are worthy of attention, though the subject is a difficult and complex one.

Some studies show that intergroup conflict resolution hinges on a particular type of training which seeks an integration of viewpoints by making warring groups realize they are dependent on one another.[2] Such a strategy tends to work more readily when both groups

---

[2] See *Intergroup Relations and Leadership,* edited by Muzafer Sherif (New York: John Wiley & Sons, Inc., 1962).

fear some external threat to both of them. This idea is not greatly different from the idea contained in the observation that members of families may fight viciously with one another but when an outsider attacks one of the family, the family abandons its differences to fight together against the intruder. It seems obvious from the analysis presented in this article, however that this strategy is operable only when prestige-authority issues are not present.

A number of researchers, teachers, and managers have begun to explore more direct methods for reducing point-of-view conflict. Some have pointed out that bringing group representatives together to explore their differences is usually doomed to failure since representatives, if they are to remain such, must be loyal to their respective groups.[3] Simple measures to increase contact also appear fruitless, because negative stereotypes end up simply becoming reinforced by the contact.

Other measures have proved more effective. Although they vary in form, almost all of these contain the following basic element: *the groups in conflict must be brought together as totalities under special conditions.*[4] The goal of all of these conditions is to reduce individual and group anxieties sufficiently so that a point of view can not only be made explicit but can be heard by those who do not share it. This procedure requires not only considerable candor between groups, but also candor within each group and within the individual himself. Naturally, sessions in which such training is supposed to take place can be extremely threatening and should be mediated by an external agent to keep threat within manageable bounds and help guide the groups into explorative rather than recriminative behavior.[5]

* * * * *

Such a pursuit, carried on openly and sincerely, cannot help but raise issues of interdepartmental ambiguity, illegitimacy, and conflicting points of view to a level where they can be re-examined and dealt with. An easy process? No. But as "old wives' tales" have told us, no remedy is without pain.

*From*

# NEW MANAGEMENT JOB: THE INTEGRATOR*

*By Paul R. Lawrence and Jay W. Lorsch*

What will be new and unique about organizational structures and management practices of business enterprises that are their industries' competitive leaders a decade from now? Because of the rapid rate of market and technological change, with the accompanying strains and stresses on existing organizational forms, managers are becoming increasingly concerned with the difficulty of reconciling the need for specialization with the need for integration of effort.

* * * * *

. . . [W]e first need to define what we mean by the term *integration.* As used in this article, integration is the achievement of unity of effort among the major functional specialists in a

---

[3] See Robert Blake and Jane S. Mouton, *Group Dynamics—Key to Decision Making* (Houston: Texas, Gulf Publishing Co., 1961).

[4] See Herbert R. Shepard and Robert R. Blake, "Changing Behavior through Cognitive Change," *Human Organization,* Summer 1962, p. 88.

[5] See Chris Argyris, *Interpersonal Competence and Organizational Effectiveness* (Homewood, Ill.: The Dorsey Press, Inc. and Richard D. Irwin, Inc., 1962).

* From "New Management Job: The Integrator," *Harvard Business Review,* vol. 45, no. 6 (November–December 1967), pp. 142–51 (excerpts).

business. The integrator's role involves handling the nonroutine, unprogrammed problems that arise among the traditional functions as each strives to do its own job. It involves resolving interdepartmental conflicts and facilitating decisions, including not only such major decisions as large capital investment but also the thousands of smaller ones regarding product features, quality standards, output, cost targets, schedules, and so on. Our definition reads much like the customary job description of any company general manager or divisional manager who has "line" authority over all the major functional departments.

Although the need for organizational integration is not new, the traditional method of using the "shared boss" as the integrator is rapidly breaking down, and a radically new approach is becoming necessary. The increasingly dynamic nature of many organizational environments is making the integrating job so important and so complex that it cannot be handled by a single general manager, no matter how capable he may be.

*        *        *        *        *

## SURVEY FINDINGS

To this point in the discussion, we have demonstrated that integrative roles are needed and are being developed in many companies. In fact, our study of ten organizations in three distinctly different industries—plastics, consumer foods, and containers—provides dramatic evidence of the importance of effective integration in any industry. This is because our research reveals a close correlation between the effectiveness of integration among functional departments and company growth and profits. However, separate integrating roles or departments are not the solution for all organizations. While formal integrative roles are highly important in R&D-intensive industries, such as plastics and consumer food products, in a comparatively stable industry, such as containers, integration can be achieved through the management hierarchy.

The important point is that in the future more organizations will be operating in rapid changing environments, and the problem of managers will be to make certain that this integrative function is effectively carried out. In order to do this, they will need to learn how to select, train, organize, supervise, and control these new integrators.

### Organization Structure

Two questions arise when we think of designing the structure of the organization to facilitate the work of integrators:

1. *Is it better to establish a formal integration department, or simply to set up integrating positions independent of one another?*
2. *If individual integrating positions are set up, how should they be related to the larger structure?*

In considering these issues it should first be pointed out that if an organization needs integrators at all, it is preferable to legitimize these roles by formal titles and missions rather than to leave them in an informal status. We derive the primary evidence on this point from an intensive study of an electronics company, where the limitations of using informal integrators are clearly revealed.[1] This research demonstrates that the effectiveness of the informal integrators is severely circumscribed when it comes to dealing with difficult interdepartmental relationships. Consider:

> In this organization the boundaries between the production and engineering departments were not well established, and there was intense competition and conflict between these two groups. The informal integrators were unable to achieve effective collaboration, at least in part because their roles were not clearly defined. Therefore, their

---

[1] Unpublished study conducted by John Seiler and Robert Katz for the Division of Research, Harvard Business School.

**EXHIBIT 1**
**Structural Solutions to the Organizational
Integration Problem**

Stable and homogeneous environment

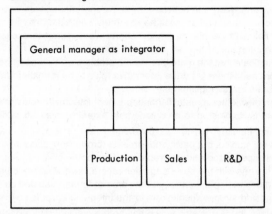

Semidynamic and heterogeneous environment

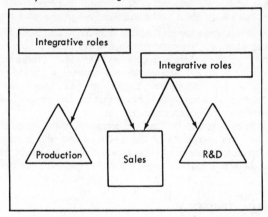

Highly dynamic and heterogeneous environment

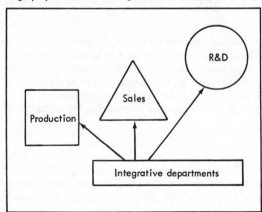

integrative attempts were often seen as inappropriate infringements on the domains of other departments.

For example, an engineering supervisor, whose own inclinations and interests led him to play a coordinating role between the two departments, was frequently rebuffed by the production personnel because he was seen as intruding into their activities. Without a clearly defined role, his integration efforts were limited to exchanging information across the interface of the two departments.

These data indicate that the more intense the problem of interdepartmental collaboration is, the more need there is for the integrative roles to be formally identified so that such activites are seen as legitimate.

The question of whether to establish independent integrative roles or to create a formal department is illuminated to a considerable extent by our data. Consider:

In the plastics industry, which has the fastest rate of technical change of the three industries we studied, the basic departments (production, sales, and research) are the most highly specialized and differentiated. Five of the six plastics companies studied, including the one with the best integration record, have what could be called "full-scale integrating departments," although they are not formally labeled as such. (See *Exhibit 1* for suggested structural solutions to the integration problem.)

In the consumer foods industry, which has both a medium rate of technical change and a medium degree of difference between basic departments, one of the two companies studied uses a full-scale "integrating department"; the other—with the better integration record—simply utilizes a set of scattered integration roles.

The container industry has the most stable technology, and thus only slight differences are perceptible between basic departments. In this industry the company with the best integration record has no formal integrators of any kind; it relies entirely on its regular line organization to do the coordinating. By contrast, a second container company, employing a full-fledged integrating department, has experienced considerable integrating difficulties. This suggests not only that the department is redundant, but that it actually impedes the coordination process.

All of this evidence indicates that the elaborateness of the integrating function should vary both with the complexity of the problems and with the size of the gap that specialization creates between the basic departments. Moreover, management should keep in mind that it is possible to get too many integrators into the act as well as too few.

## BEHAVIOR CHARACTERISTICS

Our research enables us to identify four important characteristics about the behavior of effective integrators, as well as the organizational practices that contribute to their effectiveness:

1. Integrators need to be seen as contributing to important decisions on the basis of their competence and knowledge, rather than on their positional authority.
2. Integrators must have balanced orientations and behavior patterns.
3. Integrators need to feel they are being rewarded for their total product responsibility, not solely on the basis of their performance as individuals.
4. Integrators must have a capacity for resolving interdepartmental conflicts and disputes.

*     *     *     *     *

### Decision Contribution

Although this integrator, like many of his colleagues, complains that he does not have formal authority over the other groups with whom he works, our measures of actual influence on decisions in the organizations studied indicate that all integrators, except for those in the less well-integrated container company, have a larger voice in interdepartmental decisions than their peers in functional departments. And their influence is essential in industries requiring highly specialized and well-integrated organizations, where the integrator must often initiate activities for managers in other departments.

*Personal Competence.* There is another important factor related to influence that distinguishes the integrators in effective organizations from those in less effective ones. In the more effective, the integrators are influential because of their knowledge and expertise, while in less effective organizations they are influential only because of the formal authority of their positions.

\* \* \* \* \*

These and similar comments indicate that the managers in effectively integrated organizations view the integrators as persons who have knowledge of and expertise in solving organizational problems. This personal competence appears to be the foundation on which their large voice in interdepartmental decisions rests.

*Positional Power.* In the organizations that were having difficulty in achieving integration, the tone of the functional managers' commentaries on the influence of the integrators was quite different.

\* \* \* \* \*

Comments . . . suggest that the integrators in organizations having integration problems were influential only because of the formal authority given to them by the top management and because of their proximity to top management. Other responses stressed that generally the integrators in these companies were considered less knowledgeable about industry conditions. Moreover, the specialist managers frequently volunteered disparaging remarks about the integrators' abilities and knowledge.

*Other Factors.* In planning for these integrating positions, attention must be given to placing them at levels in the organization where the incumbents will have ready access to the knowledge and information relevant to decisions. In the well-integrated organizations we studied, for example, this level was usually at the middle of the management hierarchy. Since these organizations were in dynamic, rapidly changing industries where knowledge was complex and uncertain, only those middle managers with specific problem experience had been able to master the required knowledge.

If the integrator selected has had prior work experience in two or more of the several functional departments, the specialist managers will regard him as competent because of the knowledge that his experience has provided. While persons with these ideal qualifications may be extremely scarce, it is important to recognize the necessity to fill these crucial positions. One common failing of the less well-integrated organizations is their tendency to assign young managers lacking sufficient experience in all facets of the business to these positions. Although this may provide a useful learning experience for the young managers, our evidence suggests that it really does not lead to effective integration.

## Balanced Orientation

The second important characteristic of effective integrators is that their orientations and ways of thinking strike a good balance between the extremes of the members of the specialized departments whose efforts they are integrating. For instance, our study shows that:

Research scientists think about long-term projects and issues and about solutions to scientific and technical problems.

Production managers and engineers, on the other hand, are concerned with shorter term problems, especially those that relate to an efficient and timely plant operation.

Sales personnel are also concerned with shorter term issues, but for them the important problems are those that deal with the market—that is, how to meet sales objectives, what to do about competitors' product changes, what characteristics a new product must have to meet the needs of customers, and so forth.

These differences in ways of thinking are, of course, part of what makes it difficult for these groups to collaborate effectively.

The fact that the effective integrators have balanced orientations means that they share more ways of thinking and more behavior patterns with the functional managers than those managers normally do with each other. In a sense, effective integrators speak the language of each of the specialist groups, and thus they are able to work at resolving interdepartmental conflicts. When integrators do not have balanced orientations, their ability to facilitate joint decision making between functional managers suffers. . . .

*    *    *    *    *

Our research also reveals that effective integrators tend to use an interpersonal style of behavior that falls between the two characteristic behavior orientations of specialized departments. At one extreme, sales personnel are most concerned with maintaining sound personal relationships with their colleagues in other departments. At the other extreme, production managers (and research scientists to a lesser extent) are primarily concerned with getting on with the job, even if this causes the disruption of some established relationships. Our evidence indicates that, to be effective, an integrator needs to think and act in ways which evenly balance the highly social and the highly task-oriented behavior patterns of the units he is attempting to link.

Our research further reveals that entire integrating departments are much more effective when they are intermediate in their degree of structure in relation to the specialized departments they are linking. To analyze the formalization of structure, we examined the degree to which formal rules are utilized, the average span of control, the frequency and specificity of both departmental and individual performance reviews, and the number of levels in the hierarchy.

We found, for example, that most of the formally integrated companies were in an industry where specialized departments had to develop distinctly different organizational practices to perform their respective tasks. Thus, at one extreme, the production units needed highly formalized organizational practices to perform their more routinized tasks. At the other extreme, researchers with problem-solving tasks were more effective in units that had less formalized structures. Between these extremes, the sales personnel operated most effectively with intermediate organizational practices.

When the integrators worked within an intermediate structure, they developed behavior patterns not too unlike those of the different specialists they were linking, and thus they were able to work effectively with all of them.

While our data on the need for intermediate orientations and structures are drawn from a study of integrators attempting to link research, sales, and production units, the same conclusions would seem to hold for integrators linking other functional units.

**Performance Recognition**

The third important characteristic of effective integrators is the basis on which they see themselves being evaluated and rewarded. For example, in organizations where the integrators were highly effective, they reported that the most important basis for their superior's evaluation was the overall performance of the products on which they were working. Where the integrators were less effective, the superior's evaluation was more on the basis of their individual performance.

This indicates that if integrators are to perform effectively in coordinating the many facets of complex decisions, they need to feel they are being evaluated and rewarded for the total results of their efforts. When they feel they are judged only on the basis of their performance as individuals, they may become so concerned with making decisions to please their superiors or to avoid rocking the boat that they will easily overlook what is desirable from the point of view of their total product responsibility.

## Conflict Resolution

The final characteristic of effective integrators is the mode of behavior they utilize to resolve interdepartmental conflict. It seems inevitable that such conflicts will arise in any conplex organization from time to time. So, rather than being concerned with the essentially impossible goal of preventing conflict, we are more interested in finding ways for integrators and their colleagues to handle it. Our analysis identifies three modes of behavior for resolving conflict.

*Confrontation Technique.* The first method, *confrontation,* involves placing all relevant facts before the disputants and then discussing the basis of disagreement until some alternative is found that provides the best solution for the total organization. Confrontation often involves extended discussion. . . .

\* \* \* \* \*

*Smoothing Approach.* The second technique for dealing with conflict, *smoothing,* essentially emphasizes the maintenance of friendly relations and avoids conflict as a danger that could disrupt these relations. Managers using this approach are, in effect, indicating anxiety about facing the consequences of their conflicting points of view. Such action, they feel, might not only threaten their continuing friendly relations, but even their jobs. So they smooth over their differences, perhaps by using superficial banter and kidding, and thus sidestep conflict. . . .

*Forcing Method.* The final approach, *forcing,* entails the straightforward use of power in resolving conflict. The disputing parties bring to bear whatever power or influence they have to achieve a resolution favoring their own point of view. This mode of behavior often results in a "win-lose" struggle. Unfortunately, it is often the objectives of the total organization that suffer the greatest loss. . . . Our data indicate that there is a close relationship between the effectiveness of integration in an organization and the reliance of its members on confrontation as a way to resolve interdepartmental conflict.

While confrontation showed up as a common mode of resolving conflict in all of the ten organizations we studied, the integrators and functional managers in the six most effectively integrated organizations did significantly more confronting of conflict than their counterparts in the four less well-integrated organizations. Similarly, the managers and integrators in the two organizations that had achieved a medium degree of integration were confronting conflict more often than the managers in the least effectively integrated organizations.

There is one other point worth considering: in the highly integrated organizations, we also found that the functional managers were using more forcing, and/or less smoothing, behavior than their counterparts in the less effective organizations. This suggests that, while confrontation of conflict must be the primary basis for resolving interdepartmental issues, it is also important to have a backup mode of some forcing behavior to ensure that the issue will at least be addressed and discussed, and not avoided.

\* \* \* \* \*

## Preferred Styles

In addition to measuring the integrators' motives, their preferred behavioral styles were investigated, with certain interesting results:

Effective integrators prefer to take significantly more initiative and leadership; they are aggressive, confident, persuasive, and verbally fluent. In contrast, less effective integrators are retiring, inhibited, and silent, and they avoid situations that involve tension and decisions.

Effective integrators seek status to a greater extent; they are ambitious, active, forceful, effective in communication, and have personal scope and breadth of interests. Less effective integrators are restricted in outlook and interests, and are uneasy and awkward in new or unfamiliar social situations.

Effective integrators have significantly more social poise; they are more clever, enthusiastic, imaginative, spontaneous, and talkative. Less effective integrators are more deliberate, moderate, and patient.

Effective integrators prefer more flexible ways of acting; they are adventurous, humerous, and assertive. Less effective integrators are more industrious, guarded, methodical, and rigid.

*    *    *    *    *

While American industry still needs many types of organizations, as the trend continues for more and more industries to be characterized by rapid rates of technological and market change, more organizations will be like the R&D-intensive firms described here. These firms will require both high differentiation between specialist managers in functional units and tight integration among these units. Although differentiation and integration are essentially antagonistic, effective integrators can help organizations obtain both and thus contribute to economic success. . . .

*From*

# LEADERSHIP AND MOTIVATION: A CORE CONCEPT*

## By Martin G. Evans

The question of whether a leader's behavior has an impact upon the job satisfaction and performance of the subordinate has been subjected to considerable empirical exploration. This, however, has been on a broad front rather than in any great depth. There has been a great deal of replication of Fleishman's[1] original finding that supervisory *initiation of structure* and *consideration* have an impact upon worker behavior and satisfaction. Originally it was found that satisfaction was positively related to consideration, while performance was positively related to initiation of structure. However, even in this early study, differences appeared between different types of work groups—the results were stronger for those foremen in production departments than for those in nonproduction departments. Additional work in the area has added to the confusion. A variety of studies has shown little consistency in the strength or even direction of the relationships observed.

Among the few studies that have attempted to go below the surface of the observed relationships to try to discover the conditions under which either positive or negative relationships are observed is that of Fiedler.[2] This has been a significant contribution. However, his use of a model of leadership which implies that the consideration and initiation of structure styles are the two extremes of a single continuum rather than being two orthogonal continua may have restricted its utility. Nevertheless, he found that the relationship between employee performance and supervisory behavior was moderated by aspects of the "favorableness" of the situation for the supervisor. Highly favorable situations were characterized by:

*a.* High formal power of the supervisor
*b.* High degree of liking for the supervisor by the work group
*c.* Highly structured task

---

* Reprinted by permission of *Academy of Management Journal,* vol. 13, no. 1 (March 1970). Excerpts from pp. 91–97, 99–100.

[1] E. A. Fleishman, E. F. Harris, and H. E. Burtt, *Leadership and Supervision in Industry* (Columbus, Ohio: Bureau of Educational Research, Ohio State University, 1955).

[2] F. E. Fiedler, "Engineer the Job to Fit the Manager," *Harvard Business Review* (1965), 43, 5, pp. 115–22.

Highly unfavorable situations were characterized by:

a. Low formal power of the supervisor
b. Dislike of the supervisor by the work group
c. Unstructured task

Fiedler found that in highly favorable and in highly unfavorable situations the more task-oriented (initiating structure) the supervisor then the more effective were the subordinates. Only in moderately favorable/unfavorable situations was the relationship reversed so that the more person-oriented (considerate) the supervisor the more effective the subordinates. This research has defined one set of external conditions that influence the nature of the relationship between leader and follower.

\*     \*     \*     \*     \*

## A Working Theory of Motivation

[One] . . . strand in motivation theory concerns the interrelationship between the action or behavior of the individual and his goal attainment and need satisfaction. This has been called the *Path-goal* approach to motivation. As a basic premise, the assumption is made that the individual is basically goal directed; in other words, that he will actively strive to engage in actions that he perceives as leading to his important goals. This is a simplification of the actual state of affairs; for the individual presumably has a set of goals (see above), all of which may be of importance to him, so that his choice of actions will be such as to satisfice this set of goals. However, this does not alter the basis whereby action decisions are made; i.e., the actions taken by the individual will be consistent with his perception of their instrumentality for goal attainment.

At this point we should emphasize that our initial concern is with the individual's *perception* of whether or not a particular activity helps or hurts him in the attainment of the goal. Such a perception may or may not be based upon the reality of the situation; nevertheless, the action decisions of the individual will be based upon these perceptions of path-goal instrumentality. We may, therefore, introduce the core concept of *Path-Goal Instrumentality* which is defined as the degree to which the individual perceives that a given path will lead to a particular goal.[3] We are now in a position to make some predictions about an individual's motivation to engage in specific behavior. This will be a function of the instrumentality of the behavior for his goals; and the relationship will be stronger for the more important goals of the individual. This can be summarized:

1. Motivation to engage in specific behavior =

$$f \left( \sum^{goals} \begin{array}{l} \text{(Behavior's perceived Instrumentality for goal} \times \\ \text{Goal importance)} \end{array} \right)$$

The actual frequency with which paths are followed by the individual will be a function not only of the individual's motivation to follow it, but also of the constraints on him in his choice of behavior (such as: his ability, the nature of the task, etc).[4]

2. Frequency with which a path is followed =

$$f \text{ (Motivation to follow paths/ability, freedom, etc.)}$$

This can be taken one step further; the extent to which a path is followed will, in combination with the actual path-goal instrumentality, affect the degree to which an individual's goals are

---

[3] This position has been outlined most recently (with slightly different terminology) in V. H. Vroom, *Work and Motivation* (New York: Wiley, 1964).

[4] A multiplicative relationship has been suggested by Vroom, *op. cit.*, for the moderating effect of ability: Frequency of behavior = f (Motivation × Ability).

**FIGURE 1**
**Motivation Model**

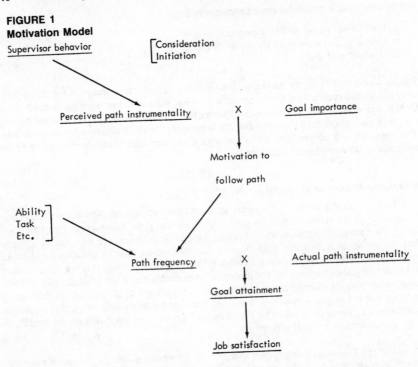

attained. In other words, by frequently taking paths which actually lead to an individual's goals there is a strong likelihood that these goals will be attained; more formally:

3. Degree of Goal Attainment =

$$f \left( \sum^{paths} (\text{Path Frequency} \times \text{Actual Path Instrumentality}) \right)$$

We suggested earlier that perceived path-goal instrumentality (which is the basis for a choice of paths) might or might not be based upon actual situations. In the ongoing organization, it is to be expected that as a result of experience, people will develop realistic perceptions of the path-goal instrumentalities; though we should be aware that both organizational and individual factors may inhibit the process of verification.[5]

The first strand of motivation theory helped us to understand the kinds of needs and goals that are relevant for motivating individual behavior. This second strand in motivation theory provides us with the relationship between action and goal attainment. This indeed sheds some light on the thorny problem of the relationship between job satisfaction and job performance.[6] In Figure 1, this is outlined diagrammatically. First, the path-goal instrumentality, in conjunction with goal importance, determines the level of motivation to follow a given path; second, this motivation level, in conjunction with environmental factors, determines the

[5] For example organizational complexity, organizational change, and managerial policies on secrecy may contribute to creating ambiguity in an individual's role requirements and hence in his perception of path-goal instrumentalities, R. L. Kahn, M. Wolfe, R. P. Quinn, J. D. Snoek, and R. A. Rosenthal, *Organizational Stress: Studies in Role Conflict and Ambiguity* (New York: Wiley, 1964); while central individual beliefs about whether the environment is essentially random in its rewards or whether such rewards are contingent upon behavior will distort the individual's perception of actual path-goal instrumentalities, J. B. Rotter, "Generalized Expectancies for Internal Versus External Control of Reinforcements," *Psychological Monographs* (1966), 80, 1 whole number 609.

[6] L. W. Porter and E. E. Lawler, "What Job Attitudes Tell About Motivation," *Harvard Business Review* (1969), 46, 1, pp. 118–26.

actual frequency with which a path is followed; third, path frequency, in conjunction with path-goal instrumentality, determines the level of goal attainment, which is a partial measure of job satisfaction. We can, therefore, see that the individual will choose a level of performance that is perceived as instrumental for the attainment of his goals. If the individual sees low performance leading to his goals, then he will be a low performer; if he sees high performance as leading to his goals, then he will be a high performer; if he is able to choose paths that lead to his goals, then he will be satisfied; if he is unable to do so, then he will be dissatisfied.

## Articulation between Supervisory Behavior and the Motivation Model

If the outline presented above is an accurate description of the motivational patterns in human behavior then the concept of *perceived path-goal instrumentality* becomes a crucial point at which influence can be exerted on the individual. To be sure, there are a variety of factors that can affect path-goal instrumentalities, but, in certain conditions, we shall consider aspects of the supervisor's behavior that impinge upon the subordinate's perceptions of the instrumentalities of his paths for his goal attainments.

Fleishmann and his associates identify two major components of supervisory behavior (*initiation of structure and consideration*) that seem to result in different patterns of subordinate behavior (in terms of both job performance and job satisfaction). These are defined as:

*Consideration* which includes behavior indicating mutual trust, respect and a certain rapport between the supervisor and his group. This does not mean that this dimension reflects a superficial "pat-on-the-back," "first name calling" kind of human relations behavior. This dimension appears to emphasize a deeper concern for group members' needs and includes such behavior as allowing subordinates more participation in decision-making and encouraging more two-way communication.

*Initiation of Structure* which includes behavior in which the supervisor organizes and defines group activities and his relation to the group. Thus, he defines the role he expects each member to assume, assigns tasks, plans ahead, establishes ways of getting things done, and pushes for production. This dimension seems to emphasize overt attempts to achieve organizational goals.[7]

Path instrumentality is the subordinate's expectation that a specific goal will be attained by following a specific path; so that, in trying to effect path-goal instrumentality, it would appear that there are three aspects involved:[8]

1. The subordinate must perceive that it will be possible for him to attain his goals. In other words, he must envisage a situation in which there exists a supply of rewards and punishments. In most formal organization situations, the supervisor is one of the sources of such a supply. It would appear that the level of *consideration* exhibited by the supervisor would affect the abundance of this source and also the appropriateness of the reward to the individual. In other words, the highly considerate supervisor is going to have a larger range of rewards (he will offer rewards in all need areas—pay, security, promotion, social and esteem) than his less considerate colleague (who will be locked in on pay and security as rewards). He is also going to ensure that these rewards are distributed selectively to·his subordinates in accordance with their individual desires, while the less considerate supervisor will not make such sophisticated discriminations among his subordinates.

---

[7] E. A. Fleishmann and E. F. Harris, "Patterns of Leadership Behavior Related to Employee Grievances and Turnover," *Personnel Psychology* (1962), 15, 43–56.

[8] This section is based upon my recent paper: M. G. Evans, "The Effects of Supervisory Behavior on the Path-Goal Relationship," *Organizational Behavior and Human Performance* (1970, 5).

2. The individual must see that his rewards and punishments (whether from an abundant and sophisticated source, or from a meager and simplistic one) are coming to him as the result of his specific behavior. In other words, there must be a perceived connection between his behavior and the rewards or punishments that he receives. It is here that *initiation of structure* by the supervisor has its impact. The supervisor who is high on initiation indicates to the subordinate the kinds of paths that he (the supervisor) wants followed and links his reward behavior to a successful following of the path. The supervisor who is low on this dimension does not indicate which paths should be followed and distributes his rewards without reference to the successful following of a path.

3. Implied in this is a third way in which supervisory behavior affects the strength of the path of instrumentality. Through his initiation of structure, the supervisor indicates those paths or activities that he thinks are appropriate to the role of the subordinate. It may be that the type of path that the superior deems appropriate is a function of the supervisor's *consideration*. This last impact is going to be very much a function of the path: presumably all supervisors see good performance as an appropriate activity for workers; whereas only those with high consideration might see "helping fellow workers" as an appropriate activity.

\*    \*    \*    \*    \*

## Implications for Management

For a management that wishes to bring about changes in the organization so as to improve worker motivation, performance, and satisfaction, and wishes to do so through the changing of leadership behavior, the initial strategy depends upon whether the two conditions are met; i.e., that a strong relationship exists between supervisory behavior and the Path-goal instrumentalities *and* a strong relationship exists between Path-goal instrumentalities and behavior and satisfaction.

If both conditions are met, then a relatively simple strategy will suffice. Any change in leadership behavior should have direct consequences for Path-goal instrumentalities and hence on worker performance and satisfaction.

If the first condition is not met (there is no relationship between leadership behavior and Path-goal Instrumentalities), the organization must investigate other aspects of the system, explore to see what variables have an impact on Path-goal Instrumentalities or inhibit the effect of supervisory behavior on Path-goal Instrumentalities—such things as the formal reward and penalty system or the nature of the work group might have this sort of impact. The organization may then decide that one of these variables is salient and that changes in this can bring about greater worker motivation; or it may decide that supervisory behavior is still salient and undertake to bring about two changes.

a. Create the conditions for a strong relationship to exist between supervisory behavior and Path-goal instrumentalities by change of the other inhibiting organizational variables, and

b. If necessary, bring about changes in supervisory behavior with resulting changes in worker motivation.

If the second condition is not met, the organization must be examined to find out what factors inhibit the appearance of this relationship. Here such variables as individual ability, the nature of the task, etc. are likely to be crucial. The procedure is then to undertake such changes as to strengthen the relationship in the second condition prior to undertaking any changes in leadership behavior.

# 4. CALIFORNIA FEDERAL SAVINGS AND LOAN ASSOCIATION

## Case Introduction

### SYNOPSIS

The California Savings and Loan Association employs 385 persons in its headquarters and nine branches. It has emphasized personalized service and has also been very efficient in the utilization of its personnel. Its management system is very decentralized at the branch level, although they are currently attempting to implement a policy change in more routine administrative service types of activities. Mr. May, the vice president of savings, is attempting to centralize the branch counselors' new account forms processing at the headquarter office. However, the plan seems to be encountering resistance at the branch level. Mr. Blackwell, the president, must decide what to do about the situation.

### WHY THIS CASE IS INCLUDED

This case illustrates the type of changes in the management system which often follows a policy of growth. With growth, the administrative procedures become more formalized and there is pressure to cut administrative costs by centralizing routine activities at the headquarters. However, such changes must consider the basic strategy of the firm on the one hand and the effect on the established social systems and motivation of individuals on the other. Thus, this case is an example of the connection among organizational strategy, management systems designed to implement strategy, and human behavioral outcomes. Resistance to changes in the management systems is another issue central to the case. Executives need to consider all of these variables in light of the trade-offs between technical efficiency, human motivation, and organizational effectiveness.

## PREDICTIVE AND DIAGNOSTIC QUESTIONS

The readings included with this case are marked (*). The author index at the end of this book locates the other readings.

1. Newman suggests that the design of the management system of an organization should be consistent with its strategy. One strategy that a small savings and loan association can have is custom or personalized service, another would be a strategy based upon large-volume administrative technologies. What sort of management system would be appropriate for each of these strategic approaches? In what ways would the management systems be similar? In what ways would they be different?

Read: *Newman, "Strategy and Management Structure."

2. Based upon the facts of the case, what is the basic strategy of the California Savings and Loan Association? What is your assessment of this strategy?

Read: *Newman, "Strategy and Management Structure." Tilles, "How to Evaluate Corporate Strategy." Drucker, *Management—Tasks-Responsibilities-Practices.*

3. What are the economic reasons for Mr. May's program to centralize the typing of new account forms at the headquarters of California Federal?

Read: Summer, "Economies of Scale and Organization Structure." Drucker, *Management—Tasks-Responsibilities-Practices.*

4. In what way does Mr. May's new procedure suggest a change in strategy for California Federal?

Read: *Newman, "Strategy and Management Structure."

5. What are the goals of Mr. Blackwell, Mr. May, and the branch managers in this case? Are these goals congruent with each other?

Read: Vancil, "What Kind of Management Control Do You Need?"

6. What are the advantages and disadvantages of Mr. May's procedure to centralize the typing of new account forms in terms of both its efficiency and its effectiveness?

Read: Vancil, "What Kind of Management Control Do You Need?"

7. Drawing from the facts of the case and the motivation theory of Hackman and others, what are likely to be the major sources of motivation for the counselors at the local branches of California Federal Savings and Loan? What are possible sources of motivation for Mr. Blackwell, the president, and Mr. May, vice president for savings?

Read: *Hackman et. al., "A New Strategy for Job Enrichment." Maslow, *Motivation and Personality.* Evans, "Leadership and Motivation: A Core Concept."

8. How is the change and procedure proposed by Mr. May likely to influence the motivations of Mr. Blackwell, Mr. May, and the counselors within the local branch?

Read: *Hackman et. al., "A New Strategy for Job Enrichment." Maslow, *Motivation and Personality.* Evans, "Leadership and Motivation: A Core Concept."

9. What are the major sources of resistance to the adoption of the new

procedure recommended by Mr. May, the vice president for savings?
Read:   *Lawrence, "How to Deal with Resistance to Change."
10. Who should make the decision as to the adoption of the new procedure developed by Mr. May?
Read:   *Lawrence, "How to Deal with Resistance to Change."

## POLICY QUESTIONS

11. What changes, if any, would you suggest that California Federal make in its strategy?
Read:   Review the readings for Questions 1 and 2 above.
12. What is the appropriate role of staff departments within California Federal in the area of introducing changes in the management system?
Read:   Review the readings for Questions 9 and 10 above.
13. What should be done about the procedure developed by Mr. May? Explain the reasons for your decision.
Read:   Review the readings for Questions 6 through 8 above.
14. What is the appropriate role of Mr. Blackwell and others in top management in introducing change within the organization?
Read:   Review readings for Questions 9 and 10 above.

# Case Text*

California Federal Savings and Loan Association, located in a medium-sized city in California, accepts savings from one class of customers who open savings accounts, and invests these with another class of customers who are seeking mortgage money—individuals buying residences, apartment houses, or making home improvements. It employs 385 people in its headquarters and nine branches. With a profit ratio higher than most savings and loan associations, the firm is known among savings and loan executives across the nation as one which has made some significant innovations in operating methods (Exhibit 1).

Its executives have published articles regarding management methods in the *S. and L. News,* and lectured at S. and L. executive programs. The president of an association in Texas says, "California S. and L. is one of the best. For example, the Savings and Loan League *Fact Book* publishes statistics on the utilization of manpower. The average number of people required to manage $1 million in assets is .53 this year for the industry as a whole. This means that one person is required to process (take in, process, loan out) $1,887,000. The California Association em-

---

**EXHIBIT 1**
**Organization Chart of California Savings and Loan Association**

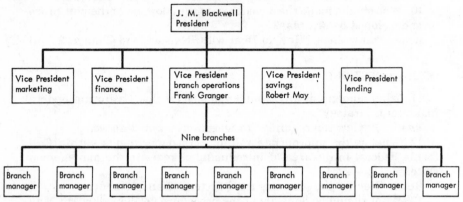

Nine branches

ployee processes $2,500,000 in assets, and they are growing faster than average by attracting new customers.

J. M. Blackwell, president of California, has this to say about his firm:

> We will be opening six new branches over the next four years. This is possible because we try very hard to find out what customers want in the way of services, and then to satisfy their needs. One of the most important factors in our success has been our organization structure. The Branch and its people are the backbone of the firm. And the counselor is the key man in our whole operation. Take for example our Colville Branch [Exhibit 2]. There are six counselors. Their function is to meet our savings customers and open savings accounts in a helpful way, displaying sufficient financial knowledge that they will be respected advisers. Their manner should leave no doubt in the customer's mind that we have a clear, forthright and efficient operation. They must perform equally well with loan customers, who expect considerable financial expertness from a professional type individual. In their outside activities in the community, they must develop respect and confidence so that prospective borrowers will come to us rather than a competitive institution. If anything, the loan function is more demanding than the savings function.
>
> There are anywhere from 5 to 9 counselors in a branch, and 66 counselors in the whole system. This is expected to grow to 95 as we open new branches.
>
> The branch manager has the duty of supervising day-to-day operations in the branch, training and developing all employees to carry out their duties properly, and acting as a two-way "fixer" between employees and the headquarters. I use that term because we want him to educate people at the bottom on how to carry out firmwide policies, and at the same time to educate the top manage-

**EXHIBIT 2**
**Organization Chart, Colville Branch**

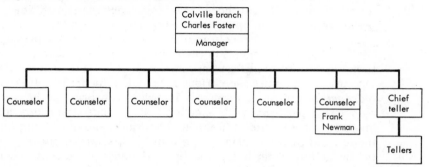

ment on any new methods or problems that arise from below. This takes some "fixing."

We all view the branch manager as having final authority about what happens in his branch; subject to the fact that he is expected to follow associationwide policies once they have been approved by the top management and the office of the president.

## Headquarters Organization

Mr. Blackwell continues:

I believe we have been ahead of the times in developing an organization for top management's making decisions. At headquarters we have five staff vice presidents, each in charge of a vital part of our total operations. These officers are supposed to concentrate their time and attention on, and become expert in, one of these key operations. For example, Bob May, vice president for savings, concentrates on developments outside the firm—what do savers want in terms of service, what are competitive institutions such as banks and insurance companies offering, how does a saver feel when he walks in our office and faces our men and our procedures, what kinds of unique methods are discovered in one of our own branches or in a competitive bank that can be applied in all other of our branches?

May's duty is therefore one of staff planning—to draw up policies for the whole firm. It is then to see that these are approved by myself, and to work with branch personnel in such a way that they see the reasons for the policy, and want to carry it out.

Other staff officers function in the same way. The finance vice president's department operates the central bookkeeping and computer service for all branches, posting customer accounts with data furnished from tellers' cages and sent in by chief tellers. The vice president for lending works with policies that guide counselors in their lending operations very much as the vice president for savings works with policies that help improve their savings operations.

We have deliberately refrained from giving headquarters various staff officers real authority over the branch managers. The vice president for branch operations is the one who has final say over matters affecting a branch and its manager. He is the principal spokesman when it comes to rewarding (with salaries and promotions) or disciplining branch personnel. The other headquarters vice presidents must use various forms of influence, or otherwise *work with* the branch managers, in order to ensure that the whole association performs with excellence in savings operations, loan operations, bookkeeping (finance) operations, and marketing (promotion and public relations) operations. This system ensures that the branch manager has at his disposal advisers and central services that are expert. They help him operate more successfully.

## Change in Method for Handling Savings Accounts

One year ago, Robert May, vice president for savings, proposed a change in procedures for opening new savings accounts. Previously, the new savings customer sat down with a counselor in the branch who explained the types of accounts available, the interest rates, and took vital information such as beneficiary in case of death, social security number, and other items listed on the customer account form (Exhibit 3). He had the customer sign the official signature card and typed the finished passbook and signature cards. During the time he was preparing the passbook, he often continued to chat with the customer sitting by his desk.

May explains how the problem of new accounts procedures arose:

> I saw a survey of savings customers done by the Savings and Loan Institute and published in their magazine. It asked what they looked for most when they opened a savings account. Three principal services were mentioned more frequently than others: free parking, no lines and congestion in the branch office, and quick, efficient service by branch personnel. After I read this, I began to think about how we could improve these three things at California S. and L. We had been averaging 120 calls a year from customers who have a complaint about savings accounts; 80 calls per year complaining about mistakes made by branch counselors in typing out passbooks and signature cards, or about having to wait too long at the branch when opening an account.

> About this same time, Hal Robinson, vice president for loans, raised a problem at our Monday Operating Committee meeting. The president and all vice presidents attend these meetings. He has always said that one loan customer of $50,000 is more important to us than 15 savings customers with balances of $3,000, to say nothing of the savings customers with $150 or $500. Though both customers are vital, we all agree with this logic. That's why Blackwell says loan customers get slight priority.

**EXHIBIT 3**

---

CALIFORNIA FEDERAL SAVINGS AND LOAN ASSOCIATION

THANK YOU—THIS IS YOUR RECEIPT   Account No. ____
                                                                        Date_____
☐New Money ☐ Transfer ☐ Change of Styling ☐ Collateral Acct.
         Check(s)   $_____
         Cash      _____
Transfer Funds   _____   TOTAL $_____


TRANSFERRED FROM _____ $_____
                              Acct. No.              Amount

                 _____ $_____
                              Acct. No.              Amount
Interest Rate_____Loan Number (if collateral ac-
count)_____
S.C. Mat. Date____Account Renewed Each____Months First Int.
Pmt. Date____
1    2    3    4    5    6    PI    FI    NI    L


☐ Book Issued ☐ Sig Card Issued ☐ SS Form Issued ☐ No Mail
            yes    no                           yes    no
Send NFH    ☐      ☐          Proxy Signed ☐      ☐
                              Office _____
                              Age Beneficiary(ies)
Successor Trustee_____ to be to Receive Funds _____
Address _____
City_____State_____ZIP_____
Social Security No._____(Underline above name of
person whose SS this is.)

   Payment Method ☐ Check ☐ Compound   ☐ Credit to Account
No. _____
Styling (Please print) _____
_____

_____

Miscellaneous comments, special instructions, etc. _____
_____

_____

                              _____
                              Customer Signature
CALIFORNIA FEDERAL SAVINGS AND LOAN ASSOCIATION
By_____
PB Color_____SS Department processing completed
by_____

Hal reported that he has received quite a number of complaints from loan customers who have to wait at the branches to see a counselor. When he followed up on these, in most instances there was a heavy load of new savings accounts that day at the branch.

Still a third reason entered in. We must maintain good public relations. If the savings customer wants to talk general subjects with the counselor, he can hardly push them out of the door. There are times when the counselor enjoys meeting people, too. He may forget his work load. We want him to be friendly. But having him type the passbook and card extends the time and provides further impetus to good conversation.

A last reason for the change was need for counselors to help branch managers balance the work load in the branch. It is impossible to hire "just the right number" of people. Sometimes one counselor will have a heavy load of loans during the day compared to loans of others. He needs help in processing loan forms or calling insurance companies on a loan. A second counselor might be asked to help. There are even times when a teller is unexpectedly absent and counselors will be asked to fill in.

For all of these reasons, I drew up a plan, submitted it to Mr. Blackwell and the Operating Committee a year ago, where it was approved unanimously. We allocated one full-time and one half-time typist at headquarters to receive all savings applications [Exhibit 3] from all branches. One of these serves as proofreader to catch any mistakes. The counselor fills out the application in legible printing, and informs the customer that he will receive his passbook by mail within two days. These are picked up at night by our regular messenger and delivered to three typists at headquarters. Rather than having 66 counselors who are diverted while doing their typing (often hunt and peck), or nine typists at branches working on this, there is now one full- and one half-time position.

### Implementation of the New System

In the year we have operated under the new system, the number of complaints has dropped from 80 to 5. This is because expert typists do the work, and we have control over quality at headquarters. Formerly there was no double check. I asked branch managers to do a check on how long new savings accounts counseling is now taking. Throughout eight branches, counseling time has dropped from an average of 30 minutes per customer to 20 minutes. Since the average counselor handles eight per day, this is more than ten man-hours a day for the whole firm.

But the system still is not functioning properly. We have one branch—Colville, managed by Charlie Foster—where counselors still do their own passbook typing, and where Foster didn't want to carry out the check. You'll see on the application form that there is a place to indicate whether the passbook was issued at the branch, or whether it is to be mailed from headquarters. This was a safety feature in case a specific customer just demanded to have his book on the spot. We also have 12 counselors scattered through other branches that issue all of their books.

These counselors, especially in slack periods when they have little to do, simply want to do the whole job. They don't see the whole firm point of view. They say that customers prefer to have the security of the passbook in their hand when they leave the branch. Charlie Foster made this point with Frank Granger (Vice president, branch operations) several times last year. To try to convince them, I sent a questionnaire to 150 of our customers asking whether they preferred picking up the passbook at the branch, or having it mailed. Eighty percent checked 'it makes no difference,' 11 percent wanted it 'at the branch,' and 9 percent wanted it mailed.

## Opinions of Branch Personnel

In interviews with the casewriter, branch personnel expressed diverse opinions:

**Frank Newman,** Counselor, Colville Branch:   I have been in this business for 16 years. I am proud of our association and work hard to make it successful, and I want satisfied customers as much as anybody. I've learned a lot dealing with people at the grass roots level. The big majority of our customers prefer to get that passbook right when they bring in their money. May's questionnaire wasn't phrased right to get the true answer. We learn much more by face-to-face contact than they do with questionnaires. I can name many customers who want the personal touch of a small institution or tangible evidence on where their money is.

**Charles Foster,** Manager, Colville Branch:   I have six counselors here, all of whom are high-caliber men. Three are young men who have joined us after the new system was installed. Three are experienced men with us several years. All agree that we must continue with the personal touch. This is one of our main competitive weapons. Let the other associations speed things up with impersonal forms—it's their mistake, not ours.

**Mike LaVerne,** Counselor, Colville Branch:   I've been here one year. After searching around after college, I'm lucky to find work I like. It looks like a career for me. The new system they suggest bothers me. It's just so much more paperwork, with things going to headquarters and then mass produced for the customer. I enjoy talking longer with the customer while I prepare the passbook. They say "hi" to me on the street when I get to know them.

**Dick Richards,** Counselor, Colville Branch:   I really don't care which system they operate under. I like my work—the two years I've been here, but a job is a job. I don't get involved in "causes" about bank efficiency or close customer contacts. I do a good day's work in a forthright manner and it seems to work. However, Charlie Foster, Mike, George and the rest [other counselors] seem convinced how we should do it at Colville. Who am I to upset things in the branch? Mr. May thinks otherwise, I gather. Who am I to upset him? I just don't care so long as I know Foster and Mr. Granger approve.

May states that the 12 counselors scattered through other branches generally give the logic illustrated above.

### Opinions of Headquarters Personnel

At the Monday Operations Committee meeting last week, May had asked Blackwell to put the new accounts system on the agenda. A condensed summary of what happened follows:

**Blackwell:** I've talked with Bob May and reviewed his evidence. It seems to me we have a problem. The number of counselors who do their own passbooks has crept up from 11 to 18 over the last year. We can save at least two professional employees by this system as we continue to open branches, and perhaps gain a significant number of customers with quicker, more accurate service. What do you men think?

**May:** (Reviewed the evidence presented in the case and requested that Frank Granger "finally just issue an order and check to see that they comply.")

**Granger:** Bob, I would go along with that except for two things. First, we do have some customers who are set in their ways and want that passbook. We don't have to turn them away if the counselors will make the right decision for those. We can have our cake and eat it too, issuing most books from headquarters but a fewer number at the branch. This takes some education to get them to do this. Second, I have to think about my branch managers. Charlie Foster is a good manager. He judges a different way. I've pointed out the new system to him and to two other managers who have counselors who do their own passbooks. They point out that with the turnover of personnel, newer counselors who don't remember the old system object to the paperwork and the interference of headquarters in branch affairs. Confidentially, I think these managers are also voicing their own dislike for the greater and greater number of uniform policies we make as we get bigger. In this case I just don't want to incur the further bad feelings of Foster and other branch managers.

After the meeting, Blackwell called May on the phone and told him that he would like to see him "for about 30 minutes tomorrow about this new account system. I want your recommendation on what, if anything, should be done in light of the opinions expressed this morning."

May reported to the case writer late that afternoon: "Damnit, I want to do the right thing. I know what the counselors ought to be doing for our long-run success. I don't want them to pull the rug from under me.

I can understand the resistance. It's more than they can expect for a staff man to solve this thing like utopia, with everybody happy. That's what some people want, I'm afraid."

# Selected Readings

*From*

## STRATEGY AND MANAGEMENT STRUCTURE*

*By William H. Newman*

\* \* \* \* \*

### Scope of Master Strategy

Strategy, as the term is used in this paper, sets the basic purposes of an enterprise in terms of the services it will render to society and the way it will create these services. More specifically, master strategy involves (*a*) picking particular product market niches that are propitious in view of society's needs and the company's resources, (*b*) selecting the underlying technologies and the ways of attracting inputs, (*c*) combining the various niches and resource bases to obtain synergistic effects, (*d*) expressing these plans in terms of targets, and (*e*) setting up sequences and timing of steps toward these objectives that reflect company capabilities and external conditions.

\* \* \* \* \*

### Integrated Management Design

Discussions of "strategy and structure" often focus on organization structure only. If the match between strategy and management design is to be fully effective, however, more than organization must be harmonized. The nature of the planning process, the leadership style and the form and location of control mechanisms are also intimately involved. This more inclusive view of management arrangements—planning, organizing, leading and controlling—we call management design.

Management designs differ. Every university is, and should be, managed in ways that are different from those used to manage the bus system that brings students to its doors. Likewise, within the university, the managerial design best suited to research laboratories is inappropriate to the cafeteria. To be sure, several common processes—organizing, planning, leading and controlling—are essential for each of these units, but as we adapt various concepts to the unique needs of each venture refinement is vital. Management sophistication is revealed in this adapting and refining of the design.

\* \* \* \* \*

\* "Strategy and Management Structure," William H. Newman, *Journal of Business Policy,* Winter 1971–72, pp. 56–66 (excerpts). Reprinted with permission from Mercury House Business Publications Ltd., London.

**TABLE 1**
**Typical Features of Management Structures for Three Types of Technology**

| Features That Distinguish Management Structures | Nature of Technology | | |
|---|---|---|---|
| | Stable | Regulated Flexibility | Adaptive |
| *Organizing:* | | | |
| Centralization versus decentralization | Centralized | Mostly centralized | Decentralized |
| Degree of division of labour | Narrow specialization | Specialized or crafts | Scope may vary |
| Size of self-sufficient operating units | Large | Medium | Small, if equipment permits |
| Mechanisms for coordination | Built-in, programmed | Separate planning unit | Face-to-face, within unit |
| Nature and location of staff | Narrow functions; headquarters | Narrow functions; headquarters and operating unit | Generalists at headquarters; specialists in operating units |
| Management information system | Heavy upward flow | Flow to headquarters and to operating unit | Flow mostly to, and within, operating unit |
| Characteristics of key personnel | Strong operators | Functional experts in line and staff | Analytical, adaptive |
| *Planning:* | | | |
| *Use of standing plans:* | | | |
| Comprehensiveness of coverage | Broad coverage | All main areas covered | Mostly "local," self-imposed |
| Specificity | Detail specified | Detail in interlocking activities | Main points only |
| *Use of single-use plans:* | | | |
| Comprehensiveness of coverage | Fully planned | Fully planned | Main steps covered |
| Specificity | Detail specified | Schedules and specs. detailed | Adjusted to feedback |
| Planning horizon | Weekly to quarterly | Weekly to annually | Monthly to three years or more |
| Intermediate versus final objectives | Intermediate goals sharp | Intermediate goals sharp | Emphasis on objectives |
| "How" versus results | "How" is specified | Results at each step specified | End results stressed |
| *Leading:* | | | |
| Participation in planning | Very limited | Restricted to own tasks | High participation |
| Permissiveness | Stick to instructions | Variation in own tasks only | High permissiveness, if results OK |

**TABLE 1 (*continued*)**

| Features That Distinguish Management Structures | Nature of Technology | | |
|---|---|---|---|
| | Stable | Regulated Flexibility | Adaptive |
| Closeness of supervision | Follow operations closely | Output and quality closely watched | General supervision |
| Sharing of information | Circumspect | Job information shared | Full project information shared |
| Emphasis on on-the-job satisfactions | Limited scope | Craftsmanship and professionalism encouraged | Opportunity for involvement |
| *Controlling:* | | | |
| Performance criteria emphasized | Efficiency, dependability | Quality, punctuality, efficiency | Results, within resource limits |
| Location of control points | Within process; intermediate stages | Focus on each processing unit | Overall "milestones" |
| Frequency of checks | Frequent | Frequent | Infrequent |
| Who initiates corrective action | Often central managers | "Production control" and other staff | Men in operating unit |
| Stress on reliability versus learning | Reliability stressed | Reliability stressed | Learning stressed |
| Punitive versus reward motivation | Few mistakes tolerated | Few mistakes tolerated | High reward for success |

## Influence of Strategy on Design

\*   \*   \*   \*   \*

*Technology: The Intervening Variable.* The best bridge between strategy and design is "technology." Here we use technology in a very broad sense to include all sorts of methods for converting resource inputs into products and service the consumers. The inputs can be labour, knowledge and capital as well as raw materials. Thus an insurance company has its technology for converting money, ideas, and labour into insurance service just as an oil company has its technology for converting crude oil and other resources into petroleum products. By extending our thinking from strategy to the technology necessary to execute that strategy, we move to *work to be done*. Once we comprehend the work to be done—both managerial and operating work—we are on familiar ground. Most of our management concepts relate directly to getting work done, and so preparing a management design to fit a particular kind of work falls within the recognized "state of the art."

The use of technology as an intervening variable produces the arrangement shown in Figure 1. To maintain perspective and to highlight key influences, strategy should focus on only a few basic ideas. Its formulation is by necessity in broad terms. We cannot jump directly from strategy to management design because we have not yet classified the array of actions that will be necessary to execute the strategy. Thinking of technology helps us to elaborate the work implications of the strategy and thereby provides us with the inputs for shaping a management design.

\*   \*   \*   \*   \*

**FIGURE 1**
**Outlook to Design**

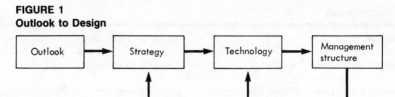

**FIGURE 2**
**Change Matrix**

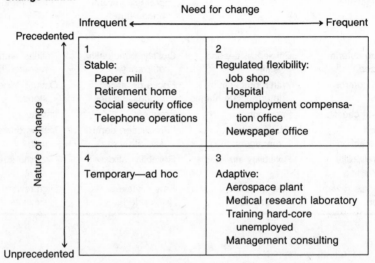

***Composite Design.*** Generally, when a department is both large and important to the strategy of the company it should be managed with a design suited to its own activity. This means that companies embracing diverse technologies should use several different managerial styles. The justification for this mixture of managerial styles lies, of course, in the improved performance of the respective departments.

Such diversity has its costs:

1. *Cooperation between Departments Becomes Increasingly Difficult.* Voluntary cooperation between groups with different values, time orientations and willingness to take risks is inevitably strained.[1] Divergent management designs add to this "cultural barrier." Because the departments are so different, we may even separate them geographically—remove research laboratories from the plants, separate mills designed for long production runs from those for short runs, and so on. When management designs of departments differ sharply,

---

[1] For an expansion of this concept of technology, see C[harles] Perrow, "A Framework for the Comparative Analysis of Organizations," *American Sociological Review* (April 1967). Other writers have explored the relation between technology and structure, but they have concentrated on the narrower concept of physical conversion of materials. See T[om] Burns and G. M. Stalker, *The Management of Innovation,* 2d ed. (London: Tavistock, 1966); J[oan] Woodward, *Industrial Organization* (London: Oxford University Press, 1965); D. H. Hickson, D. S. Pugh, and D. C. Pheysey, "Operations Technology and Organization Structure: An Empirical Appraisal," *Administrative Science Quarterly* (September 1969).

special liaison staff or other formal means for coordination is often needed. Having deliberately accentuated the difference between departments, we then add a "diplomatic corps" to serve as a communication link between them.

*2. Companywide Services Drop in Value.* With a composite design, the rotation of key personnel is impeded, budgeting is complicated, training programs fit only parts of the company, capital allocation procedures have to be tailored to different inputs and criteria. In other words, synergy arising from pooled services and reinforcing features of a management design is lacking for the company as a whole.

*3. The Task of Central Managers Is Complicated.* Understanding the subtleties of the several management designs and personally adjusting one's leadership style to each calls for unusual skill and sophistication. Most managers, often unconsciously, favour departments whose management design they find congenial.

*    *    *    *    *

## Summary

1. The interaction of two areas of management thought—master strategy and management design—offers an unusual opportunity for fruitful synthesis.

2. The "strategy and structure" approach to this synthesis should be expanded. More than organization structure is involved. Adjustments in planning, leading, and controlling, as well as organizing, are often needed to execute a new strategy; and the integration of these subprocesses into a total *management design* is vital.

3. Of course, a particular change in strategy will affect some facets of management more than others. . . .

4. Matching management design and strategy directly is difficult. A useful bridge is to focus on "technology" as the intervening variable. Here "technology" is used broadly to embrace the conversion of all sorts of resources—human and financial as well as physical —into services and goods for consumers. Fortunately, we can relate technology both to *strategy* and to *manageable* tasks.

5. One characteristic of a technology is its accommodation to changes. A matrix based on frequency of changes and their novelty helps us understand three common types of technologies: stable, regulated flexibility, and adaptive. Figure 2 gives both business and nonbusiness examples of each type. And for each type we can identify likely features of an appropriate management design. For instance:

*Stable technology* fits well with detailed planning, intermediate goals, centralization, close supervision, tight control.

*Regulated flexibility* fits well with separate planning and scheduling staff, controlled information flows, circumscribed decentralization, limited use of participative, and permissive leadership.

*Adaptive technology* fits well with planning by objective, decentralization, high personal involvement, control focused on results. (For further elaboration, see Table 1.)

6. A corollary of the proposition that management design should be varied so that it is (*a*) integrated within its parts, and (*b*) matched to specific company strategy is that no single management design is ideal for all circumstances. We cannot say, for example, that management by objectives, decentralization, participative management, or tight control are desirable in all situations. Company strategy is one of the important factors determining what managerial arrangement is optimal.

7. Turning from a total company to its constituent parts, if the preferred technologies of various departments *within* the company differ sharply, their optimal management structure will also differ. Central management is then confronted with a dilemma of either having a mismatch of technology and management design in some departments or coordinating diverse management designs.

While much refinement and amplification remains to be done, the foregoing approach to synthesizing diverse management concepts has exciting possibilities: it provides a vehicle for putting content into a "total systems" treatment of management; it helps reconcile conflicting research findings and experience about particular managerial techniques; and it suggests some very practical guidance for managers who wish to implement changes in their company strategy.

*From*

# A NEW STRATEGY FOR JOB ENRICHMENT*

*By J. Richard Hackman, Greg Oldham, Robert Janson, and Kenneth Purdy*

\*    \*    \*    \*    \*

## The Theory Behind the Strategy

*What Makes People Get Turned on to Their Work?* For workers who are really prospering in their jobs, work is likely to be a lot like play. Consider, for example, a golfer at a driving range, practicing to get rid of a hook. His activity is *meaningful* to him; he has chosen to do it because he gets a "kick" from testing his skills by playing the game. He knows that he alone is *responsible* for what happens when he hits the ball. And he has *knowledge of the results* within a few seconds.

Behavioral scientists have found that the three "psychological states" experienced by the golfer in the above example also are critical in determining a person's motivation and satisfaction on the job.

*Experienced Meaningfulness.* The individual must perceive his work as worthwhile or important by some system of values he accepts.

*Experienced Responsibility.* He must believe that he personally is accountable for the outcomes of his efforts.

*Knowledge of Results.* He must be able to determine, on some fairly regular basis, whether or not the outcomes of his work are satisfactory.

When these three conditions are present, a person tends to feel very good about himself when he performs well. And those good feelings will prompt him to try to continue to do well—so he can continue to earn the positive feelings in the future. That is what is meant by "internal motivation"—being turned on to one's work because of the positive internal feelings that are generated by doing well, rather than being dependent on external factors (such as incentive pay or compliments from the boss) for the motivation to work effectively.

What if one of the three psychological states is missing? Motivation drops markedly. Suppose, for example, that our golfer has settled in at the driving range to practice for a couple of hours. Suddenly a fog drifts in over the range. He can no longer see if the ball starts to tail off to the left a hundred yards out. The satisfaction he got from hitting straight down the middle—and the motivation to try to correct something whenever he didn't—are both gone. If the fog stays, it's likely that he soon will be packing up his clubs.

The relationship between the three psychological states and on-the-job outcomes is

\* © 1975 by The Regents of the University of California. Reprinted from *California Management Review*, vol. 17, no. 4, pp. 58–71 (excerpts), by permission of The Regents.

**FIGURE 1**

**Relationships among Core Job Dimensions, Critical Psychological States, and on-the-job Outcomes.**

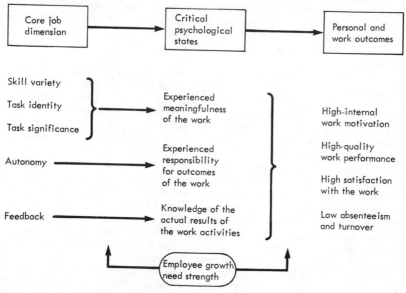

illustrated in Figure 1. When all three are high, then internal work motivation, job satisfaction, and work quality are high, and absenteeism and turnover are low.

*What Job Characteristics Make It Happen?* Recent research has identified five "core" characteristics of jobs that elicit the psychological states described above.[1-3] These five core job dimensions provide the key to objectively measuring jobs and to changing them so that they have high potential for motivating people who do them.

*Toward Meaningful Work.* Three of the five core dimensions contribute to a job's meaningfulness for the worker:

1. Skill Variety. The degree to which a job requires the worker to perform activities that challenge his skills and abilities. When even a single skill is involved, there is at least a seed of potential meaningfulness. When several are involved, the job has the potential of appealing to more of the whole person, and also of avoiding the monotony of performing the same task repeatedly, no matter how much skill it may require.

2. Task Identity. The degree to which the job requires completion of a "whole" and identifiable piece of work—doing a job from beginning to end with a visible outcome. For example, it is clearly more meaningful to an employee to build complete toasters than to attach electrical cord after electrical cord, especially if he never sees a completed toaster. . . .

3. Task Significance. The degree to which the job has a substantial and perceivable

[1] A. N. Turner and P. R. Lawrence, *Industrial Jobs and the Worker* (Cambridge, Mass.: Harvard Graduate School of Business Administration, 1965).

[2] J. R. Hackman and E. E. Lawler, "Employee Reactions to Job Characteristics," *Journal of Applied Psychology Monograph* (1971), pp. 259–86.

[3] J. R. Hackman and G. R. Oldham, *Motivation through the Design of Work: Test of a Theory,* Technical Report No. 6, Department of Administrative Sciences, Yale University, 1974.

impact on the lives of other people, whether in the immediate organization or the world at large. . . .

Each of these three job dimensions represents an important route to experienced meaningfulness. If the job is high in all three, the worker is quite likely to experience his job as very meaningful. It is not necessary, however, for a job to be very high in all three dimensions. If the job is low in any one of them, there will be a drop in overall experienced meaningfulness. But even when two dimensions are low the worker may find the job meaningful if the third is high enough.

*Toward Personal Responsibility.*   A fourth core dimension leads a worker to experience increased responsibility in his job. This is *autonomy,* the degree to which the job gives the worker freedom, independence, and discretion in scheduling work and determining how he will carry it out. People in highly autonomous jobs know that they are personally responsible for successes and failures. To the extent that their autonomy is high, then, how the work goes will be felt to depend more on the individual's own efforts and initiatives—rather than on detailed instructions from the boss or from a manual of job procedures.

*Toward Knowledge of Results.*   The fifth and last core dimension is *feedback.* This is the degree to which a worker, in carrying out the work activities required by the job, gets information about the effectiveness of his efforts. Feedback is most powerful when it comes directly from the work itself—for example, when a worker has the responsibility for guaging and otherwise checking a component he has just finished, and learns in the process that he has lowered his reject rate by meeting specifications more consistently.

*The Overall "Motivating Potential" of a Job.*   Figure 1 shows how the five core dimensions combine to affect the psychological states that are critical in determining whether or not an employee will be internally motivated to work effectively. Indeed, when using an instrument to be described later, it is possible to compute a "motivating potential score" (MPS) for any job. The MPS provides a single summary index of the degree to which the objective characteristics of the job will prompt high internal work motivation. Following the theory outlined above, a job high in motivating potential must be high in at least one (and hopefully more) of the three dimensions that lead to experienced meaningfulness and high in both autonomy and feedback as well. . . .

**Does the Theory Work for Everybody?**   Unfortunately not. Not everyone is able to become internally motivated in his work, even when the motivating potential of a job is very high indeed.

Research has shown that the *psychological needs* of people are very important in determining who can (and who cannot) become internally motivated at work. Some people have strong needs for personal accomplishment, for learning and developing themselves beyond where they are now, for being stimulated and challenged, and so on. These people are high in "growth-need strength."

Figure 2 shows diagrammatically the proposition that individual growth needs have the power to moderate the relationship between the characteristics of jobs and work outcomes. Many workers with high growth needs will turn on eagerly when they have jobs that are high in the core dimensions. Workers whose growth needs are not so strong may respond less eagerly—or, at first, even balk at being "pushed" or "stretched" too far.

Psychologists who emphasize human potential argue that everyone has within him at least a spark of the need to grow and develop personally. Steadily accumulating evidence shows, however, that unless that spark is pretty strong, chances are it will get snuffed out by one's experiences in typical organizations. So, a person who has worked for twenty years in stultifying jobs may find it difficult or impossible to become internally motivated overnight when given the opportunity.

We should be cautious, however, about creating rigid categories of people based on their measured growth-need strength at any particular time. It is true that we can predict from these measures who is likely to become internally motivated on a job and who will be less willing or able to do so. But what we do not know yet is whether or not the growth-need

**FIGURE 2**
**The Moderating Effect of Employee Growth-Need Strength**

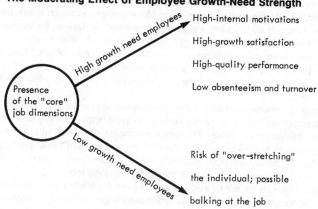

High growth need employees

High-internal motivations

High-growth satisfaction

High-quality performance

Low absenteeism and turnover

Presence
of the "core"
job dimensions

Low growth need employees

Risk of "over-stretching"

the individual; possible

balking at the job

"spark" can be rekindled for those individuals who have had their growth needs dampened by years of growth-depressing experience in their organizations.

Since it is often the organization that is responsible for currently low levels of growth desires, we believe that the organization also should provide the individual with the chance to reverse that trend whenever possible, even if that means putting a person in a job where he may be "stretched" more than he wants to be. He can always move back later to the old job—and in the meantime the embers of his growth needs just might burst back into flame, to his surprise and pleasure, and for the good of the organization.

### From Theory to Practice: A Technology for Job Enrichment

When job enrichment fails, it often fails because of inadequate *diagnosis* of the target job and employees' reactions to it. Often, for example, job enrichment is assumed by management to be a solution to "people problems" on the job and is implemented even though there has been no diagnostic activity to indicate that the root of the problem is in fact how the work is designed. At other times, some diagnosis is made—but it provides no concrete guidance about what specific aspects of the job require change. In either case, the success of job enrichment may wind up depending more on the quality of the intuition of the change agent—or his luck—than on a solid base of data about the people and the work.

In the paragraphs to follow, we outline a new technology for use in job enrichment which explicitly addresses the diagnostic as well as the action components of the change process. The technology has two parts: (1) a set of diagnostic tools that are useful in evaluating jobs and people's reactions to them prior to change—and in pinpointing exactly what aspects of specific jobs are most critical to a successful change attempt; and (2) a set of "implementing concepts" that provide concrete guidance for action steps in job enrichment. The implementing concepts are tied directly to the diagnostic tools; the output of the diagnostic activity specifies which action steps are likely to have the most impact in a particular situation.

*The Diagnostic Tools.* Central to the diagnostic procedure we propose is a package of instruments to be used by employees, supervisors, and outside observers in assessing the target job and employees' reactions to it.[4] These instruments gauge the following:

1. The objective characteristics of the jobs themselves, including both an overall indica-

---

[4] J. R. Hackman and G. R. Oldham, "Development of the Job Diagnostic Survey," *Journal of Applied Psychology* (1975), pp. 159–70.

tion of the "motivating potential" of the job as it exists (that is, the MPS score) and the score of the job on each of the five core dimensions described previously. Because knowing the strengths and weaknesses of the job is critical to any work-resdesign effort, assessments of the job are made by supervisors and outside observers as well as the employees themselves—and the final assessment of a job uses data from all three sources.

2. The current levels of motivation, satisfaction, and work performance of employees on the job. In addition to satisfaction with the work itself, measures are taken of how people feel about other aspects of the work setting, such as pay, supervision, and relationships with co-workers.

3. The level of growth-need strength of the employees. As indicated earlier, employees who have strong growth needs are more likely to be more responsive to job enrichment than employees with weak growth needs. Therefore, it is important to know at the outset just what kinds of satisfactions the people who do the job are (and are not) motivated to obtain from their work. This will make it possible to identify which persons are best to start changes with, and which may need help in adapting to the newly enriched job.

What, then, might be the actual steps one would take in carrying out a job diagnosis using these tools? Although the approach to any particular diagnosis depends upon the specifics of the particular work situation involved, the sequence of questions listed below is fairly typical.

*Step 1. Are Motivation and Satisfaction Central to the Problem?*  Sometimes organizations undertake job enrichment to improve the work motivation and satisfaction of employees when in fact the real problem with work performance lies elsewhere—for example, in a poorly designed production system, in an error-prone computer, and so on. . . .

*Step 2. Is the Job Low in Motivating Potential?*  To answer this question, one would examine the motivating potential score of the target job and compare it to the MPS's of other jobs to determine whether or not *the job itself* is a probable cause of the motivational problems documented in Step 1. . . .

*Step 3. What Specific Aspects of the Job Are Causing the Difficulty?*  This step involves examining the job on each of the five core dimensions to pinpoint the specific strengths and weaknesses of the job as it is currently structured. It is useful at this stage to construct a "profile" of the target job, to make visually apparent where improvements need to be made. An illustrative profile for two jobs (one "good" job and one job needing improvement) is shown in Figure 3.

Job A is an engineering maintenance job and is high on all of the core dimensions. . . . Job enrichment would not be recommended for this job; if employees working on the job were unproductive and unhappy, the reasons are likely to have little to do with the nature or design of the work itself.

Job B, on the other hand, has many problems. This job involves the routine and repetitive processing of checks in the "back room" of a bank. The MPS is 30, which is quite low—and indeed, would be even lower if it were not for the moderately high task significance of the job. (Task significance is moderately high because the people are handling large amounts of other people's money, and therefore the quality of their efforts potentially has important consequences for their unseen clients.) The job provides the individuals with very little direct feedback about how effectively they are doing it; the employees have little autonomy in how they go about doing the job; and the job is moderately low in both skill variety and task identity.

For Job B, then, there is plenty of room for improvement—and many avenues to examine in planning job changes. For still other jobs, the avenues for change often turn out to be considerably more specific: for example, feedback and autonomy may be reasonably high, but one or more of the core dimensions that contribute to the experienced meaningfulness of the job (skill variety, task identity, and task significance) may be low. In such a case, attention would turn to ways to increase the standing of the job on these latter three dimensions.

*Step 4. How "Ready" Are the Employees for Change?*  Once it has been documented

**FIGURE 3**

**The JDS Diagnostic Profile for a "Good" and a "Bad" Job**

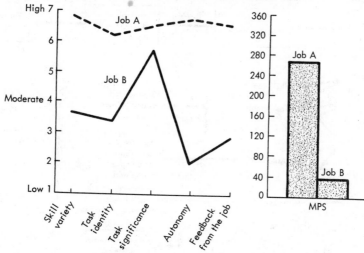

that there is need for improvement in the job—and the particularly troublesome aspects of the job have been identified—then it is time to begin to think about the specific action steps which will be taken to enrich the job. An important factor in such planning is the level of growth needs of the employees, since employees high on growth needs usually respond more readily to job enrichment than do employees with little need for growth. The JDS provides a direct measure of the growth-need strength of the employees. This measure can be very helpful in planning how to introduce the changes to the people (for instance, cautiously versus dramatically), and in deciding who should be among the first group of employees to have their jobs changed.

\* \* \* \* \*

*The Implementing Concepts.* Five "implementing concepts" for job enrichment are identified and discussed below.[5] Each one is a specific action step aimed at improving both the quality of the working experience for the individual and his work productivity. They are: (1) forming natural work units; (2) combining tasks; (3) establishing client relationships; (4) vertical loading; (5) opening feedback channels.

The links between the implementing concepts and the core dimensions are shown in Figure 4 which illustrates our theory of job enrichment, ranging from the concrete action steps through the core dimensions and the psychological states to the actual personal and work outcomes.

After completing the diagnosis of a job, a change agent would know which of the core dimensions were most in need of remedial attention. He could then turn to Figure 4 and select those implementing concepts that specifically deal with the most troublesome parts of the existing job. How this would take place in practice will be seen below.

*Forming Natural Work Units.* The notion of distributing work in some logical way may seem to be an obvious part of the design of any job. In many cases, however, the logic is one imposed by just about any consideration except job-holder satisfaction and motivation. Such considerations include technological dictates, level of worker training or experience, "efficiency" as defined by industrial engineering, and current workload. In many cases the

---

[5] R. W. Walters and Associates, *Job Enrichment for Results* (Cambridge, Mass.: Addison-Wesley, 1975).

**FIGURE 4**
**The Full Model: How Use of the Implementing Concepts Can Lead to Positive Outcomes**

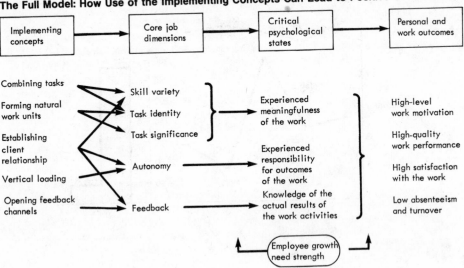

cluster of tasks a worker faces during a typical day or week is natural to anyone *but* the worker.

* * * * *

The principle underlying natural units of work, by contrast, is "ownership," a worker's sense of continuing responsibility for an identifiable body of work. Two steps are involved in creating natural work units. The first is to identify the basic work items. In the typing pool, for example, the items might be "pages to be typed." The second step is to group the items in natural categories. For example, each typist might be assigned continuing responsibility for all jobs requested by one or several specific departments. The assignments should be made, of course, in such a way that workloads are about equal in the long run. . . .

* * * * *

*Combining Tasks.* The very existence of a pool made up entirely of persons whose sole function is typing reflects a fractionalization of jobs that has been a basic precept of "scientific management." Most obvious in assembly-line work, fractionalization has been applied to non-manufacturing jobs as well. It is typically justified by efficiency, which is usually defined in terms of either low costs or some time-and-motion type of criteria.

It is hard to find fault with measuring efficiency ultimately in terms of cost-effectiveness. In doing so, however, a manager should be sure to consider *all* the costs involved. It is possible, for example, for highly fractionalized jobs to meet all the time-and-motion criteria of efficiency, but if the resulting job is so unrewarding that performing it day after day leads to high turnover, absenteeism, drugs and alcohol, and strikes, then productivity is really lower (and costs higher) than data on efficiency might indicate.

* * * * *

As a job-design principle, task combination, like natural units of work, expands the task identity of the job. For example, the hot-plate assembler can see and identify with a finished product ready for shipment, rather than a nearly invisible junction of solder. Moreover, the more tasks that are combined into a single worker's job, the greater the variety of skills he must call on in performing the job. So task combination also leads directly to greater skill variety—the third core dimension that contributes to the overall experienced meaningfulness of the work.

*Establishing Client Relationships.* One consequence of fractionalization is that the typical worker has little or no contact with (or even awareness of) the ultimate user of his product or service. By encouraging and enabling employees to establish direct relationships with the clients of their work, improvements often can be realized simultaneously on three of the core dimensions. Feedback increases, because of additional opportunities for the individual to receive praise or criticism of his work outputs directly. Skill variety often increases, because of the necessity to develop and exercise one's interpersonal skills in maintaining the client relationship. And autonomy can increase because the individual often is given personal responsibility for deciding how to manage his relationships with the clients of his work.

Creating client relationships is a three-step process. First, the client must be identified. Second, the most direct contact possible between the worker and the client must be established. Third, criteria must be set up by which the client can judge the quality of the product or service he receives. And whenever possible, the client should have a means of relaying his judgments directly back to the worker.

\* \* \* \* \*

*Vertical Loading.* Typically the split between the "doing" of a job and the "planning" and "controlling" of the work has evolved along with horizontal fractionalization. Its rationale, once again, has been "efficiency through specialization." And once again, the excess of specialization that has emerged has resulted in unexpected but significant costs in motivation, morale, and work quality. In vertical loading, the intent is to partially close the gap between the doing and the controlling parts of the job—and thereby reap some important motivational advantages.

Of all the job-design principles, vertical loading may be the single most crucial one. In some cases, where it has been impossible to implement any other changes, vertical loading alone has had significant motivational effects.

When a job is vertically loaded, responsibilities and controls that formerly were reserved for higher levels of management are added to the job. . . .

\* \* \* \* \*

*From*

# HOW TO DEAL WITH RESISTANCE TO CHANGE*

*By Paul R. Lawrence*

\* \* \* \* \*

## Roots of Trouble

The significance of these research findings, from management's point of view, is that executives and staff experts need not expertness in using the devices of participation but a real understanding, in depth and detail, of the specific social arrangements that will be sustained or threatened by the change or by the way in which it is introduced.

These observations check with everyday management experience in industry. When we stop to think about it, we know that many changes occur in our factories without a bit of resistance. We know that people who are working closely with one another continually swap

---

* From "How to Deal with Resistance to Change," *Harvard Business Review,* vol. 32, no. 3 (May–June 1954). Reprinted by permission. © 1954 by The President and Fellows of Harvard College; all rights reserved. This article was republished as a *Harvard Business Review* Classic with a "Retrospective Commentary" in January–February 1969.

ideas about short cuts and minor changes in procedure that are adopted so easily and naturally that we seldom notice them or even think of them as change. The point is that because these people work so closely with one another, they intuitively understand and take account of the existing social arrangements for work and so feel no threat to themselves in such everyday changes.

By contrast, management actions leading to what we commonly label "change" are usually initiated outside the small work group by staff people. These are the changes that we notice and the ones that most frequently bring on symptoms of resistance. By the very nature of their work, most of our staff specialists in industry do not have the intimate contact with operating groups that allows them to acquire an intuitive understanding of the complex social arrangements which their ideas may affect. Neither do our staff specialists always have the day-to-day dealings with operating people that lead them to develop a natural respect for the knowledge and skill of these people. As a result, all too often the men behave in a way that threatens and disrupts the established social relationships. And the tragedy is that so many of these upsets are inadvertent and unnecessary.

Yet industry must have its specialists—not only many kinds of engineering specialists (product, process, maintenance, quality, and safety engineers) but also cost accountants, production schedulers, purchasing agents, and personnel men. Must top management therefore reconcile itself to continual resistance to change, or can it take constructive action to meet the problem?

I believe that our research in various factory situations indicates why resistance to change occurs and what management can do about it. Let us take the "why" factors first.

**Self-Preoccupation.** All too frequently we see staff specialists who bring to their work certain blind spots that get them into trouble when they initiate change with operating people. One such blind spot is "self-preoccupation." The staff man gets so engrossed in the technology of the change he is interested in promoting that he becomes wholly oblivious to different kinds of things that may be bothering people. Here are two examples:

1. In one situation the staff people introduced, with the best of intentions, a technological change which inadvertently deprived a number of skilled operators of much of the satisfaction that they were finding in their work. Among other things, the change meant that, whereas formerly the output of each operator had been placed beside his work position where it could be viewed and appreciated by him and by others, it was now being carried away immediately from the work position. The workmen did not like this.

The sad part of it was that there was no compelling cost or technical reason why the output could not be placed beside the work position as it had been formerly. But the staff people who had introduced the change were so literal-minded about their ideas that when they heard complaints on the changes from the operators, they could not comprehend what the trouble was. Instead, they began repeating all the logical arguments why the change made sense from a cost standpoint. The final result here was a chronic restriction of output and persistent hostility on the part of the operators.

2. An industrial engineer undertook to introduce some methods changes in one department with the notion firmly in mind that this assignment presented him with an opportunity to "prove" to higher management the value of his function. He became so preoccupied with his personal desire to make a name for his particular techniques that he failed to pay any attention to some fairly obvious and practical considerations which the operating people were calling to his attention but which did not show up in his time-study techniques. As could be expected, resistance quickly developed to all his ideas, and the only "name" that he finally won for his techniques was a black one.

Obviously, in both of these situations the staff specialists involved did not take into account the social aspects of the change they were introducing. For different reasons they got so preoccupied with the technical aspects of the change that they literally could not see or understand what all the fuss was about.

We may sometimes wish that the validity of the technical aspect of the change were the sole determinant of its acceptability. But the fact remains that the social aspect is what determines the presence or absence of resistance. Just as ignoring this fact is the sure way to trouble, so taking advantage of it can lead to positive results. We must not forget that these same social arrangements which at times seem so bothersome are essential for the performance of work. Without a network of established social relationships a factory would be populated with a collection of people who had no idea of how to work with one another in an organized fashion. By working *with* this network instead of *against* it, management's staff representatives can give new technological ideas a better chance of acceptance.

**Know-How of Operators Overlooked.** Another blind spot of many staff specialists is to the strengths as well as to the weaknesses of firsthand production experience. They do not recognize that the production foreman and the production operator are in their own way specialists themselves—specialists in actual experience with production problems. This point should be obvious, but it is amazing how many staff specialists fail to appreciate the fact that even though they themselves may have a superior knowledge of the technology of the production process involved, the foreman or the operators may have a more practical understanding of how to get daily production out of a group of men and machines.

The experience of the operating people frequently equips them to be of real help to staff specialists on at least two counts: (1) The operating people are often able to spot practical production difficulties in the ideas of the specialists—and iron out those difficulties before it is too late; (2) the operating people are often able to take advantage of their intimate acquaintance with the existing social arrangements for getting work done. If given a chance, they can use this kind of knowledge to help detect those parts of the change that will have undesirable social consequences. The staff experts can then go to work on ways to avoid the trouble area without materially affecting the technical worth of the change.

Further, some staff specialists have yet to learn the truth that, even after the plans for a change have been carefully made, it takes *time* to put the change successfully into production use. Time is necessary even though there may be no resistance to the change itself. The operators must develop the skill needed to use new methods and new equipment efficiently; there are always bugs to be taken out of a new method or piece of equipment even with the best of engineering. When a staff man begins to lose his patience with the amount of time that these steps take, the people he is working with will begin to feel that he is pushing them; *this* amounts to a change in their customary work relationships, and resistance will start building up where there was none before.

The situation is aggravated if the staff man mistakenly accuses the operators of resisting the idea of the change, for there are few things that irritate people more than to be blamed for resisting change when actually they are doing their best to learn a difficult new procedure.

## Management Action

Many of the problems of resistance to change arise around certain kinds of *attitudes* that staff men are liable to develop about their jobs and their own ideas for introducing change. Fortunately, management can influence these attitudes and thus deal with the problems at their source.

**Broadening Staff Interest.** It is fairly common for a staff man to work so hard on one of his ideas for change that he comes to identify himself with it. This is fine for the organization when he is working on the idea by himself or with his immediate colleagues; the idea becomes "his baby," and the company benefits from his complete devotion to his work.

But when he goes to some group of operating people to introduce a change, his very identification with his ideas tends to make him unreceptive to any suggestions for modification. He just does not feel like letting anyone else tamper with his pet ideas. It is easy to see, of course, how this attitude is interpreted by the operating people as a lack of respect for their suggestions.

This problem of the staff man's extreme identification with his work is one which, to some extent, can only be cured by time. But here are four suggestions for speeding up the process:

1. The manager can often, with wise timing, encourage the staff man's interest in a different project that is just starting.

2. The manager can also, by his "coaching" as well as by example, prod the staff man to develop a healthier respect for the contributions he can receive from operating people; success in this area would, of course, virtually solve the problem.

3. It also helps if the staff man can be guided to recognize that the satisfaction he derives from being productive and creative is the same satisfaction he denies the operating people by his behavior toward them. Experience shows that staff people can sometimes be stimulated by the thought of finding satisfaction in sharing with others in the organization the pleasures of being creative.

4. Sometimes, too, the staff man can be led to see that winning acceptance of his ideas through better understanding and handling of human beings is just as challenging and rewarding as giving birth to an idea.

*Using Understandable Terms.* One of the problems that must be overcome arises from the fact that the typical staff man is likely to have the attitude that the reasons why he is recommending any given change may be so complicated and specialized that it is impossible to explain them to operating people. It may be true that the operating people would find it next to impossible to understand some of the staff man's analytical techniques, but this does not keep them from coming to the conclusion that the staff specialist is trying to razzle-dazzle them with tricky figures and formulas—insulting their intelligence—if he does not strive to his utmost to translate his ideas into terms understandable to them. The following case illustrates the importance of this point:

A staff specialist was temporarily successful in "selling" a change based on a complicated mathematical formula to a foreman who really did not understand it. The whole thing backfired, however, when the foreman tried to sell it to his operating people. They asked him a couple of sharp questions that he could not answer. His embarrassment about this led him to resent and resist the change so much that eventually the whole proposition fell through. This was unfortunate in terms not only of human relations but also of technological progress in the plant.

There are some very good reasons, both technical and social, why the staff man should be interested in working with the operating people until his recommendations make "sense." (This does not mean that the operating people need to understand the recommendations in quite the same way or in the same detail that the staff man does, but that they should be able to visualize the recommendations in terms of their job experiences.) Failure of the staff man to provide an adequate explanation is likely to mean that a job the operators had formerly performed with understanding and satisfaction will now be performed without understanding and with less satisfaction.

This loss of satisfaction not only concerns the individual involved but also is significant from the standpoint of the company which is trying to get maximum productivity from the operating people. A person who does not have a feeling of comprehension of what he is doing is denied the opportunity to exercise that uniquely human ability—the ability to use informed and intelligent judgment on what he does. If the staff man leaves the operating people with a sense of confusion, they will also be left unhappy and less productive.

Top line and staff executives responsible for the operation should make it a point, therefore, to know how the staff man goes about installing a change. They can do this by asking discerning questions when he reports to them, listening closely to reports of employee reaction, and, if they have the opportunity, actually watching the staff man at work. At times they may have to take such drastic action as insisting that the time of installation of a proposed change be postponed until the operators are ready for it. But, for the most part, straightforward discussions with the staff man in terms of what they think of his approach should help him, over a period of time, to learn what is expected of him in his relationships with operating personnel.

*New Look at Resistance.* Another attitude that gets staff men into trouble is the *expectation* that all the people involved will resist the change. It is curious but true that the staff man who goes into his job with the conviction that people are going to resist any idea he presents with blind stubbornness just the way he thinks they will. The process is clear: whenever he treats the people who are supposed to buy his ideas as if they were bullheaded, he changes the way they are used to being treated; and they *will* be bullheaded in resisting *that* change!

I think that the staff man—and management in general—will do better to look at it this way: When resistance *does* appear, it should not be thought of as something to be *overcome*. Instead, it can best be thought of as a useful red flag—a signal that something is going wrong. To use a rough analogy, signs of resistance in a social organization are useful in the same way that pain is useful to the body as a signal that some bodily functions are getting out of adjustment.

The resistance, like the pain, does not tell what is wrong but only that something *is* wrong. And it makes no more sense to try to overcome such resistance than it does to take a pain killer without diagnosing the bodily ailment. Therefore, when resistance appears, it is time to listen carefully to find out what the trouble is. What is needed is not a long harangue on the logics of the new recommendations but a careful exploration of the difficulty.

It may happen that the problem is some technical imperfection in the change that can be readily corrected. More than likely, it will turn out that the change is threatening and upsetting some of the established social arrangements for doing work. Whether the trouble is easy or difficult to correct, management will at least know what it is dealing with.

***New Job Definition.***   Finally, some staff specialists get themselves in trouble because they assume they have the answer in the thought that people will accept a change when they have participated in making it. For example?

In one plant we visited, an engineer confided to us (obviously because we, as researchers on human relations, were interested in psychological gimmicks!) that he was going to put across a proposed production layout change of his by inserting in it a rather obvious error, which others could then suggest should be corrected. We attended the meeting where this stunt was performed, and superficially it worked. Somebody caught the error, proposed that it be corrected, and our engineer immediately "bought" the suggestion as a very worthwhile one and made the change. The group then seemed to "buy" his entire layout proposal.

It looked like an effective technique—oh, so easy—until later, when we became better acquainted with the people in the plant. Then we found out that many of the engineer's colleagues considered him a phony and did not trust him. The resistance they put up to his ideas was very subtle, yet even more real and difficult for management to deal with.

Participation will never work so long as it is treated as a device to get somebody else to do what you want him to. Real participation is based on respect. And respect is not acquired by just trying; it is acquired when the staff man faces the reality—that he needs the contributions of the operating people.

If the staff man defines his job as not just generating ideas but also getting those ideas into practical operation, he will recognize his real dependence on the contributions of the operating people. He will ask them for ideas and suggestions, not in a backhanded way to get compliance, but in a straightforward way to get some good ideas and avoid some unnecessary mistakes. By this process he will be treating the operating people in such a way that his own behavior will not be perceived as a threat to their customary work relationships. It will be possible to discuss, and accept or reject, the ideas on their own merit.

*     *     *     *     *

## Role of the Administrator

Now what about the way the top executive goes about his own job as it involves the introduction of change and problems of resistance?

One of the most important things he can do, of course, is to deal with staff people in much the same way that he wants them to deal with the operators. He must realize that staff people resist social change, too.

*     *     *     *     *

# 5. GENERAL MACHINERY CORPORATION

---

# Case Introduction

---

## SYNPOSIS

General Machinery Corporation (GMC) is a large diversified company with 12 operating divisions and 23 manufacturing plants. Its major competitive strategy is based upon the goals of low prices and production economies made possible through the use of advanced technology. The Central Research Laboratories (CRL) of GMC play a key strategic role through the many pure and applied research projects aimed at both product and process improvements. The approval of specific research projects have been the source of uncertainty, interdepartmental tension, and has raised a number of policy issues. Dr. Hoffman, the manager of the CRL, has proposed that he be given authority to approve any research program under $100,000 and that his division be made a semiautonomous profit center. Mr. Schultz, the president of GMC, is unsure that this will resolve the basic policy problems of managing research activities for the organization.

## WHY THIS CASE IS INCLUDED

This case illustrates the necessary connection among broad company goals, the formulation of a competitive strategy, and the design of the organization for the successful implementation of the chosen strategy. Rapidly changing market and technological environments are a central aspect to policy making for an ever increasing number of firms in today's world. Companies which emphasize technological innovation are faced with the problems of directing their research effort. Central to the case are the issues of how should research resources be expended; the design questions of how research activities should relate to the rest of the organization; and who should make these strategically important decisions. Through a discussion of these issues in the context of the specific situation described in the General Machinery Corporation the reader can learn to appreciate how a general manager must use theory and judgment in the policy-making process. Also, organizations which rely heavily on research and development efforts to maintain this strategic competitive advantage have a number of unique policy problems.

## DIAGNOSTIC AND PREDICTIVE QUESTIONS

The readings included with this case are marked (*). The author index at the end of this book locates the other readings.

1.  What competitive advantages does General Machinery Corporation emphasize in the formulation of strategy? What roles does the Central Research Laboratories (CRL) play in the implementation of the GMC strategy?

    Read:   Tilles, "How to Evaluate Corporate Strategy?"
    * Ansoff and Stewart, "Strategies for a Technology-Based Business."

2.  Draw a hierarchy of goals beginning with the GMC as a whole and going down to the goals of an individual researcher within the CRL. Include the goals of Mr. Seabert, the vice president for finance, and the various group vice presidents in the hierarchy of goals. Would Vancil suggest that goal congruence exists within this organization?

    Read:   Vancil, "What Kind of Management Control Do You Need?"
    * Granger, "The Hierarchy of Objectives."

3.  In what way does the requirements for an effective research organization differ from an effective administrative organization? How might these differences lead to strain or conflict over the control and operation or research activities within GMC?

    Read:   * Litterer, "Conflict in Organization: A Re-examination."
    Seiler, "Diagnosing Interdepartmental Conflict."

4.  What problem-solving techniques would be appropriate for the financial analysis and choice of specific research projects within GMC? Would these techniques be equally useful for both applied and pure research projects undertaken by the CRL?

    Read:   * Ansoff and Stewart, "Strategies for a Technology-Based Business." Horngren, "Accounting for Management Control," pp. 356–63, 365–68.

5.  Could the problems of making decisions on specific research projects be satisfactorily handled by a matrix organizational structure or by the establishment of a project manager?

    Read:   Vancil, "What Kind of Management Control Do You Need?"
    Lawrence and Lorsch, "New Management Job: The Integrator."

6.  The Central Research Laboratories were organized as an auxiliary staff unit located under the headquarters of GMC to support the needs of the 12 operating divisions. What factors indicate that this activity should be separated from the operating divisions? Based upon the facts in the case, what are the advantages and disadvantages of placing the research function in the operating divisions?

    Read:   *Summer, "Economies of Scale and Organization Structure."

7. Mr. Hoffman's proposal essentially asks that the CRL be made into a decentralized profit center. Would this organizational design be consistent with the organizational principles favored by Mr. Schultz in the case? Explain why or why not.

> Read:   Vancil, "What Kind of Management Control Do You Need?"

8. How should the performance of the CRL be evaluated if Mr. Hoffman's proposal is accepted? How could this proposal be implemented so that the control structure of GMC could be integrated into its organizational structure?

> Read:   Vancil, "What Kind of Management Control Do You Need?"
> * Ansoff and Stewart, "Strategies for a Technology-Based Business." Newman, "Strategy and Management Structure."

9. What are the benefits and costs in terms of motivation which would result from the implementation of Mr. Hoffman's proposal? Is the answer to this question the same for the research scientists and engineers as it is for the managers of the 12 operating divisions?

> Read:   Evans, "Leadership and Motivation: A Core Concept." Maslow, *Motivation and Personality* * Gellerman, "Motivation and Productivity."

## POLICY QUESTIONS

10. What will be the effect of Mr. Hoffman's proposal on the successful implementation of the goals and strategy of GMC?

> Read:   Review the readings for Questions 1 and 2 above.

11. Would the adoption of Mr. Hoffman's proposal help to resolve the disagreements within GMC over which research projects should be funded? If not, how would you propose to manage this conflict in a constructive way so that the basic policies of the corporation might be implemented successfully?

> Read:   Review the readings for Questions 3 through 5 above.

12. How might the CRL be organized so that the control system of the corporation would be integrated into the organizational structure in such a manner that encourages goal accomplishment?

> Read:   Review the readings for Questions 7 through 9 above.

13. Assume that you are a special assistant to Mr. Schultz, the president of the company; write a letter to him which recommends a specific course of action that he should take in this case, indicating the major reasons for your recommendations.

# Case Text*

General Machinery Corporation (GMC) was founded 55 years ago, initially to produce parts for railroad locomotives. It has grown into a large diversified company with 60,000 employees, sales of $550,000,000, 12 operating (product) divisions, and 23 manufacturing plants. According to GMC president, William Schultz, the firm has been successful "because it has pursued certain main goals: lower-than-competitors' prices, economies of mass production, and higher quality than competitors' through superior technology."

**EXHIBIT 1**
**General Machinery Corporation**

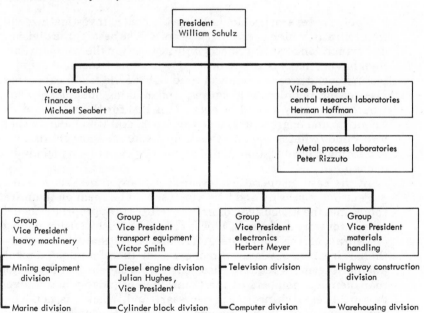

An organization chart of the company appears as Exhibit 1. Basic operating divisions (for example, diesel engine, mining equipment) are viewed by Mr. Schultz as "relatively autonomous. We expect that division managers will have the initiative to make GMC the best in their product lines. The electronic equipment division manager, for example, must

---

* Copyright 1977 by Charles E. Summer.

decide what products to bring out, what kinds of selling talents and methods he needs, and above all, how to manufacture this equipment at the lowest possible cost through mass production."

This case reports on certain problems that the company faces in carrying out its subgoals of scientific research. According to Mr. Schultz, these goals are "to develop new products ahead of competitors, and to develop new mass-manufacturing processes to keep our product quality high and our costs low. We develop these products and processes for our current operating divisions (which we call 'operating research') and for the long-range future changes in our business (we call this 'long-range research' or 'pure research')."

The problems in this case were originally suggested by Dr. Herman Hoffman, vice president in charge of the Central Research Laboratories.

### The Problem as Seen by Dr. Hoffman

Dr. Hoffman feels that the present system for operating the Central Research Laboratories (CRL) has some disadvantages for both CRL and for the company as a whole. He views the situation in this way:

> There are several problems. I am a bit tired of investigating, with my scientists, which operating projects will be best for the divisions and which long-range projects will be best for the company, and then having many of these turned down by the Executive Committee. We spend great amounts of time writing the technical proposals, getting detailed cost figures, and making judgments about where the money should be spent. It is bad for the morale of the scientists and engineers who do this work, and who judge in their own minds what is good for the company, to see their efforts come to nothing. They feel that their judgment is either being ignored or condemned.
>
> In the case of operating research, I many times know which projects have priority and how much should be spent on them. Yet sometimes the Executive Committee refuses to appropriate enough money for worthy projects. This is caused because division managers, sitting on the Committee, often are afraid that they won't get their fair share of research money. They therefore don't support another division's request. Also, it is very difficult for the two top management members of the Committee to judge when a given technical-research project is necessary and when it is not. They quite naturally must be financially oriented. Since often it is difficult to prove what the payoff for a project will be, they must wonder whether that much money should be spent. I am certainly not criticizing Mr. Seabert, the financial vice president, since he is responsible for the finances of the company. He votes to turn a project down when he judges that it is not worth the cost to the company. So does Mr. Schultz.
>
> Another kind of error is the opposite of that above. The Committee sometimes will spend too much money on a project—give it more priority than it should have. I remember a project which was

proposed to CRL by the mining equipment division. It was budgeted at $80,000 instead of $60,000, which was all that was necessary. I believe that the mining people wanted more research than was necessary, to be on the safe side. You see, they are spending my CRL research budget, and not their own money.

When it comes to long-range (pure) research, I have had a number of projects that certainly would be good for our company's growth, which have been rejected by the Executive Committee. Sometimes it is the division managers who reject the idea, and sometimes the top management managers. Again, I believe that it is unwise (and even dangerous) for such projects to be turned down. The division managers quite naturally have their own businesses to run, and cannot give the time or the expert knowledge required. We have a recent example. We at CRL see a need for increased research in surface and friction physics, and in thermodynamics. I had proposed the addition of two scientists in the first category and seven in the latter. At the Executive Committee meeting this year, six members opposed this addition.

I think that the members of the Executive Committee view CRL as an expensive overhead-cost department, always asking for money but never being able to prove what we are worth. That is what I conclude after going through years of the budget process, with our proposals scrutinized at length. Sometimes I believe that there should be more authority granted to the research vice president for saying what research will be done. The research in thermodynamics would certainly be carried out.

### Research Problems as Seen by the President

Mr. Schultz states that he sees two kinds of problems in management of Research in GMC.

First, I am concerned because we have allocated $7,000,000 for research this year, yet we will spend only $6,500,000. The board of directors established a policy that the company should spend 5 percent of sales over the years on research and development if we are to keep ahead of competitors. At current sales, this is $28,000,-000. The board further decided that this should be split between Central Research Laboratories (one quarter of the total, or 1.25 percent) and the divisions (three quarters of the total, or 3.75 percent). At current sales, CRL gets $7,000,000 for research on ideas up through the pilot-plant stage and the divisions get $21,000,000 for engineering the successful research projects into actual mass production. It is the budget of the CRL I am worried about. We know we should be spending $7,000,000 for the good of the company. The division managers and Dr. Hoffman are continuously proposing projects that they think are vital, and which total more than $7,000,000. Why is it, then, that we end up by spending less than both the board and the divisions judge is best?

CRL employs 550 people, one fourth (140) of whom are scientists and engineers. CRL is performing an absolutely vital function. We learned long ago that research pays off. We are the lowest cost manufacturer of certain types of machinery in the world—lower than Caterpillar in the United States, Fiat in Italy, and Volvo in Sweden.

CRL was put there as a central staff department to do this work because we cannot afford to have each division carry out its own research. The work we do in physics, for example, applies to many divisions at once. I expect Dr. Hoffman and his assistants to be primarily responsible for looking into all of our divisions to get ideas for improvement, and to convince division managers of the need for a specific project.

I have been doing some investigating of the unspent budget gap, trying to find why we can't get projects approved up to our target of $7,000,000. This investigation shows that the Executive Committee approved only eight out of every ten projects submitted to it in the last five years. Dr. Hoffman tells me that during the same time an average of 15 projects a year are seriously proposed by CRL, but that they never get to the formal meeting of the Executive Committee because one or more division managers react against them. Budgets for the last five years have been lower than the target (1.25 percent of sales) by from $400,000 to $700,000. The projects proposed over that period, by size, were:

| Size of Project | Percent of Total Projects |
| --- | --- |
| Less than $25,000 ................. | 20 |
| $25,000–$50,000................... | 30 |
| $50,000–$100,000................. | 20 |
| Over $100,000.................... | 30 |

Here are our official procedures. All proposals are drawn up by CRL. About 80 percent of projects are actually "seen" or initiated by CRL, while 20 percent are first mentioned by division people. Dr. Hoffman and his engineers visit with division managers throughout the year and as the embryo ideas become projects that look to Hoffman as serious prospects for next year's budget proposal, he contacts the division manager whose products are most likely to benefit from the project to see if he wants the project. The division manager may either want the project badly, be neutral on it, or oppose it. The final decision, though belongs to Hoffman. He and his engineers are the guardians of the state of our products and production processes. Nobody else will have either the interest or expertise to keep us up to date. Minutes of the Executive Committee show that 90 percent of the operating research projects have been sponsored by both Dr. Hoffman and the division manager in question, but that 10 percent have been proposed by Hoffman and supported only mildly by others.

As for pure research projects, Dr. Hoffman proposes all of these, since they are not applicable to any one division. Those are his, and I must say that neither myself nor other members of the Committee know what he is talking about sometimes.

On October 1 each year, the Executive Committee convenes for the research budge. Members include the four group vice presidents who represent the divisions under them, Mr. Seabert, financial vice president, Dr. Hoffman, and myself. We look at each research project individually to judge whether the project meets the needs of the whole corporation. It must be done this way. No one man can be expert on all the factors necessary. The group vice presidents cannot simply take their division budgets and add them up—we know from experience that they would always exceed $7,-000,000, so somebody somewhere has to establish priorities, to stay within our committed amount. Who is to do this? I cannot do this alone, because I do not know enough about research or about the divisions—I'd have to be a specialist in automobile engines as well as the television business! Dr. Hoffman has the official responsibility of recommending priorities, but he is a scientist and is not responsible for selling to hospitals or running the production lines for television tubes. Balanced Committee judgment is necessary.

What happens is that the Committe never allocates the full amount for research. I detect the feeling on the part of all of us that we don't think we've done a logical job. The divisions, as well as the CRL people, seem to resent budget sessions and feel a bit badly toward the meetings when they're finished.

## The Die Casting Project

One project that generated considerable controversy in the Executive Committee was a project to improve the quality of metal castings made in the diesel engine division. According to the proposal, CRL believed it feasible to develop two new machines to be used in casting, and a new chemical process for certain metals in the casting process.

"I cannot see why they would turn it down," says Julian Hughes, vice president of the diesel engine division. "It is absolutely necessary if we are to keep the lead among competitors. The project would only cost $140,000. Also, we worked so hard on this proposal—I'm not inclined to do that again. Finally, we are the leader now, but I know some division managers in competitive companies who are getting a great deal of research support. I was approached informally by one of these companies regarding a job last year, but of course I think GMC is my career. That is why I am concerned that we stay on top."

Herbert Meyer, group vice president for electronics, commented, "My position in the Executive Committee was against the Die Casting Project. I have respect for Hughes, Dr. Hoffman, and Victor Smith [group vice president for transportation]. But we have a large backlog of research projects in the company, many of them in electronics. I know that engine research is a necessary thing, too, and would have voted for the proposal, except that this particular one just did not sound as important as some of the rest."

Peter Rizzuto, head of the division of CRL that did the work on the proposal, says, "I think that failure of this project has set our company back in metal processing technology two years. The project might have been done, in my judgment, for $25,000 less, but Mr. Hughes felt that we needed more certainty in the outcome, and specified a series of experimental checks that I did not think necessary."

The casewriter asked Michael Seabert, financial vice president, what he thought about the project. He replied:

> First, let me say that GMC is in excellent financial condition. We are growing fast, we have sufficient cash flow to spend $10,000,000 instead of $7,000,000 if we want to, and the banks will lend us more. When the Die Casting Project came up, I listened to the various arguments. We did not need a vote, because it was opposed by three group vice presidents plus myself. It just seemed to me that the engine group were not too certain of their own argument. I am not blaming them—they must think of their group first, and try to make it the best. Other projects on the agenda seemed much more pressing to me.
>
> And then there was the $140,000 proposed by Dr. Hoffman to add two scientists in surface physics, and seven in thermodynamics. I supported him in a halfhearted way, but simply did not know enough to express my opinion clearly one way or the other.

Suggestion by Dr. Hoffman:

> I have proposed that Mr. Schultz and the board should redraw the organization chart, creating a research division from the old CRL. It would no longer be a corporate headquarters staff, but like the other operating divisions, a semiautonomous business in itself. Operating-division managers would be allowed to spend up to $100,000 for research on any one project. As long as their own division profits are to be charged for research, the total expenditure might be considerably in excess of 1.25 percent of sales. The total would vary from year to year depending on how much division managers would each want, knowing full well that (1) they must keep up with the times through research, and yet (2) that it is their budget they are spending, not CRL's.
>
> I would charge them the direct cost of the project—manpower, laboratory materials, and experimental space. I would add 15 percent for overhead costs (our actual ratio of direct costs to general laboratory offices and management), and another 5 percent for "profit." This "price" I charge to divisions would be lower than outside research businesses such as Battelle Institute in Geneva or Rand Corporation in the United States.
>
> When the demand for research services is great, I would expand my manpower and facilities. When it is less, I would contract. The

5 percent "profit" would be retained by the research division to cover minor periods when business does not support all of our personnel.

Decisions on individual projects would be made by division managers, and the Executive Committee would rule only on projects over $100,000.

As at present, scientists from the research division would suggest projects to our customer divisions, or they can suggest them to us. Whenever the division and I agree on projects less than $100,000, that is final.

For long-range pure research, the procedure would be the same, except that top management, as the customer, would decide what projects they want. There would be a very small percentage of sales, amounting to perhaps $200,000, allocated to the research division as I see fit. This money would be allocated to spend at least a portion of their time on any project that interests them in their field—very much as scientists operate in universities.

### Reaction of the President

Mr. Schultz states that he received Dr. Hoffman's proposal in general form a month ago. Since then, he has been giving it some consideration, and has obtained the thoughts of the financial vice-president. "Frankly, I am having difficulty with it. I am wondering if such a system would work as well as the one we have now."

---

# Selected Readings

---

*From*

## STRATEGIES FOR A TECHNOLOGY-BASED BUSINESS*

*By H. Igor Ansoff and John M. Stewart*

\*    \*    \*    \*    \*

### RESEARCH VERSUS DEVELOPMENT

The two concepts of "research" and "development" have become so closely linked in management thinking by the expression R&D that important differences between them are

* From "Strategies for a Technology-Based Business," *Harvard Business Review,* vol. 45, no. 6 (November–December 1967), pp. 71–83 (excerpts). Reprinted by permission. © 1967 by The President and Fellows of Harvard College; all rights reserved.

often ignored in executive decision making. This becomes particularly apparent when companies attempt to apply the lessons of their research experience to problems in development, or vice versa.

Rather than attempt to formulate a generally acceptable definition of the two concepts, we shall simply use the terms "R-intensive" and "D-intensive" to denote a tendency toward the basic and experimental on the one hand, and a tendency toward commercial product design on the other. Most companies, of course, fall somewhere in between, but they can best be described in terms of the two extremes.

*     *     *     *     *

## R-intensive

These organizations in general display six characteristics:

1. *They work with indefinite design specifications.* Since management can usually identify the problem but cannot specify the desired solution, the task of the R-intensive organization is to discover and evaluate alternative solutions, rather than to implement a single solution.

2. *They tend to "broadcast" objectives and market data among technical people, rather than channel specific kinds of information to individuals.* Being unable to present specific requirements to research, they use broadcast communications to stimulate generation of alternatives that will be consistent with top management's objectives and strategy.

3. *They are nondirective in work assignments.* Since design specifications in R-intensive companies are less definite, and technical insight and potential contribution are individual rather than group attributes, managers must permit freedom for individual initiative and progress rather than assign individuals to specific parts of a well-defined solution.

4. *They maintain a continuing project evaluation and selection process.* Research is constantly turning up alternative solutions of varying worth, and these supersede previous solutions. Moreover, a move by a competitor, or results achieved on another project, may obsolete a piece of research or change its priority. This calls for a continuing revision of the project portfolio to permit changes in the slate of projects, even within the normal routine planning period.

5. *They stress the perception of significant results.* Where a research problem has not been tightly structured, the solutions—even if found—are not always obvious. An essential skill of the technical manager is his ability to recognize technically or commercially significant results. The history of invention is replete with instances, like Carruther's discovery of nylon, where a flash of insight into the possibilities of wholly unanticipated experimental results led to great discoveries that might otherwise have been missed.

6. *They value innovation over efficiency.* Economy in performing research is less important than achieving a markedly better solution with clear market or profit advantages. Innovation is therefore prized, even when it entails the sacrifice of efficiency in organization structure, planning, or control.

## D-intensive

In contrast, these organizations can usually be recognized by four characteristics:

1. *Well-defined design specifications.* With the research essentially complete, the development objective is reasonably clear, and performance tests can be specified early during design. The technical task is not to create new alternatives but to reduce available alternatives to a single solution for implementation.

2. *Highly directive supervision.* The work to be done is highly interrelated from the beginning of design to successful testing; managers tend to specify objectives, give orders, and carefully measure performance. The relatively large number of people in the D-intensive organization—designers, test engineers, draftsmen, production engineers—also call for a more structured management approach than is required in the R-intensive company.

3. *Sequential arrangement of tasks.* Unlike the R-intensive organization where many

people can work in parallel on the whole problem or on different aspects of the same problem, the D-intensive organization requires a disciplined sequencing of tasks, with sophisticated controls to ensure that technical objectives are achieved within planned time and cost limits. Scheduling tends to be thorough and precise, as in manufacturing. When faced with trade-off decisions between efficiency and innovation, managers will usually opt for efficiency and higher output.

4. *Vulnerability to disruption by change.*    Given its relatively high manpower commitment, its sequencing of tasks, and its relative proximity to actual production in the new product development process, the D-intensive organization can be severely affected by managerial or administrative changes ordered in specifications or objectives in midstream. Recent studies by McKinsey & Company indicate that management or program changes contribute more heavily to cost, and schedule overruns, as a rule, than do engineering or technical changes—a point that often escapes the managers involved.

\*    \*    \*    \*    \*

## DOWNSTREAM COUPLING

A second important characteristic of high-technology business is the degree of *downstream coupling*—that is, the extent to which the success of the company's product introduction process depends on communication and cooperation between the R&D and the manufacturing and marketing functions, which are further "downstream" toward the customer. Clearly, industries differ in their downstream coupling requirements. Some need a great deal of information and interaction, with as little filtering as possible; others need little or none. Being aware of the coupling requirement and managing it properly not only can avert the frictions that are so frequent at the marketing-engineering interface, but also can channel the familiar conflicts between manufacturing and engineering toward more productive ends.

### Critical Balance

It is useful to distinguish three degrees of coupling, as shown in Exhibit 1—high, moderate, and low. High coupling requires close interaction among the technical, manufacturing, and marketing functions of the business. Accurate and detailed market information is essen-

**EXHIBIT 1**
**Degrees of Downstreaming Coupling**

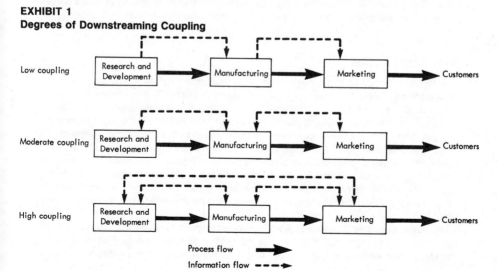

tial to adequate product line planning. The selection of R&D projects is influenced heavily by manufacturing costs, availability of raw materials, abilities of the marketing organization, and countermoves by competition. Minimizing the disruptive effect of new product introductions on manufacturing is critical. Tight control of product quality is essential to successful customer applications and minimum service engineering effort. Finally, time pressure on all functions is usually acute.

Many technically based industries require exceptionally high coupling. In specialty plastics, for example, the functions of product and process development, production, and field technical service must be closely linked by a tightly knit communication, decision, and control process—an effect that management has often vainly tried to achieve by shifting the technical service group from marketing to development, or to production, or independently to the chief executive. Some companies have completed this organizational cycle more than once.

Again, in present-day electronics, integrated circuit producers find that they must work more closely with equipment designers, field service men, and marketing planners than component suppliers ever did. Significant increases in the product coupling have made necessary corresponding increases in the management coupling of R&D with the departments downstream.

In a highly coupled organization, management is usually concerned about the downstream effect of new product introductions and about the marketing and production impact of R&D actions. The coupling-conscious management of one chemical company, wary of a proposed $3 million investment in a new chemical process developed by a recent acquisition, kept pressing for more information. The facts confirmed their misgivings: more than $20 million of additional investment would be required before the parent company's target rate of return could be achieved. The $3 million "down payment" was not approved.

In such companies, management must maintain a constant balance of influence among development, production, and technical service to the customer. If development becomes too strong, uneconomic products or processes are rammed into manufacturing, and current customer complaints must defer to future development work. If technical service is too powerful, future development is downgraded in the interest of extinguishing the fire-of-the-minute. Occasionally, manufacturing is strong enough to reject desirable product changes in the interest of maintaining high efficiencies, or to schedule output to maximize machine utilization rather than to meet customer commitments. In a highly coupled organization, correct balance among these three technically competent functions is dynamic rather than static. Changes in the company's competitive situation, technical strengths, and capacity utilization, among others, force management to keep readjusting to current conditions.

\*     \*     \*     \*     \*

## INVESTMENT RATIOS

How much should be spent on research and development? How should the investment be apportioned between basic and applied research projects? The questions are just as important at the corporate as at the national level—and they are no easier to resolve.

As yet, there is no generally accepted measure of R&D investment (taking "investment" to mean total dollar resources committed, without regard to the accounting treatment). Of late, the familiar practice of expressing R&D investment as a percentage of sales has been falling into disrepute—and rightly so, since the results of R&D are not realized immediately and, in fact, affect sales instead of being affected by them. Measures that begin, but only begin, to do justice to R&D's mission of protecting corporate assets from technical obsolescence treat the R&D investment as a percentage of total investment or of profits or cash flow.

However measured, the ratio of R&D investment/expense is important. High ratios, we may note, are characteristic of technically intensive industries such as pharmaceuticals, chemicals, and electronics; low ratio are characteristic of nonintensive industries such as food, lumber, and cement. Most industries, of course, fall between the extremes—for example, farm equipment and petroleum are near the middle of the range.

## "High" Effects

In our view, high investment ratios have four significant implications for management:

1. *They require a serious and continuous evaluation of technology procurement alternatives:*

Whether to buy technology through licensing or through hiring consultants.

Whether to buy a company in order to acquire the latest technology in an unfamiliar field.

Whether to hire top people with the specific technical competence desired.

Whether to develop additional technical competence by internal training in order to stay competitive.

Where R&D investment ratio is low, it may be possible to develop technology within the company with relatively low risk of being outpaced by competition. Higher ratios characteristically allow less lead time and make the acquisition of technology a more attractive alternative. In any case, they call for constant review of the alternatives by a corporate-level group which is aware of the pace of development inside and outside the company and which is also sensitive to significant competitive moves in the field.

2. *They usually accelerate product and process change.* This, in turn, requires an adaptive organization, which can quickly shift to new levels of efficiency and effectiveness as technology changes the work to be done. The source of the change in a high-ratio company can be either external or internal. Externally, competitors investing in the same technology may obsolete a market, a plant, or an investment—compelling the organization to respond swiftly. Internally, research and development results can produce similar pressures for change. In a company with a high R&D investment ratio, a major criterion of organization is therefore the ability to adapt to new technology without sacrificing market share or efficiency.

3. *They usually mean a dynamic product market.* Such markets, where products readily substitute for one another and where emphasis rapidly shifts from new product development to low unit cost and vice versa, impose three special requirements.

The first is clear visibility of resources, permitting management to cut off a development project quickly or to switch resources into a new technology. If it cannot foresee the implications of such decisions in terms of total corporate resources over the entire product life cycle, the company may become more deeply committed than management intended.

The second requirement is explicit strategy formulation. In a rapidly changing market, executives can lose perspective and make unwise or conflicting technical or product decisions. An explicit strategic framework permits clear definition of project alternatives and enables managers to choose more wisely among them.

The third special need is a well-developed planning system to permit the company to redirect its resources promptly and effectively. The system must be explicit, providing for control of technical resources consistent with strategy by tying R&D closely to annual corporate planning and control.

4. *They require closer supervision of technical efforts.* Since the company is highly dependent on technology for competitive survival and therefore commits proportionately more resources to the effort, the senior managers need to know more about technical problems and performance. They should be aware of the long-term corporate effects of lower level decisions and have a good grasp of the time and cost implications of particular technological developments. This is important because technology in high-ratio companies usually has a substantial effect on other functions. Thus any executive making a substantial invest-

ment in technology will need assurance that these effects are consistent with his total objective.

## "Low" Implications

In general, the effects of low R&D investment/expense ratios are the converse of those described above. Technology can be developed internally within competitive lead times—or, in some industries, purchased with the capital equipment into which technology has been incorporated by the manufacturer. Organization structure need not be highly adaptive; since technical developments are evolutionary, only occasional changes in functional structure will be needed. Resources need not be specially identified because historical accounting data on expense and investment adequately reflect the impact of product or process replacements. Finally, marketing does not have to be closely coupled with the technological functions, since marketing needs can be communicated via top management or through formal planning and control mechanisms.

*    *    *    *    *

## STATE OF THE ART

For most managers, the term "state of the art" denotes the frontier of a technology. Inside this boundary, but not beyond it, reliable and tested technical solutions are available.

However, state of the art has different implications in research and in development. For research, it denotes the frontier at which investigators seek to discover new phenomena or to devise a solution to a known problem. For development, it implies the less rarefied zone where the validity of a theory or solution has already been proved, but a successful commercial application remains to be achieved. For development, in other words, the state of the art hinges heavily on economics as well as on technology.

### Boundary Distance

How close a company's technology is to the state of the art has important implications for management planning and decision making. These implications may be considered under three headings: (1) stability, (2) predictability, and (3) precedent.

*Stability* is a function of distance from state of the art. A company working near the state-of-the-art boundary must keep trying for rapid advances like those through which it achieved its current position. At the same time, it must be alert to possible breakthroughs by competitors resulting in either a major advance in product performance or a major reduction in costs. Its market position is perpetually in jeopardy from all competitors working in the same technical area.

*    *    *    *    *

*Predictability* is low for companies near the state-of-the-art boundary. Since their researchers are working in areas of partial knowledge the nature and, even more, the timing of results are difficult to foresee. Unless the implications of low predictability are understood and allowed for, company plans can be hardly more than guesses, subject to all the vicissitudes of technical investigation.

Conversely, far from the boundary of the state of the art, where breakthroughs are unlikely, predictability is high. Specific small improvements in products or processes can be foretold with confidence and timed with a high degree of accuracy; their achievement depends on the resources invested rather than on technical innovation.

*    *    *    *    *

The implications of stability, predictability, and precedent are substantial in the areas of planning and control. Near the state of the art, a company must settle for more approximation and less precision in goals and standards. Thus planning and control systems must be tailored accordingly. In such a company, judgment is critical, and precision is often specious.

Failure to take account of these implications may be exceedingly costly. In one diversified company, an electronics division devoted to the development and marketing of highly sophisticated microwave equipment was expected to plan as far ahead and in as much detail as the industrial products divisions did. When the division manager continued to protest that the requirement was unrealistic, he was replaced by an accountant. Within 15 months, half of the technical people had left, and all momentum was gone from the R&D program.

\* \* \* \* \*

## MARKETING STRATEGY

. . . The alternatives may usefully be grouped into four major marketing strategies, recognizing that most companies will—or should—adopt a blend of these according to the requirements of their different markets or product lines:

*First to market*—based on a strong R&D program, technical leadership, and risk taking.

*Follow the leader*—based on strong development resources and an ability to react quickly as the market starts its growth phase.

*Application engineering*—based on product modifications to fit the needs of particular customers in a mature market.

*"Me-too"*—on superior manufacturing efficiency and cost control.

Each of these strategies, which we will examine more closely, has different strengths and weaknesses in particular competitive situations. Intelligent selection and execution of the appropriate strategy normally will strengthen the company's competitive posture.

### First To Market

This risky but potentially rewarding strategy has a number of important ramifications throughout the business: (*a*) a research-intensive effort, supported by major development resources, (*b*) close downstream coupling in product planning, and moderately close coupling thereafter, (*c*) high proximity to the state of the art, (*d*) high R&D investment ratio; and (*e*) a high risk of failure for individual products.

The implications of these have been discussed earlier. Taken together, they outline a clear philosophy of business. The company must recruit and retain outstanding technical personnel who can win leadership in the industry. It must see that these technical people are in close and useful communication with marketing planners to identify potentially profitable markets. It must often risk large investments of time and money in technical and market development without any immediate return. It must be able to absorb mistakes, withdraw, and recoup without losing its position in other product lines. As the nature of the market clarifies, initial plans must quickly be modified and approximation refined into precision.

Perhaps most important, top management must be able to make important judgments of timing, balancing the improved product development stemming from a delayed introduction against the risk of being second into the market. Such a company must have more than its share of long-range thinkers who can confidently assess market and competitive trends in their earliest stages and plan with both confidence and flexibility.

### Follow the Leader

This marketing strategy implies: (*a*) D-intensive technical effort, (*b*) moderate competence across the spectrum of relevant technologies, (*c*) exceptionally rapid response time in product development and marketing on the basis of finished research, (*d*) high downstream coupling of R&D with marketing and manufacturing, and (*e*) superior competitive intelligence.

The company that follows this strategy is—or should be—an organization that gets things done. It uses many interfunctional techniques, responds rapidly to change, and often seems to be in a perpetual fire drill. It has few scientists on its payroll, but some of the best development engineers available. Its senior executives are constantly concerned with maintaining the right balance of strengths among the technical, marketing, and manufacturing functions so that the company can respond effectively to the leader's moves in any of these three areas.

### Application Engineering

This strategy requires: (*a*) substantial product design and engineering resources but no research and little real development, (*b*) ready access to product users within customer companies, (*c*) technically perceptive salesmen and sales engineers who work closely with product designers, (*d*) good product-line control to prevent costly proliferation, (*e*) considerable cost consciousness in deciding what applications to develop, (*f*) an efficiency-oriented manufacturing organization, and (*g*) a flair for minimizing development and manufacturing cost by using the same parts or elements in many different applications.

The applications-engineering strategy tends to avoid innovative efforts in the interest of economy. Planning is precise, assignments are clear, and new technology is introduced cautiously, well behind the economic state of the art. Return-on-investment and cash-flow calculations are standard practice, and the entire management is profit-oriented.

### "Me-too"

This strategy, which has flourished in the past decade as never before, is distinguished by: (*a*) no research or development, (*b*) strong manufacturing function, dominating product design, (*c*) strong price and delivery performance, and (*d*) ability to copy new designs quickly, modifying them only to reduce production costs.

Competing on price, taking a low margin, but avoiding all development expense, a company that has adopted this strategy can wreak havoc with competitors following the first-to-market or follow-the-leader strategies. This is because the "me-too" strategy, effectively pursued, shortens the profitable period after market introduction when the leaders' margins are most substantial. The me-too strategy requires a "low-overhead" approach to manufacturing and administration, and a direct hard sell on price and delivery to the customer. It does not require any technical enthusiasm, nor does it aim to generate any.

\*     \*     \*     \*     \*

*From*

# THE HIERARCHY OF OBJECTIVES\*

*By Charles H. Granger*

\*     \*     \*     \*     \*

### TESTS OF VALIDITY

How can the validity of an objective be tested? What should an objective accomplish? Here are important criteria to be applied to an objective:

1. *Is it, generally speaking, a guide to action?* Does it facilitate decision making by helping management select the most desirable alternative courses of action?

2. *Is it explicit enough to suggest certain types of action?* In this sense, "to make profits"

---

\* From "The Hierarchy of Objectives," *Harvard Business Review,* vol. 42, no. 3 (May–June 1964), pp. 63–66 (excerpts). Reprinted by permission. © 1964 by The President and Fellows of Harvard College; all rights reserved.

does not represent a particularly meaningful guide to action, but "to carry on a profitable business in electrical goods" does.

3. *Is it suggestive of tools to measure and control effectiveness?* "To be a leader in the insurance business" and "to be an innovator in child-care services" are suggestive of measuring tools in a helpful way; but statements of desires merely to participate in the insurance field or child-care field are not.

4. *Is it ambitious enough to be challenging?* The action called for should in most cases be something in addition to resting on one's oars. Unless the enterprise sets objectives which involve reaching, there is a hint that the end of the road may be at hand. It might be perfectly appropriate for some enterprises which have accomplished their objectives to quietly disband. However, for an undertaking to have continuity, it needs the vitality of challenging objectives.

5. *Does it suggest cognizance of external and internal constraints?* Most enterprises operate within a framework of external constraints (e.g., legal and competitive restrictions) and internal constraints (e.g., limitations in financial resources). For instance, if objectives are to be a guide to action, it appears that American Motors, because of its particular set of constraints, should have somewhat different objectives than General Motors.

**EXHIBIT 1**
**Hierarchy of Objectives in Terms of Level of Need or Activity**

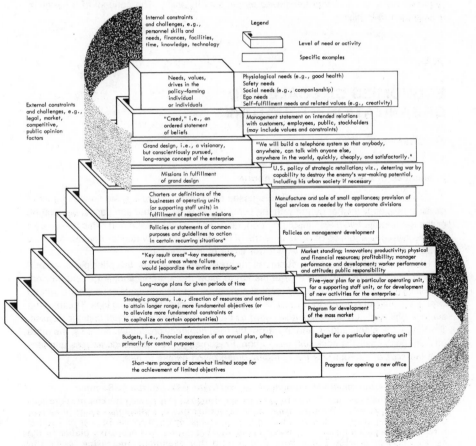

\* May occur at various organization levels.

6. *Can it be related to both the broader and the more specific objectives at higher and lower levels in the organization?* For example, are the division's objectives relatable to the corporate objectives, and in turn do they also relate to the objectives of the research department in that division?

If such tests as these are valid indications of the meaningfulness of objectives, then several further propositions become apparent. First, objectives, as aims or ends of action, are intimately involved in a complex of other important considerations or guides to action, such as definitions of the business, internal and external constraints, measurements of success, budgets, and long-range plans. Second, there is a ranking or hierarchy of objectives, proceeding in concept from the very broad to the specific. Logically, the specific or more limited objectives should not be in conflict with the broad objectives. The second proposition in particular deserves further consideration.

## COMPLETE FRAMEWORK

Much of the confusion which apparently exists about objectives can be alleviated by viewing objectives as a whole framework or complex of "aims or ends of action" and other guiding considerations. In this framework it is not helpful to think there is one overriding consideration, such as "profit," since we must also concede in the next breath that another objective is to "stay with the law." Profit may indeed be the factor to be maximized *in a particular case,* but it cannot be viewed as the sole objective. The concept of a hierarchy is illustrated in Exhibit 1.

*From*

# ECONOMIES OF SCALE AND ORGANIZATION STRUCTURE*

*By Charles E. Summer*

### Economies of Scale in Economic Theory

Economic theory has traditionally discussed economies of larger scale firms in terms of physical efficiency (higher output with the same inputs of land, labor and capital equipment, or the same output with less inputs of land, labor and capital equipment). This theory also has discussed economies of scale in terms of monetary efficiency (higher revenue with the same costs or a given revenue with lower costs of input factors).

Using the mathematics of cost curves, or break-even analyses, the principle of economies of scale stands out: with a large market to allow mass production, large and efficient machines and plants can be added (capital equipment inputs), the costs of which are spread over many units of output—thus fixed costs per unit of production become less. The long-run average unit cost curves slopes downward as the *scale* (output of product units) increases. The bigger the plants added, and the larger the total company production facilities, the more efficient (less costly) is each unit production. Presumably, the costs become less and less until the cost of coordinating the complex organization begins to rise.[1]

---

* Excerpts from unpublished manuscript, copyright 1963, Charles E. Summer.

[1] This is usually assumed away by economists, simply by stating that the cost of coordinating plants begins to rise. We know from other disciplines that this phenomena may be caused by such dysfunctions as distortion of communications, or an increase in cost of passing information between many staff departments, line executives, and operating plants, in the decision-making process. Today, we would also say that, eventually, increasing costs set in

It has also been pointed out that the degree to which economies of scale can actually be realized in practice, is dependent on two other factors: the existence of a mass market, large enough to warrant large plants and machines; and the fact that input units of capital equipment frequently are indivisible.

In regard to the last factor, take the case of an aircraft company that wishes to install a wind tunnel to test aircraft. These tunnels, which must be large enough to hold a complete airplane mock up, obviously will require a large capital expenditure. Suppose, hypothetically, that a small aircraft manufacturer entering the industry needs such a test device. A wind tunnel is not indivisible—the president of the XYZ company cannot say, "we are small, and our output isn't large enough to purchase a whole tunnel. So we will purchase ⅓ of a wind tunnel." He must, of course, go "whole hog or none." He may purchase the tunnel, and spread the $.5 million cost of it over a few airplanes, thus raising the fixed cost going into each unit of output, and probably pricing himself out of the market in competition with large companies, whose economies of scale are greater (fixed cost per unit are less). Or, he may decide not to enter the aircraft industry, but to produce smaller parts for large companies—in other words, he sees the laws of economies of scale as economic handwriting on the wall.[2] Only aircraft companies which have resources, and markets, to install large, complex capital equipment, can achieve a competitive long-run average cost curve position which is competitive.

Economists have also concerned themselves with *size* of companies. Whole plants, rather than machines, have been viewed as the basic input units of capital equipment. Similar reasoning to the wind tunnel example, where a machine was used as the input unit, has been used to show economies of scale and its relation to size of the firm.

## Economies of Scale in Organization Theory: Staff and Auxiliary Departments

Unfortunately, no literature exists which translates these principles into any realistic guides for management, when faced with the problem of adding staff and auxiliary service units to the company, or to a department of the company. It is my purpose simply to indicate along what lines such reasoning might proceed.

First, the staff or auxiliary service department should be viewed in much the same way as a machine or a plant—that is, as an input of fixed capital. If a firm's president is thinking about adding a personnel department at company headquarters, or an electronic computer service department, he is faced with the same factors as above. The market for the firm's products must be large enough to utilitze the department, and spread its output over a large number of units of product. A small bank may not be able to afford a personnel manager, or an electronic computer in bookkeeping and mailing. Additionally, though there are many combinations of service and machines that might be designed for a personnel department or data processing unit, there is a limit to which the company can buy "one half of a personnel manager," or "⅔ of a memory storage unit."

There is one difference between plant scale, and staff department scale, which should be pointed out. In the case of plants, the "market size" is the number of units or final product produced for customers—because the machines and plants are producing directly for shipment or service to customers. But in the case of staff and auxiliary service departments, the

---

because of the adverse effect of large organizations on the psychological self-actualization of individuals. This may reduce the energy and creativity released in the organization. All of these causes of increasing costs are valid, but beyond the scope of the present paper. Herein, we are interested in *economic* principles of economies of scale, as applied to organization structure, in the decreasing part of the long-run cost curve.

[2] In one interesting technological sense, he thereby becomes an "auxiliary department" of the larger company to which he sells. If the larger customer company gives the subcontractor advice on operations, this arrangement is similar to the decentralized company structure of General Electric, mentioned later. The difference is that in the latter case, departments of General Electric are divisions of a *legal* entity as well as a *technological* entity.

output of the department is an input to other *internal* company departments, instead of an input to organizations and customers *external* to the firm. In other words, the "market" or "customers" for a personnel department output are the manufacturing department, the sales department, and the central office clerical and accounting office, inside the company.

This difference has important effects on the logic which management uses to decide when to install staff and auxiliary service departments. First, it is the size of the primary operating departments (plants, sales offices, branch offices, etc.) which determines when a company can afford a staff department or auxiliary service department. Second, with the advance in specializations (in all fields from biochemistry to market research to data processing), this kind of "market," and these kinds of "economies of scale" are becoming more and more important in determining which firms survive, and what a growing company *must do,* technologically (here the word technology refers to specializations of human brains, as well as to advance in machinery).

The length of time which it takes to train and install, as a working part of the organization, a biochemist, or a corps of data systems planners and computer programmers, suggests that this kind of fixed input is even more crucial, at times, than the acquisition of plants and machines. Long-run costs are not only thoroughly committed, but they are committed in large amounts to relatively fixed blocks of input resources.

The same viewpoint can be applied at lower levels in a large firm. If management of the St. Louis sales office wishes to install a personnel clerk, or the Esso Research Laboratories in Linden, New Jersey, wishes to install a training director, or a group of patent attorneys, the basic factors are the same.

### Economies of Scale in Organization Theory: Line Departments

There is no clear-cut way to distinguish "line" and "staff" in organizations. Rather than get into details of a controversy, we can simply use the concept of "specialist" to denote the staff and auxiliary person, and the "general manager" notion as the line department.

Though Alfred Marshall made brief reference to the advantages of large firms in employing skilled general management,[3] he did not foresee the kind of developments in company organization which we have in the second half of the 20th century.

The same factors are relevant to economies of scale vis-à-vis line executives. A large unit today has a vast upward hierarchy of "coordinators," who devote time to planning and innovation, and whose marginal contribution to the firm's efficiency is spread over large volumes of output.

The most notable example is a company like General Electric, with 101 product divisions, each with a general manager, surrounded by staff and auxiliary service personnel—clerks, personnel people, training aids, etc. When the principle of indivisibility of people and machine prevents the duplication of a given service department at the division level, there are group executives with their helpers at the next level up. When indivisibility sets in even at the group vice president level, then the latest in fixed human resources (executive compensation specialists, organization planners, operations research personnel, and other "departments") are available at the corporate headquarters.

Each of these levels represents a pool composed of a general executive, with whatever staff assistance is allowed by the principle of "market" size and the principle of indivisibility.

There is no doubt but that these principles become more and more important (1) in determining the future organization and destiny of growing firms, and (2) determining the gross national product which issues forth from the manufacturing companies, banks, and hospitals of the nation. Advance in science, and in information processing will assure this.

---

[3] Alfred Marshall, *Principles of Economics,* 8th ed. (New York: The Macmillan Company, 1952), pp. 283–85.

## Limitations in Practice

In order to calculate when to add a staff or auxiliary service department, or when to add another level in the general management hierarchy, one would have to calculate the marginal productivity that the executive or specialist group provides to the line operating departments of the company. The marginal costs and revenues of the line departments, occasioned by adding a personnel department to advise them, would have to be calculated.

As most economics books point out, this is not possible in most situations. The data is not clearly available, nor can the marginal productivity and profits be clearly attributable to variations in the inputs of people and facilities. In spite of these limitations on quantification, and proof, the principles of market size (using the concept of market in this paper), indivisibility, and decreasing costs to scale, are, all three, useful logical tools of analysis in an age of rapidly advancing technology, and in an age of more complex organizations.

*From*

# MOTIVATION AND PRODUCTIVITY*

*By Saul W. Gellerman*

## The Classical Theories

\* \* \* \* \*

Alfred Adler, a one-time collaborator of Freud's who later broke with him to establish his own school of thought, has also had an important influence on our understanding of work motivation. Adler is not as well known as Freud, even among professionals; in fact, many of his ideas have become accepted today without having his name attached to them. Unlike Freud, who stressed the pleasure-seeking and life-sustaining motives, Adler placed a great deal of emphasis on the power motive. By "power" he meant the ability to require others to behave in ways that suited one's purposes. An infant actually has a great deal of power over others. As any parent can testify, a baby can cause a considerable commotion among all the adults within earshot with the merest yelp.

According to Adler, this ability to manipulate other people is inherently pleasurable. Not only does the child have a hard time unlearning it, but he may also spend a good deal of his adult life trying to recapture that blissful condition of having other people do as he wills. However, Adler did not consider the child to be merely a miniature dictator. He recognized, first of all, that power was not sought for its own sake so much as it was a refuge from the utter helplessness of childhood. Adults are the child's lifeline, and it is a life-and-death matter to the child that the adults in his world be reliable; therefore, the power motive acquires an urgency which it never quite loses even though it eventually becomes unnecessary. It is especially strong in an older child or in an adult who feels handicapped in some way in his ability to win the respect and attention of others. Such people may go to considerable lengths to command attention, thereby overcoming whatever real or imagined weakness it was that had disturbed them in the first place. In describing this process, Adler introduced two well-known terms to psychology: inferiority complex (underlying fears of inadequacy or handicap which need not necessarily have a basis in fact) and *compensation* (the tendency to exert extreme efforts to achieve the goals which the "inferiority" would ordinarily deny).

Second, Adler recognized that power was not the only way to solve the problem of helplessness. In time the growing child realizes that cooperativeness wins a more permanent

---

assurance of safety for him than power ever could, and at considerably less cost in terms of watchfulness and fear of retaliation. If the child's development proceeds normally and does not encounter too much tension, the power motive gradually transforms itself into a desire to perfect his relationships with others—that is, to make these relationships more confident, open, and helpful. Thus the mature adult would be able to move among others freely, without fear or suspicion. On the other hand, if the process were stunted somewhere along the line, perhaps by too many disappointing contacts with untrustworthy adults, the power motive would not only persist but would actually become stronger. The adult who had grown up in this way would be on guard, rarely willing to reveal very much of his plans or feelings and continually on the lookout for an advantage that would secure his position in what seemed a treacherous world.

\* \* \* \* \*

## THE COMPETENCE MOTIVE: ROBERT W. WHITE

\* \* \* \* \*

. . . White notes that the original Freudian theory, for all its complexity, is still a little too simple to account for all the facets of human behavior. Specifically, the individual is more than just a vehicle for a set of instincts; he is also an active observer and sharer of his environment. For White, one of the mainsprings of human motivation is an interest in getting to know what the world is like and in learning to get what one wants from it. Whereas Freud stressed the life-preserving and comfort-seeking instincts and Adler, going a step further, stressed the drive for power over others, White notes that people also want to understand and manipulate their physical environment (and, later on, their social environment too). In the broadest sense, they like to be able to make things happen—to create events rather than merely to await them passively.

White calls this desire for mastery "the competence motive." It can be seen even in very young infants, he believes, in the form of random fingering of objects, poking around, and feeling whatever is in reach. Later on it takes the form of exploring, tinkering, taking things apart, putting them together, and the like. As a result of years of learning his way around his own small world, learning what its possibilities are and how to exploit them, the young boy develops a certain assurance that he can handle himself equally well in the larger world he will enter as an adult. Whether his sense of competence is strong or weak depends on the balance of success and failures the boy has experienced in his pint-sized forays into the world around him. If successes have predominated, he will probably come to regard life as a fairly promising venture where a little common sense and persistence can take him a long way. On the other hand, if the failures have outweighed the successes, the boy may regard life as a hazardous game at best, one in which running risks is likely to lead to nothing but another fiasco, so that it makes more sense simply to wait for circumstances to come along and have their will with him than to try to influence them.

Because the individual can hardly avoid some kind of transactions with his environment every day, the ledger of successes and failures is altered constantly. Consequently, one's fate is never entirely sealed. There is always the possibility that a particularly fortunate set of experiences will come along to bolster a timid ego, or contrariwise an unfortunate set may knock the props out from under an overly confident one. While the emerging personality may be pretty well jelled in a number of important respects by age five, this is not true of the sense of competence: It can get off to a bad start and still develop strongly as the result of later successes.

But there is, alas, a limit to this. After a time the sense of competence is also likely to reach a sort of plateau from which it may vary somewhat but not (ordinarily) a great deal. This is because after a while the sense of competence begins to affect the likelihood of a given experience's turning into a success or a failure. The more venturesome spirits will be out trying to win things or change things, and by brushing aside obstacles and persisting toward their goals they tip the scales of chance in their favor. Meeker individuals will venture less and therefore gain less and will perhaps shrink a little too readily from obstacles. Thus the sense of competence gradually becomes a sort of self-fulfilling prophecy: The individual seldom achieves more than he expects because he does not try to achieve more than he thinks he can.

* * * * *

In adults the competence motive is very likely to express itself as a desire for job mastery and professional growth. It may therefore have a great deal to do with Herzberg's finding that the most lasting satisfactions of accountants and engineers are derived from solving difficult technical problems. The need for a suitable outlet for this motive, in a civilized society that has had most of the elemental challenges engineered out of it, may even underlie the growing tendency for people to identify themselves with their professions rather than with a particular employer or the region or group in which they were born and raised.

This job can be one of the few remaining arenas in which a man can match his skills against the environment in a contest that is neither absurdly easy nor prohibitively difficult. Where such a contest is possible, the competence motive may be exercised and considerable rewards may be enjoyed. But, where it is impossible, as in most routinized or oversuperv-ised jobs, a strong competence motive leads only to frustration, while a weak one merely encourages resignation and dependency.

Further, the sense of competence probably plays a key role in effecting job success, especially in those jobs where initiative or innovation is essential. A man who trusts his own ability to influence his environment will actually try to influence it more often and more boldly than someone who is inclined to let the environment influence him. Can it be, then, that the games and horseplay of seven- and eight-year-olds have something to do with events in the executive suite 30 years later? White's theory suggests that they may. . . .

* * * * *

## THE AFFILIATION MOTIVE: STANLEY SCHACHTER

Psychologists have been attacking the problem of human motivation from more than one angle. In addition to studying the ways in which assurance and daring evolve out of a basic sense of competence, they have turned their attention to the question of what makes some people such strikingly social creatures and why others seem to be able to spend most of their time quite happily by themselves. That most people like to be in other people's company is obvious enough, but it also seems to be true that this liking is stronger in some than in others and stronger under certain kinds of circumstances.

A promising beginning toward understanding this urge to be sociable has been made by Stanley Schachter of the University of Minnesota. . . .

* * * * *

The importance of affiliative needs is clear. . . . Yet the existence of an affiliation motive has been more or less taken for granted, so that when Schachter first began to direct serious scientific attention to it, he could find little in the way of previous research or even theorizing to guide him. It was generally assumed that affiliation could be either a means to an end or an end in itself. That is, people might seek the company of others in order to gain some kind of impersonal reward which the others meted out, such as money, favors, or protection. Or they might socialize simply because they enjoyed it. It was with this latter kind of affiliation that Schachter concerned himself: the desire to be with other people regardless of whether anything but company was apparently gained thereby.

Some previous research had touched on the question in a way. Psychologists had found that when something happens which contradicts a strongly held belief, the "believers" will tend to seek each other out with great urgency. They then go through an excited process of comparing notes, speculating about the event, and seeking explanations. Eventually some sort of consensus emerges from all this discussion, and most of the people will quickly associate themselves with it. Whether the new ideas fit the facts any better than the old ones did, or indeed whether they are very different from the old ones at all, does not seem to matter particularly. What *does* seem to matter is that one's beliefs are squared with everyone else's. There seems, in other words, to be a great deal of relief when one's thinking is shared by many others, almost as if this agreement confirmed the "rightness" and therefore the safety of one's own ideas.

\*      \*      \*      \*      \*

For Schachter, the most important element in the pattern was the reassuring effect of sharing an opinion. Apparently this kind of sharing provided a feeling that the world was understood and that therefore life was not really so dangerous after all. Evidently something more than just company was being provided by this particular form of affiliation. Socializing, in this instance, served to make life *seem* a little more manageable, a little less inexplicable, even though the shared ideas themselves might be utterly without foundation. (This probably helps to explain the unpopularity of most new ideas: They suddenly make the world seem unfamiliar!) If the pattern is not particularly rational, that does not make it any less human.

So one motive for affiliation can be the opportunity to have one's beliefs confirmed. But Schachter found himself wondering whether the discomfort of uncertainty was the only form of discomfort that would lead to affiliation or whether it was just a special case of a broader class of anxieties that would make people want to get together. To answer the question he devised an ingenious, though somewhat diabolical, series of experiments. The subjects in these experiments were those unsung heroes (heroines in this case) of most psychological research: the college sophomores who, in return for volunteering to be subjects for an experiment, are excused from a lab report.

Schachter's technique was to produce a mild state of fright by implying that his subjects would have to endure a certain amount of pain during the experiment. They endured nothing of the kind, of course; Schachter was deliberately trying to create a rather upset frame of mind. Once he had gotten his subjects sufficiently perturbed, Schachter told them that they would have to wait for further developments and gave them an opportunity to do so either alone or together. Most of them chose togetherness, despite the fact that they were strangers. At this point Schachter confessed his trick, apologized, and explained the experiment to his much-relieved subjects. He had proved his point: Misery definitely does love company.

\*      \*      \*      \*      \*

The informal work group is a way of adapting to a humiliating lack of competence in the face of a mechanized organization. The group provides some degree of reassurance: Everyone else is equally "beaten" by the system; therefore, it is less of a reflection on each individual to be beaten. Viewed in this light, the informal work group is not necessarily due to "natural" gregariousness; it may also be a defensive reaction and a symptom of deep distress.

\*      \*      \*      \*      \*

Affiliation, then, can be a simple expression of good fellowship or the symptom of a drastic loss of self-respect. (It can also be many other things: a voluntary stratagem for increasing the likelihood of obtaining certain advantages, for example.) . . .

CASE MATERIALS AND
SOCIAL SCIENCE READINGS FOR

# PART III Financial Control, Organization Structure, and Human Behavior

## ALLOCATION OF RESOURCES: AN IMPORTANT SOCIAL OBLIGATION OF MANAGERS

One of the fundamental lessons studied in economics courses is that the job of the manager is to *allocate resources.* This phrase has unfortunately degenerated in the minds of many people either (1) to the status of a meaningless, abstract cliché, or (2) to the image of a money-motivated manager driven by desires of an efficiency expert. It is even possible, as Thorsten Veblen suggested, that the manager is driven by profit and buttressed by Wall Street bankers who pressure him to forget the products he is producing and the function of those products in society.

That these things happen in poorly managed companies which do not include the public in their strategic planning, or which engage in sloppy internal financial planning, cannot be denied. However, they tend to cloud a more profound and important meaning of the verb, "to allocate resources." Namely, that in the long run those organizations are supported by society (either by legal charter or by day-to-day monetary support) which accomplish the twin goals of (1) production of a useful good or service, and (2) production of this good or service without unnecessary waste of resources. The latter is often called production with *efficiency.*

Efficiency is, therefore, a dictate of *society,* not simply a dictate of those who think like accountants, or those who are *thing*-oriented rather than *people*-oriented.

An example will help to make this concept more understandable. The Seaboard Chemical Corporation, one of the cases in Part III, is a producer of sulfuric acid. Among other fundamental forces in nature which cause this company to exist is the fact that people outside the organization want (or, as economists would say, *demand*) this product for use in drugs and medicines (Eli Lilly), in automobile tires (Goodyear), explosives (Du Pont), or hospital laboratories (Roosevelt Hospital). Fixed resources within Seaboard (such as plants and machines) must be allocated so that they produce the right quality demanded outside, the proper quantities demanded, and at the right time.

The social demand for efficiency is evident by the fact that Seaboard managers will be punished by society if they buy unnecessary equipment, hire people that sit around doing nothing, or spill and ruin raw materials stored in their inventories. There are two kinds of sanctions. First, the cost of Seaboard's product will eventually prove unacceptable to those who must pay higher prices. Second, if the rumor spreads that this is a wasteful institution, public opinion (or Ralph Nader) may urge government regulation.

Efficiency is not, then, a dirty word. It can be made dirty by poor management, but efficient allocation of resources is a pragmatic social obligation of managers. An expedient thing to do. Managers will eventually be punished if they do not discharge this obligation. For those who speak in terms of ethics, efficiency may well be a social responsibility in addition. Managers who take their ethical contribution to society seriously will in effect punish themselves if they fail to strive for efficient allocation of resources.

## FINANCIAL MANAGEMENT AS A TECHNIQUE FOR ALLOCATING RESOURCES

In the fields of accounting and finance, many techniques have been devised for trying to find "just the right amount" of various resources to assemble for the quantity of production demanded "out there." In theory, this represents an ideal. If it could actually be carried out in practice, the human beings in society would get what they want at the least possible cost and waste. Society as a whole would suffer the least possible waste of natural resources.

One of the most powerful technologies in finance for accomplishing this are the various methods for allocating fixed capital. In financial terms, this is "the investment decision." The methods all aim at telling a manager how to choose between alternatives. For example, Mr. North in Continental Electric Company has three possibilities for investing in projects that will improve the efficiency of the electric motors his division produces: purchase of a patent for a part of the motor, purchase of new machines for wiring motors, or paying his research department to develop new insulation materials. The student who puts himself or herself in North's place will learn something of "how to do it"—how to choose, based on various financial techniques.

Dover Beverage Company is faced with a different kind of resource allocation problem. It produces a popular soft drink (cola) for sale in a certain region of the United States. The Dover cola label has enjoyed success over the years as a regional brand. At the same time, Dover produces under license from National Cola the latter's own national branded cola for sale in Dover's region. The problem becomes (for Dover management) whether Dover's financial resources will yield more profit by continuing to sell both Dover and National Cola, or whether the license, which is about to expire, should be given up. Society's interest in this matter lies in the fact that Dover has limited resources, and if available labor and capital are allocated in a certain way, there will be more cola available to people in the region at less cost in consumption of labor and capital. Fortunately, financial specialists have worked out a method for investigating this kind of problem, for classifying costs to alternative lines which an organization might consider producing. This method, the "contribution method" is a tool for strategic planning—most valuable product for the least cost.

A host of other financial techniques are available to managers for allocating resources efficiently. Many who study this book and who have had training in finance and accounting will see opportunity for applying their specialty to the cases.

## FINANCIAL INFORMATION AND HUMAN PERCEPTION

When financial planning is done, considerable amounts of quantitative information are gathered, and this is summarized by certain methods. One of the important lessons managers might learn from the following cases is that these supposedly objective "facts" really do not give "impartial" answers to the problem of how to allocate resources. Human beings have a way of *interpreting* data differently. They see the cash flows through their own rose-colored (or dark gray) glasses.

For example, in the Continental Electric Company, the Electric Motor Division will meet its sales target of $12,300,000. One person views this as entirely proper, another views it as not high enough. In Dover Beverage Company, Leonard Stallings and Fred Stallings have a very different viewpoint as to whether the company should offer National Cola to the public as part of its product line. Part of the conflict between these two managers is caused by the fact that they have each selected different information on which to base their decisions. For Leonard, one set of information is *relevant,* while another set is relevant for Fred. By studying these cases, one should learn once and for all that human needs, self-interests, and organizational positions all cause various people to judge financial data differently. As a former dean of the Yale Law School once said, "the law is often determined by what the judge had for breakfast."

## USE OF MANAGEMENT INFORMATION SYSTEMS

In all of the cases in Part III, the management is trying to design an information system which will help decision makers to use scarce resources in an efficient way. Seaboard Chemical management wants to ensure that physical equipment is audited in a way that prevents waste, and furnishes data for company planning of the company's cash flow. Continental Electric management wants the right information to choose what kinds of projects will, if included in the capital budget, yield the highest returns. Dover's management needs relevant information to choose what product lines to sell. Texas-Northern Pipeline Company needs to prevent waste of oil, and minimize cost of maintenance of the line. This requires certain information to be furnished by the control system.

In using management information systems, the managements of most organizations need to solve two kinds of problems: (1) they need to design a system of information flows that balances efficiency with human motivations, and (2) they need to work out some human process for operating the system so that different people will at least support the system and make it work.

Readings attached to these cases provide knowledge of each of these aspects of an information system. Techniques such as discounted cash flows, and contribution costs, help in designing the efficiency aspect of control systems. Motivations of people involved in control systems include the need for autonomy (rather than overly restrictive controls), the possibility that controls might actually promote an individual's sense of achievement, and the fact that self-interests of parties may cause different perceptions of financial data.

Finally, those who study these cases will see possibilities for solving human problems with control systems by use of management by objectives, by participative management styles, and by constructive (rather than destructive) use of conflict.

# 6. SEABOARD CHEMICAL CORPORATION

---

# Case Introduction

---

## SYNOPSIS

Auditors from the Cleveland headquarters of Seaboard Chemical Corporation visit the Los Angeles Plant, where they judge certain items in the equipment inventory to be ruined. On return to Cleveland, they advise the controller of their judgment, who in turn requests the plant manager to write off the equipment's value ($45,000) from the asset accounts, which make up the company's balance sheet. There is disagreement between various people at the plant and at headquarters as to whether the equipment is, in fact, ruined. Actions of the parties involved are described as they relate to other individuals, and to the company organization structure.

## WHY THIS CASE IS INCLUDED

The Seaboard situation shows how the necessity for central planning (by experts) and the necessity for uniformity often conflict with the necessity for decision-making freedom at lower operating levels. The executive is faced with theories which prescribe different solutions to this problem; the "technology school" of management gives one answer, the "political school" gives another, and the "psychology school" gives a third.

In this case, a conflict appears between staff executives and line executives, and between parts of the organization structure (position descriptions of the executives involved). The various theories mentioned above all have some truth in them, and one must judge which ones apply to the specific situation.

## DIAGNOSTIC AND PREDICTIVE QUESTIONS

The readings included with this case are marked (*). The author index at the end of this book locates the other readings.

1. From the standpoint of finance (management of cash flow), why is Mr. Turner interested in having the book figures at headquarters be an accurate "symbol" or "picture" of the assets which actually exist in the real world? Or, assuming that the physical equipment will actually be needed in the following accounting period, and assuming that company headquarters must provide funds, why is he interested in such accuracy?

> Read:   * Anthony, *Management Accounting,* (Remember that the equipment is part of the capital equipment inventory.)

2. From the standpoint of the company's legal position with stockholders, and the fiduciary function of controllership, why was Turner's job description written the way it was?

> Read:   From standard texts on accounting, or auditing, study the concept of fiduciary relationship. Or, study the job description and draw your own conclusions from case facts.

3. From the viewpoint of perception theory, and certain sociological processes, why is there disagreement between the plant personnel and the headquarters personnel in Seaboard Corporation? Why might each party rely on his own job description?

> Read:   * Merton, "Bureaucratic Structure and Personality."

4. The problem of assets might be solved partially if each plant had its own corrosion engineer to appraise assets, rather than having one corrosion engineer at headquarters who works in all three plants. Why would such an organization structure not be feasible in the Seaboard Chemical Company?

> Read:   Summer, "Economies of Scale and Organization Structure."

5. From the viewpoint of that management theory which stresses technological excellence, who do you predict is most capable to make the final decision in the matter of asset condition?

> Read:   * Taylor, "Shop Management." * Veblen, *The Engineers and the Price System.* * Smith, *The Wealth of Nations.*

6. From the viewpoint of that management theory which stresses political science and "law and order," who do you predict is the most competent person (or position) to make the final decision on asset conditions?

> Read:   * Fayol, *General and Industrial Management.* * O'Donnell, "The Source of Managerial Authority." * Locke, *Concerning Civil Government.*

7. From the viewpoint of that management theory which stresses initiative, freedom, and autonomy of individual people, who in the whole hierarchy (from president to storehouse supervisor) is most qualified to make the decision on asset conditions?

> Read:   Curtice, "General Motors Organization Philosophy and Structure."

## POLICY QUESTIONS

8. Do you think any one person in the organization should decide on the condition of the equipment in the storage yard? If so, whom? If so, explain why the person you designate would have the most valid, or true, decision.

9. What specific changes would you recommend for the job descriptions of the controller and the plant manager? For any other job descriptions in the Seaboard organization?

10. Suppose answer to Question 8 is "no." What other means are available for getting a decision made which is valid or accurate?

Read:  Follett, "Constructive Conflict." Eells and Walton, *Conceptual Foundations of Business.* McGregor, *The Human Side of Enterprise.* Schein, *Process Consultation: Its Role in Organization Development.*

---

# Case Text*

---

Seaboard Chemical Corporation is a producer of sulfuric acid, employing a total of 1,640 people, with headquarters in Cleveland, Ohio. Plants are operated at Cleveland; Marcus Hook, Pennsylvania; and Los Angeles. The company is one of the older firms that produce this basic chemical.

The case concerns a problem that has arisen in the work performed at the Los Angeles plant and the work performed by the controller's department in Cleveland. Excerpts from job descriptions of the plant

**EXHIBIT 1***
**Position Description of Plant Manager, Los Angeles**

1. The plant manager shall be responsible for operating the plant profitably.
6. The plant manager shall attempt at all times to keep costs to a reasonable minimum, and to prevent waste of monetary and physical resources.
8. The plant manager's responsibility covers all operations within the plant, including direct production lines, maintenance work, and construction operations.
10. The plant manager shall have such authority over all personnel in the plant as is necessary to carry out the other responsibilities enumerated herein.

* Taken from page 16, *Organization Manual,* excerpt of certain numbered items.

---

* Copyright, 1977, Charles E. Summer.

**EXHIBIT 2***
**Position Description of Controller, Headquarters Staff**

1. The controller shall have the responsibility of conserving all assets of the company, and of protecting them from misappropriation, abuse or other conditions prejudicial to the interests of the owning stockholders.
5. The controller shall personally, or through his appointed representatives, make a periodic audit to determine the condition of company land, buildings, plants, warehouses and other fixed and current assets, and their accurate valuation.
8. The controller shall gather totals of all company assets from various locations, and all company liabilities from various locations, and consolidate these into the companywide balance sheet at the end of the year.

* Taken from page 8, *Organization Manual,* excerpt of certain numbered items.

manager and the controller appear in Exhibits 1 and 2. The general duties of other people in the plant and in the controller's department are mentioned later in the case. A simplified organization chart of the company appears in Exhibit 3.

It is the practice of Seaboard to do most of the construction of acid-processing units at each of its plants, rather than to farm out the construction of such machinery to outside construction firms. At each plant, a construction department, headed by a process (chemical) engineer, designs and constructs the various mixing vessels, pipelines, agitators, and other equipment through which raw materials are converted to finished acid. Because the materials are so corrosive, some units of machinery must be replaced as often as once a year, and many others must be replaced after a useful life of one to five years. Replacement of depreciated equipment is continuous, and construction work is treated as routine, rather than as major addition to the plant.

In order to carry out the actual building and construction of processing units, each plant has a construction department, headed by a foreman. The specifications for this position state that the man who holds the job must be a graduate process (chemical) engineer, with at least five years' experience in actual construction operations. The incumbent at Los Angeles is Bill Haley. M. M. Stevens, the plant manager at Los Angeles, says that, "Haley is unusually competent in his job, having been with us for eight years. He hasn't practiced design engineering since graduation, but he knows a lot about the practical side of construction."

Haley schedules the work, and watches the progress, of 23 construction laborers. He is also responsible for the storage of materials used in construction, though this activity has been delegated to J. K. Lemon, supervisor of the storehouse department. This department operates a warehouse for storing the hundreds of parts used regularly in the construction of units. These range from pumps worth $1,200, down to nuts and bolts worth a few cents, up to large heat exchangers that may cost $20,000 or more. In addition to warehouse space, there is a storage yard

**EXHIBIT 3**
**Partial Organization Chart of Seaboard Chemical Corporation**

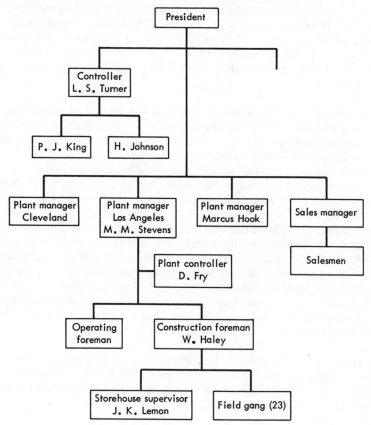

adjoining the warehouse, surrounded by a steel security fence, where large equipment is maintained in open storage.

Last August, P. J. King, a CPA and financial auditor in the controller's department in Cleveland, accompanied by Harry Johnson, an engineer-auditor employed in the same department, made their yearly visit to Los Angeles for the purpose of verifying the capital equipment on hand. This procedure had been set up so that the company controller, L. S. Turner, could have an accurate consolidated picture of the company's asset accounts to put on the balance sheet at the end of the year. King and Johnson spot-check the physical equipment in the plant, compare the equipment they inspect with the accounts kept in the plant controller's office, and either verify that the dollar amount in the account represents certain physical equipment, or advise plant personnel when they are unable to locate the specific physical equipment (asset) in the warehouse that should match a monetary asset carried on the books by the controller.

In performing this spot-check and comparison, King and Johnson found in the storage yard certain items that they inspected with close scrutiny and later decided were damaged to the point where they should be physically salvaged (sold for junk or secondhand equipment) and subtracted from the assets on the books of the plant. These items, supposedly new, cost a total of $45,000. Johnson, a specialist in metals, corrosion, and condition of equipment, drafted the following memorandum to Mr. Fry, the plant controller. The memo was signed by King as well as by Johnson.

> Our visit to Los Angeles this year has been a pleasant one, and we particularly want to thank you for the cooperation shown us by yourself and the men in your department. The only account which we believe should be adjusted is the storehouse materials account, in the amount of $45,000, and supported by the attached list. Messrs. Lemon and Haley have discussed this with us and state that the equipment is certainly in questionable condition, but that they may be able to use it in some way next year. We have, in turn, explained to them that it is in the interest of the company as a whole to have an accurate balance sheet. Only in this way can the President have the accurate information with which to run the company, and do his own planning. Since the equipment is in fact ruined, the Cleveland headquarters must provide for its replacement in next year's budget, but we cannot do this unless the accounts show the need for it. With this information, Mr. Haley said that he will go along with the decision to salvage.

After returning to Cleveland, Johnson gave a copy of this memorandum to Mr. Turner, company controller, and explained the problem of the ruined equipment. Mr. Turner then sent a routine memorandum to Mr. Fry, the last paragraph of which read:

> Would you therefore be kind enough to adjust the storehouse account downward in the amount of $45,000, so that when, in December, you send the totals in each account to Cleveland, the Controller here will have accurate figures to combine with assets of other plants for entry on the year-end balance sheet.

Fry studied the memorandum and brought up the problem with M. M. Stevens, the plant manager, at a regular Monday morning conference Stevens had set up so that he could keep abreast of financial and cost matters at the plant. Stevens had been a foreman of the blending operation for 12 years before becoming plant manager, and for the remainder of his 30 years with the company had risen from a mixer's helper up through the production operations to foreman. He had not worked in the construction department. He says, however, that, "I have watched an awful lot of construction in this plant the last 30 years, and I have a good general knowledge of the whole operation."

Stevens visited the maintenance yard along with Haley, and both men agreed that the equipment listed in the Cleveland memo was "in not too good condition." They also agreed that, "We may be able to use it next year, but we'll have to wait until then to know what shape it is in." Stevens then told Fry that an additional reason for not writing off the equipment is that, "This $45,000 will be looked at as a deduction from the profitability of this plant, and we shouldn't be blamed for it until we know definitely whether it is usable." On instruction from Stevens, Fry, on November 6th, sent the following note to Turner:

> Mr. Stevens has asked me to not write off the $45,000 worth of equipment specified in your September 14 memorandum. Therefore, the asset accounts which are listed in the attached report for balance sheet purposes reflect the fact that we are still carrying this equipment on our books.

At the writing of this case, on December 15, this is where the matter stands. In effect, the company controller, Turner, has taken the information supplied by his staff men, Johnson and King, and has requested Fry, the plant controller, to write down the equipment. Fry, on the other hand, has taken the information given him by Stevens, and the information given him by Johnson and King, and written to Turner the above memo.

# Selected Readings

*From*

## MANAGEMENT ACCOUNTING\*

*By Robert N. Anthony*

. . . As goods are purchased or manufactured, inventory is increased; as they are sold, inventory is decreased, accounts receivables are increased, and income is earned; as the receivables are collected, cash is increased; and the cycle is completed with the use of cash to pay off the payables created when purchases are made or costs incurred. Because this cycle occurs over and over again in the course of normal operations, current assets and current liabilities are often referred to collectively as *circulating capital.*

Part of the funds tied up in current assets is supplied by vendors (accounts payable) and other short-term creditors. The remainder, which is the difference between current assets and current liabilities, and which is called working capital, must come from other, more permanent sources. These other sources must also supply the funds that are tied up in the noncurrent assets. Funds supplied for these purposes are called *permanent capital.* Changes in the sources of permanent capital and the uses to which it is put are likely to be of more than ordinary interest both to management and to outsiders since they reflect

---

\* Reprinted by permission of Richard D. Irwin, Inc., Homewood, Ill., 1960 (pp. 290–92, 306).

the results of the important financial decisions that have significant long-run consequences. In order to focus on these changes, we shall not bother with the recurring movement of funds among the separate current asset and current liability accounts. The necessity for tracing these separate flows can be avoided by combining all these accounts into the single item, working capital.

## Basic Relationships

A balance sheet shows the net effect of funds transactions from the beginning of the business to the balance sheet date. The equities side shows the sources from which funds have been obtained, and the assets side shows the way in which these funds have been used. The balance sheet in Illustration 1 shows that as of the end of 1957, long-term creditors have furnished $145,000 of capital, and stockholders have furnished $394,000. Of the latter, $211,000 represents their original contribution and $183,000 represents earnings that they have permitted the company to retain in the business. The total amount of funds provided is therefore $539,000, of which $125,000 is used for working capital and $414,000 is in fixed assets.

## ILLUSTRATION 1
### Condensed Balance Sheet December 31, 1957

| Assets | | Equities | |
|---|---|---|---|
| Working capital | $125,000 | Long-term debt | $145,000 |
| | | Capital stock | 211,000 |
| | | Retained earnings | 183,000 |
| Fixed assets | 414,000 | | |
| Total Assets | $539,000 | Total Equities | $539,000 |

If all earnings were paid out in dividends and if replacements of fixed assets exactly equaled the annual depreciation charge, the amounts shown on Illustration 1 could remain unchanged indefinitely. Despite the fact that there would be numerous changes in the several current asset and current liability accounts, these could offset one another so that the total working capital could remain constant. Under these circumstances, the business would not need additional financing. But of course the balance sheet items do change; additional funds are provided, and these are put to use.

Consider the possible ways in which the company could obtain additional funds. For example, if it wished to buy a new plant: it could borrow, thus increasing long-term debt; it could sell more stock, thus increasing the Capital Stock account; it could wait until operations had generated funds, which would show up as an increase in Retained Earnings; it could use available cash, thus decreasing working capital; or it could sell some of its existing fixed assets, thus decreasing Fixed Assets. It follows, therefore, that *sources of funds are indicated by increases in equities and decreases in assets.*

Looking at the other side of the coin, what uses could the company make of additional funds that it acquired? It could add new fixed assets, it could add to working capital, it could pay off existing debt, or it could pay dividends to the stockholders, which decreases Retained Earnings. From these possibilities, it follows that *uses of funds are indicated by increases in assets and decreases in equities.*

In accordance with the dual-aspect principle, total sources of funds must equal total uses of funds. The following relationships therefore exist:

1. Sources = Uses
2. Increases in equities + decreases in assets =
   Increases in assets + decreases in equities

These same relationships can be explained in terms of debit and credit. Increases in equities and decreases in assets are both credits; increases in assets and decreases in equities are both debits. Thus, the above equation follows from the fact that changes in debits must equal changes in credits.

\*     \*     \*     \*     \*

## Diagrammatic Representation of Cash Flow

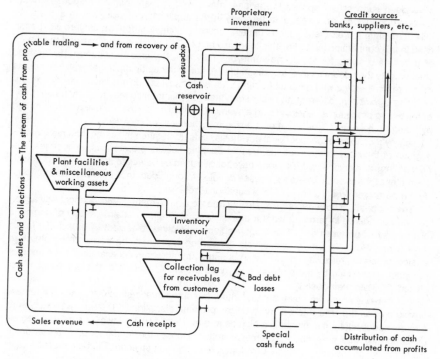

*From*

# BUREAUCRATIC STRUCTURE AND PERSONALITY*

*By Robert K. Merton*

. . . The chief merit of bureaucracy is its technical efficiency, with a premium placed on precision, speed, expert control, continuity, discretion, and optimal returns on input. The structure is one which approaches the complete elimination of personalized relationships and nonrational considerations (hostility, anxiety, affectual involvements, etc.). . . .

\*     \*     \*     \*     \*

**The Dysfunctions of Bureaucracy.**  In these bold outlines, the positive attainments and functions of bureaucratic organization are emphasized and the internal stresses and strains

* Reprinted by permission of *Social Forces*, vol. XVII (1940), pp. 560–68, by permission of the author and the publisher. (Copyright, 1940, by the University of North Carolina Press.)

of such structures are almost wholly neglected. The community at large, however, evidently emphasizes the imperfections of bureaucracy, as is suggested by the fact that the "horrid hybrid," bureaucrat, has become an epithet, a *Schimpfwort*. The transition to a study of the negative aspects of bureaucracy is afforded by the applications of Veblen's concept of "trained incapacity," Dewey's notion of "occupational psychosis" or Warnotte's view of "professional deformation." Trained incapacity refers to that state of affairs in which one's abilities function as inadequacies or blind spots. Actions based upon training and skills which have been successfully applied in the past may result in inappropriate responses *under changed conditions*. An inadequate flexibility in the application of skills will, in a changing milieu, result in more or less serious maladjustments. Thus, to adopt a barnyard illustration used in this connection by Burke, chickens may be readily conditioned to interpret the sound of a bell as a signal for food. The same bell may now be used to summon the "trained chickens" to their doom as they are assembled to suffer decapitation. In general, one adopts measures in keeping with his past training and, under new conditions which are not recognized as *significantly* different, the very soundness of this training may lead to the adoption of the wrong procedures. Again, in Burke's almost echolalic phrase, "people may be unfitted by being fit in an unfit fitness"; their training may become an incapacity.

Dewey's concept of occupational psychosis rests upon much the same observations. As a result of their day-to-day routines, people develop special preferences, antipathies, discriminations and emphases. (The term psychosis is used by Dewey to denote a "pronounced character of the mind.") These psychoses develop through demands put upon the individual by the particular organization of his occupational role.

The concepts of both Veblen and Dewey refer to a fundamental ambivalence. Any action can be considered in terms of what it attains or what it fails to attain. "A way of seeing is also a way of not seeing—a focus upon object A involves a neglect of object B." In his discussion, Weber is almost exclusively concerned with what the bureaucratic structure attains: precision, reliability, efficiency. This same structure may be examined from another perspective provided by the ambivalence. What are the limitations of the organization designed to attain their goals?

For reasons which we have already noted, the bureaucratic structure exerts a constant pressure upon the official to be "methodical, prudent, disciplined." If the bureaucracy is to operate successfully, it must attain a high degree of reliability of behavior, an unusual degree of conformity with prescribed patterns of action. Hence, the fundamental importance of discipline which may be as highly developed in a religious or economic bureaucracy as in the army. Discipline can be effective only if the ideal patterns are buttressed by strong sentiments which entail devotion to one's duties, a keen sense of the limitation of one's authority and competence, and methodical performance of routine activities. The efficacy of social structure depends ultimately upon infusing group participants with appropriate attitudes and sentiments. . . .

. . . There is a margin of safety, so to speak, in the pressure exerted by these sentiments upon the bureaucrat to conform to his patterned obligations, in much the same sense that added allowances (precautionary overestimations) are made by the engineer in designing the supports for a bridge. But this very emphasis leads to a transference of the sentiments from the *aims* of the organization onto the particular details of behavior required by the rules. Adherence to the rules, originally conceived as a means, becomes transformed into an end-in-itself; there occurs the familiar process of *displacement of goals* whereby "an instrumental value becomes a terminal value." Discipline, readily interpreted as conformance with regulations, whatever the situation, is seen not as a measure designed for specific purposes but becomes an immediate value in the life-organization of the bureaucrat. This emphasis, resulting from the displacement of the original goals, develops into rigidities and an inability to adjust readily. Formalism, even ritualism, ensues with an unchallenged insistence upon punctilious adherence to formalized procedures. This may be exaggerated to the point where primary concern with conformity to the rules interferes with the achievement of the purposes of the organization, in which case we have the familiar phenomenon of the technicism or red tape of the official. . . .

**Structural Sources of Overconformity.** Such inadequacies in orientation which involve trained incapacity clearly derive from structural sources. The process may be briefly recapitulated. (1) An effective bureaucracy demands reliability of response and strict devotion to regulations. (2) Such devotion to the rules leads to their transformation into absolutes; they are no longer conceived as relative to a given set of purposes. (3) This interferes with ready adaption under special conditions not clearly envisaged by those who drew up the general rules. (4) Thus, the very elements which conduce toward efficiency in general produce inefficiency in specific instances. Full realization of the inadequacy is seldom attained by members of the group who have not divorced themselves from the "meanings" which the rules have for them. These rules in time become symbolic in cast, rather than strictly utilitarian.

Thus far, we have treated the ingrained sentiments making for rigorous discipline simply as data, as given. However, definite features of the bureaucratic structure may be seen to conduce to these sentiments. The bureaucrat's official life is planned for him in terms of a graded career, through the organizational devices of promotion by seniority, pensions, incremental salaries, *etc.,* all of which are designed to provide incentives for disciplined action and conformity to the official regulations. The official is tacitly expected to and largely does adapt his thoughts, feelings, and actions to the prospect of this career. But *these very devices* which increase the probability of conformance also lead to an over-concern with strict adherence to regulations which induces timidity, conservatism, and technicism. Displacement of sentiments from goals onto means is fostered by the tremendous symbolic significance of the means (rules).

Another feature of the bureaucratic structure tends to produce much the same result. Functionaries have the sense of a common destiny for all those who work together. They share the same interests, especially since there is relatively little competition insofar as promotion is in terms of seniority. Ingroup aggression is thus minimized and this arrangement is therefore conceived to be positively functional for the bureaucracy. However, the esprit de corps and informal social organization which typically develops in such situations often leads the personnel to defend their entrenched interests rather than to assist their clientele and elected higher officials. . . .

It would be much too facile and partly erroneous to attribute such resistance by bureaucrats simply to vested interests. Vested interests oppose any new order which either eliminates or at least makes uncertain their differential advantage deriving from the current arrangements. This is undoubtedly involved in part in bureaucratic resistance to change but another process is perhaps more significant. As we have seen, bureaucratic officials affectively identify themselves with their way of life. They have a pride of craft which leads them to resist change in established routines; at least, those changes which are felt to be imposed by coworkers. This nonlogical pride of craft is a familiar pattern found even, to judge from Sutherland's *Professional Thief,* among pickpockets who, despite the risk, delight in mastering the prestige-bearing feat of "beating a left breech" (picking the left front trousers pocket).

. . . [T]here may ensue, in particular vocations and in particular types of organization, the *process of sanctification* (viewed as the counterpart of the process of secularization). This is to say that through sentiment-formation, emotional dependence upon bureaucratic symbols and status, and affective involvement in spheres of competence and authority, there develop prerogatives involving attitudes of moral legitimacy which are established as values in their own right, and are no longer viewed as merely technical means for expediting administration. One may note a tendency for certain bureaucratic norms, originally introduced for technical reasons, to become rigidified and sacred, although, as Durkheim would say, they are *laïque en apparence.* . . .

**Primary versus Secondary Relations.** Another feature of the bureaucratic structure, the stress on depersonalization of relationships, also plays its part in the bureaucrat's trained incapacity. The personality pattern of the bureaucrat is nucleated about this norm of impersonality. Both this and the categorizing tendency, which develops from the dominant role of general, abstract rules, tend to produce conflict in the bureaucrat's contacts with the public or clientele. Since functionaries minimize personal relations and resort to categorization, the peculiarities of individual cases are often ignored. But the client who, quite understandably, is convinced of the "special features" of *his* own problem often objects to such categorical treatment. Stereotyped behavior is not adapted to the exigencies of individual problems. The impersonal treatment of affairs which are at times of great personal significance to the client gives rise to the charge of "arrogance" and "haughtiness" of the bureaucrat. . . .

Still another source of conflict with the public derives from the bureaucratic structure. The bureaucrat, in part irrespective of his position with*in* the hierarchy, acts as a representative of the power and prestige of the entire structure. In his official role he is vested with definite authority. This often leads to an actually or apparently domineering attitude, which may only be exaggerated by a discrepancy between his position within the hierarchy and his position with reference to the public. Protest and recourse to other officials on the part of the client are often ineffective or largely precluded by the previously mentioned esprit de corps which joins the officials into a more or less solidary ingroup. This source of conflict *may* be minimized in private enterprise since the client can register an effective protest by transferring his trade to another organization within the competitive system. But with the monopolistic nature of the public organization, no such alternative is possible. . . .

*From*

# SHOP MANAGEMENT*

*By Frederick Winslow Taylor* †

. . . One of the most difficult works to organize is that of a large engineering establishment building miscellaneous machinery, and the writer has therefore chosen this for description.

Practically all of the shops of this class are organized upon what may be called the military plan. The orders from the general are transmitted through the colonels, majors, captains, lieutenants and noncommissioned officers to the men. In the same way the orders in industrial establishments go from the manager through superintendents, foremen of shops, assistant foremen and gang bosses to the men. In an establishment of this kind the duties of the foremen, gang bosses, etc., are so varied, and call for an amount of special information coupled with such a variety of natural ability, that only men of unusual qualities to start with, and who have had years of special training, can perform them in a satisfactory manner. . . .

\*    \*    \*    \*    \*

In the writer's experience, almost all shops are under-officered. Invariably the number of leading men employed is not sufficient to do the work economically. Under the military type of organization, the foreman is held responsible for the successful running of the entire shop, and when we measure his duties by the standard of the four leading principles of management referred to above, it becomes apparent that in his case these conditions are as far as possible from being fulfilled. His duties may be briefly enumerated in the following way. He must lay out the work for the whole shop, see that each piece of work goes in the proper order to the right machine, and that the man at the machine knows just what is to be done and how he is to do it. He must see that the work is not slighted, and that it is done fast, and all the while he must look ahead a month or so, either to provide more men to do the work or more work for the men to do. He must constantly discipline the men and readjust

---

* From *Scientific Management* by Frederick Winslow Taylor. Copyright © 1947. Reprinted by permission of Harper & Row, Publishers, Inc. (Excerpts from pp. 92–96, 98–100.)

† The author was an engineer at Bethlehem Steel and became consultant for many leading industries in the first two decades of this century.

their wages, and in addition to this must fix piece work prices and supervise the time-keeping.

The first of the four leading principles in management calls for a clearly defined and circumscribed task. Evidently the foreman's duties are in no way clearly circumscribed. It is left each day entirely to his judgment what small part of the mass of duties before him it is most important for him to attend to, and he staggers along under this fraction of the work for which he is responsible, leaving the balance to be done in many cases as the gang bosses and workmen see fit. The second principle calls for such conditions that the daily task can always be accomplished. The conditions in his case are always such that it is impossible for him to do it all, and he never even makes a pretence of fulfilling his entire task. The third and fourth principles call for high pay in case the task is successfully done, and low pay in case of failure. The failure to realize the first two conditions, however, renders the application of the last two out of the question.

The foreman usually endeavors to lighten his burdens by delegating his duties to the various assistant foremen or gang bosses in charge of lathes, planers, milling machines, vise work, etc. Each of these men is then called upon to perform duties of almost as great variety as those of the foreman himself. The difficulty in obtaining in one man the variety of special information and the different mental and moral qualities necessary to perform all of the duties demanded of those men has been clearly summarized in the following list of the nine qualities which go to make up a well-rounded man:

1. Brains.
2. Education.
3. Special or technical knowledge; manual dexterity or strength.
4. Tact.
5. Energy.
6. Grit.
7. Honesty.
8. Judgment or common sense.
9. Good health.

Plenty of men who possess only three of the above qualities can be hired at any time for laborers' wages. Add four of these qualities together and you get a higher priced man. The man combining five of these qualities begins to be hard to find, and those with six, seven, and eight are almost impossible to get. . . .

\*      \*      \*      \*      \*

It is evident, then, that the duties which the ordinary gang boss is called upon to perform would demand of him a large proportion of the nine attributes mentioned above; and if such a man could be found he should be made manager or superintendent of a works instead of gang boss. However, bearing in mind the fact that plenty of men can be had who combine four or five of these attributes, it becomes evident that the work of management should be so subdivided that the various positions can be filled by men of this caliber, and a great part of the art of management undoubtedly lies in planning the work in this way. This can, in the judgment of the writer, be best accomplished by *abandoning the military type of organization* and introducing two broad and sweeping changes in the art of management:

(*a*) As far as possible the workmen, as well as the gang bosses and foremen, should be entirely relieved of the work of planning, and of all work which is more or less clerical in its nature. All possible brain work should be removed from the shop and centered in the planning or laying-out department, leaving for the foremen and gang bosses work strictly executive in its nature. Their duties should be to see that the operations planned and directed from the planning room are promptly carried out in the shop. Their time should be spent with the men, teaching them to think ahead, and leading and instructing them in their work.

(*b*) Throughout the whole field of management the military type of organization should be abandoned, and what may be called the "functional type" substituted in its place. "Functional management" consists in so dividing the work of management that each man from the assistant superintendent down shall have as few functions as possible to perform. If practicable the work of each man in the management should be confined to the performance of a single leading function.

Under the ordinary or military type the workmen are divided into groups. The men in each group receive their orders from one man only, the foreman or gang boss of that group. This man is the single agent through which the various functions of the management are brought into contact with the men. Certainly the most marked outward characteristic of functional management lies in the fact that each workman, instead of coming in direct contact with the management at one point only, namely, through his gang boss, receives his daily orders and help directly from eight different bosses, each of whom performs his own particular function. Four of these bosses are in the planning room and of these three send their orders to and receive their returns from the men, usually in writing. Four others are in the shop and personally help the men in their work, each boss helping in his own particular line or function only. Some of these bosses come in contact with each man only once or twice a day and then for a few minutes perhaps, while others are with the men all the time, and help each man frequently. The functions of one or two of these bosses require them to come in contact with each workman for so short a time each day that they can perform their particular duties perhaps for all of the men in the shop, and in their line they manage the entire shop. Other bosses are called upon to help their men so much and so often that each boss can perform his function for but a few men, and in this particular line a number of bosses are required, all performing the same function but each having his particular group of men to help. Thus the grouping of the men in the shop is entirely changed, each workman belonging to eight different groups according to the particular functional boss whom he happens to be working under at the moment.

The following is a brief description of the duties of the four types of executive functional bosses which the writer has found it profitable to use in the active work of the shop: (1) gang bosses, (2) speed bosses, (3) inspectors, and (4) repair bosses. . . .


*From*

# THE ENGINEERS AND THE PRICE SYSTEM*

*By Thorstein Veblen*


. . . [T]he country's industrial system . . . is a comprehensive and balanced scheme of technological administration. Industry of this modern sort—mechanical, specialised, standardised, running to quantity production, drawn on a large scale—is highly productive; provided always that the necessary conditions of productive industry are of a well-defined technical character, and they are growing more and more exacting with every farther advance in the industrial arts. . . . [T]he mechanical technology is impersonal and dispassionate, and its end is very simply to serve human needs, without fear or favor or respect of persons, prerogatives, or politics. It makes up an industrial system of an unexampled character—a mechanically balanced and interlocking system of work to be done, the prime requisite of whose working is a painstaking and intelligent co-ordination of the processes at work, and an equally painstaking allocation of mechanical power and materials. The foundation and driving force of it all is a massive body of technological knowledge, of a highly impersonal and altogether unbusinesslike nature, running in close contact with the material sciences,

---

*Reprinted from Thorstein Veblen, *The Engineers and the Price System* (New York: The Viking Press, 1921), Chapter 5.

on which it draws freely at every turn—exactly specialised, endlessly detailed, reaching out into all domains of empirical fact.

Such is the system of productive work which has grown out of the Industrial Revolution, and on the full and free run of which the material welfare of all of the civilised peoples now depends from day to day. Any defect or hindrance in its technical administration, any intrusion or nontechnical considerations, any failure or obstruction at any point, unavoidably results in a disproportionate set-back to the balanced whole and brings a disproportionate burden of privation on all these peoples whose productive industry has come within the sweep of the system.

It follows that those gifted, trained, and experienced technicians who now are in posses-sion of the requisite technological information and experience are the first and instantly indispensable factor in the everyday work of carrying on the country's productive industry. They now constitute the General Staff of the industrial system, in fact; whatever law and custom may formally say in protest. The "captains of industry" may still vaingloriously claim that distinction, and law and custom still countenance their claim; but the captains have no technological value, in fact.

*From*

# THE WEALTH OF NATIONS*

*By Adam Smith†*

## OF THE DIVISION OF LABOUR

The greatest improvement in the productive powers of labour, and the greater part of the skill, dexterity, and judgment with which it is anywhere directed, or applied, seem to have been the effects of the division of labour.

The effects of the division of labour, in the general business of society, will be more easily understood, by considering in what manner it operates in some particular manufactures. It is commonly supposed to be carried furthest in some very trifling ones; not perhaps that it really is carried further in them than in others of more importance: but in those trifling manufactures which are destined to supply the small wants of but a small number of people, the whole number of workmen must necessarily be small; and those employed in every different branch of the work can often be collected into the same workhouse, and placed at once under the view of the spectator. In those great manufactures, on the contrary, which are destined to supply the great wants of the great body of the people, every different branch of the work employs so great a number of workmen, that it is impossible to collect them all into the same workhouse. We can seldom see more, at one time, than those employed in one single branch. Though in such manufactures, therefore, the work may really be divided into a much greater number of parts, than in those of a more trifling nature, the division is not near so obvious, and has accordingly been much less observed.

To take an example, therefore, from a very trifling manufacture; but one.in which the division of labour has been very often taken notice of, the trade of the pinmaker; a workman not educated to this business (which the division of labour has rendered a distinct trade), nor acquainted with the use of the machinery employed in it (to the invention of which the same division of labour has probably given occasion), could scarce, perhaps, with his utmost industry, make one pin in a day, and certainly could not make twenty. But in the way in which

---

* Published by Random House, Inc., in the Modern Library Series, 1937 (pp. 4–15). This citation is taken from the 1789 edition of the book.

† Adam Smith, 1723–90, Professor of Moral Philosophy at the University of Glasgow, is considered the founder of the Science of Economics.

this business is now carried on, not only the whole work is a peculiar trade, but it is divided into a number of branches, of which the greater part are likewise peculiar trades. One man draws out the wire, another straights it, third cuts it, a fourth points it, a fifth grinds it at the top for receiving the head; to make the head requires two or three distinct operations; to put it on is a peculiar business, to whiten the pins is another; it is even a trade by itself to put them into the paper; and the important business of making a pin is, in this manner, divided into about eighteen distinct operations, which, in some manufactories, are all performed by distinct hands, though in others the same man will sometimes perform two or three of them. I have seen a small manufactory of this kind where ten men only were employed, and where some of them consequently performed two or three distinct operations. But though they were very poor, and therefore but indifferently accommodated with the necessary machinery, they could, when they exerted themselves, make among them about twelve pounds of pins in a day. There are in a pound upwards of four thousand pins of a middling size. Those ten persons, therefore, could make among them upwards of forty-eight thousand pins in a day. Each person, therefore, making a tenth part of forty-eight thousand pins, might be considered as making four thousand eight hundred pins in a day. But if they had all wrought separately and independently, and without any of them having been educated to this peculiar business, they certainly could not each of them have made twenty, perhaps not one pin in a day; that is, certainly, not the two hundred and fortieth, perhaps not the four thousand eight hundredth part of what they are at present capable of performing, in consequence of a proper division and combination of their different operations.

In every other art and manufacture, the effects of the division of labour are similar to what they are in this very trifling one; though, in many of them, the labour can neither be so much subdivided, nor reduced to so great a simplicity of operation. The division of labour, however, so far as it can be introduced, occasions, in every art, a proportionable increase of the productive powers of labour. The separation of different trades and employments from one another seems to have taken place, in consequence of this advantage. This separation too is generally carried furthest in those countries which enjoy the highest degree of industry and improvement; what is the work of one man in a rude state of society, being generally that of several in an improved one. In every improved society, the farmer is generally nothing but a farmer; the manufacturer, nothing but a manufacturer. The labour too which is necessary to produce any one complete manufacture, is almost always divided among a great number of hands. How many different trades are employed in each branch of the linen and woolen manufactures, from the growers of the flax and wool, to the bleachers and smoothers of the linen, or to the dyers and dressers of the cloth! . . .

This great increase of the quantity of work, which, in consequence of the division of labour, the same number of people are capable of performing, is owing to three different circumstances; first, to the increase of dexterity in every particular workman; secondly, to the saving of the time which is commonly lost in passing from one species of work to another; and lastly, to the invention of a great number of machines which facilitate and abridge labour, and enable one man to do the work of many.

First, the improvement of the dexterity of the workman necessarily increases the quantity of the work he can perform; and the division of labour, by reducing every man's business as some one simple operation, and by making this operation the sole employment of his life, necessarily increases very much the dexterity of the workman. A common smith, who, though accustomed to handle the hammer, has never been used to make nails, if upon some particular occasion he is obliged to attempt it, will scarce, I am assured, be able to make above two or three hundred nails in a day, and those too very bad ones. A smith who has been accustomed to make nails, but whose sole or principal business has not been that of a nailer, can seldom with his utmost diligence make more than eight hundred or a thousand nails in a day. . . .

Secondly, the advantage which is gained by saving the time commonly lost in passing from one sort of work to another, is much greater than we should at first view be apt to imagine it. It is impossible to pass very quickly from one kind of work to another, that is, carried on in a different place, and with quite familiar tools. A country weaver, who cultivates a small farm, must lose a good deal of time in passing from his loom to the field, and from the field to his loom. When the two trades can be carried on in the same workhouse, the loss of time is no doubt much less. It is even in this case, however, very considerable. A man commonly saunters a little in turning his hand from one sort of employment to another. When he first begins the new work he is seldom very keen and hearty; his mind, as they say, does not go to it, and for some time he rather trifles than applies to good purpose. . . .

Thirdly, and lastly, everybody must be sensible how much labour is facilitated and abridged by the application of proper machinery. It is unnecessary to give any example. I shall only observe, therefore, that the invention of all those machines by which labour is so much facilitated and abridged seems to have been originally owing to the division of labour. Men are much more likely to discover easier and readier methods of attaining any object, when the whole attention of their minds is directed towards that single object, than when it is dissipated among a great variety of things. But in consequence of the division of labour, the whole of every man's attention comes naturally to be directed towards some one very simple object. It is naturally to be expected, therefore, that some one or other of those who are employed in each particular branch of labour should soon find out easier and readier methods of performing their own particular work, wherever the nature of it admits of such improvement. A great part of the machines made use of in those manufactures in which labour is most subdivided, were originally the inventions of common workmen, who, being each of them employed in some very simple operation, naturally turned their thoughts towards finding out easier and readier methods of performing it. . . .

All the improvements in machinery, however, have by no means been the inventions of those who had occasion to use the machines. Many improvements have been made by the ingenuity of the makers of machines, when to make them becomes the business of peculiar trade; and some by that of those who are called philosophers or men of speculation, whose trade it is not to do any thing, but to observe every thing; and who, upon that account, are often capable of combining together the powers of the most distant and dissimilar objects. In the progress of society, philosophy or speculation becomes, like every other employment, the principal or sole trade and occupation of a particular class of citizens. Like every other employment too, it is subdivided into a great number of different branches, each of which affords occupation to a peculiar tribe or class of philosophers; and this subdivision of employment in philosophy, as well as in every other business, improves dexterity and saves time. Each individual becomes more expert in his own peculiar branch, more work is done upon the whole, and the quantity of science is considerably increased by it.

It is the great multiplication of the productions of all the different arts, in consequence of the division of labour, which occasions, in a well-governed society, that universal opulence which extends itself to the lowest ranks of the people. Every workman has a great quantity of his own work to dispose of beyond what he himself has occasion for; and every other workman being exactly in the same situation, he is enabled to exchange a great quantity of his own goods for a great quantity, or, what comes to the same thing, for the price of a great quantity of theirs. He supplies them abundantly with what they have occasion for, and they accommodate him as amply with what he has occasion for, and a general plenty diffuses itself through all the different ranks of the society.

## OF THE PRINCIPLE WHICH GIVES OCCASION TO THE DIVISION OF LABOUR

This division of labour; from which so many advantages are derived, is not originally the effect of any human wisdom, which foresees and intends that general opulence to which it gives occasion. It is the necessary, though very slow and gradual, consequence of a certain propensity in human nature which has in view no such extensive utility; the propensity to truck, barter, and exchange one thing for another.

As it is by treaty, by barter, and by purchase, that we obtain from one another the greater part of those mutual good offices which we stand in need of, so it is this same trucking disposition which originally gives occasion to the division of labour. In a tribe of hunters or shepherds a particular person makes bows and arrows, for example, with more readiness and dexterity than any other. He frequently exchanges them for cattle or for venison with his companions; and he finds at last that he can in this manner get more cattle and venison, than if he himself went to the field to catch them. From a regard to his own interest, therefore, the making of bows and arrows grows to be his chief business, and he becomes a sort of armourer. Another excels in making the frames and covers of their little huts or moveable houses. He is accustomed to be of use in this way to his neighbours, who reward him in the same manner with cattle and with venison, till at last he finds it his interest to dedicate himself entirely to this employment, and to become a sort of house-carpenter. In the same manner a third becomes a smith or brazier; a fourth a tanner or dresser of hides or skins, the principal part of the clothing of savages. And thus the certainty of being able to exchange all that surplus part of the produce of his own labour, which is over and above his own consumption, for such parts of the produce of other men's labour as he may have occasion for, encourages every man to apply himself to a particular occupation, and to cultivate and bring to perfection whatever talent or genius he may possess for that particular species of business.

The difference of natural talents in different men is, in reality, much less than we are aware of; and the very different genius which appears to distinguish men of different professions, when grown up to maturity, is not upon many occasions so much the cause, as the effect of the division of labour. The difference between the most dissimilar characters, between a philosopher and a common street porter, for example, seems to arise not so much from nature, as from habit, custom, and education. When they came into the world, for the first six to eight years of their existence, they were, perhaps, very much alike, and neither their parents nor play-fellows could perceive any remarkable difference. About that age, or soon after, they came to be employed in very different occupations.

*From*

# GENERAL AND
# INDUSTRIAL MANAGEMENT*

*By Henri Fayol†*

For any action whatsoever, an employee should receive orders from one superior only. Such is the rule of unity of command, arising from general and ever-present necessity and wielding an influence on the conduct of affairs, which to my way of thinking, is at least equal to any other principle whatsoever. Should it be violated, authority is undermined, discipline is in jeopardy, order disturbed and stability threatened. This rule seems fundamental to me and so I have given it the rank of principle. As soon as two superiors wield their authority over the same person or department, uneasiness makes itself felt and should the cause persist, the disorder increases, the malady takes on the appearance of an animal organism troubled by a foreign body, and the following consequences are to be observed: either the dual command ends in disappearance or elimination of one of the superiors and organic

---

* Reprinted by permission of Sir Isaac Pitman & Sons, Ltd., London, 1959 (pp. 24–25, 68–70). (This translation is published by permission of Dunod, Editeur, 92 Rue Bonaparte (VI), Paris, owners of the French copyright.) [Translated by Constance Storrs.]

† The author was Managing Director of Commentary Fourchambault-Decazeville (French mining combine). He formed the Centre of Administrative Studies in Paris in the earliest part of the present century.

well-being is restored, or else the organism continues to wither away. In no case is there adaptation of the social organism to dual command.

Now dual command is extremely common and wreaks havoc in all concerns, large or small, in home and in State. The evil is all the more to be feared in that it worms its way into the social organism on the most plausible pretexts. For instance—

*a.* In the hope of being better understood or gaining time or to put a stop forthwith to an undesirable practice, a superior $S^2$ may give orders directly to an employee $E$ without going via the superior $S^1$. If this mistake is repeated there is dual command with its consequences, viz., hesitation on the part of the subordinate, irritation and dissatisfaction on the part of the superior set aside, and disorder in the work. It will be seen later that it is possible to by-pass the scalar chain when necessary, whilst avoiding the drawbacks of dual command.

*b.* The desire to get away from the immediate necessity of dividing up authority as between two colleagues, two friends, two members of one family, results at times in dual command reigning at the top of a concern right from the outset. Exercising the same powers and having the same authority over the same men, the two colleagues end up inevitably with dual command and its consequences. Despite harsh lessons, instances of this sort are still numerous. New colleagues count on their mutual regard, common interest, and good sense to save them from every conflict, every serious disagreement and, save for rare exceptions, the illusion is short-lived. First an awkwardness makes itself felt, then a certain irritation and, in time, if dual command exists, even hatred. Men cannot bear dual command. A judicious assignment of duties would have reduced the danger without entirely banishing it, for between two superiors on the same footing there must always be some question ill-defined. But it is riding for a fall to set up a business organization with two superiors on equal footing without assigning duties and demarcating authority.

*c.* Imperfect demarcation of departments also leads to dual command: two superiors issuing orders in a sphere which each thinks his own, constitutes dual command.

*d.* Constant linking up as between different departments, natural intermeshing of functions, duties often badly defined, create an ever-present danger of dual command. If a knowledgeable superior does not put it in order, footholds are established which later upset and compromise the conduct of affairs.

In all human associations, in industry, commerce, army, home, State, dual command is a perpetual source of conflicts, very grave sometimes, which have special claim on the attention of superiors of all ranks.

\* \* \* \* \*

Such is the system of organization as conceived by Taylor for running the workshops of a large mechanical engineering concern. It turns on the two following ideas—

*a.* Need for a staff to help out shop foremen and foremen.
*b.* Negation of the principle of unity of command.

Just as the first seems to me to be good, so the second seems unsound and dangerous.

## (a) Need for a Staff to Help out Shop Foremen and Foremen

Taylor, better than anyone else, demonstrated the complexity and weight of the responsibility laid upon the men in charge of a large mechanical engineering shop. They cannot carry out their work satisfactorily unless given help. To attain his objective, Taylor devised and carried out the foregoing procedure: sundry specialists are attached to the foreman, who absolve him from having to have special knowledge at his command, and relieve him of the innumerable interruptions which would occupy too great a part of his time. This is the work of the staff. . . . Hitherto the need has been met in a variety of ways, but rarely satisfactorily.

I consider that Taylor has rendered great service in drawing attention to the importance of such a mechanism and to the manner of instituting it.

## (b) Negation of the Principle of Unity of Command

According to Taylor the ordinary type of organization referred to somewhat scornfully by him as "military," wherein workers receive instructions from one man only—shop foreman or gang-boss—is to be abandoned. . . . According to Taylor himself some adherents to the principle of unity of command would not abjure it even at his instance. For myself I do not think that a shop can be well run in flagrant violation of this. Nevertheless, Taylor successfully managed large-scale concerns. How, then, can this contradiction be explained? I imagine that in practice Taylor was able to reconcile functionalism with the principle of unity of command, but that is a supposition whose accuracy I am not in a position to verify. In business matters, day in and day out, from top to bottom of the scalar chain, functionalism has to be reconciled with unity of command. Considerable ability is demanded and this Taylor must have had in good measure.

I think it dangerous to allow the idea to gain ground that unity of command is unimportant and can be violated with impunity. So, until things change, let us treasure the old type of organization in which unity of command is honoured. It can, after all, be easily reconciled, as recommended by Taylor, with the assistance given to superintendents and foremen.

My reservations as regards Taylor's scientific or functional management do not prevent me from admiring the inventor of high-speed steel, the pioneer of minute and precise methods in conditions of work, the energetic and adept industrialist who, having made discoveries, shrank from no effort nor spared any pains to make them of practical application, and the tireless propagandist who meant the world to profit from his trials and experiments.

*From*

# THE SOURCE OF MANAGERIAL AUTHORITY*

*By Cyril J. O'Donnell*

For four decades none of the writers in the management field inquired into the nature of authority, not even into its source. This is not strange, of course, when one considers that their main interest was in the specialization of enterprise tasks. But it is significant that none seemed to think that the right of managers to give orders would be questioned. Seeing all about them that business men, in fact, did give orders and that they were generally obeyed, that the state promulgated laws and that these were generally obeyed also—seeing these things, the facts seemed to point to acceptance of the idea that the right to issue orders must certainly rest with the business managers. Indeed, if the question had been put to them they probably would have agreed with Petersen and Plowman, who state that

"Under our democratic form of government the right upon which managerial authority is based has its source in the Constitution of the United States through the guaranty of private property. Since the Constitution is the creature of the people, subject to amendment and modification by the will of the people, it follows that society, through government, is the source from which authority flows to ownership and thence to management."[1]

* Reprinted by permission of the *Political Science Quarterly*, vol. 67, no. 4 (December 1952), pp. 573–88.

[1] Elmore Petersen and E. Grosvenor Plowman, *Business Organization and Management* (Chicago, 1949), p. 62. This is a very restricted view of the source of authority.

\* \* \* \* \*

First among the writers in the field of management theory to question this accepted doctrine was Chester I. Barnard, Harvard gradute, successful top manager of large-scale enterprises, and the author of *The Functions of the Executive.*[2] Apparently reading widely in the fields of philosophy and psychology, and being much impressed by the political theory of Harold Laski, Barnard postulates that a correct theory must be consistent with the facts and then proceeds to enumerate several instances wherein the members of an organization have refused to obey persons in authority. On the basis of these "facts" he states that ". . . the decision as to whether an order has authority or not lies with the persons to whom it is addressed, and does not reside in 'persons of authority' or those who issue these orders." This concept means, if anything, that the source of authority lies in the members of an organization, that they confer authority upon their superior by deigning to accept and act upon commands, that they may, if they wish, decide to accept orders seriatim, and that they may withdraw conferred authority at any time by refusing to obey the commands of their superiors.

\* \* \* \* \*

. . . Robert Tannenbaum[3] dubs as "formal" the authority of a manager when it is viewed as "originating at the top of an organization hierarchy and flowing downward therein through the process of delegation." He thinks of "informal" authority as a right conferred upon a manager by his subordinates. Thus, informal authority is equated with Barnard's complete concept. But Tannenbaum, as a practical matter, does not actually differ from Barnard because he says,

"The real source of the authority possessed by an individual lies in the acceptance of its exercise by those who are subject to it. It is the subordinates of an individual who determine the authority which he may wield. Formal authority is, in effect, nominal authority. It becomes real only when it is accepted."

In order to substantiate this conception of authority, Tannenbaum quotes approvingly from Barnard, Kardiner, Benne, and Simon. . . . And I may add that Selekman[4] simply cannot make up his mind on the subject so he says:

"It is true enough that the management executive must, directly or indirectly, obtain consent to his decisions from the men under him; the importance of such consent now receives ever-increasing recognition. Nonetheless, the manager still wields authority over his workers as of right—a right delegated to him by the owners of the business."

\* \* \* \* \*

Authority is the right to command or to act. It implies the possession of the power to coerce, for obviously if there were no way to enforce an order the enterprise would become disorganized and unable to achieve its purpose. To realize how clear this is, the reader should imagine what would happen in a business if workers failed to adhere to the opening and closing hours of work; if individual players on a football team decided to engage their opposites in competition at any time; . . .

\* \* \* \* \*

Now, the *order* in organized behavior implies authority—the right to command coupled with the right to coerce. Malinowski is emphatic in saying that "submission to laws as well as the power to enforce laws and rules are indispensable in human behavior."[5] Otherwise, there will only be anarchy. West is of the opinion that

*"The prime requisite and firm creator of any community life is a law or order maintained by force.* For human nature is such that, in all its most necessary social relationships, it is

---

[2] Cambridge, 1950. Succeeding quotations from Barnard are from his Chapter 12.

[3] Robert Tannenbaum, "Managerial Decision-Making," *The Journal of Business,* XXIII, 1 (January 1950).

[4] Benjamin M. Selekman, *Labor Relations and Human Relations* (New York, 1947), pp. 175–76.

[5] Bronislaw Malinowski, *Freedom and Civilization* (New York, 1944), p. 27.

subject to the permanent threat of the self-assertive impulse, which misinterprets facts, misjudges events, and then, through consequent self-justificatory passion, breaks the social bond, unless it be externally restrained. We may claim this as adequately confirmed. Nursery studies and family life confirm it. Social and natural history confirm it. Modern psychology confirms it. And finally, our common sense tends to confirm it—for all others except ourselves, which is in itself a final confirmation. Individual, group or nation-state, we cannot judge our own cause. And if we try to do so, we shall be reduced again and again to fighting for a supposed "right" against a supposed "wrong," for one set of illusions against another."[6]

*     *     *     *     *

In the case of private business enterprise the authority relationships operate in much the same way. Americans have not deprived themselves of their common-law freedom to engage in business activity. It is true that elaborate safeguards for the rights of others have been spelled out in ordinance, rule, law and constitution, but within this framework anyone can engage in business as an individual proprietorship or on a partnership basis without special permission. Since corporations are legal persons created by law, their managers exercise authority which has reached them through the chain of delegation from the people to their constitution and thence through government to its creature. But whether a manager is operating an incorporated enterprise or not, his subordinates are obliged to obey his lawful orders, as long as the employer-employee relationship exists, because the right to command issues ultimately from the collective will of the people. Neither the individual subordinate nor the trade union to which he may belong is in a position to disobey those commands. . . .

*From*

# CONCERNING CIVIL GOVERNMENT*

*By John Locke*

The great and chief end, therefore, of men uniting into commonwealths, and putting themselves under government, is the preservation of their property; to which in the state of Nature there are many things wanting.

Firstly, there wants an established, settled, known law, received and allowed by common consent to be the standard of right and wrong, and the common measure to decide all controversies between them. For though the law of Nature be plain and intelligible to all rational creatures, yet men, being biased by their interest, as well as ignorant for want of study of it, are not apt to allow of it as a law binding to them in the application of it to their particular cases.

Secondly, in the state of Nature there wants a known and indifferent judge, with authority to determine all differences according to the established law. For every one in that state of being both judge and executioner of the law of Nature, men being partial to themselves, passion and revenge is very apt to carry them too far, and with too much heat in their own cases, as well as negligence and unconcernedness, make them too remiss in other men's.

Thirdly, in the state of Nature there often wants power to back and support the sentence when right, and to give it due execution. They who by any injustice offended will seldom fail where they are able by force to make good their injustice. Such resistance many times makes the punishment dangerous, and frequently destructive to those who attempt it.

Thus mankind, notwithstanding all the privileges of the state of Nature, being but in an

---

[6] Ranyard West, *Conscience and Society* (London, 1942), p. 240.

* Encyclopaedia Britannica, Inc., William Benton, Publisher, Chicago, 1952, The Great Ideas, Vol. 35 (pp. 53–54).

ill condition while they remain in it are quickly driven into society. Hence it comes to pass, that we seldom find any number of men live any time together in this state. The inconveniences that they are therein exposed to be the irregular and uncertain exercise of the power every man has of punishing the trangressions of others, make them take sanctuary under the established laws of government, and therein seek the preservation of their property. It is this makes them so willingly give up every one his single power of punishing to be exercised by such alone as shall be appointed to it amongst them, and by such rules as the community, or those authorised by them to that purpose, shall agree on. And in this we have the original right and rise of both the legislative and executive power as well as of the governments and societies themselves.

For in the state of Nature to omit the liberty he has of innocent delights, a man has two powers. . . .

The first power—viz., of doing whatsoever he thought fit for the preservation of himself and the rest of mankind, he gives up to be regulated by laws made by the society, so far forth as the preservation of himself and the rest of that society shall require; which laws of the society in many things confine the liberty he had by the law of Nature.

Secondly, the power of punishing he wholly gives up, and engages his natural force, which he might before employ in the execution of the law of Nature, by his own single authority, as he thought fit, to assist the executive power of the society as the law thereof shall require. For being now in a new state, wherein he is to enjoy many conveniences from the labour, assistance, and society of others in the same community, as well as protection from its whole strength, he is to part also with as much of his natural liberty, in providing for himself, as the good, prosperity, and safety of the society shall require, which is not only necessary but just, since the other members of the society do the like. . . .

. . . And so, whoever has the legislative or supreme power of any commonwealth, is bound to govern by established standing laws, promulgated and known to the people, and not by extemporary decrees, by indifferent and upright judges, who are to decide controversies by those laws; and to employ the force of the community at home only in the execution of such laws, or abroad to prevent or redress foreign injuries and secure the community from inroads and invasion. . . .

# 7. TEXAS-NORTHERN PIPELINE COMPANY

---

# Case Introduction

---

## SYNOPSIS

Texas-Northern Pipeline transports liquid petroleum products in interstate commerce from oil fields and refineries in east Texas northward to the areas of St. Louis, Minneapolis, and Milwaukee. Top management of the company has developed a standard cost control system to control and evaluate the performance of division managers. Paul Wheatley, the manager of Central Division was questioned for a deviation from standard even though he was the only division which was able to keep its overall maintenance cost below the company standard. Meanwhile, other divisions which seemed to be in control actually had total costs above the company's stated objective. It is suggested that Texas-Northern delete some of the performance indicators from their control system and top management is concerned about the overall effectiveness of the management control system.

## WHY THIS CASE IS INCLUDED

Control systems in organizations with continuous process technologies are of critical importance to maintaining organizational effectiveness. The Texas-Northern Pipeline Company case offers a good example of a management control system based upon standard costing techniques. The top management's desire to have detailed control information has its effect on the attitudes, motivations, and behavior of managers who have to operate within that control environment.

This case affords the opportunity to discuss some of the relationships between the technology used by an organization and the design of an effective management control system. This relationship can be viewed from both a technical-rational and a human or behavioral perspective.

**DIAGNOSTIC AND PREDICTIVE QUESTIONS**

The readings included in this case are marked (*). The author index at the end of this book locates the other readings.

1. Texas-Northern has a continuous process technology. Newman suggests that the design of a management structure should vary depending upon whether the organization has a stable or an adaptive technology. Drawing from the facts of the case and the concepts outlined by Newman, describe the management structure used within Texas-Northern. For what type of technology is this management structure suitable?

Read: Newman, "Strategy and Management Structure."

2. Vancil offers a number of structural alternatives open to managers who design management control systems for their organizations. Based upon Vancil's concepts, how would you describe and classify the management control system of Texas-Northern? In what ways is the description used by Vancil similar to the discussion of management structures offered by Newman? In what ways are they different?

Read: *Vancil, "What Kind of Management Control Do You Need?"
Newman, "Strategy and Management Structure."

3. What are the basic sources of conflict in Texas-Northern? Is this conflict the construction type discussed by Follett? What factors either encourage or discourage the constructive outcomes described by Follett?

Read: *Follett, "Constructive Conflict." Litterer, "Conflict in Organization: A Re-Examination."

4. Compare the management control system described in the Texas-Northern Pipeline case with the eight propositions on achievement motivation offered by Stringer. In what ways does the Texas-Northern control system encourage or discourage the arousal of achievement motivation?

Read: *Stringer, "Achievement Motivation and Management Control."

5. Mr. Coriano, the president of Texas-Northern, believed in the "stretch theory" of setting performance objectives. Based upon the case facts, does this "stretch theory" seem to work? How is the use of Mr. Coriano's "stretch theory" likely to affect the arousal of achievement motivation in operating managers?

Read: *Stringer, "Achievement Motivation and Management Control."

6. The control system used within Texas-Northern was based upon the principle of management by exception. Recent writers on organizational control have been suggesting a system of management by objectives. Compare the Texas-Northern system of control with the management by objectives approach. Would Texas-Northern need to give up the principle of management by exception if they adopted a system of management by objectives? Explain.

Read: *French and Hollmann, "Management by Objectives: The Team Approach."

7. French and Hollmann call for a collaborative approach to management by objectives (MBO) rather than the one-to-one approach to MBO.

Which approach to MBO, if any, would be most appropriate for Texas-Northern?

Read:    *French and Hollmann, "Management by Objectives: The Team Approach."

8. How much participation should the top management of Texas-Northern allow in the setting of performance objectives?

Read:    *Newman and Summer, *The Process of Management: Concepts, Behavior, and Practice.*
*French and Hollmann, "Management by Objectives: The Team Approach."

9. As noted earlier, French and Hollmann call for a collaborative approach to MBO. In contrast, Stringer suggests that performance objectives should be an individual matter. What accounts for the difference of opinion expressed by these two writers? Whose opinion is likely to be most applicable to the situation described in the Texas-Northern case? Explain.

Read:    *Stringer, "Achievement Motivation and Management Control." *French and Hollmann, "Management by Objectives: The Team Approach."

10. In the Texas-Northern case, Wheatley suggested the removal of the performance standards for materials and labor (3.1, 3.2, 3.4, and 3.5 in Exhibit 2). What are the advantages and disadvantages of Wheatley's suggestion.

Read:    Newman, "Strategy and Management Structure." *Stringer, "Achievement Motivation and Management Control." *French and Hollmann, "Management by Objectives: The Team Approach."

## POLICY QUESTIONS

11. Based upon your evaluation of the overall design of the management control system used within Texas-Northern Pipeline, what advice would you give Mr. Coriano, the president, about the use of profit centers, cost centers, or revenue centers as the basis of his management control system.

Read:    Review readings for Questions 1 and 2 above.

12. How should the management control system be designed to encourage constructive conflict within Texas-Northern?

Read:    Review readings for Question 3 above.

13. Develop a list of specific recommendations outlining how the levels of performance objectives should be established within Texas-Northern. Briefly outline your reasoning used in each recommendation.

Read:    Review readings for Questions 4 through 8 above.

14. Write a letter to the president indicating exactly what he should do with Mr. Wheatley's suggested change in the control system.

Read:    Review readings for Questions 9 and 10 above.

# Case Text*

Texas-Northern Pipeline Company engages in transportation of liquid petroleum products (gasoline, jet fuel, other light oils) in interstate commerce from the oil fields and refineries in east Texas northward to the metropolitan districts of St. Louis, Minneapolis, St. Paul, and Milwaukee. This case reports on efforts by the top management of the company to control operations in each of six divisions, and to evaluate the performance of division managers. A division in this company consists of a geographic area defined by one section of the line. For example, the Central division covers a distance of 400 miles along the pipe, together with narrow right-of-way on either side, in the sates of Missouri and Iowa.

Briefly, a pipeline is operated from pumping stations at intervals along the line. The first pumping station is located at the output station of a refinery. There the product is drawn from specified storage tanks by pumpers, men who adjust the correct intake valves, draw off liquid periodically, perform chemical or color tests, and operate the pumps themselves. At each station along the line, pumpers perform the same duties. A pumping station is a complex set of machines that may cost several million dollars to construct. The pipeline itself is a costly capital investment, involving cost of pipe and construction, cost of land, and expensive maintenance. Line maintenance is important for two reasons. Break and spillage may cost several hundred thousand dollars, but shut down and delay may be equally expensive. This is due to the extremely high cost of storage—so high that the storage tank farm at a refinery might have space for only two or three days' production. The storage capacity at the receiving terminal may equal only four or five days of consumption supply. Thus if the pipeline should be stopped for emergencies, the cost of idle storage tanks is great. If the emergencies should last for five days, much more money may be lost in shutting down refineries, lost sales to customers, or damage to customers' own operations. At the Milwaukee Terminal on Lake Michigan, for example, the storage tanks hold about six days' deliveries into Great Lakes tankers. Delay beyond this limit would cost heavily in idle capital investment in ships.

"It is for all of these reasons," states A F. Coriano, Texas-Northern's president.

> that we must be extremely precise in our control of operations and costs. Essentially, the work of a pipeline is done in two categories: operations and maintenance. Reporting to the district manager are

---

**EXHIBIT 1**
**Organization Chart**

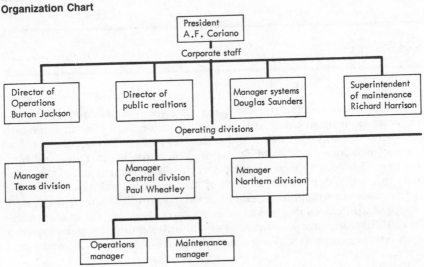

an operations manager and a maintenance manager. Each of these has reporting to him a pipeline supervisor and a pump and engine supervisor.

Two years ago, our company spent about ten months in instituting a system of objectives for the purpose of evaluating division managers. It was our general plan that Mr. Harrison, the director of maintenance here in headquarters, would draw up a list of objectives that he thought every division manager should meet if his performance is to be considered satisfactory. Mr. Jackson [director of operations] would do the same. After checking these with me for approval, they would go out to the divisions and get the approval of the six division managers. I would also have Douglas Saunders, our management systems director in headquarters, advise the operations and maintenance directors, before they went to the regions. The theory here is that if district managers have agreed in advance to a set of objective criteria, there would be no personal ugliness attached when, at the end of the year, one of the standards may not be met. It would simply be a matter of saying, "Well, we both agreed at the beginning that total pipeline maintenance costs would be not more than $630 per mile of pipeline. If it averages $700 a mile in the Southern district, that's that." It is an objective fact to be dealt with. Not a personal blame by my staff put on the divisions.

After all parties had agreed, we set up a set of sixty-two standards for all divisions, ranging all the way from the broad areas of personnel administration to public relations and operations. Here for example are 13 of the standards, in this case applicable to the maintenance function [Exhibit 2]. Or, in the case of Public Relations, we would judge the manager on such items as how many times a year

**EXHIBIT 2**
**Standards of Performance***

### 3. MAINTENANCE STANDARDS

It is the general objective of Texas-Northern Pipeline Company to maintain both pipelines and pumping stations in such condition that (1) our customers receive deliveries on time and with certainty, (2) our employees operate with safety to themselves and the public, and (3) our company achieves pipeline transportation with efficient use of resources and lack of waste. To implement these general objectives, each division manager is expected to accomplish the following standard objectives:

3.1   The labor cost for maintaining pipeline should be not more than $300 per year per mile of pipe maintained.

3.2   The materials used for maintaining pipeline should amount to not more than $280 per mile of pipe maintained.

3.3   The total cost of maintaining pipe should be not more than $630 per year per mile of pipe maintained.

3.4   The labor cost for maintaining pumps and engines should be not more than $250 per year per pump maintained.

3.5   The materials used for maintaining pumps and engines should be not more than $440 per pump unit maintained.

3.6   The total cost of maintaining pumps and engines should be not more than $670 per pump unit maintained.

3.7   Manpower used in line maintenance should be not more than 4.25 employees per 100 miles of pipeline.

3.8   Manpower used in pump and engine maintenance should be not more than 3.25 employees per 100 pump units maintained.

3.9   Materials consumed in maintenance of pumps and engines should not exceed $13,500 annually per employee.

3.10   Corrosion leaks should not exceed 35 per year per 100 miles of pipeline operated.

3.11   Accidental damage to pipelines should not exceed 4 incidents per 100 miles of pipe operated.

3.12   Unrecovered oil per leak should not exceed 75 percent of initial loss.

3.13   Warehouse turnover (except pipe) should be at least 200 percent per year.

* The list contains standards that appear in the Maintenance section of the *Standards Manual.* Other sections are Safety, Personnel Administration, Operations, Public Relations, and Management Communication. Of the 62 standards in the entire division list, 13 appear in the Maintenance section.

he visits with municipal officials in his area, how many presentations he makes at local schools, and the number of favorable items about our company that appear in local newspapers during the year.

The advantage of such a system of controls is that the top management of the company, such as myself and the financial vice president, can very quickly look across one sheet of paper to detect where there is trouble in a division. On that sheet, the six divisions are listed across the top. Down the left are listed the 62 control standards. Opposite each standard, in red, is the quantitative level expected for that item. For example, in the newspaper publicity area mentioned earlier, performance is considered satisfactory when at least two articles about Texas-Northern appear in any one year. Or, in the maintenance area [Exhibit 2] performance is satisfactory when corrosion leaks in the line do not exceed 35 per 100 miles of pipeline operated.

Under each division's column are listed the actual performance of that division. Performances rated satisfactory or above are listed in black and those below satisfactory in red. As the eye scans down a column, one can get a complete and quick picture of what went wrong in that division. Or, if one scans across columns, he can see instantly which division is performing below satisfaction and which above. This kind of document enables us to manage by exception. We do not have to have our minds filled with thousands of details and figures. The factors for success are already there. The figures are all there. The exceptions are highlighted. We can evaluate the whole company in a few hours and can have letters of inquiry going out within a day, asking why something went wrong. This is a real help to us and to the divisions.

### Setting Expense-Control Standards

During the process of setting standards, Richard Harrison included two standards that dealt with the cost of maintenance. One of these, specified that the total cost of maintaining the pipeline should not exceed $680 per mile, the other specified that the total cost of maintaining pumps and engines should not exceed $720 for each pump maintained in the district pumping stations. These standards were set by taking the average costs throughout the company for the past year. Harrison also obtained three man-months' time of one of the company's best maintenance engineers to adjust the averages slightly, based on good engineering (not historical) estimates. Both of the standards were subsequently changed.

Before Harrison took these standards to the division managers for their agreement, he met with both Coriano and Saunders to obtain their agreement. Saunders, a graduate of M.I.T. and a specialist in operations research, had been with the company for seven years and had himself spent much time out in the divisions solving operating problems. He raised the point that the two figures—total cost of maintenance in the pipeline category (3.3 in Exhibit 2) and the pump and engine category (3.6 in Exhibit 2)—were not sufficient for management control purposes.

> Maintenance [Saunders said] is a very complex matter. If we get a lump-sum figure, it will be practically useless to top management. All we could say is "Your maintenance cost is too high on pumps (or the pipeline)." We ought to include at least the following four items:
>
> 1. A standard for labor cost on line maintenance.
> 2. A standard for materials costs on line maintenance.
> 3. A standard for labor cost on pump and engine maintenance.
> 4. A standard for materials costs on pump and engine maintenance.
>
> The total cost includes more than labor and materials, but these are the major elements.

After a rather long discussion, the president said, "Well, it just seems that you two cannot agree on this matter. My own inclination is that we in headquarters must be informed—we cannot really make sense when we speak if we aren't. I believe we should include these additional items." As Harrison said afterward, "That settled that." The items were included in the finally adopted set of standards (3.1, 3.2, 3.4, and 3.5 in Exhibit 2).

Saunders called attention to one other kind of discrepancy in the control standards.

> Take a look at the two standards we would have on maintenance labor [3.1 and 3.4 in Exhibit 2]. They specify that the total labor cost of maintaining a mile of line, or in maintaining a pump, shall be a certain amount. Again, we have no way to know why labor cost is either good or bad. One district manager may be very good at finding ways to pay his labor less (less overtime, utilizing the proper grades of laborer on lower priced work, and so on), but very bad at getting his labor to be productive while they work. So we need some standards to let us know if the division manager is using his workers effectively. In addition to the total money amount spent on labor, I propose that we add two other items:
>
> 1. A standard for the actual man-hours, or people, used in pipeline work.
> 2. A standard for the actual man-hours, or people, used in pump and engine work.

These two standards later were incorporated into the finally approved set of standards (3.7 and 3.8 in Exhibit 2).

Mr. Coriano had one other suggestion to make at the meeting. He believed that most of the standards set by Harrison and Saunders were:

technically accurate. That is, they represent the best that accountants and engineers can do to represent what can and ought to happen in operation and maintenance of the line. But there is another
aspect to standards you have overlooked. They are intended to capture the attention and imagination of people whom we want to
achieve them. No man will exceed an easy goal—a pushover. How
have you set these in relation to a man's extra effort—the kind one
has to stretch to achieve?

Harrison and Saunders agreed that they had set the standards as if
a division manager and his men were working at a normal pace. "Just
what 'normal' is," Harrison said, "is not too clear. But I think it means
a man working with average energy at a job he hopes to accomplish."

Coriano said that eventually he got Harrison and Saunders to agree
to raising the achievement levels on five items.

I told them that achievement just didn't occur without challenge.
That I would be glad to spend two days of my time looking at all
the standards, working out challenging levels item by item. We
ended up, for example, by raising the level of performance on total
cost of maintaining pipeline and engines. The acceptable cost for
pipeline maintenance was lowered from $680 a mile to $630. Ditto
for pumps and engines—from $720 per pump to $670.

Later, at a meeting of all division managers, I explained that the
forces beyond our control are continuously setting standards for the
whole company that are exacting—the market forces of supply and
demand, as well as the Interstate Commerce Commission, will penalize the company unless we can keep our operations efficient and
costs down. There was a certain amount of reaction against both
the standards we put into the list and against the level we specified
for each standard. However, in the end I told them that they could
change them if they really wanted to. At that point, they all seemed
to see both the necessity for checkpoints by headquarters and for
not so easily attainable performance levels.

## Problems in Evaluation of Performance

Coriano describes how the management-by-exception system has
worked out:

We have now been operating under the standards using management by exception for three years. No system is perfect. I will give
you some examples of things we have had to contend with. I'd also
be interested in any suggestions for improving our system.

At the end of last year, Burton Jackson, our controller, sent out
a routine inquiry to Paul Wheatley, division manager in the Central
division. Under the procedures, the whole results tabulation is sent
in multiple copies to members of top management. Each of us had
some set of items to watch. Jackson watches the expense items. As

he scanned the control report, he noted that in the Central division, maintenance labor on the line was $325 per mile, entered in red. It was the only red figure in the row for line maintenance labor. All other divisions were in the black. So Jackson sent out the letter to Wheatley with a list of his exceptions. Harrison also sent his letter for exceptions in the operating section of the report, and our director of public relations sent out his letter on the public relations section.

I thought Wheatley would split a vein. He called me on the telephone and said that the system was grossly unfair. That his total cost of maintenance was under $630 per mile and that that performance was well within our other standard [3.3 in Exhibit 2]. He said that they had had a flu epidemic in Missouri last year and that this caused him to pay the nonafflicted workers overtime. He also said, "The real need of the company is to have low total maintenance cost. I performed according to the spirit of that need by doing extra hard work myself to invent ways to save on the materials factor in maintenance. I even gave special engineering time myself to devise ways of repairing the line without ordering new sections of pipe, just to save money and show a low total maintenance figure. Look at my performance on the materials cost—$220 a mile of pipe. That's pretty good [see 3.2 in Exhibit 2]."

I assured Wheatley that we are understanding when he tell us what happened about the flu epidemic and congratulated him on the good performance in materials. That didn't seem to do a lot of good. He said that as the headquarters people like Jackson and Harrison scan the reports they form impressions without knowing the facts. That under the guise of "management by exception" or "management by objective" they look for the red figures in a report, send out their letters of inquiry, and get a negative picture of his operating abilities. Of course, I assured him that the letter was one of inquiry.

Wheatley suggested that the way to correct this situation is simply to remove the standards for materials and labor [3.1, 3.2, 3.4, and 3.5 in Exhibit 2] from the control standards and the evaluation report; and to leave only the total maintenance figure [3.3 and 3.6 in Exhibit 2]. Actually, I will have to give this some more thought. That would defeat the original arguments we settled when we included them. This is one alternative for overcoming this, but I'm hoping I can achieve both Wheatley's and Saunders' objectives.

Another problem is actually in Wheatley's favor. On that total maintenance standard, his was the only district that performed within the $630 per mile of pipe. All the others were in red. We circulate the whole evaluation report to all division managers, and I got two suggestions from different divisions that this target was too high. I must admit that I don't like to see a horizontal row of figures all in red. It looks like something is wrong with the company. And the two division managers complained that it looks like there's something wrong with them. On the other hand, my "stretch" theory worked with Wheatley. His back was against the wall and he devoted a lot of creativity and energy to savings on the use of materials, just to make a good showing on his total cost. Maybe the other division managers ought to do that.

These are typical examples of the most frequent complaints. Perhaps we should take a look at the system again, to see if it needs changing.

# Selected Readings

*From*

## WHAT KIND OF MANAGEMENT CONTROL DO YOU NEED?*

*By Richard F. Vancil*

Profit centers are a major tool for management control in large industrial corporations. They possess important advantages:

1. Profitability is a simple way to analyze and monitor the effectiveness of a segment of a complex business. For example, a product division competes in the marketplace against several other companies in its industry, and also competes among other divisions in its company for an allocation of corporate resources for its future growth. Relative profitability in both types of competition is a useful decision criterion for top management.

2. Profit responsibility is a powerful motivator of men. Managers understand what profit is all about, and aggressive managers welcome the opportunity to have their abilities measured by the only real entrepreneurial yardstick.

Simple and powerful, profit centers sound like a panacea, the answer to a top manager's prayer. No wonder the concept has been so widely adopted. However, as with many a miracle drug, all too often the side effects of the medicine may be worse than the illness it was intended to cure.

\* \* \* \* \*

### CHOICE OF FINANCIAL GOALS

The cornerstone of every management control system is the concept of responsibility accounting. The basic idea is simple: each manager in a company has responsibility for a part of the total activity. The accounting system should be designed so that it yields a measurement of the financial effects of the activities that a manager is responsible for. This measurement can be stated in the form of a financial objective for each manager. Specifying that objective helps in delegating authority; a manager knows that the "right" decision is the course of action that moves him down the path toward his financial objective.

* From "What Kind of Management Control Do You Need?" *Harvard Business Review,* vol. 51, no. 2 (March–April 1973), pp. 75–85 (excerpts). Reprinted by permission. © 1967 by The President and Fellows of Harvard College; all rights reserved.

But this system does not go far enough. No single measurement, no matter how carefully constructed, can accurately reflect how well a manager has done his job. Part of the failure is simply due to the fact that corporations—and their managers—have multiple objectives. For instance, there is the matter of corporate social responsibility. Good performance toward that goal, even if measurable, cannot be added to the profit equation. Another major inadequacy of a single financial measurement is that it reflects performance during a particular time period, ignoring the effects that current actions may have on future performance. Every manager must make trade-offs between conflicting short-term and long-term needs; examples range all the way from the shop foreman who defers preventive maintenance in order to increase this month's output, but at the expense of a major breakdown next month, to the division manager who cuts his R&D budget in order to improve the year's profits but loses or delays the opportunity to introduce a profitable new product three years from now.

Despite these flaws, oversimplified financial measurements are almost universally used. The reason is not their value in evaluating a manager's performance—the faults noted are too obvious and important to ignore—but their effect on future performance. Specifying a financial objective can help a manager to think realistically about the tough decisions he must make, even if the objective does not always point the way to the right decision.

The selection of the right financial objective for each manager, therefore, can have an important effect on how he does his job. Although the range of *possible* objectives is very great, the financially measurable results of any manager's activities can usually be classified into one of the five categories of responsibility centers described in the ruled insert on page 240. As indicated, financial responsibility is simplest in the case of standard cost centers, most complex in the case of investment centers.

How should management measure the financial results achieved? It is not enough simply to say that a particular product division is a profit center; decisions are also required that specify how the profit is to be calculated, focusing in particular on how transfer prices shall be set and how the costs of services received from other organization units shall be charged against the division. Similarly, while the basic concept of an investment center is simple, it is difficult to decide which assets to include in the investment base and how they shall be valued. Therefore, although there may be only five types of financial responsibility centers, there are *many* methods of financial measurement that can be used for specific organizations.

## Criteria for Selection

Figuring out the best way to define and measure the financial performance for each manager is the corporate controller's most challenging—and analytically demanding—task. Two types of considerations affect each choice. The first is the strategy of the company: its broad objectives, the nature of the industries in which it operates, and the niche it seeks to carve for itself in each industry on the basis of its distinctive competence. The second is the organization structure of the company—the way the total task is divided among the managers to permit delegation of authority and specialization of effort.

The controller must have a thorough knowledge of his company's strategy and organization structure. He draws on this knowledge to apply two criteria for deciding which measure of financial responsibility to use for each organization unit and how it should be calculated:

*1. Fairness.* Each manager must believe that the summary financial measurement used to report on his performance is appropriate. This means he must see all of the signals he receives about his job as consistent with each other. Moreover, he must believe that the measurement encompasses all the factors he can control and excludes those over which he has no control. And he must be convinced the measurement is calculated in such a way that a "good" decision on his part will be reflected as such by the financial measurement. The "fairness" of a financial measurement is not a fact; it is a perception through the eyes of the manager to whom it applies.

*2. Goal Congruence.* The most difficult compromises that must be made in designing

## TYPES OF FINANCIAL RESPONSIBILITY

The principal types of financial responsibility can be classified as follows:

*Standard cost centers* are exemplified by a production department in a factory. The standard quantities of direct labor and materials required for each unit of output are specified. The foreman's objective is to minimize the variance between actual costs and standard costs. He also is usually responsible for a flexible overhead expense budget, and his objective, again, is to minimize the variance between budgeted and actual costs.

*Revenue centers* are best illustrated by a sales department where the manager does not have authority to lower prices in order to increase volume. The resources at his disposal are reflected in his expense budget. The sales manager's objective is to spend no more than the budgeted amounts and to produce the maximum amount of sales revenue.

*Discretionary expense centers* include most administrative departments. There is no practical way to establish the relationship between inputs and outputs. Management can only use its best judgment to set the budget, and the department manager's objective is to spend the budgeted amount to produce the best (though still unmeasurable) quality of service that he possibly can.

*Profit centers,* the focus of this article, are units, such as a product division, where the manager is responsible for the best combination of costs and revenues. His objective is to maximize the bottom line, the profit that results from his decisions. A great many variations on this theme can be achieved by defining "profit" as including only those elements of cost and revenue for which the manager is responsible. Thus a sales manager who is allowed to set prices may be responsible for gross profit (actual revenue less standard direct manufacturing costs). Profit for a product-line marketing manager, on the other hand, might reflect deductions for budgeted factory overhead and actual sales promotion expenses.

*Investment centers* are units where the manager is responsible also for the magnitude of assets employed. He makes trade-offs between current profits and investments to increase future profits. Stating the manager's objective as maximizing his return on investment or his residual income (profit after a charge for the use of capital) helps him to appraise the desirability of new investments.

a management control system have to do with varying goals.[1] When a manager is assigned a financial objective for his activities and a fair measurement of performance is determined, ideally he should be able to pursue his objective without concern for whether or not his actions are in the best interests of the corporation. But in reality, as we know, that ideal is not easy to attain. The controller, designing a management control system with a corporate-wide perspective, must ensure that managers are not working at cross-purposes. He must select objectives and measurements in such a way that a good decision by any manager is also a good decision for the corporation as a whole.

For the controller, applying these two criteria simultaneously means that he must combine the points of view of both the individual manager and the corporation. That becomes progressively more difficult as the complexity of the organization structure and the business increases. . . .

\*       \*       \*       \*       \*

---

[1] For the original statement of this problem, see Robert N. Anthony, *Planning and Control Systems: A Framework for Analysis* (Boston: Division of Research, Harvard Business School, 1965).

What varieties of control systems are possible and feasible in simple organizations? When are the criteria of fairness and goal congruence satisfied? How does a company's strategy affect the choice of a system?

## Practical Alternatives

\* \* \* \* \*

Selecting an appropriate financial measurement for this president's performance is not really a problem. He is responsible for the entire business, its profits, and the investment required. The financial responsibility of his two principal subordinates, however, is not so easily determined. The manufacturing manager, responsible for all production operations in the plant, could be charged with the responsibility of running either a standard cost center or a profit center. And the marketing manager, responsible for all sales and promotion activities, could be treated as the head either of a revenue center or of a profit center. With just two functional units, and two alternatives available for each, there are still four alternatives for the design of a management control system for this business:

| Alternative | Manufacturing | Marketing |
|---|---|---|
| 1. | Standard cost center | Revenue center |
| 2. | Standard cost center | Profit center |
| 3. | Profit center | Revenue center |
| 4. | Profit center | Profit center |

These four alternatives are not simply theoretical possibilities; each may be appropriate under different circumstances. The critical circumstances concern the nature of the key decisions to be made and the way decision-making authority is delegated in the organization.

As for the decisions, most of them involve choices in allocating resources. There are questions of *purpose* (e.g., whether incremental marketing expenditures should be used for advertising or for hiring more salesmen) and of *timing* (e.g., when a piece of production equipment should be replaced). . . . The problem is that no president can make all the decisions and that, as he delegates power to subordinates, he runs the risk they will make decisions that are different from those he would make.

Effective decision making in a functionally organized business is hampered by the fact that no subordinate has the same broad perspective of the business that the president or general manager has. Many decisions, and almost all the important ones, affect more than one function in the business. They are seen differently by managers according to the functions they manage. One possible response to this problem is not to delegate authority for important decisions below the level of general manager. Another approach is to broaden the perspective of the functional manager by delegating such authority to him and then holding him responsible for the profitability of his decisions.

The implications of the second approach can best be seen by examining a series of examples. I shall describe a company situation for each of the four design alternatives mentioned.

*1. No Profit Centers.* Company A manufactures and distributes fertilizer. It buys chemicals, minerals, and other components from large suppliers and mixes them in various combinations to produce a limited variety of standard fertilizers with specified chemical properties. These are sold to farmers in bulk. Because the quality is specified and subject to verification by chemical analysis, all producers sell at the same price and offer identical volume discounts. Transportation costs are a major factor, and Company A thus enjoys a relative advantage in its local market. Its salesmen call on purchasing agents for large corporate farms and on distributors that sell to smaller farmers. Most orders are placed well in advance of the growing season, so the mixing plant is busy several months of the year, but there is still a large seasonal peak in both marketing and manufacturing.

\* \* \* \* \*

The president of Company A is the only man financially responsible for the profit of the company. There are a limited number of key, cross-functional decisions to be made, and he makes them. One concerns the size of the sales force; another concerns the acquisition of equipment to increase the capacity or reduce the labor costs in the mixing plant. Both of these are what are called "capacity decisions." While the evaluation of alternatives for either decision is not easy, it can be handled as well or better by the president than by either of his two subordinates.

**2. Marketing Profit Centers.** Company B produces a line of branded consumer toiletries. The products are heavily advertised and made available to consumers in drugstores, supermarkets, and other retail outlets throughout the country. The marketplace is in continual turmoil as competitors jockey for consumer attention through price promotions, premium offers, and "new" formulas and "secret" ingredients announced through both media advertising and point-of-purchase promotion. The company's field sales force is small; salesmen call on distributors and purchasing agents for large retail chains. The product itself is simple to manufacture, but consistently reliable quality is considered important to maintain customer goodwill.

Marketing is where the action is in Company B. The marketing manager is responsible for profitability, which is defined as sales revenue less standard direct manufacturing costs and all marketing costs. The president of the company is very interested in the marketing function and devotes much of his time to it. At the same time, he realizes that there are a myriad of marketing decisions to be made, many of them requiring specialized knowledge of local markets and detailed current information on competitors' actions. Therefore, he needs to delegate considerable authority to the marketing manager.

The manufacturing manager, like his counter-part in Company A, is a standard cost center, responsible for standard direct costs and a variable overhead budget.

**3. Production Profit Centers.** Company C produces a line of specialty metal products sold as semifinished components, primarily to manufacturers of high-style lighting fixtures. The company has only a few dozen customers, four of which account for over 50 percent of the sales volume. The business is price-competitive; Company C's equipment is not unique, and other manufacturers are frequently asked to bid against Company C on prospective contracts. Company C is renowned, however, for it's technical skills in solving difficult manufacturing problems. Even on relatively routine contracts, the company is sometimes able to charge a slightly higher price because of its consistently high quality and its responsiveness in meeting its customers' "emergency" delivery requirements.

\*     \*     \*     \*     \*

Manufacturing is the name of the game at Company C. The manufacturing manager is responsible for profit, defined as the contribution to overhead after subtracting all direct manufacturing costs. He keeps himself informed of the backlog of orders against each type of equipment in his shop and personally reviews all bids over a nominal amount, estimating the price to quote in view of his desire for the business and his assessment of the customer's loyalty. He is also responsible for meeting his variable overhead budget.

As for the marketing manager, he is a revenue center, like his counterpart in Company A. He endeavors to use his sales force as effectively as possible to turn up attractive bidding opportunities on which the company can compete successfully.

\*     \*     \*     \*     \*

The foregoing examples, simple as they are, show how difficult it is to generalize on the question of whether or not a functional manager should be held responsible for profit. The first, most obvious, statement is that the decision turns on the nature of the business. The tangible differences between businesses and the unique tasks they imply for management must be reflected in the management control system. The challenge for the controller is to synthesize the characteristics of the business and select a financial objective for each manager that (1) motivates him to achieve the company's objectives, and (2) minimizes unnecessary conflict between managers.

\*     \*     \*     \*     \*

Product divisions are almost always treated as profit or investment centers. The responsibility of the division manager is usually broad enough so that he can conceive of his division as though it were an independent company. In addition, the scope and substance of his task and the objective he is to strive for may be delineated clearly. . . .

Now, what can functional organizations do that product divisions cannot? Functional organizations have the potential of great efficiency. The efficiency of an activity can frequently be measured in terms of the quantity of inputs required to yield one unit of output. For a great many activities, efficiency increases as the size of the activity grows—at least, up to some point where there are no further "economies of scale" to be realized. The reason that efficiency increases is that large-scale operations permit the utilization of increasingly specialized inputs. For instance, a general-purpose machine tool and a skilled operator may be able to produce 100 parts per hour; but a specially designed piece of equipment might produce 1,000 parts per hour and require no operator at all. Also, specialization of workers can yield economies of scale, as the learning curve of production workers demonstrates.

. . . While it is technically feasible to equip each plant so that it turns out one of the three products of the company, it would be a great waste to do so. Manufacturing costs would be much lower if each plant specialized in certain aspects of the manufacturing process, doing only a limited number of functions on all three products. Further, the quality of manufacturing supervision and technical services, such as engineering and quality control, is better when those activities are centralized under one manufacturing manager. Scattering such activities across three product divisions would both lower the quality of the personnel that could be afforded and reduce the efficiency of their services. Similar arguments might be made about the efficiency of the marketing organization.

What advantages are unique to product divisions? They hold out the promise of more *effective* management than is the case with functional organizations. (One way of contrasting effectiveness with efficiency is to say that efficiency means doing something right and effectiveness means doing the right something.) The benefits are harder to document or quantify, but the potential for improvement exists both in strategy formulation and in tactical decision making.

In a strategic sense, it is easier for a product division than a functional organization to focus on the needs of its customers, rather than on simply manufacturing or selling the current line of products. The division manager can develop a strategy for his particular business, finding a competitive niche for it that may be different from the strategy being pursued by other division managers with different product lines. Tactically, a product division can also be more responsive to current customer needs. The division manager has the authority to change the production schedule in response to the request of an important customer; in a functional organization, by contrast, such a request must "go through channels," which may be ponderous and time-consuming.

Finally, it can be argued that product divisions are an excellent training ground for young managers, fostering entrepreneurship and increasing the number of centers of initiative in a corporation.

A business organization must be both efficient and effective if it is to survive, be profitable, and grow. The fundamental choice in organizational design is not an either-or question, but one of achieving the best possible balance between the benefits from economies of scale and those from strategic and tactical responsiveness. One approach that is being used increasingly in a variety of settings is the matrix form of organization.

*       *       *       *       *

**Problems in responsibility.** In some businesses, both the marketing and the manufacturing functions may be highly interdependent and responsible for activities which have major effects on profits. How can the managers of the two functions be held jointly responsible?

One way is to hold each man responsible for a portion of the profits of the company, using a transfer price to permit a calculation of that profit. The determination of transfer prices in highly interdependent situations may be difficult, but it may be worth the trouble in order to motivate each manager properly.

Another approach is to use the matrix form of organization as an acknowledgment of the interdependence, and to hold each functional manager responsible for the entire profit of the business. This approach requires "double counting" of each profit dollar. In terms of Exhibit 1, the manufacturing manager would be responsible for profit, defined as sales revenues less all manufacturing costs and all direct marketing expenses, for all products manufactured in the three plants. Each plant manager might have a similar responsibility for his plant. The sum of the defined profits for the three plants would be the total contribution to corporate overhead and net profit. Each product manager would also be responsible for profits, defined in the same way, for the products in his line. The sum of the profits for the three product managers would be the same as the total profit of the three plants.

**EXHIBIT 1**
**Concept of a Matrix Organization**

| | Manufacturing Manager | | |
|---|---|---|---|
| *Marketing Manager* | *Manager Plant 1* | *Manager Plant 2* | *Manager Plant 3* |
| Manager Product A | | | |
| Manager Product B | | | |
| Manager Product C | | | |

Such a management control system may seem confusing at first, but it can be effective. The intent of double counting the profit is to make clear to all managers involved that they must work together in order to achieve their own individual objective. A profitable action which requires cooperation does not reflect to the credit of only one party, nor does it require a fictitious division of the profit between them. Both men benefit. Thus Plant Manager 1 would work with all three product managers, trying to find ways to use the facilities at his disposal in order to yield the highest profit for his plant. And Product Manager A would work with all three plant managers, attempting to utilize their resources in such a way as to maximize the profitability of his product line.

An intended effect of such a system is a certain amount of tension in the organization—an atmosphere of constructive conflict in which the managers in one function know they are working toward the same goal and must compete among themselves to cooperate with managers from the other functional area. Such conflict, if handled sensitively by a sophisticated top manager, can break down some of the parochialism of a purely functional organization without splintering it into less efficient product divisions.

Because of these potential advantages, we may see increasing use of the matrix concept in companies where functional interdependence is high and the rewards from functional specialization are too great to ignore.

\*      \*      \*      \*      \*

*From*

# CONSTRUCTIVE CONFLICT*

## By Mary Parker Follett†

. . . I wish to consider in this paper the most fruitful way of dealing with conflict. At the outset, I should like to ask you to agree for the moment to think of conflict as neither good nor bad; to consider it without ethical pre-judgment; to think of it not as warfare, but as the appearance of difference, difference of opinions, of interests. For that is what conflict means—difference. We shall not consider merely the differences between employer and employee, but those between managers, between the directors at the Board meetings, or wherever difference appears.

As conflict—difference—is here in the world, as we cannot avoid it, we should, I think, use it. Instead of condemning it, we should set it to work for us. Why not? What does the mechanical engineer do with friction? Of course his chief job is to eliminate friction, but it is true that he also capitalizes friction. The transmission of power by belts depends on friction between the belt and the pulley. The friction between the driving wheel of the locomotive and the track is necessary to haul the train. All polishing is done by friction. The music of the violin we get by friction. We left the savage state when we discovered fire by friction. We talk of the friction of mind on mind as a good thing. So in business, too, we have to know when to try to eliminate friction and when to try to capitalize it, when to see what work we can make it do. That is what I wish to consider here, whether we can set conflict to work and make it *do* something for us.

\* \* \* \* \*

There are three main ways of dealing with conflict: domination, compromise, and integration. Domination, obviously, is a victory of one side over the other. This is the easiest way of dealing with conflict, the easiest for the moment but not usually successful in the long run, as we can see from what has happened since the War.

The second way of dealing with conflict, that of compromise, we understand well, for it is the way we settle most of our controversies; each side gives up a little in order to have peace, or, to speak more accurately in order that the activity which has been interrupted by the conflict may go on. . . .

. . . Yet no one really wants to compromise, because that means a giving up of something. Is there then any other method of ending conflict? There is a way beginning now to be recognized at least, and even occasionally followed: when two desires are *integrated,* that means that a solution has been found in which both desires have found a place, that neither side has had to sacrifice anything. Let us take some very simple illustration. In the Harvard Library one day, in one of the smaller rooms, someone wanted the window open, I wanted it shut. We opened the window in the next room, where no one was sitting. This was not a compromise because there was no curtailing of desire; we both got what we really wanted. For I did not want a closed room, I simply did not want the north wind to blow directly on me; likewise the other occupant did not want that particular window open, he merely wanted more air in the room.

. . . A Dairymen's Cooperative League almost went to pieces last year on the question of precedence in unloading cans at a creamery platform. The men who came down the hill (the creamery was on a down grade) thought they should have precedence; the men who

---

\* From *Dynamic Administration: The Collected Papers of Mary Parker Follett* by H. C. Metcalf and L. Urwick. Copyright © 1942. Reprinted by permission of Harper & Row, Publishers, Incorporated. (Excerpts from pp. 30–49.)

† Miss Follett was a noted industrial psychologist in Boston in the early part of this century.

came up the hill thought they should unload first. The thinking of both sides in the controversy was thus confined within the walls of these two possibilities, and this prevented their even trying to find a way of settling the dispute which would avoid these alternatives. The solution was obviously to change the position of the platform so that both up-hillers and down-hillers could unload at the same time. But this solution was not found until they had asked the advice of a more or less professional integrator. When, however, it was pointed out to them, they were quite ready to accept it. Integration involves invention, and the clever thing is to recognize this, and not to let one's thinking stay within the boundaries of two alternatives which are mutually exclusive.

\* \* \* \* \*

Some people tell me that they like what I have written on integration, but say that I am talking of what ought to be instead of what is. But indeed I am not; I am talking neither of what is, to any great extent, nor of what ought to be merely, but of what perhaps may be. This we can discover only by experiment. That is all I am urging, that we try experiments in methods of resolving differences. . . .

The key-word of psychology today is desire. If we wish to speak of conflict in the language of contemporary psychology, we might call it a moment in the interacting of desires. Thus we take from it any connotation of good or bad. Thus we shall not be afraid of conflict, but shall recognize that there is a destructive way of dealing with such moments and a constructive way. Conflict as the moment of the appearing and focusing of difference may be a sign of health, a prophecy of progress. If the Dairymen's League had not fought over the question of precedence, the improved method of unloading would not have been thought of. The conflict in this case was constructive. And this was because, instead of compromising, they sought a way of integrating. Compromise does not create, it deals with what already exists; integration creates something new, in this case a different way of unloading. And because this not only settled the controversy but was actually better technique, saved time both the farmers and the creamery, I call this: setting friction to work, making it *do* something.

. . . What I think we should do in business organization is to try to find the machinery best suited for the normal appearing and uniting of diversity so that the difference does not stay too long crystallized, so that the pathological stage shall not be reached.

One advantage of integration over compromise I have not yet mentioned. If we get only compromise, the conflict will come up again and again in some other form, for in compromise we give up part of our desire, and because we shall not be content to rest there, sometime we shall try to get the whole of our desire. Watch industrial controversy, watch international controversy, and see how often this occurs. Only integration really stabilizes. But by stabilization I do not mean anything stationary. Nothing ever stays put. I mean only that that particular conflict is settled and the next occurs on a higher level.

\* \* \* \* \*

Having suggested integration as perhaps the way which we can deal most fruitfully with conflict, with difference, we should now consider the method by which integration can be obtained. But before we do that I want to say definitely that I do not think integration is possible in all cases. When two men want to marry the same woman, there can be no integration; when two sons both want the old family home, there can usually be no integration. And there are many such cases, some of little, some of great seriousness. I do not say that there is no tragedy in life. All that I say is that if we were alive to its advantages, we could often integrate instead of compromising. . . .

\* \* \* \* \*

If, then, we do not think that differing necessarily means fighting, even when two desires both claim right of way, if we think that integration is more profitable than conquering or compromising, the first step toward this consummation is *to bring the differences into the open.* We cannot hope to integrate our differences unless we know what they are. I will give some illustrations of the opposite method—evading or suppressing the issue.

I know a factory where, after the War, the employees asked for a 5 percent increase in wages, but it was not clear to either side whether this meant a 5 percent raise over present wages or over pre-War wages. Moreover, it was seen that neither side wished to know! The employees naturally preferred to think the former, the managers the latter. It was some time before both sides were willing to face the exact issue; each, unconsciously, hoped to win by keeping the whole problem hazy.

     \*      \*      \*      \*      \*

The first rule, then, for obtaining integration is to put your cards on the table, face the real issue, uncover the conflict, bring the whole thing into the open.

One of the most important reasons for bringing the desires of each side to a place where they can be clearly examined and valued is that evaluation often leads to *revaluation.* We progress by a revaluation of desire, but usually we do not stop to examine a desire until another is disputing right of way with it. Watch the evolution of your desires from childhood, through youth, etc. The baby has many infantile desires which are not compatible with his wish for approbation; therefore he revalues his desires. We see this all through our life. We want to do so-and-so, but we do not estimate how much this really means to us until it comes into conflict with another desire. Revaluation is the flower of comparison.

This conception of the revaluation of desire it is necessary to keep in the foreground of our thinking in dealing with conflict, for neither side ever "gives in" really, it is hopeless to expect it, but there often comes a moment when there is a simultaneous revaluation of interests on both sides and unity precipitates itself. . . .

     \*      \*      \*      \*      \*

. . . If the first step is to uncover the real conflict, the next is to take the demands of both sides and break them up into their constituent parts. Contemporary psychology shows how fatal it is to try to deal with conglomerates. I know a boy who wanted a college education. His father died and he had to go to work at once to support his mother. Had he then to give up his desire? No, for on analysis he found that what he wanted was not a college education, but an education, and there were still ways of his getting that. You remember the southern girl who said, "Why, I always thought damned Yankee was one word until I came north."

     \*      \*      \*      \*      \*

You will notice that to break up a problem into its various parts involves the *examination of symbols,* involves, that is, the careful scrutiny of the language used to see what it really means. A friend of mine wanted to go to Europe, but also she did not want to spend the money it would cost. Was there any integration? Yes, she found one. In order to understand it, let us use the method I am advocating; let us ask, what did "going to Europe" symbolize to her? In order to do that, we have to break up this whole, "going to Europe." What does "going to Europe" stand for to different people? A sea voyage, seeing beautiful places, meeting new people, a rest or change from daily duties, and a dozen other things. Now, this woman had taught for a few years after leaving college and then had gone away and led a somewhat secluded life for a good many years. "Going to Europe" was to her a symbol, not of snow mountains, or cathedrals, or pictures, but of meeting people—that was what she wanted. When she was asked to teach in a summer school of young men and women where she would meet a rather interesting staff of teachers and a rather interesting group of students, she immediately accepted. This was her integration. This was not a substitution for her wish, it was her *real* wish fulfilled.

     \*      \*      \*      \*      \*

We have been considering the breaking up of the whole-demand. On the other hand, one often has to do just the opposite; find the whole-demand, the real demand, which is being obscured by miscellaneous minor claims or by ineffective presentation. The man with a genius for leadership is the one who can make articulate the whole-demand, unless it is a matter of tactics deliberately to conceal it. I shall not stop to give instances of this, as I wish to have time for some consideration of a point which seems to me very important for business, both in dealings with employees and with competing firms, and that is the anticipation of demands, of difference, of conflict.

     \*      \*      \*      \*      \*

Finally, let us consider the chief *obstacles to integration.* It requires a high order of intelligence, keen perception and discrimination, more than all, a brilliant inventiveness: it is easier for the trade union to fight than to suggest a better way of running the factory. . . .

Another obstacle to integration is that our way of life has habituated many of us to enjoy domination. Integration seems to many a tamer affair; it leaves no "thrills" of conquest. I knew a dispute within a trade union where, by the skillful action of the chairman, a true integration was discovered and accepted, but instead of the satisfaction one might have expected from such a happy result, the evening seemed to end rather dully, flatly; there was no climax, there was no side left swelling its chest, no one had conquered, no one had "won out." It is even true that to some people defeat, as well as conquest, is more interesting than integration. That is, the person with decided fight habits feels more at home, happier, in the fight movement. Moreover, it leaves the door open for further fighting, with the possibility of conquest the next time.

Another obstacle to integration is that the matter in dispute is often theorized over instead of being taken up as a proposed activity. I think this important in business administration. Intellectual agreement does not alone bring full integration. I know one factory which deliberately provides for this by the many activities of its many sub-committees, some of which seem rather trivial unless one sees just how these activities are a contribution to that functional unity which we shall consider in a later paper.

*     *     *     *     *

A serious obstacle to integration which every businessman should consider is the language used. We have noted the necessity of making preparation in the other man, and in ourselves too, for the attitude most favorable to reconciliation. A trade unionist said to me, "Our representatives didn't manage it right. If instead of a 15 percent increase they had asked for an adjustment of wages, the management would have been more willing to listen to us; it would have put them in a different frame of mind." I don't quite see why we are not more careful about out language in business, for in most delicate situations we quite consciously choose that which will not arouse antagonism. You say to your wife at breakfast, "Let's reconsider that decision we came to last night." You do not say, "I wish to give you my criticism of the decision you made last night."

I cannot refrain from mentioning a personal experience. I went into the Edison Electric Light Company and said to a young woman at a counter. "Where shall I go to speak about my bill?" "Room D for complaints," she replied. "But I don't wish to make a complaint," I said, "I thought there was a mistake in your bill." "I think there is," I said, "but I don't wish to complain about it; it was a very natural mistake." The girl looked nonplussed, and as she was obviously speechless a man came out from behind a desk and said: "You would prefer to ask for an adjustment, wouldn't you?" and we had a chat about it.

*     *     *     *     *

I have left untouched one of the chief obstacles to integration—namely, the undue influence of leaders—the manipulation of the unscrupulous on the one hand and the suggestibility of the crowd on the other. Moreover, even when the power of suggestion is not used deliberately, it exists in all meetings between people; the whole emotional field of human intercourse has to be taken fully into account in dealing with methods of reconciliation. I am deliberately omitting the consideration of this, not because I do not feel its importance as keenly as anyone, but because in these few papers we cannot cover everything.

Finally, perhaps the greatest of all obstacles to integration is our lack of training for it. In our college debates we try always to beat the other side. . . . Managers need it just as much. I have found, in the case of the wage boards which I have been on, that many employers . . . came to these joint conferences of employers and employees with little notion of conferring, but to push through, to force through, plans *previously* arrived at, based on *preconceived* ideas of what employees are like. It seems as if the methods of genuine conference have yet to be learned. Even if there were not the barriers of an unenlightened self-interest, of prejudice, rigidity, dogmatism, routine, there would still be required training and practice for us to master the technique of integration. A friend of mine' said to me, "Open-mindedness is the whole thing, isn't it?" No, it isn't; it needs just as great a respect for your own view as for that of others, and a firm upholding of it until you are convinced. Mushy people are no more good at this than stubborn people.

*From*

# ACHIEVEMENT MOTIVATION AND MANAGEMENT CONTROL*

*By Robert A. Stringer, Jr.*

\*    \*    \*    \*    \*

A person's motivation is said to depend on three factors. First, the "basic" strength of the particular motive; second, the person's expectation that he can satisfy the motive in this situation; and third, the amount of satisfaction the person anticipates.

The final two determinants of aroused motivation are not part of a person's personality. They are not inside the person. They can be considered characteristics of the environment, because they change as the person moves from situation to situation. Different work settings signal to the individual that different kinds of satisfactions can be gained by behaving in certain ways. These signals (or cues) lead to different kinds of motivation. By understanding the varieties of human motivation, managers will be in a better position to control the activities of their subordinates.

It is assumed that every individual personality is composed of a network of these basic motives. Some of the more important motives that have been studied are:

*Need for Achievement.* The need for competitive success as measured against some standard of excellence.

*Need for Power.* The need for personal influence and control over the means of influencing others.

*Need for Affiliation.* The need for close interpersonal relationships and friendships.

*Fear of Failure.* The fear of competition or criticism when involved in an activity that is to be evaluated.

*Motives* are generally acquired during a person's early years, and they remain relatively unchanged in adult life. *Motivation,* however, is determined by the interplay between a person and his environment. Thus a man's *motivated behavior* may change radically throughout his adult life.

## ACHIEVEMENT MOTIVATION

Managers must concern themselves with *motivation to accomplish results.* When a man's motivation to achieve is aroused, accomplishment of the task will be its own best reward. The significance of achievement motivation revolves around this notion of self-reinforcing performance. When we speak of "self-motivated" men, we refer to men who are acting to satisfy their need to achieve.

It is not surprising that McClelland found high levels of achievement motivation associated with entrepreneurial behavior, innovative risk-taking, and business success.[1] Men with a high need to achieve ("high achievers") tend to:

1. Seek and assume high degrees of personal responsibility.
2. Take calculated risks.
3. Set challenging, but realistic goals for themselves.

---

\* Reprinted by permission from the November–December 1966 issue of *Personnel Administration.* Copyright 1966, Society for Personnel Administration, 485–87 National Press Building, 14th and F Streets, N.W., Washington, D.C. 20004.

[1] D. C. McClelland, *The Achieving Society* (Princeton, N.J.: D. Van Nostrand Company, Inc., 1961).

4. Develop comprehensive plans to help them attain their goals.
5. Seek and use concrete, measurable feedback of the results of their actions.
6. Seek out business opportunities where their desires to achieve will not be thwarted.

McClelland has also pointed out that environmental factors greatly influence achievement motivation.[2] . . . But what are the critical dimensions of the environment that influence motivation to achieve? Recent research has sought to answer this question.[3] The implications of this research, although tentative, seem clear. High achievers will be attracted to those business environments which offer

1. Personal responsibility for accomplishments.
2. Freedom to pursue goals by means of one's own choosing.
3. Prompt and unbiased feedback of the results of action.
4. Moderately risky situations.
5. Consistent rewards and recognition for jobs well done.

These climactic factors seem to stimulate achievement motivation in the individual. They add up to excitement and satisfaction.

## CLIMATE AND CONTROL

By creating the right kind of climate, managers can have a very definite impact on the achievement motivation of their subordinates. They can present these individuals with new sources of satisfaction and new opportunities to achieve, thereby arousing achievement motivation. Once aroused, achievement-oriented behavior will be self-rewarding. Thus, the manager need not exercise constant and forceful restraint on his subordinate's activities.

**EXHIBIT 1**

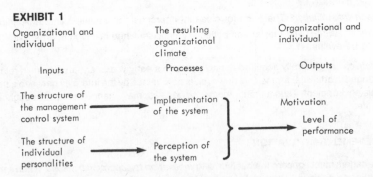

| Organizational and individual | The resulting organizational climate | Organizational and individual |
|---|---|---|
| Inputs | Processes | Outputs |

An important tool in the hands of management to influence the climate of their organizations and the motivation of their subordinates is the management control system. We will define control systems as those processes and structures by which managers assure that resources and energies are put to work serving the objectives of the organization.

Every individual interprets or perceives the control system differently, and therefore the concept of "organizational climate" is needed. When we speak of environmental influences on human motivation, we are referring to the perceived environment; that is, the climate. (See Exhibit 1.)

Climate is determined by the structure *and* the implementation of the control system, and the values and attitudes that each manager brings to the job of control. For example,

---

[2] D. C. McClelland, "Toward a Theory of Motive Acquisition," *American Psychologist,* May 1965 and "Achievement Motivation Can Be Developed," *Harvard Business Review,* November–December 1965.

[3] G. H. Litwin and R. A. Stringer, *Motivation and Organizational Climate* (Boston: Harvard Graduate School of Business Administration, Division of Research, 1968) and "The Influence of Organizational Climate on Human Motivation" unpublished monograph, 1966.

the managers in Division A might be sticklers for detail and insist on following the prescribed control procedures exactly. Managers in Division B, operating under a very similar structure, may choose to ignore a lot of the detailed rules or procedures. In this kind of organization, the two divisions may perform very differently. Why? The answers, on the surface, seem to be obvious. "People in Division A resent all the rules and regulations." Or, "Division B performs well because the workers are 'motivated' to do a better job."

Such explanations do not help the manager do his job better. Such explanations describe, rather than analyze, the causal factors involved. Analysis requires understanding. This article aims to provide a basis for better understanding of the dynamics of human motivation in work situations. We will present eight propositions about motivation to achieve.

It is assumed that there is a certain "base level" of motivation to achieve operative at the present time, but that the full potential of this achievement motivation is going unrealized. The basic strategy of these eight propositions is to program the management control processes in such a way that achievement-oriented behavior is reinforced and rewarded.

*Proposition 1. Achievement motivation will tend to be aroused if the goals of the responsibility center are made explicit.*

Achievement motivation, by definition, refers to competition with a standard of excellence. This standard may be internal (within the individual's own mind) or external (stated by the organization within which he works). By making external performance standards explicit, individuals can include them in their internal frame of reference. The specific goals and objectives of the responsibility center can become part of each individual's future plans. Personal achievement can be defined in terms of the yardsticks and measurements which are most important to the organization. . . . By making the quality standards explicit—both as to the specific level *and* the relative importance of other goals—achievement energies can be channeled into more useful pursuits.

*Proposition 2. Achievement motivation will tend to be aroused if goals represent a moderate degree of risk for the individuals involved.*

Individuals with high motivation prefer to work under conditions of moderate risk. That is, the subjective probabilities of success should be about 50–50. If goals seem to be speculative and the likelihood of success is very low, motivation to achieve will not be aroused. If the goals are too conservative and the likelihood of success is quite high, motivation will not be aroused. Moderately risky goals represent a continuing challenge, and it is this element of challenge that must be stated in the goals of the responsibility center and the goals of the individual.

Several alternatives are open to the manager in implementing this proposition. He may assess the chances of success and failure for his subordinates and impose a goal that, in his mind, seems like a moderately risky one. Or he may rely on his subordinate's judgment and opinion, and allow the subordinate some freedom in setting his goals. (See Exhibit 2.)

*Proposition 3. A higher level of achievement motivation will tend to be aroused if provision is made in the management control process for adjusting specific goals when the chances of goal-accomplishment change significantly (from the 50–50 level).*

The facts of business life are clear: environments are continually changing, and the chances of success change with each change in the environment. Even without any significant change in the environment, the odds of success may change as additional information about the tasks and the critical skills become known. A calculated risk in January may become an impossible goal by May.

To achieve flexibility, there are at least two alternatives open to management. First, the formal reward system could be adjusted to account for the risk elements of performance. Subordinates who succeeded in accomplishing goals that were judged to be 50–50 risks could be paid more than subordinates who worked toward conservative or speculative goals. A second alternative could be to have a provision for systematic review and adjustment of goals when the odds of success deviate significantly from the 50–50 criteria.

The second alternative is the most desirable. By providing for changes in the individual and responsibility center goals, the control process will be facilitating the development of achievement motivation. By forcing managers and their subordinates to examine their objec-

**EXHIBIT 2**

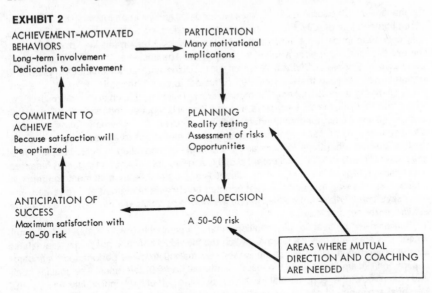

ACHIEVEMENT–MOTIVATED
BEHAVIORS
Long–term involvement
Dedication to achievement

PARTICIPATION
Many motivational
implications

COMMITMENT TO
ACHIEVE
Because satisfaction will
be optimized

PLANNING
Reality testing
Assessment of risks
Opportunities

ANTICIPATION OF
SUCCESS
Maximum satisfaction with
50–50 risk

GOAL DECISION
A 50–50 risk

AREAS WHERE MUTUAL
DIRECTION AND COACHING
ARE NEEDED

tives and by insisting that these objectives remain challenging (that is, with 50–50 odds of accomplishment), the entire climate of the organization can be injected with new excitement and achievement.

*Proposition 4.    Achievement motivation will tend to be aroused if managers are evaluated in terms of their goal-setting behaviors.*

Because of the central importance of goal-setting, the creation of an achieving climate will be furthered by zeroing in on this activity when evaluating individual managers.

We are not suggesting that managers be rewarded in proportion to their *performance* compared to the degree of risk (this idea was rejected in 3). Rather, we are suggesting that they be rewarded for setting moderately risky goals.

*Proposition 5.    Achievement motivation will tend to be aroused if individuals are given feedback of the progress they are making toward their goals.*

Empirical research has found that high achievers characteristically desire concrete feedback of the results of their actions. This feedback not only gives them achievement satisfaction, but it helps them plan ahead and set more realistic goals in the future. Further proof of this point is that high achievers tend to *seek* jobs which provide for immediate and tangible feedback, such as sales positions.

Several aspects of performance feedback are especially important. It should be (*a*) prompt, (*b*) unbiased, and (*c*) relevant. The implications of these aspects of the feedback process on management control are far-reaching.

*        *        *        *        *

*Proposition 6.    Achievement motivation will tend to be aroused if there is a climate that emphasizes individual responsibility.*

High achievers seek success, and unless they can plainly see that their success is truly theirs, little achievement satisfaction can be gained. To increase the opportunity for achievement satisfactions, the organization must place a premium on the assumption of personal responsibility at all levels of management.

In both the goal-setting and performance review process, a climate of responsibility will be created if (1) there is a "results orientation" and (2) there is sufficient "coaching." By focusing on the desired results, the entire achievement syndrome is forced upon the manager, for a *results orientation focuses on those aspects of the subordinate's behavior which are critical to his personal achievement and the achievement of the firm.* Other issues will be placed in secondary positions.

*Proposition 7. Achievement motivation will be aroused if the rewards and punishments formally provided for as part of the management control system are perceived as consistent with achievement goals.*

One consequence of the development of high levels of achievement motivation is that achievement itself becomes the most important reward. High achievers derive most of their satisfaction out of doing a good job, not out of receiving the external rewards associated with success. Formal organizational rewards are important, however, for they satisfy other personal needs and they may *symbolize success.* Thus, careful control of organizational rewards and punishments may be useful in arousing achievement.

Researchers have found that high achievers *expect to be punished* when they fail to achieve their goals. Such expectations seem to make success all the more satisfying. If organizations fail to discriminate between success and failure, or if punishments are not associated with failure to accomplish results, the entire reward system will have relatively little effect on achievement.

The fourth consideration raises important theoretical and practical questions. Rewards and punishments should be dispensed to individuals, not to groups or responsibility centers.

When rewards are given to groups rather than to individuals, personal accomplishments may be buried, making it difficult to arouse entrepreneurial spirit. A formal reward system built around individual rewards for individual accomplishments is more consistent with the six preceding propositions.

*Proposition 8. Achievement motivation will tend to be increased when there is a climate of mutual support and encouragement.*

The theoretical support for this proposition goes beyond the relatively simple concepts of achievement motivation that have been presented earlier. Briefly, it has been found that the motive, Fear of Failure (or Need to Avoid Failure), debilitates motivation to achieve. A high level of the failure motive will proportionately weaken the resultant achievement motivation.

The creation of a supportive climate tends to reduce anxiety and negate many of the dysfunctional effects that anxiety is likely to have on continued high performance. To stimulate achievement motivation, support must be task-oriented. If task-related support and encouragement is stressed, the entire organizational climate can become "self-generating." That is, *mutual support* will act as a powerful reinforcement device. Coaching, helping, informal encouragements, and other reciprocal supportive relationships can solidify the arousal effects of propositions 1 through 7.

\*     \*     \*     \*     \*

## REFERENCES

Atkinson, John W., ed. *Motives in Fantasy, Action, and Society.* Princeton, N.J.: D. Van Nostrand Company, Inc., 1958.

————. *An Introduction to Motivation.* New York: American Book Company, 1964.

Litwin, George H., and Stringer, Robert A., Jr. *Motivation and Organizational Climate.* Boston: Division of Research, Graduate School of Business Administration, Harvard University, 1968).

McClelland, David C. *The Achieving Society.* Princeton, N. J.: D. Van Nostrand Company, Inc., 1969.

McClelland, David C., and David G. Winter. *Motivating Economic Achievement.* New York: The Free Press, 1969.

Patchen, Martin. *Participation, Achievement, and Involvement on the Job.* Englewood Cliffs, N.J.: Prentice-Hall, Inc., 1970.

From

# MANAGEMENT BY OBJECTIVES: THE TEAM APPROACH*

## By Wendell L. French and Robert W. Hollmann

Study of the many books, articles, case studies, speeches, and discussions about management by objectives (MBO) indicates that most forms of this approach tend to reinforce a one-to-one leadership style. It is also apparent that MBO efforts vary from being highly autocratic to highly participative among organizations and even within some organizations. In this article we present a case and strategy for *collaborative* management by objectives (CMBO), a participative, team-centered approach. . . .

### One-to-One MBO

Let us first compare the autocratic and participative characteristics of one-to-one versions of MBO. Examples 1a through 1d in Table 1 illustrate how this form can differ along the autocratic-participative continuum. . . .

### Deficiencies in One-to-One MBO

Disregarding the likely long-range inadequacies of any autocratic form of MBO, we believe that the one-to-one mode has a number of critical deficiencies. First, one-to-one MBO does not adequately account for the interdependent nature of most jobs, particularly at the managerial and supervisory levels. Second, it does not assure optimal coordination of objectives. And third, it does not always improve superior-subordinate relationships, as is widely claimed by MBO proponents (we do not know whether a team approach always will improve relations either, but we are much more optimistic about the latter). These deficiencies pertain to all versions of one-to-one MBO, regardless of how autocratic or participative, although we believe that the deficiencies would be more salient under autocratic supervisory behavior. . . .

*Managerial Interdependence.* A number of writers have pointed out that one-to-one, superior-subordinate MBO does not recognize the interdependent or complementary nature of managerial jobs.[1] We concur with this criticism and believe that effective implementation of MBO requires a "systems view" of the organization. Each manager functions in a complex network of vertical, horizontal, and diagonal relationships, and his success in achieving his objectives is often (if not always) dependent upon the communication, cooperation, and support of other managers in this network.

\*    \*    \*    \*    \*

*Coordination of Objectives.* Another deficiency is associated with this interdependency. One of the highly touted advantages of MBO is that it results in effective coordination

* © 1975 by The Regents of the University of California. Reprinted from *California Management Review,* vol. 17, no. 3, pp. 13–22 (excerpts), by permission of The Regents.

[1] See, for example, Gerard F. Carvalho, "Installing Management by Objectives: A New Perspective on Organization Change," *Human Resource Management,* Spring 1972, pp. 23–30; Robert A. Howell, "A Fresh Look at Management by Objectives," *Business Horizons,* Fall 1967, pp. 51–58; Charles L. Hughes, "Assessing the Performance of Key Managers," *Personnel,* January–February 1968, pp. 38–43; Bruce D. Jamieson, "Behavioral Problems with Management by Objectives," *Academy of Management Journal,* September 1973, pp. 496–505; Harold Koontz, "Making Managerial Appraisal Effective," *California Management Review,* Winter 1972, pp. 46–55; and Harry Levinson, "Management by Whose Objectives?" *Harvard Business Review,* July–August 1970, pp. 125–34.

**TABLE 1**
**Objective Setting in Different Versions of MBO**

| Degree of Subordinate Influence on Objectives | Very Little | Some | Moderate | Considerable |
|---|---|---|---|---|
| Individual orientation | 1a<br>Superior prepares list of subordinate's objectives and gives it to subordinate. | 1b<br>Superior prepares list of subordinate's objectives; allows opportunity for clarification and suggestions. | 1c<br>Subordinate prepares list of his objectives; superior-subordinate discussion of tentative list is followed by editing, modification, and finalization by superior. | 1d<br>Superior and subordinate independently prepare list of subordinate's objectives; mutual agreement reached after extensive dialogue. |
| Team orientation | 2a<br>Superior prepares individual lists of various subordinates' objectives; hands out lists in group meeting and explains objectives. | 2b<br>Superior prepares unit and individual objectives; allows opportunity for questions and suggestions in group meeting. | 2c<br>Superior prepares list of unit objectives which are discussed in group meeting; superior decides. Subordinates then prepare lists of their objectives, discuss with superior; individuals' objectives discussed in team meeting with modifications made by superior after extensive dialogue. | 2d<br>Unit-objectives, including team effectiveness goals, are developed among superior, subordinates, and peers in a group meeting, usually by consensus; superior and subordinates later independently prepare lists of subordinates' objectives, reach temporary agreement; subordinates' objectives finalized after extensive discussion in team meeting. |

of objectives; that is, there is better integration (including minimization of gaps and duplication) of the objectives of all managers in the work unit. While this is certainly a desirable benefit, it must be recognized that one-to-one MBO places the responsibility for such coordination entirely upon the superior, since he is the only person in the MBO process to have formal contact with all subordinate managers. In effect, the superior is required to function as a "central processing center of objectives."

We believe that one-to-one MBO simply does not provide the opportunity for maximum coordination of objectives. The superior may be able to marginally, or even adequately, coordinate the objectives of his immediate subordinates on a one-to-one basis, but this procedure does not really do justice to the subtleties of interdependent relationships. Under such circumstances, except for information transmitted informally and sporadically between peers in on-the-job interaction, subordinate managers have little knowledge or understanding of each other's objectives. On the other hand, if these subordinates were provided with the opportunity for dynamic interactive processes in which their objectives are systematically communicated and adjusted, final objectives probably would be more effectively coordinated.

The deficiency in the coordination of objectives is magnified in cases of managers performing highly interrelated tasks but working in different departments. For example, a sales manager in a marketing division organized along product lines needs to coordinate his objectives with those of the appropriate production manager responsible for manufacturing the product. . . .

*Improved Superior-Subordinate Relationships.* The participative, or mutual involvement, form of one-to-one MBO is extolled largely for the improvement in superior-subordinate relationships it is expected to bring about. Not all research supports this claim, however. For example, Tosi and Carroll found that even after an intensive and carefully planned MBO program that stressed subordinate participation, subordinate managers did not feel that the superior-subordinate relationship had improved significantly in terms of helpfulness on the part of the superior.[2] . . .

Kerr believes that the typical organization hierarchy creates a superior-subordinate status differential that acts as a deterrent to the expected improvement in relationships.[3] For instance, when MBO is conducted in a somewhat autocratic manner the status differential inhibits the subordinate from challenging the decisions of his boss or the objectives he has established. Even in cases of greater subordinate involvement, status differences may hinder attainment of the desired ideal mutuality in the MBO process. A similar note is struck by Levinson, who believes that rivalry between a boss and his subordinate can easily impede the creation or maintenance of a positive relationship.[4] . . .

Incompatibility between the superior's role as a coach and his role as a judge may also hamper the superior-subordinate relationship. Researchers at The General Electric Company concluded that the two primary purposes of performance appraisal (performance improvement and salary adjustment) are in conflict.[5] They suggested that these two purposes could be better accomplished in two separate interviews—a proposal with which we agree. Yet even in this approach, it is easy to see the difficult position in which the superior is placed: prior to and during one interview he is expected to *constructively* evaluate the subordinate's performance and help him formulate plans for improvement, while in the second interview he is expected to *judiciously* evaluate the subordinate's performance in order to make crucial salary recommendations and to inform the subordinate of his decision. Only an exceptionally talented person could shift adroitly between these two roles (especially with the same subordinate), and it is our opinion that most managers have great difficulty doing so. Thus, an MBO program that requires the superior to have complete responsibility in performing these incompatible roles, even in separate interviews, could easily strain rather than improve superior-subordinate relationships.

## Team Collaboration in MBO

We believe that MBO could be strengthened considerably by increasing the opportunities for systematic collaboration among managers. Furthermore, MBO programs based on coop-

---

[2] Henry Tosi and Stephen J. Carroll, Jr., "Improving Management by Objectives: A Diagnostic Change Program," *California Management Review,* Fall 1973, pp. 57–66.

[3] Steven Kerr, "Some Modifications in MBO as an OD Strategy," *Proceedings,.1972 Annual Meeting,* Academy of Management, 1973, pp. 39–42.

[4] Harry Levinson, "Management by Objectives: A Critique," *Training and Development Journal,* April 1972, pp. 3–8; see also Levinson, "Management by Whose Objectives."

[5] Herbert H. Meyer, Emanual Kay, and John R. P. French, Jr., "Split Roles in Performance Appraisal," *Harvard Business Review,* January–February 1965, pp. 123–29.

**TABLE 2**
**Traditional MBO Compared with OD**

| *What Traditional (One-to-One) MBO Seems to Do* | *What OD Seems to Do* |
|---|---|
| 1. Assumes there is a need for more goal emphasis and/or control. | 1. Assumes there may be a variety of problems; a need for more goal emphasis and/or control may or may not be a central problem. |
| 2. Has no broad diagnostic strategy. | 2. Uses an "action research" model in which system diagnosis and rediagnosis are major features. |
| 3. Central target of change is the individual. | 3. Central target of change is team functioning. |
| 4. Asks organization members to develop objectives for key aspects of their jobs in terms of quantitative and qualitative statements that can be measured. | 4. Asks organization members to provide data regarding their perceptions of functional/dysfunctional aspects of their units and/or the total organization. |
| 5. Emphasizes avoidance of overlap and incongruity of goals. Assumes things will be better if people understand who has what territory. | 5. Emphasizes mutual support and help. Assumes that some problems can stem from confusion about who has what responsibilities, but also looks at opportunities for mutual help in the many interdependent components across jobs. |
| 6. Focuses on the "formal" aspects of the organization (goals, planning, control, appraisal). | 6. Initially taps into "informal" aspects of the organization (attitudes, feelings, perceptions about both the formal and informal aspects—the total climate of the unit or organization). |
| 7. Focuses on individual performance and emphasizes individual accountability. | 7. Focuses on system dynamics that are facilitating or handicapping individual, team, and organizational performance; emphasizes joint accountability. |
| 8. Stresses rationality ("logical" problem solving, man's economic motives). | 8. Legitimizes for discussion nonrational aspects (feelings, attitudes, group phenomena) of organization life as well as rationality; frequently legitimizes open exploration of career and life goals. |
| 9. Focuses on organizational end results of the human-social system (particularly as measured by "hard data") such as sales figures, maintenance costs, and so forth. | 9. Focuses on both ends and means of the human-social system (leadership style, peer relationships, and decision processes, as well as goals and "hard data"). |
| 10. Has little interpersonal-relations "technology" to assist superior and subordinate in the goal-setting and review processes. | 10. Has extensive interpersonal relations, group dynamics, and intergroup "technology" for decision making, communications, and group task and maintenance processes. |

erative teamwork and group problem solving would represent a positive step toward rectifying some of the deficiencies found in one-to-one MBO. . . .

*    *    *    *    *

. . . There are MBO programs that include systematic collaboration as an integral part of the entire process (see example 2d in Table 1). . . . In this program each team (superior and his immediate subordinates) concentrates on such matters as team-effectiveness areas, team-improvement objectives, team decision making, optimal team organization, team meeting improvements, team-effectiveness evaluation, and team-member effectiveness. Such collaborative approaches appear to have many features congruent with contemporary organization development (OD) and are qualitatively quite different from one-to-one approaches.

## MBO and OD Contrasted

One way to describe how CMBO differs qualitatively from a one-to-one approach is to contrast the one-to-one version with the emerging field of OD, which has a strong emphasis on team collaboration. Organization development in the behavioral-science meaning of the term[6] is a broader strategy for organizational improvement than is MBO, but it can include the collaborative version as we shall describe it. . . .

Some of the differences, as we see them, between the traditional one-to-one MBO and OD are shown in Table 2. . . .

. . . We would like to propose a nine-phase strategy for Collaborative MBO. Basically, the essential process is one of overlapping work units interacting with "higher" and "lower" units on overall organizational goals and objectives, unit goals and objectives, and individuals interacting with peers and superiors on role definition and individual goals and objectives.

*    *    *    *    *

## The Merits of CMBO: Research and Practice Clues

There are a number of clues to the merits of a Collaborative MBO approach (that is, the kind that has a team emphasis, is truly collaborative, and exists in a climate of mutual support and help) in research reports and in practice. . . .

Another recent study found that managers' perceptions of the supportiveness of the organizational climate and their attitudes toward MBO were significantly related.[7] A supportive climate was viewed in terms of such features as high levels of trust and confidence between superiors and subordinates, multidirectional communication aimed at achieving objectives, cooperative teamwork, subordinate participation in decision making and goal-setting, and control conducted close to the point of performance (self-control). Essentially, this climate was seen as comparable to Likert's Participative Group (System 4) management system.[8] The results of the study showed significant ($p < 0.01$) positive correlations between the supportiveness of the climate and how effective managers believed the MBO process to be. Managers' evaluations of MBO effectiveness were assessed in six areas: (1) planning and organizing work, (2) objective evaluation of performance, (3) motivation of the best job performance, (4) coordination of individual and work-group objectives, (5) superior-subordinate communication, and (6) superior-subordinate cooperation. Even more important was the significant ($p < 0.01$) positive correlation between supportiveness of the climate and managers' overall satisfaction with MBO as it related to their jobs.[9]

*    *    *    *    *

[6] Wendell French and Cecil H. Bell, Jr., *Organization Development: Behavioral Science Interventions for Organization Improvement* (Englewood Cliffs, N.J.: Prentice-Hall, Inc., 1973), p. 15.

[7] Robert W. Hollmann, "A Study of the Relationships between Organizational Climate and Managerial Assessment of Management by Objectives," unpublished Ph.D. dissertation, University of Washington, 1973.

[8] Rensis Likert, *New Patterns of Management* (New York: McGraw-Hill Book Co., 1961).

[9] Hollmann, "A Study of Relationships."

**FIGURE 1**
**A Strategy for Implementing Collaborative Management by Objectives**

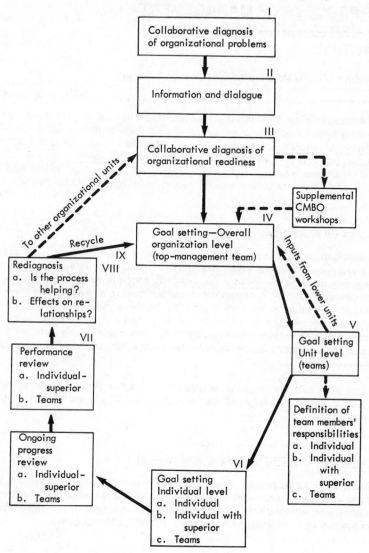

*From*

# THE PROCESS OF MANAGEMENT: CONCEPTS, BEHAVIOR, AND PRACTICE*

*By William H. Newman and Charles E. Summer*

"Participation in decision-making," however, usually has a specific meaning: that when formulating a plan, a manager draws on the ideas of his subordinates and others who will be affected by the plan. . . . Normally, there is a face-to-face discussion of a problem so that a free exchange of ideas can take place. This kind of participation requires, of course, that all participants—manager and subordinates—share a belief that the final plan will be better because the ideas of two or more persons are integrated into the decision.

\*    \*    \*    \*    \*

## DEGREES OF PARTICIPATION

A manager does not simply choose to use, or not to use, participation. In practice, we find varying degrees of influence by subordinates on decisions. Participation on a specific problem may fall anywhere between two extremes: complete delegation of the problem to a subordinate or complete centralization of decision-making, whereby the manager merely announces his conclusion and tries to get subordinates to carry out the plan. The degree of participation depends on (*a*) who initiates ideas; (*b*) how completely a subordinate carries out each phase of decision-making—diagnosing, finding alternatives, estimating consequences, and making the choice; and (*c*) how much weight an executive attaches to the ideas he receives. . . .

\*    \*    \*    \*    \*

When more than one person participates in making a decision, we often obtain these advantages: diverse knowledge, different viewpoints and biases, and complementary decision-making skills.

\*    \*    \*    \*    \*

## RECOGNIZING WHEN PARTICIPATION IS FEASIBLE

Participation is effective only when a manager is skillful in selecting problems that call for it and when he determines the degree of participation that is appropriate for the people who will be involved. No simple rule will tell him just when to utilize this potentially powerful technique, but we can identify several factors that will be helpful guides.

### Time Available for Decision

Participation requires a suggestion by one person (say, Frank), consideration of the idea by a second person (John), and John's verbal reaction to Frank. This sequence will probably be followed by a discussion of John's ideas, further consideration by Frank, and so on. Such *interaction* takes *time.*

Time can be costly in two ways: It *may* result in a decision that comes too late for strategic

---

* William H. Newman and Charles E. Summer, *The Process of Management: Concepts, Behavior, and Practice* © 1961. Reprinted by permission of Prentice-Hall, Inc., Englewood Cliffs, N.J. (Excerpts from pp. 439–48.)

effectiveness and it *always* involves an expenditure of human energies. If a crude oil pipeline breaks down, the man in charge of maintaining a flow of raw materials to the refinery served by the pipeline must act fast to arrange alternative sources of supply. At most, he has only brief consultations with other people, and he must brush aside a detailed examination of the best possible sources in making sure that the refinery can continue to operate without interruption. Participation would mean costly delays. In the following example, too, time for joint action would have meant money lost. The president of a U.S. manufacturing concern discovered on a visit to Australia that the company's sales agent was so ineffective that its reputation was suffering and new competitors were likely to enter the field. He immediately set up a new distribution arrangement while he was on the local scene without waiting to consult with his associates back home. Some toes were stepped on in the process, but everyone recognized that decisive action was more valuable in this circumstance than joint participation that would have delayed a reorganization for at least several months.

Even when there is no emergency pressure, the time required for participation may be a serious obstacle to its use. . . .

*     *     *     *     *

### Avoiding Motivational Deadlocks

A manager should think about the interests of each person he consults on a problem. The president of a chemical company, for example, was trying to decide whether the company should stop producing its own wooden boxes to pack chemicals for shipment. The Package Division of this company was large, employing 600 people—it comprised a box factory and a logging operation that cut trees to produce the boxes. In this case, the vice president in charge of the division had no experience in chemical manufacture, nor did his age and qualifications fit him for an executive position other than managing timber operations and the production of boxes and barrels. Because of the vice president's motivations and capacities, it would have been unreasonable for the president to say sincerely to this man, in effect, "Harold, we are thinking of closing up your division. I'd be greatly interested in your helping us gather facts and marshal reasons about whether this ought to be done."

Such a conflict between personal interests and company interests often arises in long-range planning. When a man has devoted his entire career to a particular product or function and has deep convictions about the importance of the activity, it may be impossible for him to think objectively and logically about a drastic curtailment of the activity or about merging it into a completely new organization structure. Once a decision has been made to move in a general direction, and a man affected by the decision has been able to reconcile himself with the inevitable, he may become a valuable participant in planning the transition. . . .

### Capacity and Willingness to Contribute

A third criterion we should pay attention to when we decide whether participation is desirable deals with the characteristics of potential participants. For instance, high *mental ability* is desirable. A participant need not be exceptional in all respects, but he needs strength in at least one of the following intellectual qualities: originality, penetrating analysis, good memory, or balanced judgment. Participation for unintelligent subordinates clearly must be restricted to limited phases of simple problems.

We have already noted that some people face new problems realistically, whereas others have a habit of withdrawing from problems, dreaming rosy dreams, becoming unduly pessimistic, failing to face facts, or resorting to other defensive mechanisms. The more *realistic* a person is, the more likely he is to be a helpful participant.

*Self-confidence* also helps make a good participant. A man with confidence in his own ideas feels freer to express them to his boss and other senior officials, even though his views may not be in harmony with what already has been said. In contrast, a highly dependent person who typically looks to others for help in solving problems is unlikely to provide fresh ideas. Moreover, such a dependent person often gets trapped by a feeling that opposition to views of a supervisor is a sign of disloyalty. Yes-men are of little help in the process of participation.

A particular problem may be so far removed from chief interests of subordinates that they are not *willing to devote effort* to participating in its solution. . . .

\*    \*    \*    \*    \*

## Economic Realities

The economic facts of life may dictate a course of action, and for a manager to invite his subordinates to consider whether that action should be taken would be near chicanery. Much research is being devoted to devising electronic machines that will sort and post checks in a bank; if a machine is developed that will cut costs of these operations in half, we should not ask the clerks now performing the operation to help us decide whether to install the new equipment. We might well seek their advice on a program of transition from the existing method to the new one, but for them the adoption of a new method should simply be treated as a given premise.

\*    \*    \*    \*    \*

## Aid to Voluntary Cooperation

Certainly in thinking about when to use participation we should also consider how much it will develop voluntary cooperation among those who actively share in the decision-making process. The participants will have an opportunity for self-expression, an increased sense of security, and the satisfaction of being an important part of a group. Such feelings foster cooperation.

Voluntary cooperation, however, should be regarded simply as a by-product. If participation cannot be justified in terms of wiser decisions, we do not recommend its use. When participation is used merely as a motivational device, employees are led to believe that their ideas are being solicited sincerely, but in fact the soliciting executive has little or no real interest in their suggestions. Such an executive will at most half-heartedly make use of the ideas. Sooner or later, the employees will sense that what is being done under the guise of participation is an attempt to maneuver them to support management's ideas and decisions. . . .

# 8. CONTINENTAL ELECTRIC COMPANY

---

# Case Introduction

---

## SYNOPSIS

The Continental Electric Company is organized by relatively autonomous product divisions for the manufacture and sale of a diverse number of electrical products. Top company management has a set of goals on which the performance of division managers is evaluated. There is a difference of opinion between top management and Mr. North, manager of the Electric Motor Division, as to whether the division has performed up to standard in the past. At the same time, Mr. North and his technical staff are faced with a choice between three investments in new technological innovation. He must recommend one of these to meet performance standards in the future. Various opinions and technical data are used to try to choose which capital investment to make.

## WHY THIS CASE IS INCLUDED

This case offers opportunity to look at the philosophy of the decentralized form of organization—what advantages it *should* have for both technological excellence and human motivation. However, the details of making decentralization work, both from a financial and a human standpoint, are not so simple as the philosophy indicates.

Particularly important are conflicts between objectives at any one time, conflicts of long- versus short-run objectives, the perceptions of human beings of the "facts" they see in attaining objectives, and the problem of generalist executives who balance objectives but who also must obtain highly technical information from staff specialists.

The case offers opportunity to understand some concepts of financial management—the relation of profits, cash flows, and time—and the relation of long-term to short-run profits.

Finally, as an advanced project, this case provides opportunity to test the place of "management science" or quantification in the coordination (concurrence, governance, agreement, etc.) of human beings in organizations. To what extent does quantification produce agreement? To what extent does it result in the *authority of fact* as opposed to the *authority of sentiment, authority of personal judgment,* or *authority of power?*

## DIAGNOSTIC AND PREDICTIVE QUESTIONS

The readings included with this case are marked (*). The author index at the end of this book locates the other readings.

1. What has the top management tried to achieve by organizing the company by product divisions rather than by functional divisions (manufacturing, sales, etc.)? Illustrate with facts from the case as to how management expects this organization will (should) affect the actions of North and his staff, as well as the economic and technical performance of the Electric Motor Division.

Read:   *Curtice, "General Motors Organization Philosophy and Structure." *Shillinglaw, *Cost Accounting.* Vancil "What Kind of Management Control Do You Need?"

2. From the viewpoint of setting economic and financial objectives, why do Richardson and Grundy view North's performance as unsatisfactory, while North views his own performance as realistic?

Read:   *Drucker, *The Practice of Management.*

3. From the two concepts of "cash flow" and "rate of return," why might Linz and Donat disagree on whether to charge the cost of the patent to current expenses or to charge it to investment?

Read:   Linz' explanation of cash flow, Exhibit 3. Anthony, *Management Accounting.* Also relate to Drucker, Question 2.

4. From the viewpoint of psychology—concepts of structural and functional factors in perception—what is causing the viewpoint of top management to differ from that of North in judging the quality of performance of the Motor Division?

Read:   *Leavitt, *Managerial Psychology,* pp. 22–26.

5. From the viewpoint of sociology—personalities of line and technical executives, and sources of authority in organizations—what might cause friction between North and Glass if the latter's project is not accepted? If we view North as a specialist on motors and Richardson as a generalist over all products, is this also true between these two "line" executives?

Read:   *Etzioni, "Authority Structure and Organizational Effectiveness."

6. Suppose the only criterion for selecting investment projects were the total profit to the company generated over the life of the project. What advantage would this have? What limitations? Which project would be selected?

7. Suppose that the only criterion for capital investment were the *average* rate of return per year from the project. What advantage would this have over the total dollar return (Question 6)? What does average

rate have to do with the payback period from each project? Which project would be selected:

Study:   The method for determining total profit, and average return, Exhibits 2, 4, 5.

8. Actually, Dr. Glass objected to the average rate of return as a selection criterion for investment projects. Examine his project, particularly the method of figuring the average. If you were in his shoes, why would you object? What factor does it leave out?

Read:   This question has to do with the limitations of an *average* as representing a series of numbers. Look at the series of yearly profits in Exhibit 5, and see why the average figure may be misleading. For those interested, review the use of the average as a statistical measure in any introductory statistics text.

## POLICY QUESTIONS

9. Which project is the best for long-run profits of Continental? Which project is best for shorter run profits?

10. Suppose you want a criterion for selecting investment projects which would measure the worth of a project—that would select between the three taking into consideration both payback period *and* amounts. What would you use, and which project would be best?

Read:   *Lewis, *Financial Controls for Management.* *Horngren, *Accounting for Management Control,* pp. 356–63, 365–68.

11. If you were North, which project would you recommend? Would this be based on (*a*) what is best for the company as a whole? (*b*) What is best for the Motor Division? (*c*) What is best for you as an employed executive in the company? How do these differ? (Think of case facts, plus the readings in Questions 1–5.)

12. From the viewpoint of both accuracy in the decision (deciding on what is best for the technology and finance of the company) and from the viewpoint of human motivation (the morale and learning of North, his staff, and top management), what methods are available for setting the financial criteria for investments, and for selecting the right project? How would these work in this case?

Read:   Newman and Summer, *The Process of Management: Concepts, Behavior, and Practice.* *McGregor, *The Human Side of Enterprise.* *Enell and Haas, *Setting Standards for Executive Performance.*

# Case Text*

## COMPANY BACKGROUND AND ORGANIZATION

Continental Electric Company is a leading producer of a wide variety of electrical products. Organizationally, it is divided into three major product groups specializing in (1) consumer products—television sets, radios, kitchen appliances, and so on; (2) industrial products—generators, motors, transformers, and so on; and (3) military products—radar and communications equipment, missile parts, and so on.

Each of these major product groups, headed by a vice president, is in turn divided into a number of related product divisions. For example, within the consumer product group there is a lighting division which produces a wide range of lamps and bulbs. There are 16 such product divisions in the company, and each is headed by a division general manager.

Since 1950, when this organization structure was adopted, the corporate management of Continental has sought to make each of the 16 divisions a semiautonomous business. (See Exhibit 1).

Edward M. Richardson, company president, described the philosophy of his organization's structure as follows:

> Along with the many benefits which come with long-scale business operation one of the most serious drawbacks can be the loss of entrepreneurial drive. . . . The organization structure of Continental Electric is designed to divide our big business into 16 little businesses. Each of my 16 general managers thinks of himself as the president of a small business. . . .
>
> Each is responsible for the long-run success of his business.
>
> *     *     *     *     *
>
> We guide the divisions by defining their broad responsibilities, or missions, in terms of total corporate goals. Within these broad guidelines they are on their own. To be sure, division performance is evaluated regularly in terms of short- and long-range criteria.
>
> These criteria are:
>
> 1.  Profitability:
>     a.  Net profit before taxes: Each division computes this for corporate review just as the company as a whole computes its income statement for stockholders' review.
>     b.  Rate of return: Net income as a percent of division assets. Again top corporate management receives the same kind of

---

figures from the divisions as the corporation must present to its stockholders.

2. Market Share: The division's percent of total industry sales.
3. Product Leadership: The degree to which the division maintains and increases the company's reputation as a technological leader in the electrical products industry.
4. Utilization of Human Resources: A series of measures are used to determine the morale and effective utilization of the division's work force.
5. Corporate Citizenship: A series of measures are used to determine whether the division is meeting its responsibilities in terms of local, state, and national needs.

Mr. Richardson went on to explain that the divisions are reviewed formally by their respective group vice presidents on a quarterly basis and annually by the corporate review board. Chaired by Richardson, the review board is made up of the company's executive vice president. F. L. Taylor, the vice president of finance, George M. Retenbush and the vice president of corporate staff, Paul D. Faust. The secretary of the board is William Lavanger who is also chief counsel.

**EXHIBIT 1**
**Relevant Portion of Organization Chart**

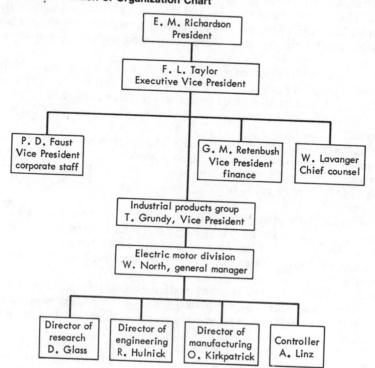

In addition to reviewing division performance, the review board also has final say on budget requests. In accord with the philosophy of decentralization, each division sets its own sales targets and develops its requests for operating funds and capital needed for more permanent divisional investments. In addition to a detailed one-year budget, the divisions also prepare three-year sales and profit forecasts which serve as a backdrop to the annual plan.

Sales targets and budget requests are reviewed by the divisions' respective group vice presidents. The group vice president does not have the authority to change the division's proposals but since he does have the authority to change divisional personnel he can exert some informal pressure if he feels that sales goals or cash requirements are out of line. However, since the success or failure of top division management is closely correlated to divisional performance, the group vice presidents tend to interfere as little as possible with division plans as long as performance is good and expectations promising.

As one group vice president put it, "The proof of who's right and who's wrong is profits. We try to let the divisions run their own show and then they stand or fall on their own decisions."

## ELECTRIC MOTOR DIVISION

The Electric Motor Division produces a variety of small fractional and one-horsepower motors. Roughly 40 percent of the division's output is sold to other divisions of Continental which use small motors in their products. The remaining 60 percent is sold to outside companies some of which use the motors in products competing with Continental products.

The "sales" within the company are made at a price based on manufacturing cost plus 8 percent markup. By way of contrast, the division's profit margin on sales to outside customers has been between 12 percent and 14 percent over full cost (manufacturing plus selling and corporate overhead).

The general manager of the Electric Motor Division, William North, is 46 years old. He has been with the company for 14 years and has been manager of the Electric Motor Division for the past five years. His performance after three years in this post was regarded by Richardson as excellent.

"We were really pleased with the way Bill improved a division that had many problems in the past," Richardson said, "and we felt at that time that in a few years Bill was slated for even bigger responsibilities. Unfortunately his last two years as divisional manager have not been as successful."

In 1961 the division fell short of realizing its estimated profit level by 18 percent. Total sales were estimated at $12 million, and the profit forecast was for $1,250,000. Actual sales came to $11,860,000, but profit was only $1,025,000.

On the basis of three-quarter results it is almost certain that the Electric Motor Division sales will rise in 1962 to the $12,300,000 level which was forecast in the profit plan for 1962. In addition, it seems equally likely that the profit objective of $1,250,000 will be met. However, Thomas Grundy, group vice president of industrial products, is not overly pleased with the division's anticipated performance in 1962.

Grundy stated:

"When Bill North took over the Electric Motor Division, we all saw bigger things in store for him. His performance from 1958–60 confirmed our confidence in him. However, in 1961 things seemed to turn sour, and this year it looks as though he will meet his profit forecast only by virtue of having reduced division expectations below what they should have been. While his sales and profits goals are higher than last year's results, they are not high enough. I warned him when he submitted his 1962 plan that I thought he should set his sights higher, but the bad year in 1961 must have scared him.

Therefore, I can't get very excited about his 1962 results for even if he reaches his objectives, I feel they were too conservative to begin with. I hope Bill is willing to present a more optimistic profit outlook for his division in 1963. If he sets his goals high enough and reaches them, he may find himself promoted in 1964. If he plays it too conservatively or fails to show a better profit picture, we'll be forced to reconsider his future with Continental.

When asked whether he had informed North about his feelings, Grundy replied, "I think Bill knows where he stands. Of course, I can't promise him anything if he does a good job nor do I want to unnerve him with threats. However, if he is the kind of executive we hope he is, he should understand his position."

When questioned about his division's performance over the past two years, North made the following observations:

Our sales and profit forecasts for 1961 reflected an anticipation on our part of wide acceptance of a new half-horsepower motor designed especially for use in lawn mowers. Doug Glass, division director of research, and Ralph Hulnick, director of engineering, did a wonderful job on the design and development of the motor. Unfortunately, in order to research projected sales targets we had to spend more than anticipated to get market acceptance. This, along with a three-week work stoppage due to a wildcat strike, pushed our operating costs above our estimates and accounted for most of the 18 percent discrepancy between projected and actual profits.

I explained this to the review board and indicated that the increased marketing expenditures would pay off in future years sales and that the stoppage was a result of a labor problem I had inherited from the previous general manager. They seemed to accept my position, but Mr. Richardson also reminded me that "you can't run a business on tomorrow's profits or yesterday's mistakes." Somehow I don't think I got through to them.

Our 1962 profit forecast may have been lower than Tom Grundy would have liked, but I think results showed our estimates to be realistic.

## DIVISION PLANS FOR 1963

In developing the 1963 profit plan for the Electric Motor Division, Mr. North is faced with a decision on three proposals for substantial capital investment put to him by his staff. Because of the size of the outlays, North feels he cannot propose more than one of these projects to corporate management.

*Proposal No. 1: Purchase of a Patent on Component Part.* The first proposal under consideration is one of several submitted by Ralph Hulnick, divisional director of engineering. All of Hulnick's proposals at this time have been included in the operating budget except this one, which will involve an outlay of $210,000 to acquire patent rights on a new component part. Hulnick estimates that this new component part, which would be used in the assembly of motors, would reduce manufacturing costs about $110,000 a year.

Unfortunately, the inventors of the part have tried for many years to find a way of producing it at a cost low enough to make its use economically feasible; as a result, Continental's legal department estimates that the patents have but three years of protection remaining. The inventors have recently solved the production problems, but lack the capital needed to take advantage of their discovery. They are, therefore, willing to sell their rights to Continental for $210,000.

Based on engineering estimates of cost savings, Hulnick and the division controller, Amos Linz, have prepared the figures summarized in Exhibit 2.

In submitting these estimates, Linz told Mr. North that he did not think it would be wise to propose this project to corporate management even though it showed a good rate of return.

"There is a slight change," Linz stated, "that Donat (the corporate controller) will make us treat the $210,000 paid for the patent as a period expense thus forcing us to absorb the cost in one year. This would help the company's cash position by reducing taxable income and taxes paid next year, but it'll really knock our reported profit down for 1963."

North requested Linz to expand on this point. Linz prepared a set of tables, accompanied by explanatory notes, showing what would happen to cash flows and reported profits if the patent purchase price was treated either as a capital investment or an operating expense. These are presented in Exhibit 3.

"As you can see," Linz explained, "as long as overall corporate profits are good enough to keep the stockholders happy, Donat is probably going to insist that we expense the $210,000 since it'll almost double the available cash flow for next year. But we're not going to see a penny of this cash until we come in with our 1964 budget. By then it's not *our* cash, but just part of the entire company's cash account, and we're but one of 16 divisions trying to get our hands on some of it."

"In a nutshell, Bill," Linz concluded, "if we propose the patent pur-

**EXHIBIT 2**
**Financial Projections for Investment in Patent (Project No. 1)**

| Year | Cost Savings before Taxes | Deprecia-tion* | Additional Taxable income | Taxes† | Additional after Tax Income |
|---|---|---|---|---|---|
| 1963 | $110,000 | $70,000 | $40,000 | $20,000 | $20,000 |
| 1964 | 110,000 | 70,000 | 40,000 | 20,000 | 20,000 |
| 1965 | 110,000 | 70,000 | 40,000 | 20,000 | 20,000 |
| | | | | | $60,000 |

* If the $210,000 payment for the patent is treated as a capital investment and depreciated over three years, the annual depreciation would be $70,000 ($210,000 ÷ 3 = $70,000).

**Profit Summary**

Total profit over life of patent = $ 60,000
Average annual profit = 20,000
Average investment = 105,000*

* Average capital tied up in 1963 (with annual depreciation of $70,000) = $175,000
Average capital tied up in 1964 (with annual depreciation of $70,000) = 105,000
Average capital tied up in 1965 (with annual depreciation of $70,000) = 35,000
Average capital tied up during project life = $315,000
Average capital tied up per year, $315,000 ÷ 3 = $105,000

$$\text{Average rate of return} = \frac{\$ 20,000}{\$105,000} = 19.00\%$$

**EXHIBIT 3**
**Purchase of Patents (Project No. 1)**
**Implications of Treating Purchase Price as Investment or Current Expense Alternative 1—Capitalizing the $210,000 Expenditure (assumes the company treats the outlay as a capital expenditure and thus "writes it off" over three years)**

| Year | (1) Extra Cost Savings before Taxes and Depreciation | (2) Depre-ciation | (3) Taxable Income | (4) Taxes (at 50 Percent Rate) | (5) After-Tax Profit | Cash Flow; Increase or Decrease in Cash Available Col. (1) − Col. (4) |
|---|---|---|---|---|---|---|
| 0 | $ 0 | $ 0 | $ 0 | $ 0 | $ 0 | $−210,000* |
| 0–1 | 110,000 | 70,000 | 40,000 | 20,000 | 20,000 | + 90,000† |
| 1–2 | 110,000 | 70,000 | 40,000 | 20,000 | 20,000 | + 90,000 |
| 2–3 | 110,000 | 70,000 | 40,000 | 20,000 | 20,000 | + 90,000 |
| | | | | | | $+ 60,000 |

* At point in time zero when the $210,000 is paid out, the only impact is $210,000 less in the "cash box."
† From point zero to one (calendar year 1963), an extra $110,000 is saved. The $70,000 in Col. (2) is not an actual outflow since depreciation is merely a partial delayed tax credit for the $210,000 that actually left the "cash box" earlier. Thus the company actually has an extra $110,000 it saves minus the $20,000 in taxes it pays, or a net cash increase of $90,000 ($110,000 − $20,000 = $90,000).

**EXHIBIT 3 (*continued*)**
Alternative 2—Expensing the $210,000 expenditure (assumes entire $210,000 is charged off in 1963, and that taxable income from other division operations will be sufficient to offset losses reported from this project)

| Year | Extra Cost Savings before Taxes | Expense to Purchase Patent | Taxable Income | Extra Taxes Saved or Paid | After Tax Profit | Cash Flow; Increase or Decrease in Cash Available |
|---|---|---|---|---|---|---|
| 0 ......... | $   0 | $   0 | $   0 | $   0 | $   0 | $−210,000* |
| 0–1 ....... | 110,000 | 210,000 | −100,000 | −50,000 | −50,000 | +160,000† |
| 1–2 ....... | 110,000 | 0 | +110,000 | +55,000 | +55,000 | + 55,000‡ |
| 2–3 ....... | 110,000 | 0 | +110,000 | +55,000 | +55,000 | + 55,000 |
|  |  |  |  |  |  | $+ 60,000 |

\* As in *Alternative Treatment 1*, at point in time zero when the $210,000 is paid out the only impact is $210,000 less in the "cash box."

† From zero to one (calendar year 1963), an extra $110,000 is saved, but if the $210,000 is treated as an expense, the division has $210,000 worth of tax credit, $110,000 of this credit is used to offset the extra income so the division "pays" no taxes on it and all $110,000 stays in the cash box.

In addition the division has $100,000 ($210,000 − $110,000 = $100,000) worth of tax credit left to apply to other division income. Thus (using a 50 percent tax rate) the division "pays" $50,000 less taxes on its other income and has an extra $50,000 left in the "cash box." The total effect of this first year is to have an extra $160,000 in the cash box:

$110,000 extra income
  50,000 taxes saved
$160,000

‡ In years two and three, $110,000 is saved each year. There is no deduction for depreciation so $55,000 is "paid out" in extra taxes, and the division ends each year with an extra $55,000 in cash having been generated.

## Comparison of Alternatives 1 and 2

*Note:* At the end of the three years (December 31, 1965), no matter which alternative is used, the company has a calculated net gain of $60,000.

*In First Year (1963):* Alternative 1 shows higher profit but lower cash available for other company uses than Alternative 2.

*In Second and Third Years (1964, 1965):* Alternative 1 shows lower profit, higher available cash than Alternative 2.

### Summarizing Results for End of 1963

| Alternative Treatment of the Expenditure | (1963) Net Profit after Taxes | 1963 Cash Flow Available for Reinvestment |
|---|---|---|
| 1. ($210,000 treated as investment) | $ +20,000 | $+ 90,000 |
| 2. ($210,000 treated as an expense) | $−50,000 | $+160,000 |

*Note:* Under Alternative 2, the company will have an extra $70,000 ($160,000 − $90,000 = $70,000) working for it for a full year, which it would not have under Alternative 1. While it is true the company will recoup this $70,000 during 1964 and 1965, at least one year's income on $70,000 will be lost to the company.

chase we may end up having to work just that much harder to show a good profit picture. Certainly, if they treat the $210,000 as an expense, our profits in 1964 and 1965 will be even better. But, remember Richardson's comment about not being able to run a business on next year's profits. It's the 1963 results they're going to judge us by."

North questioned this reasoning by asking, "Look Amos, don't you think that if they request us to expense the $210,000 outlay at the start of the year, they'll remember at the end of the year why our profits are a little lower?"

Linz' reply was: "Don't count on it, Bill. Don't forget this is only one of many many factors that is going to influence our divisional profits. And if we show lower profit forecasts because we expect them to treat the $210,000 as an expense, then Grundy [group vice president] will be all over us for not being more aggressive. If we come up with a more optimistic forecast and don't make it, the review board will treat any explanations on our part—as far as the $210,000 expense is concerned —as simply an alibi. If I were you I wouldn't take the chance on this one and put my money on Kirkpatrick's request."

**Proposal No. 2: Purchase of New Wiring Equipment.** North stated that he was not completely convinced by Amos Linz' reasoning but that he had a great deal of respect for Linz' judgment particularly in financial matters such as this. In addition, Linz has been with the company for 41 years and knows as much about company politics as anyone in the firm. Having started with the company in the accounting department as a clerk after graduation from high school, he worked his way up from the bottom. Linz is well regarded in the company, and his opinion is often sought by younger executives like North.

The project Linz advised North to include in the budget was made by Owen Kirkpatrick, director of manufacturing. Kirkpatrick has seen a piece of equipment known as the Margot-Toledo Wirer demonstrated and feels "that it could be used to automate the attachment of wire coils in the one-horsepower motors. Such automatic attachment would permit a more efficient assembly line operation, and should reduce manufacturing costs between $80,000 and $100,000 a year."

The cost of purchasing the Margot-Toledo equipment is estimated at $250,000 but Kirkpatrick stated that "even in the face of rapid changes in such automated equipment and technology, I am sure that this equipment will have at least a five-year economic life.

"I'd love to see us get that patent Ralph Hulnick's after, but if what Linz says is right and in light of my proposal's five-year life compared to the three-year life of Ralph's patent, I think we ought to put our money in the new equipment."

Working with Linz, Kirkpatrick submitted a summary of the financial estimates to North (Exhibit 4).

**Proposal No. 3: Research on Insulation Materials.** A third proposal under consideration has been put forth by Dr. Douglas Glass, division director of research. Dr. Glass who is 42, joined the company three years ago. After having taught electrical engineering at a major eastern university

## EXHIBIT 4
### Financial Projections for Investment in New Equipment (Project No. 2)

| Year | Cost Savings before Taxes | Depre- ciation* | Additional Taxable Income | Taxes† | Additional after Tax Income |
|---|---|---|---|---|---|
| 1 | $ 80,000 | $50,000 | $30,000 | $15,000 | $ 15,000 |
| 2 | 90,000 | 50,000 | 40,000 | 20,000 | 20,000 |
| 3 | 100,000 | 50,000 | 50,000 | 25,000 | 25,000 |
| 4 | 90,000 | 50,000 | 40,000 | 20,000 | 20,000 |
| 5 | 90,000 | 50,000 | 40,000 | 20,000 | 20,000 |
| | | | | | $100,000 |

* Assuming the equipment will have a five-year economic life, depreciation will be $50,000 per year ($250,000 ÷ 5 = $50,000).
† Using a 50 percent tax rate to simplify estimates.

### Profit Summary

Total profit ............... $100,000
Average profit ............ 20,000
Average investment ........ 125,000

$$\frac{20,000}{125,000} = 16.00\%$$

Average rate of return ...... $\frac{20,000}{125,000}$

for ten years, he joined the research staff of one of Continental's principal competitors where he worked for two years.

North states that he was quite happy to get Glass to join the company three years ago but soon recognized that while he had acquired the talents of a brilliant research engineer he had also taken on a strong-minded and impatient individual.

Glass explained his reasons for accepting Continental's offer as follows: "I took this job because the people I worked with on my former job should be managing a rocking chair company. They are painfully conservative, scared stiff by corporate management, and haven't listened to a new idea in ten years. I can't work in an environment like that. Things change too swiftly to sit around milking yesterday's good ideas."

Dr. Glass' largest proposal for this year's budget is the third project being considered by North. It involves embarking upon a research program designed to develop a new insulation material for use under extremely high and low temperature conditions. Success in this venture would give the division a motor which would find wide use in industry.

Dr. Glass has requested that $75,000 a year be allocated for this project for the next three years. Then if all goes well, an investment of about $100,000 will be necessary in the fourth year to begin production.

Mr. North has consulted with the group vice president of military products and the general managers of several divisions within his own group, and they are all very enthusiastic about such a breakthrough. However, none are willing to contribute to the cost of the project.

"After all," said the general manager of one division, "your division has the responsibility for updating technology in small motors. This is one of the five major criteria by which any division performance is evaluated. As much as we would like to see you come through on this project we can't see why we should subsidize you on it."

Dr. Glass, however, has taken a very strong stand for the research project.

"These other proposals are nothing but short-run cost cutting solutions to a profit problem which has long-run implications. As a division, we are dead, competitively, if we don't start moving ahead into new products and new technologies. This research cost is peanuts compared to its potential value to the company," he said, "and don't forget that product leadership is one of the goals set for us by top management."

Dr. Glass and his staff, however, are the only ones who support the project within the division. As Linz points out, "this project would take almost six years before we begin to get into the black on it. It's fine for Glass to talk about the long run, but none of us are going to be here in the long run if we don't do something about our short-term profit picture."

Based on Glass' estimates, Linz has summarized the financial outlook for the research project in Exhibit 5.

Dr. Glass feels that the benefits from his project should go well beyond eight years, but Mr. Linz is unwilling to develop financial forecasts beyond that period. In addition, Dr. Glass feels that the use of averages

**EXHIBIT 5**
**Financial Projections for Research Program (Project No. 3)**

| Year | Added Income before Taxes | Research Cost* | Depreciation† | Additional Taxable Income | Taxes Paid‡ | Additional after Tax Income |
|---|---|---|---|---|---|---|
| 1 | $      0 | $75,000 | $    0 | $−75,000 | $−37,500 | $−37,500 |
| 2 | 0 | 75,000 | 0 | −75,000 | −37,500 | −37,500 |
| 3 | 0 | 75,000 | 0 | −75,000 | −37,500 | −37,500 |
| 4 | 50,000 | 0 | 20,000 | 30,000 | 15,000 | 15,000 |
| 5 | 75,000 | 0 | 20,000 | 55,000 | 27,500 | 27,500 |
| 6 | 175,000 | 0 | 20,000 | 155,000 | 77,500 | 77,500 |
| 7 | 200,000 | 0 | 20,000 | 180,000 | 90,000 | 90,000 |
| 8 | 200,000 | 0 | 20,000 | 180,000 | 90,000 | 90,000 |
| | | | | | | $ 187,500 |

\* Assuming research cost will have to be treated as an expense and charged to period income.

† Assuming the $100,000 investment in the fourth year has a five-year economic life, depreciation will be $20,000 per year ($100,000 ÷ 5 = $20,000).

‡ Using 50 percent tax rate to simplify estimates and assuming other taxable earnings will be offset.

**Profit Summary**

Total profit.............................$187,500

Average profit..........................$ 23,438   ($187,500 ÷ 8 = $23,438)

Average Investment.....................$162,500   ($225,000 + $100,000 = $325,000
$325,000 ÷ 2 = $162,500)

Average rate of return..................$\dfrac{\$ 23,438}{\$162,500} = 14.42\%$

to compute rate of return when comparing projects such as these is deceptive. He told North in the midst of a stormy budget meeting, "I'm no financial expert but I'm sure that all these figures Amos throws around are not true measure of these projects' value."

When Amos Linz suggested that Glass stick to his research business and not meddle with financial analysis, Glass stated that "this is the same kind of ostrich thinking" he had been forced to deal with when working for Continental's competition.

A heated exchange followed, and North thought it best to call a halt to the meeting. As Linz left he turned to North and said, "Young man, you've got a real future in this company if you use your head. Every warning I gave you about the patent proposal goes double on this research project.

"Backing the research project means sacrificing between $15,000 and $25,000 of extra profits by passing up the savings on new equipment. In addition, it sticks us with a $37,500 loss per year for the next three years. I cannot see why anyone striving for a better profit picture should want to start off by throwing away roughly $60,000 in profits a year for three years."

A summary of the financial projects for the three projects prepared by Linz for North is shown below:

**Comparative Financial Projections for Three Proposals**

| Project | Payback Period* | Total Profit after Taxes | Average Rate of Return |
|---|---|---|---|
| No. 1 Patent . . . . . . . . . . . . . . . . . . . . | 2 years, 4 months | $ 60,000 | 19.00% |
| No. 2 New equipment . . . . . . . . . . . . | 3 years, 7 months | 100,000 | 16.00 |
| No. 3 Research project . . . . . . . . . . . | 6 years, 4 months | 187,500 | 14.42 |

* Using cash flow (after-tax income + depreciation), this is the length of time it takes to recover the cash outlays.

# Selected Readings

*From*

## GENERAL MOTORS ORGANIZATION PHILOSOPHY AND STRUCTURE*

*By Harlow H. Curtice†*

May I first make the point that the growth of General Motors has taken place principally over the past 35 years. This period coincides with that in which the policies and business of the corporation have functioned under the existing management organization.

In my opinion there are four principal reasons for our success. These are, first, the dynamic growth of our country; second, the even more rapid growth of the automobile industry; third, our management structure; and, fourth, our approach to problems.

> *   *   *   *   *

General Motors has grown faster than has the automobile industry as a whole. Quite obviously, we have made things that people wanted, and people in increasing numbers have bought them. . . .

General Motors has been able to offer greater dollar values in its products, and at the same time it has been able to operate efficiently to provide dividends for its shareholders and substantial sums for reinvestment in the business.

But, one may well ask why and how; and this brings me to what to my mind are the two fundamental reasons for the success of General Motors.

Both fall under the heading of what might be termed management philosophy. When this General Motors philosophy was formulated in the early 1920's—and I might add that the credit for its formulation largely goes to one man, Alfred P. Sloan, Jr.—it was unique as applied to industry. That it is no longer unique is in itself evidence of its soundness.

The first element of this philosophy has to do with organizational structure, the second with our approach to problems. Both, of course, concern people—in fact, can only be put into practice by people.

> *   *   *   *   *

To fully appreciate the revolutionary nature of the organizational structure developed by Mr. Sloan in the early 1920's, it is necessary to appraise it in the light of conditions as they existed at that time. The business enterprise which the present management took charge of in 1921 had been put together, beginning in 1908, by W. C. Durant, and it largely bore the stamp of his personality. Durant had genius as a creator and super-salesman. He was not an administrator and did not develop an effective organization. Twice under his administration the Corporation was in serious financial difficulties—first in 1910 and again in 1920.

Prior to 1921 there existed no real concept of sound management in General Motors. Operations were neither integrated nor coordinated. There was no consistent policy with

---

\* Reprinted by permission. From a Statement before the Subcommittee on Anti-Trust and Monopoly of the United States Senate Committee on the Judiciary, December 2, 1955 (pp. 5–12), "The Development and Growth of General Motors."

† Mr. Curtice was at one time President of General Motors Corporation.

respect to product programs. Frequently poor judgment was exercised in making capital expenditures and establishing production schedules. The Corporation did not have a properly developed research and engineering staff nor any sound concept of budgetary control. The central administration did not exercise adequate control over the operations of the individual divisions. There were wide variations in the competence of divisional managements. In short, the Corporation was unorganized and the individual units largely out of control.

**CHART 1**
**General Motors Percent of Industry Vehicle Sales for the Year 1921**

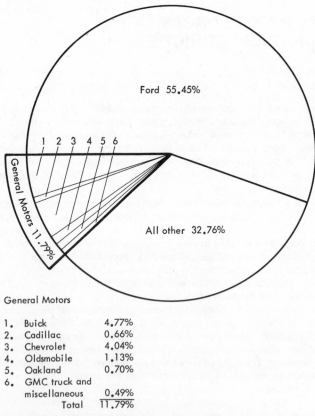

General Motors

| | | |
|---|---|---|
| 1. | Buick | 4.77% |
| 2. | Cadillac | 0.66% |
| 3. | Chevrolet | 4.04% |
| 4. | Oldsmobile | 1.13% |
| 5. | Oakland | 0.70% |
| 6. | GMC truck and miscellaneous | 0.49% |
| | Total | 11.79% |

Source: F.T.C. "Report on Motor Vehicle Industry," page 27.

It is not surprising, therefore, that [Vehicle sales for 1921: G.M., 11.79 percent; Ford, 55.45 percent; all others, 32.76 percent] was the competitive picture in 1921 when the management changed and Mr. Sloan began to put into effect the policies with respect to organizational structure which I will now outline.

Even before the crisis of 1920 materialized, Mr. Sloan was very conscious of the need in General Motors for a new and clearly defined concept of management philosophy. He had observed that much time was being consumed in solving detailed administrative problems and in meeting the critical situations which were constantly arising. He recognized that too great a concentration of problems upon a small number of executives limited initiative, caused delay, increased expense, reduced efficiency and retarded development.

He realized that centralization, properly established, makes possible directional control, coordination, specialization, and resulting economies. He also realized that decentralization, properly established, develops initiative and responsibility; it makes possible a proper distribution of decisions at all levels of management, including the foreman—with resulting flexibility and cooperative effort, so necessary to a large-scale enterprise. His objective was to obtain the proper balance between these two apparently conflicting principles of centralization and decentralization in order to obtain the best elements of each in the combination. He concluded that, to achieve this balance so necessary for flexibility of operation, General Motors management should be established on a foundation of centralized policy and decentralized administration.

Mr. Sloan's concept of the management of a great industrial organization, expressed in his own words as he finally evolved it, is "to divide it into as many parts as consistently as can be done, place in charge of each part the most capable executive that can be found, develop a system of coordination so that each part may strengthen and support each other part; thus not only welding all parts together in the common interests of a joint enterprise, but importantly developing ability and initiative through the instrumentalities of responsibility and ambition—developing men and giving them an opportunity to exercise their talents, both in their own interests as well as in that of the business."

In pursuance of that plan each of the various operations was established as an integral unit under a General Manager. Then, those operations which had a common relationship were grouped under a Group Executive for coordinating purposes. These Group Executives reported to the President who was the Chief Executive Officer.

To perform those functional activities that could be accomplished more effectively by one activity in the interest of the whole and to coordinate similar functional activities of the different operating units and promote their effectiveness, a General Staff, and in addition, Financial and Legal Staffs, were established to operate on a functional basis.

\* \* \* \* \*

Today, General Motors has two principal committees of the Board of Directors—the Financial Policy Committee, which is concerned with the financial and legal affairs of the Corporation, and the Operations Policy Committee, which deals primarily with the operating affairs of the business.

There are two additional committees of the Board of Directors, namely, an Audit Committee and a Bonus and Salary Committee, consisting of directors who are not members of management.

\* \* \* \* \*

The balance between decentralized operations, on the one hand, and coordinated control, on the other, varies according to areas. It also varies according to the temperaments and talents of executives, and the way in which they work. While the relationships of physical things are inherent in the business, it is men who establish and govern these relationships. The relationship between the Central Office Staff and the Divisional line operations may vary according to conditions and circumstances.

In summary, the organization of General Motors Corporation under the Board of Directors consists of the Financial Policy Committee and the Operations Policy Committee, supported by other committees and policy groups; staff operations; component product divisions; end product divisions; and service operations; all headed up by staff executives or general line officers who report to the Chief Executive Officer, except for the executives in charge of the financial and legal activities who report to the Chairman of the Financial Policy Committee.

\* \* \* \* \*

Such a management concept provides a continuous flow of ideas and information upward and downward through the management organization, by means of reports, meetings and conferences of both staff executives and the line executives at all appropriate levels. This results in mutual education and understanding with respect to the authority, responsibility, objectives and purposes of management at all levels from the foreman to the Chief Executive Officer. It provides interpretation and understanding of policy and procedure as it is or may be established or changed. It produces an upward flow of information with respect to situations arising in operations, full knowledge of which is necessary if appropriate changes in policy or procedure are to be accomplished intelligently and promptly. It provides maximum initiative at every managerial level and at every point requiring administrative judgment, by the men closest to all the facts of the situation having full responsibility for their decisions. Finally, it makes possible accurate and prompt appraisal and evaluation of the contribution of the individual executive at every level of management, and of the contribution as well of every divisional organization and staff operation.

Although for many years this form of decentralized industrial management was identified primarily with General Motors, in more recent years decentralized management has been adopted by other large industrial companies.

The success of General Motors is the proof of the soundness of this management philosophy and its effectiveness in its application to a large industrial organization. Testifying to this has been a growing consumer preference expressed in the purchase of General Motors products.

*From*

# COST ACCOUNTING*

*By Gordon Shillinglaw*

A company is *divisionalized* whenever certain related activities are grouped together for administrative direction and control by high-level executives. Whenever this is accompanied by the delegation to division managers of the responsibility for a segment of the company's profits, then the company is said to be *decentralized*. The hallmark of the decentralized company is its subdivision into a number of smaller, relatively self-contained entities that are equipped to operate in substantially the same manner as independent firms dependent on their own profit performance for economic survival. The creation of these semiautonomous units, often referred to as *profit centers,* has three major objectives:. . .

Perhaps the most important of these is to overcome the sheer weight of the decision-making responsibility in a large corporation. With operations spread over a vast geographical area and encompassing hundreds of products and thousands of customers, central management cannot hope to be completely and continuously in direct personal contact with every segment of the company's business. To provide flexibility and adaptability to changing conditions, it has become increasingly necessary to delegate substantial powers to executives who can maintain a closer, more detailed familiarity with individual products or markets. In other words, decentralization aims to recreate in the large organization the conditions that give life and flexibility to the small company without sacrificing the advantages of size—diversification of risk, centralized financing, and specialization in the planning and advisory functions of management.

A second objective of decentralization is to bring subordinate executives into more direct contact with the ultimate profit objectives of the firm. A strictly manufacturing executive sees all problems as production problems with a cost overlay. A marketing executive focuses his attention on sales volume and distribution cost. In a centralized organization these viewpoints come together only at the top of the pyramid. Decentralization is one way of attempting to bring them together at lower levels.

---

* Reprinted by permission of Richard D. Irwin, Inc., Homewood, Ill. 1961 (pp. 680–84, 688–89).

Closely related to this is a third objective of decentralization, namely, to provide a more comprehensive training ground for the top managers of the future. The ranks of the top executives are continually being thinned by death and retirement, and there is a need for replacements who have been schooled in various aspects of business management and are thereby better prepared to face the major problems that can be resolved only at the top-management level. This kind of experience is best obtained at lower levels where the inevitable mistakes are likely to be smaller.

\*    \*    \*    \*    \*

. . . The ideal basis for profit decentralization exists whenever a division can be relatively self-contained, with its own manufacturing and distributive facilities and relatively few transfers of product internally among divisions. In other words, decentralization is at its best whenever a division's operations come closest in scope and depth to those of separate independent companies. In these circumstances, the profit reported by each division is largely independent of operating performance in other divisions of the company, thus facilitating the interpretation of reported profits.

Unfortunately, these ideal conditions are often unattainable. Organization structure cannot be determined solely by the need for profit separability. Other factors, such as economies of common use of sales forces or facilities, may override the desirability of separating profit centers from each other. In these circumstances, the problem is to seek means of measurement and evaluation that will achieve a satisfactory compromise between conflicting objectives. Management has the task of deciding whether departures from the ideal are sufficiently serious to make profit decentralization unworkable. . . .

\*    \*    \*    \*    \*

. . . No matter how it is defined, decentralization never represents a complete delegation of authority. Even in the most decentralized companies, top management retains some vestige of authority, particularly over financing and capital expenditures. In any case, divisional autonomy is limited by the need to conform to over-all company policies and by the need for co-ordination. . . .

Both at the corporate level and within each profit center there are units that are not organized on a profit responsibility basis. These are called *service centers* or *budget centers* to distinguish them from profit centers. . . . In each of these the executive in charge is responsible for costs but not for profits. . . . Within each product division there are also staff departments, such as divisional accounting or marketing research, which act in an advisory capacity to the division managers. The managers of these departments are also responsible for costs, but they generally have no direct profit responsibilities.

\*    \*    \*    \*    \*

. . . Three criteria that divisional profit measures must meet stand out as especially important:

1. Divisional profit should not be increased by any action that reduces total company profit.
2. Each division's profit should be as independent as possible of performance efficiency and managerial decisions elsewhere in the company.
3. Each division's profit should reflect all items that are subject to any substantial degree of control by the division manager or his subordinates.

Four alternative concepts may be examined to see how well they fit these criteria:

1. *Variable profit,* or total revenues less total variable costs to make and sell.
2. *Controllable profit,* or variable profit less all the division's controllable fixed costs.
3. *Contribution margin,* or controllable profit less all other costs directly traceable to the division.
4. *Net profits,* or contribution margin less some share of general management and service center costs.

**EXHIBIT 1**
**Four Profit Concepts Illustrated**

| | |
|---|---|
| Sales . . . . . . . . . . . . . . . . . . . . . . . . . . . . . . . . . . . . . . . . . . . . . . . . . . . . . . . . . | $760,000 |

Less:

| | |
|---|---|
| Variable costs of goods sold . . . . . . . . . . . . . . . . . . . . . . . . . . . . . . . . . . . . . . | $270,000 |
| Variable divisional selling and administrative expense . . . . . . . . . . . . . . . . . . | 30,000 |
| Variable profit . . . . . . . . . . . . . . . . . . . . . . . . . . . . . . . . . . . . . . . . . . . . . . . . . . . | $460,000 |
| Less: Controllable divisional overhead . . . . . . . . . . . . . . . . . . . . . . . . . . . . . . . | 200,000 |
| Controllable Profit . . . . . . . . . . . . . . . . . . . . . . . . . . . . . . . . . . . . . . . . . . . . . . . . | $260,000 |
| Less: Fixed, noncontrollable divisional overhead . . . . . . . . . . . . . . . . . . . . . . . | 150,000 |
| Contribution margin . . . . . . . . . . . . . . . . . . . . . . . . . . . . . . . . . . . . . . . . . . . . . . . | $110,000 |
| Less: Allocation of extradivisional fixed expenses—non-controllable . . . . . . . . . . . . . . . . . . . . . . . . . . . . . . . . . . . . . . . . . . . . . . . . . . . . | 50,000 |
| Net Profit before Taxes . . . . . . . . . . . . . . . . . . . . . . . . . . . . . . . . . . . . . . . . . . . . | $ 60,000 |

*From*

# THE PRACTICE OF MANAGEMENT*

*By Peter F. Drucker*

Most of today's lively discussion of management by objectives is concerned with the search for the one right objective. This search is not only likely to be as unproductive as the quest for the philosopher's stone; it is certain to do harm and to misdirect.

To emphasize only profit, for instance, misdirects managers to the point where they may endanger the survival of the business. To obtain profit today they tend to undermine the future. They may push the most easily saleable product lines and slight those that are the market of tomorrow. They tend to short-change research, promotion and the other postponable investments. Above all, they shy away from any capital expenditure that may increase the invested-capital base against which profits are measured; and the result is dangerous obsolescence of equipment. In other words, they are directed into the worst practices of management.

To manage a business is to balance a variety of needs and goals. This requires judgment. The search for the one objective is essentially a search for a magic formula that will make judgment unnecessary. But the attempt to replace judgment by formula is always irrational; all that can be done is to make judgment possible by narrowing its range and the available alternatives, giving it clear focus, a sound foundation in facts and reliable measurements of the effects and validity of actions and decisions. And this, by the very nature of business enterprise, requires multiple objectives.

What should these objectives be, then? There is only one answer: *Objectives are needed in every area where performance and results directly and vitally affect the survival and prosperity of the business.* These are the areas which are affected by every management decision and which therefore have to be considered in every management decision. They decide what it means concretely to manage the business. They spell out what results the business must aim at and what is needed to work effectively toward these targets.

\*    \*    \*    \*    \*

* From pp. 62–64, 66, 84–87, 121, 128–131 in *The Practice of Management* by Peter F. Drucker. Copyright 1954 by Peter F. Drucker. Reprinted by permission of Harper & Row, Publishers, Inc.

There are eight areas in which objectives of performance and results have to be set:

Market standing; innovation; productivity; physical and financial resources; profitability; manager performance and development; worker performance and attitude; public responsibility.

\*     \*     \*     \*     \*

Yet, even if managing were merely the application of economics, we would have to include these three areas and would have to demand that objectives be set for them. They belong in the most purely formal economic theory of the business enterprise. For neglect of manager performance and development, worker performance and public responsibility soon results in the most practical and tangible loss of market standing, technological leadership, productivity and profit—and ultimately in the loss of business life. That they look so different from anything the economist—especially the modern economic analyst—is wont to deal with, that they do not readily submit to quantification and mathematical treatment, is the economist's bad luck; but is no argument against their consideration.

The very reason for which economist and accountant consider these areas impractical— that they deal with principles and values rather than soley with dollars and cents—makes them central to the management of the enterprise, as tangible, as practical—and indeed as measurable—as dollars and cents.

\*     \*     \*     \*     \*

"We don't care what share of the market we have, as long as our sales go up," is a fairly common comment. It sounds plausible enough; but it does not stand up under analysis. By itself, volume of sales tells little about performance, results or the future of the business. A company's sales may go up—and the company may actually be headed for rapid collapse. A company's sales may go down—and the reason may not be that its marketing is poor but that it is in a dying field and had better change fast.

A maker of oil refinery equipment reported rising sales year after year. Actually new refineries and their equipment were being supplied by the company's competitors. But because the equipment it had supplied in the past was getting old and needed repairs, sales spurted; for replacement parts for equipment of this kind have usually to be bought from the original supplier. Sooner or later, however, the original customers were going to put in new and efficient equipment rather than patch up the old and obsolescent stuff. Then almost certainly they were going to go to the competitors designing and building the new equipment. The company was thus threatened with going out of business—which is what actually happened.

\*     \*     \*     \*     \*

## The Time-Span of Objectives

For what time-span should objectives be set? How far ahead should we set our targets?

The nature of the business clearly has a bearing here. In certain parts of the garment business next week's clearance sale is "long-range future." It may take four years to build a big steam turbine and two more to install it; in the turbine business six years may be "immediate present" therefore. And Crown Zellerbach is forced to plant today the trees it will harvest fifty years hence.

Different areas require different time-spans. To build a marketing organization takes at least five years. Innovations in engineering and chemistry made today are unlikely to show up in marketing results and profits for five years or longer. On the other hand a sales campaign, veteran sales managers believe, must show results within six weeks or less; "Sure, there are sleepers," one of these veterans once said, "but most of them never wake up."

This means that in getting objectives management has to balance the immediate future— the next few years—against the long range: five years or longer. This balance can best be found through a "managed-expenditures budget." For practically all the decisions that affect the balance are made as decisions on what the accountant calls "managed expenditures"—those expenditures that are determined by current management decision rather than by past and irrevocable decisions (like capital charges), or by the requirements of current business (like labor and raw material costs). Today's managed expenditures are tommorrow's profit: but they may also be today's loss.

Every second-year accountancy student knows that almost any "profit" figure can be turned into a loss" by changing the basis of depreciation charges; and the new basis can usually be made to appear as rational as the old. But few managements—including their accountants—realize how many such expenditures there are that are based, knowingly or not, on an assessment of short-range versus long-range needs, and that vitally affect both. Here is a partial list:

Depreciation charges; maintenance budgets; capital replacement, modernization and expansion costs; research budgets; expenditures on product development and design; expenditures on the management group, its compensation and rewards, it size, and on developing tomorrow's managers; cost of building and maintaining a marketing organization; promotion and advertising budgets; cost of service to the customer; personnel management, especially training expenditures.

Almost any one of these expenditures can be cut back sharply, if not eliminated; and for some time, perhaps for a long time, there will be no adverse effect. Any one of these expenditures can be increased sharply and for good reasons, with no resulting benefits visible for a long time. By cutting these expenditures immediate results can always be made to look better. By raising them immediate results can always be made to look worse.

\*     \*     \*     \*     \*

### Balancing the Objectives

In addition to balancing the immediate and the long-range future, management also has to balance objectives. What is more important: an expansion in markets and sales volume, or a higher rate of return? How much time, effort and energy should be expended on improving manufacturing productivity? Would the same amount of effort or money bring greater returns if invested in new-product design?

There are few things that distinguish competent from incompetent management quite as sharply as the performance in balancing objectives. Yet, there is no formula for doing the job. Each business requires its own balance—and it may require a different balance at different times. . . .

\*     \*     \*     \*     \*

Any business enterprise must build a true team and weld individual efforts into a common effort. Each member of the enterprise contributes something different, but they must all contribute toward a common goal. Their efforts must all pull in the same direction, and their contributions must fit together to produce a whole—without gaps, without friction, without unnecessary duplication of effort.

Business performance therefore requires that each job be directed toward the objectives of the whole business. And in particular each manager's job must be focused on the success of the whole. . . .

\*     \*     \*     \*     \*

By definition, a manager is responsible for the contribution that his component makes to the larger unit above him and eventually to the enterprise. His performance aims upward rather than downward. This means that the goals of each manager's job must be defined by the contribution he has to make to the success of the larger unit of which he is a part. The objectives of the district sales manager's job should be defined by the contribution he and his district sales force have to make to the sales department. . . .

\*     \*     \*     \*     \*

This requires each manager to develop and set the objectives of his unit himself. Higher management must, of course, reserve the power to approve or disapprove these objectives.

But their development is part of a manager's responsibility; indeed, it is his first responsibility. It means, too, that every manager should responsibly participate in the development of the objectives of the higher unit of which his is a part. . . . He must know and understand the ultimate business goals, what is expected of him and why, what he will be measured against and how. There must be a "meeting of minds" within the entire management of each unit. This can be achieved only when each of the contributing managers is expected to think through what the unit objectives are, is led, in other words, to participate actively and responsibly in the work of defining them. And only if his lower managers participate in this way can the higher manager know what to expect of them and can make exacting demands.

*   *   *   *   *

### Self-Control through Measurements

The greatest advantage of management by objectives is perhaps that it makes it possible for a manager to control his own performance. Self-control means stronger motivation: a desire to do the best rather than just enough to get by. It means higher performance goals and broader vision. Even if management by objectives were not necessary to give the enterprise the unity of direction and effort of a management team, it would be necessary to make possible management by self-control.

So far in this book I have not talked of "control" at all; I have talked of "measurements." This was intentional. For "control" is an ambiguous word. It means the ability to direct oneself and one's work. It can also mean domination of one person by another. Objectives are the basis of "control" in the first sense; but they must never become the basis of "control" in the second, for this would defeat their purpose. Indeed, one of the major contributions of management by objectives is that it enables us to substitute management by self-control for management by domination. . . .

*From*

# MANAGERIAL PSYCHOLOGY*

*By Harold J. Leavitt*

### The Perceptual World

Most of us recognize that the world-as-we-see-it is not necessarily the same as the world-as-it-"really"-is. Our answer depends on what we heard, not on what was really said. The housewife buys what she likes best, not what is best. Whether we feel hot or cold depends on us, not on the thermometer. The same job may look like a good job to one of us and a sloppy job to another.

To specify the problem, consider the line drawing in Figure 1. This is a picture of a woman. Here are some questions about it: (1) How old is the woman at the time of the picture? (2) Does she have any outstanding physical characteristics? (3) Is she "reasonably attractive" or "downright ugly"?

Show the picture to ten other people. Do they all see the same thing? If some think she looks between twenty and thirty, does anyone think she's over fifty? If some think she's over fifty, does anyone think she's between twenty and thirty? How does one account for the conflicts? Are the differences simply differences in taste? Or in standards of beauty? Or is each person distorting the "real" world in a different way?

This old psychology-textbook picture is intentionally ambiguous. It can be seen either as

---

* From Harold J. Leavitt, *Managerial Psychology* © 1972 by The University of Chicago Press. All rights reserved. Excerpts from pp. 22–26. Reprinted by permission.

**FIGURE 1**
**Wife or Mother-in-Law**

an ugly old hag with a long and crooked nose and toothless mouth or as a reasonably attractive young girl with head turned away so that one can barely see one eyelash and part of a nose. More importantly, the picture will be based on the "facts" as they are seen by the viewer, which may be different from the "facts" seen by another viewer.

Incidentally, if the reader still sees only one of the two figures, he is getting a good feeling of what a "need" is. The tension or discomfort that one feels when he thinks he is missing something others can see or when he feels he hasn't quite closed a gap in his knowledge—that is a need. And it will probably be difficult to concentrate on reading further until he satisfies that unsatisfied need by finding the second face in the picture.

## The Influence of Our Needs on Our Perceptions

The hag picture is another demonstration of a commonplace observation, i.e., that people see things differently, that the world is what we make it, that everyone wears his own rose-colored glasses. But consider some additional questions: Whence the rose-colored glasses? Are the glasses always rose-colored? That is, does one always see what he wants to see, or does he see what he is afraid he will see, or both?

These questions are important because the primary issue of "human relations" is to consider ways in which individuals can affect the behavior of other individuals. If it is true that people behave on the basis of the perceived world, then changing behavior in a predetermined direction can be made easier by understanding the individual's present perception of the world. For if there is any common human-relations mistake made by industrial superiors in their relations with subordinates, it is the mistake of assuming that the "real" world is all that counts, that everyone works for the same goals, that the facts speak for themselves.

But if people do act on their perceptions, different people perceive things differently. How, then, is the manager, for example, to know what to expect? What determines how particular people will perceive particular things?

The answer has already been given in the preceding chapters. People's perceptions are determined by their needs. Like the mirrors at amusement parks, we distort the world in relation to our own tensions. Children from poorer homes, when asked to draw a quarter, draw a bigger than actual one. Industrial employees, when asked to describe the people they work with, talk more about their bosses (the people more important to their needs) than about their peers or subordinates, and so on.

But the problem is more complicated than that. People may perceive what is important to their needs, but does this mean people see what they want to see, or what they are afraid to see? Both wishes and fears are important to one's needs. The answer seems to be that we perceive both, but according to certain rules. We magnify a compliment from higher up in the organization but we also magnify a word of disapproval. We dream of blondes, but we also have nightmares. And sometimes we just don't pay attention at all to things that are quite relevant. We forget dentist's appointments; we oversleep when we have examinations coming up; we manage to forget to clean the basement or to call on this particular customer.

## Selective Perception

What, then are the rules of selective perception? The best answer we can give is this one: If one re-examines his memories of the past, he may find that his recall of positive, satisfying things is better than his recall of negative, unpleasant things. He may find it easier to wake early to go fishing than to get to a dentist's appointment. He may look forward, in fact, to doing pleasant, satisfying jobs but may evade mildly disturbing and unpleasant jobs. One senior executive recently commented to the author that the biggest problem he encounters with young management people is their tendency to avoid the little unpleasant decisions—like disciplining people or digging through boring and repetitive records or writing unpleasant letters. This executive felt that his younger men would be far more effective if they could learn to deal as promptly with these uncomfortable little decisions as they did with the big ones.

But we can see some sense in this selective remembering if we look for it. There are some advantages to a person in being blind to unpleasantness, even if such blindness cuts down his working effectiveness. Ignoring the unpleasant may represent more than "laziness." It may be a sensible defensive device, psychologically speaking. Thus, most people are able to ignore soft background conversation while working. In effect they are psychologically deaf to a potentially distracting part of the real world. And this defense helps them to concentrate on their work. Similarly, most people manage to ignore the threat of the hydrogen bomb and to go on eating and sleeping as though this dangerous part of the real world were not here. It can even be shown experimentally that words with unpleasant connotations tend to be recognized more slowly when exposed for very brief intervals than words with pleasant connotations.

The strange part of this defensive process, however, is that in order *not* to hear the distracting music or *not* to see the unpleasant words one must first hear and see them. One has to see the word, recognize that it is unpleasant, and reject it almost simultaneously, so that one can say, "No. I didn't see what that word was." Hence the label "defense" attached to this phenomenon—defense against the entry of preselected things mildly disturbing to one's equilibrium. So two of our rules of selective perception become: (1) see what promises to help satisfy needs, and (2) ignore mildly disturbing things.

Suppose, though, that while one is successfully ignoring background talk someone back there starts to shout; or, while one is successfully ignoring the H-bomb, an H-bomb falls on

London. At those points, when the unpleasantness becomes intense and dangerous, people stop defending and begin attacking. They stop ignoring the irritation and start directing all their attention to it. This reversal seems to happen suddenly, at some specific threshold. The distant irritation increases to a point at which it becomes so real, so imminent, and so threatening that we reverse our course, discard the blindfold, and preoccupy ourselves completely with the thing previously ignored.

This is the third rule: Pay attention to things that are really dangerous. The whole picture now begins to look like this: *People perceive what they think will help satisfy needs; ignore what is disturbing; and again perceive disturbances that persist and increase.*

This is yet a fourth step in this process. What can happen when perceived threats become even more intense and imminent? When the soldier in combat watches his buddies die around him? That one we shall consider later, in the chapter on conflict.

This process may not seem entirely logical to an outside observer, but it is quite reasonable psychologically. For this kind of self-imposed psychological blindness helps the person to maintain his equilibrium while moving toward his objectives. An organism lacking this ability to fend off minor threats might well find itself torn apart in its attempt to deal simultaneously with all of them. Or, at least, an individual unable to ignore unpleasant realities might spend so much of his energy dealing with them that he would make little progress toward his major goals. For once a person has learned to perceive a multitude of threats and dangers in his world he needs a system of defense against them. One should add, however, that some individuals may see relatively few things as dangerous and therefore have little need for defense, while for others the world holds dangers at every turn.

In the preceding chapter we suggested that a person who has encountered a relatively helpful world is likely to perceive more of his environment as potentially helpful. If, however, the world has been mostly frustrating, then more of it, and especially new things in it, will be seen as potentially dangerous. Being dangerous, they must be fended off. But, paradoxically, to be fended off they must first be seen. So to protect himself from more insecurity, the insecure person must first see the things that will provoke insecurity and then manage to deny to himself that he has seen them.

*From*

# AUTHORITY STRUCTURE AND ORGANIZATIONAL EFFECTIVENESS*

*By Amitai Etzioni*

. . . Managers are generally considered as those who have the major (line) authority because they direct the major goal activity. Experts deal only with means, with secondary activities. Therefore it is functional for them to have none, or only limited (staff), authority.

. . . Managers and experts may be differentiated from four points of view: (*a*) role structure, (*b*) personality, (*c*) background, mainly in terms of educational and occupational experience, and (*d*) normative orientations.

The *role* of the expert is to create and institutionalized knowledge. The *role* of the manager is to integrate (create or maintain) organizational systems or subsystems from the

---

* Reprinted by permission of The Graduate School of Business and Public Administration, Cornell University, Ithaca, N.Y. (*Administrative Science Quarterly,* June 1959, pp. 45–47.)

point of view of the institutional goals and needs.[1] The expert typically deals with symbols and materials (although there are many who disagree with this point of view).[2] The manager deals with people. The two role types require different *personality* types. The expert who has intensive knowledge in a limited area, tends to have a restricted perspective. The manager has extensive, though limited, knowledge of many areas, and the resulting broad perspective is essential for his role. Experts are committed to abstract ideas and therefore tend to be unrealistic, whereas managers are more practical. Managers are skilled in human relations; experts are temperamental.[3]

Managers and experts differ in *background.* Experts usually have higher educations than managers and tend to enter their first job at a later age and at higher initial salaries. They often start at relatively high positions in the hierarchy but are limited in the range of their mobility. Managers enter their first job at a younger age, with less education, and at lower positions, but they move upward faster than the experts and some of them eventually get higher than any expert.[4] Whereas many experts remain more or less restricted to the same organizational functions, the typical manager is assigned to a large variety of tasks in what is called the process of broadening.

Managers' *orientations* differ considerably from those of experts. Managers are more committed or loyal to their specific organization than are experts.[5] Experts are often primarily oriented toward their professional reference and membership groups. While managers are often committed to the organization's particular goals, experts are committed to the scientific and professional ethos regardless of the particular needs and goals of their institution.[6]

Obviously though there is a high correlation among these four variables, they are not inevitably associated. Two major mechanisms explain how the correlation is maintained. First of all there is *selective recruitment.* People with managerial personalities and background are recruited to managerial roles, and those with the personalities and education of experts tend to enter staff positions. The second mechanism is *role adaptation.* People who enter roles which are initially incompatible with their personalities often adjust to their new roles. . . .

---

[1] The roles of managers will be discussed here only with regard to the internal functions of the organization. Their roles with regard to environment will be disregarded because of space limitations.

[2] Experts can be arranged in a continuum from the less to the more skilled in human relations. Chemists, for instance, are on the average less skilled from this point of view than labor relations experts. See L. E. Danielson, "Management's Relations with Engineers and Scientists," *Proceedings of Industrial Relations Research Association,* Tenth Annual Meeting, 1957, pp. 314–21.

[3] See Robert Dubin, *Human Relations in Administration* (New York, 1951), pp. 113–38.

[4] For a comparison, see M. Dalton, "Conflicts between Staff and Line Managerial Officers," *American Sociological Review,* 15 (1950), 342–51; and C. A. Myers and J. G. Turnbull, Line and Staff in Industrial Relations, *Harvard Business Review,* 34 (July–August 1956), 113–24.

[5] For a case study which brings out this point, see A. H. Stanton and M. S. Schwartz, *The Mental Hospital* (New York, 1954).

[6] A. W. Gouldner, Cosmopolitans and Locals: Toward an Analysis of Latent Social Roles, *Administrative Science Quarterly,* 2 (1957), 444–80.

*From*

# FINANCIAL CONTROLS FOR MANAGEMENT*

*By Ralph B. Lewis*

### The Theory of Investment and Return

From the standpoint of pure theory, there is only one true method (for determining rate of return on an investment). This is the investor's method. It is also called the discount method, or present value method. All the money that is to be laid out prior to the start of operations is measured. This includes payments for plant, property and equipment and working capital as well as expenditures for research and development and other preparatory expenses. On the other hand, all of the money to be returned as profit or depreciation, i.e., cash throw-off, is likewise projected, perhaps for as long as fifteen or twenty years. The date for the start of operations is the significant key to the calculation, because this is the date used in computing present value. A number of probable rates are selected. Then using a financial table one converts all of the outlays and returns into present values: And that interest rate at which the present value of the outlays offsets the present value of the return is the true rate of return.

*From*

# ACCOUNTING FOR MANAGEMENT CONTROL**

*By Charles T. Horngren*

### DEFINITION OF CAPITAL BUDGETING

Capital budgeting is long-term planning for making and financing proposed capital outlays. Most expenditures for plant, equipment, and other long-lived assets affect operations over a series of years. They are large permanent commitments that influence long-run flexibility and earning power. Decisions in this area are among the most difficult, primarily because the future to be foreseen is distant and hard to perceive. Because the unknowable factors are many, it is imperative that all the knowable factors be collected and properly measured before a decision is reached.

The problem of measuring the potential profit of long-range investments has been receiving increased attention by management accountants. This trend is likely to grow as industrial mechanization and automation grow.

The profitability of a business decision depends on two vital factors: (1) future net increases in cash inflows or net savings in cash outflows; and (2) required investment. Thus, a chance to receive an annual return of $5,000 on a bond or stock can be judged only in

---

* *Financial Controls for Management* by Ralph B. Lewis, © by Prentice-Hall, Inc., Englewood Cliffs, N.J., 1961 (pp. 82–83).

** Charles T. Horngren, *Accounting for Management Control: An Introduction,* © 1965, excerpts from pp. 356–63, 365–68. Reprinted by permission of Prentice-Hall, Inc., Englewood Cliffs, N.J.

relationship to how much money need be committed to obtain the $5,000. If the required capital is $10,000, the $5,000 (50 percent) return may be extremely appealing. If the required investment is $1 million, the $5,000 (½ percent) return probably will be unappealing. Depending on risk and available alternatives, individuals and corporate investors usually have some notion of a minimum rate of return that would make various projects desirable investments.

The quantitative approach to management problem-solving is, generally, to estimate the effect of the alternatives on cash flows in relation to the required investments. Thus, all projects whose rate of return exceeds the minimum rate of return would be desirable, and vice versa. A project which promises a return of 25 percent would ordinarily be more desirable than one which promises a return of 12 percent. The problem of choosing the minimum acceptable rate of return (more a problem of finance than of accounting) is extremely complex. . . .

There are several different ways of approaching the capital budgeting decision. Although we shall discuss: (*a*) discounted cash flow; (*b*) payback; and (*c*) the unadjusted rate of return, we shall concentrate on discounted cash flow because it is conceptually superior to the others.

## DISCOUNTED CASH FLOW

### Time Value of Money

The old adage that a bird in the hand is worth two in the bush is applicable to the management of money. A dollar in the hand today is worth more than a dollar to be received (or spent) five years from today. This is because the use of money has a cost (interest), just as the use of a building or an automobile may have a cost (rent). *Because the discounted-cash-flow method explicitly and automatically weighs the time value of money, it is the best method to use for long-range decisions.*

Another major aspect of the cash-flow method is its focus on *cash* inflows and outflows rather than on *net income* as computed in the conventional accounting sense. . . .

There are two main variations of the discounted-cash-flow method: (*a*) time-adjusted rate of return; and (*b*) net present value. . . .

The following example will be used to illustrate the concepts:

### Example 1

A manager is contemplating the rearrangement of assembly line facilities. Because of rapid technological changes in the industry, he is using a four-year planning horizon as a basis for deciding whether to invest in the facilities for rearrangement, which should result in cash operating savings of $2,000 per year. In other words, the useful life of this project is four years, after which the facilities will be abandoned or rearranged again.

*Required:*

1. If the plant rearrangement will cost $6,074 now, that is the time-adjusted rate of return on the project?
2. If the minimum desired rate of return is 10 percent, and the planned rearrangement will cost $6,074, what is the project's net present value? How much more would the manager be willing to invest and still earn 10 percent on the project?

Requirement 1 deals with the time-adjusted rate of return, which we shall consider first.

### Time-adjusted Rate of Return

The time-adjusted rate of return has been defined as "the maximum rate of interest that could be paid for the capital employed over the life of an investment without loss on the

**EXHIBIT 1**

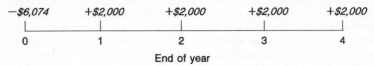

| −$6,074 | +$2,000 | +$2,000 | +$2,000 | +$2,000 |

| 0 | 1 | 2 | 3 | 4 |

End of year

**EXHIBIT 2**
**Two Proofs of Time-adjusted Rate of Return**

*Original investment, $6,074*
*Useful life, 4 years*
*Annual cash inflow from operations, $2,000*
*Rate of return (selected by trial-and-error methods), 12 percent*

Approach 1: Discounting Each Year's Cash Inflow Separately*

|  | Present Value of $1, Discounted at 12% | Total Present Value | Sketch of Cash Flows | | | | |
|---|---|---|---|---|---|---|---|
|  |  |  | 0 | 1 | 2 | 3 | 4 |
| End of Year Cash flows: |  |  |  |  |  |  |  |
| Annual savings | .893 | $ 1.786 | | $2,000 | | | |
|  | .797 | 1,594 | | | $2,000 | | |
|  | .712 | 1,424 | | | | $2,000 | |
|  | .636 | 1,272 | | | | | $2,000 |
| Present value of future inflows |  | $ 6,074† |  |  |  |  |  |
| Initial outlay | 1.000 | (6,074) | $(6,074) | | | | |
| Net present value (the zero difference proves that the rate of return is 12 per cent) |  | $ 0 |  |  |  |  |  |

Approach 2: Using Annuity Table‡

|  |  |  |  |  |  |  |  |
|---|---|---|---|---|---|---|---|
| Annual savings | 3.037 | $ 6,074 | | $2,000 | $2,000 | $2,000 | $2,000 |
| Initial outlay | 1.000 | (6,074) | $(6,074) | | | | |
| Net present value |  | $ 0 |  |  |  |  |  |

\* Present values from Table 1, Appendix II to Chapter 14 (p. 378). (Not reproduced in this book.)
† Sum is really $6,076, but is rounded.
‡ Present values of annuity from Table 2. Appendix II to Chapter 14 (p. 380). (Not reproduced in this book.)

project."[1] This rate corresponds to the effective rate of interest so widely computed for bonds purchased or sold at discounts or premiums. Alternatively, the rate of return can be defined as the discount rate that makes the present value of a project equal to the cost of the project.

The cash flows relating to our rearrangement problem are shown in Exhibit 1. The discounted cash flow analysis of these cash flows is shown in Exhibit 2. The exhibit shows that $6,074 is the present value, at a rate of return of 12 percent, of a four-year stream of inflows of $2,000 in cash. Twelve percent is the rate that equates the amount invested ($6,074) with the present value of the cash inflows ($2,000 per year for four years). In other words, *if* money were borrowed at an effective interest rate of 12 percent, the cash inflow produced by the project would exactly repay the hypothetical loan plus the interest over the four years. If the cost of capital (minimum desired rate of return on the capital) is less than 12 percent, the project will be desirable. If the cost of capital exceeds 12 percent, the cash inflow will be insufficient to pay the interest and repay the principal of the hypothetical loan. Therefore, 12 percent is the time-adjusted rate of return for this project.

\* \* \* \* \*

## Explanation of Compound Interest

The time-adjusted rate of return is computed on the basis of the cash in use from period to period, rather than on the original investment. Exhibit 3 shows that the return is 12 percent

## EXHIBIT 3
### Rationale of Time-adjusted Rate of Return

| Year | (a)<br>Unrecovered<br>Investment<br>at Beginning<br>of Year | (b)<br>Annual<br>Cash<br>Inflow | (c)<br>Return:<br>12% per<br>Year<br>(a) X 12% | (d)<br>Amount of<br>Investment<br>Recovered at<br>End of Year<br>(b) − (c) | (e)<br>Unrecovered<br>Investment<br>at End of Year<br>(a) − (d) |
|---|---|---|---|---|---|
| 1......... | $6,074 | $2,000 | $729 | $1,271 | $4,803 |
| 2......... | 4,803 | 2,000 | 576 | 1,424 | 3,379 |
| 3......... | 3,379 | 2,000 | 405 | 1,595 | 1,784 |
| 4......... | 1,784 | 2,000 | 216* | 1,784 | 0 |

\* Rounded.
*Note.* Same data as in Exhibit 14–3: Original investment, $6,074; Useful life, 4 years; Annual cash inflow from operations $2,000; Rate of return, 12 percent. Unrecovered investment at the beginning of each year earns interest for the whole year. Annual cash inflows are received at the end of each year.

of the cash invested during the year. After 12 percent of the cash invested is deducted, the remainder is the recovery of the original investment. Over the four years the cash inflow equals the recovery of the original investment plus annual interest, at the rate of 12 percent of the unrecovered capital.

## Depreciation and Discounted Cash Flow

Students are often mystified by the apparent exclusion of depreciation from discounted-cash-flow computations. A common homework error is to deduct depreciation. This is a misunderstanding of one of the basic ideas involved in the concept of the time-adjusted rate

---

[1] *Return on Capital as a Guide to Managerial Decisions,* National Association Account-ants, Research Report No. 35 (New York, December, 1959), p. 57.

of return. Discounted-cash-flow techniques and tables *automatically* provide for recoupment of the principal. Therefore, *it is unnecessary to deduct depreciation from operating cash inflows before consulting present value tables.*

In Exhibit 3, at the end of Year 1, the $2,000 cash inflow represents a 12 percent ($729) return on the $6,074 unrecovered investment at the beginning of Year 1 *plus* a $1,271 recovery of principal. The latter is similar to the depreciation provision in conventional accounting.

This difficult point warrants another illustration. Assume that a company is considering investing in a project with a two-year life and no residual value. Cash inflow will be equal payments of $4,000 at the end of each of the two years. How much would the company be willing to invest to earn a time-adjusted rate of return of 8 percent? A quick glance at the table for either the present value of $1 or the present value of an ordinary annuity of $1.00 will reveal:

Present Value of $4,000 at end of Year 1: $4,000 X .926 = $3,704
Present Value of $4,000 at end of Year 2: $4,000 X .857 =   3,428          $7,132
Present Value of annuity of $4,000 for 2 years at 8 percent: $4,000 X 1.783 = $7,132

The following is an analysis of the computations that are automatically considered in the construction of present value tables.

| Year | Investment at Beginning of Year | Oper- ating Cash Inflow | Return. @ 8% per Year | Amount of Investment Received at End of Year | Unrecovered Investment at End of Year |
|---|---|---|---|---|---|
| 1 | $7,132 | $4,000 | .08 X $7,132 = $571 | $4,000 − $571 = $3,429 | $7,132 − $3,429 = $3,703 |
| 2 | 3,703 | 4,000 | .08 X $3,703 = $297 | $4,000 − $297 = $3,703 | $3,703 − $3,703 = 0 |

A study of the above calculations will demonstrate that discounted-cash-flow techniques and tables have, built into them, the provisions for recovery of investment.

## Net Present Value

Another type of discounted-cash-flow approach may be called the net present value method. Computing the exact time-adjusted rate of return entails trial-and-error and, sometimes, cumbersome hand calculations and interpolations within a compound interest table. In contrast, the net present value method assumes some minimum desired rate of return. All expected future cash flows are discounted to the present, using this minimum desired rate. If the result is positive, the project is desirable, and vice versa.

Requirement (2) of Example 1 will be used to demonstrate the net present value approach. The problem assumes that the rearrangement will cost $6,074. Exhibit 4 shows a net present value of $264, so the investment is desirable. The manager would be able to invest $264 more, or a total of $6,338 (i.e., $6,074 + $264), and still earn 10 percent on the project.

The higher the minimum desired rate of return, the less the manager would be willing to invest in this project. At a rate of 16 percent, the net present value would be $−478 (i.e., $2,000 X 2.798 = $5,596, which is $478 less than the required investment of $6,074). (Present value factor, 2,798 is taken from Table 2.) When the desired rate of return is 16 percent, rather than 10 percent, the project is undesirable at a price of $6,074.

*    *    *    *    *

**EXHIBIT 4**
**Net Present Value Technique**

*Original investment, $6,074; Useful life, 4 years; Annual cash inflow from operations, $2,000; Minimum desired rate of return, 10 per cent*

Approach 1: Discounting Each Year's Cash Inflow Separately*

| | Present Value of $1, Discounted at 10% | Total Present Value | Sketch of Cash Flows | | | | |
|---|---|---|---|---|---|---|---|
| | | | 0 | 1 | 2 | 3 | 4 |
| **End of Year** | | | | | | | |
| **Cash flows:** | | | | | | | |
| Annual savings | .909 | $ 1,818 | | $2,000 | | | |
| | .826 | 1,652 | | | $2,000 | | |
| | .751 | 1,502 | | | | $2,000 | |
| | .683 | 1,366 | | | | | $2,000 |
| Present value of future inflows | | $ 6,338 | | | | | |
| Initial outlay | 1,000 | (6,074) | $(6,074) | | | | |
| Net present value | | $   264 | | | | | |

| | | | | | | | |
|---|---|---|---|---|---|---|---|
| Approach 2: Using Annuity Table† | | | | | | | |
| Annual savings | 3.170 | $ 6,340 | | $2,000 | $2,000 | $2,000 | $2,000 |
| Initial outlay | 1.000 | (6,074) | $(6,074) | | | | |
| Net present value | | $   264‡ | | | | | |

\* Present values from Table 1. Appendix II to Chapter 14, p. 378. (Not reproduced in this book.)
† Present annuity values from Table 2, p. 380. (Not reproduced in this book.)
‡ Rounded.

## Solution

A difficult part of long-range decision making is the structuring of the data. We want to see the effects of each alternative on future cash flows. The focus here is on bona fide *cash* transactions, not on opportunity costs. . . .

The following steps are likely to be the clearest:

*Step 1. Arrange the relevant cash flows by project, so that a sharp distinction is made between total project flows and incremental flows.* The incremental flows are merely algebraic differences between two alternatives. (There are *always* at least two alternatives. One is the *status quo,* the alternative of doing nothing.) Exhibit 5 shows how the cash flows for *each* alternative are sketched.

*Step 2. Discount the expected cash flows and choose the project with the least cost or the greatest benefit.* Both the total project approach and the incremental approach are illustrated in Exhibit 5. Which approach you use is a matter of preference. However, to develop confidence in this area, you should work with both at the start. In this example, the $8,425 net difference in favor of replacement is the ultimate result under either approach.

**EXHIBIT 5**
**Total Project versus Incremental Approach to Net Present Value (data from Example 2)**

| End of Year | Present Value Discount Factor, at 14% | Total Present Value | Sketch of Cash Flows | | | | |
|---|---|---|---|---|---|---|---|
| | | | 0 | 1 | 2 | 3 | 4 | 5 |

*Total Project Approach*

**A. Replace**

| | | | | | | | | |
|---|---|---|---|---|---|---|---|---|
| Recurring cash operating costs, using an annuity table* | 3.433 | $(102,990) | | ($30,000) | ($30,000) | ($30,000) | ($30,000) | ($30,000) |
| Disposal value, end of Year 5 | .519 | 1,557 | | | | | | 3,000 |
| Initial required investment | 1.000 | (31,000) | ($31,000) | | | | | |
| Present value of net cash outflows | | $(132,433) | | | | | | |

**B. Keep**

| | | | | | | | | |
|---|---|---|---|---|---|---|---|---|
| Recurring cash operating costs, using an annuity table* | 3.433 | $(137,320) | | ($40,000) | ($40,000) | ($40,000) | ($40,000) | ($40,000) |
| Overhaul, end of Year 2 | .769 | (7,690) | | | (10,000) | | | |
| Disposal value, end of Year 5 | .519 | 4,152 | | | | | | 8,000 |
| Present value of net cash outflows | | $(140,858) | | | | | | |
| Difference in favor of replacement | | $    8,425 | | | | | | |

*Incremental Approach*

*A–B Analysis Confined to Differences*

| | | | | | | | | |
|---|---|---|---|---|---|---|---|---|
| Recurring cash operating savings, using an annuity table* | 3.433 | $  34,330 | | $10,000 | $10,000 | $10,000 | $10,000 | $10,000 |
| Overhaul avoided end of Year 2 | .769 | 7,690 | | | $10,000 | | | |
| Difference in disposal values, end of Year 5 | .519 | (2,595) | | | | | | (5,000) |
| Incremental initial investment | 1.000 | (31,000) | ($31,000) | | | | | |
| Net present value of replacement | | $    8,425 | | | | | | |

* Table 2, p. 380. (Not reproduced in this book.)

**Analysis of Typical Items under Discounted Cash Flow**

*1. Future Disposal Values.* The disposal value at the date of termination of a project is an increase in the cash inflow in the year of disposal. Errors in forecasting disposal value are usually not crucial because the present value is usually small.

*2. Current Disposal Values and Required Investment.* There are a number of correct ways to analyze this item, all of which will have the same ultimate effect on the decision. . . . Generally, the required investment is most easily measured by offsetting the disposal value of the old assets against the gross cost of the new assets.

*3. Book Value and Depreciation.* Depreciation is a phenomenon of accrual accounting that entails an allocation of cost, not a specific cash outlay. Depreciation and book value are ignored in discounted-cash-flow approaches for the reasons mentioned earlier in this chapter.

*4. Income Taxes.* In practice, comparison between alternatives is best made after considering tax effects, because the tax impact may alter the picture. . . .

*5. Overhead Analysis.* In relevant cost analysis, only the overhead that will differ between alternatives is pertinent. There is need for careful study of the fixed overhead under the available alternatives. In practice, this is an extremely difficult phase of cost analysis, because it is difficult to relate the individual costs to any single project.

*6. Unequal Lives.* Where projects have unequal lives, comparisons may be made either over the useful life of the longer-lived project or over the useful life of the shorter-lived project. For our purposes, let us estimate what the residual values will be at the end of the longer-lived project. We must also assume a reinvestment at the end of the shorter-lived project. This makes sense primarily because the decision maker should extend his time horizon as far as possible. If he is considering a longer-lived project, he should give serious consideration to what would be done in the time interval between the termination dates of the shorter-lived and longer-lived projects.

\* \* \* \* \*

*[7.] The General Guide to Capital Budgeting Decisions.* The following decision rule, subject to the cautionary words just stated, should guide the selection of projects: The net present value method should be used, and *any* project that has a positive net present value should be undertaken. When the projects are mutually exclusive, so that the acceptance of one automatically entails the rejection of the other (e.g., buying Dodge or Ford trucks) the project which maximizes wealth measured in net present value in dollars should be undertaken.

## OTHER APPROACHES TO ANALYZING LONG-RANGE DECISIONS

\* \* \* \* \*

### Payback Method

*Payback,* or *payout,* or *payoff,* is the measure of the time it will take to recoup in the form of cash inflow from operations, the initial dollars invested. Assume that $12,000 is spent for a machine with an estimated useful life of eight years. Annual savings of $4,000 in *cash* outflow are expected from operations. Depreciation is ignored. The payback calculations follow:

$$P = \frac{I}{O} = \frac{\$12,000}{\$4,000} = 3 \text{ years} \tag{1}$$

Where $P$ is the payback time; $I$ is the initial incremental amount invested; and $O$ is the uniform annual incremental cash inflow from operations.

The payback method, by itself, does not measure profitability; it measures how quickly investment dollars may be recouped. This is its major weakness, because a shorter payback time does not necessarily mean that one project is preferable to another.

For instance, assume that an alternative to the $12,000 machine is a $10,000 machine whose operation will also result in a reduction of $4,000 annually in cash outflow. Then

$$P_1 = \frac{\$12,000}{\$4,000} = 3.0 \text{ years}$$

$$P_2 = \frac{\$10,000}{\$4,000} = 2.5 \text{ years}$$

The payback criterion indicates that the $10,000 machine is more desirable. However, one fact about the $10,000 machine has been purposely withheld. Its useful life is only 2.5 years. Ignoring the impact of compound interest for the moment, the $10,000 machine results in zero benefit, while the $12,000 machine generates cash inflows for five years beyond its payback period.

The main objective in investing is profit, not the recapturing of the initial outlay. If a company wants to recover its outlay fast, it need not spend in the first place. Then no waiting time is necessary; the payback time is zero.

*From*

# THE HUMAN SIDE OF ENTERPRISE*

*By Douglas McGregor*

Participation is one of the most misunderstood ideas that have emerged from the field of human relations. It is praised by some, condemned by others, and used with considerable success by still others. The differences in point of view between its proponents and its critics are about as great as those between the leaders of Iron Curtain countries and those of the Free World when they use the term "democracy."

Some proponents of participation give the impression that it is a magic formula which will eliminate conflict and disagreement and come pretty close to solving all of management's problems. These enthusiasts appear to believe that people yearn to participate, much as children of a generation or two ago yearned for Castoria. They give the impression that it is a formula which can be applied by any manager regardless of his skill, that virtually no preparation is necessary for its use, and that it can spring full-blown into existence and transform industrial relationships overnight.

Some critics of participation, on the other hand, see it as a form of managerial abdication. It is a dangerous idea that will undermine management prerogatives and almost certainly get out of control. It is a concept which for them fits the pattern of "soft" management exclusively. It wastes time, lowers efficiency, and weakens management's effectiveness.

A third group of managers view participation as a useful term in their bag of managerial tricks. It is for them a manipulative device for getting people to do what they want, under conditions which delude the "participators" into thinking that they have had a voice in decision making. The idea is to handle them so skillfully that they come up with the answer which the manager had in the first place, but believing it was their own. This is a way of "making people feel important" which these managers are quick to emphasize as a signifi-

---

* By permission from *The Human Side of Enterprise,* by Douglas McGregor. Copyright 1960. McGraw-Hill Book Company, Inc. (Excerpts from 124–31, 172–75.)

cant motivational tool of management. (It is important to note the distinction between making people *feel* important and *making* people important.)

Naturally, there are severe critics of this manipulative approach to participation, and they tend to conceive of all participation as taking this form.

A fourth group of managers makes successful use of participation, but they don't think of it as a panacea or magic formula. They do not share either the unrestrained enthusiasm of the faddists or the fears of the critics. They would flatly refuse to employ participation as a manipulative sales device.

Among all of these groups is a rather general but tacit agreement—incorrect, I believe—that participation applies to groups and not to individuals. None of them appears to view it as having any relationship to delegation. After all, it has a different name! Many of the strong proponents of delegation have no use whatever for participation.

In the light of all this it is not surprising that a fair number of thoughtful managers view this whole subject with some skepticism.

The effective use of participation is a consequence of a managerial point of view which includes confidence in the potentialities of subordinates, awareness of management's dependency downwards, and a desire to avoid some of the negative consequences of emphasis on personal authority. . . .

It is perhaps most useful to consider participation in terms of a range of managerial actions. At one end of the range the exercise of authority in the decision-making process is almost complete and participation is negligible. At the other end of the range the exercise of authority is relatively small and participation is maximum. There is no implication that more participation is better than less. The degree of participation which will be suitable depends upon a variety of factors, including the problem or issue, the attitudes and past experience of the subordinates, the manager's skill, and the point of view alluded to above.

\* \* \* \* \*

. . . Participation is not confined to the relationship between a first-line supervisor and his workers. It can occur between a president and his executive committee. Moreover, since there are many managerial decisions which affect a single subordinate, it is equally applicable to the individual or to the group. The kind of participation which will be utilized will vary depending upon the level of the organization as well as upon the other factors mentioned above.

\* \* \* \* \*

Since one of the major purposes of the use of participation is to encourage the growth of subordinates and their ability to accept responsibility, the superior will be concerned to pick appropriate problems or issues for discussion and decision. These will be matters of some significance to subordinates; otherwise they will see little point in their involvement. . . .

Of course, there are some risks connected with the use of participation. All significant managerial activities involve risk, and this is no exception. The usual fear is that if employees are given an opportunity to influence decisions affecting them, they will soon want to participate in matters which should be none of their concern. Managements who express this fear most acutely tend to have a very narrow conception of the issues which should concern employees. If management's concern is with the growth of employees and their increasing ability to undertake responsibility, there will of course be an expectation that employees will become involved in an increasing range of decision-making activities.

\* \* \* \* \*

In any event, there are now so many instances of the successful use of participation which has not in any discernible way weakened management's ability to manage that I can see little basis for anxiety over the issue of management prerogatives. The only conclusion I would draw is that the managements who are primarily concerned to protect their power and authority had better leave the whole matter alone.

. . . In view of the interdependence characteristic of industrial organizations there is reason for modifying the typical unilateral nature of the decision-making process. Participation, used judiciously, and in many different ways, depending upon the circumstances, offers help along these lines. It is a process which differs very little from delegation in its essential character. In fact, participation is a special case of delegation in which the subordinate gains greater control, greater freedom of choice, with respect to his own responsibility. The term participation is usually applied to the subordinate's greater influence over matters within the sphere of his superior's responsibilities. When these matters affect him and his job—when interdependence is involved—it seems reasonable that he should have the opportunity to exert some influence. . . .

Participation . . . offers substantial opportunities for ego satisfaction for the subordinate and thus can affect motivation toward organizational objectives. It is an aid to achieving integration. In the first place, the subordinate can discover the satisfaction that comes from tackling problems and finding successful solutions for them. This is by no means a minor form of satisfaction. It is one of the reasons that the whole do-it-yourself movement has grown to such proportions in recent years. Beyond this there is a greater sense of independence and of achieving some control over one's destiny. Finally, there are the satisfactions that come by way of recognition from peers and superiors for having made a worth-while contribution to the solution of an organizational problem. At lower levels of the organization, where the opportunities for satisfactions like these are distinctly limited, participation in departmental problem solving may have considerable significance in demonstrating to people how they can satisfy their own needs best by working toward organizational objectives.

Viewed thus, participation is not a panacea, a manipulative device, a gimmick, or a threat. Used wisely, and with understanding, it is a natural concomitant of management by integration and self-control.

\*    \*    \*    \*    \*

In order to create a climate of mutual confidence surrounding staff-line relationships within which collaboration in achieving organizational objectives will become possible, several requirements must be met:

1. The inadequacy of the conventional principles of unity of command and of equality of authority and responsibility must be recognized. Not only are these principles unrealistic in the modern industrial corporation, they are the source of many of the difficulties we are trying to correct. . . .

2. The primary task of any staff group is that of providing specialized help to *all levels* of management, not just to the level at which the group reports.

3. The proper role of the staff member is that of the professional vis-à-vis his clients. The genuinely competent professional recognizes (*a*) that help is always defined by the recipient and (*b*) that he can neither fulfill his responsibilities to the organization nor maintain proper ethical standards of conduct if he is placed in a position which involves conflicting obligations to his managerial "clients."

4. The central principle of managerial control is the principle of self-control. This principle severely limits *both* staff and line use of data and information collected for control purposes as well as the so-called coordinative activities of staff groups. If the principle of self-control is violated, the staff inevitably becomes involved in conflicting obligations, and in addition is required to occupy the incompatible roles of professional helper and policeman.

It may seem impractical to attempt to create a climate of staff-line relationships within the organization similar to that which characterizes effective professional-client relationships in private practice, yet this is essentially what is required. . . .

We are now in a position to consider a couple of interesting questions about the staff-line relationship. First, where is the issue of who exercises authority over whom?

With the approach suggested above, the traditional principles which define the role of staff evaporate. The professional-client relationship is an interdependent one in which neither typically exercises authority over the other although there is influence in both directions. The managerial client is dependent on the specialized knowledge and skill of the professional, but if he attempts to get the help he needs by authoritative methods he will defeat his purposes. It is not possible to obtain by command the imaginative, creative effort which distinguishes the competent professional from the glorified clerk. The manager who perceives staff members as flunkies to carry out his orders will never obtain *professional* staff help. On the other hand, the manger who perceives himself as a client utilizing the knowledge and skill of professional specialists will not attempt to achieve this purpose by relying on his authority over them.

The professional, in turn, is dependent upon his clients. Unless they accept and use his help, he has no value to the organization and therefore there is no reason for employing him. If, however, he attempts to impose "help" authoritatively (whether directly or by accepting assignments of control and coordinative responsibilities from his superiors), he places himself in the role of policeman, which is completely incompatible with the professional role.

*There is, in fact, no solution to the problem of staff-line relationships in authoritative terms which will achieve organizational objectives adequately.* Waste of human resources, friction and antagonism, elaborate and costly protective mechanisms, and lower commitment to organizational objectives are the inescapable consequences of the traditional conception of the relationship.

Second, what has happened to the distinction between line and staff? It has become evident as a result of our examination of line management's task . . . that the most appropriate roles of the manager vis-à-vis his subordinates are those of teacher, professional helper, colleague, consultant. Only to a limited degree will he assume the role of authoritative boss. The line manager who seeks to operate within the context of Theory Y will establish relationships with his subordinates, his superiors, and his colleagues which are much like those of the professional vis-à-vis his clients. He will become more like a professional staff member (although in general rather than specialized ways) and less like a traditional line manager.

The various functions within the organization differ in many ways (in the number of other functions with which they are related, for example), but not particularly in terms of the traditional line-staff distinction. All managers, whether line or staff, have responsibilities for collaborating with other members of the organization in achieving organizational objectives. Each is concerned with (1) making his own resources of knowledge, skill, and experience available to others; (2) obtaining help from others in fulfilling his own responsibilities; and (3) controlling his own job. Each has *both* line and staff responsibilities.

One consequence of this approach is the greater significance which the managerial *team* acquires at each level of organization. Much of the manager's work—be he line or staff—requires his collaboration with other managers in a relationship where personal authority and power must be subordinated to the requirements of the *task* if the organizational objectives are to be achieved. Effective collaboration of this kind is hindered, not helped, by the traditional distinctions between line and staff. The goal is to utilize the contributions of all the available human resources in reaching the best decisions or problem solutions or action strategies.

The modern industrial organization is a vast complex of interdependent relationships, up, down, across, and even "diagonally." In fact, the interdependence is so great that only collaborative team efforts can make the system work effectively. It is probable that one day we shall begin to draw organization charts as a series of linked groups rather than as a hierarchical structure of individual "reporting" relationships. . . .

*From*

# SETTING STANDARDS FOR EXECUTIVE PERFORMANCE*

## *By John W. Enell and George H. Haas*

During the seminar, it was noted by many of the panelists that the very process of formulating standards of performance can itself be of great benefit. In almost all the companies represented in this study, supervisor and subordinate work together in drawing up standards for the subordinate's job, sometimes in conference with a staff man from the personnel department. Standards developed in this manner are usually taken seriously by the executives who have had a part in their formulation; a give-and-take discussion results in a better understanding of the nature of the job expected and also of the priorities of its various segments. This formulation-by-conference method can help, too, by giving the supervisor a better understanding of the real conditions present in the subordinate's work. The seminar participants reported that, when standards were first tried in their firms, instances were found where a supervisor and his subordinate were at the outset completely at variance in their understanding of the nature of the job under consideration. This sort of misunderstanding apparently arises at every level of management. The process of correcting these conflicting views and hammering out agreement on the nature and quality of results expected on the job is an important phase of management development.

\*    \*    \*    \*    \*

Almost all the participants agreed that the executive and the subordinate must come together at some point in the process and candidly bring up—and iron out—any differences that arise. Even Robert Grover of Snap-On Tools took this point of view, despite the fact that his firm's chief standard of performance is a very detailed company-wide and departmental system of budgets. Mr. Grover remarked that the subordinate is given an opportunity to express himself when the budget for his unit is in the discussion stage. If he feels that he cannot live within his budget or produce the amount of income required of him (provided that he is in an income-producing area), he has an adequate opportunity to make his point of view clear. Once he has agreed to his budget, he must comply with it.

. . . Mr. Daffern cited one instance in which the subordinate declared that the discussion during which standards were worked out was the only time in a long work history when he had had any really frank discussion with his boss about his responsibilities and their fulfillment. . . .

---

* Reprinted by permission of the American Management Association, New York, Research Study No. 42, 1960 (pp. 16–18, 31–32).

# 9. DOVER BEVERAGE COMPANY

---

## Case Introduction

---

### SYNOPSIS

As a regional beer and soft drink bottler, Dover has established its own label and marketed a nationally branded soft drink line under license. Competition has been growing between the Dover line and the licensed products. As renewal time approaches for the license, Dover management debates both the merits of the license, as well as the appropriate analytics for making the decision about license renewal.

### WHY THIS CASE IS INCLUDED

Product line accounting is a perennial management problem. In the Dover case the student has to come to grips with the different cost concepts and the different forms of analysis which might be used to answer various management questions. In Dover, the task is asking the right management questions and matching the analytic scheme to the question. The reality of a tough competitive environment prevents the case from becoming a mere numbers exercise. The reality, as well, of conflicts within the management team complicates Dover's planning of its future.

### DIAGNOSTIC AND PREDICTIVE QUESTIONS

The readings included with this case are marked (*). The author index at the end of this book locates the other readings.

1. What business is Dover in?
Read: Drucker, *Management—Tasks-Responsibilities-Practices.* Webster, *Marketing for Managers.*

2. From what you read in the case can you identify Dover's strategy?
Read: Cannon, *Business Strategy and Policy.* Pessemier, *New Product Decisions.*

3. In what ways do the analyses by Jerry Daly and Fred Stallings differ in their classification of costs?

Read: *Horngren, *Accounting for Management Control,* pp. 250–54.

4. Beyond the issue of cost classification, in what other ways were Daly's and Stalling's analyses different?

Read: *Horngren, *Cost Accounting: A Managerial Emphasis.*

5. Did Jerry Daly use acceptable accounting techniques and definitions in his analysis?

Read: *Horngren, *Accounting for Management Control,* pp. 250–54.
*Horngren, *Cost Accounting: A Managerial Emphasis.*

6. Why did Jerry Daly recommend the "relevant cost" analysis?

Read: *Horngren, *Cost Accounting: A Managerial Emphasis.*

7. How would you respond to Fred Stallings' critique of Jerry Daly's method that it contained no built-in ruler to aid decision making?

Read: *Horngren, *Cost Accounting: A Managerial Emphasis.*

8. Was the conclusion "obvious" at the end of Fred Stallings' contribution analysis?

Read: *Horngren, *Accounting for Management Control,* p. 349.

9. What was going on between Leonard and Fred Stallings?

Read: Seiler, "Diagnosing Interdepartmental Conflict." Litterer, "Conflict in Organization: A Re-Examination."

10. How would you describe Nic Carbone's approach to managing the conflict which emerged during the May meeting? What alternative approaches might he have used?

Read: Lawrence and Lorsch, "New Management Job: The Integrator." Follett, "Constructive Conflict." Schein, *Process Consultation: Its Role in Organization Development.*

## POLICY QUESTIONS

11. Are there things going on inside or outside Dover which might prompt a strategic review?

12. What would you recommend Dover do about its strategy? Through what process (who does what)? (Review Questions 9–10.)

Read: Gilmore, "Formulating Strategy in Smaller Companies."

13. Will Dover need some product accounting analitics as part of its review? Which techniques? For what purposes? (Review Questions 1–6.)

14. What recommendations would you give Dover to manage the conflict which surfaced in both the May and June meetings? (Review Questions 7–8.)

# Case Text*

Dover's crest on a red and gold background had appeared on beer and soft drink bottles for almost a century in a northern midwest region. Three generations of the Stallings family have built the complex of four bottling plants into a well-respected regional enterprise. The current president, Leonard Stallings, 59, was particularly proud that Dover's conservative image served it well in these environmentally sensitive times. Dover was the "darling" of the environmentalists because it had never introduced the throwaway bottle or the can for its beverages. Despite almost no investment in media advertising, the Dover name seemed to be continually in the print and broadcast media. Ten years ago, the dealer relations thrust of the Dover marketing strategy was threatened by the "deposit and return" policy. The dealers, whom Dover wanted so much to cultivate, began to resist all the extra work until the "no deposit, no return" policy of Dover competitors became virtually un-American.

## May Management Meeting

It was marketing strategy that featured on the agenda of Dover's May management meeting. As was the custom, one of the department managers, John Cook, the sales manager, took his turn chairing the meeting. For the other 18 men in the room (see the organization chart in Appendix A), John Cook's report was an important one because it contained the year's first glimpse at updated market forecasts. After finishing an encouraging report on the beer market, the sales manager displayed an overhead transparency of the soft drink market development, the performance of Dover-branded products, as well as national-branded products sold by Dover under license. (Exhibit 1.)

Discussion turned first on why the market had been deteriorating for the last two years. John Cook explained that sweet drinks continued under attack by both medical doctors and dentists. He revealed his working assumptions with Exhibit 2.

"Our market share even improves slightly these days because we are proportionally better represented in the nonsweet segment which is still growing nicely." "But John," asked Leonard Stallings, "I'm more concerned over what your previous slide showed about National Products. As you know, I've just finished the negotiations over price with them and they finally agreed to our upping the price across the board 20 percent. With that development I would have thought we'd have more aggressive plans for National Products prior to our negotiating and renewing the

---
* Copyright C.E.I., Geneva, 1976. Written by Dr. J. J. O'Connell.

**EXHIBIT 1**
**Soft Drink Market**

| Year (0 = current year) | Total Market (millions of gallons) | Dover Sales (millions of gallons) | Dover Percent Share of total Market | National Product Sales (millions of gallons) | National Percent Share of Dover Sales |
|---|---|---|---|---|---|
| −10 | 22.4 | 5.5 | 24.6% | 1.3 | 24.2% |
| − 9 | 27.9 | 7.6 | 27.2 | 1.8 | 24.3 |
| − 8 | 30.9 | 8.8 | 28.5 | 2.0 | 22.7 |
| − 7 | 29.7 | 8.3 | 27.9 | 2.0 | 24.0 |
| − 6 | 35.5 | 11.0 | 30.1 | 2.1 | 19.1 |
| − 5 | 47.0 | 12.5 | 26.6 | 2.3 | 18.4 |
| − 4 | 47.5 | 19.1 | 40.2 | 2.6 | 13.6 |
| − 3 | 54.3 | 21.7 | 39.9 | 2.4 | 11.1 |
| − 2 | 57.4 | 22.8 | 39.7 | 2.8 | 12.3 |
| − 1 | 53.6 | 20.3 | 37.9 | 2.7 | 13.3 |
| 0 | 52.9 | 20.8 | 39.3 | 2.6 | 12.5 |
| + 1 | 53.9 | 21.3 | 39.5 | 2.6 | 12.2 |
| + 2 | 54.9 | 21.8 | 39.7 | 2.7 | 12.3 |
| + 3 | 56.0 | 22.3 | 39.8 | 2.8 | 12.5 |
| + 4 | 57.1 | 22.8 | 39.9 | 2.8 | 12.3 |
| + 5 | 58.4 | 23.3 | 39.9 | 2.9 | 12.4 |

**EXHIBIT 2**
**Soft Drink Market Structure (in percent)**

| | Years | | | | | | | | |
|---|---|---|---|---|---|---|---|---|---|
| | −3 | −2 | −1 | 0 | +1 | +2 | +3 | +4 | +5 |
| Sweet drinks | | | | | | | | | |
| Noncola | 76.5 | 76.7 | 77.0 | 76.2 | 75.6 | 75.0 | 74.5 | 74.0 | 73.5 |
| Cola | 7.1 | 6.8 | 6.8 | 6.8 | 6.9 | 7.0 | 7.0 | 7.0 | 7.0 |
| Noncarbinated | 4.7 | 4.5 | 4.0 | 3.9 | 3.8 | 3.7 | 3.6 | 3.5 | 3.4 |
| Nonsweet drinks | 11.7 | 12.0 | 12.2 | 13.1 | 13.7 | 14.3 | 14.9 | 15.5 | 16.1 |

license agreement with them next year. How can I go back to them with such a flat projection for the proposed life of the license?"

"Dad," said Fred Stallings, operations vice president, "We've been losing so much money on National Products for so long that many of us would be just as happy to forego the privilege of distributing their products. Besides, the cola market is going nowhere. Show the picture, John."

The sales manager explained:

**EXHIBIT 3**
**Cola Market**

| Year | Total Soft Drink (millions of gallons) | Share Percent for Cola | Total Cola Sales (millions of gallons) | National Cola Sales (millions of gallons) | National Percent Share of Cola Market |
|------|------|------|------|------|------|
| −3 | 54.3 | 7.1% | 3.86 | 1.44 | 37.3% |
| −2 | 57.4 | 6.8 | 3.90 | 1.44 | 36.9 |
| −1 | 53.6 | 6.8 | 3.64 | 1.40 | 38.5 |
| 0 | 52.9 | 6.8 | 3.60 | 1.33 | 35.8 |
| +1 | 53.9 | 6.9 | 3.72 | 1.38 | 37.1 |
| +2 | 54.9 | 7.0 | 3.84 | 1.43 | 37.2 |
| +3 | 56.0 | 7.0 | 3.92 | 1.45 | 37.0 |
| +4 | 57.1 | 7.0 | 4.00 | 1.48 | 37.0 |
| +5 | 58.4 | 7.0 | 4.01 | 1.50 | 37.4 |

**EXHIBIT 4**
**Mix of National Products at Dover (millions of gallons)**

| Year | Cola | Red | Green | Total National Products Sales |
|------|------|------|------|------|
| −6 | .988 | .853 | .282 | 2.123 |
| −5 | 1.158 | .887 | .299 | 2.344 |
| −4 | 1.564 | .764 | .226 | 2.554 |
| −3 | 1.444 | .813 | .165 | 2.422 |
| −2 | 1.436 | 1.236 | .128 | 2.800 |
| −1 | 1.396 | 1.212 | .088 | 2.696 |
| 0 | 1.370 | 1.180 | .075 | 2.625 |
| +1 | 1.375 | 1.250 | -0- | 2.625 |
| +2 | 1.425 | 1.275 | -0- | 2.700 |
| +3 | 1.450 | 1.300 | -0- | 2.750 |
| +4 | 1.475 | 1.325 | -0- | 2.800 |
| +5 | 1.500 | 1.350 | -0- | 2.850 |

The picture would look slightly different for the regional cola market if Dover really had all of National's cola business in the region. If we added in the business the Dairy Co-op does in cans of National Cola plus the business allocated by National in the southeastern corner of the territory to Shamrock Bottlers, National really has a 50 percent share of the cola market in the region. Ten years ago National had 55 percent. Recently, American cola plus the two local colas have been splitting the remainder of the market and stealing some of National's share.

"But," interrupted the President, "the National line is more than cola. Give the complete picture, John."

"That's an interesting way to announce a strategic decision!" shouted Leonard Stallings. "What the hell happens to National Green next year? It took you guys just three years to kill National Green after jumping right on top of them with a Dover substitute. Congratulations! That bright move really strengthens my hand as I go in to renegotiate the license. Good work!!!"

After an awkward pause, Frederick Stallings spoke up to his father. "National's been out to kill off our Dover Red since they came right in on top of us ten years ago. We've simply been more effective in the recent head-to-head competition on Green. You don't deny that it's uneconomic for us to handle National Green at this year's volume. The $136,000 in gross sales doesn't come near covering our costs of special handling. I decided with John Cook's group that we'd be better off without National Green."

**EXHIBIT 5**
**Revenue Forecast for National Products (price held to current year new price)**

| Year | Cola | Red | Green | Total |
|---|---|---|---|---|
| −1......... | $1,828,500 | $1,604,750 | $130,000 | $3,563,250 |
| 0 ........ | 2,275,250 | 1,952,750 | 135,750 | 4,363,750 |
| +1......... | 2,279,000 | 2,076,250 | 0 | 4,355,250 |
| +2......... | 2,355,500 | 2,112,500 | 0 | 4,468,000 |
| +3......... | 2,391,750 | 2,148,250 | 0 | 4,540,000 |
| +4......... | 2,427,750 | 2,183,750 | 0 | 4,611,500 |
| +5......... | 2,462,250 | 2,217,500 | 0 | 4,679,750 |

As he had done so often in the past 30 years, Nic Carbone, bottling manager, attempted to pour oil on troubled waters,

I don't know about the rest of you, but I get tired of conclusions based on assumptions. I have no idea what you, Fred, are assuming as special handling costs for National Green. Unlike National Cola and Red, Green comes in one bottle size. We don't worry about special packaging for fountain syrups or three bottle sizes like the rest of the National line. Why don't we specify our assumptions and then agree on what accounting conventions we will all use? Right now, we all have unstated assumptions and private numbers. Dover is getting like my uncle's shoe factory in Italy with three or four sets of books, each to be dragged out for its own special purpose. Why don't we wait until the June management meeting which Norman [Norman Stallings, accounting manager, brother of the president] chairs? Norman and Jerry [Jerry Daly, control manager] can surface the assumptions floating around about National Products and they can bring in clean numbers on which we all agree, especially those tricky overhead allocation numbers. Norman's agenda can be on product line accounting. Don't you think that's what we should do, Freddie?

The Wallaces [Harry, Dover Line sales manager, and Joseph, Plant A manager] and I worked up those numbers a couple of weekends ago at the fishing camp. Possibly, we could work with Norm and Jerry in preparing for the June meeting.

Thanks, Frederick! Jerry and I can handle the job ourselves. We'll consult with you, of course. We'll send our analysis to everyone a week in advance of the June meeting.

In a calm voice again, the president reacted to Nic's idea. "Nic's right, as usual. We need some agreed product line accounting analysis on which to base the discussion of whether to renew the National license. Agreed, then . . . Norman and Jerry straighten us out on the 26th. Anything else, John, before we adjourn this meeting?"

"No, except Norman should know that the forecasts I used today are consensus numbers of our three operating departments. Other than that, the meeting's over. Thank you!"

As the executives filed out of the conference room, Leonard Stallings spoke in a stage whisper to Richard Cuff: "Are you still sales manager for the National line?"

## Preparation of the June Management Meeting

Norman Stallings and Jerry Daly met on the Monday following the May meeting to plan the analysis promised for the June meeting. Jerry Daly proposed that the only analysis of value in the go/no-go decision on the National line would be a "relevant cost" analysis. After long discussion of alternative or substitute analyses, Mr. Stallings finally agreed that Jerry's proposal was most responsive to the president's specific mandate. Another hour was spent defining terms and carefully planning who was to be interviewed and in what sequence. Mr. Stallings was eager to keep a low profile in the preparation and presentation of the analysis, "in order to preserve my independence as chairman of the June meeting." Nonetheless, Mr. Stallings offered to meet at 5 P.M. every other day until the analysis was complete. Jerry Daly took care to combine data gathering and explanation of the "relevant cost" analysis as he went from office to office. He took the trouble of going right down to the bottling lines in three plants, riding delivery trucks, and visiting supermarket outlets with Dover salesmen. By the time Norman Stallings approved his memorandum for distribution on June 17, Jerry Daly was convinced he had done a professional accounting job with all the diplomacy possible (see the Memorandum in Appendix B).

The evening after receiving the Daly memorandum, Frederick Stallings discussed the analysis with the Wallace brothers as they car-pooled toward their suburban neighborhood. All agreed that Jerry Daly had done a first-class job. The only complaint on the numbers came from Joe Wallace. "Jerry was clever. Once you accepted his definitions, there was damn little room for contest on the numbers. Yet, even in my plant, we would notice the departure of the National line. There'd be less hard work, fewer setups on the bottler for those three nonstandard bottle sizes, and in general less jackassing of someone else's bottles and cases around our plant. All such grief is defined out of Jerry's analysis."

"So, we grant him the definitions and numbers," said Fred, "but, I still don't buy the conclusion. If I understand the analysis, you'd keep National products if you had one dollar of profit after all relevant costs. There's no ruler built into the analysis to say whether the profit generated with Jerry's routine is large enough to bother about. In some way, you have to compare National to Dover soft drinks and beer. You can't do it with Jerry's analysis. Our contribution analysis may need some cleaning up, but at least it shows what National contributes to general overheads compared to our own soft drinks and beer. Tomorrow night let's bring our papers home and spend some time at the camp this weekend. We have some of Jerry's allocation decision rules and John's new forecasts, so we should get some generally acceptable results. Any allocations we're not sure of, Harry, you can check with Jerry on Monday. If we get clean copy done by Tuesday, we can send our analysis to the group. They'd still have two days before the meeting to digest it."

Fred and the Wallaces spent much of Saturday and Sunday on their contribution analysis. In the course of the weekend they made seven phone calls to Dover colleagues and two to Jerry Daly. Some late work on Monday readied the memorandum for Tuesday typing and distribution (see Appendix C).

## The June Management Meeting

After some mock congratulations by Nic Carbone to the assembled managers for reducing Dover's multiple sets of accounting books to two, Norman Stallings opened the meeting by asking Jerry Daly to answer questions about his memorandum. The first to speak up was Dick Cuff, National Products sales manager. "Am I right in assuming that my salary is not a relevant cost in your analysis?"

"That's right. You yourself said you spent virtually all your time handling both Dover and National products in the eastern metropolitan district. Leo Roberts and Harry Wallace confirmed that your real job is a district sales manager, not a product sales manager. One of you used the expression 'pure cosmetics for National's sake' in describing your position title."

Dick Cuff continued:

> Thanks, Jerry, I just wished to establish the fact that I have nothing personal to win or loose on this National license decision. On that understanding, I want to pick up the challenge Mr. Stallings gave me at the very end of the last meeting. Both your numbers, Jerry and Fred, are interesting but irrelevant. No one has done any serious thinking from National's point of view or from our competitors' points of view. Let me show you what I mean.
>
> As National, I'd be fed up with Dover. You refuse to carry my full line or my complete packaging on any one item. Dover is National's toughest competitor in noncola products. To get coverage in this region, National has to have three or four licensees. Furthermore,

Dover more and more drops special marketing for National. You are even phasing out the special National car and truck fleet. Dover marketing philosophy is to *push* via the dealers, whereas National's philosophy is to *pull* the product from the dealers by stimulating customer demand. From National's viewpoint Dover is getting to be more foe than friend.

The Dairy Coop already has National in cans. True, the Coop doesn't have the same dealer coverage Dover has but that can change. Milk sales are not increasing, so the Coop is running scared for the long pull. Right now money is no problem for them. For National, the Coop would be an aggressive noncompetitor, willing to push the whole line in all packaging forms. Why shouldn't National switch to Coop and sign even a sweetheart contract for the first three or five years while Coop builds bottling capacity?

Fitzgerald Bottlers is another possibility for National. They're not making any money on their own cola label even though they have some 20 percent of the market. We all know they'd just as soon concentrate on beer. The National license would be an elegant way out of their own cola business. National loses a competitor as it gains a licensee eager to utilize his newly idle cola bottling line.

I can even see National backing Shamrock Bottlers from down south. Shamrock has always had eyes on Dover territory anyway. They know one another and Shamrock has not been throwing tantrum fits of independence as Dover has.

So, Dover is not on top of the heap. National has attractive alternatives. Competitors are eager and able to take the National business. How about Dover? My position is that we need the National license no matter what the numbers say. Until I hear a Dover strategy with different dimensions than today, I'm convinced the National license is needed if only for defensive purposes. If we drop National we end up with more overcapacity both in production and administration than we now have. Overcapacity breeds an unhealthy psychology. We'd lose the prestige image associated with a nationally advertised line. We might even lose our National products specialists in Plants B and C. We lose control over National as a competitor. We don't have foolproof control over them now, but it's a damn sight more than nothing. Our dealers—our special friends—lose part of their beverage service from Dover as supplier. We become less important in their eyes.

Instead of playing with the finery of accounting, we should be spending our time defining tactics for retaining the National license.

"Well done, Dick!" shouted Leonard Stallings as he joined in the applause with Nic Carbone, Ben Ford, Ed Hunter, Frank Stevens, and Martin Frankel. "I didn't think you'd roll over and play dead!"

After the room quietened down, Fred Stallings turned to his uncle, Norman Stallings, and asked: "Was our agenda for this meeting product line accounting, or wasn't it?"

**APPENDIX A**
**Organization Chart**

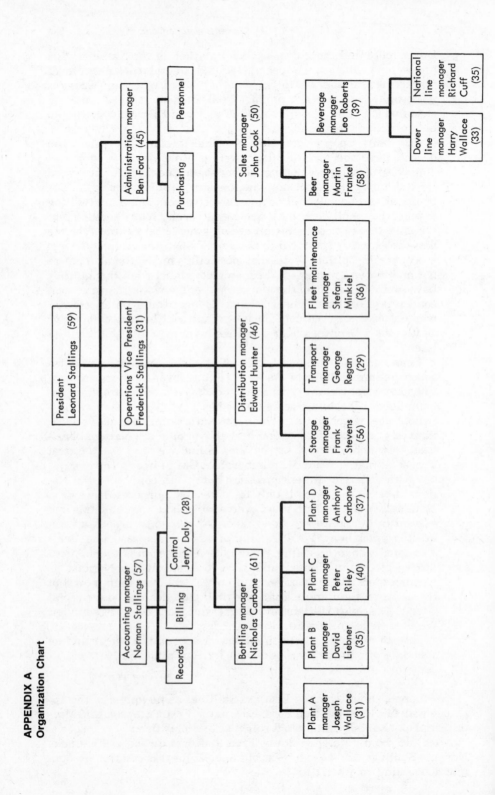

# APPENDIX B

**MEMORANDUM**

TO:   Management Group
FROM:   Jerry Daly, Control
DATE:   June 17
RE:   Relevant Cost Analysis

In preparation for the June management meeting, attached please find the "relevant cost analysis" concerning which I have spoken to each person involved. Definitions and assumptions accompany the analysis. Further detail is available in my office.

Let me repeat the principle of this analysis. In deciding whether or not to renew the National license, we wish to see what if any real profit we forego by dropping the line. Revenue is given in the agreed forecast. We charge against that revenue only those costs which would disappear if and when National were dropped. The plant lights stay on whether we produce National or not, so electricity is not a relevant cost. A maintenance man spending 10 percent of his time on the National production line cannot be dismissed if National drops nor is it obvious that incremental new work will automatically fill his day. Therefore the 10 percent of his salary is not a relevant cost. No general administration expenses will cease if National's dropped, so they are not relevant here.

*Conclusion:* There is significant and growing pretax profit after relevant costs in National products. Until such time as management plans reveal competitive demand for resources now committed to National products, it makes little sense to drop the National line.

## Relevant Cost Analysis

| | | | | Year | | | |
|---|---|---|---|---|---|---|---|
| | -1 | 0 | +1 | +2 | +3 | +4 | +5 |
| Gross revenue | $3,563,250 | $4,363,750 | $4,355,250 | $4,468,000 | $4,540,000 | $4,611,500 | $4,679,750 |
| Direct variable costs | −2,229,750 | −2,584,250 | −2,522,500 | −2,577,250 | −2,607,000 | −2,639,750 | −2,664,250 |
| | $1,333,500 | $1,799,500 | $1,832,750 | $1,890,750 | $1,933,000 | $1,971,750 | $2,015,500 |
| Direct fixed costs | − 379,974 | − 388,352 | − 373,765 | − 343,198 | − 328,650 | − 323,251 | − 309,085 |
| | $ 953,526 | $1,411,148 | $1,458,985 | $1,547,552 | $1,604,350 | $1,648,499 | $1,706,415 |
| Allocated joint costs | − 496,276 | − 614,398 | − 609,735 | − 621,052 | − 635,600 | − 640,999 | − 655,165 |
| | $ 457,250 | $ 796,750 | $ 849,250 | $ 926,500 | $ 968,750 | $1,007,500 | $1,051,250 |
| Capital costs | − 148,000 | − 196,750 | − 183,500 | − 187,250 | − 189,000 | − 190,750 | − 190,750 |
| Annual profit after all relevant costs | $ 309,250 | $ 600,000 | $ 665,750 | $ 739,250 | $ 779,750 | $ 816,750 | $ 860,500 |
| Percent profit on sales | 8.7% | 13.7% | 15.3% | 16.5% | 17.2% | 17.7% | 18.4% |

*Notes:*

1.  A relevant cost is one that disappears or is productively absorbed elsewhere if and when the National line is dropped.

2.  Direct variable costs (discounts, rebates, excise taxes, raw materials, bottle loss, distribution expense) are those directly varying with liquid or bottle volume of National products separately . . . some diminution expected in coming years as the mix of bottle sizes changes more toward the larger size.

3.  Direct fixed costs (dedicated National selling units in two metropolitan locations) are those annual lump commitments of salary or other expenses specifically for National products (including cooperative advertising on 50/50 basis with National) . . . it had been planned that these units and activities would be gradually reduced each year in favor of joint marketing as occurs in the two nonmetropolitan districts.

4.  Allocated joint costs (only in Plants B and C where significant National bottling occurs. . . . National use of Plant A is restricted to partial, singleshift, use of one bottling line . . . Plant D is not involved in National production) are fractions of ongoing expenses traceable to National (see table of current year allocation of relevant joint costs of Plants B and C for example).

5.  Capital costs (on receivables and inventory of raw material, bottles, pallets, cases, and finished goods) are 14 percent per annum on the financial resources committed to National exclusively . . . no capital costs on fixed assets like machinery or trucks because no such freed asset has a foreseen alternative economic use or is already fully depreciated like the dedicated vehicles in the metropolitan districts.

## Current Year Allocation of Relevant Joint Costs (Plants B and C)

| | Plant B Budget | Percent Allocated to National | Plant C Budget | Percent Allocated to National | Total Allocated to National |
|---|---|---|---|---|---|
| Production | | | | | |
| Manual | | | | | |
| sorting........... $139,258 | | 100%* | $104,250 | 80.0%* | $222,650 |
| Bottling............. xxx | | 0 | $364,500 | 25.0%† | $ 91,125 |
| Water costs........ $191,250 | | 7.4%‡ | $113,750 | 19.4%‡ | $ 36,275 |
| Maintenance | | | | | |
| and cleaning ...... $380,963 | | 3.6%§ | $ 80,250 | 33.3%‖ | $ 40,538 |
| Storage and Distribution: | | | | | |
| Truck fuel | | | | | |
| and physical | | | | | |
| handling ......... $521,807 | | 18.6% # | $334,000 | 38.0% # | $223,810 |
| | | | | | $614,398 |

\* By observation.
† One dedicated line can be shut and people let go.
‡ A function of bottle number and mix.
§ A function of National bottle volume share.
‖ A function of National bottle volume share and the reduced load because of closing dedicated line.
# A function of National bottle volume share and the manning of decicated vehicles which can be dropped.

# APPENDIX C

**MEMORANDUM**

TO:  Management Group
FROM:  F. Stallings, J. Wallace, H. Wallace
DATE:  June 22
RE:  Contribution Analysis

In order to complete the picture presented in Jerry Daly's excellent June 17th memo, we offer a comparative analysis of Dover beer, Dover soft drinks, and National products. No special definitions are necessary. Standard business language is used. John Cook's consensus forecasts have been adopted, as have Jerry Daly's allocation decision rules. No basis for allocation was incorporated without discussing the matter with Jerry Daly and the individuals involved.

The detailed analysis is shown in short form.
*Conclusion:* Obvious!

**Contribution Analysis (current year)**

|  | Dover Beer | Dover Soft Drinks | National Products | Total |
|---|---|---|---|---|
| Volume (gallons) ......... | 20,050,000 | 17,704,566 | 2,625,000 | 40,379,566 |
| Percent ................. | 49.6% | 43.8% | 6.6% |  |
| Gross revenue .......... | $43,814,000 | $23,486,500 | $4,364.000 | $71,664,500 |
| Percent ................. | 61.1% | 32.8% | 6.1% |  |
| Contribution* ........... | $ 5,430,500 | $ 3,916,250 | $ 452,250 | $ 9,799,000 |
| Percent ................. | 55.4% | 40.0% | 4.6% |  |
| Percent contribution on sales.............. | 12.5% | 17.0% | 10.4% | 13.7% |
| Contribution per gallon ............ | 27.1 | 22.1 | 17.2 | 24.3 |

* To cover general and administrative overhead.

## Contribution Analysis (current year)

| | Dover Beer | Percent | Dover Soft Drinks | Percent | National Products | Percent |
|---|---|---|---|---|---|---|
| Gross reserve | $43,814,000 | 100.0 | $23,486,500 | 100.0 | $4,364,000 | 100.0 |
| Excise tax and discounts* | 21,705,750 | 49.5 | 6,291,000 | 26.8 | 980,500 | 22.5 |
| | 22,108,250 | 50.5 | 17,195,500 | 73.6 | 3,383,500 | 77.5 |
| Raw material* | 6,881,750 | 15.7 | 3,845,750 | 16.4 | 1,220,250 | 28.0 |
| | 15,226,500 | 34.8 | 13,349,750 | 57.2 | 2,162,250 | 49.5 |
| Bottling and maintenance† | 2,859,250 | 6.5 | 3,046,500 | 13.0 | 459,250 | 10.5 |
| | 12,367,250 | 28.3 | 10,303,250 | 44.2 | 1,703,000 | 39.0 |
| Storage and distribution‡ | 4,611,750 | 10.5 | 4,407,750 | 18.8 | 892,250 | 20.4 |
| | 7,755,500 | 17.8 | 5,895,500 | 25.4 | 810,750 | 18.6 |
| Marketing and product development§ | 2,325,000 | 5.3 | 1,979,250 | 8.4 | 358,500 | 8.2 |
| | $ 5,430,500 | 12.5 | $ 3,916,250 | 17.0 | $ 452,250 | 10.4 |
| Contribution to cover general and administrative overhead | | | | | | |

* Where costs are not fully direct, allocation is on the basis of volume in gallons.
† Where costs are not fully direct, allocation is on the basis of recorded man-hours on bottler per product.
‡ Where costs are not fully direct, allocation is on the basis of volume in bottles.
§ Where costs are not fully direct, allocation of marketing is by volume in gallons, allocation of product development is divided by volume in gallons between Dover beer and Dover soft drinks.

# Selected Readings

*From*

## ACCOUNTING FOR MANAGEMENT CONTROL*

*By Charles T. Horngren*

### CONTRIBUTION APPROACH

#### Contribution Approach versus Traditional Approach

The major difference between the traditional and the contribution approaches is the tendency of the traditional approach to emphasize a *functional-cost* classification as opposed to a classification by *cost behaviors.* Hence, the traditional income statement has the following pattern:

```
Sales................................................... xx
Less manufacturing cost of goods sold
  (including fixed manufacturing overhead)...................... xx
Gross profit ............................................. xx
Less selling and administrative expenses ........................ xx
Operating income .......................................... xx
```

In contrast, the contribution approach stresses cost behavior as the primary classification scheme:

```
Sales ................................................... xx
Less variable costs:
  Manufacturing........................................ xx
  Selling............................................... xx
  Administrative....................................... xx      xx
Contribution margin ....................................... xx
Less fixed costs:
  Manufacturing........................................ xx
  Selling............................................... xx
  Administrative....................................... xx      xx
Operating income.......................................... xx
```

---

* Charles T. Horngren, *Accounting for Management Control: An Introduction,* 3d Edition, © 1974, excerpt from pp. 250–254. Reprinted by permission of Prentice-Hall, Inc., Englewood Cliffs, N.J.

**EXHIBIT 1**
**Comparison of Contribution Approach with Traditional (Functional) Approach**

SAMSON COMPANY
Contribution Income Statement
For the Year Ending December 31, 19x2
(in thousands of dollars)

| | | |
|---|---:|---:|
| Sales | | $20,000 |
| Less variable expenses: | | |
| Direct material | $ 7,000 | |
| Direct labor | 4,000 | |
| Variable indirect manufacturing | 1,000 | |
| Total variable manufacturing cost of goods sold | $12,000 | |
| Variable selling expenses | 1,000 | |
| Variable administrative expenses | 100 | |
| Total variable expenses | | 13,100 |
| Contribution margin | | $ 6,900 |
| Less fixed expenses: | | |
| Manufacturing | $ 3,000 | |
| Selling | 2,000 | |
| Administrative | 900 | |
| | | 5,900 |
| Operating income | | $ 1,000 |

SAMSON COMPANY
Traditional (Functional) Income Statement
For the Year Ending December 31, 19x2
(in thousands of dollars)

| | | |
|---|---:|---:|
| Sales | | $20,000 |
| Less manufacturing cost of goods sold: | | |
| Direct material | $7,000 | |
| Direct labor | 4,000 | |
| Indirect manufacturing costs | 4,000 | |
| | | 15,000 |
| Gross profit | | $ 5,000 |
| Selling expenses | $3,000 | |
| Administrative expenses | 1,000 | |
| Total selling and administrative expenses | | 4,000 |
| Operating income | | $ 1,000 |

Note that the traditional statement does not show any contribution margin. Although the manufacturing-, selling-, and administrative-cost classifications could also be further subdivided to show variable and fixed classifications, this subdivision is not typical. The omission of a contribution margin raises analytical difficulties in the computation of the impact on net income of changes in sales. Fixed manufacturing overhead, under traditional procedures, is unitized and assigned to products. Hence, unit costs and gross-profit figures include fixed overhead that must be removed for a short-run cost-volume-profit analysis.

The contribution approach stresses the lump-sum amount of fixed costs to be recouped before net income emerges. This highlighting of total fixed costs helps to attract management attention to fixed-cost behavior and control when both short-run and long-run plans are being made. Keep in mind that advocates of this contribution approach *do not maintain that fixed costs are unimportant or irrelevant;* but they do stress that the distinctions between behaviors of variable and fixed costs are crucial for certain decisions.

\*       \*       \*       \*       \*

## Advantages of Contribution Margins and Ratios

The advantages of knowing the contribution margins and ratios of divisions and product lines may be summarized as follows:

1. *Contribution-margin ratios* often help management decide on which products to push and which to de-emphasize or tolerate only because of the sales benefits that relate to other products.

2. *Contribution margins* are essential for helping management to decide whether a product line should be dropped. In the short run, if a product recovers more than its variable costs, it may be making a contribution to overall profits. This information is provided promptly by the contribution approach. Under the traditional approach, the relevant information is not only difficult to gather, but there is a danger that management may be misled by reliance on unit costs that contain an element of fixed overhead.

3. Contribution margins may be used to appraise alternatives that arise with respect to price reductions, special discounts, special advertising campaigns, and the use of premiums to spur sales volume. Decisions such as these are really determined by a comparison of the added costs with the prospective additions in sales revenue. Ordinarily, the higher the contribution-margin ratio, the better the opportunity for sales promotion; the lower the ratio, the greater the increase in volume that is necessary to recover additional sales-promotion commitments.

4. When desired profits are agreed upon, their attainability may be quickly appraised by computing the number of units that must be sold to secure the wanted profits. The computation is easily made by dividing the fixed costs plus desired profits by the contribution margin per unit.

5. Decisions must often be made as to how to utilize a given set of resources (for example, machines or materials) most profitably. The contribution approach furnishes the data for a proper decision, because the latter is determined by the product that makes the largest total contribution to profits.

\*       \*       \*       \*       \*

*From*

# COST ACCOUNTING: A MANAGERIAL EMPHASIS*

*By Charles T. Horngren*

## RELEVANT COSTS AND THE CONTRIBUTION APPROACH TO DECISIONS

In this chapter we turn to costing for special nonrecurring decisions, such as the addition or deletion of a product line, the manufacture or purchase of direct materials (make or buy), the acceptance or rejection of a special order, the replacement of equipment, and countless others. Teamwork among executives is commonly used in reaching these decisions, which are often fusions of the thinking of engineers, economists, production managers, sales managers, mathematicians, and accountants. Cost analysis is nearly always needed, and that is why the cost accountant plays an important role in these special decisions.

\*     \*     \*     \*     \*

## THE ACCOUNTANT'S ROLE IN SPECIAL DECISIONS

### Relevance and Accuracy

Accountants have an important role in the decision-making process, not as the decision makers themselves, but as collectors and reporters of relevant information. Many managers want the accountant to offer recommendations about a decision, even though the final choice always rests with the operating executive.

Relevance and accuracy are not identical concepts. *Relevance* means pertinence to the decision at hand. Figures are relevant if they guide the manager toward the decision that harmonizes with top-management objectives. Ideally, the information should be *relevant* (valid or pertinent) and *accurate* (precise). However, figures may be accurate but irrelevant, or inaccurate but relevant.

### Qualitative and Quantitative Factors

The consequences of each alternative may be divided into two broad categories, *qualitative* and *quantitative*. Qualitative factors are those whose measurement in dollars and cents is difficult and imprecise; yet a qualitative factor may easily be given more weight than the measurable cost savings.

\*     \*     \*     \*     \*

Quantitative factors are those that may more easily be reduced to terms of dollars and cents, such as projected alternative costs of materials, direct labor, and overhead. The accountant, statistician, and mathematician increasingly try to express as many decision factors as possible in quantitative terms. This approach tends to reduce the number of qualitative factors to be judged.

## MEANING OF RELEVANCE

### The Nature of Decision Making

Because the nature and method of decision making are examined in depth elsewhere, we will not dwell on them here. Nevertheless, decision making deserves scrutiny because

---

\* Charles T. Horngren, *Cost Accounting: A Managerial Emphasis,* 3d Edition, © 1972, excerpts from pp. 349–353, 355, 358–360, 368–369, 943–953. Reprinted by permission of Prentice-Hall, Inc., Englewood Cliffs, N.J.

it should be the fundamental focus of cost accounting. Decision making is a goal-seeking process; to decide is to choose from among a set of alternative courses of action in light of some objective. The decision maker must (*a*) recognize why a choice is necessary; (*b*) delineate the set of alternative courses of action; (*c*) evaluate the alternatives; and (*d*) pick a course of action.

Every decision deals with the future—whether it be ten seconds ahead (the decision to adjust a dial) or eighty years ahead (the decision of where to locate a factory). A decision always involves a prediction. Therefore, the function of decision making is to select courses of action for the future. There is no opportunity to alter the past.

Note too that the set of alternative actions and the objective of the decision are also predictions. In selecting a set of alternatives, the decision maker (hereafter often referred to as a manager) must predict that the set contains the best of the possible alternatives. That is, the manager may choose the best alternative in a given set, but he might have come closer to his objective had he picked an alternative that was overlooked and was excluded from the set he considered. For example, a manager may choose between Machines A and B and completely overlook the availability of Machine C, which may be the best alternative.

Moreover, the manager may have chosen the wrong objective. For example, the basic goal may be to maximize the market value of the common shares. The manager may think that the best way to accomplish this is to maximize earnings per share, so he uses this yardstick as his objective. But perhaps in this case a better way to maximize market value is to maximize the net cash flow available for dividends. Hence, he may err in a decision because he predicted incorrectly by selecting an inferior objective.

The manager needs a method for making a choice among different courses of action. This method is frequently called a *decision model*. A *model* is an abstraction and depiction of the relationships among the recognized objects in a particular concrete situation; it emphasizes the key interrelationships and often excludes some unimportant factors. Models have many forms and purposes: They may be descriptive or predictive; verbal, physical, or mathematical; dynamic or static; and so on. For instance, accounting systems and financial reports are financial models of an organization's operations. A *decision model* provides a conceptual representation that enables the manager to measure the effects of alternative actions.

### Relevance as Defined Here

The words *information* and *data* have a variety of meanings in both the popular and the technical literature. For our purposes, information is that subset of data that is likely to alter a decision maker's prediction. Exhibit 1 sketches the decision process and uses an illustration of a decision to rearrange plant facilities. Accounting records show that past direct-labor costs were $2 per unit. No wage-rate changes are anticipated, but the rearrangement is expected to reduce direct-labor usage by 25 percent. Direct-material costs of $5 per unit will not change under either alternative.

The somewhat elaborate mechanism shown in Exhibit 1 seems unnecessary for this decision. After all, the analysis in a nutshell is:

*Relevant Costs per Unit*

|  | Do not Rearrange | Rearrange |
|---|---|---|
| Direct labor............ | $2.00 | $1.50 |

If all other considerations are a standoff, and the objective is to minimize costs, then rearrangement is the more desirable alternative.

Note that the method used for making the decision per se (the decision model) necessitated a comparison of *expected future costs* that will *differ* under alternatives. The $2

**EXHIBIT 1**
**Decision Process and Role of Information**

The decision is whether to invest in the rearrangement of plant facilities. The objective is to minimize costs.

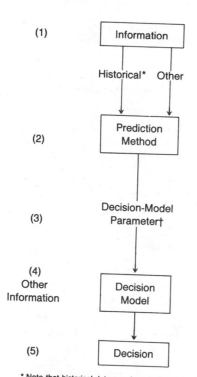

(1)

Historical direct-labor costs were $2 per unit. No wage-rate changes are expected, but the rearrangement is expected to reduce direct labor usage. Direct-material costs were $5 per unit, and will not be affected by the rearrangement.

(2)

Use the information together with an assessment of probabilities as a basis for predicting the future costs of direct labor and direct materials. Direct-labor usage is expected to decline by 25 percent.

(3)

*Cost Comparison per Unit*

| | Do not Rearrange | Rearrange |
|---|---|---|
| Direct labor....... | $2.00 | $1.50 |

(4)
Other Information

The *expected future* costs are the outputs of the prediction method and are inputs of the decision model together with other quantitative and qualitative information. For example, the effect of the rearrangement on worker morale may be a qualitative consideration.

(5)

\* Note that historical data may be relevant for prediction methods.
† Historical data are never relevant per se for decision models. Only those expected future data that are different are really relevant. For instance in this example, direct labor makes a difference and direct material does not. Therefore, *under our definition here*, direct material is irrelevant.

direct-labor charge may be the same as in the past, and the past records may have been extremely helpful in preparing the $2 forecast. The trouble is that most accountants and managers view the $2 past cost as the future cost. But the crucial point is that the $2 is an expected future cost, not a past cost. *Historical costs in themselves are irrelevant to the decision per se, even though they may be the best available basis for predicting future costs.*

The direct-material costs of $5 per unit are expected future costs, not historical costs. Yet these future costs are irrelevant because they will not differ under alternatives. There may be no harm in preparing a comparative analysis that includes both the relevant direct-labor-cost forecast and the irrelevant direct-material-cost forecast:

*Cost Comparison per Unit*

| | Do not Rearrange | Rearrange |
|---|---|---|
| Direct materials........ | $5.00 | $5.00 |
| Direct labor .......... | 2.00 | 1.50 |

However, note that we can safely ignore the direct-material cost, because it is not an element of difference between the alternatives. The point is that irrelevant costs may be included in cost comparisons for decisions, provided that they are included properly and do not mislead the decision maker. A corollary point is that concentrating solely on relevant costs may eliminate bothersome irrelevancies and may sharpen both the accountant's and the manager's thinking regarding costs for decision making. A key question in determining relevance is, "What difference will it make?"

In summary, the chart below shows that relevant costs for decisions are expected future costs that will differ under alternatives. Historical costs, although helpful in predicting relevant costs, are always irrelevant costs per se:

|  | | |
|---|---|---|
| *Past Costs* | | *Expected Future Costs* |
| *(often used as a guide for prediction)* | | |
| | | *Do Not* | |
| | | *Rearrange* | *Rearrange* |
| | | $5.00* | $5.00* |
| Direct materials . . . . . . . . . . . . . . $5.00 | | | Second Line of |
| | | | Demarcation |
| | | - - - - - - - - - - - - | |
| Direct labor. . . . . . . . . . . . . . . . . 2.00 | | 2.00 | 1.50 |

First Line
of
Demarcation in a Conceptual
Approach to Distinction Between
"Relevant" and "Irrelevant"

\* Although these are expected future costs, they are irrelevant because they are the same for both alternatives. Thus, the second line of demarcation is drawn between those costs that are the same for the alternatives under consideration and those that differ: *only* the latter are relevant costs *as we define them.*

\*    \*    \*    \*    \*

### Short Run and Long Run

Do not jump to the conclusion that all variable costs are relevant and all fixed costs are irrelevant. This preconceived attack may be handy, but it is far from being foolproof. For instance, in this special-order example, although the selling costs are variable, they are irrelevant because they are not affected by this special order.

Economists and accountants agree that if the length of time under consideration becomes long enough, no type of cost is fixed. Yet management is faced with the task of making decisions when the length of time under consideration is short enough so that many conditions and costs are fixed. What role should fixed costs play in decision making? No categorical answer may be given to this question. About the most useful generalization is that fixed costs should be considered when they are expected to be altered, either immediately or in the future, by the decision at hand.

\*    \*    \*    \*    \*

### Dropping a Product Line

Assume that a company has three product lines, all produced in one factory. Management is considering dropping Product C, which has consistently shown a net loss. The predicted income statements follow:

|  | Product | | | |
|---|---|---|---|---|
|  | A | B | C | Total |
| Sales............................ | $500,000 | $400,000 | $100,000 | $1,000,000 |
| Variable expenses.................. | 295,000 | 280,000 | 75,000 | 650,000 |
| Contribution margin................. | $205,000 (41%) | $120,000 (30%) | $ 25,000 (25%) | $ 350,000 (35%) |
| Fixed expenses (salaries, depreciation, property taxes, insurance)................. | 165,000 | 90,000 | 45,000* | 300,000 |
| Operating income.................. | $ 40,000 | $ 30,000 | $ (20,000) | $ 50,000 |

\* Includes product-line supervisor's salary of $20,000.

Assume that the only available alternatives are to drop Product C or to continue with Product C. Assume further that the total assets invested will not be affected by the decision. Thus, the issue becomes one of selecting the production combination that will provide maximum profits. Comparisons follow:

| Income Statements | Keep Product C | Drop Product C | Difference |
|---|---|---|---|
| Sales.................. | $1,000,000 | $900,000 | −$100,000 |
| Variable expenses ....... | $ 650,000 | $575,000 | −$ 75,000 |
| Fixed expenses.......... | 300,000 | 280,000 | − 20,000 |
| Total expenses ..... | $ 950,000 | $855,000 | −$ 95,000 |
| Operating income........ | $ 50,000 | $ 45,000 | −$ 5,000 |

The data above reveal that dropping unprofitable Product C would make matters worse instead of better. Why? Because all the fixed expenses would continue except for the $20,000 that would be jarred loose through discharging supervisory help. Product C now contributes $25,000 toward the coverage of fixed overhead; thus, the net effect of dropping Product C would be to forego the $25,000 contribution in order to save the $20,000 salaries. The result would be a $5,000 drop in overall profit, from $50,000 to $45,000.

Another important alternative besides the two discussed above is the possibility of dropping Product C, keeping the supervisor, and using the vacant facilities to produce, say, Product A to satisfy its expanding demand. If this happened, and if sales of Product A are expanded by $100,000, income would increase by $16,000, as follows:

|  | Total, Keep Product C | Total, Drop C, Produce More A | Difference | |
|---|---|---|---|---|
|  |  |  | Drop C | More A |
| Sales................ | $1,000,000 | $1,000,000 | −$100,000 | +$100,000 |
| Variable expenses ..... | $ 650,000 | $ 634,000 | −$ 75,000 | +$ 59,000 |
| Fixed expenses........ | 300,000 | 300,000 | | |
| Total expenses .. | $ 950,000 | $ 934,000 | −$ 75,000 | +$ 59,000 |
| Operating income...... | $ 50,000 | $ 66,000 | −$ 25,000 | +$ 41,000 |

Note that a shortcut solution to this problem could be found by concentrating on the differences shown in the two right-hand columns of the tabulation. These make up the final $16,000 difference in net income.

Note further that, with given facilities and given fixed expenses, the emphasis on products with higher contribution margins apparently maximizes operating income. Although this may be true in many instances, the matter is not quite that simple, as our next section demonstrates.

### Contribution per Unit of Constraining Factor

When a multiproduct plant is being operated at capacity, decisions must often be made as to which orders to accept. The contribution approach supplies the data for a proper decision, because the the latter is determined by the product that makes the largest *total* contribution to profits. This does not necessarily mean that the products to be pushed are those with the biggest contribution-margin ratios per unit of product or per sales dollar. The objective is to maximize total profits, which depend on getting the highest contribution margin per unit of the *constraining* (*scarce, limiting,* or *critical*) *factor.* The following example may clarify the point. Assume that a company has two products:

|  | Product (per unit) | |
| --- | --- | --- |
|  | A | B |
| Selling price | $10 | $15 |
| Variable expenses | 7 | 9 |
| Contribution margin | $ 3 | $ 6 |
| Contribution-margin ratio | 30% | 40% |

At first glance, B looks more profitable than A. However, if you were the division manager, had 1,000 hours of capacity available, and knew that you could turn out 3 units of A per hour and only 1 unit of B per hour, your choice would be A, because it contributes the most margin *per hour,* the constraining factor in this example:

|  | A | B |
| --- | --- | --- |
| Contribution margin per hour | $ 9 | $ 6 |
| Total contribution for 1,000 hours | $9,000 | $6,000 |

The constraining factor is the item that restricts or limits the production or sale of a given product. Thus, *the criterion for maximum profits, for a given capacity, is the greatest possible contribution to profit per unit of the constraining factor.* The constraining factor in the example above may be machine-hours or labor-hours. It may be cubic feet of display space; in such cases, a ratio such as the contribution-margin ratio is an insufficient clue to profitability. The ratio must be multiplied by the stock turnover (number of times the average inventory is sold per year) in order to obtain comparable measures of product profitability.

\*    \*    \*    \*    \*

### SUMMARY

The accountant's role in special decisions is basically that of a technical expert on cost analysis. His responsibility is to see that the manager is supplied with relevant data for guiding decisions.

To be relevant to a particular decision, a cost must meet two criteria: (*a*) it must be an expected *future* cost: and (*b*) it must be an element of *difference* between alternatives. The key question is, "What difference does it make?" If the objective of the decision maker is to maximize long-run net income, all *past* (*historical*) costs are irrelevant to any *decision* about the future.

The role that past costs play in decision making is an auxiliary one; the distinction here should be definitive, not fuzzy. Past (irrelevant) costs are useful because they provide empirical evidence that often helps sharpen *predictions* of future relevant costs. But the expected future costs are the *only* cost ingredients in any decision model per se.

The ability to distinguish relevant from irrelevant items and the use of the many contribution approach to cost analysis are twin foundations for tackling many decisions.

In decisions about activity evels (the special order, make or buy, and adding or dropping a product line), there may be a temptation to say that variable costs are always relevant and that fixed costs are always irrelevant. This is a dangerous generalization, because fixed costs are often affected by a decision. For example, plans to buy a second car for family use should be most heavily influenced by the new set of fixed costs that would be encountered. Conceivably, if the total family mileage were unaffected, the variable costs could by wholly irrelevant.

For a given set of facilities or resources, the key to maximizing net income is to obtain the largest possible contribution per unit of constraining factor.

Generally, in cost analysis it is advisable to use total costs, not unit costs, because unitized fixed costs are often erroneously interpreted as if they behaved like variable costs. A common activity or volume level must underlie the comparison of equipment.

The book value of old equipment is always irrelevant in replacement decisions. Disposal value, however, is usually relevant.

Incremental or differential costs are the differences in total costs under each alternative.

Opportunity cost is the maximum contribution that is foregone by using limited resources for a particular purpose. The use of opportunity cost is a practical means of reducing the alternatives under consideration: the solution reached is still the same as that given by a more complete "total-alternatives" approach. The decision maker says, "There are many alternatives that I want to reject without conducting a thorough analysis. Therefore, I shall take the best of these, compute its contribution, and use that as the cost of the scarce resource [copper in the example] when I explicitly analyze the remaining alternatives."

* * * * *

## GLOSSARY

[Editor's Note: These definitions are drawn from the full glossary at the end of C. T. Horngren's book.]

**Allocation.** Assigning one or more items of cost or revenue to one or more segments of an organization according to benefits received, responsibilities, or other logical measures of use.

**Absorption Costing.** That type of product costing which assigns fixed manufacturing overhead to the units produced as a product cost. Contrasts with direct costing.

**Capacity Costs.** An alternate term for *fixed costs,* emphasizing the fact that fixed costs are needed to provide operating facilities and an organization ready to produce and sell at a planned volume of activity.

**Committed Costs.** Those fixed costs arising from the possession of plant and   equipment and a basic organization and, thus, affected primarily by long-run   decisions as to the desired level of capacity.

**Contribution Approach.** A method of preparing income statements which separates variable costs from fixed costs in order to emphasize the importance of cost behavior patterns for purposes of planning and control.

**Direct Costing.** That type of product costing which charges fixed manufacturing overhead immediately against the revenue of the period in which it incurred, without assigning it to specific units produced. Also called *variable costing* and *marginal costing.*

**Discretionary Costs.** Those fixed costs that arise from periodic, usually yearly, appropriation decisions that directly reflect top-management policies. Also called *managed costs* and *programmed costs.*

**Factory Overhead.** All factory costs other than direct labor and direct material. Also called *factory burden, indirect manufacturing costs, manufacturing overhead,* and *manufacturing expense* (the latter is a misnomer).

**Fixed Cost.** A cost which, for a given period of time and range of activity called the relevant range, does not change in *total* but becomes progressively smaller on a *per unit* basis as volume increases.

**Functional Costing.** Classifying costs by allocating them to the various functions performed, such as warehousing, delivery, billing, and so forth.

**Imputed Cost.** A cost that does not appear in conventional accounting records and does not entail dollar outlays. A common example is the inclusion of "interest" on ownership equity as a part of operating expenses.

**Incremental Cost.** The difference in total cost between two alternatives. Also called *differential cost* and *relevant cost.*

**Joint Cost.** A cost which is common to all the segments in question and which is not clearly or practically allocable except by some questionable allocation base. Also called *common cost.*

**Joint Product Costs.** Cost of two or more manufactured goods, of significant sales values, that are produced by a single process and that are not identifiable as individual products up to a certain stage of production known as the *split-off point.*

**Opportunity Cost.** The maximum alternative earning that might have been obtrained if the productive good, service, or capacity had been applied to some alternative use.

**Out-Of-Pocket Costs.** Costs which entail current or near-future outlays for the decision at hand.

**Separable Cost.** A cost directly identifiable with a particular segment.

**Shutdown Cost.** A fixed cost which continues to be incurred even when there is no activity (production).

**Relevant Data for Decision Making.** Expected future data which will differ as between alternatives.

**Sunk Cost.** A cost which has already been incurred and which, therefore, is irrelevant to the decision-making process. Also called *historical cost.*

**Unit Cost.** A total cost divided by some related base, such as labor hours, machine-hours, or units of product.

**Variable Cost.** A cost which is uniform *per unit,* but which fluctuates *in total* in direct proportion to changes in the related total activity or volume.

*From*

# ACCOUNTING FOR MANAGEMENT CONTROL*

*By Charles T. Horngren*

### Intelligent Analysis of Relevant Data

The accounting system should produce information that leads managers toward correct decisions regarding either evaluation of performance or selection among courses of action. Intelligent analysis of costs is often dependent on explicit distinctions between cost behavior patterns, which is more likely to be achieved via the contribution approach than via traditional methods. The general tendency toward indiscriminate full-cost allocations raises analytical dangers.

> **Example.** A bakery distributed its products through route salesmen, each of whom loaded a truck with an assortment of products in the morning and spent the day calling on customers in an assigned territory. Believing that some items were more profitable than others, management asked for an analysis of product costs and sales. The accountants to whom the task was assigned allocated all manufacturing and marketing costs to products to obtain a net profit for each product. The resulting figures indicated that some of the products were being sold at a loss, and management discontinued these products. However, when this change was put into effect, the company's overall profit declined. It was then seen that, by dropping some products, sales revenues had been reduced without commensurate reduction in costs because the joint manufacturing costs and route sales costs had to be continued in order to make and sell remaining products.

The foregoing example demonstrates the importance of knowing how various costs behave.

---

\* Charles T. Horngren, *Accounting For Management Control: An Introduction,* 3d Edition, © 1974, excerpt from p. 349. Reprinted by permission of Prentice-Hall, Inc., Englewood Cliffs, N.J.

CASE MATERIALS AND
SOCIAL SCIENCE READINGS FOR

# PART IV Decision Making, Management Science, and Human Behavior

## ORIGINS OF MANAGEMENT SCIENCE

One approach to managerial decision making has been variously called "operations research," "management science," or "quantitative methods." Courses under one or more of these labels now occupy an important place in the curriculum of schools of administration. The field of management science is characterized principally by a certain set of problems to which are applied mathematics and statistics or the logic of the payoff matrix. The problems of finance and accounting already covered in Part III also use numbers and quantities. That one group of problems and techniques has come to be called "finance" and another group of problems has come to be called "operations research/management science" is partly a result of historical accident. Finance and accounting were developed by those interested in planning and recording investment decisions of the type already seen in Continental Electric Company; or in planning and recording the current operating expense budget.

The origins of management science courses are well known. The British government, in World War II, needed fast solutions to a number of action problems it faced in defending the British Isles. It called upon a group of academic men from several disciplines. Not only mathematicians, but also sociologists and other specialists were asked to apply the fundamental *phenomena* from their particular fields, and to apply the *methods* of science, to practical managerial problems. In the United States, the U.S. government established a similar effort, among other places, at the Johns Hopkins University.

In its early usage, "operations research" meant "research into operating problems." It carried a heavy bias toward looking at operating problems first, and then seeing what content or methods from various sciences might be applicable to those problems. It also meant drawing on a variety of physical and social sciences. In these two respects, the

331

early meanings of management science were not unlike the approach used throughout all six parts of the present volume.

But shortly after its inception, management science took on a somewhat different meaning, both to its practitioners and to curriculum builders in schools of administration. It became dominated by mathematics and quantification. We have already seen in the introductory chapters that quantification has been *one* of the key attributes of science, and that this has certain powerful advantages for controlling nature. Today's management science departments in schools of administration mostly offer courses which specialize in applied mathematics. The Institute of Management Sciences is composed primarily of staff men in industry and professors in universities who are specialists in mathematical techniques.

## POWER AND LIMITATIONS OF SCIENCE IN MANAGEMENT

In an age of larger and more complex organizations, it seems vital that most managers must have some knowledge and skill in solving those kinds of problems that lend themselves to mathematical decision making. Readers will recognize as they study the whole book that (1) management science of the mathematical variety is only *one* of the ways in which to use the various physical and social sciences in management, and that (2) it is perhaps more accurate to say "use of *science in management*" than it is to imply that there is such a thing as one *science of management.* Management, or policy (action) decision making is a *profession* which draws on many scientific disciplines. It puts emphasis on policy decisions first, and science as a technique second. It requires the attitudes of a professional who recognizes both the powers and limitations of science, who recognizes that different sciences can actually prescribe conflicting action solutions to him, and who has skill in balancing and reconciling such conflicts. Carrying through the theme set for *The Managerial Mind* in the introductory chapters, it will be the purposes of Part IV:

1.  To examine some of the mathematical and statistical techniques that are used by managers in action (policy) problems.
2.  To show the advantages of such techniques as well as their limitations in practice. Particularly, human behavior, the subject of psychology and sociology, often determines when mathematical rationality will work and when it will not.
3.  To develop the attitude that managerial decision making almost always involves a trade-off (compromise, balance) between rational factors of management science, on the one hand, and human factors, on the other.
4.  To gain some skill, through case practice, in tailoring a professional decision to the particular operations of a certain firm and its specific people; in effect, making the above trade-offs.
5.  To show how decision techniques from mathematics operate as one factor which determines the organization *structure* of the enterprise.

## THE PHILOSOPHICAL IMPORTANCE OF MANAGEMENT SCIENCE

Before studying more about managerial use of mathematical techniques, the manager has a right to ask, "Why are these techniques ultimately important—why are they *good*?" This is a philosophical question. A question of what is good in life.

One importance has to do with the dictates of society outside the firm. We shall not repeat here the material from the introductions to Parts II and III. The argument is similar in the case of managerial uses of all rational sciences, and particularly similar to use of financial techniques in Part III. In summary, society depends on (1) the production of goods and services and (2) at an acceptable level of efficiency. The manager who does not operate his or her organization with these two goals in mind might suffer two kinds of penalties. First, he or she may in fact find that society "out there" no longer supports him and the organization in legal charter terms, in terms of public attitudes, or in terms of day-to-day monetary payments. In the last analysis, nobody wants to waste the natural resources of society when efficient ways exist to get the same products with less waste of the labor force and raw materials. In addition, those who have ethical beliefs about the responsibilities of managers to society will penalize themselves if they run sloppy organizations that are wasteful. Managers must, as it pointed out in Part VI, observe social dicta about the good life *other than* efficiency and production, but this does not mean that they can at the same time abrogate the latter responsibilities.

## EXAMPLES OF QUANTITATIVE TECHNIQUES AND MANAGERIAL PROBLEMS

One of the earliest mathematical techniques applied to work in organizations is that of work measurement. It does not employ as sophisticated techniques of mathematics as "the new management science." In fact, it is the product of an earlier movement called "scientific management." But the traditional nature of this set of techniques should not cloud the fact that work measurement is widely used through the world in the 70s. In terms of manufacturing applications, hardly a factory can be found in the developed countries of Europe, Japan, Russia, and the United States which does not make some use of such techniques. In developing countries such as India, this trend is likewise noticeable.

The extension of such techniques to nonmanufacturing enterprise continues to progress. The Family Service Association of America, for example, has been in effect told by some Community Chest charity boards across the nation that their social case workers are not efficient when compared to other agencies such as workers in the poverty program or the Boy Scouts. Many who disperse funds for charity have intimated that unless the family counseling agencies use some form of work measurement to show how much actual service is rendered for the money spent, they may get less funds: funds will be put to a use where the public gets more efficient social service. The Metropolitan Life Insurance Company, along with other companies in the industry, has consistently applied work measurement to paper work as contrasted with physical production in a factory. And the Czechoslovakian government quite recently has sponsored research to apply the concept to many types of endeavor in order to help raise the gross national product.

The more glamorous techniques developed recently are used in other cases in Part IV. The owner of the Sea Breeze Motel experiments with probability theory in order to see how many reservations he must take. Because many customers make reservations and then do not show up, he tries to predict how many "no shows" there will be so that he can decide how many reservations to take. Neither the motel owner nor society wins if scarce resources are invested in empty rooms.

In Midwest Hardware Manufacturing Company, the managers struggle with a particular type of problem faced by managers in various kinds of business—the inventory problem, as it is referred to in operations research literature. They use probabilities and formulas to tell them how much of their resources to tie up in finished goods inventories and inventories of raw materials and semifinished products kept on hand.

In Western Office Equipment Company, the top management is concerned with determining just the right number of sales agents to employ in order to sell the most office equipment at the least cost in human power. They want to know how many sales representatives are required in Salt Lake City, San Francisco, Vancouver, and Seattle. A management science staff specialist, recently graduated from a school of administration, takes on the job of applying marginal economics to this problem. Since the amount of resources required in every branch depends in part on that in every other branch, he must have a notion of systems analysis if he is to be successful.

## MANAGERIAL (POLICY) DECISION MAKING

Sometimes the application of mathematical techniques, and the logic of the pay-off matrix, are called "decision making." This is a perfectly acceptable usage of the term provided that one recognizes that this is a *particular kind* of decision making. As one professor of English literature once said in a curriculum committee meeting at Columbia University, "I don't understand how you can call this operations research course simply decision making in general. I, too, am teaching decision making. Students who gain profound insights about human nature through study of literature can make wiser decisions in the future."

Decision making by use of quantitative techniques is a form of decision making which attempts to reduce the factors in a decision to rational alternatives (strategies, courses of action), to isolate those variables which can be measured, and to manipulate numbers so that the weight of the various factors indicate which alternative to choose. In order to comply with the second of these steps, most administrative applications measure more "thing" factors than they do "people" factors. In order to comply with the third step, most applications reduce all factors in a decision to costs or revenues, or both.

Thus, management science tends to have in common with the older scientific management, the goal of technological efficiency. That this is a worthy goal has already been established.

But this book is addressed to policy formulation, or managerial decision making in a broader sense. While it is hoped that an important byproduct of studying Part IV will be *knowledge* of valuable mathematical tools, it is also hoped that another byproduct will be *knowledge* of some valuable concepts (nonquantifiable) about human behavior, politics in organizations, and ways of coordinating organizations.

If these are byproducts, then what is the principal product? It is skill, ability, and judgment of the individual human brain in making sense of both at once, in thinking through the whole problem. It is seeing how "things" are related to "people," when mathematical techniques will work and when they will not, how quantified rational facts must be traded off against nonquantifiable human nature and organizational politics. These, together with the relevant knowledge of techniques and theories, are equally important in *The Managerial Mind.*

## MANAGEMENT INFORMATION SYSTEMS

The term "Management Information System" (frequently abbreviated to M.I.S.) means any collection of original data which is summarized, or manipulated, in a certain way that has *meaning* to a manager desiring to know "what is going on" with operations. For example, an income statement is an aggregate of thousands of separate debits and credits, specifically aggregated under certain concepts, or categories: "gross sales" *less* "cost of goods sold" *equals* "gross profit" *less* "selling and administrative expenses" *equals* "net profit before taxes." This statement has *meaning* in that (1) the manager can see whether costs are near or far from being equal to sales (if they are more than sales, the company will cease to exist!), and (2) the manager can see whether the company is purchasing and manufacturing (cost of goods sold) efficiently or whether selling and administrative activities are detracting from efficiency.

In one sense, all of the cases in Part IV show some manager trying to either design, or use, an information system. The Sea Breeze Motel manager needs figures which mean something about reservations, and help him solve the problem of guests who make reservations but do not show up. He designs a system for gathering facts and summarizing them in categories like "probability of no shows," or "lifetime value of a loyal guest." The Midwest Hardware Manufacturing Company manager needs figures that help him decide how much inventory of parts he should carry to produce a gas furnace control unit. He designs a system that summarizes such things as "order lot size," and "number of orders per month," or "carrying cost of safety stock." Western Office Equipment Company's president needs figures which help him decide how many sales representatives to hire in Los Angeles or San Francisco. He designs a system that summarizes "marginal contribution of a salesman."

One case, the Farnsworth Company, shows the management of the Paper Products Division trying to design a M.I.S. for the whole division. The readings with that case provide some guidelines for designing such a system. The case itself shows why human beings must be considered simultaneously with techniques of M.I.S. if the final information system is to succeed.

# 10. SEA BREEZE MOTEL, INC.

---

## Case Introduction

---

### SYNOPSIS

A graduate of a university program in hotel administration builds a new motel on Cape Cod. During the first season's operation, there is a considerable problem of "no-shows"—people who make reservations and then do not honor them. This often results in loss of revenues. In order to overcome this problem, the owner of the motel employs a consultant in operations research who recommends an optimum strategy, that of taking 12 reservations for a ten-room facility. During the second season's operation, the motel operates under this strategy. However, in the judgment of the owner, the formula or model is not working, and he wonders whether to use it in the third season.

### WHY THIS CASE IS INCLUDED

The Sea Breeze case enables one to see both the power of scientific approaches in the practice of management and the limitations of this approach. It forces the policy maker to decide whether a management science approach will be utilized in the formulation of firm policy or whether he will place more reliance on judgment or intuition.

### DIAGNOSTIC AND PREDICTIVE QUESTIONS

The readings included with this case are marked (*). The author index at the end of this book locates the other readings.

1. From the viewpoint of economics, why is it so important to Heenan to have the rooms filled to capacity at all times?

Prepare: Using your own analytical ability, think about the fixed costs such as investment in buildings and furnishings. Convert these costs to a formula that will yield fixed cost per unit of output.

337

2. Why did Heenan "decide right then and there that there must be a way for me to solve the problem more reliably than just by guessing"? Why did Imhoff have inner self-confidence that he could solve the problem by mathematics or "management science"?

Read: The concept of "convergent phenomena" and the section on "Physical Science" in Chapter 2 of *The Managerial Mind.*

3. Why do you think that Heenan "obeyed" Imhoff—or, in what sense did Imhoff have "authority" over Heenan? The same question might be asked as to why the journal article had "authority" or "influence" over Heenan.

Read: *General Electric Co., *Professional Management in General Electric.* *Moore and Tumin, "Specialists and the Ignorance of Non-Specialists." *Simon, Smithburg, and Thompson, *Public Administration.*

4. Why didn't the facts of the world correspond to the mathematical prediction—that is, why did the motel units fill less than predicted in June and more than predicted in July? Why did Heenan consider Shields as part of the "model" which didn't work?

Read: Chapter 2 of *The Managerial Mind,* and the section on *"Ceteris Paribus* in Social Science" in Chapter 3.

## POLICY QUESTIONS

5. If you were in Heenan's place, what would you do about the reservation policy in the coming season?

# Case Text*

Since his graduation from the Cornell University School of Hotel Administration, Dave Heenan had been the owner-manager of the Sea Breeze Motel in Harwichport, Massachusetts, on Cape Cod. With funds furnished from an administered inheritance, Heenan initiated the construction of the lavish, ten-suite complex in the late autumn three years ago.

An early completion date of the following March 23 further enabled Heenan to solicit customers for the oncoming season—beginning June 1 and terminating September 10. Heenan intended to supplement his seasonal earnings at Sea Breeze by assisting his cousin in the management of the Royal Palms Hotel during the winter months.

Since the rate per suite was set at $40 a day, and because the motel has only ten units, Heenan sought to segment the motel's market to upper

---

* Copyright 1977 by Charles E. Summer. Names of persons, associations, firms, and places have been disguised.

income families and to make his accommodations conducive to repeat trade over the years. Although competition on the Cape was fierce for this type of clientele, Heenan initiated measures to appeal to the appropriate market.

First, Heenan—with the assistance of experienced classmates and friends of his father—sought out and received the highest possible rating, "AAA," from the Certification Board of the New England Hotel and Motel Association (NEHMA). Knowledgeable persons in the hotel-motel industry had pointed out to Heenan that the possession and maintenance of "AAA" would be probably the most important factor in attracting desirable occupants.

In addition, Heenan embarked on a promotional campaign designed to attract wealthy vacationers. By advertising in the travel sections of the *Boston Globe,* the *Christian Science Monitor,* and appropriate national and regional media and by personally selling a carefully selected group of travel agents, Heenan felt that he had made significant headway in promoting the Sea Breeze image.

However, upon returning to Harwichport in May two years ago Heenan soon became aware that full-season occupancy of individual customers would be most difficult to achieve in the early stages of operations. The majority of early reservations received were for various periods ranging from three nights to two months. Moreover, the average duration appeared to be somewhere between one to two weeks. With this in mind, Heenan readied the Sea Breeze for the reception of its first guest in June.

While he considered the first summer's operations as favorable for the most part, Heenan realized that if his existing facilities were to be expanded annually, greater revenues and/or reduced operating costs would have to be generated. What bothered Heenan most was the so-called "no-show" problem. In a significant number of instances, people who had previously reserved a specific Sea Breeze suite neither arrived to fill their reservations nor notified management in advance of their cancellations.

Initially, Heenan thought about establishing a minimum advance deposit to protect against "no-show" losses, but he soon dropped the idea after recognizing that such a requirement would foster a host of inhibitory effects in the minds of potential upper income occupants. As a result, Heenan adopted a policy of holding reservations until 3 P.M. of the specified day to protect against possible losses. This arbitrary deadline, he thought, would best afford sufficient customer convenience while, at the same time, hopefully enable management ample time within which to rent the rooms of canceled reservations. But in practice over a period of weeks, marked customer irritation was voiced by those unable to each Harwichport by early afternoon, and since it was extremely difficult to rent "no-show" rooms late in the day, it soon became evident that such a policy was unwise. Nevertheless, feeling that "no-shows" were making serious inroads on the motel's profitability, Heenan saw no other course of action but to retain the 3 P.M. deadline.

It was not until Heenan's attendance at the annual assembly of hotelmen in the late fall of the same year, that a workable solution to the "no-show" dilemma seemed imminent. Originated some years ago to serve the dual role of congregating hotel executives and informing them of updated managerial methods and techniques, the assembly provided a forum for the discussion—formally and informally—of a wide variety of operational problems.

In his association with other managers, Heenan found that an ever increasing percentage of hotelmen minimized the risk of "no-shows" with a procedure of accepting more reservations than the number of rooms available. The strategy is directed at placing the motel in the optimal position of receiving sufficient reservations to fill available rooms after "no-show" reservations are deducted. Moreover, the motel's calculated demand for rooms, based on the "estimated valid" reservations (those remaining after the elimination of an estimated percentage of "no-shows"), is equated to the fixed supply of rooms.

In practice, there are costs associated with the adoption of such a strategy. For example, if the demand for rooms is underestimated, there will result vacant rooms with a consequential loss of rental revenues. Or, if the demand for rooms is overstated, there will no doubt be a loss of those highly dissatisfied customers who are rejected lodging in spite of their reservations.

Bob Fuller, manager of the Pipe Manor Lodge in Lake Placid, New York, and one of Heenan's most respected classmates from Cornell, suggested that Heenan should make use of some modern operations research techniques for solving the "no-show" problem. He explainnd that, in operations research terms, the proprietor of a motel might adopt various "strategies" or alternatives of action. These strategies, in the last analysis, are different numbers of reservations the proprietor might wish to accept. For example, given the fixed number of ten suites at Sea Breeze, Heenan might have one strategy of accepting 11 reservations, a second strategy of accepting 12 reservations, or a third strategy of accepting 13 reservations. In Heenan's later calculations, when he drew up a decision matrix (Table 2), these strategies were listed down the left column as row headings.

Fuller went on to explain that the other critical determinant of what he should do about "no-shows" were various "states of nature" that he might encounter—things over which he has little control. "You can control the number of reservations, through your strategy, but you cannot control what all of those customers will do—whether they will cancel or simply not show up. Therefore, why not view the actual number of customers which in fact arrive as various states of nature, and then calculate which strategy will yield the least cost to Sea Breeze due to "no-show" customers."

Fuller also recommended that Heenan read an article entitled "Decision Theory Applications to the No-Show Problem" in a recent edition of a hotel trade publication. After reading this article, Heenan said, "I decided right then and there that there must be a way for me to solve this problem more reliably than just by guessing. I got in touch with a large consulting firm in Boston, and they referred me to Jim Imhoff, an individual who does operations-research-type consulting. The big firm frankly said my project was not as large or complex as they generally take on."

Heenan arranged to return from Florida in the spring a year ago, and he arranged with Imhoff to come to Harwichport to gather data from his records. This Imhoff did, and according to Heenan, "We worked well together. Jim kept asking questions and I would supply what I could. I even enlisted the help of three other motels out here to furnish data, in return for which we agreed to let them read the report." Imhoff's memorandum to Heenan appears as Exhibit 1.

**EXHIBIT 1**

Mr. David Heenan
Sea Breeze Motel
Harwichport, Massachusetts

Dear Dave:

I know that you are anxious to receive this final report, so that you can proceed with accepting reservations for the summer season. I have enjoyed working on this project, and hope that you will feel free to call on me again if you have further questions. I have discussed the problem with my partner before coming to the final conclusion.

The purpose of this report is to give you our final recommendation as to how many reservations you should accept, and to explain how we arrived at this figure. Let me, therefore, begin with this recommendation:

Sea Breeze Motel should accept 12 reservations for the existing ten-suite facility, if optimum season profit is to be realized.

I know that you have been referring to this final figure as "the magic number." Here it is. But I should like to explain how we arrived at this so that it won't seem like magic. Rather, it is an orderly attempt to gather concrete factual information and then to use certain mathematical techniques to arrive at costs, revenues, and final profit. I'm fully aware that you know much of what we're doing from our past conversations. However, let me devote the rest of this report to summarizing the steps we went through.

Essentially, two different cost figures had to be determined: (*a*) the cost of a vacant room (given a "no-show"); and (*b*) the cost of the anticipated lifetime loss of a good customer if he is denied admission, even with a reservation (because of an overstated demand estimate). The former statistic was easily derived; it was simply the daily loss of revenues of a single vacant suite, or $40. However, to determine the latter expense, we had to analyze the

**EXHIBIT 1 (*continued*)**

financial record of the past season. Initially required was the average customer stay at Sea Breeze, which was found to be ten days. At the set rate of $40 per day, we calculated that some $400 in rentals were generated during this period. Furthermore, desirous of a 10 percent profit return on gross rentals, we calculated a net profit of $40 for any base period.

To project the expected lifetime customer value, it was necessary to determine the probability of one's returning to Sea Breeze in the following year. Although the infancy stage of your operations did not provide available historical information, files of the NEHMA revealed that approximately an 80 percent probability of return could be anticipated for motels comparable to the Sea Breeze. Stated otherwise, the probability that a guest will return for $n$ years in $(0.80)^n$—or Lifetime value of a customer = (Net profit base) + (Pr. return next year)

(Net profit base) $+ \ldots +$ (Pr. return $n$ years) $\cdot$ (Net profit)

For Sea Breeze then—

$$\text{Lifetime value} = \$40 + (0.80) \cdot (40) + (0.64) \cdot (40) + \ldots + (0.80)^n \cdot (40) = \underline{\underline{\$200}}$$

In summary, the expected lifetime revenue stream at Sea Breeze for the average customer was found to be $200. However, recognizing the present value of money, we discounted the above statistic (by 10 percent yearly) in order to establish the true present worth to the motel.

$$\text{Lifetime value adjusted} = \$40 + \frac{(0.80) \cdot (40)}{1.10} + \frac{(0.64)\,(40)}{1.21} +$$

$$\ldots \frac{(0.80)^n\,(40)}{(1.10)^n} = \underline{\underline{\$90.09}}$$

Moreover, Sea Breeze would probably lose the entire $90.09 for any customer who, despite a reservation, has been turned away for his vacation stay.

To calculate the probabilities of the requisite states of nature, we first determined the probability of a "no-show" and then the total number of reservations. You were able to obtain "no-show" statistics over a five-year period from three comparable motels on Cape Cod. These records indicated that 25 percent of all reservations were of a "no-show" variety. Given the total nummer of reservations, we utilized the binomial probability distribution to calculate probabilities of the various numbers of "no-shows."

For $R$ (reservations), the probability of $n$ ("no-shows") is:

**EXHIBIT 1 (*continued*)**

$$\frac{R\,(R-1)\,(R-2)\,\ldots\,(R-n+1)}{n\,(n-1)\,(n-2)\,\ldots\,(2)\quad(1)}\,(0.25)^n(0.75)^{R-n}$$

For example, given ten suites, we considered how many reservations over ten you might best be advised to accept. If 11 reservations were taken, the probability of one "no-show" (the optimal solution) could be determined as follows:

$$\text{Pr. 1 no-show} = \frac{11}{1}\,(0.25)^1(0.75)^{10} = 0.1459 = 15\%$$

Simply stated, there is roughly a 15 percent chance that if one "extra" reservation were accepted, the two ever present costs—loss of rentals and loss of lifetime customer value—would be erased.

Proceeding in this manner, we computed the probabilities of "no-shows" under various acceptance strategies, letting $R$ equal the number of reservations:

**TABLE 1**
**Probability**

| "No-Shows" | $R = 11$ | $R = 12$ | $R = 13$ |
|---|---|---|---|
| 0 | 0.0422 | 0.0317 | 0.0238 |
| 1 | 0.1549 | 0.1267 | 0.1029 |
| 2 | 0.2581 | 0.2323 | 0.2059 |
| 3 | 0.2581 | 0.2581 | 0.2517 |
| 4 | 0.1721 | 0.1936 | 0.2097 |
| 5 | 0.0803 | 0.1032 | 0.1258 |
| 6 | 0.0268 | 0.0401 | 0.0559 |
| 7 | 0.0064 | 0.0115 | 0.1186 |
| 8 | 0.0011 | 0.0024 | 0.0047 |
| 9 | 0.0001 | 0.0004 | 0.0009 |
| | | | 0.0001 |
| | 1.000 | 1.000 | 1.000 |

Finally, having computed the probabilities of the various states of nature (the number of "no-shows," over which you have no control), and the necessary costs we calculated the resultant payoffs. By utilizing the matrix in Table 2 which blends the costs and probabilities of selected reservation strategies, we found that the minimum expected cost—hence, the optimal solution—was attained when $R = 12$.

By adopting a policy of accepting 12 reservations for ten rooms, the Sea Breeze would follow the safest and surest possible course of action. In short, the least cost (over time) of such a policy would be $63.69 as compared with the more costly strategies of $R = 11$ and $R = 13$.

**EXHIBIT 1** (*concluded*)

**TABLE 2**

| "No-Shows" | 0 | 1 | 2 | 3 | 4 | 5 | 6 | 7 | 8 | 9 | Expected Cost US $ |
|---|---|---|---|---|---|---|---|---|---|---|---|
| Probability | 0.0422 | 0.1549 | 0.2581 | 0.2581 | 0.1721 | 0.0803 | 0.0268 | 0.0064 | 0.0011 | 0.0001 | $75.75 |
| strategy: R=11 | $ 90.09 | 0 | $40 | $80 | $120 | $160 | $200 | $240 | $280 | $320 | |
| Probability | 0.0317 | 0.1267 | 0.2323 | 0.2581 | 0.1936 | 0.1032 | 0.0401 | 0.0115 | 0.0024 | 0.0004 | $63.69 |
| strategy: R=12 | $180.18 | $ 90.09 | $ 0 | $40 | $ 80 | $120 | $160 | $200 | $240 | $280 | |
| Probability | 0.0238 | 0.1029 | 0.2059 | 0.2517 | 0.2097 | 0.1258 | 0.0559 | 0.0186 | 0.0047 | 0.00009 | $73.66 |
| strategy: R=13 | $270.27 | $180.18 | $90.09 | $ 0 | $ 40 | $ 80 | $120 | $160 | $200 | $240 | |

*Note:* If there are zero "no-shows" with one reservation too many, the cost is the lifetime value of a customer ($90.09).

According to the recommendation, the Sea Breeze Motel should accept 12 reservations for any given period, so long as the facility contains ten suites. Imhoff explained over the telephone, after Heenan had received the report, that no solution "will allow you to eat your cake and have it, too. You can't have completely satisfied every single customer and at the same time satisfied your desire for every dollar of profit. But 12 reservations will give the best balance—the optimum profit."

Assured that this policy would remedy the "no-show" predicament at Sea Breeze, Heenan announced his intention of accepting 12 reservations for ten suites during single time intervals of the oncoming seasons. For the first few weeks of the motel's operations last season, Heenan was pleased with the relative effectiveness of his newly stated reservations program. It was true that customers were turned away on some occasions because of overacceptance, while on others, vacant rooms resulted because of underestimated "no-shows." However, Heenan believed that these costs would be exceeded by the additional revenues gained in reserving the two extra suites.

During the remaining months of last season, however, a series of incidents occurred which caused considerable trouble, in Heenan's words, "for the smooth operations of Sea Breeze Motel, and for its reputation."

In July, Cape Cod was plagued with an unusually bad weather situation. Fog, haze, and below normal temperatures resulted in a decreased tourist business for the entire area and in a high rate of cancellations and "no-shows" for Sea Breeze. Given ten motel units, and 31 days in July, the motel would be fully occupied if the management received payment for 310 unit/days. However, for the month as a whole, paying guests occupied units only for 186 unit/days. This is the equivalent of having six units occupied for the 31-day period, instead of the full ten units. On inspection of his records, Heenan found that almost exactly half of these unoccupied unit/days were accounted for by "no-shows"—in other words, of the four units remaining unoccupied throughout July, two of these could be traced to occasions when people did not cancel their reservations. On numerous occasions, because of the quality of his property, Heenan had the opportunity of renting to tourists who, defying the weather, stopped in between 10 A.M. and 2 P.M. to see if they could stay overnight. Believing in his reservation system, he turned these potential guests away.

Just the opposite happened in August. Instead of having many cancellations and "no-shows," the Sea Breeze found that everyone seemed to want to carry through his vacation plans. Even though Table 1 in Imhoff's report indicates that there is only a 3 percent chance that there will be no "no-shows" if 12 reservations are accepted, there were in fact nine days on which reservation guests arrived for all 12 reservations.

One additional event in August troubled Heenan a great deal. On the weekend of August 14th, one of those nine times when all 12 reservations appeared for actual occupancy, a particularly important guest was refused his room. Mr. Foster Shields, executive secretary of the New England Motel Managers Association, arrived with a reservation made in May. He arrived just before the latest reservation hold time (3 P.M.). The desk clerk apologized for the error in bookings, and offered to help him obtain suitable accommodations elsewhere.

Shields later wrote to Heenan and informed him that the committee on certifications could lower his rating from "Triple A" to a lower category, possibly "BCC." Heenan knew that with the luxury nature of his property, such an action would seriously impair the image of his motel, and he knew that loss of qualitative status is reported in trade journals which are read widely by travel agencies.

On closing the Sea Breeze and going to Florida last fall, Heenan took with him the day-by-day records of the season. He wanted to study the records and compare them with the Imhoff report, to see what to do about a reservation policy for the motel in the coming season.

As of the time this case is written, early this year, Heenan states:

> I have got to decide whether to try to operate under this system this year, whether to junk the whole thing and accept only ten reservations to match my facilities, or whether to hire Jim Imhoff again to see if he can work the bugs out of the system. Somehow I know that the thing can be solved better than just by guessing—I had faith in what Bob Fuller said, what I read in the journal, and what Jim Imhoff can do as a man with knowledge I don't have. At the same time, I think I fell between the chairs last summer. I alienated guests in August too much, I lost too much profits in July, and that problem with Shields is a sticky one. Incidentally, I did visit with Shields personally and things are temporarily OK. He is thoroughly pleased with everything he knows or has seen regarding Sea Breeze. That's the one thing that saves us. I showed him all of the calculations and tried to explain what I'm trying to do—to match a really excellent facility with good management. I don't think he understood what I was talking about but he agreed to let me inform him this month (March) what I intend to do regarding customer satisfaction through a good reservation system. One thing is certain: I've got to decide what to do about reservations for this season; this is a better year for tourist and vacation expenditures than ever.

# Selected Readings

*From*

## PROFESSIONAL MANAGEMENT IN GENERAL ELECTRIC*

### MEASURING

Of the four elements of the work of a professional manager, the element of measuring has been given too little inventive attention. Conversely, this is an area in which rapid advances will be made if the area is given the attention which it deserves. The feed-back of adequate measurements into the other areas of a manager's work closes the cycle and makes dynamic progressive achievement possible. What would a sailor on the high seas do without a compass? How can a manager make wise decisions if he does not have adequate, timely facts about the working situation? The more completely, accurately, and promptly he can be kept informed, the wiser and surer his decisions can be.

\*    \*    \*    \*    \*

The work of managing inherently involves exercising judgment as a basis for making decisions. Judgment, which is in essence appraisal, is in turn a function of the facts and information on which it is based. It is the manager's task, in a business enterprise, or component, to make decisions as occasion requires, and on the best information available at the time. If only qualitative appraisal, rooted in general experience or beliefs, is feasible, it is still essential to weigh and to decide. But the professional manager's job is to function through the authority of knowledge rather than of rank. Hence, the more he can "measure," the more he can ask sound, balanced, objective, and persuasive questions and when appropriate, make decisions of corresponding clarity and acceptability. As a manager develops professional skill, the advantages of seeking "measured facts" in more and more areas is increasingly realized. With modern knowledge of mathematics and statistics, and with modern tools and machines or computers to apply them, the opportunities to "measure" increasingly more complex situations are simultaneously enhanced. Hence, the areas can be minimized where reliance is on opinion and qualitative judgment alone because the appraisal factors can be stated and worded in terms which are more and more measurable.

\*    \*    \*    \*    \*

In *The New York Times* for January 31, 1954, Secretary of the Treasury George M. Humphrey is quoted as saying, "There are no hard decisions, just insufficient facts. When you have the facts, the decisions come easy."

The scientific method involves analysis and synthesis that are directed toward the simplification of concepts and the statement of generalizations or principles. The situations in which we find ourselves tend to become unmanageable, unless the simplification process keeps pace with the rapidly growing volume and complexity of observed facts. The first four

---

* By permission from *Professional Management in General Electric,* Book Three, *The Work of a Professional Manager,* copyright 1954 by the General Electric Company. (Excerpts from pp. 109–10; 142–43.)

chapters of this book give an orderly arrangement of the ideas that appear pertinent and of significant importance in the WORK OF A PROFESSIONAL MANAGER. By the very arrangement of these ideas, simplification of concept is achieved.

Zay Jefferies has observed that if the simplification processes keep pace with the complicating processes, "individuals with a given ability can expect to go forward indefinitely without becoming casualties of their own complexity."

The true search of the people of the world is for order, not chaos. Managing should be the science of bringing the kind of order which nature exhibits all about us; and of doing so by applying a process of rational organization to the relationships in which men associate. This is our deep need. As individuals we show little or no more capacity or ability or emotional steadiness than the able men among our forebears. Yet, unfolding science brings new complexities, and it is the manager's job to match them with patterns of simplicity, which will win the comprehension and the acceptance of the individual men whose work is being managed. . . .

*From*

# SPECIALISTS AND THE IGNORANCE OF NON-SPECIALISTS\*

*By Wilbert E. Moore and Melvin M. Tumin*

The function of ignorance that is most obvious, particularly to the cynical, is its role in preserving social differentials. However, a purely cynical view is likely to overlook the extent to which the continuity of any social structure depends on differential access to knowledge in general, and, *a fortiori,* to specialized knowledge of various kinds. In many instances, of course, the counterpart of ignorance on the part of the outsider is *secrecy* on the part of the possessor of knowledge. Some of the outstanding examples of this general function of ignorance are summarized in the following paragraphs.

*The Specialist and the Consumer.* Ignorance on the part of a consumer of specialized services (for example, medical or legal advice) helps to preserve the privileged position of a specialized dispenser of these services. This is in some measure a by-product of the division of labor, and theoretically the same persons may occupy super-ordinate or subordinate positions as one or another service or skill is demanded. However, there are both theoretical and empirical bases for concluding that some persons whose skills are both scarce and functionally important will occupy a generalized superior position.[1] Although that status is not solely the product of the ignorance of others, in concrete instances it is partially maintained by such ignorance.

One evidence of the function of ignorance of as a preservative of privileged position lies in the situation where the consumer acquires, through continuous exposure to the services of the specialist, a sense of his own ability to deal with his problems, and thus to dispense with the services of the specialist (*e.g.,* when we learn how to treat common colds, simple fevers, and bruises, and where we learn how to send stern notes concerning contractual obligations). Thus the range of situations in which the special services are believed to be required is altered from the original position.

\* By permission from "Some Social Functions of Ignorance," *American Sociological Review,* vol. 14 (December 1949), pp. 788–89. Copyright by the American Sociological Society.

[1] Kingsley Davis and Wilbert E. Moore, "Some Principles of Stratification," *American Sociological Review,* vol. 10 (April 1945), pp. 242–49.

On the other hand, the specialist commonly develops devices to protect himself against this sort of attrition. A common device is that of specialized and possibly esoteric vocabulary, or the use of instruments and techniques not intrinsically required for the solution but seemingly so.

However, the central point remains that real or presumed differential knowledge and skills are inherently necessary to maintain mutually satisfactory relationships between specialist and consumer. . . .

*From*

# PUBLIC ADMINISTRATION*

*By Herbert A. Simon, Donald W. Smithburg, and Victor A. Thompson*

From a psychological standpoint the exercise of authority involves a relationship between two or more persons. On the one side we have a person who makes proposals for the action of others. On the other side we have a person who accepts the proposals—who "obeys" them. Now a person may accept another's proposals under three different sets of circumstances:

1. He may examine the merits of the proposal, and, on the basis of its merits become convinced that he should carry it out. We shall exclude such instances of acceptance from our notion of authority, although some writers on administration have called this the "authority of ideas."

2. He may carry out the proposals without being fully, or even partially, convinced of its merits. In fact he may not examine the merits of the proposal at all.

3. He may carry out the proposal even though he is convinced it is wrong—wrong either in terms of personal values or of organizational values or both.

We will treat both the second and third cases as instances of the acceptance of authority. Of course in any actual instance all three of the "pure types" of acceptance listed above may be combined in various proportions. In actual practice authority is almost always liberally admixed with persuasion. . . .

\*    \*    \*    \*    \*

Because the person who accepts proposals may do so for a variety of motives, there will be seen in any organization a number of different types of authority relationship, corresponding to these different motives for acceptance. . . .

People accept the proposals of persons in whom they have great confidence. In any organization there are some individuals who, because of past performance, general reputation, or other factors, have great influence or authority. Their proposals will often be accepted without analysis as to their wisdom. Even when the suggestions of such a person are not accepted, they will be rejected reluctantly and only because a stronger authority contradicts them.

The authority of confidence may be limited to a special area of competence in which a person has acquired a reputation. . . .

\*    \*    \*    \*    \*

. . . The willingness to accept authority on the basis of confidence, both within and outside organizations, goes even one step further. Not only is the layman generally unable

* Reprinted from *Public Administration* by Herbert A. Simon, Donald W. Smithburg, and Victor A. Thompson. Copyright 1950 by Herbert A. Simon, Donald W. Smithburg, and Victor A. Thompson. Reprinted by permission of Alfred A. Knopf, Inc.

to judge the quality of the advice he is getting from the specialist, but he often is in no position to judge the competence of the specialist, except on the basis of certain superficial and formal criteria that give the specialist his *status*.

. . . [T]here are at least two kinds of status, which may be called *functional status* and *hierarchical status*. It is with functional status that we are concerned at the moment. A person has functional status in a particular area of knowledge when his decisions and recommendations in that area are accepted as more or less authoritative.

In the established professions, status is generally conferred on the basis of standards developed by the profession itself. The M.D. degree is conferred on the young doctor by the medical profession (acting through an "accredited" medical school). Law and engineering degrees and the certificate of the public accountant are awarded in much the same way. In other cases, job experience in a particular field confers functional status in that field. A person with long experience in a professional position in the Interstate Commerce Commission may acquire status as a transportation economist.

\*     \*     \*     \*     \*

. . . Confidence can be a powerful support for hierarchical as well as for nonhierarchical authority. A subordinate will much more readily obey a command of a superior if he has confidence in the intelligence and judgment of that superior or if he believes that the superior has knowledge of the situation not available to himself.

In particular, where a problem requiring decision affects the work of several units in an organization, the superior who has hierarchical authority in the formal organization plan over all the units involved is often accepted as the person best located—because he has the "whole picture"—to make the decision. Hence, the coordinating functions that are commonly performed by those in hierarchical authority are based, in part at least, upon the authority of confidence—upon the belief of subordinates that the superior is the best informed about the situation as a whole.

\*     \*     \*     \*     \*

The most generally recognized weapon of the superior is the sanction—the ability of the superior to attach pleasant or unpleasant consequences to the actions of the subordinate. . . .

\*     \*     \*     \*     \*

The relationship of the authority of sanctions with the organizational hierarchy can be viewed from a more general standpoint. When a person joins an organization he is accepting a system of relationships that restricts his individuality or his freedom of action. He is willing to do so because he feels that, in spite of the organizational restraints, being a member of the organization is preferable to other alternatives available to him. To continue as a member of the organization, he must continue, to some extent, to abide by the complex of procedures which constitutes the organization. Although, increasingly, the power to discharge an employee is not lodged in any specific superior (because of merit systems, central personnel offices, labor unions, etc.) nevertheless, the power resides somewhere in the organization, being, in fact, one of its working procedures. The sanctions discussed in this section are increasingly *organization* sanctions, brought into play through the working procedures of the organization, and not the special prerogatives or powers of *individial superiors*. . . .

. . . For the most part the authority of sanction rests on the behavior responses that are induced by the *possibility* that a sanction may be applied. An organization member is seldom presented with an ultimatum "to do so and so or suffer the consequences." Rather, he anticipates the consequences of continual insubordination or failure to please the person or persons who have the ability to apply sanctions to him, and this anticipation acts as a constant motivation without expressed threats from any person. . . .

\*     \*     \*     \*     \*

There is another reason why employees accept the proposals of other organization members—a reason less rationalistic but probably more important than the desire to avoid the organization sanctions discussed above. People accept "legitimate" authority because they feel that they *ought* to go along with the "rules of the game."

. . . [T]hroughout their development to maturity and after, people are educated in the beliefs, values, or mores of society. They learn what they ought to do and what they ought not to do. One of the values with which they are indoctrinated is that a person should play according to the rules of the game. This ethic is acquired very early. When a child enters a ball game in the sand lot he does not expect the game to be altered at various points to suit his convenience. Rather he expects to adjust his behavior to the rules of the game. Although there may be disputes as to what the rule is on some point, once this is established, the proposition that he should abide by the rule is unquestioned.

Likewise, when people enter organizations most of them feel that they ought to abide by the rules of the game—the working procedures of the organization. These working procedures define how the work will be done; how working problems will be solved when they arise; how conflicts will be settled. They prescribe that on such and such matters the individual will accept the suggestions of this or that person or organization; secure the advice of such and such unit; clear his work with so and so; work on matters that come to him in such and such a way; etc.

The working procedures of an organization prescribe that the individual member will accept the proposals of other members in matters assigned to them. This acceptance is one of the rules of the game which he feels he should abide by. Thus, individuals in organizations also accept the authority of other persons because they think they *ought* to accept it.

*     *     *     *     *

. . . The working relationships in an organization designated by the term "hierarchy" constitute a particular organization procedure for handling the authority of legitimacy. Acceptance of the working procedures of an organization by a member includes acceptance of the obligation to go along with the proposals of an hierarchical superior, at least within a limit of toleration—the "area of acceptance." Thus, whether the other reasons for obedience are operating or not (confidence, identification, or sanctions), organization members will feel that they ought to obey their superiors. Legitimacy is one of the most important sources of the authority of the hierarchical superior.

The feeling that hierarchical authority is legitimate is immensely strengthened by previous social conditioning. Hierarchical behavior is an institutionalized behavior that all organization members bring to the organization with them. Like the players in the Oberammergau Passion Play who begin to learn their roles in early childhood, "inferiors" obey "superiors" because they have been taught to do so from infancy, beginning with the parent-child relationship and running through almost constant experience with social and organizational hierarchies until death brings graduation from this particular social schooling. Hierarchical behavior involves an inferior-superior role-taking of persons well versed in their roles. "Inferiors" feel that they ought to obey "superiors"; "superiors" feel that they ought to be obeyed.

Our society is extremely hierarchical. Success is generally interpreted in terms of hierarchical preferment. Social position and financial rewards are closely related to hierarchical preferment, as also are education and even perhaps romantic attainment. Advancement up a hierarchy is generally considered a sign of moral worth, of good character, of good stewardship, of social responsibility, and of the possession of superior intellectual qualities.

Hierarchy receives a tremendous emphasis in nearly all organizations. This is so because hierarchy is a procedure that requires no training, no indoctrination, no special inducements. It rests also entirely on "pre-entry" training—a training so thorough that few other organization procedures can ever compete with it. Furthermore, hierarchy is a great simplification. . . .

# 11. WESTERN OFFICE EQUIPMENT COMPANY

---

## Case Introduction

---

### SYNOPSIS

The company manufactures and sells office equipment through four regional offices in the western portion of the United States. Charles Porter, the president, applies a number of up-to-date management techniques in order to promote economic success for the company. Particularly, he employs corporate staff men specializing in management science applications to plan a new management control system. In allocating manpower (sales force) between Vancouver, Salt Lake City, San Francisco, and Los Angeles, policies and decision rules are developed to guide top managers and regional managers in deciding both where to locate new salesmen and how many to hire in each locality. The top management is faced with what seem to be powerful advantages of the system but also with serious disadvantages. Some of the latter seem to be technical dangers of the system. Others appear in the form of human conflict between corporate headquarters and geographic division managers.

### WHY THIS CASE IS INCLUDED

The case offers opportunity to see and understand, in a real-life action situation:

1. The place of objectives in long-range or strategic planning; the need for goals, the need for balance between conflicting goals, and the conflict between long- and short-run goals.
2. A decision-making process among top managers of a company: president, corporate staff, and division line managers.
3. The advantages and disadvantages of management science as a tech-

352

nique of corporate management, and as an integral part of a management control system. Specifically, marginal analysis and quantification applied to setting of decision rules.
4. Both the technological and human factors which cause conflict between executives in a larger system (the company) and a smaller component system (its branches).
5. The advantages of more sophisticated methods of management to society, as well as to an individual company.

Finally, the case offers opportunity to take a managerial viewpoint, and to construct better methods of using management science. In this pursuit, judgment between a number of diverse variables must be used. There is no final "scientific" way of solving such judgmental problems.

## DIAGNOSTIC AND PREDICTIVE QUESTIONS

The readings included with this case are marked (*). The author index at the end of the book locates the other readings.

1. From the viewpoint of management theory and strategic planning, of what importance in the future success of Western Office Equipment company is Porter's statement that "we redefined the objectives of the company to include growth in four districts: Salt Lake, San Francisco, Vancouver, and Los Angeles," and his redefinition of how much manpower is required in each location?

Read:   Tilles, "How to Evaluate Corporate Strategy." Drucker, *The Practice of Management.*

2. Why is the creation of the new position of manager of operations analysis an important matter in designing the organization structure of Western Office Equipment Company?

Read:   Smith, *The Wealth of Nations.*

3. Why is Porter's search for "some guiding standards that can be applied over the years, to tell us when to hire salesmen and where to put them," an effective managerial way of thinking?

Read:   Tilles, "How to Evaluate Corporate Strategy." Jerome, *Executive Control—The Catalyst.*

4. Consider the methods used by Olson in arriving at the $133,333 control standard. Then look at the four action decisions he states, beginning "(1) reduce the sales force in Salt Lake from. . . ." Why might Olson and Porter have high motivation to install these action recommendations? Recall especially Porter's opening statement at the meeting of district managers.

Read:   Rapoport and Drews, "Mathematical Approach to Long-Range Planning." Gellerman, *Motivation and Productivity.*

5. If scientific methods (in this case economics) yield action decisions that Porter and Olson believe in (Question 4), and if the efficiency of this company is in the interest of society, why do Ralph Hudson in Salt Lake and James Fulmer in San Francisco not "see the light"? Can they not share in the enthusiasm for an efficient Western Office Equipment Company through the power of science and rational decision making?

Read:   *Miller and Starr, *Executive Decisions and Operations Research.* *Maslow, *Motivation and Personality.*

6. Read carefully Porter's explanation of how the districts might grow in the future by having the manufacturing plants lower their costs to 60 percent of sales (or 60 cents of every sales dollar), instead of the present 70 percent. Do you see another reason which might add to Fulmer's and Hudson's frustration in trying to have their own districts grow in total sales or total number of salesmen employed?

Read:   Leavitt, *Managerial Psychology*, pp. 317–25. Those who wish additional insight into the answer to this question may consult in the library, *Managerial Psychology* by Harold J. Leavitt, University of Chicago Press, 2d. ed., 1964, pp. 16–21, 24–26. Leavitt discusses the concept of dependency of one individual on another individual or organization, and the resultant frustration this might cause.

7. Get clearly in your own mind how this company situation involves a conflict (1) between headquarters and subsidiary district managements and (2) between those responsible for direct selling and those in other parts of the company such as manufacturing. In what sense can this be considered a "win-lose" or "zero-sum" conflict? What are the attributes of this kind of conflict, and what are the implications for whether or not the conflict can be resolved?

Read:   *Litterer, "Conflict in Organization: A Re-Examination."

## POLICY QUESTIONS

8. At least in theory, there is a way for Porter to think about achieving an efficient company and achieving good morale on the part of all company personnel at the same time. What kind of ideal or theoretical approaches are available?

Read:   Follett, "Constructive Conflict." Newman and Summer, *The Process of Management: Concepts, Behavior, and Practice.*

9. Another approach is what some people call a more courageous, forceful decisiveness on the part of Porter or Roberts as they exercise the leadership function. What would Porter do under this kind of theory?

Read:   Jennings, "Business Needs Mature Autocrats." Odiorne, *How Managers Make Things Happen.* O'Donnell, "The Source of Managerial Authority."

10. One modern means of dealing with the cost problem *and* the morale of district managers would be what is called *organization development.* What would Porter do if he used this approach?

Read:   *French, "Organization Development Objectives, Assumptions and Strategies." Leavitt, *Managerial Psychology*, pp. 317–25.

11. Considering all factors suggested in the above questions, what would you do if you were president of Western Office Equipment Company?

Read:   *Beard, *Public Policy and the General Welfare.*

# Case Text*

Western Office Equipment Manufacturing Company was founded in Salt Lake City, Utah, for the purpose of making and selling steel utiliy shelving used in offices and warehouses. Today it is still a family-owned company, though with the retirement of the founder six years ago, a professional manager, Charles F. Porter, was employed as president. The company still makes its original line of steel shelving but has added a diverse line of medium-priced desks, chairs, bookcases, and other small furniture. Porter says, "We have never tried to compete with high-quality manufacturers—our customers are medium and smaller companies who want serviceable furniture at a good price." Current sales volume is $3,830,000.

## MODERNIZATION UNDER MR. PORTER'S DIRECTION

Since he assumed the presidency, Charles Porter has, in the words of one member of the founding family,

> . . . Measured up to our expectations. Before he came to our head-quarters in Salt Lake City, the company was successful mostly by trial and error. We had developed a good line of products, and our salesmen were good. We were selling in Salt Lake, San Francisco, and Vancouver. Those places were chosen somewhat by accident. The founder was originally from Seattle, worked for an eastern competitor and knew those districts well. He had 15 salesmen when he retired, all reporting to Mr. Roberts, the marketing vice president here in in Salt Lake. Several years ago, we entered Los Angeles on a very modest basis because we hired an excellent salesman who knew customers and the market there. Today, Porter has organized the 15 company salesmen into four district offices, with one of the senior men serving as district manager. He has also added new products to the line, set up accounting and profit controls, and enabled us to compete as we never have before with companies that are much larger than ours. In short, our objective is to grow, and Porter is the man we depend on for that.

## ALLOCATION OF SELLING EFFORT

Among other ways of improving the company, the effective allocation of salesmen to territories has been one of Porter's concerns.

---

* Copyright 1977 by Charles E. Summer.

After I joined the firm [Porter said], there were many things to do. I did not have time to look into the matter of selling effectiveness. Sam Roberts, the marketing vice president, and I looked at the statistics on selling as the company began to grow. We set the policy that the company should add salesmen to a district as long as the average sales per salesman in the district did not fall below $250,-000.

The current allocation of salesmen by district, the average sales per salesman, and the total sales volume are shown in Exhibit 1.

**EXHIBIT 1**
**Current Annual Sales Volume\* and Salesmen Distribution by District**

| District | Number of Salesmen | Total Sales Volume | Average Sales Volume per Salesman |
|---|---|---|---|
| Salt Lake City . . . . . . 4 | | $1,060 | $265 |
| Los Angeles. . . . . . . . 1 | | 250 | 250 |
| San Francisco . . . . . . 6 | | 1,500 | 250 |
| Vancouver . . . . . . . . . 4 | | 1,020 | 255 |
| Totals† . . . . . . . . 15 | | $3,830 | |

\* All amounts given in thousands of dollars.
† Average sales per salesman for the company as a whole: 3,830/15 = 255.3, or $255,300.

Porter continued:

We have 15 salesmen—6 in San Francisco, 4 each in Salt Lake City and Vancouver, and 1 in Los Angeles. Several months ago, we redefined the objectives of the company to include growth in four districts. Salt Lake City handles Nevada, Wyoming, Colorado, Idaho, and Montana. San Francisco handles central California; and Vancouver handles British Columbia, Washington, and Oregon. The really important decision has been to enter the Los Angeles market on a full-scale basis.

John Olson has been with us as manager of operations analysis for three years. He specialized in finance and operations research at Stanford and has done very much to analyze our plant facilities by using modern quantitative methods. I have asked him to analyze the selling effort with this objective in mind: How can we allocate salesmen in districts so that (1) we get the most sales from our total sales force, and (2) we employ the least number of salesmen to achieve this volume? In other words, I wanted him to establish some standard that will tell us how many men to hire and where to put them to get the most volume. The company is growing more complex, and we need some guide that can be applied over the years—I do not want rule-of-thumb assignment on the basis of who a particular salesman is. Decisions have to be made for the business as a whole, and over a period of years.

## OLSON'S ANALYSIS AND RECOMMENDATIONS

John Olson spent the first month of his analysis visiting with district managers in the four districts. In each case he explained to them that his purpose was to forecast statistics on potential sales in the district under differing manpower assumptions. For example, he would ask the San Francisco manager to study with him market-potential figures from trade associations, statistics on number and types of businesses in the district, and other materials that he had worked up and brought with him. Then he asked the manager to use his own knowledge of territories, distances between customers, severity of competition by other companies, and other information. Finally, he and the manager jointly dicussed both the territory characteristics and the market-research data.

Olson described the results:

> In each case, we arrived at the estimates in Exhibit 2. Look at San Francisco. You will see that if Western employs only one salesman, we would sell $400,000. If two, $750,000; if five, $1,430,000. The incremental amount sold by each salesman decreases as you add salesmen in a district because the first salesman gets the best customers, the shortest distances to cover, and other advantages. With only one salesman, we would skim the cream off the market. Each time we add another salesman, we either take less desirable customers or raise the cost of reaching customers, or both. In fact, you can see in the column marked "marginal" the incremental amount of sales volume generated by adding one more salesman in each territory.
>
> Notice, too, that the amount that can be sold by each salesman varies by district. The first salesman in San Francisco will sell $400,000, but the first one in Los Angeles will sell only $250,000. These inter-district differences are caused by various factors— there may be more competition in one market than in another, or the distance between cities and customers may be greater and so the result will be fewer calls per day.
>
> Once having determined these figures, the next step was to discover a way of measuring what a salesman is worth to the company. In financial terms, what is his contribution to the company profit picture? It costs the company an average of $40,000 a year to support a salesman. From the records, I found that this does not vary much by districts. At a conference between myself, Sam Roberts, and the district managers, we compared figures on Salesmen's performance and agreed that for our company and our line of products there is very little difference in salesmen's capabilities. We have some differences, but salesmen are very similar in output.
>
> Given this $40,000 cost, what does the salesman produce in profit contribution? Well, we very carefully got accounting figures to show that the total cost of delivering products to customers (except the cost of salesmen) was 70 percent of sales. This means that the sales-

**EXHIBIT 2**
**Potential Sales Volume* by District, in Relation to Number of Salesmen**

| Number of Salesmen | Salt Lake City | | | Los Angeles | | | San Francisco | | | Vancouver | | |
|---|---|---|---|---|---|---|---|---|---|---|---|---|
| | Total Sales | Average Sales | Marginal Increment | Total Sales | Average Sales | Marginal Increment | Total Sales | Average Sales | Marginal Increment | Total Sales | Average Sales | Marginal Increment |
| 1 | $ 450 | $450 | $450 | $ 250† | $250 | $250 | $ 400 | $400 | $400 | $ 350 | $350 | $350 |
| 2 | 850 | 425 | 400 | 480 | 240 | 230 | 750 | 375 | 350 | 650 | 325 | 300 |
| 3 | 960 | 320 | 110 | 690 | 230 | 210 | 1,050 | 350 | 300 | 900 | 300 | 250 |
| 4 | 1,060† | 265 | 100 | 860 | 215 | 170 | 1,300 | 325 | 250 | 1,020† | 255 | 120 |
| 5 | 1,150 | 230 | 90 | 1,000 | 200 | 140 | 1,430 | 286 | 130 | 1,100 | 220 | 80 |
| 6 | 1,200 | 200 | 50 | 1,110 | 185 | 110 | 1,500† | 250 | 70 | 1,140 | 190 | 40 |

* All amounts given in thousands of dollars.
† Denotes current sales volume.

man is adding 30 percent of sales as his part of the contribution to profits. Now here is the important point. We will break even if a salesman sells $133,333 worth of merchandise. Thirty percent of $133,333 is $40,000. If the salesman sells just that, he pays (in revenues) for himself. Anything beyond that is a contribution to profits. Stated in reverse, if his sales fall below $133,333, he is paid more than he contributes.

This is known as incremental analysis. In economics we learn that any resource may be evaluated this way. That is, a company should add additional units of any resource up to the point where marginal cost exceeds marginal revenue.

Now to apply this to Western's sales force, we must look at the marginal column for each district (see Exhibit 2). In the Salt Lake district, the second salesman will add $400,000 to sales, but the third will add only $110,000. Or in Los Angeles, the third salesman will add $210,000.

|  | Current Volume (000) | Planned Volume (000) |
|---|---|---|
| Salt Lake district | $1,060 | $ 850 |
| Los Angeles district | 250 | 1,000 |
| San Francisco district | 1,500 | 1,300 |
| Vancouver district | 1,020 | 900 |
| Total for company | $3,830 | $4,050 |

Finally, we can convert all of the analysis to total profits for Western.

| | |
|---|---|
| Sales with new allocation | $4,050,000 |
| Sales volume at present | 3,830,000 |
| Increase in sales volume | $ 220,000 |
| Profit margin (multiply) | .30 |
| Additional profit | $ 66,000 |

The incremental analysis shows that the company should take the following actions, based on the standard of $133,333:

1. Reduce the sales force in Salt Lake district from the present four salesmen to two.
2. Increase the sales force in Los Angeles district from one man to five.
3. Decrease the number of salesmen in San Francisco from six to four.
4. Decrease the salesmen in Vancouver district from four to three.

You will also notice that the total sales force comes out to be 14, instead of the present 15. The reason is that there is nowhere we can put a fifteenth salesman that he will produce the standard sales volume to break even.

Other managerial decisions are also solved by applying this standard. For example, here are the new sales volume quotas compared to the old sales performance figures for each district.

## TOP MANAGEMENT APPROVAL

John Olson kept Charles Porter informed throughout his analysis, giving reasoning identical with that presented to the casewriter. At the conclusion, using easel charts, he presented the complete report to Porter and the board of directors. At that time, one board member said that it looked to him as if one could not draw conclusions about what a salesman could sell until he knew the specific salesman. "Some salesmen simply are better than others." Porter answered that while there will be deviations, a company cannot plan its structure of divisions, including where offices will be located and the size of the sales force, on the basis of one salesman's characteristics. "If he leaves the company, we would have no logical and rational plan."

Porter questioned Olson on how the division managers would receive the new plan and standard. He specifically wanted to know if Olson had obtained their agreement. Olson replied:

> I have their complete agreement that our company must plan where to add salesmen on an economic basis. All managers agreed that, for the sake of our competitive position, we must do this. Also, in my meetings with division managers they each helped to draw up the amounts that would be sold by each additional salesman in their regions. In other words, the marginal and total sales figures in Exhibit 2 are their estimates as much as mine.

The board, noting that both the added $66,000 of profits and the expansion into the more profitable market of Los Angeles (from $250,000 sales to $1,000,000) were consistent with the company's growth goal, approved the new plan. On recommendation of Porter, it set a target of three years for transfer of salesmen and buildup to the new district quotas.

Porter then made an implementation plan. He stated that he

> knew that there would be considerable upset among the salesmen and the district managers. In consultation with Sam Roberts, we decided to transfer two men each from Salt Lake and San Francisco to Los Angeles. One of the salesmen in Vancouver will have to be terminated. We decided on him because he only has two years to go until retirement.
>
> Nevertheless, there are times in managing a business when you have to take steps that aren't too popular. It may cause some anxiety in our company temporarily, but five years from now everyone will be operating on the new plan as if it were always that way.

## REACTIONS OF FIELD PERSONNEL

A meeting of district managers was held at the Fairmont Hotel in San Francisco to explain the new financial and selling plan. Porter thought it best not to mail the plan in advance, but simply to explain all of the details on a face-to-face basis. "I thought it necessary to explain the whole thing at once. Only in this way could we get a meaningful understanding of it. If we mailed it in advance, the managers may have focused on only one part or aspect of the whole plan."

Porter opened the meeting by calling attention to the goal of the company to grow, using the most modern management and selling methods available.

> I'm sure that each of you want our company to use our resources to produce the best products at lowest cost to the customer. In this way, we will always be able to stay efficient and come out ahead of competition. For this reason, I know you will want to understand thoroughly a new plan for district realignment—one that is based on the markets "out there"—that takes best advantage of where the customers are whom we can serve in the most efficient way. I'm sure, too, that you are interested in the fact that we have set as our goal our company becoming a leading supplier in the Rocky Mountain and West Coast states. We will no longer simply put our efforts into districts as they have grown up, often somewhat by accident, over the years.

Later, John Olson gave a complete summary of the reasoning behind the new moves, as well as a summary of his analytical methods. At the conclusion, Porter stated that there was plenty of time for questions. "I certainly want you district managers to feel free to question John or me, so that you can satisfy yourself that you know what we are doing and why."

Robert Perry, the manager-salesman from Los Angeles, stated that he had been waiting for months for the go-ahead signal to expand sales there. "The market is there just waiting to be sold. Within three years we will show those larger national firms how to sell."

Ralph Hudson asked Olson why it made sense to transfer two of his salesmen, thus decreasing his sales force by 50 percent, when his four salesmen were averaging $265,000 sales each.

> You and I both agree [Olson said] that salesmen who are doing above $133,000 are making money for the company. The average salesman in the Salt Lake district is not only doing over that, but our average salesman is selling more than that of any other district. It just doesn't seem logical, from the company's viewpoint, to cut down from over $1,000,000 sales to $850,000. Why, I would be giving away customers to competition.

Porter clarified at length the reasoning that Olson had reported in the case. "But I don't think we really got across. Ralph said that he of course would be willing to do what is best for the company, but the tone of his voice and the relative lack of enthusiasm seemed negative."

James Fulmer said that he had just recently started new sales training programs in San Francisco and instituted a new kind of advertising at the same cost as his previous campaigns.

> In this way, I will eventually get those fifth and sixth salesmen up above $133,000 in production. It may take a couple of years, but I can do it. I believe that you should leave the six salesmen in San Francisco. In fact, though your production forecasts are correct, and I helped draw them up, I had no idea you would draw these kinds of conclusions for them.

Both Hudson and Fulmer questioned how their districts could grow if the company were actually cutting out salesmen and lowering the sales targets, which implied cutting out customers.

Porter explained:

> Actually, I see three ways. First you can make better use of sales training and promotion campaigns to raise the marginal sales of each salesman. These are examples of ingenious new methods that can be invented within your own districts. When that contribution level goes above $133,000 you can bet that Olson and I will be quick to add salesmen.
>
> The other method of growth is a little harder to explain. You see, in a complex business, one part actually depends on another part. One of the factors we have used in the standard is the cost of goods sold (excluding cost of supporting a salesman). That is today 70 percent. It is determined by efficiency in our manufacturing plants as well as efficiency in the central office overhead. In short, all of the cost elements in the profit-and-loss statement. Now in the long run, if we strive for efficiency here to the point where, say, our cost of goods sold is 60 percent, and if we keep our price and volume to the customer the same, the salesmen's contribution will go up to 40 percent of sales instead of 30 percent. That would immediately lower our salesmen's break-even point to $100,000 ($40,000 divided by .40). You can see that, right at the present, the two added salesmen in Salt Lake would be justified, as would six in Los Angeles, five in San Francisco, and four in Vancouver.
>
> The same kind of effect would exist if we passed this new efficiency on to the customer in the form of lower price. Our volume would increase, the selling contribution would go up (and the break-even point down). Manufacturing contribution would go down.
>
> Balancing a complex business like ours is a difficult matter. I'm saying that your contribution depends in part on how efficient our plants and headquarters are. We will work on these other opera-

tions as hard as we can. When their efficiency raises the contribution of the salesmen you can bet we will be quick to grow in each and every territory. But in the meantime, it is sometimes necessary to actually hurt one part of the business (for example, the Salt Lake or San Francisco selling branches) to increase overall efficiency. In the long run, it will pay off.

At this point in the meeting, all three managers (with the exception of Robert Perry from Los Angeles) asked a wide variety of questions, most of which, according to Olson, were actually phrased as arguments against the plan. For example, "You don't think you can transfer both Dolan and Franklin to Los Angeles, do you?" Or "Why can't you keep our customers in Vancouver and cut your manufacturing costs now, instead of hurting us in the market place?"

The meeting adjourned at seven in the evening, two hours later than planned. Porter described the results of the meeting.

I told them that in view of their objections, we would declare a temporary suspension of the plan. That we would have another meeting in 60 days to discuss it again. I have a lot of faith in Olson's abilities and am certain in my own mind that the plan is good for the company's growth objectives. Right now, I am wondering what to do, and how to get the plan into effect with the support of the district managers. Their own good work is, of course, vital to a company like ours.

**EXHIBIT 3**
**Organization Chart**

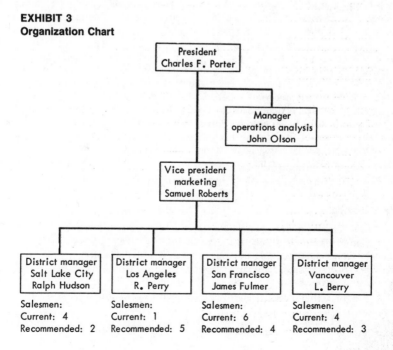

# Selected Readings

*From*

## EXECUTIVE DECISIONS AND OPERATIONS RESEARCH*

*By David W. Miller and Martin K. Starr*

### Goals of the Role

People play many roles. Each role can be associated with its own objectives. Individuals simplify their decision problems by establishing for themselves these multiple objectives instead of just one basic objective. Most people, for example, will establish some kind of objective for themselves in the area of their professional activities. They will usually have other objectives relating to their interpersonal relationships; e.g., father, husband, son. They will also have objectives regarding their relationship to society as a whole, e.g., political activity or public-spirited work. They will often have some objectives regarding their leisure activities. And, of course, we can continue and obtain quite a catalogue of the different areas in which people are likely to set themselves some kind of objectives. It appears that most people handle their decision problems in a particular field of activity by ignoring the objectives of other fields of activity. Thus, a business executive will solve his decision problems in business—for example, what position he will accept—in terms of his professional objective.

Even within a single field of activity an individual has many different roles. An executive reports to his boss and in turn has people reporting to him. His position in the organization determines the extent of his responsibility and the importance of decisions he must make. The goal of the executive is strongly tied to the complex image he has of his role. Although no two executives have the same situations, the similarity of goals which they share as a group causes us to speak about executive goals. However, similarity should not blind us to the differences. In the same way, for convenience, we group employee goals, ownership goals, salesmen's goals, and so on. There is a certain relevant pattern of goal-seeking within each of these groups. It is hardly necessary to expand on what these might be. On the other hand, it is an observable fact that sometimes there is a conflict between the objectives of several groups to which the individual belongs.

### Suboptimization

. . . Whenever there is no conflict between objectives, the individual can proceed to solve his decision problems separately. As long as the action taken to achieve either objective is independent of the other, he can do this. However, when objectives are dependent, the optimization of one can result in a lower degree of attainment for all the others. This condition is known as *suboptimization*. For example, an executive may decide to take a new position on the basis of his professional objectives. The new job, however, entails extremely long

* *Executive Decisions and Operations Research,* David W. Miller and Martin K. Starr © 1961 by Prentice-Hall, Inc., Englewood Cliffs, N.J. (pp. 38–42, 45–47, 50).

hours and much traveling. Assume that the new job is optimal in terms of the executive's professional objective. The fact that the time he can now spend with his family is sharply reduced may have such adverse effects that he will find that his optimization in terms of one objective has produced a result which is very much less than optimal in terms of all his objectives.

The same notion of suboptimization is involved in the effects on the decision problem of the fact that we lead our lives through time and that we have only very imperfect ability to foresee the future. This means that any decision problem can be solved only in terms of the knowledge and situation obtaining currently. But the action chosen may, and probably will, have effects on the decision-maker's situation for a considerable period in the future. An optimal action at one time may, therefore, turn out to have been a very inferior suboptimization in terms of a longer period of time.

* * * * * *

It is quite clear that we can never really achieve optimization. Over time, unexpected events can change what had appeared to be an optimal decision into an inferior decision. There is almost no reversibility in decision systems. Generally speaking, by the time we find out that a decision was not a good one, we cannot return to the state which prevailed before the decision had been made. Consequently, decision systems should provide the best possible predictions of future expectations. And in addition, decision systems should not commit us to irrevocable action for very long periods of time. And so we reach the conclusion that a *sequential decision process* permits maximum flexibility with respect to both objectives and actions.

## Bounded Rationality

. . . We have been using the word "optimum," and some other forms of the same word, rather loosely. In fact, it is important to note that people rarely make a prolonged effort to achieve the optimum action in any realistic decision problem facing them. To paraphrase John Maurice Clark, people simply don't have such an irrational passion for dispassionate rationality. Furthermore, there are good reasons why they shouldn't. All of the reasons have reference to the exorbitant complexity of any realistic decision problem. Three main aspects of this complexity should be noted.

First, consider the point just made, that an optimum decision made at one point in time is only suboptimum in terms of subsequent times. . . . .

. . . Second, there are an enormous number of possible choices of action (strategies, as we have called them) and any attempt to obtain information on all of them would be self-defeating.

. . . Third, there are virtually innumerable factors outside the control of the decision-maker (we call them states of nature) which may affect the outcome of his decision.

. . . The net effect of these limitations on human decision-making procedures has been observed and neatly summarized by Herbert Simon in his "principle of bounded rationality." According to this principle human beings seldom make any effort to find the optimum action in a decision problem. Instead, they select a number of possible outcomes of their available strategies which would be good enough. Then they select a strategy (choose an action) that is likely to achieve one of the good-enough outcomes. Thus, the executive looking for a new job makes no effort to discover all possible jobs from which he can then select the best (optimum) one. Instead, he decides what he wants from a job in terms of his various objectives. Then he searches for a job that will provide him with the things he wants, e.g., a certain income, satisfactory working conditions, chances for advancement. He does not try to find that one job somewhere in the world which might give him the optimum. The principle of bounded rationality is a neat way to describe the actual procedure of human beings involved in the decision problems of life, and it succinctly reminds us not to assume any irrational extremes of rationality.

* * * * * *

## Organizational Problems of Suboptimization

. . . Under what conditions does suboptimization arise in business? Of course we can answer that it arises whenever an action has an effect on several different objectives simultaneously. But this is merely to state the same thing in different words. In fact, there is no general answer to this question. The best that can be done in any specific decision problem is to utilize intuition, experience, and all available methodology to endeavor to see whether actions intended for one purpose have any probable effects on other objectives. If they do then it follows that the problem is one that involves a possible conflict of objectives and it must be handled with this fact in mind.

It should be explicitly noted that no genuine problem of a conflict of objectives can be reconciled by expressing all the possible outcomes in terms of the utility measure for one of the objectives. Now, it is fortunate that many decision problems of business can be framed in terms such that the possible outcomes can be measured in dollars. But it is by no means the case that all business objectives can be expressed in dollars. If, to take an instance, workers' attitudes could be measured in dollars, then it would follow that all possible outcomes in the area of workers' attitudes could be expressed in dollars. The total objective need only be stated as the maximization of profit. We would not require a special description of workers' attitudes. No such easy solution to the problem of conflicting objectives is usually available. . . .

Looking at the bright side, there are a great number of important decision problems that do not involve any conflict of objectives. For any one of these we can attempt to optimize with no fear of difficulties arising from suboptimization. In particular, we can state that, at the minimum, a business must attempt to optimize its situation with regard to each specific objective as long as it does not affect adversely its situation with regard to any other objective. This construction is a variant of an idea introduced in a different context by the Italian economist and sociologist, Vilfredo Pareto. Pareto was concerned with the problem of what should govern the actions of society if it is assumed that the utilities of the various individuals composing the society cannot be compared. By utility we mean the subjective value that each individual subscribes for the various goods and services available. Under these circumstances society cannot act to achieve the greatest total utility because this idea has no meaning for the stated conditions. Pareto suggested that society should then try to achieve at least an optimum such that each individual had the maximum utility possible without subtracting anything from anyone else's utility. In other words, if society can act so as to increase one individual's total utility without taking anything away from anyone else, then it should do so. A condition where this has been accomplished is known as *Paretian optimality.*

The problem with which Pareto was dealing arises because there is no common standard of measure of value between individuals. And this is precisely analogous to the problem of multiple objectives with which we are dealing. Our problem arises because there is no common measure of value for the various objectives. If there were one common measure we could formulate one objective rather than several. Therefore we can state, along with Pareto, that any business should always attempt to achieve a condition of Paretian optimality with regard to its various objectives.

\* \* \* \* \*

Business organizations are subject to still another kind of suboptimization problem. Whereas a real person is a unit that is more or less indecomposable, the fictitious person of the business corporation is usually made up of a number of different departments or divisions. The successful functioning of the business demands the integration of the efforts of the various departments that compose it. The achievement of any of the business objectives requires that the various departments should each achieve some departmental objectives. But, by the very nature of things, departments are likely to have considerable autonomy and it can happen that the objectives they set are not in accord with the over-all business objectives. It can also happen that the actions of one department have an effect on the situation of other departments such that an optimal strategy for one department in terms of its own objectives deleteriously affects other departments and, hence, the entire business. Both of these kinds of situations represent other variants of the suboptimization problem.

*        *        *        *        *

. . . We can now look at illustrations of suboptimization where two parts of the company are in conflict with each other. For example, a division's objective of achieving the best possible profitability record may lead it to purchase parts from competitors rather than from another division of the same company. This may lower the profitability of the division that normally supplies parts. As another aspect of the inventory problem, a sales manager's objective of getting the largest possible sales may lead him to want a large inventory so that all orders can be promptly filled. This might be in conflict with the controller's objective of tying up a minimum of capital in inventory. Which one is in the best interests of the business? As a final example, a production department uses less steel by cutting down on the upper limit of the tolerances to which it machines a part. This results in a higher number of rejects of the finished assembly and an eventual complete redesign of the product with no appreciable gain in quality.

All of these examples serve to demonstrate the crucial importance of the suboptimization problem. Once again we could raise the question: When does this kind of problem arise? And once again, there is no general answer. Being aware of the problem we must rely on common and uncommon sense to help us to discover which particular decision may exemplify it. Fortunately, the majority of the forms of this kind of suboptimization problem involve objectives that can be expressed in quantitative form, so many of these problems can be resolved by methods which we will be discussing at length below. Thus, for example, the problem of inventory size and the conflicting interests of the sales manager and the controller can generally be resolved by expressing all the costs in dollars and solving the decision problem in terms of the over-all business objective of minimizing costs. This simple statement may make it seem easy. It isn't, as we know from the problem of the small-plant manager. How can we express the loss of dignity which he experiences as a result of being out of stock more often than he would like? Similarly, how do we represent the loss of customer goodwill that results from being out of inventory on an item that the customer wants immediately? Nonetheless, despite some difficulties, these kinds of problems can often be satisfactorily resolved.

*From*

# MOTIVATION AND PERSONALITY*

*By A. H. Maslow*

## A THEORY OF HUMAN MOTIVATION

### THE BASIC NEEDS

#### The Physiological Needs

The needs that are usually taken as the starting point for motivation theory are the so-called physiological drives. Two recent lines of research make it necessary to revise our customary notions about these needs: first, the development of the concept of homeostasis, and second, the finding that appetites (preferential choices among foods) are a fairly efficient indication of actual needs or lacks in the body.

---

* From pp. 80–94 from *Motivation and Personality,* 2d. ed. by A. H. Maslow. Copyright © 1970 by Abraham H. Maslow. Reprinted by permission of Harper & Row Publishers Inc.

Homeostasis refers to the body's automatic efforts to maintain a constant, normal state of the blood stream. Cannon . . . has described this process for (1) the water content of the blood, (2) salt content, (3) sugar content, (4) protein content, (5) fat content, (6) calcium content, (7) oxygen content, (8) constant hydrogen-ion level (acid-base balance), and (9) constant temperature of the blood. Obviously this list can be extended to include other minerals, the hormones, vitamins, etc.

Young . . . has summarized the work on appetite in its relation to body needs. If the body lacks some chemical, the individual will tend (in an imperfect way) to develop a specific appetite or partial hunger for that food element.

Thus it seems impossible as well as useless to make any list of fundamental physiological needs, for they can come to almost any number one might wish, depending on the degree of specificity of description. We cannot identify all physiological needs as homeostatic. That sexual desire, sleepiness, sheer activity, and maternal behavior in animals are homeostatic has not yet been demonstrated. Furthermore, this list would not include the various sensory pleasure (tastes, smells, tickling, stroking), which are probably physiological and which may become the goals of motivated behavior.

\* \* \* \* \*

Undoubtedly these physiological needs are the most prepotent of all needs. What this means specifically is that in the human being who is missing everything in life in an extreme fashion, it is most likely that the major motivation would be the physiological needs rather than any others. A person who is lacking food, safety, love, and esteem would most probably hunger for food more strongly than for anything else.

If all the needs are unsatisfied, and the organism is then dominated by the physiological needs, all other needs may become simply nonexistent or be pushed into the background. It is then fair to characterize the whole organism by saying simply that it is hungry, for consciousness is almost completely preëmpted by hunger. All capacities are put into the service of hunger-satisfaction, and the organization of these capacities is almost entirely determined by the one purpose of satisfying hunger. The receptors and effectors, the intelligence, memory, habits, all may now be defined simply as hunger-gratifying tools. Capacities that are not useful for this purpose lie dormant, or are pushed into the background. The urge to write poetry, the desire to acquire an automobile, the interest in American history, the desire for a new pair of shoes are, in the extreme case, forgotten or become of secondary importance. . . .

Another peculiar characteristic of the human organism when it is dominated by a certain need is that the whole philosophy of the future tends also to change. For our chronically and extremely hungry man, Utopia can be defined simply as a place where there is plenty of food. He tends to think that, if only he is guaranteed food for the rest of his life, he will be perfectly happy and will never want anything more. Life itself tends to be defined in terms of eating. Anything else will be defined as unimportant. Freedom, love, community feeling, respect, philosophy, may all be waved aside as fripperies that are useless, since they fail to fill the stomach. Such a man may fairly be said to live by bread alone.

. . . It is quite true that man lives by bread alone—when there is no bread. But what happens to man's desires when there *is* plenty of bread and when his belly is chronically filled?

*At once other* (*and higher*) *needs emerge* and these, rather than physiological hungers, dominate the organism. And when these in turn are satisfied, again new (and still higher) needs emerge, and so on. This is what we mean by saying that the basic human needs are organized into a hierarchy of relative prepotency.

One main implication of this phrasing is that gratification becomes as important a concept as deprivation in motivation theory, for it releases the organism from the domination of a relatively more physiological need, permitting thereby the emergence of other more social goals. The physiological needs, along with their partial goals, when chronically gratified cease to exist as active determinants or organizers of behavior. They now exist only in a potential fashion in the sense that they may emerge again to dominate the organism if they are thwarted. But a want that is satisfied is no longer a want. The organism is dominated and its behavior organized only by unsatisfied needs. If hunger is satisfied, it becomes unimportant in the current dynamics of the individual.

This statement is somewhat qualified by a hypothesis to be discussed more fully later, namely, that it is precisely those individuals in whom a certain need has always been satisfied who are best equipped to tolerate deprivation of that need in the future, and that furthermore, those who have been deprived in the past will react differently to current satisfactions than the one who has never been deprived.

## The Safety Needs

If the physiological needs are relatively well gratified, there then emerges a new set of needs, which we may categorize roughly as the safety needs. All that has been said of the physiological needs is equally true, although in less degree, of these desires. The organism may equally well be wholly dominated by them. They may serve as the almost exclusive organizers of behavior, recruiting all the capacities of the organism in their service, and we may then fairly describe the whole organism as a safety-seeking mechanism. Again we may say of the receptors, the effectors, of the intellect, and of the other capacities that they are primarily safety-seeking tools. Again, as in the hungry man, we find that the dominating goal is a strong determinant not only of his current world outlook and philosophy but also of his philosophy of the future. Practically everything looks less important than safety (even sometimes the physiological needs, which being satisfied are now underestimated). A man in this state, if it is extreme enough and chronic enough, may be characterized as living almost for safety alone.

*   *   *   *   *

Another indication of the child's need for safety is his preference for some kind of undisrupted routine or rhythm. He seems to want a predictable, orderly world. For instance, injustice, unfairness, or inconsistency in the parents seems to make a child feel anxious and unsafe. This attitude may be not so much because of the injustice *per se* or any particular pains involved, but rather because this treatment threatens to make the world look unreliable, or unsafe, or unpredictable. Young children seem to thrive better under a system that has at least a skeletal outline of rigidity, in which there is a schedule of a kind, some sort of routine, something that can be counted upon, not only for the present but also far into the future. Child psychologists, teachers, and psychotherapists have found that permissiveness within limits, rather than unrestricted permissiveness is preferred as well as *needed* by children. Perhaps one could express this more accurately by saying that the child needs an organized world rather than an unorganized or unstructured one.

*   *   *   *   *

Confronting the average child with new, unfamiliar, strange, unmanageable stimuli or situations will too frequently elicit the danger or terror reaction, as for example, getting lost or even being separated from the parents for a short time, being confronted with new faces, new situations, or new tasks, the sight of strange, unfamiliar, or uncontrollable objects, illness, or death. Particularly at such times, the child's frantic clinging to his parents is eloquent testimony to their role as protectors (quite apart from their roles as food givers and love givers).

From these and similar observations, we may generalize and say that the average child in our society generally prefers a safe, orderly, predictable, organized world, which he can count on, and in which unexpected, unmanageable, or other dangerous things do not happen, and in which, in any case, he has all-powerful parents who protect and shield him from harm. . . .

That these reactions may so easily be observed in children is in a way a proof of the fact that children in our society feel too unsafe (or, in a word, are badly brought up). Children who are reared in an unthreatening, loving family do *not* ordinarily react as we have described above. In such children the danger reactions are apt to come mostly to objects or situations that adults too would consider dangerous.

The healthy, normal, fortunate adult in our culture is largely satisfied in his safety needs. The peaceful, smoothly running, good society ordinarily makes its members feel safe enough from wild animals, extremes of temperature, criminal assault, murder, tyranny, etc. Therefore, in a very real sense, he no longer has any safety needs as active motivators. Just as a sated man no longer feels hungry, a safe man no longer feels endangered. . . .

* * * * *

## The Belongingness and Love Needs

If both the physiological and the safety needs are fairly well gratified, there will emerge the love and affection and belongingness needs, and the whole cycle already described will repeat itself with this new center. Now the person will feel keenly, as never before, the absence of friends, or a sweetheart, or a wife, or children. He will hunger for affectionate relations with people in general, namely, for a place in his group, and he will strive with great intensity to achieve this goal. He will want to attain such a place more than anything else in the world and may even forget that once, when he was hungry, he sneered at love as unreal or unnecessary or unimportant.

In our society the thwarting of these needs is the most commonly found core in cases of maladjustment and more severe psychopathology. Love and affection, as well as their possible expression in sexuality, are generally looked upon with ambivalence and are customarily hedged about with many restrictions and inhibitions. Practically all theorists of psychopathology have stressed thwarting of the love needs as basic in the picture of maladjustment. Many clinical studies have therefore been made of this need, and we know more about it perhaps than any of the other needs except the physiological ones. Suttie . . . has written an excellent analysis of our "taboo on tenderness."

One thing that must be stressed at this point is that love is not synonymous with sex. Sex may be studied as a purely physiological need. Ordinarily sexual behavior is multidetermined, that is to say, determined not only by sexual but also by other needs, chief among which are the love and affection needs. Also not to be overlooked is the fact that the love needs involve both giving *and* receiving love. . . .

## The Esteem Needs

All people in our society (with a few pathological exceptions) have a need or desire for a stable, firmly based, usually high evaluation of themselves, for self-respect, or self-esteem, and for the esteem of others. These needs may therefore be classified into two subsidiary sets. These are, first, the desire for strength, for achievement, for adequacy, for mastery and competence, for confidence in the face of the world, and for independence and freedom.[1] Second, we have what we may call the desire for reputation or prestige (defining it as repect or esteem from other people), status, dominance, recognition, attention, importance, or appreciation. These needs have been relatively stressed by Alfred Adler and his followers, and have been relatively neglected by Freud. More and more today, however, there is appearing widespread appreciation of their central importance, among psychoanalysis as well as among clinical psychologists.

---

[1] Whether or not this particular desire is universal we do not know. The crucial question, especially important today, is, Will men who are enslaved and dominated inevitably feel dissatisfied and rebellious? We may assume on the basis of commonly known clinical data that a man who has known true freedom (not paid for by giving up safety and security but rather built on the basis of adequate safety and security) will not willingly or easily allow his freedom to be taken away from him. But we do not know that this is true for the person born into slavery.

Satisfaction of the self-esteem need leads to feelings of self-confidence, worth, strength, capability, and adequacy, of being useful and necessary in the world. But thwarting of these needs produces feelings of inferiority, of weakness, and of helplessness. These feelings in turn give rise to either basic discouragement or else compensatory or neurotic trends. An appreciation of the necessity of basic self-confidence and an understanding of how helpless people are without it can be easily gained from a study of severe traumatic neurosis . . .

From the theologians' discussion of pride and *hubris,* from the Frommian theories about the self-perception of untruth to one's own nature, from the Rogerian work with self, from essayists like Ayn Rand . . . , and from other sources as well, we have been learning more and more of the dangers of basing self-esteem on the opinions of others rather than on real capacity, competence, and adequacy to the task. The most stable and therefore most healthy self-esteem is based on *deserved* respect from others rather than on external fame or celebrity and unwarranted adulation.

## The Need for Self-Actualization

Even if all these needs are satisfied, we may still often (if not always) expect that a new discontent and restlessness will soon develop, unless the individual is doing what he is fitted for. A musician must make music, an artist must paint, a poet must write, if he is to be ultimately at peace with himself. What a man *can* be, he *must* be. This need we may call self-actualization. . . .

This term, first coined by Kurt Goldstein . . . , is being used in this book in a much more specific and limited fashion. It refers to man's desire for self-fulfillment, namely, to the tendency for him to become actualized in what he is potentially. This tendency might be phrased as the desire to become more and more what one is, to become everything that one is capable of becoming.

The specific form that these needs will take will of course vary greatly from person to person. In one individual it may take the form of the desire to be an ideal mother, in other it may be expressed athletically, and in still another it may be expressed painting pictures or in inventions.[2]

The clear emergence of these needs usually rests upon prior satisfaction of the physiological, safety, love, and esteem needs.

## The Preconditions for the Basic Need Satisfactions

There are certain conditions that are immediate prerequisites for the basic need satisfactions. Danger to these is reacted to as if it were direct danger to the basic needs themselves. Such conditions as freedom to speak, freedom to do what one wishes so long as no harm is done to others, freedom to express oneself, freedom to investigate and seek for information, freedom to defend oneself, justice, fairness, honesty, orderliness in the group are examples of such preconditions for basic need satisfactions. Thwarting in these freedoms will be reacted to with a threat or emergency response. These conditions are not ends in themselves but they are *almost* so since they are so closely related to the basic needs, which are apparently the only ends in themselves. These conditions are defended because without them the basic satisfactions are quite impossible, or at least, severely endangered.

If we remember that the cognitive capacities (perceptual, intellectual, learning) are a set

---

[2] Clearly creative behavior, like painting, is like any other behavior in having multiple determinants. It may be seen in innately creative people whether they are satisfied or not, happy or unhappy, hungry or sated. Also it is clear that creative activity may be compensatory, ameliorative, or purely economic. It is my impression (from informal experiments) that it is possible to distinguish the artistic and intellectual products of basically satisfied people from those of basically unsatisfied people by inspection alone. In any case, here too we must distinguish, in a dynamic fashion, the overt behavior itself from its various motivations or purposes.

of adjustive tools, which have, among other functions, that of satisfaction of our basic needs, then it is clear that any danger to them, any deprivation or blocking of their free use, must also be indirectly threatening to the basic needs themselves. Such a statement is a partial solution of the general problems of curiosity, the search for knowledge, truth, and wisdom, and the ever-persistent urge to solve the cosmic mysteries.

We must therefore introduce another hypothesis and speak of degrees of closeness to the basic needs, for we have already pointed out that *any* conscious desires (partial goals) are more or less important as they are more or less close to the basic needs. The same statement may be made for various behavior acts. An act is psychologically important if it contributes directly to satisfaction of basic needs. The less directly it so contributes, or the weaker this contribution is, the less important this act must be conceived to be from the point of view of dynamic psychology. A similar statement may be made for the various defense or coping mechanisms. Some are directly related to the protection or attainment of the basic needs, others are only weakly and distantly related. Indeed, if we wished, we could speak of more basic and less basic defense mechanisms, and then affirm that danger to the more basic defenses is more threatening than danger to less basic defenses (always remembering that this is so only because of their relationship to the basic needs).

### The Desires to Know and to Understand

The main reason we know little about the cognitive impulses, their dynamics, or their pathology, is that they are not important in the clinic, and certainly not in the clinic dominated by medical-therapeutic tradition, i.e., getting rid of disease. The florid, exciting, and mysterious symptoms found in the classical neuroses are lacking here. Cognitive psychopathology is pale, subtle, and easily overlooked, or defined as normal. It does not cry for help. As a consequence we find nothing on the subject in the writings of the great inventors of psychotherapy and psychodynamics, Freud, Adler, Jung, etc. Nor has anyone yet made any systematic attempts at constructing cognitive psychotherapies.

Schilder is the only psychoanalyst I know in whose writings curiosity and understanding are seen dynamically. Among the academic psychologists Murphy, Wertheimer, and Asch . . . have treated the problem. So far, we have mentioned the cognitive needs only in passing. Acquiring knowledge and systematizing the universe have been considered as, in part, techniques for the achievement of basic safety in the world, or for the intelligent man, expressions of self-actualization. Also freedom of inquiry and expression have been discussed as preconditions of satisfactions of the basic needs. Useful though these formulations may be, they do not constitute definitive answers to the questions as to the motivational role of curiosity, learning, philosophizing, experimenting, etc. They are at best no more than partial answers. . . .

*From*

# CONFLICT IN ORGANIZATION:
# A RE-EXAMINATION*

*By Joseph A. Litterer*

## FUNCTIONS AND VARIABLES

\*    \*    \*    \*    \*

While doubtless some forms and certain degrees of conflict are dysfunctional or "unhealthy," other types, to certain degrees, are useful. The questions then are how much conflict is functional and where are the limits beyond which it becomes dysfunctional. The problem before us is therefore much more complex than previously. At one time the ideal amount of conflict was zero and the common decision was "eliminate it." Now the questions are what are the limits within which conflict is useful and how does one manage conflict.

. . . Our approach instead will be from the point of view of examining what conflict is and identifying the organizational elements that produce it. If we are to manage conflict within reasonable boundaries, it is to these elements that we have to look to find the levers and handles with which to do the job.

### Functions of Conflict

. . . Perhaps one of the most important functions cited by a number of investigators[1] is that conflict initiates a search for some way to resolve or ameliorate the conflict and therefore leads to *innovation* and *change*. It should be noted at the same time that conflict not only leads to a search for change but it also makes change more acceptable, even desirable.

Closely related with the above is the observation that a conflict energizes people to activity, sometimes just to reduce the conflict and its concurrent displeasures, at other times because the conflict gives a zest to certain activities.

Conflict with an organization can be an essential portion of a cybernetic system. It often occurs at the point at which some other systems within the organization are functioning inadequately and therefore calls attention to these problem areas and generates a search for solutions or improvements. Conflict often leads to shifts or reallocations of existing or future rewards or resources, thereby fundamentally changing important aspects of the organization. Budget allocation and union-management conflicts are among many widely recognized.

\*    \*    \*    \*    \*

### Definition of Conflict '

\*    \*    \*    \*

Our definition of conflict, . . . is that conflict is a *type of behavior which occurs* when two or more parties are in opposition or in battle *as a result* of a perceived relative deprivation from the activities of or interacting with another person or group.

---

* Reprinted with permission from the *Academy of Management Journal,* vol. 9, no. 3 (September 1966), excerpts from pp. 179-83.

[1] Melville Dalton, *Men Who Manage* (New York: John Wiley & Sons, 1959); Peter Blau and William R. Scott, *Formal Organizations* (San Francisco: Chandler Publishing Company, 1962); James G. March and Herbert A. Simon, *Organizations* (New York, John Wiley & Sons, 1959).

## FOUR CONFLICT SITUATIONS

The organizational causes of conflict are numerous. The particular organizational elements which lead to conflict do not bring this result about directly. Instead they create conditions which affect the perception and motivation of organizational members in such a way that conflict results. There are then a set of intervening variables which transform structural forms into behavioral outputs. The many organizational structures which produce conflict seem to feed four principal types of intervening variables or organizational situations. . . .

### Win-Lose Situations

This intervening variable develops when two people or two units have goals which cannot exist simultaneously. Surprisingly, organizations set up many circumstances which lead to this condition. This is commonly witnessed in inspection situations. The inspector is hired to find errors but errors are someone else's output. Therefore every time the inspector finds an error justifying his position's existence and opening the opportunity for praise and reward, someone else is losing. The latter's output is shown to be inadequate and his rewards are endangered. . . .

Inspection is one type of win-lose situation. There are others not so obvious, however. Not long ago a major airline was faced with considerable conflict between two of its managers at a western city. Upon investigation it was found that the Sales Manager, in order to increase his sales volume, wanted to provide certain services for customers. These, however, would be provided by the employees and from the budgets of the Ramp and Services Manager. There was considerable effort to decentralize and promote as much autonomy for individual managers as possible and handsome bonus systems were set up on certain standards of individual managerial performance. If the Sales Manager could increase his sales he would have many advantages. Conversely, if the Ramp Services Manager could keep his costs down he too would have many rewards coming to him. Hence the problem, and the conflict; the Sales Manager could not get his bonus unless the Ramp Services Manager were to forego some of his own. This condition, although not always clearly recognized, exists in many organizations where reward systems are based upon individual performances which are not independent but are very much interdependent.

### Competition over Means Utilization

In this area, conflict occurs not over goals which may be similar, but stems from the fact that there are differing ideas as to what means are appropriate or who will have the means. French has shown that conflicts over the means to goal accomplishment are more disruptive of group cohesiveness than conflicts over differing goals.[2]

Another common source of conflict involves shared dependence on limited resources and scheduling problems.[3] Those that center on budgetary decisions, allocation of capital resources and the efforts made by certain departments to assure themselves that adequate supplies of scarce personnel are provided by the personnel department are recognized and common.

Scheduling problems are often not as clearly recognized and are perhaps more common. A common situation is cited by Whyte in a plant where a group of women workers was asked to participate in establishing new work norms.[4] As might be expected from previous studies, the standards they established were actually above those the industrial engineering depart-

---

[2] John R. P. French, Jr., "The Disruption and Cohesion of Groups," *The Journal of Abnormal and Social Psychology,* vol. 36 (1941), pp. 361–77.

[3] March and Simon, *op. cit.,* p. 122.

[4] William Foote Whyte, *Money and Motivation* (New York: Harper & Brothers, 1955).

ment would have provided. However, worker-set performance standards 30–50 percent over engineering standards, instead of being a satisfactory situation, created numerous problems. The department following this one faced an avalanche of material which created considerable pressure. Departments preceding this one were placed under considerable pressure to produce more. Employees in these and other departments hearing of the high earnings in the initial department complained about inequities. The engineering department felt humiliated at having so badly misjudged workable standards. Management at several levels, seeing all these events, felt that somehow things were out of control and that their position was being eroded.

## Status Incongruency

As often neglected but extremely pervasive influence on behavior stems from the fact that people want to know where they stand relative to others, that is, what their status is. This might not be too much of an issue if there were but one standard for evaluating a person. But actually there are numerous status hierarchies and one's position is never the same on them all. Further, it is often changing.

One set of status problems in industry arises from the impact of changing technology. Men who entered companies years ago and rose slowly through the ranks often feel that seniority and age justify fairly high status positions. However, they may find themselves superseded by younger men moved into higher level positions because their more recent technical training better fits them to cope with modern business problems. Working for someone younger than themselves and with less seniority, these men feel their status has been eroded and often accept this with little grace.

*     *     *     *     *

## Perceptual Differences

It has long been recognized that people who look at things differently often come into conflict. In organizations, people see things differently for a variety of reasons, among them locational factors. It is frequently observed that people in different functional departments will tend to have different views of what is good for the company and how things are to be done. The classic conflicts between marketing and production over such things as delivery times, quality and lengths of production runs are well known. People in these departments not only perform different types of work but also interact with different publics. Marketing people interact most frequently with people outside the company, customers and competitors; those in manufacturing interact mostly with other departments within the company or with the union. These differences in systemic linkages and activities lead to differences in perception of considerable magnitude.[5]

Hierarchal location also has an impact. The problems seen by the first line supervisor, faced with the enormous pressures of day-to-day operations, are quite different from those of the managers two and three levels above whose time perspectives are greater and whose pressures take a different form and come from different quarters. . . .

---

[5] See for example, DeWitt C. Dearborn and Herbert A. Simon, "Selective Perception: A Note on Departmental Identification of Executives," *Sociometry,* vol. 21 (1958) pp. 140–44.

*From*

# ORGANIZATION DEVELOPMENT OBJECTIVES, ASSUMPTIONS AND STRATEGIES*

*By Wendell French*

Organization development refers to a long-range effort to improve an organization's problem solving capabilities and its ability to cope with changes in its external environment with the help of external or internal behavioral-scientist consultants, or change agents, as they are sometimes called.

\*    \*    \*    \*    \*

**Objectives of Typical OD Programs.**    Although the specific interpersonal and task objectives of organization development programs will vary according to each diagnosis of organizational problems, a number of objectives typically emerge. These objectives reflect problems which are very common in organizations.

1.  To increase the level of trust and support among organizational members.
2.  To increase the incidence of confrontation of organizational problems, both within groups and among groups, in contrast to "sweeping problems under the rug."
3.  To create an environment in which authority of assigned role is augmented by authority based on knowledge and skill.
4.  To increase the openness of communications laterally, vertically, and diagonally.
5.  To increase the level of personal enthusiasm and satisfaction in the organization.
6.  To find synergistic solutions[1] to problems with greater frequency. (Synergistic solutions are creative solutions in which 2 + 2 equals more than 4, and through which all parties gain more through cooperation than through conflict.)
7.  To increase the level of self and group responsibility in planning and implementation.[2]

\*    \*    \*    \*    \*

**Relevancy to Different Technologies and Organization Subunits.**    Research by Joan Woodward[3] suggests that organization development efforts might be more relevant to certain kinds of technologies and organizational levels, and perhaps to certain workforce characteristics, than to others. For example, OD efforts may be more appropriate for an organization devoted to phototype manufacturing than for an automobile assembly plant. However, experiments in an organization like Texas Instruments suggest that some manufacturing efforts which appear to be inherently mechanistic may lend themselves to a more participative, open management style than is often assumed possible.[4]

However, assuming the constraints of a fairly narrow job structure at the rank-and-file

---

\* © 1969 by The Regents of the University of California. Reprinted from *California Management Review*, vol. XII, no. 2, pp. 23–29, 32, by permission of The Regents.

[1] Cattell defines synergy as "the sum total of the energy which a group can command." Daniel Katz and Robert L. Kahn, *The Social Psychology of Organizations* (New York: John Wiley & Sons, 1966), p. 33.

[2] For a similar statement of objectives, see "What is OD?" *NTL Institute: News and Reports from NTL Institute for Applied Behavioral Science,* II (June 1968), 1–2. Whether OD programs increase the overall level of authority in contrast to redistributing authority is a debatable point. My hypothesis is that both a redistribution and an overall increase occur.

[3] Joan Woodward, *Industrial Organization: Theory and Practice* (London: Oxford University Press, 1965).

[4] See M. Scott Myers, "Every Employee a Manager," *California Management Review*, X (Spring 1968), 9–20.

level, organization development efforts may inherently be more productive and relevant at the managerial levels of the organization. Certainly OD efforts are most effective when they start at the top. Research and development units—particularly those involving a high degree of interdependency and joint creativity among group members—also appear to be appropriate for organization development activities, if group members are currently experiencing problems in communicating or interpersonal relationships.

***Basic Assumptions.*** Some of the basic assumptions about people which underlie organization development programs are similar to "Theory Y" assumptions[5] and will be repeated only briefly here. However, some of the assumptions about groups and total systems will be treated more extensively. The following assumptions appear to underlie organization development efforts.[6]

### About People

Most individuals have drives toward personal growth and development, and these are most likely to be actualized in an environment which is both supportive and challenging.

Most people desire to make, and are capable of making, a much higher level of contribution to the attainment of organization goals than most organizational environments will permit.

### About People in Groups

Most people wish to be accepted and to interact cooperatively with at least one small reference group, and usually with more than one group, e.g., the work group, the family group.

One of the most psychologically relevant reference groups for most people is the work group, including peers and the superior.

Most people are capable of greatly increasing their effectiveness in helping their reference groups solve problems and in working effectively together.

For a group to optimize its effectiveness, the formal leader cannot perform all of the leadership functions in all circumstances at all times, and all group members must assist each other with effective leadership and member behavior.

### About People in Organizational Systems

Organizations tend to be characterized by overlapping, interdependent work groups, and the "linking pin" function of supervisors and other needs to be understood and facilitated.[7]

What happens in the broader organization affects the small work group and vice versa.

What happens to one subsystem (social, technological, or administrative) will affect and be influenced by other parts of the system.

The culture in most organizations tends to suppress the expression of feelings which people have about each other and about where they and their organizations are heading.

Suppressed feelings adversely affect problem solving, personal growth, and job satisfaction.

The level of interpersonal trust, support, and cooperation is much lower in most organizations than is either necessary or desirable.

---

[5] See Douglas McGregor, *The Human Side of Enterprise* (New York: McGraw-Hill Book Company, 1960), pp. 47–48.

[6] In addition to influence from the writers of McGregor, Likert, Argyris, and others, this discussion has been influenced by "Some Assumptions About Change in Organizations," in notebook "Program for Specialists in Organization Training and Development," NTL Institute for Applied Behavioral Science, 1967; and by staff members who participated in that program.

[7] For a discussion of the "linking pin" concept, see Rensis Likert, *New Patterns of Management* (New York: McGraw-Hill Book Company, 1961).

"Win-lose" strategies between people and groups, while realistic and appropriate in some situations, are not optimal in the long run to the solution of most organizational problems.

Synergistic solutions can be achieved with a much higher frequency than is actually the case in most organizations.

Viewing feelings as data important to the organization tends to open up many avenues for improved goal setting, leadership, communications, problem solving, intergroup collaboration, and morale.

Improved performance stemming from organization development efforts needs to be sustained by appropriate changes in the appraisal, compensation, training, staffing, and task-specialization—in short, in the total personnel system.

*Value and Belief Systems of Behavioral Scientist-Change Agents.* While scientific inquiry, ideally, is value-free, the applications of science are not value-free. Applied behavioral scientist-organization development consultants tend to subscribe to a comparable set of values, although we should avoid the trap of assuming that they constitute a completely homogenous group. They do not.

One value to which many behavioral scientist-change agents tend to give high priority, is that the needs and aspirations of human beings are the reasons for organized effort in society. They tend, therefore, to be developmental in their outlook and concerned with the long-range opportunities for the personal growth of people in organizations.

A second value is that work and life can become richer and more meaningful, and organized effort more effective and enjoyable, if feelings and sentiments are permitted to be a more legitimate part of the culture. A third value is a commitment to an action role, along with a commitment to research, in an effort to improve the effectiveness of organizations.[8] A fourth value—or perhaps a belief—is that improved competency in interpersonal and intergroup relationship will result in more effective organizations.[9] A fifth value is that behavioral science research and an examination of behavioral science assumptions and values are relevant and important in considering organizational effectiveness. While many change agents are perhaps overly action-oriented in terms of the utilization of their time, nevertheless, as a group they are paying more and more attention to research and to the examination of ideas.[10]

The value placed on research and inquiry raises the question as to whether the assumptions stated earlier are values, theory, or "facts." In my judgment, a substantial body of knowledge, including research on leadership, suggests that there is considerable evidence for these assumptions. However, to conclude that these assumptions are facts, laws or principles would be to contradict the value placed by behavioral scientists on continuous research and inquiry. Thus, I feel that they should be considered theoretical statements which are based on provisional data.

This also raises the paradox that the belief that people are important tends to result in their being important. The belief that people can grow and develop in terms of personal and

---

[8] Warren G. Bennis sees three major approaches to planned organizational change, with the behavioral scientists associated with each all having "a deep concern with applying social science knowledge to create more viable social systems; a commitment to action, as well as to research . . . and a belief that improved interpersonal and group relationships will ultimately lead to better organizational performance." Bennis, "A New Role for the Behavioral Sciences: Effecting Organizational Change," *Administrative Science Quarterly*, VIII (Sept. 1963), 157–158; and Herbert A. Shepard, "An Action Research Model," in *An Action Research Program for Organization Improvement*, pp. 31–35.

[9] Bennis, "A New Role for the Behavioral Sciences," 158.

[10] For a discussion of some of the problems and dilemmas in behavioral science research, see Chris Argyris, "Creating Effective Relationships in Organizations," in Richard N. Adams and Jack J. Preiss, eds., *Human Organization Research* (Homewood, Ill.: The Dorsey Press, 1960), pp. 109–23; and Barbara A. Benedict et al., "The Clinical Experimental Approach to Assessing Organizational Change Efforts," *Journal of Applied Behavioral Science* (November 1967), 347–80.

organizational competency tends to produce this result. Thus, values and beliefs tend to be self-fulfilling, and the question becomes "What do you choose to want to believe?" While this position can become Pollyannaish in the sense of not seeing the real world, nevertheless, behavioral scientist-change agents, at least this one, tend to place a value on optimism. It is a kind of optimism that says people can do a better job of goal setting and facing up to and solving problems, not an optimism that says the number of problems is diminishing.

It should be added that it is important that the values and beliefs of each behavioral science-change agent be made visible both to himself and to the client. In the first place, neither can learn to adequately trust the other without such exposure—a hidden agenda handicaps both trust building and mutual learning. Second, and perhaps more pragmatically, organizational change efforts tend to fail if a prescription is applied unilaterally and without proper diagnosis.

***Strategy in Organization Development: An Action Research Model.*** A frequent strategy in organization development programs is based on what behavioral scientists refer to as an "action research model." This model involves extensive collaboration between the consultant (whether an external or an internal change agent) and the client group, data gathering, data discussion, and planning. While descriptions of this model vary in detail and terminology from author to author, the dynamics are essentially the same.[11]

Figure 1 summarizes some of the essential phases of the action research model, using an emerging organization development program as an example. The key aspects of the model are diagnosis, data gathering, feedback to the client group, data discussion and work by the client group, action planning, and action. The sequence tends to be cyclical, with the focus on new or advanced problems as the client group leans to work more effectively together. Action research should also be considered a process, since, as William Foote Whyte says, it involves ". . . a continuous gathering and analysis of human relations research data and the feeding of the findings into the organization in such a manner as to change behavior."[12] (Feedback we will define as nonjudgmental observations of behavior.)

Ideally, initial objectives and strategies of organization development efforts stem from a careful diagnosis of such matters as interpersonal and intergroup problems, decision-making processes, and communication flow which are currently being experienced by the client organization. . . .

This initial diagnosis, which focuses on the expressed needs of the client is extremely critical. . . . In the absence of a skilled diagnosis, the behavioral scientist-change agent would be imposing a set of assumptions and a set of objectives which may be hopelessly out of joint with either the current problems of the people in the organization or their willingness to learn new modes of behavior. In this regard, it is extremely important that the consultant hear and understand what the client is trying to tell him. This requires a high order of skill.[13]

Interviews are frequently used for data gathering in OD work for both initial diagnosis and subsequent planning sessions, since personal contact is important for building a cooperative relationship between the consultant and the client group. . . .

Data gathering typically goes through several phases. The first phase is related to diagnosing the state of the system and to making plans for organizational change. This phase may utilize a series of interviews between the consultant and the key client, or between a

---

[11] For further discussion of action research, see Edgar H. Schein and Warren G. Bennis, *Personal and Organizational Change through Group Methods* (New York: John Wiley & Sons, 1966), pp. 272–74.

[12] William Foote Whyte and Edith Lentz Hamilton, *Action Research for Management* (Homewood, Ill.: Richard D. Irwin, 1964), p. 2.

[13] For further discussion of organization diagnosis, see Richard Beckhard, "An Organization Improvement Program in a Decentralised Organization," *Journal of Applied Behavioral Science*, II (January–March 1966), 3–4, "OD as a Process," in *What's Wrong with Work?*, pp. 12–13.

**FIGURE 1**
**An Action Research Model for Organization Development**

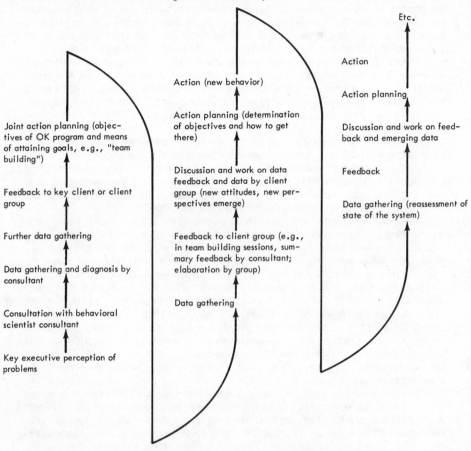

few key executives and the consultant. Subsequent phases focus on problems specific to the top executive team and to subordinate teams. (See Figure 2.)

\*    \*    \*    \*    \*

***Laboratory Training and Organization Development.*** Since organization development programs have largely emerged from T-group experience, theory, and research, and since laboratory training in one form or another tends to be an integral part of most such programs, it is important to focus on laboratory training per se. As stated earlier, OD programs grew out of a perceived need to relate laboratory training to the problems of ongoing organizations and a recognition that optimum results could only occur if major parts of the total social system of an organization were involved.

\*    \*    \*    \*    \*

Ordinarily, laboratory training sessions have certain objectives in common. The following list, by two internationally known behavioral scientists,[14] is probably highly consistent with the objectives of most programs:

---

[14] Schein and Bennis, p. 37.

**FIGURE 2**
**Organization Development Phases in a Hypothetical Organization**

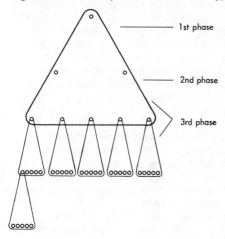

1st phase. Data gathering, feedback, and diagnosis—consultant and top executive only.

2nd phase. Data gathering, feedback, and revised diagnosis—consultant and two or more key staff or line people.

3rd phase. Data gathering and feedback to total top executive team in "team-building" laboratory, with or without key subordinates from level below.

4th and additional phases. Data gathering and team-building sessions with 2nd or 3rd level teams.
Subsequent phases. Data gathering, feedback, and interface problem-solving sessions across groups.
Simultaneous phases. Several managers may attend "stranger" T-Groups; courses in the management development program may supplement this learning.

## Self Objectives

Increased awareness of own feelings and reactions, and own impact on others.
Increased awareness of feelings and reactions of others, and their impact on self.
Increased awareness of dynamics of group action.
Changed attitudes toward self, others, and groups, i.e., more respect for, tolerance for, and faith in self, others, and groups.
Increased interpersonal competence, i.e., skill in handling interpersonal and group relationships toward more productive and satisfying relationships.

## Role Objectives

Increased awareness of own organizational role, organizational dynamics, dynamics of larger social systems, and dynamics of the change process in self, small groups, and organizations.
Changed attitudes toward own role, role of others, and organizational relationships, i.e., more respect for and willingness to deal with others with whom one is interdependent, greater willingness to achieve collaborative relationships with others based on mutual trust.
Increased interpersonal competence in handling organizational role relationships with superiors, peers, and subordinates.

## Organizational Objectives

Increased awareness of, changed attitudes toward, and increased interpersonal competence about specific organizational problems existing in groups or units which are interdependent.
Organizational improvement through the training of relationships or groups rather than isolated individuals.
Over the years, experimentation with different laboratory designs has led to diverse criteria for the selection of laboratory participants. Probably a majority of NTL-IABS human relations laboratories are "stranger groups," i.e., involving participants who come from differ-

ent organizations and who are not likely to have met earlier. However, as indicated by the organizational objectives above, the incidence of special labs designed to increase the effectiveness of persons already working together appears to be growing. Thus terms like "cousin labs," i.e., labs involving people from the same organization but not the same subunit, and "family labs" or "team-building" sessions, i.e., involving a manager and all of his subordinates, are becoming familiar. Participants in labs designed for organizational members not of the same unit may be selected from the same rank level ("horizontal slice") or selected so as to constitute a heterogeneous grouping by rank ("diagonal slice"). Further, NTL-IABS is now encouraging at least two members from the same organization to attend NTL Management Work Conferences and Key Executive Conferences in order to maximize the impact of the learning in the back-home situation.[15]

\* \* \* \* \*

*Summary Comments.* Organization development efforts have emerged through attempts to apply laboratory training values and assumptions to total systems. Such efforts are organic in the sense that they emerge from and are guided by the problems being experienced by the people in the organization. The key to their viability (in contrast to becoming a passing fad) lies in an authentic focus on problems and concerns of the members of the organization and in their confrontation of issues and problems.

Organization development is based on assumptions and values similar to "Theory Y" assumptions and values but includes additional assumptions about total systems and the nature of the client-consultant relationship. Intervention strategies of the behavioral scientist-change agent tend to be based on an action-research model and tend to be focused more on helping the people in an organization learn to solve problems rather than on prescriptions of how things should be done differently.

Laboratory training (or "sensitivity training") or modification of T-group seminars typically are a part of the organizational change efforts, but the extent and format of such training will depend upon the evolving needs of the organization. Team-building seminars involving a superior and subordinates are being utilized more and more as a way of changing social system rapidly and avoiding the cultural-distance problems which frequently emerge when individuals return from stranger labs. However, stranger labs can play a key role in change efforts when they are used as part of a broader organization development effort.

Research has indicated that sensitivity training generally produces positive results in terms of changed behavior on the job, but has not demonstrated the link between behavior changes and improved performance. Maximum benefits are probably derived from laboratory training when the organizational culture supports and reinforces the use of new skills in ongoing team situations.

Successful organization development efforts require skillful behavioral scientist interventions, a systems view, and top management support and involvement. In addition, changes stemming from organization development must be linked to changes in the total personnel subsystem. The viability of organization development efforts lies in the degree to which they accurately reflect the aspirations and concerns of the participating members.

In conclusion, successful organization development tends to be a total system effort; a process of planned change—not a program with a temporary quality; and aimed at developing the organization's internal resources for effective change in the future.

---

[15] For further discussion of group composition in laboratory training, see Schein and Bennis, pp. 63–69. NTL-LABS now include the Center for Organization Studies, the Center for the Development of Educational Leadership, the Center for Community Affairs, and the Center for International Training to serve a wide range of client populations and groups.

*From*

# PUBLIC POLICY AND THE GENERAL WELFARE*

*By Charles A. Beard*

"Every enterprise in the Great Society itself, as well as the Great Society itself, rests upon administration. Industry on a large scale depends upon organization—upon the management of large numbers of employees of different crafts and arts and the disposition of material goods. In some industries, the administration organization is national and even international in its range. Thousands, hundreds of thousands, of men and women must be brought together and distributed among various departments of production. They must be graded in a vast economic hierarchy, with skilled engineers and managers at the top and the simple day laborers at the bottom. They must be assigned specific and appropriate tasks in the operation of the organization. They must be directed, controlled."

"The state in the Great Society, like the private corporation, also rests upon administration."

* Charles A. Beard, *Public Policy and the General Welfare,* copyright © 1941, Holt, Rinehart & Winston, Inc. Reprinted by permission. (Excerpts from pp. 148 *et seq.*)

# 12. MIDWEST HARDWARE MANUFACTURING COMPANY

---

## Case Introduction

---

### SYNOPSIS

Recently, Midwest Hardware Manufacturing Company was in the midst of a substantial expansion program designed to increase its capacity to meet the steadily increasing demand for its products. Midwest's management was determined to finance the expansion with internally generated funds, and was therefore seeking all possible means to maximize its allocation of the cash available. A survey of current inventory control practices indicates that a large amount of funds can be released from the inventory account for more productive allocation elsewhere. Also, a revamped method of ordering component parts for assembly would bring significant savings in operating expenses. A mathematical model is used to compute optimum inventory levels and optimum purchase lot sizes.

In connection with this program, the new inventory control system was adopted and implemented. Some three months later, when the new system is evaluated by Midwest's management, results appear quite disappointing. Predicted benefits have not been realized, and some unforeseen problems have arisen. Management must decide whether the new system should be continued, modified, or abandoned.

### WHY THIS CASE IS INCLUDED

Midwest's concern over the short supply of working capital—concentrating on internally generated cash as the source of funds—and the best use of such funds—allocation to inventory, receivables, fixed assets, and so on—highlights the influence of economic and financial matters on policy making. Not only does the adequacy of the sources of funds set parameters, or boundaries, around the alternatives open to management, but the same factor also acts as a stimulant and pressure to plan carefully and design effective policies for the allocation of funds.

Analyzing the use of the mathematical model for inventory control has value of itself, but this case raises the larger issue of the benefits and limitations of scientific rationality (operations research techniques) in business policy formulation. Science is pitted against "judgment." The utilization of techniques of scientific rationality affects the relationships among people and even alters organization structure, the unshared expertise of the specialist further complicates the traditional line-staff conflicts. The issue of the desirability and feasibility of subordinate participation in management decisions and action is also raised. Finally, the case offers the opportunity to examine the economic theory relating to the use of overhead departments in various size enterprises (here considering the new inventory system comparable to the introduction of a service department or overhead unit).

## DIAGNOSTIC AND PREDICTIVE QUESTIONS

The readings included with this case are marked (*). The author index at the end of this book locates the other readings.

1. In what way has the short supply of funds affected the policy making of Midwest's management? Recall from the case that Mr. Gilbert, the president, pointed to the strain on working capital caused by recent expansion moves. Relate this concern to Maxon's comment: "I've always felt that we have far too much cash tied up in inventories of components awaiting assembly."

Read:   Anthony, *Management Accounting.*

2. What are the advantages of Maxon's "science" as compared to Iverson's "judgment"?

Read:   *Taylor, "Principles of Scientific Management."

3. In modifying its inventory controls the management of Midwest went through at least six phases: (*a*) search for ways of increasing the available working capital, (*b*) investigation of the Iverson inventory control system, (*c*) computation of optimum stock levels and reorder quantities, (*d*) explanation of the new system and training of personnel, (*e*) implementation and administration of the new system during shakedown period, (*f*) evaluation of results. To what extent did all the interested parties participate in this process as a whole? What advantages—if any—could be gained by having subordinate participation in each phase of the process? Are there reasons which would make participation impossible or undesirable in specific phases?

Read:   McGregor, *The Human Side of Enterprise.* Newman and Summer, *The Process of Management: Concepts, Behavior, and Practice.* *Odiorne, *How Managers Make Things Happen.* Jennings, "Business Needs Mature Autocrats."

4. Was Maxon's role in the entire process one of a line manager or a staff specialist? What should his role have been? It has been said that knowledge is power. (Francis Bacon, 1561–1626, *Religious Meditations*

—*Of Heresies:* "Nam et ipsa scientia potestas est." Knowledge itself is power.) Does this in any way dictate what role Maxon, as an expert in operations research will necessarily play in the organization?

   Read:   *Hobbes, *Leviathan.* *Lasswell and Kaplan, *Power and Society.* *Carr et al., *American Democracy in Theory and Practice.* Etzioni, "Authority Structure and Organizational Effectiveness."

   5. As the implementation of the new system evolved, should Mr. Gilbert have been able to predict that Iverson would feel he was "the guy in the middle" between Hennessey and Maxon? If so, should he have insisted that Iverson take orders from one superior

   Read:   Fayol, *General and Industrial Management.* Taylor, "Shop Management." McGregor, *The Human Side of Enterprise.*"

   6. Reasoning from the logic of the scientific inventory method and its use in Midwest, why didn't Maxon's new system produce the results hoped for? Recall that at the executive committee's last meeting Hennessey stated he could see many practical difficulties which Maxon's figures did not show (e.g., low morale, quality deterioration, component C stamping costs, etc.).

   Read:   *Buffa, *Modern Production Management.* Miller and Starr, *Executive Decisions and Operations Research.* Lindblom, "The Science of 'Muddling Through.'"

   7. In studying the formalization, rationalization, or bureaucratization of organizations, sociologists have developed the notion of the dysfunctions of bureaucracy—unforeseen and undesirable consequences resulting from efforts to formalize procedures, rules, structure, and so on. Would a knowledge of this notion have helped Gilbert anticipate such things as the hoarding of parts by the foremen and the interdepartment "wars"? Would it have helped him to design preventive policies?

   Read:   Merton, "Bureaucratic Structure and Personality."

## POLICY QUESTIONS

   8. Knowing Midwest's need for more working capital, what other ways seem feasible for dealing with the problem—other than Maxon's effort to release cash from inventories and cut operating costs? (See Question 1 and its readings.)

   9. Could you have done anything with the operations research technique itself to make the Maxon inventory model conform better to the concrete circumstances of the Midwest situation? (See Question 6 with its attached readings.)

   10. If you had been Gilbert, the president, would you have directed Maxon's efforts any differently? Why? Or, why not? (See Questions 3, 4, 5, and 7 with their attached readings.) As president, would you have encouraged more participation of subordinates in the design and implementation of the new system? In which—if any—of the six phases of the process (identified in Question 3) would you have desired more participation?

   11. Had you been Maxon, would you have handled your relationship

with Iverson any differently? Why? Or, why not? (See Question 3 and its attached readings.)

12. What should Gilbert do now about the inventory control system?

# Case Text*

## THE COMPANY AND ITS PRODUCTS

Midwest Hardware is an old-line, well-known manufacturer of hardware, plumbing supplies, spigots, valves, and other construction accessories for residential and industrial use. The assembly, finishing, and testing of its products comprise the bulk of the company's manufacturing operations. Only a small portion of the components are manufactured by Midwest itself, the majority being purchased from a relatively few nearby suppliers, most of whom are located in the same city as Midwest's plant. Almost every supplier of components had been doing business with Midwest for many years, and relations have generally been close and satisfactory between the company and its suppliers.

Annual sales volume has been fairly stable at around $28 million for the past seven years, and the work force has averaged some 300 employees. Thomas Gilbert, Jr., Midwest's president, believes that, although the company has not grown much in the past few years, it has established an outstanding reputation for quality and dependability of its products. To support his claim that the company is among the leaders in its field, he cites the fact that Midwest currently has a full year's backlog of orders on many of its products. Mr. Gilbert has recently initiated an expansion program, designed to increase manufacturing capacity by additions to plant space, machinery, and equipment. This expansion program was spurred by a rising level of regional construction activity and by market surveys forecasting a doubling of the demand for Midwest's products within the next eight years.

At the monthly meeting of the executive committee in April, Mr. Gilbert reviewed the progress of the expansion program to date, and concluded with the comment that growth was indeed exciting and satisfying, but its resultant strain on working capital was becoming evident. The balance of the meeting was devoted to discussion of working capital needs and conservation. John W. Maxon, the company's controller, emphasized the importance of conserving internally generated cash funds by minimizing the use of scarce cash on nonessentials. "As a prime example of what I mean," Maxon stated, "I've always felt that we have far too much cash tied up in inventories of components awaiting assembly. A whole battery of new techniques have been developed in so-called

---

* Copyright 1977 by Charles E. Summer.

Operations Research, designed to minimize inventory costs; yet we're still flying by the seat of our pants when it comes to our inventories. I firmly believe that some hard thinking and close calculating can yield pretty impressive savings in this area."

Joseph Hennessey, vice president-production, agreed that some savings might be achievable, but pointed out that production personnel had neither the time nor the mathematical backgrounds to apply O. R. methods to inventory problems. It was then agreed that Maxon would undertake an investigation of Midwest's present inventory controls and then present any recommendations he may have at the next meeting.

## PRESENT METHOD OF COMPONENT INVENTORY CONTROLS

All component inventories in the plant are under the control of Peter Iverson, head foreman in charge of assembly, manufacturing, and receiving. Iverson initiates all orders for components—whether manufactured in the plant or purchased outside—and has been doing so for many years. He relies primarily on frequent inspections of inventories on hand, observations of "how things stood in each department," and periodic checks with his foremen and their requirements. Whenever Iverson judges the time is ripe, he enters a buy or make order for the needed component. Over the years Iverson has established a standard order size, in terms of number of units, for each component used.

Thus order quantities are held constant for each item, while the frequency of placing orders will vary with the rate at which components are taken into production. Since output rates and product mixes have historically been quite stable, there has been a high degree of constancy in the frequency of orders for each major component. The ordering procedure followed by Iverson is, in effect, a variant of the traditional "two bin" system, under which inventories are physically divided between two separate bins or storage areas. As one bin is exhausted, a standard-size lot order is placed, while withdrawals are continued from the second bin. Iverson believes that operating results confirm the soundness of his inventory control system: "There may be some talk about me playing it extra-safe, but Mr. Hennessey or anybody else will tell you that we've *never* been out of stock on any part we needed in all the years I've been in charge of the inventory."

## ANALYSIS OF PRESENT CONTROL SYSTEM

At the May meeting of the executive committee (consisting of the president and all the department heads), Maxon was ready to present the findings of his investigation of Iverson's present component inventory controls. He reported that he had a detailed analysis of the components needed for a typical Midwest product—a gas furnace control unit—referred to as "GFC-5" on the company's product line lists.

The GFC-5 unit is assembled from five components (labeled A through E in all exhibits), of which four were purchased, and one was manufactured by Midwest. Exhibit 1 presents a simplified product flow chart for

**EXHIBIT 1**
**Product Flow and Relevant Organization Chart**

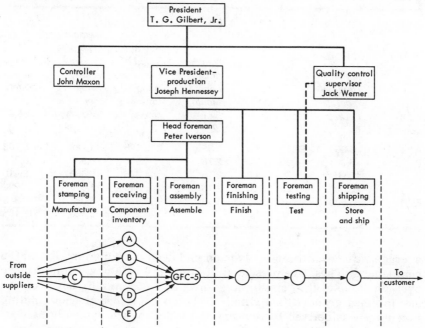

the GFC-5 superimposed on an organization chart identifying relevant supervisory personnel. Also shown is the monthly requirement of each component for meeting current output levels of 5,000 GFC-5 units per month (see Exhibit 2).

Maxon distributed copies of his analysis sheets to all participants in the meeting (reproduced on Exhibits 3 and 4).

Referring to Exhibit 3, the analysis of Iverson's present practices, Maxon explained that he had calculated—from accounting records—the

**EXHIBIT 2**
**Monthly Component Requirement for 5,000 Units of GFC-5 per Month**

| Component | Number Needed for Each GFC-5 | Net Monthly Requirement | Monthly Requirement Including Allowance for Rejects, Waste | Unit Cost | Make or Buy |
|---|---|---|---|---|---|
| A .......... 1 | | 5,000 | 5,000 | $9.50 | B |
| B .......... 1 | | 5,000 | 5,000 | 4.00 | B |
| C .......... 2 | | 10,000 | 10,900 | 1.75 | M |
| D .......... 4 | | 20,000 | 22,000 | .23 | B |
| E .......... 1 | | 5,000 | 5,000 | .95 | B |

**EXHIBIT 3**
**Components for GFC-5 Present Inventory Levels and Ordering Practices**

| Component | (1) Monthly Requirement in Units (D) | (2) Unit Cost (P) | (3) Order Lot Size in Units (Z) | (4) Number of Orders per Month $\left(\dfrac{D}{Z}\right)$ | (5) Average Value of Circulating Inventory $\left(\dfrac{Z}{2} \times P\right)$ | (6) Average Value of Inventory Actually Carried from Accounting Records | (7) Average Value of "Safety Stock" (Col. 6— Col. 5) |
|---|---|---|---|---|---|---|---|
| A......... | 5,000 | $9.50 | 1,900 | 2.63 | $ 9,025 | $14,728 | $ 5,703 |
| B......... | 5,000 | 4.00 | 1,800 | 2.78 | 3,600 | 6,802 | 3,202 |
| C......... | 10,900 | 1.75 | 5,000 | 2.18 | 4,375 | 6,985 | 2,610 |
| D......... | 22,000 | .23 | 8,000 | 2.75 | 920 | 1,612 | 692 |
| E......... | 5,000 | .95 | 5,000 | 1.00 | 2,375 | 3,323 | 948 |
| | | | | | $20,295 | $33,450 | $13,155 |

average value of inventories Iverson had been carrying for each GFC-5 component. (These are presented in Column 6.) He next computed the average value of the "circulating" inventory (Column 5), based on the assumptions graphed in Exhibit 4. Maxon explained that circulating inventory was derived by dividing the order lot size typically used by Iverson (Column 3) by two, thereby getting the average inventory of each component needed to meet the monthly requirements of the assembly operation. He then multiplied these units of circulating inventory (Column 5). By subtracting average value of "safety stocks" presently being carried (Column 7).

"Exhibit 3 tells us," said Maxon, "that we've had an average of $33,450 (Column 6) tied up in components for the GFC-5, and that of this amount an average of $13,155 (Column 7) was never circulated into production,

**EXHIBIT 4**
**Schematic Diagram of Inventory Model**

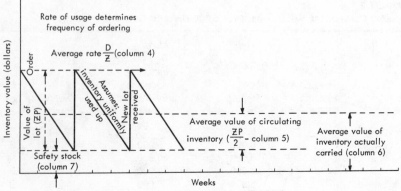

Note: Symbols and Columns Numbers refer to Table in Exhibit 3.

but was tied up permanently as a safety cushion against a possible run-out. Safety stocks are in effect equivalent to an insurance premium against runouts, and it's my contention that we're paying a high premium to cover an almost negligible risk. Quantitative analysis tells us that in setting up levels of safety stocks we must balance the cost of carrying this stock against the *cost* and *probability* of a runout on any component. The cost of running out of any component is usually tough to estimate, since it requires placing a value on the cost of missed sales and production downtime. In our case, I think it's reasonable to place this cost at close to zero. With a year's backlog of orders we're not liable to lose *any* sales, and with our flexible assembly schedules there's no reason for any downtime due to missing parts. We can easily switch assembly to other products until the missing parts come in. Furthermore the *probability* of running out, in our case, is just about negligible. Our suppliers are highly reliable; they are very close to us and will do their darndest to deliver right on time. We could, theoretically, get by with no safety stocks whatsoever, but I'd say a stock of one or two days' production would be ample."

## PROPOSED CONTROL SYSTEM

Maxon proceeded to outline the proposed inventory control system he had developed, as tabulated in Exhibit 5. By comparing Exhibits 3 and 5, he pointed out that his analytical approach to the problem achieved significant reductions in the levels of both "circulating" (Column 5 versus Column 12) and "safety" (Column 7 versus Column 13) stocks, so that the total component inventory for the GFC-5, carried by Midwest, was reduced in value from an average of $33,450 to $19,291 (Column 6 versus Column 14).

Safety stocks were reduced to a level representing one to two days' production for the reasons cited by Maxon in criticizing the present system. Circulating inventories were reduced by the application of a computing technique which establishes optimum order lot sizes for each component. By balancing the cost of placing and receiving an order against the cost of carrying the parts in inventory, this technique establishes the size of lots to be ordered so as to minimize total inventory costs.

"After quite a bit of digging around," said Maxon, "we've calculated that it costs us $11 to place a purchase order, inspect, receive, and store it in place. In the illustration worked out in Exhibit 5 we have used the symbol $C_1$ to indicate these ordering costs. On the other hand, we figure that it costs us 19 cents a year for every dollar we have tied up in inventory—this is based on our cost of capital of 12 percent, plus an additional 7 percent representing insurance, space charges, loss, waste, etc. In the illustration worked out in Exhibit 5 we have used the symbol $C_2$ to indicate these carrying costs. We use both these values, for the $C_1$ and $C_2$ factors, in the equations we set up to determine optimum lot size. Any of you who are interested in the methods used can follow the example in Exhibit 5.

"Now let me show you that the proposed inventory control system will

**EXHIBIT 5**
**Components for GFC-5 Optimal Inventory Levels and Lot Sizes—as Proposed by Controller's Office**

| Components | (8) Monthly Requirement in Units (D) | (9) Unit Cost (P) | (10) Optimal Order Lot Size in Units (Ẑ) | (11) Number of Orders per Month $\left(\frac{D}{Z}\right)$ | (12) Average Value of Circulating Inventory $\left(\frac{Z}{2} \times P\right)$ | (13) Average Value of "Safety Stock" (1–2 Day's Production) | (14) Average Value of Inventory to Be Carried (Col. 12 + Col. 13) |
|---|---|---|---|---|---|---|---|
| A ......... | 5,000 | $9.50 | 860* | 5.81 | $ 4,085 | $3,800 | $ 7,885 |
| B ......... | 5,000 | 4.00 | 1,300 | 3.85 | 2,600 | 1,600 | 4,200 |
| C ......... | 10,900 | 1.75 | 2,900 | 3.76 | 2,537 | 1,225 | 3,762 |
| D ......... | 22,000 | .23 | 11,500 | 1.91 | 1,322 | 460 | 1,782 |
| E......... | 5,000 | .95 | 2,700 | 1.85 | 1,282 | 380 | 1,662 |
| | | | | | $11,826 | $7,465 | $19,291 |

\* Illustration of method of determining optimal order lot size

*Component A*

$$\text{Optimum Lot Size } \hat{Z} = \sqrt{\frac{2DC_1}{PC_2}}$$

where: $C_1$ = cost of ordering, receiving, inspecting, etc. = $11.00 per order;
   $C_2$ = .016 since cost of carrying inventory = 19% of its value per year, or

$$\frac{.19}{12} = .016 \text{ per month.}$$

For Component A:

$$\hat{Z}_A = \sqrt{\frac{2 \times 5,000 \times 11}{9.50 \times .016}} = \sqrt{723,684} = 851 \text{ units}$$

Rounding off: $\hat{Z}_A = 860$ *units* — inserted in Row A, Column 10, above. In similar fashion, optimal lot sizes are calculated for components B, C, D, and E.

yield a number of significant benefits, both immediate and long-run.

"Initially, we should have a significant amount of cash released from inventory to help us in our problems with working capital. Just by reducing the average value of the GFC-5 inventories from the present $33,450 (Column 6) to the proposed $19,291 level (Column 14), we will immediately release some $14,000 of sorely needed cash. This is about 42 percent of the cash we not have tied up in GFC-5 components. If a like percentage can be drawn out of all our inventories, I would guess we're talking about something in the order of $100,000 added to our working capital. That ain't hay in any league.

"We can also put dollar and cents signs on savings on ordering and carrying costs. The proposed system will allow us to cut our operating expenses. First, Exhibit 6 compares the order and carrying costs of the *circulating component inventories* under the present system run by Iverson and our proposed system. Again, we use the GFC-5 components as our example. Monthly savings in costs of this type amount to $71.27 (Column 21). Second, Exhibit 7 compares the carrying costs of the *safety*

**EXHIBIT 6**
**Comparison of Order and Carrying Costs of "Circulating" Component inventories (present and proposed methods)**

Total inventory costs, $TC = \dfrac{DC_1}{Z} + \dfrac{ZC_2}{2}$

$\underbrace{\dfrac{DC_1}{Z}}_{\substack{\text{Total ordering}\\\text{cost per month}}} + \underbrace{\dfrac{ZC_2}{2}}_{\substack{\text{Total carrying}\\\text{cost per month}}}$

where $\left.\begin{array}{l} C_1 = \$11.00 \\ C_2 = .016 \end{array}\right\}$ see Exhibit 5

| Com-ponent | Present Method | | | Proposed Method | | | |
|---|---|---|---|---|---|---|---|
| | (15) Order Cost $\frac{D}{Z} \times 11.00$ (Col. 4)×(C₁) | (16) Carrying Cost $\frac{ZP}{2} \times .016$ (Col. 5)×(C₂) | (17) Total Cost (per Month) (15 + 16) | (18) Order Cost $\frac{D}{Z} \times 11.00$ (Col. 11)×(C₁) | (19) Carrying Cost $\frac{ZP}{2} \times .016$ (Col. 12)×(C₂) | (20) Total Cost (per Month) (18 + 19) | (21) Saving in Total Cost (per Month) (17 − 20) |
| A | $ 28.93 | $144.40 | $173.33 | $ 63.91 | $ 65.36 | $129.27 | $44.06 |
| B | 30.58 | 57.60 | 88.18 | 42.35 | 41.60 | 83.95 | 4.23 |
| C | 23.98 | 70.00 | 93.98 | 41.36 | 40.59 | 81.95 | 12.03 |
| D | 30.25 | 14.72 | 44.97 | 21.01 | 21.15 | 42.16 | 2.81 |
| E | 11.00 | 38.00 | 49.00 | 20.35 | 20.51 | 40.86 | 8.14 |
| | $124.74 | $324.72 | $449.46 | $188.98 | $189.21 | $378.19 | $71.27 |

**EXHIBIT 7**
**Comparison of Carrying Costs of "Safety Stocks" (present and proposed methods)**

| Present Method | | Proposed Method | | |
|---|---|---|---|---|
| *(22)* | *(23)*<br>*Annual*<br>*Carrying* | *(24)* | *(25)*<br>*Annual*<br>*Carrying* | |
| *Average Value*<br>*of "Safety*<br>*Stock"*<br>*(See Col. 7)* | *Cost of*<br>*"Safety*<br>*Stock"*<br>*($13,155 \times C_2$)* | *Average Value*<br>*of "Safety*<br>*Stock"*<br>*(See Col. 13)* | *Cost of*<br>*"Safety*<br>*Stock"*<br>*($7,465 \times C_2$)* | *(26)*<br>*Annual Savings*<br>*(23–25)* |
| $13,155 | $2,499.45 | $7,465 | $1,418.35 | $1,081.10 |

**EXHIBIT 8**
**Summary of Annual Savings in Operating Costs by Using the Proposed System Instead of the Present System**

| *(27)*<br>*Annual Savings in Ordering*<br>*and Carrying Costs of the*<br>*Circulating Component*<br>*Inventories*<br>*(Col. 21 $\times$ 12 Months)* | *(28)*<br><br><br>*Annual Savings in Carrying*<br>*Costs of "Safety Stocks"*<br>*(Col. 26)* | *(29)*<br><br>*Total Annual Savings in*<br>*Operating Costs under*<br>*Proposed System*<br>*(Col. 27 + Col. 28)* |
|---|---|---|
| $855.24 | $1,081.10 | $1,936.34 |

*stocks* under the present Iverson system and our proposed system. Annual savings here amount to $1,018.10 (Column 26). Exhibit 8 summarizes these two aspects of the savings on operating expenses. Notice that the total annual saving is in excess of $1,900 for the GFC-5 components alone (Column 29). Assuming comparable results in all our other products, I'd guess at annual savings of over $15,000—certainly an attractive piece of change to pick up without any extra work, effort or investment on our part. It's simply a byproduct of using scientific methods to determine the proper inventory levels and reorder quantities."

In response to Mr. Gilbert's concern that suppliers may raise their unit prices as a result of the reduced order sizes, Maxon replied that he had already checked out several of the key suppliers. "They'll go along with us, and will hold their prices even on smaller individual orders as long as our annual purchases run at about the same volume we've been giving them. They're just as anxious as we are to see us expand our sales volume, and just as quickly as possible."

Maxon's proposals were discussed at some length, and it was unanimously agreed that he should proceed to implement his suggestions as rapidly as possible. Hennessey again questioned the competence of his production personnel and their ability to devote the necessary time needed to install the new system. He did not foresee any problems, however, in their operating with the system once installed. "That means, John," said Hennessey to Maxon, "that it'll be up to you to get the thing going and do all the necessary missionary work. I'll certainly tell my boys to cooperate with you fully." Maxon was quite agreeable to undertaking the task and stated he would proceed as rapidly as possible.

## IMPLEMENTATION OF NEW SYSTEM

By early June, Maxon had completed his calculations for all major components used by Midwest, and had prepared a set of procedure outlines and guide sheets for implementation of the new ordering system. On June 4 he called a meeting of all foremen and inventory clerks at which Joe Hennessey was also present. Maxon outlined Midwest's urgent need for working capital in its current expansion program. He then proceeded to explain the importance of establishing optimum order lot sizes and minimal safety stock levels. Maxon distributed the same exhibit sheets he had used in his presentation at the executive committee meetings, although his explanations were given on a more elementary level. "Don't worry too much about the formulas and tables," he suggested, "the most important thing you should note is the savings the company is going to get out of this new system. I know it'll mean writing up more orders per month than you've been doing so far, but the cost of this extra work is all allowed for in the calculations we've made and, as you see, we come out well ahead of the game."

Hennessey initiated the discussion of Maxon's presentation by stating that he too was anxious to achieve any possible savings, and that as far as he could see Maxon's ideas appeared to make good sense. "You fellows will be dealing with this new system, and you're familiar with our inventory problems," he told the group, "so let's hear your reactions to Mr. Maxon's proposals." In the discussion that followed most foremen felt they were not qualified to evaluate the mathematical computations involved and, with various degrees of reservation, agreed that the new system deserved a trial. Pointing out that Iverson would be in charge of the system, when installed, Hennessey asked for any suggestons he might have. "For a guy who had trouble with high school math" Iverson replied, "I can't claim that I understand all the figures. It doesn't seem to me that I've been loading up too heavy on parts, but I guess I could've been. I guess I was just naturally more concerned with the smooth running of the shop than with the theoretical costs involved." Iverson, after pointing out that he couldn't really tell how things would work out from just looking at tables of figures, agreed he would do his best to adapt to the new system.

Maxon spent the next two weeks distributing lists of proposed inventory levels and reorder lot sizes for all major components to the foremen and clerks involved. He devoted as much time as he could to explaining the lists and procedures to Iverson, and overseeing the ordering of any specific components which happened to come up during his visits with Iverson. While Maxon was devoting much of his time to the inventory system installation, he found that some of his other duties were being unavoidably neglected. He was, therefore, quite relieved when, toward the end of June, he felt that Iverson and the other foremen were acquiring the necessary familiarity and competence in the new system and could be safely left to their own devices. Before returning to a full-time pursuit of his controller's duties, Maxon set up a monthly summary form to be maintained by Iverson's chief clerk. The form was designed to show monthly average inventory levels and reorder quantities, by components, from which Maxon could compute actual reductions and savings for comparison with the newly set standards. Maxon felt that it would probably take three to four months for the new procedures to "shake down." Accordingly, he informed Mr. Gilbert that he would be ready to present the results of his drive on component inventories at the October meeting of the executive committee.

During the "shakedown" period, Mason made it his business to pay Iverson a visit or two a month and to ask how things were coming along. Iverson reported that he was doing his best to follow the new inventory procedures whenever his day-to-day production problems permitted it. He made a few attempts to point out some of those production problems, which seemed to be increasing in recent weeks. Maxon, conscious of his limited competence in production problems, and careful not to overstep his functional authority, suggested that Iverson discuss his manufacturing problems with Hennessey, "one of the best production men in our industry." After one of Maxon's visits, Iverson turned to his stamping foreman and said: "Boy, am I the guy in the middle! Hennessey tells me my troubles all come from this inventory system and to see Maxon, and Maxon tells me to go see Hennessey. One way or another I'm as busy as a one-armed paperhanger."

## THE NEW SYSTEM REVIEWED

At the October meeting of the executive committee Mr. Gilbert called on John Maxon to present his scheduled evaluation of the new inventory procedures installed in June. Maxon reported that he was most disappointed in the results to date. His summary records showed that some reduction in inventory levels was indeed achieved, but that it was a long way from the goals he had established. Using the GFC-5 components again as a typical example, Maxon reported that average inventory levels were reduced by only about $5,000, as against the goal of $14,000 computed in his original presentations. Monthly total costs of ordering and carrying inventories showed an almost negligible reduction, well below the $1,900 annual rate predicted. The reasons for this disappointing performance, Maxon pointed out, were quite self-evident from his summary records. Iverson had only cut back his "safety stocks" by some $3,500 (instead of the proposed $5,690), and had adopted the recommended optimum order lot size in only 40 percent of his reordering. "The solution is as obvious as the cause of the failure," claimed Maxon. "Iverson is just not competent to be in charge of a system which requires some understanding of mathematical techniques and at least some appreciation of costs. Sure, Iverson can understand a price-tag of $9.50 on each 'A' component he orders, but he just has no idea of how much it costs us to have it lying around. If we're ever going to succeed in putting some of the modern mathematical techiques to work for us, we've got to have people who understand what it's all about. It is my recommendation that we pull Iverson off the inventory control job and put in some bright kid who's had some accounting or record-keeping experience. This inventory thing isn't the only modernization in plant methods that we're going to have, so we might as well face the issue and put in some people who can move with the times."

Hennessey strongly objected to Maxon's analysis of the situation. Iverson, he pointed out, was a top-notch foreman who knew his job and had demonstrated his ability to perform it for many years. The fault was not in Iverson's handling of the system, but in the system itself. "Now that we've had a few month's experience with it," Hennessey stated, "I can see many practical problems which John's figures didn't show."

"In the first place, since John's system was put in we've had several runouts on components needed for assembly. Now I know that we can theoretically switch assembly jobs around so as not to run into any downtime, but in practice my people aren't used to being shifted around without notice. They just didn't expect runouts, and as a result this switching around gets them upset and rattled. I've even noticed some secret hoarding of parts by foremen—something we've never had before. In addition every time we get hit by a runout, I find myself in the middle of interdepartmental wars. The assembly department blames ordering and receiving for disrupting their work schedules, ordering blames assembly for late requisitioning, and the shipping room—with the sales department on their neck—scream blue murder at everybody in the place when they have no finished units to ship. These frictions and hassles are really knocking down morale.

"Now in the past few weeks I've also had Jack Werner [quality control supervisor] almost constantly on my back. He's complaining bitterly about a tremendous increase in the percent rejects we're turning out. Even though I know Jack's a real nut on quality, his figures really shook me up. I started checking up and I can see the reason for these figures. Aside from the effect of the disturbances on my people, I find that Iverson just isn't giving sufficient supervision to his departments. He's constantly chasing around with his inventory and ordering problems, putting out brush fires and trying to keep the peace; so he just isn't there when he's needed.

"Another thing that's causing trouble is John's lot size for Component 'C' which we turn out in our stamping department. We used to order 5,000 units at a time, which meant scheduling about two runs of it a month. [Actually an average of 2.18 per month, see Exhibit 3, Column 4.] Now John wants it ordered in 2,900-unit lots. This means we've got to set up the job four times a month—twice as often as before—and that's double the trouble and expense. Maybe we're saving some money in 'C' inventories under the new system, but we're sure throwing it away in the stamping department.

"As far as I'm concerned, this whole trial run convinces me that we're saving pennies and throwing away dollars. I can't show you any neat figures of how much runouts, frictions, quality troubles, and disruptions are costing us in dollars and cents, but I'm convinced it's well over anything John can save us in inventory costs. I'm for going to some simpler and more practical inventory ordering system. The fancy stuff is probably good for the real big companies, with their computers and experts, but just doesn't work in an outfit our size."

Mr. Gilbert believed that the arguments presented should be studied in detail by him before making a decision on the inventory procedures to be followed. He did not feel it was worthwhile to take up the entire executive committee's time with further discussion of the issue, and accordingly set up a meeting with Maxon and Hennessey at his office for the following day. He suggested they give the matter further thought and bring whatever additional data they could develop in support of their position.

Turning to Maxon, the president remarked with a smile, "Just don't show me too much with high-level differential equations which you know I can't handle."

Upon returning to his office, Hennessey told Iverson, who was waiting for him, "I really let them have it, Pete. Maxon was trying to nail you with it, but I wasn't having any. You know, after this whole hassle, I believe there's something to cleaning up and formalizing our inventory systems. We don't need any fancy accounting stuff, but I think we can improve on what we had. Let's you and I get together Monday to work something out."

---

# Selected Readings

---

*From*

## PRINCIPLES OF SCIENTIFIC MANAGEMENT*

*By Frederick Winslow Taylor*

President Roosevelt, in his address to the Governors at the White House, prophetically remarked that "The conservation of our national resources is only preliminary to the larger question of national efficiency."

The whole country at once recognized the importance of conserving our material resources and a large movement has been started which will be effective in accomplishing this object. As yet, however, we have but vaguely appreciated the importance of the "larger question of increasing our national efficiency."

* From *Scientific Management* by Frederick Winslow Taylor. Copyright © 1947. Reprinted by permission of Harper & Row, Publishers, Inc. (Excerpts from pp. 5–8, 40–41.)

We can see our forests vanishing, our water-powers going to waste, our soil being carried by floods into the sea; and the end of our coal and our iron is in sight. But our larger wastes of human effort, which go on every day through such of our acts as are blundering, ill-directed, or inefficient, and which Mr. Roosevelt refers to as a lack of "national efficiency," are less visible, less tangible, and are but vaguely appreciated.

We can see and feel the waste of material things. Awkward, inefficient, or ill-directed movements of men, however, leave nothing visible or tangible behind them. Their appreciation calls for an act of memory, an effort of the imagination. And for this reason, even though our daily loss from this source is greater than from our waste of material things, the one has stirred us deeply, while the other has moved us but little.

As yet there has been no public agitation for "greater national efficiency," no meetings have been called to consider how this is to be brought about. And still there are signs that the need for greater efficiency is widely felt.

The search for better, for more competent men, from the presidents of our great companies down to our household servants, was never more vigorous than it is now. And more than ever before is the demand for competent men in excess of the supply.

*    *    *    *    *

In the past the man has been first; in the future the system must be first. This in no sense, however, implies that great men are not needed. On the contrary the first object of any good system must be that of developing first-class men; and under systematic management the best man rises to the top more certainly and more rapidly than ever before.

This paper has been written:

*First.* To point out, through a series of simple illustrations, the great loss which the whole country is suffering through inefficiency in almost all of our daily acts.

*Second.* To try to convince the reader than the remedy for this inefficiency lies in systematic management, rather than in searching for some unusual or extraordinary man.

*Third.* To prove that the best management is a true science, resting upon clearly defined laws, rules and principles, as a foundation. And further to show that the fundamental principles of scientific management are applicable to all kinds of human activities, from our simplest individual acts to the work of our great corporations, which call for the most elaborate cooperation. And, briefly, through a series of illustrations, to convince the reader that whenever these principles are correctly applied, results must follow which are truly astounding.

This paper was originally prepared for presentation to The American Society of Mechanical Engineers. The illustrations chosen are such as, it is believed, will especially appeal to engineers and to managers of industrial and manufacturing establishments, and also quite as much to all of the men who are working in these establishments. It is hoped, however, that it will be clear to other readers that the same principles can be applied with equal force to all social activities: to the management of our homes; the management of our farms; the management of the business of our tradesmen, large and small; of our churches, our philanthropic institutions, our universities, and our governmental departments.

*    *    *    *    *

The first illustration is that of handling pig iron, and this work is chosen because it is typical of perhaps the crudest and most elementary form of labor which is performed by man. The work is done by men with no other implements than their hands. The pig iron handler stoops down, picks up a pig weighing about 92 lbs., walks for a few feet or yards and then drops it on the ground or upon a pile. This work is so crude and elementary in its nature that the writer firmly believes that it would be possible to train an intelligent gorilla so as to become a more efficient pig-iron handler than any man can be. Yet it will be shown that the science of handling pig iron is so great and amounts to so much that it is impossible for the man who is best suited to this type of work to understand the principles of this science, or even to work in accordance with these principles without the aid of a man better educated than he is. And the further illustrations to be given will make it clear that in almost all of the mechanic arts the science which underlies each workman's act is so great and amounts to so much that the workman who is best suited actually to do the work is incapable (either through lack of education or through insufficient mental capacity) of understanding this science. This is announced as a general principle. . . .

*From*

# HOW MANAGERS MAKE THINGS HAPPEN*

*By George S. Odiorne*

### Management Is Not a Passive Art

*        *        *        *        *

A manager is more than a problem solver. He's a goal setter. Without waiting for others to ask him, he envisions things that should happen, and thinks through some possible paths by which the goal can be reached. At this stage he has few, if any, people who would agree with him that the goal is possible. Because he's active in deed as well as thought, however, he converts them into action in his plan, and enlists their talents toward reaching the goal which he dreamed up. Before long he has a full scale movement afoot and people become ego-involved in his goal just as if they themselves had thought of it.

*        *        *        *        *

### Making Growth a Company Goal

. . . [A] few dominant trends seem to emerge. One of these is that *company growth* is one present day goal which seems to spur executive action and make things happen. This has some important implications for the company which wants to grow. It also has a great deal of relevance to the building manager—or the one who's arrived—who has talents for making things happen and seeks ample opportunity to demonstrate his prowess along these lines.

Studies by the Stanford Research Institute of several hundred companies with records of growth show that there are several traits which are common to most of them. . . .

*        *        *        *        *

Stanford's studies also showes that those companies which have growth patterns have been led by management of great moral courage in making decisions in favor of growth and sticking with them to make the growth occur. . . .

. . . [The manager has] the heavy responsibility for spurring others to overcome their own inertia. . . . He's got to be able to move projects and people off dead center and get them rolling toward his goals. He's got to generate enthusiasm for these goals so that people adopt them as their own, with the result that they generate enthusiasm on their own part for getting there. He must further instill a desire to excel and do the job fully and without mistakes or altering. To do this demands several traits in the action-getting manager which he must assiduously cultivate at the risk of failure.

1. He's going to have to maintain optimism if he's going to overcome inertia. Most managers who make things happen have ego drives that push them on personally, and unbounded optimism and confidence that others will ultimately see his vision of what's to be accomplished despite repeated defeats and failures.

* *How Managers Make Things Happen,* George S. Odiorne. © 1961 by Prentice-Hall, Englewood Cliffs, N.J. (pp. 4–11, 37–38, 52–53).

2. He needs a sound knowledge of people to impel them to produce and create. He needs to know what incentives are required to get action from others, and to have some artistry in using them.

3. He needs a certain callousness in demanding high standards of performance from others who are helping him. The manager with an overdeveloped sense of sympathy and understanding of failure will usually "usurp all of the dirty jobs for himself while others stand about and marvel at his performance," as David Moore puts it.

\*    \*    \*    \*    \*

## Profit Requires Action

Being a successful manager in a commercial and industrial enterprise means a profit-minded one. Conversely, it's the profit-minded manager at any level who stands the best change of moving upward. This is more than simple avarice, or single minded love of money for itself. It's largely because profit is a universal standard for measurement that is easily grasped by managers and quite clearly understood by those who judge his performance.

It's entirely possible that someday a more commonly held standard will come along, for example—service; but it must always meet the standard which profit has become—immediate, easy to caluclate, universally accepted. Profit, for all the criticisms leveled against it, is the best available instrument and standard of managerial success and organizational performance. With adaptations it applies to any organization, even in Soviet Russia.

We hear a great deal of pious foolishness written and said about profit. At the annual congress of industry of the NAM each winter, solemn and quite pompous words are uttered in defense of this mysterious lubricant which causes the wheels of industry to turn. To some it becomes a divinely inspired instrument which it becomes sacrilegious to damn. This of course is not the point here.

\*    \*    \*    \*    \*

*Profit, then, is more than an accounting term. It's a positive creation and standard of measuring effectiveness of management action and decision making.*

\*    \*    \*    \*    \*

. . . Profit is the result almost wholly of the *actions of managers* who exercise initiative and leadership of a dynamic nature, and of the people who respond to this leadership to carry through toward the goals of the organization. .

There is probably no company in business today which couldn't be out of business through lack of profit inside of ten years if its management attempted to conduct its affairs simply through mechanical application of administrative practice, at the expense of the more vital, personal, and human application of individual leadership.

\*    \*    \*    \*    \*

. . . The most pernicious trait a manager can have when faced with obstacles is indecisiveness. Very often this is explained away as a need for mature consideration of the situation, but actually indecision is the result of the mind slipping away into inappropriate or trivial matters. He may find that ordering a new desk or settling a squabble between two secretaries is much more intriguing than writing the order, or picking up the telephone to announce the decision. The obstacle hurdler makes his decision when he can—and the sooner the better.

\*    \*    \*    \*    \*

Equally vital among the qualities of the obstacle breaker is that of using people without becoming sentimentally overinvolved with their successes or failures. A survey of fifty company presidents by two graduate students at the School of Business at Micigan showed that such things as fraternal connections and other sentimental ties rated last among these executives' considerations when picking men for positions of leadership.

\*    \*    \*    \*    \*

Despite his concern with meeting the needs of others and meeting the basic needs of people, the action-getter has developed a tough-mindedness. For one thing, as Chris Argyris, management researcher of Yale, has put it, he has "a high tolerance for frustration." He can plug through all sorts of red tape without blowing his top when he has to. He frequently endures the delays and runarounds of committees and clearances with spartan endurance. He is patient where such patience is the only possible way of getting the final payoff that he seeks.

This patience isn't submissiveness, however, and when the time for patience is past and more direct action is called for, the action-minded manager is willing to be ruthless. When the choice is between maintaining old relationships and getting the job done he is always ready to decide in favor of the job. Stepping on people's corns isn't his first choice, but he does it firmly if the occasion demands.

       *     *     *     *     *

The action-minded manager is probably tough-minded in his relations with people, too. He's willing to stick by his people through their honest mistakes—or to chop off heads as the need arises. He assumes that men are made of tough stuff and will work hard and take heavy blows as a price of making a living and contributing to the success of the business. He will urge on a man who is working at less than his best abilities.

He is liberal with recognition for good work, and equally liberal with a reverse kind of recognition for the people who aren't performing up to their capacities. People over their heads in their jobs find this action-minded man a fearsome figure, one who will certainly drive them to perform things they hadn't thought possible, or face up to the fact that they have no great future in the organization until they do.

He's tough-minded, too, in being willing to pay the prices for personal success. Long hours, hard work, and man-killing travel schedules are the way of life for him. He concentrates on his job with a fury and singleness of purpose that reduces other things to a lesser role. This doesn't mean he's inhuman or a dull grind. . . .

*From*

# LEVIATHAN (CHAPTER X, OF POWER, WORTH, DIGNITY, HONOUR, AND WORTHINESS)

*By Thomas Hobbes\**

The power of a man, to take it universally, is his present means to obtain some future apparent good, and is either original or instrumental.

*Natural* power is the eminence of the faculties of body, or mind; as extraordinary strength, form, prudence, arts, eloquence, liberality, nobility. *Instrumental* are those powers which, acquired by these, or by fortune, are means and instruments to acquire more; as riches, reputation, friends, and the secret working of God, which men call good luck. For the nature of power is, in this point, like to fame, increasing as it proceeds; or like the motion of heavy bodies, which, the further they go, make still the more haste.

The greatest of human powers is that which is compounded of the powers of most men, united by consent, in one person, natural or civil, that has the use of all their powers depending on his will; such as is the power of a Commonwealth: or depending on the wills of each particular; such as is the power of a faction, or of diverse factions leagued. Therefore to have servants is power; to have friends is power: for they are strengths united.

---

\* Thomas Hobbes, 1588–1679, made significant contributions to political science through *Leviathan,* his major work.

Also, riches joined with liberality is power; because it procureth friends and servants: without liberality, not so; because in this case they defend not, but expose men to envy, as a prey.

Reputation of power is power; because it draweth with it the adherence of those that need protection.

So is reputation of love of a man's country, called *popularity,* for the same reason.

Also, what quality soever maketh a man beloved or feared of many, or the reputation of such quality, is power; because it is a means to have the assistance and service of many.

Good success is power; because it maketh reputation of wisdom or good fortune, which makes men either fear him or rely on him.

Affability of men already in power is increase of power; because it gaineth love.

Reputation of prudence in the conduct of peace or war is power; because to prudent men we commit the government of ourselves more willingly than to others.

Nobility is power, not in all places, but only in those Commonwealths where it has privileges; for in such privileges consisteth their power.

Eloquence is power; because it is seeming prudence.

Form is power; because being a promise of good, it recommendeth men to the favour of women and strangers.

The sciences are small powers; because not eminent, and therefore, not acknowledged in any man; nor are at all, but in a few, and in them, but of a few things. For science is of that nature, as none can understand it to be, but such as in a good measure have attained it.

Arts of public use, as fortification, making of engines, and other instruments of war, because they confer to defence and victory, are power; and though the true mother of them be science, namely, the mathematics; yet, because they are brought into the light by the hand of the artificer, they be esteemed (the midwife passing with the vulgar for the mother) as his issue.

*From*

# POWER AND SOCIETY*

*By Harold D. Lasswell and Abraham Kaplan*

. . . The circulation of a leadership varies inversely with the disparity between its skills and those of the rank and file.

This is one of Michels' basic theses, elaborated throughout his study of *Political Parties:* "the leader's principal source of power is found in his indispensability." Every organization rests on a division of labor, and hence specialization. And to the degree that distinctive skills are involved the specialist becomes indispensable. The leader is such a specialist.

"The leaders cannot be replaced at a moment's notice, since all the other members of the party [or other group] are absorbed in their everyday occupations and are strangers to the bureaucratic mechanism. This special competence, this expert knowledge, which the leader acquires in matters inaccessible, or almost inaccessible to the mass, gives him a security of tenure. . . (1915, 84)."

What is fundamental is that the possession of certain values is a requisite of leadership, and that these values are nontransferable. (Leadership resting on a transferable value could

* Reprinted by permission of the Yale University Press, New Haven, Conn., 1950 (pp. 157–59).

be replaced by effecting the transfer.) Skill is the most striking of the nontransferable values; but there are others as well. Thus prestige is an important requisite of leadership not readily transferable. Hence stability of leadership will also vary with the disparity in the respect accorded the leaders and the rank and file. And the same will be true with regard to personal characteristics (for instance, prowess) on which leadership in a given case might be based.

As a consequence, the major threat to the leadership is provided, not by the rank and file itself, but by potential rivals for leadership with the requisite skills and other qualities.

"Whenever the power of the leaders is seriously threatened, it is in most cases because a new leader or a new group of leaders is on the point of becoming dominant, and is inculcating views opposed to those of the old rulers of the party. . . . It is not the masses which have devoured the leaders: the chiefs have devoured one another with the aid of the masses (1915, 164–5)."

As a further consequence of the skill conditions, a leadership is rarely completely replaced by its rivals. In criticism of Pareto's "theory of the circulation of elites" Michels points out that "in most cases there is not a simple replacement of one group of élites by another, but a continuous process of intermixture, the old elements incessantly attracting, absorbing, and assimilating the new" (1915, 378). The rival leaderships are indispensable to one another as well as to the group. The new leadership cannot dispense altogether with the skills and experience of the old, nor can the old better maintain its favorable power position than by extending to rivals a restricted share in their own power. Hence

"very rarely does the struggle between the old leaders and the new end in the complete defeat of the former. The result of the process is not so much a 'circulation des élites' as a 'reunion des élites,' an amalgam, that is to say, of the two elements (1915, 177)."

Throughout even the most revolutionary changes a stable administration core remains, which is the more prominent the more specialized are the skills it possesses.

*From*

# AMERICAN DEMOCRACY IN THEORY AND PRACTICE*

*By Robert Carr, Marver H. Bernstein, and Donald H. Morrison*

The highly technological character of American civilization makes it possible through the mass-circulation newspaper and magazine and the magic of radio and television, to bring essential information concerning social problems to every citizen and thereby to encourage the formation of intelligent public opinion. At the same time, it renders the problems themselves so complex and difficult that there arises a question concerning the ability of even an educated and informed citizenry to think about these problems intelligently and rationally. For example, two of the greatest issues of our time—finding satisfactory systems for the social control of atomic energy and space weapons and satellites—are made almost impossibly difficult. . . . The machine age is placing a strain upon the democratic process in this respect. It is clear that if the democratic system is to survive, increasing attention must be paid to such a basic point as bringing essential information concerning the social problems of a technological age to the people so that the process of forming public opinion may be carried forward.

*    *    *    *    *

Mention of dissemination of information by the government raises the issue whether public officers in a democracy should try to influence public opinion or should only be influenced by it. Public officers in a democracy must show a high sensitivity to public opinion. But it is also clear that they must often provide strong leadership as public opinion takes shape on a difficult issue. For example, where the President possesses expert information concerning such matters as the international situation or economic trends within the country, which information in his judgment seems to necessitate the following of particular policies, he must do his best to shape a favorable public opinion in support of these policies.

*From*

# MODERN PRODUCTION MANAGEMENT*

*By Elwood S. Buffa*

In a sense, inventories make possible a rational production system. Without them we could not achieve smooth production flow, obtain reasonable utilization of machines, reasonable material handling costs, or expect to give reasonable service to customers on hundreds of items regarded as "stock" items. At each stage of both manufacturing and distribution, inventories serve the vital function of *decoupling* the various operations in the sequence beginning with raw materials, extending through all of the manufacturing operations and into finished goods storage, and thence to warehouses and retail stores. Between each pair of activities in this sequence, inventories make the required operations enough independent of each other that low cost operations can be carried out. Thus, when raw materials are ordered, a supply is ordered that is large enough to justify the out-of-pocket cost of putting through the order and transporting it to the plant. When production orders to manufacture parts and products are released, we try to make them big enough to justify the cost of writing the orders and setting up machines to perform the required operations. Otherwise, order writing and setup costs could easily become prohibitive. Running parts through the system in lots also tends to reduce handling costs because parts can be handled in groups. . . .

*    *    *    *    *

Unfortunately, the inventory question is not a one-sided one, which is precisely why inventories are a problem in the operation of a production system. If there were not an optimal level to shoot for, there would be no problem. Anyone could follow the simple rule: "Make inventories as big as possible." Inventories require that invested capital be tied up, and, therefore, there is an appropriate opportunity cost associated with their value. Not only that, they require valuable space and absorb insurance and taxation charges. . . .

Thus, we have one set of costs that are fixed by the purchase or production order size and another set of costs which increase with the level of inventory. The first set of costs exert a pressure toward large purchase and production lots to reduce unit order writing and setup costs to a reasonable level. The second set of costs exerts a pressure toward small lots in order to maintain inventory costs at reasonable levels. . . .

\*    \*    \*    \*    \*

We have been discussing inventory controls as if they could be set up independently of the production system, inferring criteria, or measures of effectiveness, that do not reflect the effect of inventories on production programs and on the control of general levels of production. This independence is unrealistic because there are interactions between these problems. Inventory policy must fit in with schedules to produce a *combined* minimum cost of operation rather than a minimum for inventories alone. . . .

\*    \*    \*    \*    \*

Production and inventory control are one subject, because any partitioning of the problems in this area that does not consider both will likely result in a suboptimum solution. The development of economic lot sizes is a good example of this. This concept holds in the narrower sense, but when interactions with production fluctuations are taken into account, other basic schemes of control may exhibit superior overall cost characteristics. There may be other interactions. For example, how does the length of a production run affect learning time and therefore, labor cost? Perhaps this effect is insignificant for some situations, but it is known to be important in many others. Do lot size formulations account for this effect? What other interactions are not accounted for? We are witnessing some of the difficulties in attempting mathematical solutions to problems of restricted definition.

# 13. FARNSWORTH COMPANY

---

# Case Introduction

---

## SYNOPSIS

In the process of designing a management information system for the new product division level in a paper company that grew by acquisition, a questionnaire is sent to one of the recently acquired companies. The local data processing supervisor discusses the questionnaire with his boss, the controller. An upset controller brings the questionnaire to the general manager who delays its completion and return beyond the deadline.

## WHY THIS CASE IS INCLUDED

In the Farnsworth case the logic of system integration and control via information confronts the reality of individual needs and subsystem independence. The reader can explore the causal chain from strategy to structure to processes (information flow, control, and so on. The case permits the testing not only of the logic for a particular kind of change but also the logic of the process of change itself.

## DIAGNOSTIC AND PREDICTIVE QUESTIONS

The readings included with the case are marked (*). The author index at the end of this book locates the other readings.

1. Are Mr. Fersterberg and his divisional staff going about the design of the divisional M.I.S. (control system) in an effective way?

Read:  Vancil, "What Kind of Management Control Do You Need?"
  Lawrence, "How to Deal with Resistance to Change."

2. In management terms, after years of relative independence, what is Mr. Perry fearing from what he saw in the questionnaire?

Read:   *Sampson, The Sovereign State of ITT. *Jerome, *Executive Control—The Catalyst.*

3. Does Ansoff's concept of "synergy" (particularly "management synergy") help help in understanding the logic of Farnsworth in dealing with its acquired companies?

Read:   *Ansoff, *Corporate Strategy: An Analytical Approach to Business Policy for Growth and Expansion.*

4. Could you have predicted a structural change at Farnsworth, given its growth pattern?

Read:   Chandler, *Strategy and Structure.*

5. Recall that Mr. Perry says: "I should have been clever enough to see the writing on the wall." What predictions might he have made after the recent changes in structure and people.

Read:   Leavitt, *Managerial Psychology,* pp. 317–25. Lawrence and Lorsch, "New Management Job: The Integrator."

6. Why did Mr. Perry use the expression "Captain Manager" in place of "General Manager"?

Read:   Maslow, *Motivation and Personality.* Litterer, "Conflict in Organization: A Re-Examination."

7. Did John Sanford experience "unity of command" in this case? Over whom does David Sammons have "functional authority?"

Read:   Fayol, *General and Industrial Management.* Taylor, *"Principles of Scientific Management."*

## POLICY QUESTIONS

8. As an adviser to Mr. Fersterberg, what would you recommend concerning the design of the new divisional M.I.S.? (Review your answers to Questions 1, 2, 5, and 6.)

9. What should Mr. Perry do himself at the end of the case?

10. What should Mr. Perry advise Mr. Sanford to do at the end of the case? (Review your answer to Question 8.)

11. If you were Mr. Sanford, what would you do at the end of the case?

---

# Case Text*

---

The Farnsworth Company was founded in 1905 as a logging and timber company, cutting its own trees and converting them to lumber in its own sawmills. The founder of the company was seriously committed to the strategy that one company should own both trees (which were cut

---

* Copyright 1976, C.E.I., Geneva. Written by Dr. J. J. O'Connell.

by the logging department) and sawmills (which were operated by the lumber department). In this sense, the company was vertically integrated from the very beginning.

Over the years, the "Farnsworth Group" has grown by acquiring other companies, all of which are related to wood products. It administers these subsidiary divisions from "Group Headquarters" in Chicago.

The company has vertically integrated between, and within, each of its three main divisions. The Forestry Products Division supplies trees and wood chips to the Paper Products Division. It supplies a different kind of tree derivative to the Paper Board (Container) Division. Within the Forestry Products Division, the Logging Department sells logs to the Lumber Department, as raw materials for the latter's sawmills; and to the Plywood Department, as raw material for its Plywood and Door factory. Both of these departments sell to the Forestry Products Division's Modular Home Department.

Within the Paper Products Division, the Pulp Department converts logs and chips to wood pulp and sells this to the Fine Paper Department. This department is still called Learner Brothers Paper Company. Located in Hartford, Connecticut, it is one of nine departments which produce different paper products: fine paper, sanitary paper, printing paper, newsprint, and coarse paper stock for industrial wrapping materials. All of these divisions were independent companies prior to acquisition by the Farnsworth Group.

### The M.I.S. Project

Recently, the Executive Committee of the Paper Products Division made a decision to improve the Management Information System of the entire division. In the words of Paul Fersterberg, vice president and general manager of the Paper Products Division, "there are certain advantages enjoyed by a company which puts the five product groups (fine, coarse, newsprint, and so on) together in one company, as Farnsworth has done with its nine paper companies. For one thing, we can coordinate the right amount of raw materials flowing from one department to another. For another, we can often find some excellent operation which has been discovered in one department and make use of it, at little additional cost, in another department.

"But to make decisions of this kind, which affect more than one department, we need a management information system which shows us what is going on in the division as a whole—we cannot make those decisions if each department is a separate company, reporting figures a different way, and with no attention to *interdepartmental* (as opposed to intradepartmental) economies."

Fersterberg recognized that one cannot change the entire accounting, statistical and other information systems overnight. He therefore asked the Group Headquarters if his division could "borrow one of your specialists on Management Information Systems. We would like to have him on detached service here in our Atlanta Headquarters, to help devise the new system."

In due time, David Sammons was sent by the Chicago Headquarters to Atlanta, to serve in this capacity. "I recognize I must go glowly in this project," Sammons says. "The first step is simply to find out what kind of accounting, statistical and other information records are being kept, and what they are used for."

Following this thinking, Sammons devised a questionnaire which he sent to the data processing manager on the staff of each of the nine subsidiary paper departments.

### The M.I.S. Questionnaire

John Sanford, supervisor, data processing department, received the following letter from the new Paper Division headquarters in Atlanta, on February 17:

> Mr. John Sanford
> Data Processing Department
> Learner Brothers Paper Company
> Constitution Plaza
> Hartford, Connecticut
>
> Dear Mr. Sanford,
>
> As agreed in the Executive Committee of the Paper Division, I am carrying out a survey on M.I.S. among the nine companies in the Division. I am on loan to the Division from Group Headquarters just until the Division completes its staffing search internally, and, if necessary, externally. My involvement at this stage may contribute to the objectives of the yet-to-be developed Divisional M.I.S.: "(*a*) to better serve the individual and common needs of the division companies; (*b*) to make possible the coordination and synergy-seeking efforts of Group Headquarters." I have the Headquarters perspective, am now forming a view of the world from the division level, and I need your help in getting an accurate picture of the company level. The enclosed questionnaire is self-explanatory. At a later stage, someone from the Divisional M.I.S. Project Team will visit your company. In the name of our Paper Division Vice-President, Mr. Paul Fersterberg, I thank you in advance for your assistance.
>
> Sincerely,
>
> David Sammons
> Divisional M.I.S. Project Leader

Just for laughs, John Sanford weighed the questionnaire on his secretary's postage scale: 28 ounces! He read the cover sheet.

MANAGEMENT INFORMATION REQUIREMENTS FOR
PAPER PRODUCTS DIVISION

*Explanatory notes on the questionnaire:*
Two of the stated steps in the objective of the study are:

1.  Define compatibility among division companies, between companies and the division, and between companies and the group.
2.  Determine the information compatibility requirements.

In order to accomplish these steps it is necessary to analyze:

1.  The number of operational units that exist in the division in the most limited definition possible, that is, the business stream at a site location.
2.  The size of these units in information terms.
3.  How the units relate to each other, to the company, to the division and to the group.
4.  The type of systems and hardware that exist in the units.

The questionnaire has been designed in modular form and comprises the following 12 sections:

1.  General
2.  Balance Sheet and P. +L.
3.  Fixed Asset Accounting
4.  Budgeting/Costing
5.  Billing/Accounts Receivable
6.  Purchasing/Accounts Payable
7.  Customers
8.  Product
9.  Market
10.  Distribution
11.  Sales Organization
12.  Payroll

Depending entirely on the structure of your company, it may be necessary to complete several copies of one or all of the sections for each location. In such cases use the copy provided as a blank master.

Would you please ensure that the completed questionnaires are returned to David Sammons, Divisional MIS Project Leader, Paper Products Division, Atlanta, by Monday, March 8.

Since Sammons referred to the approval of the Paper Division Executive Committee, John Sanford figured that the Learner Brothers General Manager, Franklin Perry, agreed that he fill in the questionnaire. That surprised him! In the four and a half years that Learner Brothers had been a member—by acquisition—of the Farnsworth Group, Mr. Perry had jealously protected the independence promised in the acquisition agreement. He always said that a strong ROI was the best defense. In Farnsworth's forward integration strategy, Learner Brothers was not a unique acquisition.

Five of the nine companies in the year-old Paper Products Division were acquisitions of companies in the coarse paper, fine paper, printing paper, sanitary paper, and newsprint fields. Learner Brothers was unique as the only one of the nine in the fine paper sector. Farnsworth had used a similar move "from trees to consumer products" in the other two divisions: forestry products, and paper board products.

John Sanford, in his nine years with Learner Brothers grew to like the small-company atmosphere and credited Mr. Perry with maintaining it despite the acquisition by Farnsworth. Just to check his own reading of the situation, John brought the questionnaire in to his boss, Frank Meadows, the controller. Together they paged through the questionnaire. Certain of the items appeared to be straightforward, like Section 1.3—Data Processing Capability.

---

Please indicate processing method for the following head office systems, using the following key:

   a.  Fully manual.
   b.  Manual/accounting machine.
   c.  Manual/accounting machine/computer.
   d.  Accounting machine/computer.
   e.  Fully computerized.
   f.  Not applicable.

| | | | |
|---|---|---|---|
| 1.3.1 | order entry ———— | 1.3.10 | material utilization —— |
| 1.3.2 | sales reporting ———— | 1.3.11 | fixed-asset accounting — |
| 1.3.3 | billing ———— | 1.3.12 | purchased inventory |
| 1.3.4 | accounts receivable—— | | recording———— |
| 1.3.5 | inventory recording —— | 1.3.13 | purchased inventory |
| 1.3.6 | production planning, | | control ———— |
| | scheduling ———— | 1.3.14 | accounts payable——— |
| 1.3.7 | inventory control——— | 1.3.15 | general ledger ——— |
| 1.3.8 | payroll ———— | 1.3.16 | costing ———— |
| 1.3.9 | labor utilization ———— | 1.3.17 | P. + L. reporting ——— |
| | | 1.3.18 | other (————)——— |

---

John Sanford expressed more concern over his filling in Section 1.8—Future Information Requirements.

---

| | |
|---|---|
| 1.8.1 | What do you consider to be the major weaknesses in your present MIS? |
| 1.8.2 | To correct these difficulties what projects do you have: |
| 1.8.2.1 | approved |
| 1.8.2.2 | under study |
| 1.8.2.3 | planned for future study |

For a different reason, John pencilled a big question mark next to Section 1.15—Record Count.

---

How many unique accounting records are maintained in your accounting system (exclude the individual transaction levels and customer and supplier levels).

|  |  | *Currently* | *In Five Years* |
|---|---|---|---|
| 1.15.1 | below 500 | — | — |
| 1.15.2 | 500 – 1,000 | — | — |
| 1.15.3 | 1,000 – 2,000 | — | — |
| 1.15.4 | 2,000 – 5,000 | — | — |
| 1.15.5 | over 5,000 | — | — |

---

The controller dog-eared the page covering Section 4.29—Changes in Costing System.

---

How would a major amendment to your costing system impact on other systems. Please list systems affected (e.g., inventory recording, purchasing, stores, fixed assets, payroll, maintenance control, planning, etc.). Use the following scale in assessing the degree of impact:

   a.  Complete reorganization.
   b.  Major reorganization.
   c.  Significant reorganization.
   d.  Minimal reorganization.

| *System* | *Degree of Impact* |
|---|---|
| 4.29.1 ...................... | — |
| 4.29.2 ...................... | — |
| .         .  ...................... | — |
| .         . | . |
| .         . | . |

---

By the time that John and Frank Meadows got to the Receivables section under number 5, the controller was drumming the table furiously with the fingernails of his right hand.

---

5.15   What percentage of your invoices are on the following payment terms:

|  |  | *Percentage* |
|---|---|---|
| 5.15.1 | Less than 15 days | — |
| 5.15.2 | 15 to 30 days | — |
| 5.15.3 | 30 to 50 days | — |
| 5.15.4 | 60 to 90 days | — |
| 5.15.5 | 90 to 120 days | — |
| 5.15.6 | Over 120 days | — |
| 5.16 | What percent of bad debt loss did you have last year? | |

5.19  If the division were to use an IBM 370–145 for weekly tele-
processing the listing of your aged receivables over $5,000,
what change would that require at your end? (Check all relevant items.)

15.19.1 ———————— Major hardware investment.

15.19.2 ———————— Minor hardware investment.

15.19.3 ———————— Major software investment.

15.19.4 ———————— Minor software investment.

15.19.5 ———————— No real investment required.

Before John could ask a question, the Controller was barrelling out of
his office toward Mr. Perry's office with the questionnaire in hand.
Strangely, neither Frank Meadows nor Franklin Perry mentioned the
questionnaire to John in the weeks that followed. He had almost forgotten the matter when he received the following telex on March 16 from
David Sammons in Atlanta: "We are moving ahead with functional and
hardware specification at division level but we badly need the company
input from you. Can we expect it this week?"

When interviewed during that same week in mid-March, Learner's
General Manager, Franklin Perry, spoke of the opportunity he had had
fourteen months ago of taking the Paper Products Division Vice Presidency. "I thought it would be a non-job, coordinating unimportant matters. When Fersterberg took the job last February, I began to wonder. He
had been running Farnsworth's own biggest paperboard company.
Clearly, he was being groomed for big things. Maybe I was too close to
this product division evolution to see what was going on. Hell, this started
out three years ago as a product coordination project group at Farnsworth headquarters. They spent five times as much time discussing paper chemistry as they did the business of making or selling paper. To be
honest, I guess we all made sure that's what would happen by the kind
of guys we nominated.

"Now look what's happening! Fersterberg is adding paper experience
to his command of paperboard . . . won't be long before he's ready to sit
in a bigger chair. Even this sharpie, Sammons, when he finishes nosing
into every paper company in this division, he will move on to set up M.I.S.
in the Paperboard Division, and then to the Forestry Products. He'll not
only have the grass-roots knowledge but he'll have a network of familiar
faces in key slots. Know where he's headed, I bet? The group controller,
Malcolm Honiss, is getting so old that his chair is getting cool already.
Malcolm has been a great asset during this acquisition binge. He never
let them buy a bad company. That's why he could be satisfied with getting quarterly variance reporting from me on a not-very-detailed P. & L.
He's been a wise old fox but the new generation probably looks on him
as a pussy cat.

"You know, the irony of this affair shows in this letter I got yesterday
from Fersterberg. Look at this paragraph:

My staff tells me that you have the most experienced M.I.S. man in
the Division in your company. The personnel files your people pro-

vided to my office even show he's something of an expert in tele-processing. That's a skill our M.I.S. project team could use for about three weeks. I assume you will have no objection to our borrowing him for three weeks in April 2.

"Here I sit, holding up the Sammons questionnaire, and they want to steal one of my key guys.

"I should have been clever enough to have seen the writing on the wall. Sure, we in the Paper Division Executive Committee approved a 'need and feasibility study for divisional M.I.S. hardware and software.' But I never saw this questionnaire before. When I see someone asking about weekly reports of aged receivables—and I only get monthly exception reporting—I understand what's in the wind. Look at the sentence I underlined in last year's annual report. In announcing the three new product divisions, the president called it a 'decentralization'. That sure as hell isn't what it looks like from my chair."

"My wife asked me how I felt this morning and I said: 'like the Captain Manager of Learner Brothers.' "

---

# Selected Readings

---

*From*

## THE SOVEREIGN STATE OF ITT*

*By Anthony Sampson*

### THE MOVING FINGER

On the last Monday of every month, a Boeing 707 takes off from New York to Brussels, with sixty ITT executives aboard, including Geneen or one of his deputies, with a special office rigged up from him to work in. They stay in Brussels for four days, inside their own company capsule, spending most of their time in one of the marathon ITT meetings.

A meeting is a weird spectacle, with more than a hint of Dr. Strangelove. One hundred and twenty people are assembled in the big fourth-floor room, equipped with cool air-conditioning, soft lighting and discreet microphones. The curtains are drawn against the daylight, and a big screen displays table after table of statistics. Most of the room is taken up with a huge horse-shoe table, covered in green baize, with blue rocking armchairs and names in front of each chair, with a bottle of mineral water and a book of accounts. On the chairs sit the top men of ITT from all over Europe, like diplomats at a conference: in the middle are the senior vice-presidents. Among them, swivelling and rocking to and fro in his armchair, surveying the faces and gazing at the statistics, is an owlish figure behind a label saying Harold S. Geneen.

---

* Copyright © 1973 by Anthony Sampson. From the book, *The Sovereign State of ITT.* Reprinted with permission of Stein and Day, publishers. Excerpts from pp. 91–92, 116–20.

A low voice, from one of the controllers, intones the salient facts about each batch of figures; and as the voice talks, a small, sharp arrow appears on the screen, alongside the relevant figure. Some of the figures have brackets round them, indicating a loss, and there the arrow lingers specially long (it seems almost like an extension of Geneen's finger). From time to time, Geneen's voice, also very low, interposes with a question; why has a target not been reached, why is an inventory figure too high? The managing director justifies himself tensely and briefly: "We're already looking into that, Mr. Geneen." Geneen nods, or swivels round, or utters some mild reproof. The arrow moves on to the next incriminating figure.

The meetings, whether in Brussels or New York, are the central ordeal of the ITT discipline, the test that its men are attuned to the openness of the system. As Geneen explained to me, it is not enough for him to see the accounts; he must see the expression of the man that gives them, and how he gives them. The words "I want no surprises" are always there, in the background. If there *is* a surprise, the reaction is immediate; a task force will be immediately appointed, perhaps two or three task forces unaware of each other, to find out the reason, to supply a solution. For a newly-joined manager—and specially from a company newly acquired by ITT—the ordeal can be terrifying; there are stories of one man fainting as he walked in, and of another rushing out to get blind drunk for two days.

*    *    *    *    *

The most gruelling sessions come each year in September and October, when Geneen and his court come over to Brussels for several weeks, for the annual Business Plan Review. From ten in the morning, sometimes till well after midnight, Geneen or his deputy sits in the swivel chair in the air-conditioned room and watches each managing director come forward with his presentation of his plan. He cross-examines each one in front of his colleagues, who are encouraged to join in the ritual. "We all said to each other 'what a farce!'," said one ex-managing director, "but you must have this theatrical atmosphere to force you to think."

*    *    *    *    *

. . . Geneen takes the capitalist system to its logical limits, and for any ambitious businessman, it is an anticlimax to retreat back from those limits.

## THE REGIME OF REASON

To rule over his thousand companies, Geneen developed his unique system of controls. From his years as an accountant, studying other men's mistakes, he was determined that *his* organisation should never get out of hand. Geneen's system was to become famous far outside ITT; it became the subject of study in business schools, in magazine articles, and in management courses all over America and Europe. . . .

. . . Geneen was constructing a system of management which, he was confident, would long outlive him; like Alfred Sloan, the founder of General Motors who was one of his heroes (and who, like Geneen, put his company before everything), he was building for posterity.

It sounds, as he describes it, more like a system for ruling the world than for ruling a company. When I met him, I asked him about the question of the bigness of business; wasn't there a point at which companies got too big? He asked what I meant about being big: ITT, when you looked at it, was really a group of companies, many of them quite small, which were held together by a common logic, a system of reason. But wasn't it too big to be controlled by one man? No, he wasn't controlling it, he explained, he was only teaching people how to do it; once they had learnt the system, others could work it just as well; when you've seen it work, he said—with missionary fervour in his voice—you realise it's *the only way.* But didn't the size of a vast corporation, I went on, have a diminishing effect on individuals—particularly young people? No, he said, people in inefficient small companies weren't happy—there's nothing satisfying about inefficiency. ITT can release people's full resources, can show them how to work rationally. As for young people, he went on, what do *they* know about work, and making jobs? They're a problem that he was glad to leave to the next generation.

He insists, again and again, that his system is based on nothing more sinister than logic. It is, as he says, the only way. In his 1971 annual report he restated once again his philosophy:

> More than 200 days a year are devoted to management meetings at various organisational levels throughout the world. In these meetings in New York, Brussels, Hong Kong, Buenos Aires, decisions are made based on logic—the business logic that results in making decisions which are almost inevitable because all the facts on which the decisions must be based are available. The function of the planning and the meetings is to force the logic out into the open where its value and need are seen by all. That logic cannot be legislated or ordered. It comes as a natural process.

He runs the company, he likes to explain, not by giving orders, but by uncovering the facts. "The real tyrant here," said one New York executive, "isn't Geneen; it's the facts and figures. What makes Geneen mad is to discover someone trying to hide his mistakes. What makes him happiest is for someone to come to him and admit his failure; I've seen people fortify their positions that way." Geneen impresses all his colleagues by his ability to ferret out the true "unshakeable facts" about a company or a product, uncovering layers of false facts before he reaches the truth; and it is this, perhaps more than anything, which has made ITT more proof against disasters than other conglomerates. In 1965 Geneen produced a short homily for his staff called *Facts:* "Effectively immediately I want every report specifically, directly and bluntly to state at the beginning a summary containing the following facts in this order. . . ." He proclaimed that the highest art of professional management requires the literal ability to "smell" a "real fact" from all others. All his staff, he insisted, must become connoisseurs of "unshakeable fact," and warned them: "You will hear a lot more of this term, 'unshakeable facts' as we go forward."

The very diversity of the ITT empire makes it easier—so their managers argue—to control it objectively. As one of them put it: "If you're responsible for only one product, like cars or hotels, you get emotionally involved; you get to like them too much." ITT executives are taught not to make things, but to make money (engineers, with their hopeless pride in perfection, are their villains).

Lacking this sense of involvement with solid objects, they are forced more single-mindedly back on to their own ambition and ability to make profits. Nor is the organisation of ITT reassuring in psychological terms; "It's not a good company," as one of them said, "for people who like a structured world; you may think you're in charge of something, but you'll soon find out that there are two or three other men working on the same thing."

It is implicit in Geneen's whole system that no man is given full responsibility for anything; and the more senior the managers, the more they are subject to inspection, checking and cross-checking. The managing director of a huge subsidiary may appear to be his own master; but each department will be supervised by the experts from head office—experts on products, accounting, public relations, quality control or real-estate—who have their own direct lines to the top. Like all despotisms, ITT is based on a system of divide and rule; but the divisions can be justified in the name of profits. In each monthly report and at each monthly meeting, the senior managers have to report the "red flag items" which indicate a prediction gone wrong, a surprise unforeseen. As soon as the red flag goes up, the experts will move in and "swarm over him." Or, to use another ITT phrase, "Geneen unleashes the pack."

As the basic safeguard, Geneen has his special band of comptrollers, in each of the companies, reporting directly to the chief comptroller in New York, an accountant of legendary thoroughness called Herb Knortz, one of the few men who dares argue openly with Geneen. From his vantage point, checking all the movements of inventories, profits, receivables, Knortz can detect the first signs of incipient losses, excessive stocks or unprofitable products, and if the local managing director has failed to notice them, he will be in trouble.

*     *     *     *     *

From

# EXECUTIVE CONTROL—THE CATALYST*

*By William Travers Jerome, III*

### KINDS OF CONTROL

The word "control" has the serious shortcoming of having different meanings in different contexts. Most of these meanings are negative ones that connote such things as faultfinding or obedience by subordinates to instructions emanating from superiors. That "control" should evoke these meanings is unfortunate. . . . Control in any broad management sense bespeaks a planned rather than haphazard approach by a society to the employment of both its human and material resources. Control represents those forces that make it possible for any organized activity, whether public or private, to function purposefully. . . .

Control in its broad or managerial sense . . . can be quite appropriately defined as "the presence in a business of that force which guides it to a predetermined objective by means of predetermined policies and decisions."[1] By "force" presumably is meant (1) management's conviction of the importance of continuous and systematic planning and (2) availability of the skills necessary to perform the planning (i.e., controlling) properly. . . .

Those with engineering backgrounds . . . seem to regard modern systems of managerial control as "strikingly similar to simple servomechanisms of the electromechanical type." Since electromechanical control systems are designed to maintain a level of performance (e.g., temperature) between predetermined limits, it is assumed that "preventiveness is the essential attribute of a control system. . . . The existence of a control system is justified by its ability to enforce its norms. Precision in the determination of norms is of elemental importance in industrial control."[2] Such a concept of control is highly appropriate for machines or some shop operations. It is far too rigid and uncompromising a concept, however, for the world of people.

For a proper perspective of the meaning of control, it is important to recognize that a whole host of important but relatively mundane controls lie outside of management's customary scope and concern. These other kinds of control help to set a precise pattern of rules and procedures, not unlike those of . . . servomechanisms, . . . to expedite the handling of a firm's routine operations. This particular pattern is known in the accounting trade as the "system of internal control." . . . It should prove both interesting and suggestive simply to classify controls on the basis of the *use* to which a given control is put. The following classification might result:

1. *Controls used to standaridize performance* in order to increase efficiency and to lower costs. Included might be time and motion studies, inspections, written procedures, or production schedules.

2. *Controls used to safeguard company assets* from theft, wastage, or misuse. Such controls typically would emphasize division of responsibilities, separation of operational, custodial, and accounting activities, and an adequate system of authorization and record keeping.

---

* From *Executive Controll—The Catalyst* by Wm. Travers Jerome III. Copyright ©1961 by John Wiley & Sons, Inc. Reprinted by permission. Excerpts pp. 31–34.

[1] "The Planning and Control Concept," *The Controller,* September 1954, p. 403.

[2] J. V. McKenna, "The Basic Theory of Managerial Control," *Mechanical Engineering,* vol. 77, no. 8 (August 1955), pp. 180 ff.

3. *Controls used to standardize quality* in order to meet the specifications of either customers or company engineers. Blueprints, inspection, and statistical quality controls would typify the measures employed to preserve the integrity of the product (or service) marketed by the company.

4. *Controls designed to set limits within which delegated authority can be exercised without further top management approval.* Organization and procedure manuals, policy directives, and internal audits would help to spell out the limits within which subordinates have a free hand.

5. *Controls used to measure on-the-job performance.* Typical of such controls would be special reports, output per hour or per employee, internal audits, and perhaps budgets or standard costs.

6. *Controls used for planning and programming operations.* Such controls would include sales and production forecasts, budgets, various cost standards, and standards of work measurement.

7. *Controls necessary to allow top management to keep the firm's various plans and programs in balance.* Typical of such controls would be a master budget, policy manuals, organization manuals, and such organization techniques as committees and the use of outside consultants. The overriding need for such controls would be to provide the necessary capital for . . . operations and to maximize profits.

8. *Controls designed to motivate individuals within* a firm to contribute their best efforts. Such controls necessarily would involve ways of recognizing achievement through such things as promotions, awards for suggestions, or some form of profit sharing. . . .

Certain similarities and dissimilarities in these techniques at once appear. For example, there is a preventional or compliance aspect characteristic of the controls in groupings 1 through 3. This grouping consists of the controls used to standardize performance, to safeguard assets, and to insure quality. These controls are really in the nature of directives or procedures that must be followed. Compliance with these is not left to the discretion of anyone using them. Instead, the effectiveness of performance will be judged primarily by the degree of compliance attained.

The second grouping, on the other hand, consists of controls that are intended to provide some elements of latitude to those who are affected by them. They are useful in helping to set the goals, to plan the work, to appraise the performance, and to set the tone for the firm's activity. These controls consist of the remainder of the items on the preceding list. These are the controls designed to set limits for delegated authority, to set norms against which performance can be measured, to facilitate company planning, to keep overall company balance in the interest of optimizing company objectives, and to motivate action.

This "control" classification is striking primarily in the way a number of these controls appear to belong appropriately in either of these two major groupings. Standard costs or budget, for example, can be used to compel compliance. Thus, they provide the means for management to set the desired level of performance expected of subordinates. Variance of actual from anticipated performance is the signal built into these techniques for flagging possible investigation of the reasons for deviations.

Standard costs, and particularly budgets, are also the principal techniques for reflecting a firm's plans. They provide a method for a given level of management to gauge its own performance. These uses are constructive as they encourage both self-evaluation and the forward look.

Control techniques such as budgets that are interchangeable between the two groupings provide ample room for misunderstanding. When budgets are regarded as "planning," it is questionable whether they should be used to compel compliance. Thus, the score envisioned by a golfer on the first tee is not the same as what he intends to set for his bets! Or, as a further example, when internal auditing is sold to lower levels of management on constructive grounds, its compliance or policeman's role must be exercised with considerable restraint.

There is a second significant thing about the preceding classification. All these control techniques, except for those in the final classification, have one thing in common: each can measure performance.

In other words, each of the controls listed serves as a norm or standard of conduct. Against this standard, actual performance can be compared. Unless such comparison is made, the standards have limited value.

Another way to say this is that "control" is not something intrinsic to a given technique any more than "measurement" is inherent in a given yardstick. "Control" comes from the conscious use of such devices to influence action. This influence (or control) may be in terms of either or both: (1) the thought, the analysis, the planning, and the cooperative effort that go into constructing particular norms or yardsticks, and (2) the corrective action taken when a comparison of results with the projected performance indicates the need.

Controls governing routine and repetitive operations stress compliance, as mentioned earlier. Their primary function, therefore, is to serve in the area of internal control.

Management controls, on the other hand, serve both as a measure of performance and as conditioners of the firm's working environment. The attitudes of planning and of self-evaluation are particularly powerful influences in a firm, for they are among the key forces that contribute to decisive and continuous progress. This capability of any given executive control to motivate constructive action is by all odds its most important characteristic. This contrasts with the compliance or command feature of other types of control.

*From*

# CORPORATE STRATEGY: AN ANALYTICAL APPROACH TO BUSINESS POLICY FOR GROWTH AND EXPANSION*

*By H. Igor Ansoff*

### SYNERGY AND CAPABILITY PROFILES

. . . In this chapter we begin to explore *synergy,* which is one of the major components of the firm's product-market strategy. It is concerned with the desired characteristics of fit between the firm and its new product-market entries. In business literature it is frequently described as the "2 + 2 = 5" effect to denote the fact that the firm seeks a product-market posture with a combined performance that is greater than the sum of its parts.

\*    \*    \*    \*    \*

. . . We shall derive a method for qualitative estimation of joint effects. In the process it will be shown that measurement of synergy is similar in many ways to what is frequently called "evaluation of strengths and weaknesses." In synergy, *joint* effects are measured between two product-markets; in strength and weakness evaluation, the firm's competences are rated relative to some desired performance level. The former contributes to the decision to make a new entry; the latter, to the decision to exploit certain strengths or to remedy certain deficiencies within the firm. Thus the difference is largely one of viewpoint.

\*    \*    \*    \*    \*

## Concept of Synergy

. . . Each product-market makes a contribution to the overall profitability of the firm. Each product brings in annual sales of $S$ dollars. Operating costs of $O$ dollars are incurred for labor, materials, overhead, administration, and depreciation. To develop the product, to provide facilities and equipment, and to set up a distribution network, an investment of $I$ dollars must be made in product development, tooling, buildings, machinery, inventories, etc.

The annual rate of return, ROI, on product $P$, can be written in the form

$$\text{ROI} = \frac{S_1 - O_1}{I_1}$$

Expressed in words, the formula states that the return on investment from a product can be obtained by dividing the difference between operating revenues and costs during a period by the average investment which is needed to support the product. A similar expression can be written for all products in the product line: $P_1, P_2, \ldots, P_n$.

If all the products are unrelated in any way, the total sales of the firm will be

$$S_T = S_1 + S_2 + \ldots + S_n$$

And similarly for operating costs and investment

$$O_T = O_1 + \ldots + O_n$$
$$I_T = I_1 + I_2 + \ldots + I_n$$

The return on the investment for the firm as a whole will be

$$(\text{ROI})_T = \frac{S_T - O_T}{I_T}$$

This condition obtains whenever the revenues, the operating costs, and the investments are unrelated. Therefore, their totals can be obtained through simple summations. In practice this is very nearly true in an investment firm which holds unrelated securities, or in a holding company in which there is no interaction among the operating units. A picture of the total profitability is obtained through a simple consolidation of the individual statements.

In a majority of firms, advantages of scale exist under which a large firm with the same total sales as a number of small firms can operate at a cost which is lower than the sum of the operating costs for the separate enterprises. The investment in a large firm can be similarly lower than a simple sum of the respective investments. Using symbols, this is equivalent to saying that for

$$S_s = S_T$$

we have

$$O_s \leqslant O_T$$
$$I_s \leqslant I_T$$

where subscript $s$ denotes the respective quantities for an integrated firm and subscript $t$, the sum for independent enterprises.[1] As a result, the potential return on investment for an integrated firm is higher than the composite return which would be obtained if the same dollar volumes for its respective products were produced by a number of independent firms:

---

[1] The symbol $\leqslant$ means less than or equal to; the symbol $\geqslant$ means greater than or equal to.

$$(ROI)_S > (ROI)_T$$

A similar argument can, of course, be made by keeping the total investment fixed. In this case

$$S_S \geq S_T$$
$$O_S \leqq O_T$$
$$I_S = I_T$$

For a given level of investment, a firm with a complete product line can usually realize the advantages of higher total revenues and/or lower operating costs than competing independent firms.

The consequences of this joint effect are clearly very far-reaching. A firm which takes care to select its products and markets so as to optimize the effect has great flexibility in choosing its competitive stance. It can gain a larger share of the market by lowering prices, it can choose to make a larger investment in research and development than its competitors, or it can maximize its ROI and attract growth capital to the firm. All this can be done while remaining fully competitive with firms whose product-markets are not as carefully chosen.

### Types of Synergy

This effect which can produce a combined return on the firm's resources greater than the sum of its parts is frequently referred to as "2 + 2 = 5." We shall call this effect *synergy*. . . . One way to classify the several types of synergy is in terms of the components of the ROI formula:

*1. Sales Synergy.* This can occur when products use common distribution channels, common sales administration, or common warehousing. Opportunity for tie-in sales offered by a complete line of related products increases the productivity of a sales force. Common advertising, sales promotion, past reputation can all have a multiple payoff for the same dollar spent.

*2. Operating Synergy.* This is the result of higher utilization of facilities and personnel, spreading of overhead, advantages of common learning curves, and large lot purchasing.

*3. Investment Synergy.* This can result from joint use of plant, common raw materials inventories, carryover of research and development from one product to another, common tooling, common machinery.

*4. Management Synergy.* Although not immediately apparent from the formula, this type is an important contributor to the total effect. As will be shown below, management in different types of industry faces different strategic, organizational, and operating problems. If upon entering a new industry management finds the new problems to be similar to the ones it has encountered in the past, it is in a position to provide forceful and effective guidance to the newly acquired venture. Since competent top-level management is a scarce commodity, very positive enhancement of performance can result in the combined enterprise. Thus synergy will be strong.

If, on the other hand, the problems in the acquired area are new and unfamiliar, not only will positive synergy be low, but there is a distinct danger of a negative effect of top-management decisions. For example, management of a firm in the defense industry would be at an actual disadvantage if it attempts, without prior experience, to assume responsibility for pricing and advertising decisions in a higher competitive consumer area, such as the cigarette or the automobile industry.

This example points to the fact that management synergy, as well as the other types, can be negative as well as positive. An attempt at joint use of a facility which is not suited for manufacturing of a new product (e.g., use of airframe factories for consumer aluminum products), or of an organization which is not set up to perform a new function (e.g., use of

**TABLE 1**
**Functional Synergy between Industry Groups**

| Diversifying Industry | New Industry | | | |
|---|---|---|---|---|
| | Functional Capability | Defense-Space | Producers | Consumers |
| Defense-Space | GM<br>R&D<br>Mfg.<br>Mkt. | High<br>High<br>High<br>High | High<br>Moderate<br>Low<br>Low | Moderate<br>Low<br>Negative<br>Negative |
| Producers | GM<br>R&D<br>Mfg.<br>Mkt. | High<br>Moderate<br>Low<br>Low | High<br>High<br>High<br>High | Moderate<br>Low<br>Low<br>Low |
| Consumers | GM<br>R&D<br>Mfg.<br>Mkt. | Moderate<br>Low<br>Negative<br>Negative | Moderate<br>Low<br>Low<br>Low | High<br>High<br>High<br>High |

Legend:
GM—general management.
R&D—research and development.
Mfg.—manufacturing.
Mkt.—marketing.

\* Note: This table is from H. I. Ansoff and J. F. Weston, "Merger Objectives and Organization Structure," *Review of Economics and Business*, August 1963, pp. 49–58.

a consumer sales organization to sell to industrial customers) can result in total profitability which is *lower* than the combined profitability of two independent operations.

Table 1 demonstrates the possibility of negative synergy through a comparison of competences in the principal functional areas found in typical firms in different industry groups. For purposes of comparison we are assuming that a firm in one of the groups shown in the first column diversifies into an industry group shown in the first line.

It is seen that the best carryover of functional competence will occur in general management, where many practices and skills in accounting, finance, industrial relations, and public relations are common among industries. However, even here the differences in the competitive environment and in basic resource allocation problems have led us to give unequal ratings to different pairs of industrial areas. In manufacturing and marketing where organizational forms, cost controls, and individual skills become more specified, greater differences in synergy appear among the groups. The differences become so great between space defense and consumer groups as to create potentially negative synergy.

It should be noted that the above table describes *potential* (rather than actual) synergy. Whether the indicated joint effects will, in fact, materialize depends on the manner in which the new acquisition is integrated into the parent organization . . .

**Startup Synergy and Operating Synergy**

As discussed above, the synergistic effect can be measured in either of two ways: by estimating the cost economics to the firm from a joint operation for a given level or revenue, or by estimating the increase in net revenue for a given level of investment. In this section we shall take the first approach and discuss the nature of synergy through analysis of cost economies and diseconomies.

Acquisition of a new product-market area goes through two successive phases, startup and operating. In addition to identifiable physical costs, such as the costs of facilities and inventories, the costs associated with startup include the highly intangible costs of learning a new kind of business: setting up a new organization, establishing new rules and procedures, hiring new skills and competences, paying for mistakes in developing organizational relationships and for early bad decisions made in unfamiliar business environment, and costs of gaining customer acceptance. Although these are one-time costs, most of them are not capitalized, but charged to operating expense during the startup period. They are difficult to pinpoint, since many of them are not identified (no firm is likely to have a special account labeled "management blunders made in startup"), but are evident only indirectly through substandard operating efficiencies.[2] During the period in which they are incurred they put the firm at a disadvantage with respect to the established competitors in the field, since the latter no longer incur any of these costs.

Whether the firm will, in fact, have to incur these startup costs depends on how well its skills and resources are matched to the requirements of the new product-market area. If the required new capabilities are very different from those of the firm, then, as discussed earlier, cost diseconomies may result in any of the major functional areas. Thus startup in new business can have potentially negative as well as positive synergy; a firm with positive synergy will have a competitive advantage over a firm which lacks it.

\*    \*    \*    \*    \*

. . . During the startup phase, synergy can occur in two forms: in the form of dollar savings to the firm thanks to the existence of competences appropriate to the new line of business, and in the form of time savings in becoming fully competitive.

The second category of costs incurred in a new entry is the costs of a going concern: the operating costs and the investment required to support the operation. Here two basic effects operate to produce synergy. One is the advantage of scale—many operations will produce at a lower unit cost when the total volume is increased. For example, purchasing in large quantities offers the advantage of discounts; production in large quantities makes possible more efficient methods and procedures and hence lower direct costs. Many other well-known examples can be given.

A more subtle effect in synergy is a distribution of the burden of overhead expenses over a number of products. This arises from the fact that most overhead functions require a certain minimum level of effort for a wide range of business volume. If volume can be added through a type of diversification which makes use of the existing overhead services, economies will be effected in both the new and the old business. For example, a sales management and administration function must be staffed regardless of whether the firm has one product or a full line; the same research must be conducted regardless of whether it supports one or many products (so long as the products are all based on the same technology).

If top-management talent in a firm is not fully utilized in running the present business, and if its training and experience are relevant, it can provide the most critical ingredient to the new operation. Unfortunately, this potentially strongest component of synergy is also most difficult to measure. Many diversification histories can be cited in which an erroneous estimate was made, either through failure to realize that top management was already fully committed and that new responsibilities resulted in a thin spread of talent or through failure to realize that new business called for different types of talent and experience and that synergy, in fact, did not exist.

---

[2] This is one major reason for the difficulty encountered in determining marginal cash flows for new product-market entries.

CASE MATERIALS AND
SOCIAL SCIENCE READINGS FOR

# PART V Leadership and Organization Development

## LEADERSHIP AS AN IMPORTANT FUNCTION OF MANAGEMENT

In previous parts of the book, we see that managers are concerned with certain key tasks which they perform. These tasks are important functions in the organization if the organization goals are to be achieved. They are functions in the sense that the heart has a certain function if the physical body is to achieve its purposes: walking, talking, or thinking. Part II examined the tasks of strategic planning and organization design. Part III centered on the allocation of resources (principally fixed resources) through financial planning and control. Part IV turned to allocation of resources (principally day-to-day operating labor force and materials) by use of management science.

In each of these tasks and functions, it was our purpose not only to understand something of the specific tasks (e.g., organization design or scientific decision making), but also more importantly to see how that task related to other organizational tasks with which the manager must cope: financial control was related to the way he or she designs the organization structure; decision making was related to human behavior.

In Part V, we will be changing the center of attention. Instead of centering on *things,* such as organization goals and operating technology, with subsidiary and allied interest in how this relates to *people,* we shall center on the people side of the managerial system and ask how human behavior is affected by technology or how human behavior affects technology.

The particular kind of human behavior we are interested in is leadership. This concept has meant many things to many people. It has been studied by historians (does history make the man, or does the man make history?), sociologists (charismatic versus legal leaders), small group sociologists (is there such a thing as one leader, or is leadership shared? and is authoritarian or democratic leadership more effective?), and political scientists (are monarchies, oligarchies, or democracies best?).

For our purposes, leadership is the sum total of (1) the day-to-day actions of a manager as he or she attempts to influence others in ways that help the organization achieve its goal, and (2) actions that help the manager to find out when to change organizational goals, internal operations, or policies. Leadership may be exercised by anyone in the organization who is interested in doing this—from the bottom of the pyramid to the top. In fact, the concept allows a subordinate in the hierarchy to become a leader in relation to his or her boss. But throughout all ages, the function of leadership and the task itself has been recognizably present in the relatively few who are most interested and most successful in this kind of behavior. In organizations from the Catholic Church to the Chase Manhattan Bank or the Black Panthers, this means the managers.

## EXPEDIENT OBLIGATIONS AND SOCIAL RESPONSIBILITY OF LEADERS

It is one of the central theses of this book that the manager who is able to think through the *reality* of action problems (to diagnose what is going on in the technical system and the people system) in some depth, who knows some of the managerial techniques for coping with one's organizational world, and who is skilled in using one's own brain to apply both of these kinds of knowledge, will be more successful with people *and* things.

Only managers who are informed and skilled can discharge either their expedient obligations or their ethical responsibilities. For example, it is one who can understand the motivations of people in the Manco Corporation, who understands the technology of its Systems Department, and who is acquainted with techniques or authority, integrative behavior, or organization development methods, that can use his or her mind best to cope in day-to-day relations with others. This kind of manager also has a higher probability of being respected by others as one who is able to cope. The manager is "obliged" through necessity of expediency to use what knowledge he or she can to make informed judgments. Otherwise the organization will not be as successful and leadership actions "won't work" as well. Either there will be defective technology and efficiency, or there will be messy human relations, or both. And for those who feel ethical responsibilities to operate an excellent company for society, or to operate an organization in which human beings are treated with dignity, such informed judgments and actions are the surest way to fulfill them.

## CONCEPTS AND THEORIES OF HUMAN BEHAVIOR

The readings in Part V include a number of concepts and theories from the behavioral sciences that aid the manager in understanding the human system. Sociologists have devoted much time and research to the concept of *roles*, the recurring (habitual) actions of an individual, interrelated with the repetitive (habitual) action of others so that one can predict what will happen between the people playing the roles. The concept is (not surprisingly) roughly analogous to the various roles in a theatre performance or a movie. The roles in an organization, *together,* form the social system of the company. Understanding of the role of the company president in British Commercial Investments, Ltd., in relation to the role of the general manager of its subsidiary, Harrogate Asphalt

Products Ltd., will help the student to understand why these managers act the way they do, and enable one to see possibilities for a more productive leadership pattern.

Psychologists have contributed much to the understanding of basic human needs, as well as to the understanding of the games people play (in the form of defense mechanisms) in organizations. These insights may well enable one, as president of Parkerville, Ltd., to understand better why an important company committee operates as it does.

In the four cases in Part V, one may also see how different managerial values and attitudes affect how one manager acts differently from another. . . some may be motivated to do a good job for the company, others may be motivated to do a good job for themselves, and still others may seek power, prestige, or simply companionship on the job.

In most of the cases in Part V we see some form of human conflict. Perhaps this is not so unusual, since organized life implies that one person must be somehow related to other people around him or her. Nature seems to make each human being different from each other human being, and in order for people to arrive at a concurrence about any joint undertaking, a process of conflict and conflict resolution is always present. One question is—what kinds of conflict are positive (helping people learn to work together) and what kinds are negative (destructive to learning). Allied to this is another question: What kinds of leadership action promote positive conflicts and eliminate negative conflicts? As we study conflict between managers in Manco Corporation, between conglomerate president and local company president in Harrogate Asphalt Products Ltd., or between headquarters and subsidiary in Bergen Metalfabrik, we will want to distinguish between different kinds of conflict and their causes, as well as between alternative leadership actions that might be used in the specific situation. Readings interspersed with these cases will help to identify such things as causes of conflict and actions for conflict resolution.

## PRACTICES AND TECHNOLOGIES OF LEADERSHIP

It is one thing to see in theory how human beings behave in organizations. It is a somewhat different thing to see the details—the concrete facts—of how managers in the cases behave in their day-to-day dealings with others. Mr. Lampton in Harrogate Asphalt Products Ltd., seems to use a combination of strategic competence and authority. Executives in Bergen Metalfabrik temporarily turn over at least part of the leadership to organization development consultants, who use team building techniques. To see the practices of these men in action helps one to learn a deeper and more concrete meaning for leadership styles like "participation," "team building," or "technical competence."

## TRAINING (OR) LEARNING AS A LEADERSHIP STYLE

One of the cases in Part V, Parkerville, Ltd., offers a rare opportunity to understand how training programs might be used as a leadership style by some managers. It is important to understand that what is "training" to the professor or manager who designs a program is, from the standpoint of the student in a program, "learning." Therefore, either "training" or "learning" sometimes comes within our definition of leadership.

In the Parkerville case, the committee which sets up a training program has certain goals in mind. Its members, mostly operating executives, want the participants in the program to learn certain skills, attributes, or knowledge. In other words, they expect to exert influence over the future behavior of the managers who attend the program. At the same time, the director of personnel, and the outside professor/consultant who design the program, have *another* and *different* set of goals. They expect to exert influence toward different skills and attitudes, and therefore to influence future behavior of the participants in a different way.

The case offers opportunity, in addition, to understand something of the *process* through which people go when they learn new attitudes or skills. Knowledge of this process may itself help the manager in trying to perform the leadership function.

# 14.  HARROGATE ASPHALT
PRODUCTS LTD. (AR)

---

# Case Introduction

---

**SYNOPSIS**

British Commercial Investments, Ltd. (BCI), is an industrial holding company with headquarters in London. With 16 subsidiary companies which engage in a wide variety of industrial activities, the parent company is in the process of changing its philosophy from that of an investment banker, buying stocks in companies, to that of a conglomerate which takes active interest in managing the companies it buys.

Based on recommendations of a BCI staff analyst (who later becomes president of BCI), BCI acquires Harrogate Asphalt Products Company—a company located some distance from London, and which has a record of successful performance.

Soon after the acquisition, it became apparent that Mr. Lampton, BCI executive representative on Harrogate's board, disagreed markedly with Mr. Denham, the president of Harrogate. Denham, who had been relatively autonomous in operating the company, became increasingly subject to control by headquarters. The case describes the actions of both men as they attempt to operate the subsidiary company.

**WHY THIS CASE IS INCLUDED**

This case offers an opportunity to view some of the management problems centering around the acquisition of a subsidiary. The reader can see how differences in policy, management practices, and personality variables all provide special strains on both the holding company executives as well as subsidiary management personnel. Questions of policy evaluation, conflict on both the individual and the total company level, and organization structure are raised. In this last area, the structural questions center on decisions concerning whether or not to merge two subsidiary organizations, the type of interaction between the headquarters company and the subsidiary, and the role of the boards of directors for subsidiary organizations. All of these questions should be of special interest given the current merger movement and trends toward industrial centralization.

## DIAGNOSTIC AND PREDICTIVE QUESTIONS

The readings included with this case are marked (*). The author index at the end of this book locates the other readings.

1. Seymour Tilles defines a strategy as a set of goals and major policies. As such, a strategy determines how a corporation relates to its environment. What are the strategies of BCI and Harrogate Asphalt Products Ltd., as expressed by Mr. Lampton and Mr. Denham? Are they internally consistent? Using the framework provided by Tilles, evaluate the strategy of the corporation from the perspective of both BCI and Harrogate.

Read:   *Tilles, "How to Evaluate Corporate Strategy."

2. The strategy of an organization also determines what kind of synergy can be exploited. In order to utilize the effects of synergy, management selects activities that are mutually reinforcing so that the output of the total system is greater than the sum of the outputs of the activities taken singly. What are the prospects for synergy resulting from the planned merger between Harrogate and the Trowbridge Company? Are there other potential sources of synergy suggested in the case?

Read:   Ansoff, *Corporate Strategy: An Analytical Approach to Business Policy for Growth and Expansion.*

3. Some theories of business behavior suggest that there is a considerable difference in the organization, structure, and behavior of owner- and manager-controlled firms. What changes in ownership and control occurred in this case? What changes in strategy relating to staffing, diversification, and management is BCI trying to bring about in Harrogate?

Read:   *Monsen and Downs, "A Theory of Large Managerial Firms."

4. Initially the role of the managing director of Harrogate was defined by Stanley, Denham, and the organizational "culture" of an independent Harrogate. After the merger, a new organizational "culture" was established under corporation law such that the role definition of the managing director was strongly influenced by BCI top management.

Look closely at the behavior of all parties in the case. Then try to write a few sentences which describe: (a) the new role of Lampton in the BCI-Harrogate organization, (b) the new role of Sample in this organization, and (c) The new role of Denham in the BCI-Harrogate organization.

Read:   *Katz and Kahn, *The Social Psychology of Organization.*
        Levinson, "Role, Personality, and Social Structure in the Organizational Setting."

5. Why did Lampton feel that he must shift from a passive role of investment banker to the more active role of a professional manager? Do you think this change was beneficial to the company and to society?

Read:   Friedman, "A Friedman Doctrine: The Social Responsibility of Business Is to Increase Its Profits." Eells and Walton, *Conceptual Foundations of Business,* pp. 185 et. seq.

6. What do the role expectations established by BCI management for the BCI nominee director do to the authority structure of subsidiary corporations? Is the change of authority legitimate? On what grounds?

Read: *Drucker, *The Future of Industrial Man.* Etzioni, "Authority Structure and Organizational Effectiveness." O'Donnell, "The Source of Managerial Authority"; see also readings for Question 5 above.

7. Why did Mr. Lampton refuse to discuss issues on an informal basis with Mr. Denham? What do you think was Mr. Lampton's objective for insisting that these issues be brought before a formal meeting of the board of directors?

Read: *Hampton, Summer, and Webber, *Organizational Behavior and the Practice of Management.* Evan, "Organization Man and Due Process of Law."

8. What changes in motivation might be expected for Mr. Lampton, Mr. Denham, and Mr. Sample as a result of the changed authority structure and evolving status and roles of these three men as discussed in the case?

Read: Maslow, *Motivation and Personality.* Gellerman, *Motivation and Productivity.*

9. Mr. Lampton stated that he was against the authoritarian approach of Mr. Denham. Did he mean by this statement that he favored the participative approach to management?

Read: McGregor, *The Human Side of Enterprise.*

10. What is Lampton's perception of a *policy decision* in a large corporation located in current British or American society? How might this explain his "doubt that Denham ever made real policy decisions?" Didn't Denham discontinue unprofitable operations, make laborsaving technical improvements ahead of his competitors, and otherwise operate a profitable company?

Read: Leavitt, *Managerial Psychology,* pp. 22–26.

11. How might Lampton's concept of "policy decisions" contribute to conflict between himself and Denham? What other sources of conflict can be found in the case?

Read: Litterer, "Conflict in Organizations: A Re-Examination."

## POLICY QUESTIONS

12. Assume that you are a member of the planning staff of BCI headquarters. Outline the rationale as well as a recommendation relation to (*a*) the approval or disapproval of the Harrogate-Trowbridge merger, (*b*) if you recommend approval, how would you go about "merging" the management of these two subsidiaries.

(See Questions 1, 2, and 3 above.)

13. Analyze and evaluate the consistency of the BCI policy as it relates to (*a*) the role of the BCI nominee director on subsidiary boards, (*b*) the requirement for "in-depth" staffing at the subsidiary level, and (*c*) the initiation of merger decisions at the BCI headquarters level.

(See Questions 4 and 5 above.)

14. Assume that you are a management analyst reporting directly to the president of BCI. Analyze the decision-making structure of BCI and Harrogate and prepare a letter for the president indicating a summary of the results and any recommendations that you may feel necessary.

   Read:   Curtice, "General Motors Organization Philosophy and Structure." Shillinglaw, *Cost Accounting.*

15. Assume that you are a consultant to Mr. Lampton in this case. What advice would you give him concerning his relationships with Mr. Denham and for other managing directors of subsidiaries in the future? Outline a number of possible approaches to the problem as you see it in this particular case and deduce the likely consequences of each before making a final suggestion to Mr. Lampton.

   (See Questions 6 through 11 above.) One additional approach would be to suggest that Lampton secure the services of a consultant in organization development. See Schein, *Process Consultation: Its Role in Organization Development.*

# Case Text*

## COMPANY BACKGROUND

This case concerns the financial and managerial relationships between two companies: British Commercial Investments, Ltd. (BCI), an industrial holding company located in London, and Harrogate Asphalt Products, Ltd., located in Frampton, a small town in Yorkshire near Harrogate.

BCI, Ltd., started life as the Pentiling Rubber Plantations, Ltd., a Malayan rubber company. The directors decided to diversify out of the politically risky area of their operations, and acquired a number of small- to medium-sized private companies, mainly in the United Kingdom. Twelve years ago, the last of Pentiling's rubber plantations was disposed of and the company was renamed British Commercial Investments, Ltd. The BCI group now comprises some 16 subsidiary companies, with operations ranging from the manufacture of oil drilling equipment to electrical components and from special steel fabrication to the construction of agricultural buildings.

Mr. Henry Lampton, the managing director of BCI, described the group's progress as follows:

> Our subsequent growth, due partly to the acquisition of new subsidiaries and partly to internal expansion has been pretty satisfac-

* Copyright 1968, l'Institut pour l'Etude des Méthodes de Direction de l'Enterprise (IMEDE), Lausanne, Switzerland. The original version of this case has been revised and edited for use in this book.

tory. Our gross tangible assets have increased in the last seven years from £9,000,000 to £31,000,000, and our pretax profits from £900,000 to £3,400,000. This large growth has caused us to institute increasingly elaborate systems for forecasting financial requirements and planning to meet them. We have instituted what we call the BCI Three-Year-Forecast, which involves much forward thinking in detail. This kind of planning is accepted as essential in modern company planning, but even if it wasn't, something very similar would be needed to ensure the continued strength of BCI.

Furthermore, our present investment effort is directed mainly toward internal expansion by existing subsidiaries, and the acquisition of no new subsidiaries, unless they complement technologically those we already have. These two efforts—growth from within and acquisition of related companies, are what will produce the kind of profit we are interested in.

We have been trying recently to provide additional help to our subsidiary companies. In today's world, we do not think that they can expand to their full potential, without some help from central advisory services provided by BCI central staffs. Until very recently, however, we were rather diffident about providing these services to give specialized advice in particular fields; it would be fatal to try to force them on unwilling subsidiary managements. But recently, the success of our operations-research group, the welcome accorded to the monthly economic bulletins of our chief economist, and the demand for the services of our BCI Marketing Advisor, all attest the need felt by subsidiary managers. Only in the last three weeks, Mr. J. F. Roberts has joined our staff as computer adviser and has begun to familiarize himself with existing EDP Installations and projects. We have been too slow in recognizing the part that EDP techniques will play in the future. We hope to provide companies individually too small to justify their own EDP units with access to facilities, and to reduce costs for all by organizing a coordinated network available on a BCI-wide basis.

It is, however, a part of our philosophy that our subsidiaries should be of a size that they can support their own local functional staff of a high caliber. We are not suffering under the delusion that we can operate a large central-services team capable of resolving the local problems of such a diverse organization. Our advisory staff is used as catalysts.

Finally, I would like to say something about the services rendered to subsidiary operating companies by our BCI nominee director. We like to think that the personalities, experience and sometimes wider contacts that our directors have, are an important source of help to managements of BCI subsidiary companies.

In an interview with Mr. E. M. Jackson, another executive of BCI, the casewriter was told that

BCI maintains a [nonexecutive] director on the board of each of its subsidiaries, usually as chairman. Although nonexecutive, the BCI nominee normally visits each of his two or three companies about once a week, or twice every three weeks. The BCI nominee typically has had considerable industrial experience before joining our organization, either with a firm of accountants or management consultants, or with some other industrial corporation in an executive capacity. Many of them have university education, and have also attended advanced management programs such as the Administrative Staff College at Henley, Harvard Business School, Stanford Business School, or IMEDE in Lausanne.

After this statement by Jackson, Lampton continued.

The position of a BCI nominee director involves a rather heavy responsibility. We are not bankers, interested only in the financial aspects of the business. We are not there to take a normal dividend and let it go at that. In some financial holding companies, the local managements have the idea that they are entirely self-sufficient, except for dividends. At the same time, the directors nominated by the parent company to the boards of those subsidiaries create the impression that they are banker types—somewhat superior to getting into real operating problems. I personally believe that, in some such holding companies, the headquarters managers are being supine—they sit there with talent that could add to operations, but they make no contribution. Specifically, I am certain that in this day of complex technology and society, the director has a moral responsibility to help his managers in subsidiary companies—to encourage them to do planning for the future, to aid them in selecting and staffing their operations, and to give advice in areas where the director has talent or knowledge.

I can give you one example. In June, one year ago, BCI acquired the L.M. Trowbridge Company from the Trowbridge family. This company specializes in construction projects using asphalt products—parking lots, tennis courts, large industrial asphalt areas. It is to the benefit of everyone—BCI, Harrogate (which produces asphalt materials) and Trowbridge managers, and employees of both companies—to merge the operations of the two companies [Harrogate and Trowbridge]. In this way, both will be more profitable, enjoy more growth, and stand a much better chance of survival in the British economy. This autumn we are going to form a company to hold both Harrogate and Trowbridge, in the interest of better all round operations. The move was, inevitably, initiated by the BCI nominee chairman; the managers of Harrogate and Trowbridge don't have the same chance of standing back and taking an overall view of their operations. Without our BCI man, the merger would never have come about.

This shows how far we have moved from our position when BCI was still mainly involved in Malayan plantations and when our United Kingdom subsidiaries were regarded merely as diversified investments to be bought and sold; managerial responsibilities rested wholly with the underlying unit. Gradually we have come to acknowledge that this is an untenable position, and have taken on full responsibility for the underlying units, while allowing them a very wide degree of local autonomy in the main areas of their businesses.

## THE ACQUISITION OF HARROGATE

Seven years ago, Mr. Jack Stanley, a man of 82, approached a member of BCI management in London, with the idea that BCI might be interested in acquiring Harrogate Asphalt Products, Ltd., as part of the BCI group. Lampton, now managing director of BCI, was then 31 years old, lived in Birmingham, and was the BCI Midlands representative. He was assigned the job of doing a management evaluation of the Harrogate Company for possible acquisition.

Excerpts from Lampton's management and operating appraisal appear as Exhibit 1. It will be seen from that exhibit that his general conclusion was that Harrogate represented an excellent investment. He based this on a thorough analysis of finances, management, marketing, production, and raw material procurement. He also found that the Harrogate management had sold the less profitable coal business 14 years ago, concentrated on the more profitable asphalt operations, introduced a revolutionary technological process 11 years ago, and expanded production and sales.

## THE FIRST FIVE YEARS OF OPERATION

As of the time this case is written, BCI has owned Harrogate Asphalt for seven years. During the first year, the board of directors of Harrogate consisted of Jack Stanley, Paul Denham, and Gerald Kemp, a full-time executive in BCI who was assigned as the parent company representative. More information on these men appears in Exhibit 1.

During those years, Henry Lampton was serving as BCI representative in the Midlands and as nominee director of two BCI subsidiaries located near Birmingham. Nevertheless, Lampton recalls certain things which he knew went on during the first five years:

> In that period, the new equipment installed from Mason and Grant gave Harrogate an overwhelming competitive advantage in a business mainly served by fairly small companies, with the result that profits, sales, and return on new capital increased dramatically. Here is a company whose return on net worth was among the highest of any BCI company. Nevertheless, in my judgement, there were definite signs of trouble. Stanley died at the end of the second year. This left the BCI director and Paul Denham. About a year later, these two directors recommended as the third director Roger Sample, a young man who was hired by Denham six years ago (in the second year of our ownership). I'll have more to say about him later, but I acknowledged Roger from the first time I met him to be

a capable chap, though his experience in Harrogate was limited.

The Board meetings of those days consisted of a rather formal, cut-and-dried reporting of figures, once a month.

The casewriter, at this point, asked, "Was Paul Denham making the policy decisions?" Mr. Lampton responded:

If there were any policy decisions being made—though I doubt there were.

Also, in about the second year, Harrogate suddenly found itself with a strike on its hands. Denham was at loggerheads with the union[1] and he was at a loss as to what to do. The BCI director had to go up there and deal with the union, and a settlement was reached. As I recall, Denham simply gave up and said that he could not deal with them.

Also, Denham operated by turning up at eight in the morning, opening the mail, then sitting in the sales (internal) office for two hours, returning to his own office where he would incarcerate himself and merely look at figures of past performance. He rarely went to see customers off site, or saw customers when they came in.

## OPERATIONS IN THE PAST TWO YEARS

About two and a half years ago, while some other changes were being made in BCI organization, Lampton, at age 35, returned from Birmingham to the BCI London head office as a director of BCI; at the same time he was also assigned to the board of Harrogate. The remainder of this case covers the past two years of his relationships with the latter company. Incidentally, Lampton, just recently, was named managing director of BCI Industries. Lampton described his experience with Harrogate:

I arrived on the scene of this highly successful company (60 percent on net worth is remarkable by any criteria) full of youthful bounce, and asking why they don't look at the situation in the building-products industries for growth, I knew that the company was doing no real forward planning, and that with the addition of a lot of hard work along this line the company could do much better. I also had a certain amount of goodwill and ambition—and the knowledge that I would have a delicate time with Paul Denham.

But I soon found that it was an unusual company. I saw a managing director making £15,000 a year, but no other men of responsibility. His four top men, including Roger Sample, were making £3,000 or under. This came as a surprise—here was an outstandingly successful company, profit wise (£600,000), with no staff in depth. In fact, in addition to Roger Sample, the only talent I could see was a good production assistant who had just given notice of his termination.

---

[1] In Lampton's appraisal report (Exhibit 1) it is shown that there was no union at the time of acquisition of Harrogate.

I'm going to give you a number of facts about what happened during those two years, but first let me say that I am not adverse to local autonomy—I believe it is best—but not for one local autocrat. Let me also say that my relationship with Denham was a good relationship, personally speaking, but when I tried to bring some things up for improvement, around the board table (I had instituted more frequent board meetings, and insisted that we discuss company policy problems, rather than just review figures of past performance), he did not want to discuss them. Instead, he would say, "This is not a matter for formal board—why don't you come around to my office and let's talk about it informally." Nevertheless, I thought that all three board members (including Sample) should be in on important matters, and that there should be formal board meetings where responsible action could be taken.

Let me give you an example. Our operators in the plant were getting very high piece-rates, but it was physically very hard work, 58 hours a week, and two one-and-a-half week holidays that had to be split, one and a half weeks in summer and one and half in winter: anyone absent without a doctor's note got instant dismissal. When Denham asked me not to bring this up in the board, but to come to his office, I said, "No! This is a board matter." I could see that these conditions would mean trouble, and Roger Sample was telling me—not as a moral issue at all, but as a practical issue—we couldn't keep things this way. For my own part, I regarded it as a practical issue and a moral issue. In a way, we were blackmailing the workers with high pay and not providing opportunity for recreation. They were spending money in considerable amounts in gambling and drinking (this seemed to be a problem in the town). So I proposed that we allow them to take their two one-and-a-half-week holidays together, thus affording more of a real holiday and rest away from the job.

As I persisted in placing this matter before the board, Denham finally said, "I don't want any part of this discussion. If you want to make board policy, do it." Notice that he wasn't saying, "I am the managing director, I will think and be responsible about this." Instead, he was abdicating the managing directorship to us.

I mentioned Roger Sample. Denham had hired him five years ago from a local construction firm, and he subsequently became production manager. Although he had rather narrow experience working locally up there in Yorkshire, he is a man of talent. He knew I thought highly of him, but he was reticent with me at first, because he didn't know what kind of game I was playing. He did not have much confidence in pushing his ideas, because when Denham resisted, he did not know if I would back him. Gradually, however, we established a relationship of trust. It came about through situations like the following. On my side, I could see great need for looking beyond the narrow confines of present products and processes. The company needed market research and research on new technology. On Roger's side, he had been reading magazines of the industry and had become aware of some new processes that were being developed in Sweden. He wanted to go there to investigate, but had been forbidden by the managing director. Later, I raised this at the board table, but Denham's reaction was, "Don't let's meddle outside the company now. We have a system that is producing high profit." Why he took this attitude I don't know. I suspect that the real trouble lay in the fact that Denham had been outgrown by the company he managed, and he was afraid that anything new might put him still further out of his depth. Harrogate's very success was against him.

Some time later, the accountant for the plant quit. I think it was because he was mistreated by Denham. At this point, I tried to get Denham to go out and find a really topflight managerial accountant —one who could think and plan rather than simply be an audit clerk. As things proceeded, I could see that Denham just wasn't capable of doing this, so I persuaded him that we should go out and hire an outside firm of consultants to do the recruiting. The consultants presented four candidates for our approval. I was party to interviewing them. We rejected two immediately, and there were two left in my opinion, who were suitable. About this time, I left to attend the 13-week Advanced Management Program of Harvard University in the United States. When I returned, I found to my amazement that he had rejected both of them and instead hired a local accountant at £1,800 a year, rather than the £4,000-man I had envisaged.

About this time I recognized that Paul Denham was a man who was going to reject any sort of idea, and any sort of talent, that he was not familiar with. I was utterly disenchanted with what he was doing. When I got back from Harvard, Paul Denham also recognized that I was a chap who was going to stick to his guns. I could see trouble ahead and was determined to do something about it, even though the company's profit record continued to be outstanding.

The last remark reminded the casewriter of something said by E. M. Jackson, another BCI executive, who read the first draft of this case at the request of Mr. Lampton. Mr. Jackson said that, during the Harrogate affair,

Lampton knew that Denham must go and yet he was very conscious that the company's success was in some measure due to the tremendous pace that Denham set for the company in earlier years. Indeed, the competitive edge that Harrogate had gained came largely from the fact that the company utilized its machines so intensively—the credit for which, at any rate initially, was Denham's.

Mr. Lampton continued:

At the second Board meeting after I returned, Roger Sample brought up a subject that I had encouraged him to study (I had encouraged him to look at all facets of the business). Our office staff had very high turnover. The staff was working on Saturday mornings, but there was no need, no work, for this. When Roger proposed that Saturday morning hours be eliminated, Paul again said he wanted no part of it. He wasn't even fighting it. I suspect it was because he knew it was going to be put into effect anyway.

At any rate, I was intent on pursuing this to some sort of conclusion. The meeting became heated and intense. Denham said, "Hell, why do we waste our time on these matters—go out and find out what the order position is and lets get down to work." At this point, and in front of Roger, I blew my top. "This is real business," I said, "and if we don't pursue it we have a real crisis."

After this incident, which took place about a year ago, Lampton came back to London and wrote to Denham the letter that appears as Exhibit 3, and that requests Denham to come to London for a meeting. "I felt that it was stupid to keep this up," Lampton said, "and that we must resolve it somehow. Anyway, Denham had not once been to London in the six years we owned the company. I always invited him to the annual dinner we hold for subsidiary managing directors, but he always accepted and then sent a last minute excuse. The night before the meeting was to take place here at head office, Paul Denham telephoned to say that he was not feeling well."

## EXHIBIT 1
### Excerpts from a Financial and Managerial Appraisal of Harrogate Asphalt Products, Ltd., by Henry Lampton

This appraisal was written by Henry Lampton seven years ago, shortly before the acquisition of Harrogate. All quoted material in this exhibit (in italics) is from the Lampton appraisal; all other comments are those of the case writer.

DIRECTORS AND PERSONNEL

P. DENHAM (Age 48, Managing Director and Secretary, salary £4,000-plus.)

*Mr. Denham has spent the last 25 years with Mr. Stanley and has grown up with the business. Originally, he was responsible for the coal distribution concern (sold eight years ago), but has been the prime mover in the expansion of Harrogate materials over the past ten years.*

*As will be appreciated later in the report, despite the rapid growth of this company, it is still relatively easy to administer and Denham has a tight personal control over it.*

*He has a very pleasant personality. He is a strict disciplinarian and is respected for it. As the company is in a rural area and there is a very low labor turnover, Denham regards the employees with Edwardian paternalism.*

*He has three sons at public school, the eldest (at 16) works in the company during vacations. Denham hopes one of the three will join him in the business later.*

*His remuneration has risen rapidly and it is intended that in future he should have a basic salary of £4,000 per annum and a commission of 2½ percent on all net profits over £100,000 per annum.*

P. JENKINS (Age 35, Works Manager, salary £1,600.)

He has spent all his life in the asphalt product industry and joined Harrogate 18 months ago from Dackman products of Nottingham. Denham has a high regard for his technical ability, but believes he is rather weak and immature in his handling of employees (this may well be because Denham himself is "ever present").

He appeared to be rather shy, but showed great enthusiasm when explaining production methods and new developments.

K. WARREN (Age 32, Transport Manager, salary £1,600.)

Most of the day-to-day problems in this company are not concerned with production, but rather with transport of finished goods. Until recently this has been done entirely with hired vehicles, and Warren has been responsible for handling this. To deal with 60 or 70 hired vehicles requires considerable tact, patience, humor, planning ability, and downright strength. Warren appears to have these qualities in full. He was in the Royal Navy prior to joining Harrogate some five years ago.

J. NIXON (Age 45, Sales and Production Planning Manager, salary £1,700.)

Nixon was not met, but from the way Denham referred to him he was a weak member of the management team. He evidently does his work well enough in a pedestrian way, but has not much strength of personality or many ideas."

\*      \*.      \*      \*      \*

Jenkins, Warren, and Nixon are regarded by Stanley and Denham as future board members, but it would appear that Warren is the only one who is likely to grow to sufficient stature.

OUTSIDE STAFF

In this section, Mr. Lampton pointed out that the workers in the plant earn very good wages compared to general conditions in British industry. The wages are exceptionally high in relation to the surrounding agricultural area. Wages of between £30 and £40 per week were due to the fact that when the new revolutionary production machinery was purchased 11 years ago, neither the manufacturer of the machinery nor the Harrogate management knew that it would be so productive. Piece-rates were established based on what the machines were estimated to produce, but these were "grossly wrong."

*The company (in the event wisely) did not change these rates, but reserved the undisputed right to trim all production units to a bare minimum of labor. As the company has constantly expanded, no surplus labor has been laid off, but merely transferred to new units.*

*Needless to say, at these rates competition for jobs at Harrogate is very high. There was an intensely "brisk" air about the whole place. It is nonunion labour. There is no pension scheme. Hours worked are long (normally 07:30 to 18:30) and annual holidays are split, a week in the summer and another in the winter. The work is arduous, and in the winter, conditions are not good by the very nature of the business. As the rates are all fixed by team output there is no room for individual slacking. Relations with management appear to be good. Total labour force has risen rapidly in the past year to around 100.*

FINANCE AND OPERATIONS

After presenting a profit and sales summary (Exhibit 2), Mr. Lampton, among others, made the following points:

1. The increase in gross profits has been due primarily to the introduction of new manufacturing equipment.

2. The productivity of labor could be still further reduced if one operation were not necessary. "Through the engineering firm of Mason and Grant, secret experiments are taking place with a mechanism that must be changed only once daily, instead of once with each batch of product. This would mean that each large machine could be filled automatically, cutting out one man's work on each of the five lines (at £1,500-plus per annum per line)." Mr. Lampton also made the point that "the finished product is a very strong and high quality job. Harrogate's products withstood the British Standard tests to a very satisfactory degree."

3. In the area of purchasing and supply logistics, Harrogate has a favorable location for securing raw materials economically. Because production is increasing very rapidly (75 percent in the past year), one of the company's principal raw material suppliers suggested to Denham that a subsidiary transport company could be set up to pick up raw materials, rather than have them shipped by the vendor. This subsidiary company has been set up with Stanley and Denham as directors. A significant cost saving in raw materials has been achieved. The company has its own electricity substation. "Overall, there is no problem with regard to raw materials."

4. In storage, and in distribution, Harrogate is regarded "as an excellent call" because large amounts of finished product can be handled and loaded in a short time. Use of modern materials handling equipment (the company owns, for example, 40 forklift trucks and 20,000 pallets) has made this possible. Also, the company has bought five flat lorries and intends over the years to build up to its own fleet. However, management indicates that they will still use contractors for uneconomic trips and in emergency.

**EXHIBIT 2**
**Selected Financial and Operating Results, Harrogate Asphalt Products, Ltd.**

| Years Ago | Sales* | Profits before Taxes* |
|---|---|---|
| 14 . . . . . . . . . . . . . £ | 31,000 | n.a. |
| 13 . . . . . . . . . . . . | 55,000 | £ 22,000 |
| 12 . . . . . . . . . . . . | 83,000 | 28,000 |
| 11 . . . . . . . . . . . . | 110,000 | 39,000 |
| 10 . . . . . . . . . . . . | 178,000 | 62,000 |
| 9 . . . . . . . . . . . . | 224,000 | 87,000 |
| 8 . . . . . . . . . . . . | 361,000 | 136,000 |
| 7 . . . . . . . . . . . . | 520,000 | 150,000 |
| 6 . . . . . . . . . . . . | 867,000 | 260,000 |
| 5 . . . . . . . . . . . . | 1,053,000 | 310,000 |
| 4 . . . . . . . . . . . . | 1,096,000 | 300,000 |
| 3 . . . . . . . . . . . . | 1,638,000 | 450,000 |
| 2 . . . . . . . . . . . . | 1,922,000 | 595,000 |
| 1 . . . . . . . . . . . . | 2,050,000 | 600,000 |
| Present . . . . . . . . | 2,500,000 | 750,000 (estimated) |

* Figures are rounded to nearest £1,000.

CURRENT PROGRESS AND FUTURE PROSPECTS

In this section, Mr. Lampton pointed out that productive capacity has increased significantly. He cites the month of June in each of the last four years, showing that production, in tons, had progressed from 5,600 in the first year, to 8,000, 10,000, and

17,700 in the successive three years. A new production line, together with machines, has been set up in the last three months (adding 950 tons to usage of raw materials). Sales the last ten months have increased to £452,400 as compared with £301,900 in the same period last year.

*The reason for the company's success is probably due to its geographical position (both for raw materials and markets), the fact that it invested early in revolutionary production machinery (outside engineers reckon that Harrogate has more of this machinery than anyone else, but Denham has no proof of this), very efficient management (mainly by Denham) and because it is supplying a material in increasing demand over the past decade.*

*The future looks good. This is a first-class company and should prove an excellent investment for BCI.*

**EXHIBIT 3**
**Letter from Lampton to Denham**

Mr. Paul Denham, Managing Director
Harrogate Asphalt Products, Ltd.
Frampton, Yorkshire

Dear Paul,

I have given myself some cooling time since our last meeting to consider its implications. I believe that it is most important that you and I meet away from Harrogate to discuss both the future of the business and the way in which you and I can operate together constructively for its good.

Could you come to see me and have lunch on Tuesday 2nd August, Thursday 4th, or Friday 5th. At the moment I have these days free from outside appointments.

Yours,

Henry Lampton

# Selected Readings

*From*

# HOW TO EVALUATE CORPORATE STRATEGY*

*By Seymour Tilles*

### DYNAMIC CONCEPT

A strategy is a set of goals and major policies. The definition is as simple as that. But while the notion of a strategy is extremely easy to grasp, working out an agreed-upon statement for a given company can be a fundamental contribution to the organization's future success.

In order to develop such a statement, managers must be able to identify precisely what is meant by a goal and what is meant by a major policy. Otherwise, the process of strategy determination may degenerate into what it so often becomes—the solemn recording of platitudes, useless for either the clarification of direction or the achievement of consensus.

### Identifying Goals

Corporate goals are an indication of what the company as a whole is trying to *achieve* and to *become*. Both parts—the achieving and the becoming—are important for a full understanding of what a company hopes to attain. . . .

\*    \*    \*    \*    \*

Achieving. In order to state what a company expects to achieve, it is important to state what it hopes to do with respect to its environment.

\*    \*    \*    \*    \*

Becoming. If you ask young men what they want to accomplish by the time they are 40, the answers you get fall into two distinct categories. There are those—the great majority—who will respond in terms of what they want to *have*. This is especially true of graduate students of business administration. There are some men, however, who will answer in terms of the kind of men they hope to *be*. These are the only ones who have a clear idea of where they are going.

The same is true of companies. For far too many companies, what little thinking goes on about the future is done primarily in money terms. There is nothing wrong with financial planning. Most companies should do more of it. But there is a basic fallacy in confusing a financial plan with thinking about the kind of company you want yours to become. It is like saying, "When I'm 40, I'm going to be *rich*." It leaves too many basic questions unanswered. Rich in what way? Rich doing what?

---

The other major fallacy in stating what you want to become is to say it only in terms of a product. The number of companies who have got themselves into trouble by falling in love with a particular product is distressingly great.[1] Perhaps the saddest examples are those giants of American industry who defined their future in terms of continuing to be the major suppliers of steam locomotives to the nation's railroads. In fact, these companies were so wedded to this concept of their future that they formed a cartel in order to keep General Motors out of the steam locomotive business. When the diesel locomotive proved its superiority to steam, these companies all but disappeared.

The lesson of these experiences is that a key element of setting goals is the ability to see them in terms of more than a single dimension. Both money and product policy are part of a statement of objectives; but it is essential that these be viewed as the concrete expressions of a more abstract set of goals—the satisfaction of the needs of significant groups which cooperate to ensure the company's continued existence.

\*     \*     \*     \*     \*

## Role of Policy

A policy says something about *how* goals will be attained. It is what statisticians would call a "decision rule," and what systems engineers would call a "standing plan." It tells people what they should and should not do in order to contribute to achievement of corporate goals.

A policy should be more than just a platitude. It should be a helpful guide to making strategy explicit, and providing direction to subordinates. Consequently, the more definite it is, the more helpful it can be. "We will provide our stockholders with a fair return," is a policy no one could possibly disagree with—or be helped by. What *is* a fair return? This is the type of question that must be answered before the company's intentions become clear.

The job of management is not merely the preparation of valid policies for a standard set of activities; it is the much more challenging one of first deciding what activities are so strategically significant that explicit decision-rules in that area are mandatory. No standard set of policies can be considered major for all companies. Each company is a unique situation. It must decide for itself which aspects of corporate life are most relevant to its own aspirations and work out policy statements for them. . . .

\*     \*     \*     \*     \*

## Need to Be Explicit

The first thing to be said about corporate strategy is that having one is a step forward. Any strategy, once made explicit, can quickly be evaluated and improved. But if no attempt is ever made to commit it to paper, there is always the danger that the strategy is either incomplete or misunderstood.

Many successful companies are not aware of the strategy that underlies their success. It is quite possible for a company to achieve initial success without real awareness of its causes. However, it is much more difficult to successfully *branch out into new ventures* without a precise appreciation of their strategic significance. This is why many established companies fall miserably when they attempt a program of corporate acquisition, product diversification, or market expansion.

Another reason for making strategy explicit is the assistance it provides for delegation and for coordination. To an ever-increasing extent, management is a team activity, whereby groups of executives contribute to corporate success. Making strategy explicit makes it far easier for each executive to appreciate what the over-all goals are, and what his own contribution to them must be.

---

[1] See Theodore Levitt, "Marketing Myopia," *Harvard Business Review,* July-August 1960, p. 45.

## MAKING AN EVALUATION

Is your strategy right for you? There are six criteria on which you base an answer. These are:

1. Internal consistency.
2. Consistency with the environment.
3. Appropriateness in the light of available resources.
4. Satisfactory degree of risk.
5. Appropriate time horizon.
6. Workability.

&ast; &ast; &ast; &ast; &ast;

*1. Is the Strategy Internally Consistent?* Internal consistency refers to the cumulative impact of individual policies on corporate goals. In a well-worked-out strategy, each policy fits into an integrated pattern. It should be judged not only in terms of itself, but also in terms of how it relates to other policies which the company has established and to the goals it is pursuing.

&ast; &ast; &ast; &ast; &ast;

*2. Is the Strategy Consistent with the Environment?* Consistency with the environment has both a static and a dynamic aspect. In a static sense, it implies judging the efficacy of policies with respect to the environment as it exists *now.* In a dynamic sense, it means judging the efficacy of policies with respect to the environment *as it appears to be changing.* One purpose of a viable strategy is to ensure the long-run success of an organization. Since the environment of a company is constantly changing, ensuring success over the long run means that management must constantly be assessing the degree to which policies previously established are consistent with the environment as it exists now; and whether current policies take into account the environment as it will be in the future. In one sense, therefore, establishing a strategy is like aiming at a moving target: you have to be concerned not only with present position but also with the speed and direction of movement.

&ast; &ast; &ast; &ast; &ast;

*3. Is the Strategy Appropriate in View of the Available Resources?* Resources are those things that a company *is* or *has* and that help it to achieve its corporate objectives. Included are money, competence, and facilities; but these by no means complete the list. In companies selling consumer goods, for example, the major resource may be the name of the product. In any case, there are two basic issues which management must decide in relating strategy and resources. These are:

What are our critical resources?
Is the proposed strategy appropriate for available resources?

Let us look now at what is meant by a "critical resource" and at how the criterion of a resource utilization can be used as a basis for evaluating strategy. . . .

The essential strategic attribute of resources is that they represent action potential. Taken together, a company's resources represent its capacity to respond to threats and opportunities that may be perceived in the environment. In other words, resources are the bundle of chips that the company has to play with in the serious game of business.

From an action-potential point of view, a resource may be critical in two senses: (1) as the factor limiting the achievement of corporate goals; and (2) as that which the company will exploit as the basis for its strategy. Thus, critical resources are both what the company has most of and what is has least of.

The three resources most frequently identified as critical are money, competence, and physical facilities. . . .

&ast; &ast; &ast; &ast; &ast;

## Achieving the Right Balance

One of the most difficult issues in strategy determination is that of achieving a balance between strategic goals and available resources. This requires a set of necessarily empirical, but critical, estimates of the total resources required to achieve particular objectives, the rate at which they will have to be committed, and the likelihood that they will be available. The most common errors are either to fail to make these estimates at all or to be excessively optimistic about them.

*     *     *     *     *

Another place where optimistic estimates of resources frequently cause problems is in small businesses. Surveys of the causes of small-business failure reveal that a most frequent cause of bankruptcy is inadequate resources to weather either the early period of establishment or unforeseen downturns in business conditions.

It is apparent from the preceding discussion that a critical strategic decision involves deciding: (1) how much of the company's resources to commit to opportunities currently perceived, and (2) how much to keep uncommitted as a reserve against the appearance of unanticipated demands. This decision is closely related to two other criteria for the evaluation of strategy: risk and timing. . . .

### 4. Does the Strategy Involve an Acceptable Degree of Risk?

*     *     *     *     *

. . . Our concern here is not with these quantitative aspects but with the identification of some qualitative factors which may serve as a rough basis for evaluating the degree of risk inherent in a strategy. These factors are:

1.  The amount of resources (on which the strategy is based) whose continued existence or value is not assured.
2.  The length of the time periods to which resources are committed.
3.  The proportion of resources committed to a single venture.

*     *     *     *     *

### 5. Does the Strategy Have an Appropriate Time Horizon?   A significant part of every strategy is the time horizon on which it is based. A viable strategy not only reveals what goals are to be accomplished; it says something about *when* the aims are to be achieved.

Goals, like resources, have time-based utility. A new product developed, a plant put on steam, a degree of market penetration, become significant strategic objectives only if accomplished by a certain time. Delay may deprive them of all strategic significance. . . .

In choosing an appropriate time horizon, we must pay careful attention to the goals being pursued, and to the particular organization involved. Goals must be established far enough in advance to allow the organization to adjust to them. Organizations, like ships, cannot be "spun on a dime." Consequently, the larger the organization, the further its strategic time horizon must extend, since its adjustment time is longer. . . .

*     *     *     *     *

If a strategy cannot be evaluated by results alone, there are some other indications that may be used to assess its contribution to corporate progress:

The degree of consensus which exists among executives concerning corporate goals and policies.

The extent to which major areas of managerial choice are identified in advance, while there is still time to explore a variety of alternatives.

The extent to which resource requirements are discovered well before the last minute, necessitating neither crash programs of cost reduction nor the elimination of planned programs. The widespread popularity of the meat-axe approach to cost reduction is a clear indication of the frequent failure of corporate strategic planning.

*From*

# A THEORY OF LARGE MANAGERIAL FIRMS*

## By R. Joseph Monsen, Jr., and Anthony Downs

. . . In most of the largest and most significant modern firms, ownership and management are functions carried out by two entirely separate groups of people. Even management itself is really a combination of functions carried out by different groups. Thus the entity normally referred to as *the firm* has in fact become a number of different subentities. The people in each of these subgroups within the firm are still primarily motivated by self-interest. However, their changed relationship to the firm as a whole has changed the way in which their self-interest leads them to behave regarding the firm's profits. Therefore, our theory is really nothing more than the application of the self-interest axiom in traditional theory to a new type of firm: one is which ownership is separate from management; and management itself consists of a bureaucratic hierarchy containing several layers.

Our two central hypotheses can be stated as follows:

1. *Owners desire to have each firm managed so that it provides a steady income from dividends and gradual appreciation of the market price of the stock.*
2. *Managers act so as to maximize their own lifetime incomes.*

Since these two hypotheses are the foundations of our whole analysis, we will examine each in detail.

*   *   *   *   *

## Summary

1. We have proposed a modified theory of the firm to explain the behavior of large, diffused-ownership firms, which we refer to as *large managerial* firms. This theory assumes that ownership and management are essentially separate, and that each such firm is so large that its management hierarchy contains at least three types of managers: top, middle, and lower. We postulate that both owners and managers act in their own self-interest by pursuing the following goals:

*a. Owners* are basically *satisficers* who desire uninterrupted dividends and a steady rise in the price of the firm's stock. Their remoteness from the firm's actual affairs makes it impossible for them to press for profit-maximizing behavior.

*b. Managers* are "economic men" who *desire to maximize their own lifetime incomes* (which includes both monetary and non-monetary elements), principally by obtaining rapid promotions as a result of pleasing their superiors in the firm.

2. The behavior of large managerial firms deviates from the profit maximization posited by the traditional theory of the firm for the following reasons:

*a.* The large size of such firms requires them to develop *bureaucratic management* structures which cannot be perfectly controlled by the men in charge of them. In particular, these structures tend to (i) provide biased information to top management which reflects its own desires and ideas too strongly and (ii) only partially carry out the orders issued by top management. These tendencies cause systematic deviations from whatever goals the organization is ostensibly pursuing. They exist in large owner-managed firms as well as large

* R. Joseph Monsen, Jr., and Anthony Downs, "A Theory of Large Managerial Firms." Reprinted with permission from the *Journal of Political Economy,* © by The University of Chicago Press, 1965. (vol LXXIII, no. 3, June 1965. Excerpts from pp. 224–25; 236;231–35.)

managerial firms, since they result from sheer size. In essence, such deviations are caused by divergences of goals *within* management; that is, between middle and lower management on the one hand and top management on the other. These goal divergences are able to influence the firm's behavior because large size both compels top managers to delegate authority to their subordinates and prevents them from checking up completely on how that authority is used. This behavior of the firm which is not optimal from the viewpoint of the top man can be caused *either* by size alone (technical inefficiency) or by a combination of size and divergent goals (technical plus motivational inefficiency).

*b.* The separation of ownership and management limits owners to being satisficers instead of maximizers; hence managers aim at achieving steady growth of earnings plus gradually rising stock prices instead of maximum profits. As a result, large managerial firms are more cautious; spend less on "crash" research programs; experience less variability of profits; have larger expense accounts; evidence more conciliation in dealings with government, unions, and the public; and probably grow more slowly than they would if they sought to maximize profits. In essence, these outcomes result from the divergence of goals *between* owners and top management set forth in paragraph 1 above. The size and structure of the firm both compel owners to delegate authority to top management and prevent them from checking up fully on its performance or imposing their own goals upon top management.

## IMPLICATIONS OF THE THEORY REGARDING BEHAVIOR OF MANAGEMENT

Now that we have set forth our basic theory and examined the bureaucratic context of managerial decision-making, we will explore the theory's implications regarding the behavior of managers at various levels within the firm.

### A. Top-Management Behavior

*Top Management's Promotional Strategy.* The best way for top management to maximize its own lifetime income is to "keep the stockholders happy." This normally involves three basic policies:

*a. Carefully screening all information which is forwarded to stockholders or the public at large* so that it reflects an outstanding management performance. . . .

*b. Directing the firm toward achievement of constant or slightly rising dividends plus steadily increasing stock prices.* However, top management need only attain a "satisfactory" rate of stock-price growth, not a "maximum" one.

*c. Maintaining a "public image" of competence by avoiding controversy and criticism.* Public criticism of the firm or controversy about its policies tends to contradict this "image" and raise doubts in the minds of the stockholders about the wisdom of retaining the existing top management.

\*    \*    \*    \*    \*

Thus the attention of management is focused on stock *prices* rather than *earnings* (profits), which are viewed as means to obtain higher stock prices rather than as ends in themselves. Therefore, if top management must choose between (*a*) maximizing profits over a given period by accepting fluctuating earnings, or (*b*) achieving total profits by maintaining steadily rising annual earnings, it will normally choose the latter. Therefore, diffused-ownership firms will experience less *variability of earnings* than firms which try to maximize profits.

. . . Other implications of our hypothesis and forecasts consistent with it concerning top management behavior are as follows:

*a.* Research and development expenditures are more likely to be budgeted for steady yearly growth than for "crash" expansion of promising innovations.

*b.* Diffused-ownership firms will exhibit a strong predilection for diversification of products, especially through merger, as a means of reducing risks taken on any one product or line of products. Since diversification through merger tends to reduce the rate of return on capital, owner-managers would be less likely to adopt such policies.

*c.* Financing rapid expansion through additional stock offerings is less likely to be used by top management in diffused-ownership firms than by owner-managers. In many cases, the original owners of a firm which expands rapidly use sales of common stock to "buy themselves out" of the corporation, thus capitalizing on their original ownership interest. Managers whose only stock comes from stock options are more likely to adopt internal financing, bank borrowing, or bond issues for such financing so as not to dilute their own interests. . . .

*d.* Top management will be much more sensitive to public, union, and government criticism than owner-managers would be. Hence top managers will be more conciliatory in their public dealings than might be required for profit maximization.

*e.* Top managers will use their roles in the firm to enhance their own personal prestige and stature. As a result, they will contribute to local causes and participate in community affairs more than they should from a purely profit-maximizing point of view.

*f.* In order to stabilize future profits, avoid controversy, and prevent adverse publicity, top management may make concessions to labor unions more readily than owner-managers would. . . .

*g.* Expense accounts are likely to be more extravagant in managerial firms than they would be if managers really maximized returns to owners. . . .

*h.* Managerial firms are likely to respond more slowly to declines in profits than they would if they really pursued profit maximization. Since managers wish to preserve their personal prerogatives (such as large expense accounts) and do not suffer directly from lower profits, they will be willing to "ride out" a sudden decline in profits without cutting back expenditures in the hope that it will be temporary. In contrast, true profit maximizers would exhibit no such inertia but would immediately alter their existing behavior patterns. However, if lower profits continue, even managerial firms will adjust their behavior so as to avoid having lower yearly earnings cause any decline in stock prices (if possible).

## B. Middle-Management Behavior

*1. The Organizational Setting.* Middle managers are those operating executives under top management who are responsible for carrying out various specialized tasks within the firm. Middle managers are normally paid for their performance primarily by salaries and bonuses and secondarily by expense accounts and other untaxed perquisites.

*2. Middle Management's Promotional Strategy.* The best way for middle managers to maximize their lifetime incomes is to increase the size of those incomes by being promoted to higher-paying positions within the firm or in other firms. Since their promotions are determined by the recommendations of their superiors, their efforts to obtain promotion consist essentially of doing whatever will most please and impress their superiors, regardless of the effects of their actions upon the profits of the firm.

\*     \*     \*     \*     \*

## C. Lower-Management Behavior

*1. The Organizational Setting.* Lower managers are those supervisory personnel at the foreman or comparable level who have direct authority over production or lowest-level clerical personnel. They are normally paid for their performance by salaries and bonuses. Their salaries are partly based on seniority and longevity in the firm, and their bonuses are based on achieving production or quality goals. Normally, lower managers have little expectation of being promoted in middle or top management because the educational standards for those higher echelons are beyond their capabilities.

*2. Lower Management's Promotional Strategy.* The best way for lower managers to maximize their lifetime incomes is to seek promotions up to the highest attainable lower-management level and then to hold on to what they have achieved. Often their performances can be accurately measured objectively by means of production quotas, quality checks, costs accounting, etc. Thus the efforts of lower management are more intensively directed at meeting objective performance criteria than is the case with middle and top management.

   *3. Implications of Lower-Management Behavior.* Lower managers are risk-avoiders of a high order. Their aim is primarily to retain their present positions by meeting quotas and avoiding gross errors. In this echelon are the classic bureaucrats who never violate the rules and fear to "stick their necks out." As with middle management, the result is undoubtedly a lower level of creativity, innovation, and risk-taking than would occur in a firm perfectly organized to maximize profits.

*From*

# THE SOCIAL PSYCHOLOGY OF ORGANIZATION*

*By Daniel Katz and Robert L. Kahn*

**THE TAKING OF ORGANIZATIONAL ROLES**

\*     \*     \*     \*     \*

**Definition of Role Behavior**

   Generically, role behavior refers to the recurring actions of an individual, appropriately interrelated with the repetitive activities of others so as to yield a predictable outcome. The set of interdependent behaviors comprise a social system or subsystem, a stable collective pattern in which people play their parts.

   When we abstract some of the essential persisting features from the specific acts comprising role behavior we speak of roles. For example, we can speak of the role of the quarterback on a football team in general terms of play selection without specifying the particular signals he barks to his teammates or the specific plays with which they respond. This general description applies to roles both within and outside formal organizations. . . . In formal organizations many of the functionally specific behaviors comprising the system are specified in written and coded presentations. Moreover, in formal organizations the roles people play are more a function of the social setting than of their own personality characteristics. The basic criterion, then, for studying role behavior is to identify the relevant social system or subsystem and locate the recurring events which fit together in converting some input into an output. This can be done by ascertaining the role expectations of a given set of related offices, since such expectations are one of the main elements in maintaining the role system and inducing the required role behavior.

**The Process of Role-Sending**

   All members of a person's role set depend upon his performance in some fashion; they are rewarded by it, judged in terms of it, or require it in order to perform their own tasks. Because they have a stake in his performance they develop beliefs and attitudes about what he should and should not do as part of his role. The prescriptions and proscriptions held

   \* From *The Social Psychology of Organization* by D. Katz and R. L. Kahn. Copyright©1966 by John Wiley & Sons, Inc. Reprinted by permission. Excerpts pp. 174–80, 182, 186–87.

by members of a role set are designated *role expectations,* in the aggregate they help to define his role, the behaviors which are expected of him. The role expectations held for a certain person by a member of his role set will reflect that member's conception of the person's office and of his abilities. The content of these expectations may include preferences with respect to specific acts and personal characteristics or styles; they may deal with what the person should do, what kind of person he should be, what he should think or believe, and how he should relate to others. Role expectations are by no means restricted to the job description as it might be given by the head of the organization or prepared by some specialist in personnel, although these individuals are likely to be influential members of the role sets of many persons in the organization.

The mention of influence raises additional issues of definition and theory. Role expectations for any given office and its occupant exist in the minds of members of his role set and represent standards in terms of which they evaluate his performance. The expectations do not remain in the minds of members of the role set, however. They tend to be communicated in many ways; sometimes as direct instructions, as when a supervisor describes to a subordinate the requirements of his job; sometimes less directly, as when a colleague expresses admiration or disappointment in some behavior. The crucial point (for our theoretical view) is that the activities which define a role are maintained through the expectations of members of the role set, and that these expectations are communicated or "sent" to the focal person.[1] In referring to role expectations as sent, we are following the formulation of Rommetveit (1954). He refers to members of a role set as role senders, and to their communicated expectations as the *sent role.*

The numerous acts which make up the process of role-sending are not merely informational. They are attempts at influence, directed at the focal person and intended to bring about conformity to the expectations of the senders. Some of these influence attempts (for example, those from superiors) may be directed toward the accomplishment of formally specified responsibilities and objectives of office.

Others (perhaps from peers or subordinates) may be directed toward making life easier or more pleasant for the senders themselves, in ways which contravene official requirements.

Thus each individual in an organization acts in relation to and in response to the expectations of the members of his role set, not because those expectations constitute some mentalistic field of forces but because they are expressed in explicit behavioral ways. . . .

. . . Every attempt at influence implies consequences for compliance or noncompliance. In organizations, as we have seen, these commonly take the form of sanctions—gratifications or deprivations which a role sender might arrange for the focal person, depending on his having conformed to the sender's expectation or not. The concept of legitimacy, and its acceptance by organizational members, makes the actual use of such sanctions infrequent. Members obey because the source and substance of the command are legitimate. The availability and visibility of sanctions are important, however, whether or not they are used or even threatened. The strengthening or role-sending with the possibility of sanctions is the major basis for gaining compliance with the requirements of formal organization.

\*    \*    \*    \*    \*

## The Received Role

To understand the response of any member of an organization to the complex pattern of role-sending addressed specifically to him, we must regard the organization from the vantage point of his office. When we do so, we see that the members of his role set and the influential pressures which they direct to him are part of his objective environment. To consider his compliance with or deviation from his sent role, however, takes us immediately

---

[1] The term *focal person* will be used to refer to any individual whose role or office is under consideration.

beyond the objective organization and environment. Each individual responds to the organization in terms of his perceptions of it, which may differ in various ways from the actual organization. In the immediate sense, the individual responds not to the objective organization in his objective social environment but to that representation of it which is in his psychological environment.

The objective organization and the psychological organization of a person may or may not be congruent, depending on his ability and opportunity to perceive organizational reality. Thus for each person in an organization there is not only a sent role, consisting of the influential and communicative acts of the members of his role set, there is also a *received role,* consisting of his perceptions and cognitions of what was sent. How closely the received role corresponds to the sent role is an empirical question for each focal person and set of role senders, and will depend upon properties of the senders, the focal person, the substantive content of the sent expectations, the clarity of the communication, and the like.

It is the sent role by means of which the organization communicates to each of its members the do's and don'ts associated with his office. It is the received role, however, which is the immediate influence on his behavior and the immediate source of his motivation for role performance. Each sent expectation can be regarded as arousing in the focal person a motivational force of some magnitude and direction. This is not to say that these motivational role forces are identical in magnitude and direction with the sent influence attempts that evoked them. When sent-role expectations are seen by the focal person as illegitimate or coercive, they may arouse strong resistance forces which lead to outcomes different from or even opposite to the expected behavior. It is such processes, repeated for many persons over long periods of time, that produce the persistent component of unintended effects in organizational behavior. Pressures to increase production sometimes result in slowdowns. Moreover, every person is subject to a variety of psychological forces in addition to those stimulated by pressures from his role set in the work situation. Role-sendings are thus only a partial determinant of his behavior on the job.

Additional and important sources of influence in role-taking are the objective, impersonal properties of the situation itself. In some situations the taking of roles may be aided by the nature of the task and the previous experience of the individual with respect to similar tasks. The soldier in combat seeks cover when under fire not so much because of the expectations of members of his role set as because of the demands of the situation. The man on the assembly line tightens the belt on the passing car both because he has been told that it is his job and because the structuring of his work situation is a constant reminder of what he is supposed to do. People can be conditioned to play their roles by cues other than those of the communicated expectations from other system members. Nevertheless, in most organizations, role behavior is largely dependent upon role sending.

In addition to the motivational forces aroused by sent expectations and other cues, there are important internal sources of motivation for role performance. For example, there is the intrinsic satisfaction derived from the content of the role. The concert pianist has many motives which lead him to give performances; one of them is probably the intrinsic psychological return from exercising a hard-won and valued skill. But there is, in addition to intrinsic satisfaction in expressing valued abilities, another kind of "own force" important in the motivation of role behavior. In a sense each person is a "self-sender," that is a role sender to himself. He too has a conception of his office and a set of attitudes and beliefs about what he should and should not do while in that position. He has some awareness of what behaviors will fulfill his responsibilities, lead to the accomplishment of organizational objectives, or further his own interests. He may even have had a major part in determining the formal responsibilities of his office, especially if he occupies a line or staff position well up in the hierarchy.

Moreover, some of the persisting motives of the individual are likely to include the sector of organizational behavior. Through a long process of socialization and formal training within the organization and in the larger culture of which it and he are parts, he has acquired a set of values and expectations about his own behavior and abilities, about the nature of human organizations and the conditions for membership in them. In short, as Miller (1962), Dai (1955), and others have observed, the person has an occupational self-identity and is motivated to behave in ways which affirm and enhance the valued attributes of that identity. He comes to the job in a state of what we have previously referred to as role-readiness, a state which includes the acceptance of legitimate authority and compliance with its requests, a compliance which for many people extends to acts which they do not understand and which may violate many of their own values. . . .

**Multiple Roles and Multiple Activities.** An organization is a complex arrangement of many collective cycles of behavior, some of which intersect, others of which are tangential to one another, while still others are connected only indirectly. In other words, the organization is made up of many subsystems. The common treatment of *role* and *office* tends to oversimplify this complexity by neglecting the fact that one office can be located in a number of such role subsystems and that one individual can be involved in many organizational subsystems.

Let us examine more closely the meaning and implications of these assertions. The basic unit of organizational life is the *molar unit of behavior,* the behavioral cycle. This is what we mean by *an activity:* a recurring behavior sequence which has organizational relevance, is held in the form of role expectations by some members of the role set, and which affords some sense of closure on completion. For example, taking four bolts out of a barrel and using them to fasten the left rear fender of an automobile to the body is an activity on the assembly line.

*A role consists of one or more recurrent activities* out of a total pattern of interdependent activities which in combination produce the organizational output. Role, unless otherwise qualified, will refer to a set of such activities within a single subsystem of the organization and within a single office.

*An office is a point (location) in organizational space* defined by one or more roles (and thereby one or more activities) intended for performance by a single individual. It locates the individual in relation to his fellows with respect to the job to be done and the giving and taking of orders.

The simplest organizational arrangement occurs when one activity defines role and office. Thus, the job of assembly-line operator No. 23 might consist of the one activity described in the previous example, bolting on the left rear fender. That activity defines the role, and the office is merely the point in organizational space associated with that role and activity.

The situation can become more complex in any of several ways:

Multiple activities may be defined into a single role.
Multiple roles may be defined into a single office.
Multiple offices may be held by a single person.

*    *    *    *    *

## The Role Episode

Our description of role-sending and role-receiving has been based on four concepts: *role expectations,* which are evaluative standards applied to the behavior of any person who occupies a given organizational office or position; *sent role,* which consists of communications stemming from role expectations and sent by members of the role set as attempts to influence the focal person; *received role,* which is the focal person's perception of the role-sendings addressed to him, including those he "sends" to himself; and *role behavior,* which is the response of the focal person to the complex of information and influence he has received.

These four concepts can be thought of as constituting a sequence or role episode. The first two, role expectations and sent role, have to do with the motivations, cognitions, and behavior of the members of the role set; the latter two, received role and role behavior, have

**FIGURE 1**
**A Model of the Role Episode**

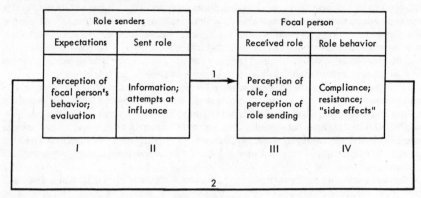

to do with the cognitions, motivations, and behavior of the focal person. A model of the role episode is presented in Figure 1.

These three additional classes of variables—organizational, personality, and interpersonal—can be conveniently represented in an enlargement and extension of Figure 1. That figure presented a causal sequence: role expectations (I) lead to a role-sending (II), which leads to received role (III), which leads to behavior in response to the role as received (IV). That figure and the sequence it represents also forms the core of Figure 2.

The circles in Figure 2 represent not the momentary events of the role episode, but enduring states of the organization, the person, and the interpersonal relations between focal

**FIGURE 2**
**A Theoretical Model of Factors Involved in the Taking of Organizational Roles**

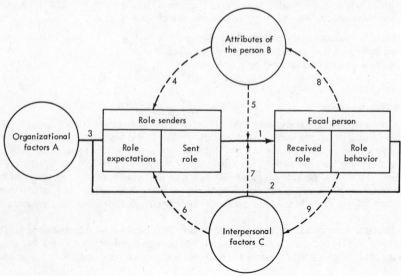

person and role senders. Such enduring properties are for the most part abstractions and generalizations based upon recurrent events and behaviors. For example, characterizing a relationship as supportive means simply that the parties to the relationship have behaved in a supportive manner toward one another on a sufficient number of occasions so that we feel justified in inferring supportiveness as a quality of the relationship. Such repetitions and patterns of events provide the basis and context within which each new occurrence can best be understood.

To a considerable extent the role expectations held by the members of a role set—the prescriptions and proscriptions associated with a particular office—are determined by the broader organizational context. The technology of the organization, the structure of its subsystems, its formal policies, and its rewards and penalties dictate in large degree the content of a given office. What the occupant of that office is supposed to do, with and for whom, is given by these and other properties of the organization itself. Although human beings are doing the "supposing" and rewarding, the structural properties of organization are sufficiently stable so that they can be treated as independent of the particular persons in the role set. For such properties as size, number of echelons, and rate of growth, the justifiable abstraction of organizational properties from individual behavior is even more obvious.

*From*

# THE FUTURE OF INDUSTRIAL MAN*

*By Peter F. Drucker*

Legitimate power stems from the same basic belief of society regarding man's nature and fulfillment on which the individual's social status and function rest. Indeed, legitimate power can be defined as rulership which finds its justification in the basic ethos of the society. In every society there are many powers which have nothing to do with such a basic principle and institutions which in no way are either designed or devoted to its fulfillment. In other words, there are always a great many "unfree" institutions in a free society, a great many inequalities in an equal society, and a great many sinners among the saints. But as long as that decisive social power which we call rulership is based upon the claim of freedom equality or saintliness, and is exercised through institutions which are designed toward the fulfillment of these ideal purposes, society can function as a free, equal or saintly society. For its institutional structure is one of legitimate power.

This does not mean that it is immaterial whether non-decisive powers and institutions of a society are in contradiction to its basic principles. On the contrary, the most serious problems of politics arise from such conflicts. And a society may well feel that a non-decisive institution or power relationship is in such blatant contrast to its basic beliefs as to endanger social life in spite of its non-decisive character. The best case in point is that of the American Civil War when the chattel-slavery of the South was felt to endanger the whole structure of a free society. Yet the decisive power of ante-bellum America was undoubtedly legitimate power deriving its claim from the principle of freedom, and exercised through institutions designed and devoted to the realization of freedom. American society did thus function as a free society. It was indeed only because it functioned as such that it felt slavery as a threat.

What is the decisive power, and the decisive institutional organization in any society cannot be determined by statistical analysis.

---

Nothing could be more futile than to measure a society by counting noses, quoting tax receipts or comparing income levels. Decisive is a political, and that means a purely qualitative, term. The English landed gentry comprised never more than a small fraction of the population; furthermore, after the rise of the merchants and manufacturers it had only a very modest share of the national wealth and income. Nevertheless, down to our times it held the decisive social power. Its institutions were the decisive institutions of English society. Its beliefs were the basis for social life; its standards the representative standards; its way of life the social pattern. And its personality ideal, the gentleman, remained the ideal type of all society. Its power was not only decisive; it was legitimate power.

Equally, laws and constitutions will rarely, if ever, tell us where the decisive power lies. In other words, rulership is not identical with political government. Rulership is a social, political government largely a legal category. The Prussian Army between 1870 and 1914 was, for instance, hardly as much as mentioned in the Imperial German Constitution; yet it undoubtedly held decisive power and probably legitimately. The government was actually subordinated to the army, in spite of a civilian and usually antimilitaristic Parliament.

*    *    *    *    *

Finally, it should be understood that legitimacy is a purely functional concept. There is no absolute legitimacy. Power can be legitimate only in relation to a basic social belief. What constitutes "legitimacy" is a question that must be answered in terms of a given society and its given political beliefs. Legitimate is a power when it is justified by an ethical or metaphysical principle that has been accepted by the society. Whether this principle is good or bad ethically, true or false metaphysically, has nothing to do with legitimacy which is as indifferent ethically and metaphysically as any other formal criterion. Legitimate power is socially functioning power; but why it functions and to what purpose is a question entirely outside and before legitimacy.

Failure to understand this was responsible for the confusion which made "legitimism" the name of a political creed in the early nineteenth century. The European reactionaries of 1815 were, of course, absolutely within their rights when they taught that no society could be *good* except under an absolute monarch; to have an opinion on what is desirable or just as basis of a society is not only a right, it is a duty, of man. But they were simply confusing ethical choice with functional analysis, when they said no society could *function* unless it had an absolute monarch. And they were probably wrong when they proclaimed the dogma that only absolute monarchy were *legitimate*. . . .

The functional analysis as to what is legitimate power does not in any way prejudge the ethical question of the individual's right or duty to resist what he considers pernicious power. Whether it is better that society perish than that justice perish is a question outside and before functional analysis. The same man who maintains most vigorously that society can function only under a legitimate power may well decide that society is less of a value than certain individual rights or beliefs. But he cannot decide, as the Legitimists did, that his values and beliefs *are* the socially accepted values and beliefs because they *ought* to be.

Illegitimate power is a power which does not derive its claim from the basic beliefs of the society. Accordingly, there is no possibility to decide whether the ruler wielding the power is exercising it in comformity with the purpose of power or not; for there is no special purpose. Illegitimate power cannot be controlled; it is by its nature uncontrollable. It cannot be made responsible since there is no criterion of responsibility, no socially accepted final authority for its justification. And what is unjustifiable cannot be responsible.

For the same reason, it cannot be limited. To limit the exercise of power is to fix the lines beyond which power ceases to be legitimate; that is, ceases to realize the basic social purpose. And if power is not legitimate to begin with, there are no limits beyond which it ceases to be legitimate.

No illegitimate ruler can possibly be a good or wise ruler. Illegitimate power invariably corrupts; for it can be only "might," never authority. It cannot be a controlled, limited, responsible, or rationally determinable power. And it has been an axiom of politics—ever since Tacitus in his history of the Roman emperors gave us one case study after another—

that no human being, however good, wise or judicious, can wield uncontrolled, irresponsible, unlimited or rationally not determinable power without becoming very soon arbitrary, cruel, inhuman and capricious—in other words, a tyrant.

For all these reasons a society in which the socially decisive power is illegitimate power cannot function as a society. It can only be held together by sheer brute force—tyranny, slavery, civil war. Of course, force is the ultimate safeguard of every power; but in a functioning society it is not more than a desperate remedy for exceptional and rare diseases. In a functioning society power is exercised as authority, and *authority is the rule of right over might*. But only a legitimate power can have authority and can expect and command that social self-discipline which alone makes organized institutional life possible. Illegitimate power, even if wielded by the best and the wisest, can never depend upon anything but the submission to force. On that basis a functioning, institutional organization of social life cannot be built. Even the best tyrant is still a tyrant.

*From*

# ORGANIZATIONAL BEHAVIOR AND THE PRACTICE OF MANAGEMENT*

*By David Hampton, Charles Summer, and Ross Webber*

### THE MOTIVATION OF EXECUTIVES TO POLITICAL ACTION

The motivations which cause executives to design technological systems, to convert them to systems of authority, and (in some cases) to engage in strategic actions intended to influence others can be further analyzed into (1) the value (attitude) of technological necessity, (2) the desire to be head of an organization, (3) the competitive urge and the will to conquer, (4) the urge to creative action, (5) the need for symmetry as a means of security, and (6) the pragmatic position—"it works." Each of these will be discussed separately.

### The Attitude of Technological Necessity

Technological necessity was discussed in Chapter 7. Without being repetitious, let us recall that phenomenon.[1] We start with the fact that in industrially developed societies, specialization has progressed to a profound degree. Man and his family are dependent on the roundabout production process for almost everything they require in the form of material needs. The days of the nearly sufficient Vermont farm are gone forever, and one of society's great unwritten mores is what Galbraith has called "the paramount position of production." Whether in the United States or in Soviet Russia, the society has provided both "ethical" and "monetary" institutions which reward the executive when his organizational system is efficient, and which punish him when it is inefficient. Granted that there are sometimes other motivations which operate to prevent him from striving for *maximum* organizational efficiency, there are nevertheless powerful material and non-material pressures which cause him to put a high value on organizational efficiency.

---

* Excerpts from *Organizational Behavior and the Practice of Management* by David R. Hampton, Charles E. Summer, and Ross A. Webber. Copyright © 1968 by Scott, Foresman and Company. Reprinted by permission.

[1] The description of the technological system in Chapter 7 of *Organizational Behavior and the Practice of Management,* including the powerful statements of Veblen, Friedman, and Beard, gives added emphasis to the necessity for both technological planning and political action.

This means, among other things, that the internal technological system of the firm or department—the rational division of this system into parts (specializations) and the rational relating of one of these parts to others (planning the input-output system)—must be (1) designed (an act of rule formulation) and that (2) it must be cloaked with the symbols of authority and legitimacy.

In addition to this social belief in production and prevention of waste, together with rewards and penalties which cause executives to *learn* this value, there is undoubtedly the factor of training and education of the man himself. Stated simply, if one goes to business school or engineering school and learns finance, operations research, marketing, or any of the sub-fields of administration, this stored knowledge with its symbolic representation is a form of "invested capital" in one's own life and career. It represents one's functional importance in society—his repertoire of actions that help him cope with life in an industrial and economic world. This commitment no doubt reinforces the original social value attached to planning and implementing an efficient, "well run," "high quality" organization.

**The Desire to Be Head of an Organization**

Some people, particularly those who rise to high positions in organizations, have found that the way to get what they want and to be secure in getting it in the future, is to rely on getting into positions of status and power. This is where we get the familiar phrase "empire building." Schumpeter, the great sociologist-economist, characterized the entrepreneur this way:

> "In the breast of one who wishes to do something new . . . there is the dream and the will to found a private kingdom. . . . The modern world really does not know any such positions, but what may be attained by industrial or commercial success is still the nearest approach to medieval lordship possible to modern man. Its fascination is specially strong for people who have no other way of achieving social distinction. The sensation of power and independence loses nothing by the fact that both are largely illusions."[2]

Of course, this motivation comes to different people in degrees. In moderation, it is functional for the individual executive and functional for the organization. Running throughout much of the more accepted management literature is an implication that the executive has a degree of this motivation. When Chester Barnard . . . gives us the principles of cooperative action, we can see at least his self-confidence in creating a system for large numbers of people to live in and to follow in their behavior. This same might be said of Fayol's explanation of discipline and unity of command, of the casual way in which Newman lays out the purposes of standing policies and procedures, and of the tone in which Cordiner presents General Electric's vast philosophy for governing the behavior of 281,000 employees. Even Wilfred Brown, head of Glacier Metal Company in England, who brought industrial psychologists from Tavistock into his company, shows a high degree of self-confidence in his role as the most important single person responsible for instituting a specific "new order" for governing behavior within the firm.

In extreme cases, this desire to achieve a position of status and power can be dysfunctional for both the executive and for the organization. In literature, we have the "King Lear" syndrome, in which the desire for keeping one's status and prerogatives was so strong that decisions made by the King were finally unworkable with resulting disintegration of his own personality and rebellion by his subjects. Or, we need look only to Hitler in Germany to see

---

[2] Joseph A. Schumpeter, *Theory of Economic Development* (Cambridge, Mass.: Harvard University Press, 1934), pp. 84–94.

the results of one imbued with maintaining personal office and power—resulting in organizational decisions which would not work.

A number of modern sociologists have cited cases where executives so focused on the rule system and the prerogatives of office, that they almost ignore changing needs of customers, of technology, or of other *facts* which should be considered in dynamic decision-making. . . .

## Competition and the Will to Conquer

But Schumpeter gives us another set of motivations, which have some verification in subsequent studies in clinical psychology:

> "Then there is the will to conquer: the impulse to fight, to prove oneself superior to others, to succeed for the sake, not of the fruits of success, but of success itself. From this aspect, economic action becomes akin to sport—there are financial races, or rather boxing matches . . ."[3]

This motivation, too, comes parceled to differing executives in differing degrees. And here, too, moderation may well be functional for both the organization and the individual executive.

We recall from Gellerman's summary of "The Power Motive" as "The Power Motive" as conceptualized by the psychoanalyst, Adler . . . , that all men may have some of this type of motivation. And in economics, the very essence of "free enterprise" has been the competitive instinct. Too little of this motivation may result in one's being a follower but not a leader, and too much may result in pathological or dysfunctional outcomes. . . . Bennis and Shepard . . . clearly [show] that, in their orientations toward authority, some people tend to have formed habitual behavior patterns of dependency, others of counter-dependency, and still others of "independency."

In extreme cases, we should not discount the possibility that the *executive* can be the one who plays Berne's deadly game, "Now I've Got You You Son of a Bitch." . . . If he plays for the rules *per se,* without regard for the reality of decisions, and if his primary motivational repertoire consists of the one strategy to check up on people, to "place the blame," this seems the proper diagnosis.

## The Urge to Creative Action

A third executive motivation often cited in the literature is aptly put by Schumpeter:

> "[In addition to the dream of a private kingdom, and the will to conquer] there is the joy of creating, of getting things done, or simply of exercising one's energy and ingenuity. . . . Our [executive] type seeks out difficulties, changes in order to change, delights in ventures."[4]

Schumpeter goes on to explain that there *would be no leaders* if there were not some people who possess certain mental characteristics which enable them to get outside of their routine way of living in the organization. There are three reasons why, for many human beings, it is difficult to create new things and get things done. First, there is great risk—mental risk—in doing something new, in which the outcome is unknown. Action must be taken without working out all of the details, and success depends partly upon *Intuition*. Therefore, there is a lack of objective information "out there." Secondly, even if there were not objective insecurity out there, there is subjective insecurity for the human mind to do something new.

---

[3] Ibid.

[4] Ibid.

"In the breast of one who wishes to do something new, the forces of habit rise up to bear witness against the embryonic project. A new and *another kind* of effort of will is necessary. This mental freedom presupposes a great surplus force over the everyday demand and is something peculiar and by nature rare."[5] Thirdly, even if one can overcome the two obstacles above, there is a reaction of the social environment against one who wishes to do something new. For all of these reasons, we take the position in the present chapter that the men who actually engage in political action—who actively make rules, and who engage in dynamic action to get them instituted—are motivated in part by these kinds of feelings. Remembering the Maslow theory of human motivation. . . , we see that such men are engaging in a kind of self-fulfillment—and they have found a way of life to do this, that of political action.

At a number of points in this book, we have seen that there is another kind of executive who relies on the existing rules to achieve security and status, who "goes by the book," who is satisfied by the feeling of importance of office and title, and whose mental reactions are similar to the less innovating individual described above. That there are such executives cannot be denied. They are motivated by the two first of Schumpeter's forces (empire ruling and the will to conquer), but not especially by the third.

### Symmetry as a Means to Security

Mental security—"peace of mind"—results in part when a person lives in an orderly world, in which "everything is in its place," and in which there are few unexpected events. If you expect that your class will begin at 10 o'clock and that there will be an examination on Chapters 3–7 in the book, think what it does to your feelings of security if the professor shows up at 10:30, or if he gives the examination on Chapters 5–8!

This kind of motivation operates for both general (line) executives and for specialist (staff) executives. In the former case, sociologists have pointed out that many executives have "a demand for control," and that this causes them to make rules for uniformity, or standards for measuring results. Given the necessity for technological coordination, the executive is much more secure if he can predict what people will do in the organization, and if he has uniform standards and policies so that all parts and people don't have to be viewed individually. Throughout the readings by Barnard. . . , Newman, Cordiner, and Brown, we see the need expressed in orderly procedures, policies and standards.

In the case of staff specialist executives, this need is expressed in the desire to formulate business operations on the basis of certain *known* bodies of knowledge. The finance specialist is much more secure in his thinking if he has tools of marginal analysis or discounted cash flow to apply to investment decisions or pricing problems. The marketing specialist's mind is much more at ease if there are known ways of predicting consumer motivation or of choosing advertising media. And the Operations Research specialist, through use of formulas for inventory control, can do his work much more securely than if he had to face entirely new projects, without models for approaching them. This kind of motivation is clear . . . when staff men are sometimes given "functional authority."

Thus, both general executives and specialist executives have an additional reason for formulating standing plans and rules, and for instituting them in organizations. Such rules enable them to pursue their careers, and use their minds, and with less mental strain and frustration than if there were no systems, rules, and order.

### The Pragmatic Position—"It Works"

A final reason why executives engage in political action is that all human beings need law and order in an interdependent organization, and the executive recognizes either explicitly or intuitively that he *can* take such action.

This has already been explained . . . on more than one level analysis. Lock's philosophi-

---

[5] Ibid.

cal explanation of human passion, Presthus' emphasis on reduction of anxiety among peers, and Gouldner's explanation of how rule systems reduce anxiety between superiors and subordinates all confirm that the executive can, if he does so wisely, govern human behavior through formulation of systems of law and order.

The many other studies in this book which show that people react to authority systems in ways which are dysfunctional should, however, serve as a warning. The phrase "if he does so wisely" is an important one. Later in this chapter, we will examine how the technological rule system is converted to legitimate law and order.

## DESIGNING THE TECHNOLOGICAL SYSTEM

It may seem odd that in a chapter on political action, we begin with a section called "Designing the Technological System." Does this not sound like engineering or economics instead of politics? The answer lies in the fact that the technological system—the organization output goals, the system of working parts, and the input-output relationships between them—are at one and the same time the technical work operations to be performed by each part of the organization, and the rules of human conduct which the part (person, department) should follow. . . .

# 15. BERGEN METALFABRIK, A/S

---

## Case Introduction

---

### SYNOPSIS

A medium-sized Norwegian manufacturing company experiences difficulty in building relationships between headquarters and the newly merged international subsidiaries in Sweden, Denmark, Germany, Italy, and Switzerland. The director of human resources uncovers uneasiness in both headquarters and subsidiaries and decides, with the president, to engage a consultant to assist with a team-building activity during the first top management meeting planned for early 1972 in Sweden. The consultant recommends using an organization development technique called "force field analysis." While the meeting is being planned, the company acquires another major division. The management team from the new division joins the other managers for the team-building exercise during the top management meeting. In work groups with representation from headquarters, divisional, and subsidiary levels a diagnosis of the headquarters-subsidiary relationship is performed and recommendations for remedial action are presented. The consultant leaves the top management meeting ambivalent over the results.

### WHY THIS CASE IS INCLUDED

Though the field of organization development is now over a decade old, few cases exist which document blow by blow, as it were, the organization development process. In the Bergen Metalfabrik case the readers can examine an organization's need for change and analyze the decision process which led to responding to the need with a particular form of consulting intervention. The organization development consulting style and the organization development technique of "force field analysis," can be observed in action. The reader can test his or her own ideas for change against the consultant's in light of the immediate and the likely future results of the organization development activity.

462

## DIAGNOSTIC AND PREDICTIVE QUESTIONS

The readings included with this case are marked (*). The author index at the end of this book locates the other readings.

1. Why is it not surprising that Bergen Metalfabrik experiences some difficulties in headquarters-subsidiary relationship at this stage of its history?

2. What was Nils Guren communicating to Vince Matthews in his September 3rd letter when he asks advice on an *"organization development* project"?

Read:   French, "Organization Development Objectives, Assumptions, and Strategies."

3. Is it clear that Nils Guren and Vince Matthews adapt and behave according to the values and assumptions of organization development?

Read:   French, "Organization Development Objectives, Assumptions, and Strategies."

4. Describe the consulting style of Vince Matthews. What other styles might he have used? Did his style fit the circumstances at Bergen Metalfabrick?

Read:   *Schein, *Process Consultation: Its Role in Organization Development.* *Kolb and Frohman, "An Organizational Development Approach to Consulting."

5. Why did not the plenary session work as smoothly as Vince Matthews had hoped? What accounts for what the planning director calls "shallowness"?

Read:   McGrath, *Social Psychology: A Brief Introduction.*

6. Why did Vince Matthews want to see the president before the exercise?

Read:   Levinson, "Role, Personality, and Social Structure in the Organizational Setting."

7. The president has been described as an entrepreneur and has led an aggressive growth drive in the past seven years. Did the organization development approach suit his personal style?

Read:   Odiorne, *How Managers Make Things Happen.* *Jennings, "Business Needs Mature Autocrats."

8. Do you see any evidence of change in Bergen Metalfabrik as you review the output of the group work? What do you predict will happen in headquarters-subsidiary relationships in the coming year? What are the bases of your prediction?

## POLICY QUESTIONS

9. Would you have done anything differently if you were Nils Guren? Vince Matthews? The president?

10. What should Vince Matthews suggest at the end of the case?

11. If you were the president, what would you do now that the exercise is over?

# Case Text*

On September 10, Dr. Vincent Matthews received a letter from a Norwegian Director of human resources he had met some seven months earlier in a management development seminar.

> Bergen Metalfabrik, A/S
> Bergen, Norway
> 3 September 1971

Dr. Vincent Matthews
Paris, France

Dear Vince:

May I ask your advice on someone to help us with an organization development project on headquarters-subsidiary relationships next January? We have heard good things about Edward Carey in Switzerland and Fred Post in Belgium. How about Peter Williams in England? How about your own availability? Could you recommend any other first class organization development consultants in Europe?

Many thanks for your big help!

> Regards,

> Nils Guren
> Director of Human Resources

Vincent Matthews recalled that Nils Guren worked for a 60-year-old medium-sized, Norwegian, family-owned firm which had recently gone multinational by acquiring several subsidiaries throughout Europe. Annual growth in the firm exceeded 10 percent but integration of the newly merged units had not yet been accomplished. The president and majority owner of the firm showed an entrepreneurial flair, but not until recently had there been concentration on the internal management of the emerging multinational enterprise. Nils Guren had joined the firm as director of human resources, just a year and a half ago after several years as training officer for an employer's federation and lecturer in psychology at the university. Vincent Matthews remembered Nils Guren as a probing and well-informed professional The prospect of working with him

---

on the headquarters-subsidiary organization development project was attractive to Vincent Matthews so he responded as follows:

Paris, France
13 September 1971

Mr. Nils Guren
Director of Human Resources
Bergen Metalfabrik, A/S
Bergen, Norway

Dear Nils:

Thank you very much for your letter of September 3, 1971.

You sound like you are planning an exciting meeting for your company on the topic of "headquarter-subsidiary relations." The organization development approach is most appropriate for this kind of task. I agree with you that the consultant you use must be first class.

I know Edward Carey very well. We have worked together in the States prior to coming here and we have worked here together in the recent past. He operates very well with executive groups and has the age and experience to be perfectly credible in such a sensitive task. I am not sure, however, Edward has direct experience in such an organization development approach but I have every confidence he could package it well.

I also know Fred Post from having worked with him on our research on teaching methods this past year. He is younger than Edward but he has already cumulated much experience with executives in his short career. He is formally trained by NTL [1] and knows the organization development material singularly well. If your group would accept his relative youth, he would be qualified to do the job.

I am sorry to say that I do not know Peter Williams first hand so I will not comment on his capacity.

There are two other men in Belgium who could do the job well. Pierre Lefol is French but has very good English. He too is NTL trained and has done organization development work with client firms, in France especially. He has the age and experience to be immediately credible.

Wayne Burke is another good prospect. We worked together in the States for several years prior to his coming to Europe. He is first class. He has done such things for companies here and in the States and if he has time could perform very well.

The other English-speaking trainers I know in Europe do not have sufficient European exposure for me to recommend them at this time, It would be inappropriate to use a North American who is not yet culturally sensitized.

---

[1] National Training Laboratories.

I have done such organization development work both here and in the States. I am particularly fascinated by the relationship issue between such units as headquarters-subsidiaries or information Operations Research staff and company client groups. It is in these contexts where I have done my work.

Do not feel any obligation to give me first priority because you have written to me but simply be advised that I think I could do the job and might be able to fit it into my schedule if the timing is right. There is one week in January which is impossible for me (16–21 January).

I hope you have in hand the six book series on organization development from Addison-Wesley. The authors included are Blake-Mouton, Lawrence-Lorsch, Walton, Bennis, Schein, and Beckhard.

You should also have in hand the book by Gordon Lippit entitled *Organizational Renewal* (Appleton Century Crofts, 1969). Finally, you will want to consult the new book by Chris Argyris, *Intervention Theory and Method* (Addison-Wesley, 1970).

I hope these comments are useful to you in your planning.

Sincerely,

Vincent Matthews

On September, Vincent Matthews received the following telex from Nils:

Att: Vince Matthews          24 Sept. 71
Thanks for good news. Would be pleased to work with you. Next step could be discussion between us in Paris. Do you have time in near future? Regards
Nils Guren—Bergen

An exchange of telexes led to a meeting in Vincent Matthew's office in Paris on October 8th. The meeting lasted some five hours. Vincent Matthews' notes summarize the main points discussed.

### Notes of 8 October Meeting with Nils Guren

1. Nils outlines the organization with the warning that positions and people are shifting rapidly.

Just about 5,000 were employed in Bergen Metalfabrik in 1971, two thirds in Division A where 75 percent of the sales were generated. Consolidated sales volume in 1970 had been almost 50 million. The product lines from Divisions A and B have many common engineering and production characteristics but serve different customer needs through different distribution systems.

The Bergen Holding Company comprised two product divisions unrelated to Division A or B products in technology, market or any other

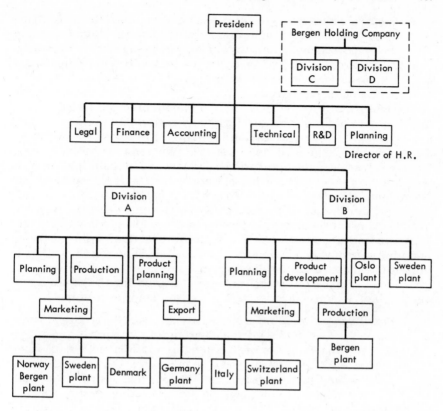

way. The president and his family held majority ownership in the holding company and operated it virtually independently of Bergen Metalfabrik. In 1970, the holding company had sales of $10 million.

The newest of the subsidiaries in Division A was the small sales company in Italy which had just been added a month ago. The German subsidiary had been added less than a year ago as had the minority interest in the Swiss company. The Danish and Swedish subsidiaries both had been part of Bergen Metalfabrik for over ten years but each started as a profit center just last year when the company was divisionalized.

2. The concern for improving the headquarters-subsidiary relationship started with the director of human resources but the president gave the project highest priority. Nils Guren had picked up many—often emotional—comments from managers in the subsidiaries concerning the unsatisfactory relations with headquarters. The subsidiary managers often did not know what headquarters wanted and found report requests from headquarters to be burdensome. Headquarters was seen to be unresponsible to the subsidiaries' requests for technical and marketing help. Similarly, headquarters executives cited cases of poor communications and unresponsiveness from the subsidiaries.

3. About 40 executives (19 from headquarters and 21 from various subsidiaries) would be brought to neutral territory in Ronneby Brunn, Sweden, for a two and one-half day top management meeting on January 13–14, 1972. One full day of that meeting was to be committed to the organization development project. The rest of the time would be devoted to corporate planning activities.

4. Under Nils Guren's aegis, Bergen Metalfabrik had begun experimenting with organization development by beginning managerial grid seminars. Only 30 executives had participated in phase one seminars, some in public sessions, some in a special pilot session within the company. A full-scale managerial grid program would probably be launched within a year as soon as the appropriate materials were translated into Norwegian. However, neither this program nor the other educational efforts within Bergen Metalfabrik seemed adequate to cope with the headquarters-subsidiary issue. Prompt and specific action was thought desirable and necessary. The full-scale introduction of the corporate planning system would be retarded if remedial action were not taken to improve headquarters-subsidiary relationships.

5. Three proposed approaches were discussed for the organization development exercise during the January top management meeting.

*a.* Small groups would work on various phases of the strategy formulation process (surveying the environment for threats and opportunities, analyzing the firm's strengths and weaknesses, objective setting, etc.) The groups would be mixed representation of headquarters and subsidiary personnel. As deemed desirable we could provide process feedback on the group meetings and/or sessions on team building.

*b.* Homogeneous small groups could begin a social perception audit by describing (each from its own perspective) the relationship between headquarters and subsidiaries. Each group would also predict the description to be given by the other group. In plenary session the descriptions and predictions would be shared and discussed. Disagreements would be revealed and misunderstandings straightened out. Critical road blocks for the relationship would be identified so that mixed small groups could design action plans to improve the relationship.

*c.* Mixed small groups could engage in a force field analysis whose dependent variable would be "headquarters-subsidiary cooperation." Each group would list the forces conducive to cooperation and the forces standing in the way of cooperation. The results would be displayed in plenary session and the highest priority items on each list identified for attention in an action plan to be designed in the small groups.

6. The strategy planning exercise was rejected because it was too indirect and because it was thought premature to involve this group in so sensitive an exercise at this stage of dramatic change in the company. The social perception audit was rejected because it was too confron-

tive and uncontrollable. The more reticent Scandinavians might be threatened by the assignment.

The force field analysis was selected because of the balance built right into the force field exercise. A man could risk being negative because he could recoup quickly by adding a positive item. Nils Guren saw benefit in each man being able to manage his own risks even if this meant some of the deeper data never were revealed. In the long run, he insisted, more good would be done by taking small controlled steps than by forcing emotional confrontation.

7. Nils Guren asked Vince Matthews to make a concrete proposal and design the instrument to Nils Guren:

Paris, France
4 November 1971

Mr. Nils Guren
Director of Human Resources
Bergen Metalfabrik, A/S
Bergen, Norway

Dear Nils:

I am sorry for the delay in getting back to you. I hope you find the enclosed documents satisfactory. It would help if you or one of your colleagues would pretest the force field analysis instrument and let me see the results.

Also, of course, feel free to alter the instrument to give better examples or explanation. Does the organization development program plan seem to make sense?

I am in Malmö on the second and third of December just in case we should get together either there or in Copenhagen.

Hoping to hear from you soon, I am,

Sincerely,

Vincent Matthews

Encl.: Organization development program schedule and force field analysis instrument

### Organization Development Program Plan

| Activity | Time |
|---|---|
| I. *Introduction*—Vince Matthews will describe the exercise and the forms and respond to questions. | 15 minutes 1:30–1:45 |
| II. *Individual exercise*—Each executive will fill in the force field analysis. | 60 minutes 1:45–2:45 |

III.    *Small group discussion*—Six-man groups will discuss the individual data with the purpose of devel-
oping a group consensus. They record their con-           120 minutes
sensus on flip chart pages.                               3:15–5:15

IV.    *Plenary discussion*—All the participants gather to
hear the reports from group representatives. The
separate group lists are combined to one master
list.
Then the items are ranked—at least the top three          120 minutes
forces in each of the four categories.                    7:00–9:00

V.    *Small group discussion*—Newly mixed groups
(different than in step III) of six men each take the
ranked master list of forces and design action
plans (suggestions) to reinforce driving forces and
remove or mitigate restraining forces. Sugges-            90 minutes
tions are recorded on flip charts.                        9:00–10:30

VI.    *Plenary discussion*—All participants gather to
hear the individual group reports.
The President presides and responds in two ways:
    A.   Where possible he supports good ideas.
    B.   In most cases he refers the suggestions to a
       follow-up project team (made up of both
       headquarters and subsidiary representa-
       tives) for further study.
The project team will be asked to submit a prog-          90 minutes
ress report by April 1st to all participants.             10:30–12:00

## FORCE FIELD ANALYSIS ON HEADQUARTERS/ SUBSIDIARY COOPERATION

### Instructions

Please record on the following pages your views on the forces influencing the relationships between Bergen headquarters and subsidiaries. We
will be describing the *present* situation.

Certain forces (*driving forces*) will be helping or facilitating the effectiveness of communication and coordination in the relationship. Some
of these *driving forces* will be external to the company and others will
be internal to the company. Examples of each appear on the pages that
follow.

Other forces (*restraining forces*) will be hindering or blocking the
effectiveness of communication and coordination in the relationship.
Again, some of these *restraining forces* will be external to the company
and others will be internal to the company.

In some cases, a particular force may be both driving and restraining
when viewed from different perspectives.

After individually filling in the force field analysis, we will discuss the data in small groups and then in a plenary session.

The exercise may be visualized as follows:

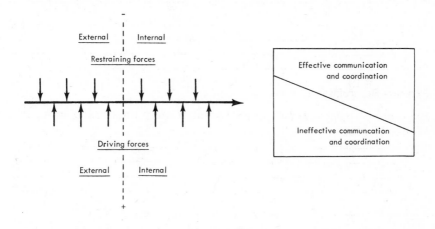

Name_____

## External Driving Forces

Example:   The economics of TELEX communication has reduced the cost of frequent communication.

1. _____
   _____
   _____
   _____

2. _____
   _____
   _____
   _____

3. _____
   _____
   _____
   _____

## Internal Driving Forces

Example:   People in headquarters and the subsidiaries are getting to know one another better.

1. _____
   _____
   _____
   _____

2. _____
_____
_____
_____

3. _____
_____
_____
_____

## External Restraining Forces

Example:   Physical separation prevents timely interaction on urgent matters.

1. _____
_____
_____
_____

2. _____
_____
_____
_____

3. _____
_____
_____
_____

## Internal Restraining Forces

Example:   Reporting forms and procedures have not yet been fully standardized.

1. _____
_____
_____
_____

2. _____
_____
_____
_____

3. _____
_____
_____
_____

Nils Guren responded by inviting Vince Matthews for a three-hour meeting in a Copenhagen hotel on December 2nd to review the program and examine the pretest results of the force field instrument.

**Notes of 2 December Meeting with Nils Guren**

1. Bergen Metalfabrik recently purchased a company in Norway almost the size of Division A, which roughly coincides with the product line of Division C of the Bergen holding company. Plans are not complete, but it is likely that the new company will not be fully integrated into Bergen Metalfabrik. Rather it and Division C will probably be run independently except for the sharing of some headquarters' administrative services. In any event, since the new unit "Norco" has a profit center structure like Division A, Norco executives will participate in the top management meeting, including the headquarters-subsidiary exercise.

2. The group at Ronneby Brunn will now have 55 members, many of whom will be meeting one another for the first time. The group will be composed as follows:

| | |
|---|---|
| Headquarters . . . . . . . . . . . . . . . | 9 |
| Division A | |
|   Division level. . . . . . . . . . . . . . | 8 |
|   Subsidiary level. . . . . . . . . . . . | 13 |
| Division B. . . . . . . . . . . . . . . . . . | 11 |
| Division C + Norco | |
|   Division level. . . . . . . . . . . . . . | 10 |
|   Subsidiary level. . . . . . . . . . . . | 4 |

3. Since Division B really has no subsidiaries, that 11-man group will do its own force field analysis on intradivisional communications. They will not report back during the plenary session but will rather observe and add comments where appropriate. Their reporting and action planning will be handled within their divisional meeting on Saturday, January 15, by Nils Guren. This group will work in Norwegian.

4. Simultaneous interpretation will be used at Ronneby Brunn because many headquarters people speak only Norwegian and many subsidiary people speak no Norwegian.

5. The exercise will be renamed "Analysis of Factors Influencing Headquarters-Subsidiary Cooperation." Nils found some resistance to the physical or engineering analogy in the term "force field analysis." For the same reason, the diagram will be omitted from the instrument.

6. Rather than just ask for five "issues" under each of the four headings in the instrument, we decided to ask for issues plus specific examples. Nils thought the more specific data would help in preparing the action plan.

7. The president preferred that Vince Matthews chair the final session and that the division general managers from Division A and Norco join him on a panel to respond to the action program suggestions. Nils reported that the president would be more comfortable with this arrangement. There is no disagreement with proposed procedure to submit the action program suggestions to a project team which will report back by early spring to the whole top management group.

8. Vince Matthews expressed some uneasiness to Nils Guren that he

had had no chance to meet the president to discuss the organization development exercise with him. Nils said he knew the president well enough to sense that he understood the risks and potential payoffs of the exercise and that he was fully committed to it. Since it was inconvenient to arrange a meeting prior to going to Ronneby Brunn, it was agreed that Vince would lunch with the president on the first day of the meeting and that they could continue discussions while the groups were working on the analysis.

Vince Matthews left the Copenhagen meeting somewhat unsettled because of the significant changes in group composition and because of the awkwardness of having parallel but different exercises going with Division A and Division C plus Norco and Division B. On the plane to Sweden, he reviewed the pretest results which Nils had given him. Those results are summarized in Appendix A. He found many of the comments superficial but he thought the group work at Ronneby Brunn would produce better analytic work.

Vince Matthews had no further contact with Nils Guren until he arrived at Ronneby Brunn on the evening of 12 January. They set right to work to make the assignments to six groups, taking care to have representation of all three levels in each group—headquarters, divisions, and subsidiary. For the first set of groups, there was no crossing of divisional lines. In the second set of groups, for the action programming phase, mixed groups were composed of Division A and Norco personnel. Care was taken not to have direct superior-subordinate pairs in the same group where possible. Reporters were appointed for each group without regard to status in the group hierarchy. The Division B group stayed the same throughout. The rest of the evening was spent in arranging logistics for the conference room, a large rectangular room permitting four seats on either side of a center isle in each of seven rows.

The morning session on Thursday began by the president's remarks in Norwegian. Vince Matthews listened to the English interpretation and made the following notes.

### Notes on President's Remarks—13 January

1. We are in the midst of a drive for internationality. Multinationality is a conscious objective.
2. Our problems, particularly in Division A and Norco, arise because of lack of contact and poor information flow between headquarters and subsidiaries. We will work on this later in our meeting.
3. It is no surprise that we have some problems since we have grown tenfold in seven years.
4. We want to improve communications so we can have bigger units and more cooperation.
5. In our newly enlarged group we plan to look for synergies in centrally managed activities rather than leave all decisions to the divisional level.
   *a.* We will coordinate finance to permit economies.
   *b.* We will standardize personnel policies to permit faster career

movement, to encourage early responsibility for young managers, and to facilitate our programs of promoting from within
and intercountry transfer.

   *c.* We will standardize in our management techniques, management system, and in our information system.

6. Being Norwegian by origin presents some problems:
   *a.* Language barrier.
   *b.* Geographically far from the center of activities.
   *c.* Underdeveloped capital market.

At some future time we could control the company from some other
location.

7. There are good points in being from a small country:
   *a.* Ease of contacting the highest government officials.
   *b.* Being Scandinavian allows trade with the Comecon countries.
8. Our objectives for the future are:
   *a.* Continued quantitative growth.
   *b.* Vertical integration.
   *c.* An extended product range.

As Vince Matthews listened to the interpreter, he became uneasy with
the artificial block to the communication represented by the earphones
and the interpreter's evident difficulty in catching the full message with
its business jargon. He feared that he grasped only two thirds of what
the president said. In light of the forthcoming headquarters-subsidiary
exercise, he wondered how the group received the president's assertion,
of impending centralization of a number of management decisions and
policies. He hoped for some feedback when the president threw the floor
open for questions and discussion but only one man rose to ask a question
about company prospects in light of the newly enlarged common market.
After a period of silence, the president handed the meeting over to the
planning director who began a description of the new planning system.
Vince Matthews decided it was best to write out the remarks he was to
make after lunch to guarantee that the interpreter could prepare for
accurate translation into Norwegian.

## Vince Matthews' Introductory Remarks

  I. *Introduction*

    A. Nothing unusual about working on headquarters-subsidiary
relationship. A concern for all firms at some stage depending
on:

      1. Rate of growth.
      2. Type of growth.
        *a.* Internal expansion.
        *b.* Expansion by acquisition.
      3. Degree of multinationality.
      4. Complexity of product line.

    The time is right now for Bergen + Norco to focus on
headquarters-subsidiary relationship because of the:

       1.  Fast growth.

       2.  Expansion by acquisition.

       3.  Recent multinationality.

       4.  Growing complexity of product lines.

    B.  Focus not so much on problem solving but opportunity seizing. What we do here is a direct support for the growth objectives announced this morning. The men in this room are undoubtedly *smart* as individuals. We approach our task as a group to see if we cannot become *wise*.

       1.  A smart man is a man who can get himself out of all sorts of problems.

       2.  A wise man never gets into the problems in the first place. As a group, we will try to do maintenance on the relationship between headquarters and subsidiaries, but we will try to be wise enough to do *preventive* maintenance.

    C.  This part of the top management meeting is a minor theme. The major theme focuses on *doing the right things.* In our part, we focus on *doing things right.* Obviously, it matters little how well we do things if we do the wrong things. The two themes are related, but, clearly, priority must go to planning the right growth strategies. When that's done, our organization development effort is in the right focus.

  II.  *What we are going to do:*

    A.  Describe the present relationship between headquarters and subsidiaries.

    B.  Analyze why the relationship is the way it is . . . what factors support good communications and coordination and what factors stand in the way of good communications and coordination.

    C.  Search for opportunities to improve the relationship in the future.

  III.  *How we are going to proceed:*

    A.  We will work in the next 24 hours as individuals, in small groups, and in this plenary meeting.

    B.  We will document our progress at each step.

(Vincent Matthews then went on to explain the instrument and the time schedule.)

It had been impossible for Vince Matthews to lunch with the president, but they met with Nils Guren and the division general managers from Division A and Norco while the rest of the group was doing the first phase of the analysis. The man representing Norco was in transition to the position of director of corporate planning. His successor at Norco was too new to the company to be anything more than an observer. The new planning director began the meeting by predicting the groups would not focus on relations with headquarters but rather on relations with the plants or the divisional administration. The president concurred in this prediction. While no one expressed any concern over the outcome, all showed enthusiasm and curiosity over what would be said. Vince Matthews outlined the role of the panel which was to receive the action plan suggestions in the last session. The panel was to be supportive rather than evaluative and was to indicate actions already under way or contemplated on the issues raised. All agreed that the project team, which was to be appointed to coodinate and "package" the action suggestions into specific action programs, should report to the appropriate unit—headquarters or division—and issue a progress report to the whole top management group prior to June 1, 1972. Names were selected for the six-man project team, representative of each level in both Division A and Norco. For logistical ease, the project team was to meet in Bergen under the lead of Nils Guren, even though this meant that only two non-Norwegians would be on the team. Throughout this meeting, Vince Matthews frequently felt left out when discussion and side comments occurred in Norwegian.

When the six groups began discussing the analyses done individually, Nils Guren and Vince Matthews circulated the syndicate rooms. Only one group experienced definitional problems and had to be encouraged to relax the formalities and get on with the task. Lively and rather full participation characterized each group. One of the Scandinavian languages, rather than English, seemed most frequently used in the discussions. One group asked if they could meet in the sauna. Nils gave the okay but the group never left its meeting room.

After dinner, each group reporter summarized the goup consensus, using flip chart graphics. Vince Matthews taped the flip chart sheets to the wall after each spoke. Clarifying questions were invited but only one was raised. Aside from two or three bursts of laughter the room was rather silent. During the presentations, the president and planning director whispered to one another frequently in the front row.

When all the flip chart sheets were displayed, Vince Matthews asked the group to pick the top three priority items in each of the four categories: external driving factors, internal driving factors, external restraining factors, internal restraining factors. He indivated the items should be controllable by Bergen/Norco and issues on which the group could design action recommendations. The selected items would be typed overnight and distributed to the second set of work groups for action programming in the morning.

Vince Matthews asked the group to begin by choosing the high priority external driving factors. No response. Long pause. Vince Matthews suggested an item which seemed common to several groups. No response. Finally, one man offered a suggestion. Vince Matthews asked if the group concurred. No response. So it proceeded through the second of the lists of driving factors. Four men made all the contributions from the floor and, except for occasional *Sotte voce* remarks by the president and planning director like "that's not important," the room was quiet. Since it was the hour designated for finishing the two more lists that remained for discussion, Vince Matthews called a five-minute stretch break. Nils Guren encouraged numbers of the group to gather around the displayed lists so they could prepare suggestions for the next priority items. Nils took Vince aside and said the lists were not visible from the back of the room. He thought this accounted for the lack of participation.

After the break, Vince Matthews began by summarizing the next list prior to asking for suggestions. The response came somewhat more quickly but five or six men remained the only contributors. In 45 minutes, the priority list was finished and the group broke up.

Nils took Vince to the bar for a drink. Vince admitted he was frustrated and disappointed but Nils tried to lift his spirits by attributing the lack of participation to the technological problem of visibility and the fatigue of the group. Vince insisted the exercise design packed too much into the evening session and prevented him from being of more help to the group. He could not digest the 200 or more items reported by the work groups in a way that would facilitate the task of drawing up the priority list. They agreed they could do no more prior to the morning session so they merely gave the list to the typist for reproduction.

### Priority List of Driving and Restraining Factors

    I.  Internal restraining factors.
        A.  Information problems (quantity and quality).
            1.  Slow and inaccurate reporting.
            2.  Not enough information inside and between functions.
            3.  Lack of sufficient information from the top level.
        B.  Delayed and unqualified feedback.
        C.  Inventory of corporate human resources.
        D.  Conflict of interests.
        E.  Integration of new subsidiaries.
   II.  External restraining forces.
        A.  Language training.
        B.  Different quality demands.
  III.  Internal driving forces.
        A.  Standardization.
        B.  Exchange of know-how (technical).
        C.  Common principles for planning and reporting.
  IV.  External driving forces.
        A.  Image of the group.
        B.  Availability of data processing.
        C.  Standardization.

At nine in the morning, the groups began developing action plans to reinforce the driving factors and remove or mitigate the restraining forces. Each group was encouraged to select items from the list to concentrate on rather than attempt to respond to all 13 items. Again, the small group discussions seemed lively and the plenary session began with much buzzing in the room. Frequently, as each group reporter summarized his group's recommendations, laughing and random comments spread through the room. The president and planning director whispered frequently in their position at the panel table with the Division B managing director and Vince Matthews. With redundancies removed, the suggestions appear in outline form below:

1. *Standardized information:*
    a. Produce manual of policies on finance, distribution, guarantees, technical changes, reporting procedures, and simplified price list.
    b. Assure that all technical drawings at least are in English.
    c. Compile a frequently updated directory of headquarters' personnel, including organization chart for reference.
    d. Translate all information from headquarters or divisions into the local language of the subsidiary.
    e. Set specific time limit for responding to telexes.
    f. Standardize currency units for all reports.
    g. Use more visuals in all reports.
2. *Information from headquarters and divisions:*
    a. Reports comparing subsidiary performance should be issued quarterly to all subsidiaries by division.
    b. Announcements of major business decisions or appointments should be made at the same time to all company units before public dissemination.
    c. Divisions should work out procedures to prevent delayed and/or unqualified feedback to subsidiary inquiries especially concerning product development and quality control.
    d. Headquarters should require from subsidiaries no more information than the subsidiaries find useful in managing their own units.
    e. Employ management by objectives in such a way that discussed and agreed objectives are the basis for follow-up and corrective action.
3. *Information meetings:*
    a. Managers and controllers across units should meet regularly to discuss relative standing of the units.
    b. Functional meetings should be held twice a year to avoid the commander-troop mentality.
4. *Inventory of corporate human resources:*
    The director of human resources should prepare a computerized file of Bergen/Norco managers and specialists, showing alternative personnel for each position. Include profile data and current project memberships. Include as well outside potential human resources. Issue a human resources policy.
5. *Conflict of interest:*
    Make a top-level decision to resolve the conflict of interest among subsidiaries in Norco.
6. *Integration of new subsidiaries:*
    a. The director of planning should head a project team to develop a merger integration plan.
    b. There should be a checklist of problems arising in merger integration after the recent experience in Italy.

7.  *Language training:*
    The company should institute language course using appropriate technology and possibly rewarding managers who demonstrate increased language facility in English.
8.  *Management information system:*
    a.  A project team should develop a better sales forecasting system and factory planning and control system.
    b.  Headquarters and subsidiary EDP practices should be studied and unified.
    c.  Study the feasibility of centralizing EDP for the whole group via data lines.
9.  *Image of the group:*
    a.  Get more publicity in trade papers, radio, television, and international trade fairs.
    b.  Have technical papers presented at professional meeting by Bergen/Norco personnel.
    c.  Improve relations with bankers and major customers by stressing the quality of products and the quality of our people.

After the presentations were completed, the president called for a break in order for the panel to prepare its response. The three panelists agreed on a division of labor depending on whether the suggestion was more relevant to headquarters or one of the two divisions. When the group was reconvened, the president began by expressing thanks for the suggestions and committing the company to appropriate action. He announced some immediate responsible action like calling the people concerned with the conflict of interest case to a luncheon meeting. He also agreed to the formation of a number of the project teams recommended and promised immediate action on such items as the new corporate directory.

The other two panelists continued in the same spirit by committing their organizations to action or by underlining relevant work already in progress. Vincent Matthews announced the coordinating project team membership and explained its mandate of digesting the recommendations with all the backup data from the exercise and constructing a composite action plan for submission to the relevant company units. A progress report from the coordinating project team was promised to the whole top management group before 1 June.

Before closing the meeting for lunch, Vince Matthews gave the group the following feedback on its performance in the exercise:

> What more could a consultant ask from such an exercise than that change has already begun. From what I have observed the Bergen/Norco group is well on its way not only to do the right things but also to do things right.
>
> How was the performance in the exercise? The quality of small group work was excellent. Everyone seemed active and involved. The groups were productive.
>
> The quality of analysis varied from group to group but overall

coverage was wide-ranging and rather deep in some places. One is left with the feeling, however, that some things have been unsaid.

The work in the plenary session was rather unproductive. Many in the room remained passive. Why? Altogether we were too large a group for this kind of task especially given the geography of this room where each individual saw more backs than faces. Last evening we tried too much. Aside from the difficulty of seeing the flip chart displays, we attempted to comprehend some 200 lines of data without prior preparation. The group could not do the processing quickly enough nor could I singificantly help the group in its efforts. Any outside observer would comment that few people took risks during these plenary sessions. I would not consider that unusual since you did not know one another very well. One does not know the magnitude of risk one is taking in a group unless familiarity with colleagues allows a prediction of their likely response. Finally, the technology of simultaneous interpretation made the setting overly formal. Many people had to use second or third languages to discuss very important matters. In those circumstances, you are to be congratulated for doing so well.

For myself, I am frustrated that my language limitations prevented me from getting as fully involved in the exercise as is my custom. I am grateful, however, for your gracious hospitality and generous cooperation.

As the meeting adjourned, the planning director leaned over to Vince Matthews and asked: "Do such groups always stay on the surface? I do not think they got down to the real issues. They were too general and philosophical." Vince Matthews started to respond but the president interrupted: "How did the panel do?" Vince Matthews had only time to say: "Couldn't have been better" before the president pumped his hand, saying "thanks, and good-bye!"

Nils Guren came up with apologies for not having formally thanked Vince Matthews in front of the group. He expressed his own thanks and his conviction that the exercise went well. There was little time to talk further since Nils had to prepare for his own presentation after lunch and Vince had to catch a plane to Paris. They parted with the agreement to sit down soon and analyze the experience.

As Vince Matthews took the taxi to the airport, he tried to sort out his mixed feelings. The performance of the panel was immensely better than he could have hoped and yet he had to grant the planning director's assertion that the analysis and recommendations were somewhat superficial and unresponsive to the specific mission of the exercise. Vince could not predict very well the outcome of the coordinating project team nor the follow-up of headquarters or divisions. He wondered if the exercise could not have been better designed, or more radically, if something different should not have been done from the beginning or at least from the point at which the character of the top management meeting changed with the addition of Norco.

# APPENDIX A

## PRETEST RESULTS OF THE FORCE FIELD ANALYSIS (H1 AND H2 ARE HEADQUARTER'S MANAGERS AND S1 AND S2 ARE SUBSIDIARY'S MANAGERS)

### External Driving Forces

H1    Standardization in technical specifications in today's Europe.

H1    The threat from large multinational companies motivates smaller ones to unite and "communicate."

H1    Development in the field of transportation.

H2    The rapid and good traffic connections between different countries (flights).

H2    The telephone connections have been better and better during last to three years (especially Italy).

H2    Development of dictating machines in connection with phone calls.

S1    Automatic telephone network in Europe equals faster contact today.

S2    Automatic dialing telephones inside some part of group area.

S2    Generally rising level of English language knowledge all over in Europe.

S2    Transportation improving, air freight and container transportation.

S2    Lowering customs plus passport plus barriers.

S2    All businessmen are reading the same magazines today.

### External Restraining Forces

H1    Language difficulties.

H1    Lack of common European standard.

H1    Lack of trained "internationalists."

H1    Growing isolationism (problems in financing, currency transfer, etc.).

H2    Geographic distances.

H2    Patriotism.

H2    Different technical development.

H2    Different laws in different countries.

### Internal Driving Forces

H1    Basically a common language (in Scandinavia).

H1    Valuable exchange of know-how.

H1    Necessity to acquire export outlets in order to grow to a level sufficient for survival.

H2    Uniform information systems in different functions (budgeting, reporting, etc.).

H2   Personal contacts.
H2   Policy group meetings (we have had only two).
H2   Exchange of personnel between group companies especially between Norway and other countries.
H2   Norweigian employees in group companies.
S1   Willingness to solve common problems.
S1   Personal ambition.
S2   Some personal contacts are forming.


## Internal Restraining Forces

H1   Differences in standards.
H1   Factory almost totally Norwegian speaking.
H1   Nationalist pride.
H1   Lack of skill in operating in present scale.
H2   Lack of knowledge of group companies. We are not information minded.
H2   Bad knowledge of main languages.
H2   Lack of knowledge about organization (who is who).
H2   Low educational level in some of local companies.
H2   There does not exist any internal education within the corporation.
H2   Nonhuman climate, especially in Norway.
S1   Language barrier. English is supposed to be the official language which is "foreign" to everyone. From the international point of view, still the best choice. Terminology has to be straightened out.
S1   Lack of knowledge of the other end of the communication line. More personal contact wanted. By the same token, better information regarding systems and organization wanted.
S1   National feelings among employees might affect the communication negatively. The multinational idea not always accepted. The feeling of the multinational group does not really exist at the headquarters either.
S1   Starting up of new projects is often formed via questionnaires which do not have the full explanation of background and aim of the project. First reaction: negative.
S2   Lack of personal contacts between headquarters and subsidiaries.
S2   Not very often given "why's" for different policies.
S2   The need to sell a product which you do not know fully and are not able to believe in fully.
S2   Difficult to give promises when others are depending on you.
S2   Organization divided into profit centers, therefore corporate views are forgotten now and then.
S2   Language barrier: Norwegian language.
S2   Poor planning: we are not accustomed to function as a whole—plans have to be made upon loose promises . . . lack of education and experience.

S2   Overemphasis upon economics and forgetting all other things . . . results are demanded without giving needed resources, facilities, etc.

S2   Long line and many links between the factory and customer and much buck-passing.

S2   Bias of wanting all solutions used within corporation to be of Norwegian origin.

S2   Exaggerated fright to tell things when they are negative . . . lack of correct information . . . lack of feedback, planning, and time table.

---

# Selected Readings

---

*From*

## PROCESS CONSULTATION: ITS ROLE IN ORGANIZATION DEVELOPMENT*

*By Edgar H. Schein*

### INTRODUCTION

This book is about a special kind of consultation which I am calling *Process Consultation* (P-C)—what it is, and what role it plays in organizational development (OD).

\*   \*   \*   \*   \*

Process consultation, . . . involves the manager and the consultant in a period of *joint* diagnosis. The process consultant is willing to come into an organization without a clear mission or clear need, because of an underlying assumption that most organizations could probably be more effective than they are if they could identify what processes (work flow, interpersonal relations, communications, intergroup relations, etc.) need improvement. A closely related assumption is that no organizational form is perfect, that every organizational form has strengths and weaknesses. The process consultant would urge any manager with whom he is working not to leap into an action program, particularly if it involves any kind of changes in organizational structure, until the organization itself has done a thorough diagnosis and assessment of the strengths and weaknesses of the present structure.

The importance of *joint* diagnosis derives from the fact that the consultant can seldom learn enough about the organization to really know what a better course of action would be for that *particular group* of people with their *particular* sets of traditions, styles and personalities. However, the consultant can help the manager to become a sufficiently good diagnostician himself, and can provide enough alternatives, to enable the manager to solve the problem. This last point highlights another assumption underlying P-C: problems will stay solved longer and be solved more effectively if the organization solves its own problems;

---

\* Edgar H. Schein, *Process Consultation: Its Role in Organization Development,* 1969, Addison-Wesley, Reading, Mass. Excerpts from pp. 3, 5–7, 9.

the consultant has a role in teaching diagnostic and problem-solving skills but he should not work on the actual concrete problem himself.

\* \* \* \* \*

Process consultation . . . focuses on joint diagnosis and the passing on to the client of diagnostic skills. The consultant may recognize early in his work what some of the problems are in the organization and how they might be solved. He does not advance them prematurely, however, for two reasons. One, he may be wrong and may damage his relationship with the client by a hasty diagnosis which turns out to be wrong. Two, he recognizes that even if he is right, the client is likely to be defensive, to not listen to the diagnosis, to misunderstand what the consultant is saying, and to argue with it.

It is a key assumption underlying P-C that the client must learn to see the problem himself, to share in the diagnosis, and to be actively *involved* in generating a remedy. The process consultant may play a key role in helping to sharpen the diagnosis and in providing alternative remedies which may not have occurred to the client. But he encourages the client to make the ultimate decision as to what remedy to apply. Again, the consultant does this on the assumption that if he teaches the client to diagnose and remedy situations, problems will be solved more permanently and the client will be able to solve new problems as they arise.

It should be emphasized that the process consultant may or may not be expert in solving the particular problem which is uncovered. The important point in P-C is that such expertise is less relevant than are the skills of involving the client in self-diagnosis and helping him to find a remedy which fits his particular situation and his unique set of needs. The process consultant must be an expert in how to diagnose and how to develop a helping relationship. He does not need to be an expert on production, marketing, finance, and the like. . . .

> P-C is a set of activities on the part of the consultant which help the client to perceive, understand, and act upon process events which occur in the client's environment.

The process consultant seeks to give the client "insight" into what is going on around him, within him, and between him and other people. The events to be observed and learned from are primarily the various human actions which occur in the normal flow of work, in the conduct of meetings, and in formal or informal encounters between members of the organization. Of particular relevance are the client's own actions and their impact on other people.

It should be noted that this definition brings in several new concepts and assumptions, relating in general to what one looks for in making one's *diagnosis*. The important elements to study in an organization are the human processes which occur. A good diagnosis of an organizational problem may go beyond an analysis of such processes but it cannot afford to ignore them. By implication, the process consultant is primarily an expert on processes at the individual, interpersonal, and intergroup levels. His expertise may go beyond these areas, but it must at the minimum include them. Improvement in organizational effectiveness will occur through effective problem finding in the human process area, which in turn will depend upon the ability of managers to learn diagnostic skills through exposure to P-C.

I am not contending that focusing on human processes is the *only* path to increasing organizational effectiveness. Obviously there is room in most organizations for improved production, financial, marketing, and other processes. I am arguing, however, that the various functions which make up an organization are always mediated by the interactions of people, so that the organization can never escape its human process. . . . As long as organizations are networks of people, there will be processes occurring between them. Therefore, it is obvious that the better understood and better diagnosed these processes are, the greater will be the chances of finding solutions to technical problems which will be accepted and used by the members of the organization.

*From*

# AN ORGANIZATION DEVELOPMENT
# APPROACH TO CONSULTING*

*By David A. Kolb and Alan L. Frohman*

The model for planned change presented below will be most appropriate if the consultant's interventions in the client system are placed in the context of a total organizational development program. Here, organizational development refers not to the content of the consultant intervention but to the manner in which it is carried out. More specifically, an intervention is an organizational development intervention if:

1. It is not undertaken as an isolated event but rather with consideration for its impact on the organization as a total system. That is, it is part of a total plan for organization improvement.[1]

2. It is directed not only at solving the organization's immediate problem but also at improving the organization's ability to anticipate and solve similar problems. The result is an increase in the ecological wisdom of the organization through improvement of its ability to survive and grow in its environment.

While there may be some consulting relationships for which this organizational development approach is not appropriate, it is our observation that much of the dissatisfaction with consulting interventions arises from a failure to deal with these two issues.

## Model for Planned Change

\*    \*    \*    \*    \*

The model focuses on two central issues which are highly interrelated. One concerns the relationship between client and consultant. To whom in the client organization does the consultant relate? Who influences whom? How open will the client and the consultant be with each other? The second concerns the nature of the work. How is the problem defined? What solutions are considered? It is typically the second issue that receives the most attention from consultants even though relationship factors also strongly affect the course and outcome of consulting work. These two issues can be considered within the framework of a dynamic, seven-stage model of the planned change process: scouting, entry, diagnosis, planning, action, evaluation, and termination (see Figure 1). These stages are by no means clear cut in practice. They may occur sequentially or simultaneously. However, the articulation of each stage provides a convenient way for the consultant to conceptualize and recognize the stages in his practice.

In the figure, the arrows connecting the stages illustrate the general developmental nature of the model. The first feedback loop, from planning to entry, defines the need for continuing renegotiation with the client in the light of diagnosis and planning activities. The second loop, from evaluation to planning, defines the need for using the evaluations of previous actions to modify planning activities. The central issues in the consulting process and their implications are summarized below for each stage in the change process. Successful intervention is the client system and implementation of change is directly related to the successful resolution of these issues.

---

[1] Beckhard, *Organization Development: Strategies and Models.* Reading, Mass., Addison-Wesley, 1969, p. 100. Beckhard defines organization development as "an effort (1) *planned,* (2) *organization-wide,* and (3) *managed from the top,* to (4) increase *organization effectiveness* and *health* through (5) *planned interventions* in the organization's 'processes', using *behavioral-science* knowledge."

**FIGURE 1**
**Process of Planned Change**

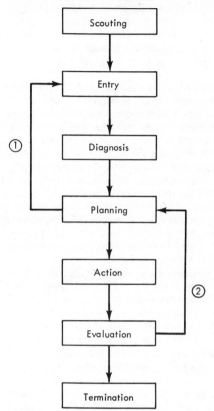

*Scouting.*  In the scouting phase, neither the client nor the consultant has committed himself to working with the other. Each is free to explore the potential relationship in order to obtain some preliminary data about the other. The client system is searching for resources and solutions to its problems. An invitation to a consultant to work with the client is based on the client's perception that the consultant can help in some way.

The consultant is also scouting his own interests, values, and priorities in order to decide whether this client system is one with which he wants to work. Often the first scouting goal is to answer the question: What about their perception of the problem and myself led them to contact me? An investigation of the client's actions prior to calling the consultant can be helpful here. . . .

In making his decision, the consultant may want to look at the following characteristics of the client system: (1) major resources, (2) major limitations, (3) important social and cultural norms and values, (4) major subsystems within the overall system (departments, divisions, subsidiaries), (5) gross interrelationships among major subsystems, (6) attitudes toward change, authority, outsiders, (7) relationship between client system and other systems in its environment (competitors, neighbors, regulating agencies), and (8) motivation of the client system to improve itself. In assessing these characteristics there is, of course, some danger of stereotyping the client as a result of insufficient evidence. Detailed assessment in most cases will have to wait until the diagnosis stage.

The most important result of this preliminary assessment is the choice of a formal entry point in the client system. In choosing an appropriate one, the interrelationships among the various units of the system are especially important. The acceptance and implementation of change most often requires that the recognized power structure of the system be used to establish the change. If one's initial contacts are with the deviant members of the organization, they may be very willing to accept a change for the system. But they are also likely to have little influence with the established authorities in the system.

*   *   *   *   *

*Entry.* Once the entry point has been selected, the consultant and the client system, through the entry representative, begin to negotiate a contract. In its use here, the word "contract" implies more than a legal document agreed upon at the outset of the project.[2] The contract will define if and how the succeeding stages of the planned change process will be carried out. The emphasis is on a continuing process of sharing the expectations of the consultant and the client system and agreeing on the contributions to be made by both parties. Mark Frohman has listed 10 areas in which agreement over expectations is important in order to develop an effective working relationship.[3] (1) the consultant's and the client's goals for the project, (2) broad definition of the problem (to be redefined as the relationship progresses), (3) relationship of the problem to the overall system, (4) client resources and abilities applicable to the problem, (5) consultant resources and abilities applicable to the problem, (6) broad mode of approach to the problem, (7) nature of the consultant/client relationship, (8) expected benefits for the client, (9) expect benefits for the consultant, and (10) ability of one party to influence the other.

Perhaps the most important issue in the negotiation process is power—gaining the influence necessary to work effectively in the client system. The four primary sources of power are: (1) legitimately constituted authority in the system, (2) expert power (the prestige of the consultant or the compelling logic of a solution, for example), (3) coercive power, and (4) trust-based power (the informal influence that flows from collaborative problem definition and solution). While in most cases all four types of power are used, trust-based power is particularly critical to the success of those planned change efforts where the system's formal power structure is the cause of the problem to be solved.

*   *   *   *   *

As the planned change process progresses and new information is gathered, it may be necessary to renegotiate the contract (see Figure 1). For example, the nature of the problem may change, the resources needed for its solution may increase or decrease, the consultant's particular expertise may become more or less relevant to the client system. As the diagnosis and planning stages proceed, the entry point into the client system may have to shift or expand to include those parts of the system which are affected by and/or responsible for the problem.

*Diagnosis.* The diagnostic phase focuses on four elements: the client's felt problem, the client's goals, the client's resources, and the consultant's resources. Starting the diagnosis with the client's felt problem means something more than simply copying his words. It involves appreciating the client system's culture and language, seeing events the way the client sees them. This empathy on the part of the consultant facilitates his ability to meet the client's needs and insures the client's involvement in the diagnostic process.

The first step in defining the specific problem to be attacked is to identify the subpart(s) of the system where the problem is located and interrelationships between the subpart and the other parts of the system. This is necessary in order to anticipate the effect of a change in one part of the system on other aspects of the system's functioning. If more and/or different problems are identified as the diagnosis progresses, the client and consultant can

---

[2] E. Schein, *Process Consultation: Its Role in Organization Development.* Reading, Mass., Addison-Wesley, 1969.

[3] M. Frohman, "Conceptualizing a Helping Relationship," Ann Arbor, Institute for Social Research Center for Research on Utilization of Scientific Knowledge, 1968 (mimeo).

assign priorities and focus attention on the most important problem or the problem which must be solved before other problems can be attacked.

The second step is to define the goals of the client system. What is the desired state toward which the client is striving? If goals are operationally defined, they can give direction to a meaningful, lasting solution of the problem and can place the problem in the context of the organization's total development.

The third and fourth elements assessed in the diagnostic processes are the client's and the consultant's resources for improving the situation. One particularly important variable to consider is motivation and readiness for change on the part of both the client system and the consultant. Is the client system really committed to solution of the problem? Are the key individuals responsible for implementing the change committed? What are the consultant's motives—prestige, genuine desire to help, scientific experimentation? The consultant should look especially for resources internal to the client system which can be developed and utilized to solve the problem. In this way the development of internal resources is accelerated and dependency on the consultant is reduced.

\* \* \* \* \*

***Planning.*** The creation of plans for change should proceed cooperatively with the client to insure that the plans are appropriate to his needs, and that he will understand them and be committed to their execution. The first planning step is to define the specific behavioral objectives to be achieved by the change. . . . The formulation of specific objectives also makes the evaluation task easier.

Once clear-cut objectives have been established, alternative solutions or change strategies can be generated. Later, when choosing among the alternatives, an attempt should be made to simulate the consequences of each action plan. This can be done simply by thinking through the implications of each change strategy, or by using more sophisticated simulation methods.

Each alternative can be classified on two dimensions: the source of power used to implement the intervention (formal power, expert power, coercive power, and trust-based power) and the organizational subsystem to which the intervention is addressed. The six organizational subsystems are . . .

1. The People Subsystem . . .

   \* \* \* \* \*

2. The Authority Subsystem . . .

   \* \* \* \* \*

3. The Information Subsystem . . .

   \* \* \* \* \*

4. The Task Subsystem . . .

   \* \* \* \* \*

5. The Policy/Culture Subsystem . . .

   \* \* \* \* \*

6. The Environmental Subsystem . . .

   \* \* \* \* \*

The four sources of power and the six organizational subsystems can be combined to form a checklist to be used by the consultant when planning or executing any action intervention. The primary purpose of the checklist is to remind the consultant that a change in one subsystem will affect other organizational subsystems. The list can be useful for selecting the best leverage point and for identifying the other subsystems most likely to be affected by the intervention.

\* \* \* \* \*

The checklist can also be useful for identifying the sources of power available for bringing about change and for determining which source, or combination of sources, is the most appropriate for the type of intervention planned. Certain combinations may not be enough to implement even the most optimal plan. . . .

***Action.***   In the action phase, the best change strategy developed in the planning phase is implemented. If the work of the previous four phases has been done well, the action plan should proceed smoothly. Hitches or problems can usually be traced to unresolved issues in the early phases: a failure to diagnose the system adequately, a failure to anticipate all the consequences of the action in the planning phase. If these errors are not so great as to disrupt the total change effort, they can become useful "critical incidents" for learning about the client system.

\*     \*     \*     \*     \*

***Evaluation.***   The tradition in the scientific evaluation of change projects has been to separate the evaluation phase from the action phase. To insure unbiased results, an independent researcher is often hired to evaluate the change efforts. While this approach has some benefit from the standpoint of scientific objectivity, it has some cost in terms of the effective implementation of change. It should be clear from our model that we see the evaluation phase as an integrated part of the change process.

\*     \*     \*     \*     \*

To decrease the dependency on the consultant and develop within the client system the ability to use the information generated for self-analysis, the client should monitor the progress of the action phase and evaluate the data himself. The results of the evaluation stage determine whether the change project moves to the termination stage or returns to the planning stage for further action planning and perhaps to the entry stage for further contract negotiation with the client.

***Termination.***   The consultant-client relationship is by definition temporary. Yet most consulting relationships are conceived to bring about some permanent or far-reaching improvement in the client system's functioning. The issue of termination must therefore be given attention throughout the relationship. In the initial entry contract, the conditions of termination should be discussed and a tentative agreement reached. These conditions should be continually open for renegotiation and become clearer as the relationship progresses.

\*     \*     \*     \*     \*

## On the Developmental Nature of the Consulting Process

In closing, we would like to share some of our speculations about the developmental regularity of the seven stages outlined above. Following Erikson's child developmental model,[4] Figure 2 depicts a developmental matrix. The vertical axis defines the seven stages of the consulting processes in developmental order; the horizontal axis designates the actual behavior of the consultant. The white boxes represent the "normal" developmental path of a consulting relationship as outlined in the paper. On this path, the consultant resolves the issues of the scouting stage before proceeding to the issues of the entry stage; he then resolves these issues before confronting diagnosis issues, and so on.

Horizontal movement in the matrix represents a fixation—a failure to resolve the issues of one stage before proceeding to the next. The consultant represented by arrow 1, for example, has not resolved the scouting issue of selecting an appropriate entry point. Thus, he is forced in the entry stage to continue his search for a point of entry under the pretext of negotiating a contract. Vertical movement in the matrix represents arrested development—a failure to confront the issues of the next stage. Consultant 2, for example, may see an entry point, but for some reason he is reluctant to press forward toward a contract with the client. Perhaps the most common case of arrested development occurs in the action-evaluation stages (consultant 2'). In this case, the consultant, for a complex set of reasons, cannot bring himself to evaluate his actions and so continues these actions with his client.

Another typical consulting strategy can be examined in this matrix. Some consultants—the planner (arrow 3) the action specialist (arrow 4), and the evaluator (arrow 5), for exam-

---

[4] See E. Erikson, *Childhood and Society.* New York, Norton, 1950.

**FIGURE 2**
**Developmental Model of Consultation Process**

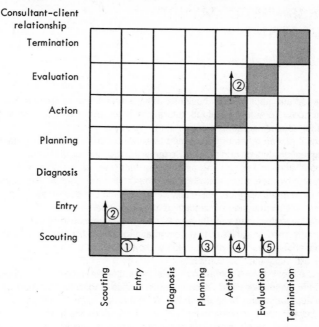

Consultant behavior

ple—see themselves as specialists. These inexperienced consultants may choose to ignore the fact that their speciality is but one part of the client system's problem solving process. The result is a plan that is not seen by the people with the power to implement it (scouting is ignored) or a plan that has no commitment from the people who are to carry it out (entry issues are ignored) or a plan that is inappropriate for the client (diagnosis is ignored). Similar problems can be identified in evaluation studies. The action specialist, however, can cause the most difficulty.

Consultants can become so committed to their particular "bag," be in sensitivity training, achievement motivation, or information systems, that they become salesmen for their "product" rather than consultants whose commitment is to organizational development. It is often these salesmen who most lament the organization's resistance to change.

The consultant-client relationship, like any human relationship, can never be reduced to a set of mechanistic rules. We believe, however, that consulting relationships can be improved and organizational changes better implemented if consultant and client attend to the issues and problems raised in each of the seven developmental stages. This model provides no pat answers, but it will hopefully supply some guideposts along the often confusing and difficult path to organization improvement.

*From*

# BUSINESS NEEDS MATURE AUTOCRATS*

## By Eugene E. Jennings

The democratic approach to business administration and leadership seems to have reached its apex. To some people its future is subject to much doubt. What these critics refer to as its veneer has been cracking for at least five years.

Substantial research has been devoted to seeking a pattern of management which will yield the highest production and morale. So far as the research data are concerned, evidence today is insufficient to warrant the assumption that there is a single approach to better performance. Why then, after enjoying for some 30 years a gradual and somewhat unexpected increase in acceptance, especially verbal, should the democratic approach now be subject to doubts? What kind of executives do we now need and want?

The social scientists can wait for answers to these questions but businessmen cannot. If the commonly held assumption that democratic executive procedures are most effective is being challenged, business needs to know the nature of the challenge and what kind of procedures are suggested as substitutes.

One of the most difficult things to understand is the meaning of democracy, especially in terms of the business system. A common technique is to define the opposite approach, that is, the autocratic, and base the definition of the democratic on that.

The *autocratic approach* means that group members are dependent on a single person. That person—called leader, executive, supervisor, etc.—so behaves that he makes himself the key to all group action and eventually becomes indispensable. His need to dominate is expressed by keeping the group acting as individuals and on a personal basis with him. This means usually that communication is kept to the minimum of administrative necessity except insofar as it is through him and focused upon him. Because he becomes and remains the focus of group attention, he is a firm believer in the indispensability of a good leader, such as he tries to be.

The *democratic approach* in many respects is the direct opposite. The individuals in the group, including the leader, are so closely knit that cohesion sometimes disguises who actually is running things. The leader seeks to evoke maximum participation and involvement of every member in determining group activities and objectives. He so leads the group that the result of the joint effort is not ascribable to his own virtues and superiority.

In short, the autocrat recognizes the superiority of the individual over the group, whereas the democrat recognizes the superiority of the group over himself.

There are differences of view in other regards as to how the democrat and the autocrat behave, but these definitions are generally acceptable. My own research could not find evidence that the autocratic type or democratic was superior; but criticism of the democratic, sometimes called human relations, approach which began five years ago is gaining in strength.

In 1953 Douglas McGregor of M.I.T., then president of Antioch College, warned that business was confused about human relations. He described as a major error of management the assumption that personnel administration consisted largely in dealing with human relations problems. He said that this was looking at the subject as a repair job, instead of a way to prevent the need for repairs. Since then other writers and observers have continued

---

* Reprinted by permission of *Nation's Business,* Chamber of Commerce of the United States, Washington, D.C., September 1958.

the attack on human relations as being essentially a tool by which management manipulates people into the desired patterns of productivity and comformity. These writers see considerable moral and intellectual degradation and degeneration as a result of the human relations exploitation approach.

Since the human relations approach has had such lofty ideals and high verbal acceptance, it is to be expected that these critics will find numerous and severe opponents. Already a defense seems to have taken shape. Some defenders, believing that the many advocates of human relations have failed to make clear just what they are talking about, have tried to relieve the misunderstanding and confusion by suggesting that the underlying theme of the human relations approach is an attempt to understand people as they really are and to accept them as such. The theme is that better understanding of the problems of people at work, of discovering ways for making work a more rewarding experience, will likely create positive benefits for all concerned.

This implies that management should so manage that the workers' purposes and the firm's purpose are mutual and complementary. Translated in the language of the critics of the manipulation-conformity thesis, this means that the unique strengths of the democratic work process can be used as positive forces for accomplishing the objective aims of the large organization: that is, making a profit.

In theory this might be logical, desirable and perhaps even necessary, but it covers up an underlying problem that may turn out to be an insurmountable contradiction. This problem is how to include in an autocratic system the democratic urges of the subordinate and inferior members of that system.

There are opposing drives here that go far deeper than changing manifest behavior to accommodate and compromise forces that are in conflict with each other.

One may question whether executives are psychologically able to allow the group to participate in decisions affecting both them and the larger organization. I have found that by and large the typical executive does not have the psychological capacity to integrate to this extent even if he wanted to.

Even appearing to give lip service and some degree of credence to the democratic approach in such things as decision-making and policy formulation is almost beyond the psychological capacity of most executives.

The difficulty becomes plain once we recognize what the typical executive is really like. Robert McMurry, senior partner of McMurry, Hamstra & Co., a Chicago-based personnel consulting firm, has supplied a good description. He says that most executives are likely to be hard-driving, egocentric entrepreneurs who came up in careers where they have had to keep the power in their hands. They may be veterans and victors in the give-and-take, no-quarter, in-fighting for position of power within the business. Instead of participative management, Mr. McMurry describes business as a "benevolent autocracy" wherein the top man stresses the desirability of humanistic management but remains undeniably the strong man. This diagnosis would suggest that the democratic approach is basically a result of some kind of external pressure and not a manifestation of inner conviction on the part of executives. The possibility is that the democratic approach will from here on be attacked more openly by executives themselves and repudiated by a regression to a firmer autocratic approach.

*   *   *   *   *

. . . [M]ore democracy was bound to be urged upon executives if for no other reason than that a democratic society, believing in certain dignities of the individual, will constantly exert a force to have these dignities accepted in the most inaccessible crevices. This external pressure upon management, plus the demands of large-scale organization for group decision-making, caused some degree of acceptance of the human relations approach.

Even so, this surge to group decision-making came relatively quickly. When some 69 executives of leading firms were interviewed by this writer, the general reaction was that they use group decision-making for getting acceptance of their decisions—not necessarily for getting better decisions. This reaction is in part a result of the failure of social scientists to come up with an adequate definition of what the new executive, who is bending somewhat to this pressure of democratic participation, should be.

In overthrowing previous authoritarian concepts of leadership the social scientists have failed to offer a new management pattern that is, 1, commonly agreed upon by them, 2, commonly understood by executives, and, 3, sufficiently motivating to these executives.

*    *    *    *    *

Consultants who are to some extent both observers and practitioners must offer rather arbitrary advice even though they know science will not yet affirm it. When I am placed in this role my answer has been that the type of executive needed is the polished autocrat. That is to say, the business system seems to be perfectly set up today for the individual who wants to run with the ball but who at the same time makes the team feel needed. He makes decisions, he controls and dominates individually and with emphasis on personal influence but he does not arouse animosity. Historians often call him . . . a man who walks with a firm, but quiet step.

*    *    *    *    *

In presenting this model of leadership to businessmen I have had considerable concurrence that the firm but quiet type is becoming increasingly necessary. Some of the most eminent businessmen have this attribute about them.

Whether the polished, mature autocrat has replaced the crude type is still an academic question because our idealistic eyes sometimes indicate that more executives are less autocratic today than yesterday. What is a good bit of insight, although not yet supported by research, is that there must be dominance of the majority by a few and that these few must make decisions on behalf of themselves or the majority, or both, and that consultation with the majority is seldom feasible.

What is feasible is that the few appear to be humanitarian, conscientious and open minded. They generate not necessarily love or hate, but respect and a little, but not too much, fear.

They do not, however, consult any more than necessary to get acceptance. When they do it is with other power individuals who, when allied with them, will bring the advantages of their leadership.

That these polished autocrats are useful and necessary to society is attested to by the fact that they are numerously found in some of our most democratic institutions. I have found them in religious, social work agencies, and charitable organizations.

They are in educational, political, and economic organizations. They represent at best the attempt to respond as administratively as possible to the democratic urges of a mass culture.

But such a response is only possible to a degree. That degree, I believe, qualifies them to be called Mature Autocrats.

# 16. MANCO CORPORATION

## Case Introduction

### SYNOPSIS

During the formative years of the management systems department of a consumer specialities manufacturing and marketing company, the staff witnesses three major reorganizations. In the last four years, the organization moves from a specialization by function (systems analysts and programmers) to specialization by customer (internal operating divisions like Marketing, Finance, Manufacturing, and R&D). The "generalists" in management systems serve the operating divisions in project groups headed by systems project administrators. This latter position evolves from a liaison and coordination role to a formal, supervisory role with accountability for the project itself and the project personnel involved in the new, integrated, staff service.

A former specialist, who is promoted to the systems project administrator position, seems to resist the newly integrated approach. He leaves the organization, and one of his former subordinates runs into serious trouble with an important EDP system for an operating division. A systems project administrator who had not previously been involved with the faulty system nor its designer assumes responsibility for both. Arrangements are made to correct the system. The systems project administrator "is very troubled" over what to do with the system's designer in view of his superior's statement: "I'm not sure where he fits in . . . do what you have to do."

### WHY THIS CASE IS INCLUDED

The brief history of the management systems department records the interplay between the individual and organization structure. It is instructive to trace the development of role demands and the relationship between such role demands and perceived roles of those involved in the case. The history of the management systems department also points to the interdependence of people, structure, and technology—no one of the factors is altered in an organizational change effort without affecting the other two. There is opportunity to explore the degree of openness in interpersonal relationships and how this affects executive decisions. Finally, the case poses the issue of due process for the white-collar or management employee—that is, the degree of protection the employee has from unilateral behavior of superiors, especially when he works for a succession of different superiors with seemingly different criteria for acceptable performance.

## DIAGNOSTIC AND PREDICTIVE QUESTIONS

The readings included with this case are marked (*). The author index at the end of this book locates the other readings.

1. In an economic sense, what was Manco trying to accomplish in the 1963 reorganization of the management systems department? Keeping in mind the two concepts of specialization and coordination, trace the impact of the reorganization on the customer account computer system.

Read: *O'Connell, "Beyond Economics: Coordinomics," Part I.

2. Trace the interdependencies of people and structure during the 1963–66 period of growth and change in the management systems department of the Manco Corporation. Should top management have been able to predict the "people impact" of the structural changes and the "structure impact" of the personnel changes?

Read: *Leavitt, *Managerial Psychology,* pp. 317–25.

3. Using the social psychology conceptual schema for role development, trace the impact of the 1963 reorganization on the behavior (role performance) of the specialists in programming and the specialists in systems. What were the new role demands for each class of specialist? For the newly appointed systems project administrators?

Read: *Levinson, "Role, Personality, and Social Structure in the Organizational Setting."

4. Using the theoretical model of interpersonal relations analyze the relations between the following pairs as they are pictured and as they develop in the case: Carson-Wallace, Wallace-Roberts, Roberts-Carson, Behrens-Wallace, Behrens-Jonas, Jonas-Roberts, Carson-Jonas. Do you find perception "errors" in any of these relationships? If so, why do the individuals misperceive one another?

Read: *McGrath, *Social Psychology: A Brief Introduction.*

5. Trace the development of Wallace's self-concept and Roberts' self-concept. Relate each self-concept to role performance by using the bridging construct of role concept.

Read: The readings assigned in the two previous questions.

6. When Wallace's job was eliminated in a reorganization of Behrens' unit, Jonas raised the issue of the "very involved system for placing unsatisfactory performers on warning. . . ." He said: "That system's supposed to protect the employee." Does Jonas voice a legitimate concern? What are the consequences of what Jonas calls "a completely arbitrary system?" Does Roberts have due process protection?

Read: *Evan, "Organization Man and Due Process of Law."

**POLICY QUESTIONS**

7. From what has happened to Wallace and Roberts in the Manco Company do you find cause to revise the appraisal system? If so, what would you recommend?

8. Would you have planned or implemented the Manco reorganizations any differently? If so, how?

9. If you were Behrens, what would you do at the end of the case? If you were Carson? If you were Jonas?

10. In one sense, the systems analysts prior to the reorganization four years ago were staff integrators. They were supposed to visit the marketing division or manufacturing division client, for example, and learn his operations. They then began to design the new system for the client—coming back to the systems division and working with the specialist programmers (who were to put the new system in computer language). After the reorganization, each systems analyst was supposed to know *both* the client management system *and* programming. Both the individual systems man and the project administrator were supposed to *integrate* the client needs with the computer program.

What advise would you give the company as to improving their method of integrating? This might be advice on the organization structure (whether to revert to systems department integrators, or whether to maintain the present structure wherein every man is an integrator, or to increase the integrating activities of the project administrator).

Read:  Lawrence and Lorsch, "New Management Job: The Integrator."

# Case Text*

The Manco Corporation serves the consumer field with a broad line of high-quality specialty products. Most of the corporation's 6,000 employees work in Saginaw, Michigan, the headquarters and main plant location. Manco, with the other nine leading companies in its field, invests heavily in R&D and relies more on product innovation than on the protection of its numerous patents. Manco's $200 million sales volume is made up of about 75 percent domestic sales and 25 percent foreign sales. Growth over the past half-dozen years has averaged somewhat over 5 percent a year, and profit margins have stayed well in excess of 10 percent before tax.

One of the staff support groups serving the expanding and ever more sophisticated management is the management systems department. The

* Copyright 1977, J. J. O'Connell.

partial organization chart of the Manco Corporation in Exhibit 1 shows the position of this department as of June of last year.

## THE MANAGEMENT SYSTEMS DEPARTMENT

The 55 professional people in the management systems department serve all the operating divisions of the corporation as part of the central staff reporting to Elkin Parker, the vice president of Manco's Administrative Division, through Harold Simken, the director of administrative services.

The department is responsible for performing a broad range of internal consulting activities. The management systems department's major efforts are concentrated in the design and maintenance of computer-based information systems. Project work is also conducted in the areas of organization planning, operations research, general systems design, and standard operating procedures.

All management systems work is conducted on a project request basis. For example, the customer account system mentioned later resulted from a problem first seen by Ned O'Donnell, manager of the physical distribution department, which in turn is a part of the Sales Division of the company. O'Donnell and the vice president for sales had long wanted a method for keeping customer charge accounts more accurately, and a method for processing these with great speed. They had called the management systems department for help.

The systems department thus forms a central service unit for the whole company. The company has a rule that only if a major operating division requests assistance on its own initiative can work actually commence in the systems department. This rule is designed so that the systems analysts will assume the role of consultants to the other divisions of the company, rather than to assume the active role of managing the operating divisions either by initiating their plans, or by controlling and acting as policemen. According to Simkin, "this means that the systems department is somewhat like a small business seeking customers. We are here to perform services for the operating departments. They must feel a need for our service and, in effect, hire us to perform them. They're also in the position of not buying our services if the services don't genuinely contribute to solving their problems."

After another division requests assistance, the project request is jointly reviewed by the management systems department manager and his five unit supervisors so that a priority might be assigned to the project. The considerable project backlog has made it necessary for managers within the department to devote substantial time to identifying the most important projects.

The organization of management systems (Exhibit 1) reflects Harold Simken's and Walter Davis' strong interest in maintaining satisfactory and stable relationships with all company divisions. Three systems units—the international-marketing unit, the financial-manufacturing unit, and the R&D-administrative unit—form the core of the department. Each unit performs work for two company divisions on a continuing

**EXHIBIT 1**
**Partial Manco Organization Chart (June of last year)**

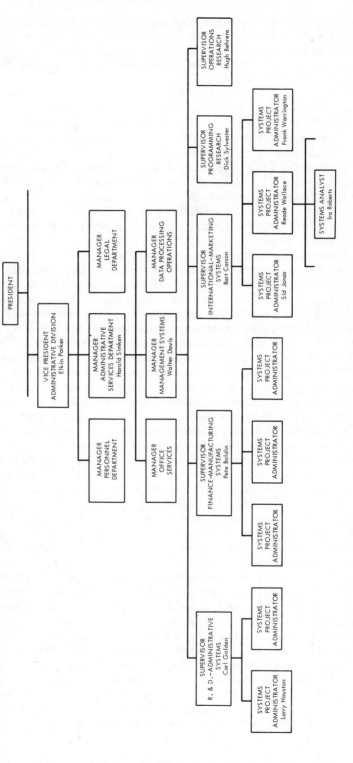

basis. The operations research and programming research units provide technical support to the three systems units. Operations research and programming research personnel often work on those systems projects which require very specialized skills, and they are frequently involved in nonproject development work.

The mix of project work and personnel within each of the three systems units is determined by the pattern of project requests made by the various Manco divisions. The potential for meaningful systems design work and the receptivity of key managers vary from division to division. These differences create demands for divergent sets of skills in the three systems units. Project requests from the Research and Development Division, for example, involve the computerized retrieval of scientific information on laboratory experiments. On the other hand, systems work for the Administrative Division primarily consists of issuing and revising standard operating procedures. As a result of these project demands the R&D—administrative unit has two distinct types of analysts—programmers and standard procedure specialists.

The requests made by the International and Marketing Divisions demand a still wider set of skills in the international-marketing systems unit. This unit has been involved in large-scale simulations of domestic and international distribution networks, organizational studies of the Marketing Division and several international branches, and other complex systems studies. Since these projects usually require skills different from either programming or procedure work, the international-marketing systems unit employs management scientists and organizational planning specialists, as well as programmers and systems analysts.

Within each systems unit, there are two or three systems project administrators, who handle the day-to-day administrative activities of the systems units. Each project administrator is responsible for specific departments in one or two Manco divisions. Thus, in the international-marketing systems unit, one project administrator is responsible for projects in the market research and promotion planning departments, while another supervises project work for the sales, advertising, and general promotion departments. The systems project administrator is, in essence, a working first-line supervisor. From a supervisory standpoint, the project administrators supervise client project requests, plan and schedule work loads, administer salary, and appraise performance of their subordinates. In addition, they spend approximately one third of their time actually performing some of the more complex project work.

The present management systems department was formed during a June reorganization four years ago, which combined all systems and programming activities. Prior to the reorganization, separate systems and programming sections existed. Most of the analysts believed that the reorganization was precipitated by management's dissatisfaction with the divided responsibility for projects, which so often called for both systems and programming work. There had been an increasing number of complaints concerning the inability of the two sections to meet deadlines for converting systems from manual to computer processing. The systems analysts believed that the programmers were at fault for not adhering to schedules. The programmers contended that the systems analysts did not appreciate the magnitude and complexity of the programming task. Because of this lack of understanding, argued the programmers, the systems analysts made unrealistic calendar commitments to the divisional managers responsible for the particular system.

The reorganization was also designed to eliminate the discontent among systems analysts and programmers over advancement opportunities. As a result of the reorganization, the positions of management systems manager and unit supervisor were upgraded to higher salary classifications. The new position of systems project administrator was created one level below the unit supervisor level. In the two years following the reorganization, eight former senior system analysts and senior programmers were elevated to systems project administrators.

In the spirit of the reorganization, the systems analysts working for each systems project administrator were expected to perform both systems and programming activities. Initially the interests and assignments of most analysts corresponded to their previous specialty—systems or programming. Salary increases and promotions in the new organization, however, were designed to reward the generalist—the man who was able and willing to do both systems and programming and demonstrated this in project work. The hiring and training of new employees were also geared to produce this new breed of systems analysts.

## THE INTERNATIONAL-MARKETING SYSTEMS UNIT

The supervisor of the international-marketing systems unit (see Exhibit 1) is Bart Carson. Carson, who had transferred into systems from the Manufacturing Division nine years ago, is generally considered by his peers to be the most experienced and talented systems supervisor. Although his experience before the reorganization had been confined to the systems section, he has been very positive about the new integrated approach of the reorganization. Carson has made conscious efforts to give his analysts diversified exposure and gradually has begun to develop what is regarded as a well-rounded unit within the context of the new management systems job responsibilities.

One of the three systems project administrators reporting to Carson years ago in the summer was Reade Wallace. Carson had given Wallace responsibility for project work in the International Division and the distribution department of the Marketing Division. Wallace, who had joined the company eight years ago after obtaining his MBA degree, had been regarded as a mainstay of the pre-reorganization systems section. He had specialized in organization planning, standard operating procedures, and general systems work. Wallace's associates noted that his diplomacy and tact had enabled him to establish excellent rapport with several key managers in the company, in general, and in the International Division, in particular. Harold Simken, manager of administrative services, and Walter Davis, manager of management systems, were keenly interested in generating new international project work, and they both often spoke of how much they valued Wallace's interpersonal skills.

After the reorganization but before his promotion to systems project administrator, Wallace had made it clear to Bart Carson, systems supervisor, that he had no desire to get involved in EDP or management science projects. He preferred to continue his concentration in organizational planning and general administrative systems and said so publicly. Wallace was, in fact, the only analyst after the reorganization who overtly resisted Carson's plan for development. Consequently, Wallace's promotion to systems project administrator in October of the following year had been a very controversial move. To many analysts, the promotion represented a flagrant violation of the criteria established for the systems project administrator position. Some analysts attributed the move to pressure exerted on Carson by Simken and/or Davis.

## MANAGEMENT SYSTEMS DEPARTMENT EXPANDS

The management system department experienced rapid growth in the two-year period after reorganization, expanding from a personnel complement of 30 analysts to one of 55 analysts. One source of new people was the company's management training program, a rotational program consisting of several six- to eight-week assignments in various Manco divisions.

Among the trainees in this program was Ira Roberts, a former high school teacher who had taught for four years. As he completed the program a year ago last December, Roberts' record showed he had created favorable impressions throughout the company during his rotational assignments. Roberts' first permanent position was as management systems analyst in Bart Carson's international-marketing unit, reporting to Reade Wallace. Roberts had performed poorly on the programming aptitude test administered to all prospective management systems employees. He had received a B— on the exam, lower than anyone currently in the department. The independent psychological consulting firm, which administers the test, placed Roberts in the "Not Recommended" category on the analysis accompanying his test score. Since Roberts' principal work was to be in the general systems area, Carson and Wallace agreed that Roberts' personal strengths offset his relatively weak performance on the aptitude test. Carson and Wallace planned to increase Roberts' exposure to programming at some later date.

Roberts' first assignment was to develop a small-scale system to centralize information on grants to foundations and charities made by various company departments. His second project involved procedural work with various company divisions to insure companywide compliance with new federal legislation affecting the sale of company products. After some training in network scheduling techniques, Roberts performed admirably in developing a PERT chart to plan and schedule the introduction of Manco's first product in the Australian market. Co-workers observed Roberts working yeoman's hours, and the manager of the new Australian Branch was unstinting in his praise of Roberts and his network schedule.

Roberts' performance during his first year in systems was formally appraised by Wallace last January. He noted the following strengths:

1. Quick mind.
2. Ability to shoulder responsibility.
3. Works well with others.
4. Loyal and excellent attitude toward the company.
5. Documents work well and is both cost and profit conscious.

Wallace listed project planning as Roberts' major area for improvement. He rated Roberts satisfactory overall and concluded the appraisal by discussing his potential:

> Roberts handles work very well and has high potential. Could develop into one of our better senior analysts with a bit more programming experience.

At the bottom of the appraisal sheet in the section entitled "Promotability," Wallace checked off "Promotable within two years." The only rating superior to this was "Promotable immediately." The appraisal was reviewed and signed by Carson, in accordance with company policy.

During the early part of this year, the personnel department notified Roberts that several managers in the company were interested in offering him positions in their departments. These offers of employment in the public relations, distribution, and personnel departments were transmitted through the company's formal system for recruiting internal candidates. Each of these opportunities represented a promotion for Roberts. While these advancement opportunities all appeared attractive, Roberts expressed enthusiasm for his work in systems and was reluctant to leave. When he discussed the situation with Wallace and Carson, they both spoke optimistically about his future progress and their plans for him. Roberts decided to turn down the various internal opportunities and remain in management systems.

On April 1 of this year Wallace and Carson jointly announced that Roberts had been promoted from management system analyst to senior management systems analyst.

## THE CUSTOMER ACCOUNT COMPUTER SYSTEM (CACS) PROJECT

As part of his plan to increase Roberts' programming experience, Wallace assigned him in April to a major EDP project, under the direction of another analyst. The basic purpose of this project was to create a computerized information system of all retail and wholesale accounts that distributed a major section of the product line. The system was designed to assist in processing orders during the hectic fall and winter sale periods. A secondary objective was to use the system for recording salesmen's call activities. The system was scheduled to go "on-line" in the fall.

In May, the project was dealt a serious setback when the senior systems analyst leading the project resigned from the company. Wallace decided to have Roberts direct the project and assigned a new analyst to assist him. Between May and September, Roberts worked feverishly to complete the system. He worked a considerable amount of overtime each week, including six Saturdays during the summer months. Throughout this period, he assured Wallace and Carson and the management of the distribution department that the system would be ready to go into operation by September 1.

In the midst of Roberts' efforts on the CACS project, corporate organization changes affected the management systems department.

## THE CORPORATE REORGANIZATION

In July, another major corporate reorganization was announced. The objectives of the reorganization were the separation of planning activities from operations and the introduction of a strong profit center philosophy.

As a result of the reorganization, some key management changes occurred in the management systems department. Walter Davis, manager of the department, was appointed director, organization and policy planning, on the new corporate staff. Carl Golden, supervisor of the R&D—administrative systems unit, joined Davis' staff as manager of organization planning.

Bart Carson replaced Davis as management systems manager (see Exhibit 2). Dick Sylvester, previously supervisor, programming research, was named to direct a new management research group. The three systems units were merged into two new units, reporting to Pete Boldin and Hugh Behrens. Behrens, who has previously served as supervisor, operations research, assumed responsibility for Carson's international-marketing systems unit and for all R&D systems. The administrative systems would henceforth be designed by the new corporate staff group headed by Walter Davis and Carl Golden. Boldin retained responsibility for all financial and manufacturing systems.

## THE JULY–OCTOBER PERIOD

After the initial excitement generated by the announcement of management appointments, management systems activities continued with no major changes in direction. Carson and his two direct subordinates, Boldin and Behrens, conferred regularly to establish project objectives for next year, plan the impending conversion to a 360 computer, and develop a new project control system.

Behrens' four systems project administrators (Sid Jonas, Frank Warrington, Larry Houston, and Reade Wallace) found him more conservative and less communicative than Carson, and yet by late summer they felt they had good rapport with him. Behrens started with Manco as a programmer seven years ago, and had since served in various capacities in the programming section, systems section, and operations research section. He was credited with conducting the company's most successful operations research effort—a large-scale simulation of the entire Manco distribution network. His several diverse skills had enabled him to establish an excellent reputation throughout the corporation.

Behrens called informal meetings of his four systems project adminis-

**EXHIBIT 2**
**Partial Manco Organization Chart (August of this year)**

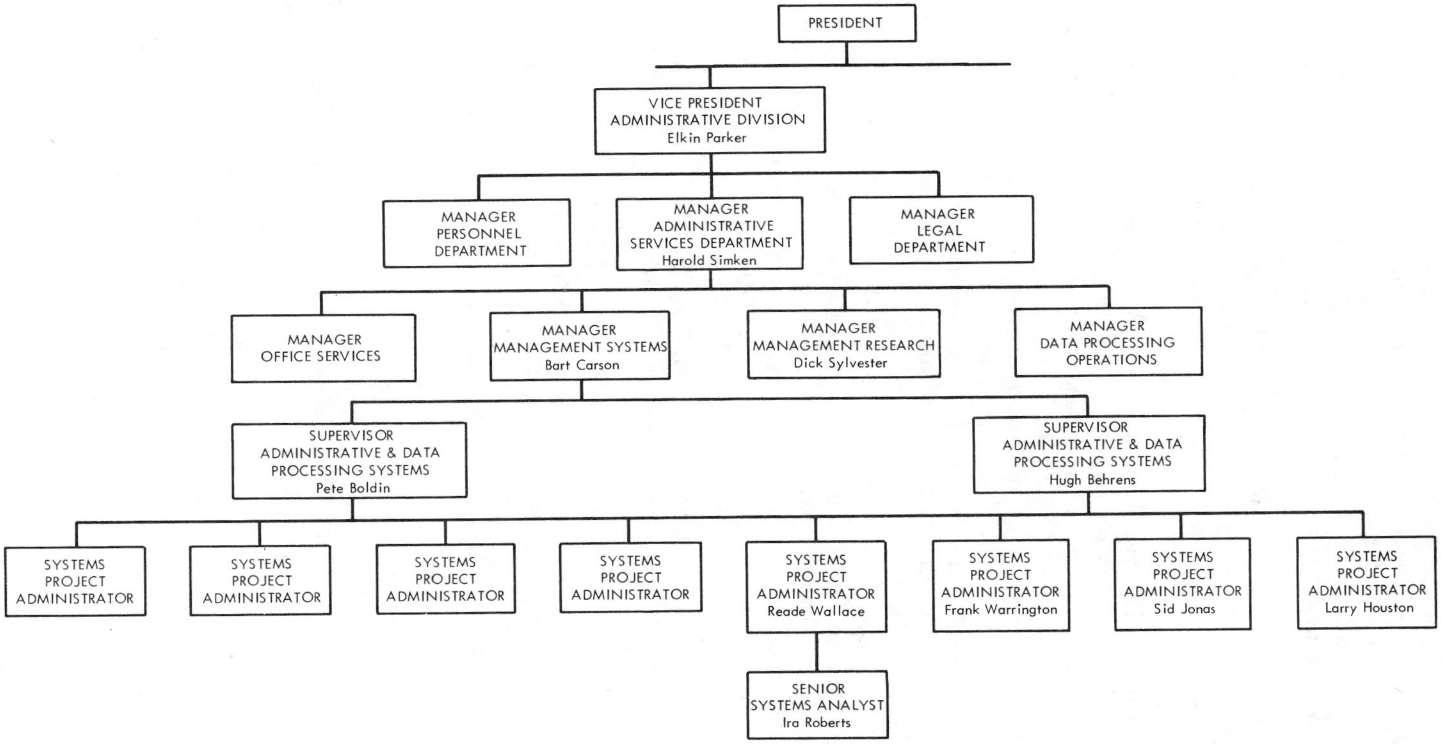
PRESIDENT
VICE PRESIDENT ADMINISTRATIVE DIVISION Elkin Parker
MANAGER PERSONNEL DEPARTMENT
MANAGER ADMINISTRATIVE SERVICES DEPARTMENT Harold Simken
MANAGER LEGAL DEPARTMENT
MANAGER OFFICE SERVICES
MANAGER MANAGEMENT SYSTEMS Bart Carson
MANAGER MANAGEMENT RESEARCH Dick Sylvester
MANAGER DATA PROCESSING OPERATIONS
SUPERVISOR ADMINISTRATIVE & DATA PROCESSING SYSTEMS Pete Boldin
SUPERVISOR ADMINISTRATIVE & DATA PROCESSING SYSTEMS Hugh Behrens
SYSTEMS PROJECT ADMINISTRATOR
SYSTEMS PROJECT ADMINISTRATOR
SYSTEMS PROJECT ADMINISTRATOR
SYSTEMS PROJECT ADMINISTRATOR
SYSTEMS PROJECT ADMINISTRATOR Reade Wallace
SYSTEMS PROJECT ADMINISTRATOR Frank Warrington
SYSTEMS PROJECT ADMINISTRATOR Sid Jonas
SYSTEMS PROJECT ADMINISTRATOR Larry Houston
SENIOR SYSTEMS ANALYST Ira Roberts

trators whenever he felt it necessary to review plans or communicate information. These hour-long meetings occurred about every two weeks during the late summer and early fall.

On October 18, Behrens called a 1:30 meeting of his systems project administrators. The only unusual aspect of the scheduling was the short two-hour notice. When the group assembled, they noted that Behrens, who was typically a very calm individual, seemed upset. Warrington, Jonas, and Houston were also surprised to see that Wallace was not present. Behrens began the meeting by announcing:

> I've called you together to tell you that our unit has been reorganized as of this afternoon. Reade Wallace's job has been eliminated and he is leaving the company today. Sid Jonas will pick up Reade's responsibilities for all systems and management science projects in International. Ira Roberts will report to you, and we'll continue to recruit for a replacement for Ira's predecessor on the CACS project. Frank will handle all EDP projects for International. Barbara Mellor and Murray Hankins [Wallaces's other analysts] will report to you.

Jonas was the first to speak after a long silence. "Does that mean that Reade was fired due to unsatisfactory performance?" "No," replied Behrens, "Reade was doing a satisfactory job, but we no longer had a position for him in our organization." Jonas reacted sharply to Behrens' answer:

> Now, how can you do a thing like that? We have a very involved system for placing unsatisfactory performers on warning for 30 to 90 days and advising them that they will be canned if they don't shape up. You just subverted the whole system by reorganizing him out of a job. That system's supposed to protect the employee. Now all of the analysts will think that this is a completely arbitrary system and the axe can fall on them any time. We all know that Reade was deficient in certain respects. Why don't you call a spade a spade?

Interrupting, Behrens said:

> Hold on a minute, Sid. Some of your points are valid, but you don't have all the facts. First of all, Wallace did get severance pay amounting to over $5,000. More important, we talked to all the personnel experts, and they said it would be in his best interest to do it this way. The company can give him a good reference without any black marks on his record. And, as an aside, we tried to place him elsewhere in the company. Distribution and International were interested, but because of the budget cutbacks throughout the company, they couldn't afford someone at his salary level. It's been my most traumatic experience since I've been with the company. What more can I say?

Jonas was preparing to resume the verbal battle but thought better of it and added, "I'm sorry, Hugh, but I don't agree. I'm probably unfair arguing with you over this since Reade only worked for you for three months. It's Bart Carson who's responsible, and I plan to tell him that I think the whole situation was handled poorly." With that the meeting was adjourned.

## THE CUSTOMER ACCOUNT COMPUTER SYSTEM FAILS

Following the announcement of Wallace's departure, Jonas and Warrington met with their newly assigned analysts to review work loads and project plans. The main topic during the first meeting between Jonas and Roberts on October 20 was the CACS project. Roberts first explained the system to Jonas, pointing out its objectives and major features. He explained that the system began operating in September, although a few "bugs" still had to be ironed out. Roberts expressed confidence that the system would be operating smoothly before too long.

The CACS project seemed to be moving toward final completion when Jonas was called into Behrens office on Thursday, November 9. Behrens informed Jonas that one of the scheduled computer runs for the CACS project had produced incorrect results and Ned O'Donnell, the distribution department manager, had phoned a complaint to Bart Carson. Behrens expressed the fear that there might be some major problem with the entire system. Jonas suggested they speak to Roberts. Behrens phoned Roberts, requesting that he come to his office. Roberts explained that the error in sales totals resulted from 50 duplicate records on the master file. He had scheduled a computer printout of the master file so that the clerks in the distribution department could correct the errors. He assured Jonas and Behrens that he would take care of the problem.

The master file printout was checked by the distribution clerks on Monday, November 13, and Tuesday, November 14. On the 15th, Ned O'Donnell asked Harold Simken, manager of administrative services, to come to his office. When Simken arrived, he saw that O'Donnell had several hundred pages of a computer report on his desk. O'Donnell began to shout at Simken, "Harold, you see this printout? You know how much it's worth? This much!" And with that O'Donnell stuffed the printout in the waste basket. O'Donnell continued, "What's wrong with your damn department? If it's not one kind of mistake, it's another. Now that guy has gone and dropped all of our accounts in Northern California from the file. I can't make any sense out of this."

Simken returned to his office and asked to see Jonas, since Carson and Behrens were both out of the office. Carson was at a week-long management training session, and Hugh Behrens was attending a seminar in operations research. Simken gave Jonas a monotone hello when he entered and asked him what he was doing about the CACS situation. Jonas identified the various problems as best he could and reviewed the instructions he had given Roberts. Simken listened without comment until Jonas was through and then began to speak in a very stern voice. "Sid, I know you weren't involved in this system from the start, and you aren't responsible for these problems. But, it's yours now, and I'm holding you responsible for correcting this mess. Now, get busy on this and keep me informed of your progress."

When Behrens returned to the office the following morning, he was treated to a similar—in his words—"severe harangue," from Simken. Behrens decided to form a task force of himself, Pete Boldin, Jonas, and Roberts to conduct a comprehensive review of the system. After a three-day review, Behrens submitted a report to Carson and Simken, outlining the various technical problems and the proposed remedial action. The review had made it clear to Jonas and Behrens that Roberts did not have the technical EDP expertise to direct a project as complex as CACS. Moreover, some aspects of the system were misrepresented to marketing management in that the system was touted as a panacea for all of distribution's information problems. The cost of the system was vastly underestimated. Original estimates for development costs and annual operating costs were $14,000 to $19,000 and $8,500 to $14,000. Actual development costs exceeded $32,000, while annual operating costs zoomed to $30,000.

When Jonas and Behrens reviewed the report, Behrens began to discuss Roberts' capabilities:

> Sid, we really gave you a personnel problem. That review convinced me that Roberts is not capable of senior analyst performance. There's no question about his technical deficiencies as far as I'm concerned. We know he wasn't a technical whiz but, if that wasn't bad enough, he did a terrible job of directing the project. There's no evidence of any planning. He missed every deadline, and I'm not sure he properly represented the critical status of the system to marketing or us. He probably didn't know how bad off he really was. You better think about how you're going to use him in the future. Given the type of things we expect from you in the future, I'm not sure where he fits in.

Jonas raised some questions about the apparently poor supervision and direction which Roberts had received from Wallace. Behrens agreed that this was a consideration. Behren's secretary interrupted to remind him of a meeting, and he abruptly ended the discussion, "Well, give it some thought, Sid, and let's discuss it in a few days."

On Wednesday, November 22, Jonas arranged a session with Carson and Behrens to discuss the Roberts situation. Jonas opened the discussion by summarizing his position for Carson:

> Bart, I've given this issue considerable thought, and I'm very troubled by it. I'm not reluctant to be a so-called "tough-minded manager" and place Roberts on warning for unsatisfactory performance. The problem with this approach is that it's the easy way out because it avoids the real troubling issues. Someone in this organization has to accept responsibility for the things that were said to Roberts six months ago. We told him that his future was very bright

in systems and dissuaded him from accepting other jobs in the company. In fact, we promoted him in a relatively short span of time. In retrospect, that was the wrong decision. He's better suited for less technical work, such as personnel or public relations. So far, he hasn't demonstrated that he can perform at a senior level. And, don't forget, one big reason for his poor performance was the lack of proper supervision from Wallace.

If you want me to, I'll try to compensate for our past errors by getting back to basics and developing Roberts the right way. But I can't do this if you're not willing to adjust your expectations of my group. Hugh thinks that Roberts doesn't fit into my operation. So now it seems that if I try to develop one of my less adequate subordinates, I don't meet my technical responsibilities. If I stick to the technical goals, I ship Roberts out the door.

Carson answered:

Sid, I don't want you to worry about things that were said to Roberts before he started working for you. Perhaps we were premature in promoting him. I'll accept responsibility for all of that. We expect big things of you, and you need the proper blend of skills in your group. It's very easy for Hugh and me to sit here and tell you what to do. But, if we did that, we'd impair your development as a supervisor. All I can say is do what you have to do.

# Selected Readings

*From*

## BEYOND ECONOMICS: COORDINOMICS*

*By Jeremiah J. O'Connell*

The word economics is taken from the two Greek words *oikos* and *nemein*. Oikos means "household" and *nemein* means "to manage." The root meaning of the word economics, therefore, is "to manage a household." In the economics of business enterprise we concentrated on the specialized segments or segmented departments of the corporation. Historically, the emphasis has been on efficiency within functional departments—a concentration on the area described by each of the boxes on the organization chart. Each box was a household, so to speak, to be managed in such a way that, within the confines of that functional box on the organizational chart, we achieved all the efficiencies produced by specialization and derived all the benefits from economies of scale or size. Now, in the

---

* Excerpt from Keynote Address at the Eighth Annual Systems Conference of the Southwest, Dallas, Texas, May 9, 1966.

mature business enterprise it seems we are approaching the point of diminishing returns to our efforts at managing these segmented compartments of the organization. We are at a point now where the emphasis is shifting in the quest for efficiency to inter-departmental cooperation and coordination—that is, to a concentration on managing the spaces between the boxes on the organization chart. We are at the point where there are greater returns to an investment spent on achieving coordination among the functional departments of an organization than to an investment spent on improving the operations in any one of the functional departments.

Historically, when we spoke of systems, we behaved as if the organization were a mechanical system, that is, that the whole was nothing other than and nothing different from the sum of the several, functionally specialized, parts of the organization. Systems today have come to mean something organic rather than mechanical—that is, the whole is something other than and something in addition to the sum of the functionally specialized parts. In this sense, then, we have moved beyond economics—the management of separate households—to coordinomics—the managements of the process of coordination. Economics had us focus on the compartments of the organization; coordinomics would have us focus on the spaces between the compartments in the organization. . . .

*From*

# MANAGERIAL PSYCHOLOGY*

*by Harold J. Leavitt*

### THE VOLATILE ORGANIZATION: EVERYTHING TRIGGERS EVERYTHING ELSE

In this first chapter in Part IV, we have just one purpose—to encourage the reader to think about organizations not just as simple, static charts or as milling collections of people or as smoothly oiled man-machine systems but as rich, volatile, complicated but understandable systems of *tasks, structures, tools,* and *people* in states of continuous change.

Toward that purpose, consider the following example:

> If, as a manager, you have a rather complicated problem, you may want to call in a consultant for help. Suppose the problem is a typically hard one: one of your larger field units is turning in much poorer results than all your forecasts had predicted.
>
> So you call in the partner in charge of the local office of one of the reputable older consulting firms—the largest in town. They contract to take on the problem and send some people out to the unit to collect information.
>
> When they finally come in with a report, you scan it and then turn to the recommendations. They recommend the following: (1) You need tighter controls. (2) Job relationships need to be reorganized and redefined; job descriptions need to be rewritten with greater precision (to get rid of squabbles about overlapping authority). (3) The functional form of organization they now have down there ought to be switched over to a product form. (4) In fact, that unit has grown so big that it ought to go through a partial decentralization itself, with a lot more authority given to the product managers. (5) You need a thorough methods analysis. The number of reports that are being generated now is excessive. There is wasteful duplication of effort and communica-

tion. You ought to streamline the organization's procedures. (6) And you may have to move a few people out, too. There is too much fat in the organization, and so on.

If you are a manager with a experimental turn of mind and a pocket full of money, you will decide not to act on this consultant's report yet. You decide, instead, to knock on the door of another consultant and get a second independent assessment.

You had gotten to know the first firm by now. You had found that the people in it were active in the Society for the Advancement of Management, and highly experienced in business organization. You note, with some discomfort, that this second firm professes different allegiances and displays other pedigrees. This second group is active in the Operations Research Society, and the Institute for Management Sciences. Its experiences in industry really are not as extensive as those of number-one firm, but it has done a lot of recent military work, and its senior people all have Ph.D's. It looks like a group of whiz kids. But they have cut their hair and they sound reasonable, so you hire them to look into the same problems.

They send their people out to the unit, and they, too, come up with a report. But their conclusions are different. Instead of recommending modifications in the *structure* of the organization, they recommend modifications in the *technical* and *analytic* methods being used. They are technologists who think technological improvement is the means to the best of all possible worlds. They want to linear program the inventory control methods being used in that division, and to automate the purchasing operation. They want to modify the information flows, so that decisions can be made at different points in the organization, and faster. And instead of job descriptions and organization charts as their tools, their pockets are full of computers and long equations. You will have to hire some hot-shot college boys if you want to carry out their recommendations; because neither you nor any of your top people can fully understand them.

But if you are *really* an experimental manager, and if you pockets are really full of gold, and if you don't satisfy easily, you call in the only other consulting firm in town. Its members are Ph.D. types, too. Their offices aren't very elaborate, either. Their affiliations are different, again. They are members of the American Psychological Association, and/or members of the consultant network of the National Training Laboratories. They are clinical or social psychological types. And they view the world from the human side. They don't carry computers in their back pockets, or write job descriptions, or draw organization charts. Their favorite tools are the meeting, the discussion, the face-to-face group, and the open-ended interview.

So you hire them and let them and take a look at your difficult unit. And they too come up with a report. But their report is different again. It argues that the solution to unit *X*'s problem lies in changing the attitudes and interrelations of the people in that unit. Morale is low, they say. Apathy is high. People are constricted and anxious, afraid to speak up or take risks. What you organization needs is more *openness,* more *participation,* more *involvement,* more *creativity.*

So their recommendation is that you work on the people end of the problem. They want you to set up a series of "laboratory" training programs, in which you take groups of your people from division *X* out to a country club for a week at a time to talk things over; to open up valid communication among themselves; to express what they really feel; and to develop much more mutual trust and confidence.

Probably you could go on experimenting, but the board members are giving you strange looks by now, and the people in unit *X* are really up in the air. So you decide to stop there and take a look at what you have. Which of the three firms' recommendations should you follow up? Since you are the manager, we'll leave it to you to answer that question.

But though we can't answer it, let's not leave it quite there. As of right now we have a situation that looks like this:

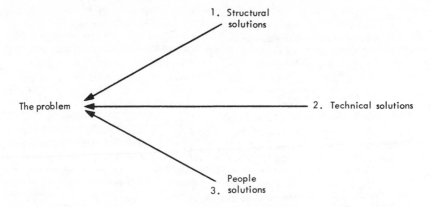

We have one group that wants to solve the problem of unit *X* by working on *structure*, by changing the organization chart and the locations of authority and responsibility. We have another group that's going to solve the same problems *technologically*, by improving the analytic quality of decisions and applying new techniques for controlling and processing information. And we have a third group that's going to solve the very same problems humanly, by working on persons and interpersonal relations. But there is one more important point that needs to be made here, before you decide which one of these to use. They aren't mutually exclusive. The point is that the diagram above is incomplete. Because no one of these actions will affect the way the task of division *X* gets done without also involving each of the other points on that chart. *Structure* and *technology* and *people* are not separable phenomena in organizations. If we hire the structurally oriented firm, and if we decentralize the unit, or if we change the present allocation of responsibilities, it will not only affect the problem but will also affect (perhaps adversely) people's attitudes and interpersonal relations. We will have to draw an arrow like this:

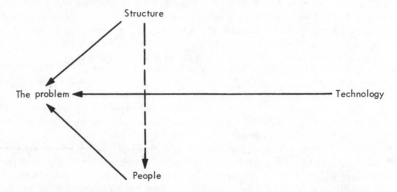

If you tighten controls, for example, some people may get angry or uncomfortable. If you switch from a functional to a product organization form, there will be new problems of interpersonal relations.

And if we play with the organization structure we will also get some effects on *technology*. The kinds of techniques that are now appropriate in a highly decentralized scheme—the accounting techniques for example—may have to be very different than those appropriate for highly centralized organizations.

And similarly, if we hire the technically oriented consulting firm, and go on to introduce the computer and new information flows, then we can darn well expect effects not only on the way the job gets done but also on structure and on people. If we can centralize information in locations where we couldn't centralize before, we will find decisions being made and responsibilities being taken in different places than they were being taken before. And while we may be talking about de-centralization, that new information system may be pushing us toward centralization. We may also find that the kinds and numbers of people we need in our new, technically sophisticated organization may be quite different from the kind and number of members we needed before. Moreover some things that were done judgmentally and thoughtfully are now pretty well programmed, so that essentially they can be done by the machine—with some consequent effects on the attitudes and feelings of persons.

Finally, if we move in on the people side, hiring the human relations firm, we will encourage people to be more open and more valid in their communication, encourage people to take more responsibility, and encourage people to interact more with other members of the organization. If we do these things, let us not for a moment think that we can do them without exerting great pressure on our existing organizational structure. The authority system will change and so will the status system. And we will exert pressure on technology too. The newly freedup people may want new tools or the abolition of old ones that have been technically useful but are psychologically frustrating.

And so we end up with a diagram that looks like this:

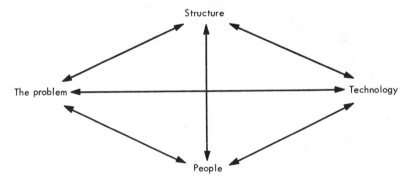

In this one everything feeds back on everything else, so that although we started out to worry only about the relationship between structure and task, or technology and task, or people and task, we must end up worrying about the effects of changes in any one on all of the others. Some of those changes may be very helpful, but some may be negative. And the manager has to somehow diagnose the secondary and tertiary effects of action in any one of these areas.

For organizations do not stand still. If we inject something into one part of the system bells begin to ring and lights begin to go on all over the system, often in places we hadn't counted on and at times we hadn't expected.

This is not to say that the complexity of the organization is so great that we can never tell what will happen when we do something. It is only to say that an organization is complex enough to make any simple structural or technical or human model inadequate. But we have made a lot of progress in understanding the complexities in the last few decades. We now know a good deal more about ways of acting on structure or people or technology; and we know somewhat more about how they are wired to one another. We now know a good deal more about ways of acting on structure or people or technology; and we know somewhat more about how they are wired to one another. There is real progress in the organizational world. The three classes of consulting firms in our example should not be taken as an indication that things have gone to pot. On the contrary they are an indication of how much we have learned about organizations. And about how much we now know of ways to change or modify them.

The practitioner in each of these three realms may be oversold on his own product. He may be overly enthusiastic about all that can be done by changing structure, or technology, or people. Each may be partially and understandably blind to the perspectives of the others. But the manager need not be blind. He has lots more to work from than he did in the days when we so naïvely believed that the simple line drawing on the organization chart actually did capture the essence of our live, volatile organization.

## In Summary

Organizations can be thought of as lively sets of interrelated systems designed to perform complicated tasks. We can try to manipulate at least three dimensions of those systems in order to get the performance of tasks changed or improved. We can manipulate the organization structure—which means we can manipulate the communication system or the authority and power system, or the system of work flows and processes. We can manipulate the tools and techniques used in the system—which means we can provide new and better hammers or new and better information-processing devices. And we can enter from the people side, to change bodies, or attitudes, or interpersonal relations—which means we can change the training and skills of our people, or the numbers of people involved, or the kinds of people we hire.

But we must never for a moment forget that when we tamper with any one of these three variables, structure or technology or people, we are likely to cause significant effects on the others, as well as on the task.

*From*

# ROLE, PERSONALITY, AND SOCIAL STRUCTURE IN THE ORGANIZATIONAL SETTING*

*By Daniel J. Levinson*

### "Social role" as a unitary concept

The concept of role is related to, and must be distinguished from, the concept of social position. A position is an element of organizational autonomy, a location in social space, a category of organizational membership. A role is, so to say, an aspect of organizational physiology; it involves function, adaption, process. It is meaningful to say that a person "occupies" a social position; but it is inappropriate to say, as many do, that one occupies a role.

There are at least three specific senses in which the term "role" has been used, explicitly or implicitly, by different writers or by the same writer on different occasions.

a. Role may be defined as the *structurally given demands* (norms, expectations, taboos, responsibilities, and the like) associated with a given social position. Role is, in this sense,

---

* This abridgment from the article of the same title is from *Journal of Abnormal Psychology,* vol. 58 (1959), pp. 171–80. Copyright 1959 by the American Psychological Association. Reprinted by permission.

something outside the given individual, a set of pressures and facilitations that channel, guide, impede, support his functioning in the organization.

b. Role may be defined as the member's *orientation* or *conception* of the part he is to play in the organization. It is, so to say, his inner definition of what someone in his social position is supposed to think and do about it. Mead (1934) is probably the main source of this view of social role as an aspect of the person, and it is commonly used in analyses of occupational roles.

c. Role is commonly defined as the *actions* of the individual members—actions seen in terms of their relevance for the social structure (that is, seen in relation to the prevailing norms). In this sense, role refers to the ways in which members of a position act (with or without conscious intention) *in accord with or in violation of a given set of organizational norms.* Here, as in (*b*), role is defined as a characteristic of the actor rather than of his normative environment.

Many writers use a definition that embraces all of the above meanings without systematic distinction, and the shift, explicitly or implicitly, from one meaning to another. The following are but a few of many possible examples.[1]

\* \* \* \*

In short, the "unitary" conception of role assumes that there is a 1:1 relationship, or at least a *high degree of congruence,* among the three role aspects noted above. In the theory of bureaucratic organization, the rationale for this assumption is somewhat as follows. The organizationally given requirements will be internalized by the members and will thus be mirrored in their role-conceptions. People will know, and will want to do, what is expected of them. The agencies of role socialization will succeed except with a deviant minority—who constitute a separate problem for study. Individual action will in turn reflect the structural norms, since the appropriate role-conceptions will have been internalized and since the sanctions system rewards normative behavior and punishes deviant behavior. Thus, it is assumed that structural norms, individual role-conceptions and individual role-performance are three isomorphic reflections of a single entity: "the" role appropriate to a given organizational position.

It is, no doubt, reasonable to expect some degree of congruence among these aspects of a social role. Certainly, every organization contains numerous mechanisms designed to further such congruence. At the same time, it is a matter of common observation that organizations vary in the degree of their integration; structural demands are often contradictory, lines of authority may be defective, disagreements occur and reverberate at and below the surface of daily operations. To assume that what the organization requires, and what its members actually think and do, comprise a single, unified whole is severely to restrict our comprehension of organizational dynamics and change.

\* \* \* \* \*

## ORGANIZATIONALLY GIVEN ROLE-DEMANDS

The role-demands are external to the individual whose role is being examined. They are the situational pressures that confront him as the occupant of a given structural position. They have manifold sources: in the official charter and policies of the organization; in the traditions and ideology, explicit as well as implicit, that help to define the organization's purposes and modes of operation; in the views about this position which are held by mem-

---

[1] An argument very similar to the one made here is presented by Gross, Mason, and McEachern (1958) in a comprehensive overview and critique of role theory. They point up the assumption of high consensus regarding role-demands and role-conceptions in traditional role theory, and present empirical evidence contradicting this assumption. Their analysis is, however, less concerned than the present one with the converging of role theory and personality theory.

bers of the position (who influence any single member) and by members of the various positions impringing upon this one; and so on.

*    *    *    *    *

In attempting to characterize the role-requirements for a given position, one must therefore guard against the assumption that they are unified and logically coherent. There may be major differences and even contradictions between official norms, as defined by charter or by administrative authority, and the "informal" norms held by various groupings within the organization. Moreover, within a given status group, such as the top administrators, there may be several conflicting viewpoints concerning long range goals, current policies, and specific role-requirements. In short, the structural demands themselves are often multiple and disunified. Few are the attempts to investigate the sources of such disunity, to acknowledge its frequency, or to take it into conceptual account in general structure theory.

It is important also to consider the specificity or *narrowness* with which the normative requirements are defined. Norms have an "ought" quality; they confer legitimacy and reward-value upon certain modes of action, thought and emotion, while condemning others. But there are degrees here. Normative evaluations cover a spectrum from "strongly required" through various degrees of qualitative kinds of "acceptable," to more or less stringently tabooed. Organizations differ in the width of the intermediate range on this spectrum. That is, they differ in the number and kinds of adaptation that are normatively acceptable. The wider this range—the less specific the norms—the greater is the area of personal choice for the individual. While the existence of such an intermediate range is generally acknowledged, structural analyses often proceed as though practically all norms were absolute prescriptions or proscriptions allowing few alternatives for individual action.

There are various other normative complexities to be reckoned with. A single set of role-norms may be internally contradictory. In the case of the mental hospital nurse, for example, the norm of maintaining an "orderly ward" often conflicts with the norm of encouraging self-expression in patients. The individual nurse then has a range of choice, which may be narrow or wide, in balancing these conflicting requirements. There are also ambiguities in norms, and discrepancies between those held explicitly and those that are less verbalized and perhaps less conscious. These normative complexities permit, and may even induce, significant variations in individual role-performance.

The degree of *coherence* among the structurally defined role-requirements, the degree of *consensus with which they are held, and the degree of individual choice* they allow (the range of acceptable alternatives) are among the most significant properties of any organization. In some organizations, there is very great coherence of role-requirements and a minimum of individual choice. In most cases, however, the degree of integration within roles and among sets of roles appears to be more moderate.[2] This structural pattern is of especial interest from a sociopsychological point of view. To the extent that the requirements for a given position are ambiguous, contradictory, or otherwise "open," the individual members have greater opportunity for selection among existing norms and for creation of new norms. In this process, personality plays an important part. . . .

### Role-Facilities

In addition to the demands and obligations imposed upon the individual, we must also take into account the techniques, resources, and conditions of work—the means made available to him for fulfilling his organizational functions. . . .

*    *    *    *    *

---

[2] The reduced integration reflects in part the tremendous rate of technological change, the geographical and occupational mobility, and the diversity in personality that characterize modern society. On the other hand, diversity is opposed by the standardization of culture on a mass basis and by the growth of large-scale organization itself. Trends toward increased standardization and uniformity are highlighted in Whyte's (1956) analysis.

## PERSONAL ROLE-DEFINITION

### Individual (and Modal) Role-Conceptions

The nature of a role-conception may perhaps be clarified by placing it in relation to an ideology. The boundary between the two is certainly not a sharp one. However, ideology refers most directly to an orientation regarding the entire organizations (or other) structure—its purposes, its modes of operation, the prevailing forms of individual and group relationships, and so on. A role-conception offers a definition and rationale for one position within the structure. If ideology portrays and rationalizes the organizational world, then role-conception delineates the specific functions, values, and manner of functioning appropriate to one position within it.

*    *    *    *    *

. . . After all, individual role-conceptions are formed only partially within the present organizational setting. The individuals' ideas about his occupational role are influenced by childhood experiences, by his values and other personality characteristics, by formal education and apprenticeship, and the like. The ideas of various potential reference groups within and outside of the organization are available through reading, informal contacts, etc. There is reason to expect, then, that the role-conceptions of individuals in a given organizational position will vary and will not always conform to official role-requirements. Both the diversities and the modal patterns must be considered in organizational analysis.

### Individual (and Modal) Role-Performance

This term refers to the overt behavioral aspect of role-definition—to the more or less characteristic ways in which the individual acts as the occupant of a social position. Because role-performance involves immediately observable behavior, its description would seem to present few systematic problems. However, the formulation of adequate variables for the analysis of role-performance is in fact a major theoretical problem and one of the great stumbling blocks in empirical research.

Everyone would agree, I suppose that role-performance concerns only those aspects of the total stream of behavior that are structurally relevant. But which aspects of behavior are the important ones? And where shall the boundary be drawn between that which is structurally relevant and that which is incidental or idiosyncratic?

One's answer to these questions probably depends, above all, upon his conception of social structure. Those who conceive of social structure rather narrowly in terms of concrete work tasks and normative requirements, are inclined to take a similarly narrow view of role. In this view, role-performance is simply the fulfillment of formal role-norms, and anything else the person does is extraneous to role-performance as such. In this view, role-performance is simply the fulfillment of formal role-norms, and anything else the person does is extraneous to role-performance as such. Its proponents acknowledge that there are variations in "style" of performance but regard these as incidental. What is essential to *role*-performance is the degree to which norms are met.

A more complex and inclusive conception of social structure requires correspondingly multi-dimensional delineation of role-performance. An organization has, from this viewpoint, "latent" as well as "manifest" structure; it has a many-faceted emotional climate; it tends to "demand" varied forms of interpersonal allegiance, friendship, deference, intimidation, ingratiation, rivalry, and the like. If characteristics such as these are considered intrinsic properties of social structure, then they must be included in the characterization of role-performance. My own preference is for the more inclusive view. I regard social structure as having psychological as well as other properties, and I regard as intrinsic to role-performance the varied meanings and feelings which the actor communicates to those about him. Ultimately, we must learn to characterize organizational behavior in a way that takes into account, and helps to illuminate, its functions for the individual, for the others with whom he interacts, and for the organization.

It is commonly assumed that there is great uniformity in role-performance among the members of a given position. Or, in other words, that there is a *dominant, modal pattern of role-performance corresponding to the structural requirements*. The rationale here parallels that given above for role-conceptions. However, where individual variations in patterns of role-performance have been investigated, several modal types rather than a single dominant pattern were found. . . .

Nor is this variability surprising, except to those who have the most simplistic conception of social life. Role-performance, like any form of human behavior, is the resultant of many forces. Some of these forces derive from the organizational matrix; for example, from role-demands and the pressures of authority, from informal group influences, and from impending sanctions. Other determinants lie within the person, as for example his role-conceptions and role-relevant personality characteristics. Except in unusual cases where all forces operate to channel behavior in the same direction, role-performance will reflect the individual's attempts at choice and compromise among diverse external and internal forces.

\*       \*       \*       \*       \*

## ROLE-DEFINITION, PERSONALITY, AND SOCIAL STRUCTURE

\*       \*       \*       \*       \*

Clearly, individual role-conception and role-performance do not emanate, fully formed, from the depths of personality. Nor are they simply mirror images of a mold established by social structure. Elsewhere, . . . I have used the term "mirage" theory for the view, frequently held or implied in the psychoanalytic literature, that ideologies, role-conceptions, and behavior are mere epiphenomena or by-products of unconscious fantasies and defenses. Similarly, the term "sponge" theory characterizes the view, commonly forwarded in the sociological literature, in which man is merely a passive, mechanical absorber of the prevailing structural demands.

Our understanding of personal role-definition will remain seriously impaired as long as we fail to place it, analytically, in *both intra-personal and structural-environmental contexts.* That is to say, we must be concerned with the meaning of role-definition both for the individual personality and for the social system. A given role-definition both for the individual personality and for the social system. A given role-definition is influenced by, and has an influence upon, the *psyche* as well as the *socius.* If we are adequately to understand the nature, the determinants, and the consequences of role-definition, we need the double perspective of personality and social structure. The use of these two reference points is, like the use of our two eyes in seeing, necessary for the achievement of depth in our social vision.

*From*

# SOCIAL PSYCHOLOGY: A BRIEF INTRODUCTION*

*By Joseph E. McGrath*

## THE PERCEPTION OF OTHER PEOPLE

Oliver Wendell Holmes (1809–1894) once described a famous conversation between John and Henry in which six "persons" took part: John, as John knew himself; John, as he was known to Henry; the "true" John, as he was known only to God; and the equivalent trio of Henrys.

This same basic insight into the special nature of interpersonal perception was reflected in the work of early sociologists, notably in Cooley's (1902) concept of the "looking-glass self" and in George Mead's (1934) concepts of the two selves, the "I" and the "me." Both men pointed out that the child first develops an awareness of himself as an entity separate and distinct from his environment because *other people* respond to him as a separate, autonomous object. If there were no other people, we would have no self concept. As an individual develops a concept of "self," he becomes aware of himself as an object of his own perception (Mead's "me"), as distinct from himself as the perceiver (Mead's "I"). Furthermore, his own evaluation of himself arises as a *reflection of others' evaluation of him.* Thus, argued Mead and Cooley, the very heart of the individual's personality, his own concept, arises in the first instance and develops through time by the process of social interaction with other people.

Since these early formulations, there has been much research and theory on the nature and consequences of interpersonal perceptions. One whole school of psychotherapy . . . is built upon Mead's premise that the self concept is crucial to adjustment and that self evaluation changes in response to changes in others' evaluations of oneself. On this premise, the crux of therapy is to provide the patient with a consistently warm and accepting social environment, thus providing a proper climate for him to reorient his self concept. Recently, Fiedler and his coworkers . . . have shown that interpersonal perceptions are related to the individual's adjustment. In a large study of both military and college living groups, they found that individuals who see themselves as similar to others with whom they have close associations and who are seen as similar by those "significant others" show better personal adjustment than persons for whom this is not the case.

Newcomb . . . points out that our perceptions of other people are closely tied to our attitudes on matters related to those people. We tend to agree with those we like and like those with whom we agree. We also tend to disagree with those we dislike and dislike those with whom we disagree. Newcomb has formalized these ideas in a theoretical model that summarizes many of the concepts in this area. Newcomb's model deals with two persons (A and B) engaged in interaction about one or more objects (Xs), which can be ideas, physical objects, or other people. The set of attitudes which A and B have about each other and about the X's constitutes a system of interrelated parts. This set of attitudes is a system because the parts are interdependent, and when one part changes other parts are likely to show compensating changes. In fact, Newcomb postulates that there are certain states of the system (patterns of attitudes) which constitute *balanced* or *equilibrium* states. These balanced states are: mutual attraction between A and B, along with agreement about X's; and mutual rejection between A and B along with disagreement about X's. All other states (such

* From Chapter Five from *Social Psychology: A Brief Introduction* by Joseph E. McGrath. Copyright © 1964 by Holt, Rinehart and Winston, Inc. Reprinted by permission of Holt, Rinehart and Winston, Inc.

as disagreement with mutual attraction) are unstable states and will tend toward one or another of the equilibrium patterns.

Underlying this "objective" system or pattern are attitudes of two "subjective" A-B-X systems, one for A and one for B. A's subjective system includes his attitudes toward B and toward X and his *perceptions* (estimates) of B's attitudes toward himself (A) and toward X. B's subjective system includes the corresponding attitudes and perceptions. The same kinds of balanced states (perceived agreement with positively attractive others, and perceived disagreement with negatively attractive others) and the same tendency toward system balance hold for the subjective systems as for the objective A-B-X system. These systems of interpersonal relationships are shown in Figure 1.

**FIGURE 1**

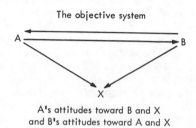

The objective system

A's attitudes toward B and X
and B's attitudes toward A and X

The subjective systems

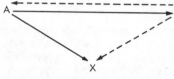

From A's point of view

A's attitudes toward B and X
and A's perceptions (estimates)
of B's attitudes toward A and X

From B's point of view

B's attitudes toward A and X
and B's perceptions (estimates)
of A's attitudes toward B and X

Diagram of Newcomb's A-B-X Model of Systems of Interpersonal Relationships. A and B represent two persons; X represents an object about which A and B are communicating or toward which A and B are co-orienting. Solid arrows represent actual attitudes of one person toward the other or toward X. Arrows run from holder of the attitude to target of the attitude. Broken-line arrows represent estimates by one person of the other persons' attitudes; for example, B———————→ X represents A's estimate of B's attitude toward X.

Thus, Newcomb is saying that the famous John and Henry conversation includes two other "persons" besides the six listed by Holmes, namely: John as John believes Henry sees him; and Henry's perception of how John sees Henry. Newcomb is also postulating that these interpersonal perceptions are interdependent with John's and Henry's own attitudes about the topics of their interaction and with their perceptions of each other's attitudes. Thus, at a more general level, he postulates that interpersonal attitudes, interpersonal perceptions, and attitudes toward other objects are all interdependent with one another, tend to be compatible, and tend to change together as a system.

*From*

# ORGANIZATION MAN AND DUE PROCESS OF LAW*

## By William M. Evan

*The ideology of the "organization man," as it bears on industrial organizations, has at least two irrelated structural sources: (a) the unstructured character of the work of junior and middle managers which is conducive to the use of subjective criteria of performance appraisal, and (b) an authority structure devoid of a mechanism to insure "procedural due process of law." It is hypothesized that this ideology has largely dysfunctional consequences from the viewpoint of the individual executive, the industrial organization, and society as a whole. Two potential countervailing forces are considered: the professionalization of management and the institutionalization of norms of procedural due process. Some research implications of this analysis are noted.*

\*     \*     \*     \*     \*

By comparison with the unionized manual worker, whose occupational rights are protected by the grievance machinery provided by the collective bargaining agreement, the junior or middle manager is at a distinct disadvantage: lacking the right of appeal, he is at the mercy of the decisions of his immediate superior who, in his decisions regarding his subordinates, may function simultaneously as judge, jury, and prosecutor.[1] From this perspective, the organization man appears to be a member of a "new proletariat" in present-day American industry. He does not have the protection of an outside occupational organization, such as unionized employees do; nor does he have a code of professional ethics to govern his relationships with his superordinates, his peers, and his subordinates; nor does he have the protection of "colleague control," as professionals do, to counteract "hierarchical control." Since the nature of his work makes objective evaluation of performance difficult, and since he lacks the right of appeal, he is, therefore, highly motivated to fulfill his superior's expectations—even at the expense of his own ideas and wishes—in order to insure a positive appraisal and the associated rewards. However, to fulfill his superior's expectations, which are often ambiguous, he learns to avoid any actions which he suspects might displease his superior. Such actions may range from joining or not joining the Masons[2] to the choice of style of clothing. The organization man's process of adapting himself to the expectations and behavior patterns of his superior and of relinquishing, if necessary, his own preferences and judgments may be likened to the conformity patterns experimentally observed by Sherif and Asch. Subjects faced with an ambiguous and unstructured situation—as in the case of the auto-kinetic effect—tend to adjust their statements of perceptions to one another;[3] and some subjects faced with an unambiguous and structured situation relinquish their true statement of perceptions of reality in favor of a false statement of perceptions made by others.[4]

---

\* Reprinted from *American Sociological Review*, vol. 26, no. 4 (August 1961).

[1] "There is no final escape from dependency if the superior is the ultimate authority, with no appeal beyond his interpretation or ruling. Unless there is some outside authority to which the subordinate can appeal, he never can be entirely safe in his dependency or quite able to develop a real independence." Mason Haire, *Psychology in Management* (New York: McGraw-Hill Book Co., 1956), p. 67.

[2] Cf. Melville Dalton, *Men Who Manage* (New York: John Wiley & Sons, Inc., 1959), pp. 178–81.

[3] Muzafer Sherif, "Group Influences upon the Formation of Norms and Attitudes," in Eleanor E. Maccoby, Theodore M. Newcomb, Eugene L. Hartley (eds.), *Readings in Social Psychology* (New York: Henry Holt & Co., 1958), pp. 219–32.

[4] Solomon E. Asch, "Effects of Group Pressure upon the Modification and Distortion of Judgments," in Maccoby, Newcomb and Hartley, op. cit., pp. 174–83.

In brief, the ideology of the organization man has at least two interrelated sources: occupational and organizational. Occupationally, the amorphous character of managerial work encourages the use of subjective criteria for evaluating performance, including a pattern of sponsorship or patronage and a concern for the organizational loyalty of subordinates. Organizationally, in the absence of norms of procedural due process of law, such as the right to appeal the decision of a superordinate, junior and middle managers are encouraged to become "conformists," developing an over-sensitivity to the expectations of superordinates in order to insure positive appraisal and corresponding rewards. Otherwise put, the ideology of organization man is an adaption to certain normless elements in the work situation of junior and middle managers.

## SOME CONSEQUENCES OF THE IDEOLOGY OF THE ORGANIZATION MAN

The consequences of the ideology of the organization man are presumably—in the absence of systematic data—largely dysfunctional from the viewpoint of the individual executive as well as from the viewpoint of the industrial organization and society at large. Several illustrative and hypothetical dysfunctions will be considered.

From the standpoint of the individual executive as well as the organization, the ideology tends to inhibit original and creative effort which, by definition, departs from prevailing practices, and hence runs the risk of not being approved by a superordinate. Accordingly, the industrial organization must increasingly rely on staff specialists for new ideas rather than on line management. This entails a loss to the organization of a potential source of valuable innovations—which is not to gainsay the advantages of having staff specialists concern themselves principally with problems of innovation.

Another consequence of this ideology for the individual as well as for the organization is the paradoxical combination of high job immobility with high job insecurity. By definition, the organization man's loyalty induces him to devote his entire career to his organization. He has a "local" rather than a "cosmopolitan" orientation; in other words, his reference group in his organization rather than the occupation of management which transcends a given organization. This tends to result in a high degree of job immobility among executive personnel. From the point of view of the organization, low turnover may be highly advantageous, provided the manager's performance is judged to contribute to the organization's effectiveness. In the event that his performance is judged to interfere with the organization's attainment of its goals, the organization may transfer him to an innocuous position, induce him to resign, or dismiss him.[5] In the absence of due process of law for junior and middle managers, and we might even add top managers, those who are judged undesirable for whatever reasons—relevant or irrelevant—may be discharged without an opportunity for a fair hearing.

Another consequence of the ideology which is dysfunctional for the organization is the tendency of the organization man to restrict upward communication to material which is calculated to enhance his self-image and simultaneously not threaten the superordinate in any way. On the basis of studies of experimentally created hierarchies, we would expect that organization men who are upwardly mobile—and this is presumably true of the bulk of junior and middle managers—would be strongly motivated to censor upward communication to insure positive appraisal and corresponding rewards.[6] Such action, of course, complicates the planning and coordination problems of top management.

Yet another effect of the ideology on the individual executive, related to job insecurity and the pressures for restriction of upward communication, is the tendency for discrepancies

---

[5] Cf. Perrin Stryker, "How to Fire an Executive," *Fortune,* vol. L (October 1954), pp. 116–17, 178–92.

[6] Cf. Harold H. Kelley, "Communication in Experimentally Created Hierarchies," *Human Relations,* vol. IV (February 1951), pp. 39–56; Arthur R. Cohen, "Upward Communication in Experimentally Created Hierarchies," *Human Relations,* vol. XI (February 1958), pp. 41–53.

to develop between overt and covert behavior. Covert nonconformity occurs provided the probability of the discovery of such action is low. Where covert nonconformity does not occur, we may expect to find covert disbelief in the legitimacy of the authority exercised by the superior together with overt behavioral conformity. The resulting degree of cognitive dissonance, due to the discrepancy between overt conformity and covert disbelief, on the part of the organization man may be considerable. To reduce the resulting dissonance, the organization man can convince himself that his overt behavior is quite satisfactory after all, i.e., by changing his cognitions so that they are consonant with his overt behavior.[7]

The effect of the ideology of the organization man on society as a whole is probably more elusive than its effects on the individual manager and on the industrial organization, though nonetheless real. As a result of the premium put on cautious behavior calculated not to offend the preferences and expectations of a superior, the organization man may tend to transfer this behavior pattern and principle of behavior to his community life and engage in only "conformist" activity. This approach to community life lessens the chances of success-fully coming to grips with new and complex social problems requiring innovative rather than "conformist" behavior. The consequences of this ideology for society as a whole may be especially marked in view of the recent efforts by corporations to encourage management to increase their participation in community affairs.

A related effect of the ideology may be observable in family values and childrearing patterns of the organization man. The values of seeking approval from superiors, of "team-work," and of "togetherness" may be transplanted from the corporation to the family.[8]

## POTENTIAL COUNTERVAILING FORCES TO THE IDEOLOGY OF THE ORGANIZATION MAN

Two potential countervailing forces to the ideology of the organization man are the institutionalization of norms of procedural due process of law for corporate management and the professionalization of management.

As yet it is difficult to discern any evidence for the institutionalization of norms of due process within corporate management. It is possible, however, that such a development may be stimulated by the need for resolving conflicts between staff and line management. The high frequency of such conflicts, in the absence of unionization among staff specialists, may be conducive to the growth of norms of procedural due process. Such a development could pave the way for the extension of this institution to all corporate management.

Another source of influence favoring an extension of procedural due process is external to the corporation. There is a growing awareness of the need for restricting the powers of the corporation. In particular, it is being argued that courts and the legislatures should extend constitutional guarantees of procedural due process to the corporation[9] or that corporations should develop their own "supplementary constitutional systems."[10] The venerable doctrine of due process, which dates back at least to the Magna Carta, includes a complex of procedural safeguards against the exercise of arbitrary and unlimited power.[11] These norms seek to insure that disputes are resolved impartially and fairly. This complex of norms includes the right of all parties to a conflict to be heard, the right to confront witnesses, to cross-examine them, and to introduce evidence in one's behalf. . . . Another potential

---

[7] Leon Festinger, *A Theory of Cognitive Dissonance* (Evanston, Ill.: Row, Peterson & Co., 1957), pp. 1–31.

[8] Daniel R. Miller and Guy E. Swanson, *The Changing American Parent: A Study in the Detroit Area* (New York: John Wiley & Sons, Inc., 1958).

[9] Adolph A. Berle, Jr., *The 20th Century Capitalist Revolution* (New York: Harcourt, Brace & Co., 1954), pp. 77 ff.

[10] Benjamin M. Selekman, "Power and Morality in Business," in Dan H. Fenn, Jr., *Management's Mission in a New Society* (New York: McGraw-Hill Book Co., 1959), pp. 317–19.

[11] Rodney L. Mott, *Due Process of Law* (Indianapolis, Ind.: Bobbs Merrill Co., 1926), pp. 1–29.

countervailing force to the ideology of the organization man is the professionalization of management. In spite of the plethora of discussions for several decades about the professionalization of management, there has been very little progress in this direction. . . .[12]

\* \* \* \* \*

Either of the two potential countervailing forces to the ideology of the organization man may be conducive to the development of the other. As between these two possible developments it appears more likely that professionalization of management will be conducive to the institutionalization of norms of due process than the reverse.

Short of the institutionalization of the norms of procedural due process for junior and middle management, several other mechanisms may upon inquiry prove to have an equivalent function. The first is the institutionalization of the right of job transfer within a company. This would enable a manager, finding himself in an unsatisfactory authority relationship with his superior, to overcome this problem without suffering the consequences of adjustment to an arbitrary superior.

A related mechanism is "job rotation." To the extent that this becomes an institutionalized procedure, it affords the executive an opportunity to manifest his abilities to more than one superior and in different organizational situations, which in turn increases the chances of a more objective appraisal of his talents.

A third mechanism which might be a functional substitute for the norms of due process is an increase in the opportunities for intercompany mobility. One of the major impediments to such mobility is the absence of vested pension rights. This discourages job changes because of the financial loss entailed. The vesting of pension rights for executives—such as already exists among university professors—if it should ever develop, would probably betoken a significant measure of progress toward the professionalization of management. Only an occupation with "cosmopolitan" values would encourage the institutionalization of such a practice.

---

[12] See, for example, Henry C. Metcalf (ed.), *Business Management as a Profession* (Chicago: A. W. Shaw Co., 1927); Howard R. Bowen, "Business Management: A Profession?" *Annals of the American Academy of Political and Social Science,* Vol. 297 (January 1955), pp. 112–17.

# 17. PARKERVILLE, LTD.

---

## Case Introduction

---

### SYNOPSIS

After designing and implementing two successful in-company management training programs for lower and middle-level managers, the management development director receives permission from the Management Development Committee to offer a program for senior, "high-promotables." All goes well with the design team, which includes an external consultant, until the personnel director reminds the team of a condition imposed by the committee. For the first time at Parkerville, data about the program participants' managerial potential was to be collected within the new program. Reaction to the innovation of assessing participants within an educational program places the management development director under personal, professional, and organizational stress. Symbolizing the strong reaction is the consultant's threat to withdraw from the program if the participant assessment idea is implemented.

### Why This Case Is Included

In the Parkerville, Ltd. case we see the potential conflict between the process of identifying and the process of developing the company's top leaders for the future. Both the idealist and pragmatist confront learning theory, professional values of educators, and the unavoidable necessity of picking out the "high fliers." The case also reminds us that committees develop—often in an unplanned and unexamined way—a leadership or managerial style.

### DIAGNOSTIC AND PREDICTIVE QUESTIONS

1. Psychologically, how can you explain Tom Foster's ignoring the Management Development Committee's request for assessment in the new program?

Read:  Leavitt, *Managerial Psychology* pp. 22–26. Maslow, *Motivation and Personality.*

2. Why would the Managerial Development Committee require assessment of the executives in the new program? And what options did it have to achieve this objective?

Read:  *Leavitt, *Managerial Psychology* pp. 87–104.

3. Analyze the leadership style of the Management Development Committee (and of Mr. Streeter as its chairman).

Read:  *Tannenbaum and Schmidt, "How to Choose a Leadership Pattern."

4. What is there about the learning process for executives that makes Dr. Webber so concerned over the "distraction of assessment"?

Read:  *Schein, Management Development as a Process of Influence."

5. What is there in Dr. Webber's role as distinct from Tom Foster's or Mr. Streeter's that prompted him to react as "devil's advocate" on the proposal to evaluate and assess the executives in the educational program?

Read:  Levinson, "Role, Personality and Social Structure in the Organizational Setting." Katz and Kahn, *The Social Psychology of Organizations.*

6. Dr. Webber's letter poses his conflict with the Management Development Committee's "innovation," as a win-loose situation, do you agree?

Read:  Litterer, "Conflict in Organization: A Re-Examination."

## POLICY QUESTIONS

7. As a prospective participant in the new program, what policy would you like to see Parkerville adopt on assessment in in-company education? Why?

8. As Tom Foster, write a policy statement on assessment in education. This policy should be one under which you would like to work as a course organizer and instructor. (Carefully re-read the lunch conversation in the case.)

9. What should Tom Foster's next step be at the end of the case? Think of both tactics and arguments.

10. As Mr. Streeter, propose a policy statement which would guide participants, instructors, sponsoring executives, organizers and anyone involved in in-company education in the matter of the collecting, or using of various kinds of evaluative or assessment data.

11. As chairman of the Management Development Committee what process should Mr. Streeter use to get the decision reviewed and either confirmed or revoked? (Review your answer to Question 3.)

12. How should Mr. Streeter and the Management Development Committee achieve their objective of assessing the candidates for general management positions? (Review your answer to Question 2.)

# Case Text*

Tom Foster found himself in a conflict. As management development director of Parkerville, Ltd., a United Kingdom-based integrated chemical company, he had satisfying success of late in introducing in-company training courses. Starting bottoms-up, he offered one basic course for young managers early in their first supervisory assignment and followed that with a project-based educational experience for high potentials, average age 35. Both program initiatives were well-received by the Management Development Committee chaired by Tom Foster's boss, Fred Streeter, the personnel director, and comprised of seven directors of operating or staff divisions. In the two years since the Management Development Committee approved the two programs, three sessions of the first and two of the second received wide acclaim from the participants and their sponsoring divisions.

On this success record, Tom Foster and his two colleagues in the Management Development Department launched the third program idea, this time for men already identified as candidates for higher managerial positions. This group, in their early 40s, represented the future of the company. Again, the Management Development Committee welcomed the new program and agreed in principle to its being offered in the next fiscal year. In its memorandum for approval, the Management Development Committee noted that the participants should be informed that their program performance would be assessed just as their managerial performance was assessed in their normal jobs. It was this line which gave Tom Foster the problem. Never before had assessment of participant arisen in considerations about the Parkerville in-company education programs.

Initially, the reference to assessment was ignored as Tom Foster and his two colleagues set about designing the new program. Feeling less experienced in designing programs for senior managers, they sought assistance from a business school professor, Dr. Donald Webber, who had for many years designed and taught in programs for senior executives. After two meetings in May and July, the design team met in October at Parkerville headquarters to finalize the program content and faculty. They worked through most of Wednesday until a meeting at 3 o'clock in Mr. Streeter's office where Dr. Webber was to meet the personnel director for the first time.

Tom Foster introduced Dr. Webber to Mr. Streeter and then took the occasion to brief Mr. Streeter on the design team's progress in preparing the program for the following spring. Mr. Streeter agreed with the new

---

* Copyright C.E.I., Geneva, 1976. Written by Dr. J. J. O'Connell.

developments and then asked: "How are you going to do the assessment in the program? I don't see any place in your program design for assessment activities nor do I see any provision for observers?"

Dr. Webber tried to catch Tom Foster's eye to get some hint on what Mr. Streeter meant. Prior to that moment, there had been no mention of assessment in any of the three design meetings. In the awkward moment of silence, Mr. Streeter turned toward Dr. Webber for a reply. Without the chance of checking with Tom Foster, Dr. Webber said: "I was not aware assessment was planned in the program. Given the opportunity, I would like to play devil's advocate on the idea."

Mr. Streeter: "Our Management Development Committee expressly requested that this new program include assessment." He reached for his file on the program and drew out the committee's memorandum. "Here's the Committee's instructions," he read: "Arrangements should be made within the program to assess the potential of the participants. The participants should be aware that their program performance will be assessed just as their managerial performance is assessed in their normal jobs."

Looking at Tom Foster, Mr. Streeter continued: "If we are not going to do assessment in the new program, I will have to raise the matter again with the committee. As I mentioned to you after the committee's meeting on the program, it was Dr. Rickers (technical director) who argued for the assessment idea. When such a careful scientist raises an issue of this kind within the committee, he has substantial influence."

Standing and moving to the large window overlooking the duck pond in the headquarters garden, Mr. Streeter continued reflectively: "Before coming to Parkerville, when I was with the engineering company, I participated in in-company educational programs in the role of an observer. It was hard work but I found that I learned an enormous amount about people in the process."

After another awkward pause, Dr. Webber cautiously raised some objections to mixing assessment and education. As Dr. Webber spoke, Tom Foster's mind hardly registered the arguments challenging his boss' and the committee's innovation on assessing participants in the new company program. At the moment, he wasn't so much bothered by the theoretical, moral, or even practical problems of assessment in education programs. He felt low because the issue had arisen at all to disturb the smooth flow of design and implementation of this third new program which would be such a fitting capstone to his career as he approached retirement in nine months. As he dragged his attention back to Dr. Webber's words, he noticed Mr. Streeter paying close attention and even occasionally seeming to agree. Before Tom knew it, Mr. Streeter was shaking Dr. Webber's hand and saying: "Thank you; we'll think this matter over and talk about it among ourselves next week."

The walk down the long corridor from Mr. Streeter's office was silent until Tom Foster and Dr. Webber were in the stairwell on the way down to the Management Development Department.

"I was taken back by this issue of assessment. This was the first time I heard of this feature in the program. I tried to catch your eye in there so we would be synchronized in our responses. Without knowing your position I had to follow my own reasoning. I hope I didn't speak too strongly."

"I'm sorry you got this surprise. We probably should have talked this assessment business through with you in advance but, frankly, we figured the matter would just disappear if we didn't raise it in our program design. It just didn't seem important enough to worry about. You did the right thing with Mr. Streeter."

Back in the Management Development Department with the other two management development officers, John Carr and Jim Porter, Tom Foster told what happened. Both seemed disappointed. John took a position immediately: "We can't assess these men in the program! My men in the project course worry about confidentiality as they work within various departments in gathering facts and opinions for their reports. They're not so much worried about themselves being evaluated but about being seen as evaluators of those who are cooperating as data sources. If our education efforts get tainted with this evaluation image, I bet our project sources dry up fast. Curiously, Dr. Rickers has sponsored two projects already and is eager for his third."

Jim spoke from the experience with the three sessions of the basic course. "The issue of evaluation always comes up in some phase of each program. Usually, there is some humorous remark made about grades going back to the boss but 90 percent of these young guys know us personally and trust us when we say there's no evaluation. Our credibility with that group, even the alumni, may be shot if we become evaluators in the senior course. The company never asked for evaluations before, why start now?" Tom replied: "We have to admit, the senior course is different in important ways. We can't hide from the fact that big promotion decisions will be made about these men in the near future. There's more at stake. Remember too that we are using six board level executives as speakers in the new program. Why do you think each so readily agreed to participate? These new program participants are the future of the business and the top people don't miss the point."

"That means," said Jim, "that we may be put in the evaluator's spot whether we design assessment into the program or not. If there is such interest in the potential of these me, I can well imagine us facing an inquisition on their program performance by the executive group. What do we do then?"

At that stage, Dr. Webber had to leave for another appointment in the city. The meeting broke up without a decision on next steps in designing the new program. The assessment issue was left hanging. Tom Foster walked Dr. Webber to his car in the parking lot and asked: "Would you be willing to write down your reactions to mixing assessment and education in a letter to me? It may help as we try to sort out our tactics for the meeting with Mr. Streeter next week." Agreeing to do so, Dr. Webber said: "Good-bye," and drove off.

Tom left the office Wednesday in a distracted mood and carried the distraction through his efforts on Thursday to finalize the department's budget for the next year. He realized that the budget for the senior program would itself not be adequate as originally established if assessment were to be included. Without finally deciding what to do, he increased the program budget by 20 percent as a hedge just so he could meet the deadline for submission of departmental budget proposals. This increase required the reduction of the "miscellaneous" line item to almost zero in order to stay within the target total he had tentatively agreed with Mr. Streeter.

On Friday Tom was scheduled to attend a regional meeting of the National Trainers Association in the city. He seized the occasion at lunch to test the issue of assessment with a number of professional colleagues from other companies. Tom asked the four men (Mark Gunning from a rubber company, Gerard Graham from a chemical company, Frank Stevens from a ball bearing company, and Larry Bennett from a tobacco company) at his table how they handled management requests for assessment or evaluation data about in-company program participants.

Mark Gunning jumped in first. "We do evaluation of participants in our programs and everybody knows it. We're all big boys. We don't hide from the fact that we continually face evaluation in business life. A course is part of real life, not an isolated greenhouse for nuturing delicate blossoms which will quickly wilt in face of wind and sun. I write a standard evaluation of the participants to the director of personnel, comparing one against the other in course performance. The director of personnel then has a double check on the potential review done by each man's boss. I try to get the same data from the external schools where we send our executives. Many academics are reluctant but in some places I have my sources."

**Gerard Graham:** Do you reveal which ones pinched waiters and which ones pinched waitresses or the average time each one spent bending the elbow at the bar?

**Mark Gunning:** Of course not, don't be ridiculous!

**Gerard Graham:** I'm serious! The social behavior of participants may be more important in promotion decisions than how men react to artificial exercises in a classroom setting. Those are the kinds of questions I get at least.

**Tom Foster:** How do you answer?

**Gerard Graham:** It depends on who asks. Some questions are easily deflected. Politically, I can't avoid a direct question from the managing director. Besides, I trust him to use the information sensibly. Okay, in some cases I feel awkward in answering questions I can't duck but that's life.

**Mark Gunning:** You guys bother me with such a discussion! Tom asked about assessment and evaluation, not about passing on back fence gossip.

**Frank Stevens:** That's a fine distinction I wish more managers would make. In our programs we have a policy against assessment or evaluation and a policy against our training people passing on their own observations on any aspect of participant performance or behavior. If someone slips and asks us about a participant we answer blandly: "Joe was a fine participant." Normally, the questioner gets the message and backs off. This is a terribly sensitive issue for participants no matter what Mark says about being "big boys." I remember one instance where a visiting lecturer casually used our managing director's first name when addressing the group. He later tried to get groups to use a feedback instrument during a group exercise and the participants simply revolted. He insisted and the participants ganged up on him by marking "average" on all his measurement scales, ruining his statistics and largely destroying the benefit of the exercise. The poor visitor never knew what hit him until I pointed out later how his use of the M.D.'s first name changed his role with the group from the neutral outsider to the suspect insider. This professor's usefulness to us has been compromised so that we can't use him any longer.

**Mark Gunning:** Sounds like a really healthy and mature environment you have there!

**Larry Bennett:** I know what Frank is trying to say. It's a pregnancy issue. You're either seen as an evaluator or you're not. I've tried to be a purist. In fact, I have been a purist in this matter. Yet, I feel guilty just as Gerard implied he sometimes does when he reluctantly answers questions about participants he cannot politically avoid. You're damned if you do, damned if you don't. I recall one instance which still haunts me. I was asked about a former participant at the time when he was up for promotion to the top position in a Latin American country where expatriates had to cope daily with very sensitive relations with host country nationals. I deflected the question with the "Joe is a nice boy" response, all the time realizing that Joe unquestionably demonstrated a superior attitude and an intolerance for developing country nationals right within our in-company seminars. I held my tongue; Joe got the job and within nine months had made such a mess of the situation that he was relieved and shortly left the company. I'll never know if my feedback would have prevented his promotion, but I must live with the feeling that my purist attitude may have permitted Joe to agonizingly fail and may have seriously affected the company's chances of successfully doing business in that country. If the situation arose again, I'm not so sure I'd be the purist.

By coffee time, Tom noticed that the discussion was getting increasingly heated and emotional. Obviously, he had opened Pandora's box and out popped "guilt," "politics," "ethics," and so on. The discussion didn't give him any peace of mind over the weekend. On Monday he tried to convey both the message and the feeling tone to his two colleagues in the department. As they were discussing how to raise the matter and what position to take with Mr. Streeter and the Management Development Committee, Tom's secretary brought in Dr. Webber's letter.

Mr. Thomas Foster
Management Development Department
Parkerville, Limited

Dear Tom:

Many thanks to you and your colleagues for the fine day at Parkerville. I trust there was sufficient output to justify the investment.

You asked me to write a few lines about assessment within education programs. First, some distinctions. Pure assessment activities within a potential identification system can be enormously valuable and highly professional. Forgotten in history is the fact that this was a U.K. innovation some 35 years ago. The Americans developed the idea in the meantime so that numerous companies run assessment centers (AT&T, Sears, SOHIO, etc.). The technology returned to the United Kingdom seriously three years ago when the men of Sussex University began research and consultancy on the matter. Now, Sussex is the best European center for such issues.

Pure management education, whether in-company or external, contains no hidden nor formal assessment data collection for use in the potential identification system by a participant's superiors or their staff. Three qualifiers ought to be added here, especially for in-company programs. Lecturing company executives will form impressions of participants during their brief encounter in class but this is mutually accepted for what it is—a small sample, personal impression, analogous to what happens at any business lunch. Participants will get rather good data about one another which may legitimately influence careers in succeeding years. This is accepted as a legitimate analogy to any project work where men interact and learn about one another. Finally, and most importantly, the participant gathers much information about himself relative to men who are an acceptable reference group. This information is used by each participant as he influences his own potential identification process.

The mixed assessment/education activity should be subdivided between hidden and announced assessment. Hidden assessment in education should be—and is—dismissed as unethical and unprofessional!

Announced assessment in education has been tried occasionally and considered successful over the long run in only one setting to my knowledge, in an American company. It works there because: (1) the practice fits both the company culture and the national culture; (2) the company has invested initially and continuously in the expensive process of identifying relevant criteria on which to observe and assess; (3) the participants know as they begin their careers in the company that promotion will be dependent on participation in the assessment/education activity; (4) the staff includes competent psychologists as well as executives; (5) the educational programs have built-in time for formal assessment activities as in an assessment center; (6) no program ends without time for each participant to receive professional feedback and counselling with the promise of professional follow-up; (7) the announced company policy states that no executive promotion may be made without consultation with the program director and through him his staff; (8) external and internal faculty are chosen for their willingness and competence to contribute both to education and assessment.

Other efforts to get a higher return on investment in education by mixing it with announced assessment seem consistently to reveal an inadequate potential identification system or relative ignorance of an existing potential identification system, coupled with a hair-raising naivete on the consequences for the learning process. Further, few of the experimentors have given adequate consideration to the eight reasons why the American company case works relatively well. To understand the negative consequences on learning, one must consider some of the theoretical issues in adult education. For an *adult* to learn (knowledge, attitudes, skills) he must go through a phase of at least considering discarding some of the prior things he brought to the learning experience. As Kenneth Boulding, the economist, wisely says: "Wisdom is the discarding of knowledge!" In an evaluative setting, an executive must avoid the psychological dissonance of believing for a minute that the competences which earned him a seat in a seminar could be questioned. He defends what he is and never discovers what he may become. He doesn't learn himself nor is he an open resource for another's learning. He becomes simply an advocate for himself as a promotable product. The feeling in the room in such situations reminds me of the posturing of peacocks in a mating dance.

One consequence heatedly discussed by professional educators in companies is the impact on their own lives and careers from involvement in assessment in education. Such educators become organizationally isolated as company spies. It gets lonely drinking alone! They carry guilt at giving assessments of men on inadequate sample observations and at answering questions which obviously require them to break confidences and violate privacy. They feel unavoidably irresponsible because data they pass on (since they themselves are not the decision makers) may be misinterpreted or taken out of context by a succession of men getting second or third hand data.

My observation is that the mixed education/assessment model is roundly rejected by most professionals and well-informed executives. Certainly, in my client firms the matter has been discussed and education is separated from assessment by any company I am personally familiar with in Europe. At our school we feel so strongly on the issue that we have an announced policy of not honoring a request for assessment data no matter from whom it comes.

After discussion here, it is decided that I as a school representative will withdraw from your seminar if the mixed assessment/education model is chosen. Our credibility as educators is jeopardized too much to be party to such an exercise. If you should choose the pure assessment approach, you are well advised to consult the professionals at Sussex who have an enormous comparative advantage over us in this matter. If you choose the pure educational model, I am delighted to continue the relationship.

If this issue is not adequately covered in the above comments, I could go into more detail about theory, morality, or practicality at your convenience.

Sincerely,

Dr. Donald Webber
Professor of
Organization Behavior

# Selected Readings

*From*

## MANAGERIAL PSYCHOLOGY*

*By Harold J. Leavitt*

### THE ASSESSMENT OF PEOPLE: ONE APPLICATION OF PERSONALITY THEORY

Two equally appropriate subtitles might have been attached to this chapter. One could have been: "How not to be snowed by test salesmen." The other might have been: "How not to be snowed by anti-test salesmen." For management people are under attack from two fronts: from those who offer tests as a solution to selection problems and from those who attack tests as unethical, unscientific, and anti-individualistic.

This last chapter in part 1, then, is devoted to a practical problem: the problem of assessment.

### The Scope of the Assessment Problem

People in industry continually need to forecast the behavior not only of the economy, of competition, of prices, but also of one another. "Assessment," "selection," and "evaluation" are all varieties of people-forecasting.

Both professionals and laymen have frequently failed miserably in forecasting how people will behave in specified jobs. One reason is the difficulty of the job. If our earlier chapters were right, what has to be predicted is the result of a complex maze of hard-to-specify

---

* From Harold J. Leavitt, *Managerial Psychology*, 3d edition. © 1972 by The University of Chicago Press. All rights reserved. Excerpts from pp. 87–93, 95–104.

interrelated forces. Forecasting the behavior of one individual is much like trying to predict exactly what pattern of cracks will result when a particular thrower throws a particular ball against a particular pane of glass. We can be fairly certain that the glass will crack. But we seldom know enough about the ball, the air currents, the thrower, and the particular pane to be sure about the directions and lengths of the cracks that will result.

Nevertheless, we cannot escape in industry from the problem of having to assess people for tasks. Every job assignment that a manager makes includes the requirement that he assess the people available against the job he has in mind.

\*　　\*　　\*　　\*　　\*

So assessment is not limited to "formal" problems like selecting new employees or rating the qualifications of old ones, nor is it limited to the assessment of personality. It must necessarily involve assessment of knowledge, experience, education, and many other aspects of the person.

For the formal phases, like personnel selection and merit rating, a good deal of research and experience is available. Every executive in industry these days is aware of personality tests, patterned interviews, personnel-rating forms, and the like. Underlying each of these is a large (but not large enough) body of theory and empirical research. Unfortunately no comparable amount of work has been done on the day-to-day problems of assessment to help the business executive make increasingly accurate spot judgments about other people. Even so, some useful things are coming to be known. So, when the boss asks, "well, what did you think of him?" the executive can honestly say something more than, "He's a nice guy" or "I don't like him."

## Formal Methods of Selection and Evaluation

One can single out at least three more or less separate formal approaches to the selection and evaluation of personnel for industry. Looked at right now, the separations among the three are indistinct, for they have been growing together. But historically, each has made its way over a different route.

*Pencil-and-Paper Tests and the Empirical Method.* The first approach, one largely American in origin, can be roughly labeled the "pencil-and-paper-test approach." The great bulk of short intelligence tests, aptitude tests, etc. belong under this heading. So too, for the most part, do standard interview forms, most merit-rating scales, fitness reports, and the like. Until recently, they were mostly tests of specific skill or abilities, like numerical ability, finger dexterity, and so on.

\*　　\*　　\*　　\*　　\*

The pencil-and-paper position is this: The task of selecting people for jobs is a task of predicting in advance how people will behave. Clearly, then, what is required are some measurable advance predictions and some corresponding measurements, taken at some later time, of how people actually performed.

\*　　\*　　\*　　\*　　\*

. . . The problem is not whether the predictions make sense, but whether they predict. If they predict, they are useful; if they do not predict, they are not useful.

For the pencil-and-paper approach is itself a method of measurement rather than a theory of man's behavior. Any theorist of any persuasion may use it. Some test items may be based on a theory of physiognomy, some on Freudian psychodynamics, some on the color of a man's shoes. In actual practice, the current pencil-and-paper personality tests used in business derive largely from a semibehavioristic theory of personality. They have been, until recently, notable for their failure to include "deep" areas of personality.

This pencil-and-paper method has a great many advantages and some practical disadvantages. It has the huge advantage of quantification and empiricism. It also has dollar advantages. Pencil-and-paper tests, once standardized, are easy to manufacture, administer, and score. Professional testers are often needed only in the developmental stages because administration can usually be turned over to trained, but not professional, technicians. Such devices are not very time consuming, so that large numbers of people can be tested, frequently in groups of indefinite size, at reasonable costs.

Perhaps the greatest disadvantage of such procedures is that they are designed for statistical, rather than individual, prediction. That is, they are most useful in making predictions about the behavior of large numbers of people rather than about particular individuals.

\* \* \* \* \*

This tendency of pencil-and-paper methods to predict en masse rather than individually raises two questions. The first is an ethical question and perhaps a specious one. Is it "right" to turn any job applicant away, even if he is only one in a hundred, who would have been perfectly competent if he had been hired? Is it "fair" to the applicant to so depersonalize him that he becomes simply a score among hundreds of scores, his fate inexorably tied to a numerical system? Perhaps these are valid questions, and perhaps it is somehow more fair to tie an applicant's fate to the rose-colored perceptions of a nonquantitative interviewer. It would seem, however, that the ethical issue properly attaches to the whole selection problem itself, not to the issue of selection by tests.

The second question that can be asked is about the utility of pencil-and-paper devices at higher organizational levels, where the number of applicants for particular positions may be small. The usual statistical indexes of validity do not apply to very small samples. So if the task is to select assistant general managers rather than typists, the utility of the method is sharply reduced.

*Projective Tests and the Clinical Method.*  A second approach to formal selection lays much more emphasis on the dynamics of personality, much less on empirical validity. The approach may be labeled, somewhat unfairly, the projective approach. Projectives are much more "head doctor" techniques than pencil-and-paper tests. They are European in origin, springing theoretically from Freud and technically from the Swiss psychiatrist Rorschach. They build on the internal, perceptual frame of reference talked about in chapter 3, assuming that one can get a valid picture of a person quickly by assessing the way he projects his personality onto some standard, ambiguous parts of the world. All projectives contain these elements of standardization and ambiguity. The "questions" on the Rorschach test are some standardized ink blots that the subject is asked to describe. The tester then interprets the number, quality, and variety of the subject's responses against the tester's theory of personality and against his and others' experience with the responses of other people to the same blots.

Similarly, in the Thematic Apperception Test, the subject is asked to tell stories about a standard series of pictures. The tester records the stories and the subject's behavior. He then interprets the subject's personality in the light of the themes used in his stories.

The end result of a battery of projective tests, then, is not a numerical score comparing subject X with other subjects. It is a verbal report assessing the subject's dominant needs and ambitions, his tolerance of frustrations, his attitudes toward authority, the major conflicts that seem to be operating in his personality, and so on. Given such a report, a manager clearly must decide for himself whether the tester's judgment deserves heavy weighting in the final decision.

\* \* \* \* \*

One important industrial advantage of projectives is also, their scientific weakness. They are essentially individualistic, and they cannot be easily "proved" right or wrong, even by their proponents. Projectives, therefore, push decision-making back to where it belongs anyway, into the hands of management. The projective tester says to the manager, in effect, "Here is my expert judgment of John Jones. You have your judgment of him to which you can now add mine. I have tried to add information to your fund of relevant information, but I cannot guarantee that my judgment will be right. You make the decision."

\* \* \* \* \*

Unlike the pencil-and-paper tests, projectives seldom get to the stage at which they can be scored by technicians, because the interpretation always remains individual. The judgment of the tester is a large factor. When management buys pencil-and-paper tests, it buys a quantitative tool from which most subjective elements of interpretation have been eliminated. Any honest technician counting up the yeses and noes on an interest inventory will come up with the same score as any other honest technician. Not so with honest projective testers. The professional judgment of the test administrator plays a far more important part than the projective tests themselves in determining what comes out. In effect, then, when management buys projective tests, it buys the tester, just as when one buys a chest X ray, one buys the judgment and of the interpreting physician rather than the plate itself.

Projectives are expensive. Although efforts are being made to standardize and simplify them for mass administration, they remain largely one-at-a-time tests. A professional tester may spend eight hours or more testing and interpreting a single subject. Consequently, projectives have entered industry at the level at which they are most likely to be both useful and worth the money—at the executive level where pencil-and-paper tests are relatively useless.

Management's only bases for determining whether projectives are worth the investment are, first, its own opinion of the tester it has hired, and, second, *its experience over time in relating the actual behavior of applicants with the predictions that testers have made.*

\* \* \* \* \*

Managers sometimes react against these qualifications, wishing for more "practical," black-and-white[1] decisions. Realistically, though, selecting an executive is not a black-and-white problem. It is not usually true that people simply succeed or fail. They succeed or fail "if," or they would have succeeded or failed "but." They might have succeeded if they had worked for another kind of superior, or if management had given them a little looser or a little tighter rein, or if they had been provided with a high-powered assistant, or if the job description had been rewritten so that the new man was given more responsibility in area A and less in area B. For success on a job, especially a decision-making managerial job, is not a function of personality alone but of a personality in an environment. . . .

\* \* \* \* \*

If a projective tester, therefore, can start management worrying about whether to put a new employee to work for systematic department-head Smith or for loose, easy-going department-head Jones, that in itself may be a considerable service to the company.

***Sociometric Methods.*** Sociometrically, people are not assessed by tests or by testers but by other people: peers or subordinates or superiors. The "buddy rating" system used by the military in the Second World War is a typical sociometric device. A platoon of potential officer candidates, for example, trains together for several weeks. Then each member is asked to nominate the three men he thinks would make the best combat officers and the three he thinks would make the worst combat officers. They might be asked, too, to rate their buddies on honesty or intelligence or sense of humor or any of a number of other characteristics. Positive and negative votes received by each man are totaled and a score assigned to that man. The score represents his peers' joint estimate of his aptitude for a particular job.

\* \* \* \* \*

. . . When, sociometrically, one simply asks men to make an overall judgment of one another, one is, in a way, automatically taking the wholeness of personality into account.

This coin has another side. When data consist of the general feelings of some people about some other people, the dangers of distortion are many. Such distortions may be partially eliminated by using large numbers of judgments. Although the judgment made by one platoon member may be far off base, the judgments of fifty platoon members are reasonably valid—at least more valid, as World War II experience showed, than many paper-and-pencil tests, rating scales, and even military-school grades.

Sociometric methods have been used in a variety of ways for a variety of purposes.

---

[1] Here is an example of how our perceptions are influenced by our times. When I first wrote this, "black-and-white" popularly meant "clear and definitive." Now it also has racial meaning. So I'll leave it in, since *both* meanings are relevant here.

Sometimes one asks several judges to observe and listen to a group of applicants talking to one another. The judges sit on the periphery and observe the applicants. They then decide which one of the applicants would best perform a particular job. A number of variations of this "leaderless group" method are in current use.

\* \* \* \* \*

. . . . Sociometric methods, especially buddy ratings, are something like the voting process. Voting democracy in industry carries many dangers for traditional managerial "prerogatives" and for the whole power balance within an organization. If operators are allowed to select their own foremen, managers will argue, political plots and fixed "elections" may not be far behind. Selection by "popularity," they add, will replace selection by ability, despite the fact that research to date has shown that such ratings are not popularity contests.

### The Assessment Center

Despite these objections, sociometric methods are taking hold, particularly in executive selection. Several major companies have, in the last few years, established assessment centers for their executives, either as separate entities or as parts of management development centers.

These assessment centers typically lean heavily on sociometric measurements of several kinds. Usually they work like this:

Some small numbers of middle- to high-level executives are brought together at a special site for, say, three days. The assessment staff includes one or two professionals—psychologists usually—and several senior line executives who arrive in advance for a short period of training in assessment procedures. This assessment staff then puts the "subject" executives through a series of tests and exercises. The tests may be conventional ones—pencil and paper or projectives. The exercises have a sociometric flavor. Groups of the subject executives are given, for example, a group task—a company problem—and asked to discuss it and put forth some recommendations. This discussion is observed by the senior executive staff, often with one senior executive particularly observing just one or two subject executives as they debate and discuss the issue. This process is repeated in several forms, several times, with the seniors building up their observations of each man relative to the others.

Usually peer assessments are added. Subject executives are asked to rate one another on a collection of factors.

At the end of the three days, the whole batch is put together. The staff talks over each man, using observations, peer ratings, test scores, and anything else available, and makes an assessment of his executive potential and, usually, of his development needs.

Sometimes all these data are kept confidential in the center files. Usually they are fed back to each man in a series of interviews; occasionally they are made available to the boss of the man in question.

Technically the process is probably quite effective. It uses a team approach to assessment, exploiting "soft" observational data as well as more hard-nosed test scores. It provides good training in observation and evaluation for the senior executives who work as staff members.

On the other hand, are there ethical problems that such schemes generate? Of course. May we ask the reader to ponder those broader concerns for himself? For example, is it proper to subject a man to three days of assessment, whether he wants it or not? May an executive not want it? Is refusal really possible? What about the findings? Who sees them? What are they used for? How long do they remain in the personnel file?

### Day-to-Day Assessment of People

People directing an organized human effort must necessarily spend some of their time making judgments about the fitness of certain members for certain tasks. Some judgments can be formalized, but it is at an informal, day-to-day level that most assessment goes on.

Top management informally, gradually, imperceptibly, perhaps even unconsciously, decides that Jones looks like presidential timber and that Smith is never likely to go anywhere.

* * * * *

. . . A man's capacity to judge probably correlates positively with the extent to which he can view the outside world undistortedly, i.e., it correlates with his own security and self-knowledge. For judging is one kind of problem-solving. It can be reduced to three phases: determining what information is necessary to make a judgment; obtaining that information, usually through communication with other persons; evaluating that information into a judgment. Each of these processes is likely to be as good as the judge's own internal information-processing system.

The first, deciding what information is relevant, requires also that we ask: "Relevant for what?" Is he being considered for a specific job? What kind of a job? Working with whom? And so on. If we can get a good psychological picture of the task, we may be able to isolate the kinds of psychological information that would be relevant in a personality.

* * * * *

### Getting Information about a Person

A good deal of information about A can be obtained by talking to B or C. A good deal more can be gotten by talking to A. If the judge has lived closely and intimately with his subject, the process of gathering additional information to make a new judgment is minimal. He probably knows all he needs to know, and his task is to order it against the problem for which the judgment is being made and to try to extricate himself from his prejudices. If one is dealing with a relative stranger, however (and it is in this category that most problems of assessment reside), then gathering information is a major part of the problem.

* * * * *

In industry "subjective" personal assessment may lead an organization always to find new people like the old ones. "Good" people may become people that today's management likes. And the people today's management likes may well be people like today's management. Subjective, personalized assessment, with little reference to the question of assessment-for-what, may indeed ultimately yield an in-group of "all-alike" people. But since all-alike people may be able to work together better than all-different people, an organization may, under certain conditions, profit from just such prejudice. For example, one can argue that in a period of growth and youth an all-alike team has many advantages; later in an organization's life the same subjective prejudices may be stifling to the birth of new ideas.

There is another side to this picture. When people are being assessed and know it, they behave in ways they think will evoke the best assessment. If a personnel interviewer asks Mr. X, "How do you get along with people?" his answer might be, "Oh, just fine. I like people etc., etc., etc." But if a psychiatrist for whose services Mr. X was paying asked him the same question an hour later, his answer might be different: "Well, Doc, that's just the problem. Some people don't seem to pay any attention to me etc., etc., etc." This truism, that people play to their audiences, is frequently overlooked in industrial interviewing.

* * * * *

These thoughts about day-to-day evaluations of other people are general and incomplete. Ultimately, after all, an evaluation of one person by another is a judgment and nothing more. A good judge needs all the information he can get from all the sources he can find. To an extent, scales, forms, and categories can be helpful. But no "system" provides a means for escaping from one's own lack of sensitivity or understanding in making such judgments. There are no formulas that can rule the judge out of the judging equation.

### Assessment and the Atmosphere of the Organization

Drawing from earlier chapters, we can predict that people in an organization will try to evoke the best assessment they can get. They will (and should) try to stack the cards in their own favor. More than that, however, we can predict that they will have mixed feelings about assessment, both resenting it and seeking it out. We should expect resentment because assessment is a threat to independence and autonomy. But we should also expect people to "want to know where they stand," to want to know whether they are loved and thought well of by those on whom they depend.

From the managerial point of view, then, the problem of assessment is more than a problem of technique. The tests, the interviews, the other ritualistic paraphernalia of assessment, are only a small part of the problem. The bigger parts raise questions like these: Shall we consciously assess our people? Shall we formalize the process? Shall we report back results? All results? Or only "good" ones? Who shall assess? Superiors only? Or peers? Or subordinates? What is to be assessed? Personality or performance? Shall we build a work environment permeated with an atmosphere of assessment?

This book can offer no pat answers to such questions. There are none.

### In Summary

Three general approaches to formal assessment have been described: pencil-and-paper tests, projectives, and sociometric methods. Each has its own advantages and costs. Pencil-and-paper devices are relatively cheap and relatively standardized, but their use is largely limited to mass-selection situations. Projectives go deep and are rich in the material they dredge up, but subjective, individualistic, expensive, and poorly validated. Sociometrics are easy and relatively valid but carry serious implications for the power relationships in an organization.

Day-to-day assessing of people is a more difficult problem. It can be helped by a set of categories for thinking about personality, by utilizing modern interviewing techniques, and by increasing one's insight into oneself.

The larger questions of assessment are not "how" questions but questions of "why" and "how much."

*     *     *     *     *

*From*

# HOW TO CHOOSE A LEADERSHIP PATTERN*

*By Robert Tannenbaum and Warren H. Schmidt*

*     *     *     *     *

The net result of the research findings and of the human relations training based upon them has been to call into question the stereotype of an effective leader. Consequently, the modern manager often finds himself in an uncomfortable state of mind.

Often he is not quite sure how to behave; there are times when he is torn between exerting "strong" leadership and "permissive" leadership. Sometimes new knowledge pushes him in one direction ("I should really get the group to help make this decision"), but at the same time his experience pushes him in another direction ("I really understand the problem better than the group and therefore I should make the decision"). He is not sure when a group decision is really appropriate or when holding a staff meeting serves merely as a device for avoiding his own decision-making responsibility.

---

* From "How to Choose a Leadership Pattern," *Harvard Business Review,* vol. 36, no. 2 (March–April 1958) pp. 95–100 (excerpts). Reprinted by permission. © 1958 by The President and Fellows of Harvard College; all rights reserved.

The purpose of our article is to suggest a framework which managers may find useful in grappling with this dilemma. First we shall look at the different patterns of leadership behavior that the manager can choose from in relating himself to his subordinates. Then we shall turn to some of the questions suggested by this range of patterns. For instance, how important is it for a manager's subordinates to know what type of leadership he is using in a situation? What factors should he consider in deciding on a leadership pattern? What difference do his long-run objectives make as compared to his immediate objectives?

## RANGE OF BEHAVIOR

Exhibit 1 presents the continuum or range of possible leadership behavior available to a manager. Each type of action is related to the degree of authority used by the boss and

**EXHIBIT 1**
**Continuum of Leadership Behavior**

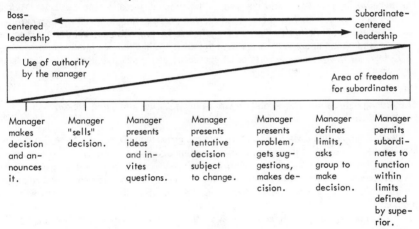

to the amount of freedom available to his subordinates in reaching decisions. The actions seen on the extreme left characterize the manager who maintains a high degree of control while those seen on the extreme right characterize the manager who releases a high degree of control. Neither extreme is absolute; authority and freedom are never without their limitations.

Now let us look more closely at each of the behavior points occurring along the continuum:

### The Manager Makes the Decision and Announces It

In this case the boss identifies a problem, considers alternative solutions, chooses one of them, and then reports this decision to his subordinates for implementation. He may or may not give consideration to what he believes his subordinates will think or feel about his decision; in any case, he provides no opportunity for them to participate directly in the decision-making process. Coercion may or may not be used or implied.

### The Manager "Sells" His Decision ·

Here the manager, as before, takes responsibility for identifying the problem and arriving at a decision. However, rather than simply announcing it, he takes the additional step of persuading his subordinates to accept it. In doing so, he recognizes the possibility of some resistance among those who will be faced with the decision, and seeks to reduce this resistance by indicating, for example, what the employees have to gain from his decision.

### The Manager Presents His Ideas, Invites Questions

Here the boss who has arrived at a decision and who seeks acceptance of his ideas provides an opportunity for his subordinates to get a fuller explanation of his thinking and his intentions. After presenting the ideas, he invites questions so that his associates can better understand what he is trying to accomplish. This "give and take" also enables the manager and the subordinates to explore more fully the implications of the decision.

### The Manager Presents a Tentative Decision Subject to Change

This kind of behavior permits the subordinates to exert some influence on the decision. The initiative for identifying and diagnosing the problem remains with the boss. Before meeting with his staff, he has thought the problem through and arrived at a decision—but only a tentative one. Before finalizing it, he presents his proposed solution for the reaction of those who will be affected by it. He says in effect, "I'd like to hear what you have to say about this plan that I have developed. I'll appreciate your frank reactions, but will reserve for myself the final decision."

### The Manager Presents the Problem, Gets Suggestions, and Then Makes His Decision

Up to this point the boss has come before the group with a solution of his own. Not so in this case. The subordinates now get the first chance to suggest solutions. The manager's initial role involves identifying the problem. He might, for example, say something of this sort: "We are faced with a number of complaints from newspapers and the general public on our service policy. What is wrong here? What ideas do you have for coming to grips with this problem?"

The function of the group becomes one of increasing the manager's repertory of possible solutions to the problem. The purpose is to capitalize on the knowledge and experience of those who are on the "firing line." From the expanded list of alternatives developed by the manager and his subordinates, the manager then selects the solution that he regards as most promising.[1]

### The Manager Defines the Limits and Requests the Group to Make a Decision

At this point the manager passes to the group (possibly including himself as a member) the right to make decisions. Before doing so, however, he defines the problem to be solved and the boundaries within which the decision must be made.

\*    \*    \*    \*    \*

### The Manager Permits the Group to Make Decisions within Prescribed Limits

This represents an extreme degree of group freedom only occasionally encountered in formal organizations, as, for instance, in many research groups. Here the team of managers or engineers undertakes the identification and diagnosis of the problem, develops alternative procedures for solving it, and decides on one or more of these alternative solutions. The only limits directly imposed on the group by the organization are those specified by the

---

[1] For a fuller explanation of this approach, see Leo Moore, "Top Much Management Too Little Change," *Harvard Business Review,* January–February 1956, p. 41.

superior of the team's boss. If the boss participates in the decision-making process, he attempts to do so with no more authority than any other member of the group. He commits himself in advance to assist in implementing whatever decision the group makes.

## KEY QUESTIONS

As the continuum in Exhibit 1 demonstrates, there are a number of alternative ways in which a manager can relate himself to the group or individuals he is supervising. At the extreme left of the range, the emphasis is on the manager—on what *he* is interested in, how *he* sees things, how *he* feels about them. As we move toward the subordinate-centered end of the continuum, however, the focus is increasingly on the subordinates—on what *they* are interested in, how *they* look at things, how *they* feel about them.

When a business leadership is regarded in this way, a number of questions arise. Let us take four of especial importance:

Can a boss ever relinquish his responsibility by delegating it to someone else?

\*     \*     \*     \*     \*

Should the manager participate with his subordinates once he has delegated responsibility to them?

\*     \*     \*     \*     \*

How important is it for the group to recognize what kind of leadership behavior the boss is using?

\*     \*     \*     \*     \*

Can you tell how "democratic" a manager is by the number of decisions his subordinates make?

\*     \*     \*     \*     \*

## DECIDING HOW TO LEAD

Now let us turn from the types of leadership that are *practical* and *desirable*. What factors or forces should a manager consider in deciding how to manage? Three are of particular importance:

1. Forces in the manager.
2. Forces in the subordinates.
3. Forces in the situation.

We should like briefly to describe these elements and indicate how they might influence a manager's action in a decision-making situation.[2] The strength of each of them will, of course, vary from instance to instance, but the manager who is sensitive to them can better assess the problems which face him and determine which mode of leadership behavior is most appropriate for him.

### Forces in the Manager

The manager's behavior in any given instance will be influenced greatly by the many forces operating within his own personality. He will, of course, perceive his leadership problems in a unique way on the basis of his background, knowledge, and experience. Among the important internal forces affecting him will be the following:

*1. His Value System.* How strongly does he feel that individuals should have a share in making decisions which affect them? Or, how convinced is he that the official who is paid

---

[2] See also Robert Tannenbaum and Fred Masarik, "Participation by Subordinates in the Managerial Decision-Making Process," *Canadian Journal of Economics and Political Science,* August 1950, pp. 413–18.

to assume responsibility should personally carry the burden of decision making? The strength of his convictions on questions like these will tend to move the manager to one end or the other of the continuum shown in Exhibit 1. His behavior will also be influenced by the relative importance that he attaches to organizational efficiency, personal growth of subordinates, and company profits.[3]

*2. His Confidence in His Subordinates.* Managers differ greatly in the amount of trust they have in other people generally, and this carries over to the particular employees they supervise at a given time. In viewing his particular group of subordinates, the manager is likely to consider this knowledge and competence with respect to the problem. A central question he might ask himself is: "Who is best qualified to deal with this problem?" Often he may, justifiably or not, have more confidence in his own capabilities than in those of his subordinates.

*3. His Own Leadership Inclinations.* There are some managers who seem to function more comfortably and naturally as highly directive leaders. Resolving problems and issuing orders come easily to them. Other managers seem to operate more comfortably in a team role, where they are continually sharing many of their functions with their subordinates.

*4. His Feelings of Security in An Uncertain Situation.* The manager who releases control over the decision-making process thereby reduces the predictability of the outcome. Some managers have a greater need than others for predictability and stability in their environment. This "tolerance for ambiguity" is being viewed increasingly by psychologists as a key variable in a person's manner of dealing with problems.

The manager brings these and other highly personal variables to each situation he faces. If he can see them as forces which, consciously or unconsciously, influence his behavior, he can better understand what makes him prefer to act in a given way. And understanding this, he can often make himself more effective.

**Forces in the Subordinate**

Before deciding how to lead a certain group, the manager will also want to consider a number of forces affecting his subordinates' behavior. He will want to remember that each employee, like himself, is influenced by many personality variables. In addition, each subordinate has a set of expectations about how the boss should act in relation to him (the phrase "expected behavior" is one we hear more and more often these days at discussions of leadership and teaching). The better the manager understands these factors, the more accurately he can determine what kind of behavior on his part will enable his subordinates to act more effectively.

Generally speaking, the manager can permit his subordinates greater freedom if the following essential conditions exist:

If the subordinates have relatively high needs for independence. (As we all know, people differ greatly in the amount of direction that they desire.)

If the subordinates have a readiness to assume responsibility for decision making. (Some see additional responsibility as a tribute to their ability; others see it as "passing the buck.")

If they have a relatively high tolerance for ambiguity. (Some employees prefer to have clear-cut directives given to them; others prefer a wider area of freedom.)

If they are interested in the problem and feel that it is important.

If they understand and identify with the goals of the organization.

If they have the necessary knowledge and experience to deal with the problem.

---

[3] See Chris Argyris, "Top Management Dilemma: Company Needs versus Individual Development," *Personnel,* September 1955, pp. 423–34.

If they have learned to expect to share in decision making. (Persons who have come to expect strong leadership and are then suddenly confronted with the request to share more fully in decision making are often upset by this new experience. On the other hand, persons who have enjoyed a considerable amount of freedom resent the boss who begins to make all the decisions himself.)

The manager will probably tend to make fuller use of his own authority if the above conditions do *not* exist; at times there may be no realistic alternative to running a "one-man show."

The restrictive effect of many of the forces will, of course, be greatly modified by the general feeling of confidence which subordinates have in the boss. Where they have learned to respect and trust him, he is free to vary his behavior. He will feel certain that he will not be perceived as an authoritarian boss on those occasions when he makes decisions by himself. Similarly, he will not be seen as using staff meetings to avoid his decision-making responsibility. In a climate of mutual confidence and respect, people tend to feel less threatened by deviations from normal practice, which in turn makes possible a higher degree of flexibility in the whole relationship.

### Forces in the Situation

In addition to the forces which exist in the manager himself and in his subordinates, certain characteristics of the general situation will also affect the manager's behavior. Among the more critical environmental pressures that surround him are those which stem from the organization, the work group, the nature of the problem, and the pressures of time. Let us look briefly at each of these:

*Type of Organization.* Like individuals, organizations have values and traditions which inevitably influence the behavior of the people who work in them. The manager who is a newcomer to a company quickly discovers that certain kinds of behavior are approved while others are not. He also discovers that to deviate radically from what is generally accepted is likely to create problems for him.

\* \* \* \* \*

*Group Effectiveness.* Before turning decision-making responsibility over to a subordinate group, the boss should consider how effectively its members work together as a unit.

\* \* \* \* \*

*The Problem Itself.* The nature of the problem may determine what degree of authority should be delegated by the manager to his subordinates. Obviously he will ask himself whether they have the kind of knowledge which is needed. It is possible to do them a real disservice by assigning a problem that their experience does not equip them to handle.

Since the problems faced in large or growing industries increasingly require knowledge of specialists from many different fields, it might be inferred that the more complex a problem, the more anxious a manager will be to get some assistance in solving it. However, this is not always the case. There will be times when the very complexity of the problem calls for one person to work it out. . . .

\* \* \* \* \*

The key question to ask, of course, is: "Have I heard the ideas of everyone who has the necessary knowledge to make a significant contribution to the solution of this problem?"

*The Pressure of Time.* This is perhaps the most clearly felt pressure on the manager (in spite of the fact that it may sometimes be imagined). The more that he feels the need for an immediate decision, the more difficult it is to involve other people. In organizations which are in a constant state of "crisis" and "crash programming" one is likely to find managers personally using a high degree of authority with relatively little delegation to subordinates. When the time pressure is less intense, however, it becomes much more possible to bring subordinates in on the decision-making process.

\* \* \* \* \*

*From*

# MANAGEMENT DEVELOPMENT AS A
# PROCESS OF INFLUENCE*

## By Edgar Schein

The continuing rash of articles on the subject of developing better managers suggests, on the one hand, a continuing concern that existing methods are not providing the talent which is needed at the higher levels of industry and, on the other hand, that we continue to lack clear-cut formulations about the process by which such development occurs. We need more and better managers and we need more and better theories of how to get them.

In the present paper I would like to cast management development as the problem of how an organization can influence the beliefs, attitudes, and values (hereafter simply called attitudes) of an individual for the purpose of "developing" him, i.e., changing him in a direction which the organization regards to be in his own and the organization's best interests. Most of the existing conceptions of the development of human resources are built upon assumptions of how people learn and grow, and some of the more strikingly contrasting theories of management development derive from disagreements about such assumptions.[1] I will attempt to build on a different base: instead of starting with assumptions about learning and growth, I will start with some assumptions from the social psychology of influence and attitude change.

\*   \*   \*   \*   \*

. . . Attitudes are generally organized and integrated around the person's image of himself, and they result in stabilized, characteristic ways of dealing with others. The suggestion of the need for change not only implies some criticism of the person's image of himself, but also threatens the stability of his working relationships because change at this level implies that the expectations which others have about him will be upset, thus requiring the development of new relationships. . . .

\*   \*   \*   \*   \*

Given these general assumptions about the integration of attitudes in the person, it is appropriate to consider influence as a process which occurs over time and which includes three phases:

*1. Unfreezing.* An alternation of the forces acting on the individual, such that his stable equilibrium is disturbed sufficiently to motivate him and to make him ready to change; this can be accomplished either by increasing the pressure to change or by reducing some of the threats or resistances to change.

*2. Changing.* The presentation of a direction of change and the actual process of learning new attitudes. This process occurs basically by one of two mechanisms: (*a*) *identification*[2]—the person learns new attitudes by identifying with and emulating some other person who holds those attitudes; or (*b*) *internalization*—the person learns new attitudes by being placed in a situation where new attitudes are demanded of him as a way of solving problems which confront him and which he cannot avoid; he discovers the new attitudes essentially for himself, though the situation may guide him or make it probable that he will discover only those attitudes which the influencing agent wishes him to discover.

*3. Refreezing.* The integration of the changed attitudes into the rest of the personality and/or into ongoing significant emotional relationships.

In proposing this kind of model of influence we are leaving out two important cases—the

---

\* From *Industrial Management Review,* vol. II, no. 2 (May 1961). Reprinted by permission.

[1] These phases of influence are a derivation of the change model developed by Lewin (1947).

[2] These mechanisms of attitude change are taken from Kelman (1958).

individual who changes because he is *forced* to change by the agent's direct manipulation of rewards and punishments (what Kelman calls "compliance") and the individual whose strong motivation to rise in the organizational hierarchy makes him eager to accept the attitudes and acquire the skills which he perceives to be necessary for advancement. I will ignore both of these cases for the same reason—they usually do not involve genuine, stable change, but merely involve the adoption of overt behaviors which imply to others that attitudes have changed, even if they have not. In the case of compliance, the individual drops the overt behavior as soon as surveillance by the influence agent is removed. Among the upwardly mobile individuals, there are those who are willing to be unfrozen and to undergo genuine attitude change (whose case fits the model to be presented below) and those whose overt behavior change is dictated by their changing perception of what the environment will reward, but whose underlying attitudes are never really changed or refrozen.

I do not wish to imply that a general reward-punishment model is incorrect or inappropriate for the analysis of attitude change. My purpose, rather, is to provide a more refined model in terms of which it becomes possible to specify the differential effects of various kinds of rewards and punishments, some of which have far more significance and impact than others. For example, as I will try to show, the rewarding effect of approval from an admired person is very different in its ultimate consequences from the rewarding effect of developing a personal solution to a difficult situation.

\* \* \* \* \*

[Editor's Note: The author goes on to apply the model to Communist brainwashing, the training of a nun, and the initiation of a fraternity brother.]

The kind of model which has been discussed above might best be described by the term "coercive persuasion." The influence of an organization on an individual is coercive in the sense that he is usually forced into situations which are likely to unfreeze him, in which there are many overt and covert pressures to recognize in himself a need for change, and in which the supports for his old attitudes are in varying degrees coercively removed. It is coercive also to the degree that the new attitudes to be learned are relatively rigidly prescribed. The individual either learns them or leaves the organization (if he can). At the same time, the actual process by which new attitudes are learned can best be described as persuasion. In effect, the individual is forced into a situation in which he is likely to be influenced. The organization can be highly coercive in unfreezing its potential influence targets, yet be quite open about the direction of attitude change it will tolerate. In those cases where the direction of change is itself coerced (as contrasted with letting it occur through identification or internalization), it is highly unlikely that anything is accomplished other than surface behavioral change in the target. And such surface change will be abandoned the moment the coercive force of the change agent is lessened. If behavioral changes are coerced at the same time as other unfreezing operations are undertaken, actual influence can be facilitated if the individuals finds himself having to learn attitudes to justify the kinds of behavior he has been forced to exhibit. The salesman may not have an attitude of cynicism toward his customers initially. If, however, he is forced by his boss to behave as if he felt cynical, he might develop real cynicism as a way of justifying his actual behavior.

## Management Development: Is It Coercive Persuasion?

Do the notions of coercive persuasion developed above fit the management development situation? Does the extent to which they do or do not fit such a model illuminate for us some of the implications of specific management development practices?

*Unfreezing.* It is reasonable to assume that the majority of managers who are being "developed" are not ready or able to change in the manner in which their organization might desire and therefore must be unfrozen before they can be influenced. They may be eager to change at a conscious motivation level, yet still be psychologically unprepared to give up certain attitudes and values in favor of untried, threatening new ones. I cannot support this assumption empirically, but the likelihood of its being valid is high because of a related fact which is empirically supportable. Most managers do not participate heavily in decisions which affect their careers, nor do they have a large voice in the kind of self-development in which they wish to participate. Rather, it is the man's superior or a staff specialist in career development who makes the key decisions concerning his career (Alfred, 1960). If the individual manager is not trained from the outset to take responsibility for his own career and given a heavy voice in diagnosing his own needs for a change, it is unlikely that he will readily be able to appreciate someone else's diagnosis. It may be unclear to him what basically is wanted of him or, worse, the ambiguity of the demands put upon him combined with his own inability to control his career development is likely to arouse anxiety and insecurity which would cause even greater resistance to genuine self-assessment and attitude change.[3] He becomes preoccupied with promotion in the abstract and attempts to acquire at a surface level the traits which he thinks are necessary for advancement.

*     *     *     *     *

The essential elements to unfreezing are the removal of supports for the old attitudes, the saturation of the environment with the new attitudes to be acquired, a minimizing of threat, and a maximizing of support for any change in the right direction. In terms of this model it becomes immediately apparent that training programs or other activities which are conducted in the organization at the place of work for a certain number of hours per day or week are far less likely to unfreeze and subsequently influence the participant than those programs which remove him for varying lengths of time from his regular work situation and normal social relationships.

Are appraisal interviews, used periodically to communicate to the manager his strengths, weaknesses and areas for improvement, likely to unfreeze him? Probably not, because as long as the individual is caught up in his regular routine and is responding, probably quite unconsciously, to a whole set of expectations which others have about his behavior and attitudes, it is virtually impossible for him to hear, at a psychological level, what his deficiencies or areas needing change are. Even if he can appreciate what is being communicated to him at an intellectual level, it is unlikely that he can emotionally accept the need for change, and even if he can accept it emotionally, it is unlikely that he can produce change in himself in an environment which supports all of his old ways of functioning. This statement does not mean that the man's co-workers necessarily approve of the way he is operating or like the attitudes which he is exhibiting. They may want to see him change, but their very expectations concerning how he normally behaves operate as a constraint on him which makes attitude change difficult in that setting.

On the other hand, there are a variety of training activities which are used in management development which approximate more closely the conditions necessary for effective unfreezing. These would include programs offered at special training centers such as those maintained by IBM on Long Island and General Electric at Crotonville, N.Y.; university-sponsored courses in management, liberal arts, and/or the social sciences; and especially workshops or laboratories in human relations such as those conducted at Arden House, N.Y., by the National Training Laboratories. . . .

*     *     *     *     *

The practice of rotating a manager from one kind of assignment to another over a period of years can have some of the same unfreezing effects and thus facilitate change. . . .

*     *     *     *     *

Another example of how unfreezing can be facilitated in the organizational context is the practice of temporarily reducing the formal rank and responsibilities of the manager by making him a trainee in a special program, or an apprentice on a special project, or an assistant to a high-ranking member of the company. . . .

*     *     *     *     *

---

[3] An even greater hazard, of course, is that the organization communicates to the manager that he is not expected to take responsibility for his own career at the same time that it is trying to teach him how to be able to take responsibility for important decisions!

. . . In all of the illustrations of organizational influence we have presented above, change was defined as being a means of gaining status—acceptance into Communist society, status as a man or a fraternity brother, salvation, etc. If participants come to training programs believing they are being punished, they typically do not learn much.

*   *   *   *   *

The above discussion is intended to highlight the fact that some management development practices do facilitate the unfreezing of the influence target, but that such unfreezing is by no means automatic. Where programs fail, therefore, one of the first questions we must ask is whether they failed because they did not provide adequate conditions for unfreezing.

*   *   *   *   *

*Changing.* Turning now to the problem of the mechanisms by which changes actually occur, we must confront the question of whether the organization has relatively rigid prescribed goals concerning the direction of attitude change it expects of the young manager, or whether it is concerned with growth in the sense of providing increasing opportunities for the young manager to learn the attitudes appropriate to ever more challenging situations. It is undoubtedly true that most programs would claim growth as their goal, but the degree to which they accomplish it can only be assessed from an examination of their actual practice.

Basically the question is whether the organization influences attitudes primarily through the mechanism of identification or the mechanism of internalization. If the development programs stimulate psychological relationships between the influence target and a member of the organization who has the desired attitudes, they are thereby facilitating influence by indentification but, at the same time, are limiting the alternatives available to the target and possibly the permanence of the change achieved. If they emphasize that the target must develop his own solutions to ever more demanding problems, they are risking that the attitudes learned will be incompatible with other parts of the organization's value system but are producing more permanent change because the solutions found are internalized. From the organization's point of view, therefore, it is crucial to know what kind of influence it is exerting and to assess the results of such influence in terms of the basic goals which the organization may have. If new approaches and new attitudes toward management problems are desired, for example, it is crucial that the conditions for internalization be created. If rapid learning of a given set of attitudes is desired, it is equally crucial that the conditions for identification with the right kind of models be created.

One obvious implication of this distinction is that programs conducted within the organization's orbit by its own influence agents are much more likely to facilitate identification and thereby the transmission of the "party line" or organization philosophy. On the other hand, programs like those conducted at universities or by the National Training Laboratories place much more emphasis on the finding of solutions by participants which fit their own particular needs and problems. . . .

*   *   *   *   *

*Refreezing.* Finally, a few words are in order about the problem of refreezing. Under what conditions will changed attitudes remain stable, and how do existing practices aid or hinder such stabilization? Our illustrations from the non-industrial setting highlighted the importance of social support for any attitudes which were learned through identification. Even the kind of training emphasized in the National Training Laboratories programs, which tends to be more internalized, does not produce stable attitude change unless others in the organization, especially superiors, peers, and subordinates, have undergone similar changes and give each other stimulation and support, because lack of support, because lack of support acts as a new unfreezing force producing new influence (possibly in the direction of the original attitudes).

If the young manager has been influenced primarily in the direction of what is already the company philosophy, he will, of course, obtain strong support and will have little difficulty maintaining his new attitudes. If, on the other hand, management development is supposed to lead to personal growth and organizational innovation, the organization must recognize the reality that new attitudes cannot be carried by isolated individuals. The lament that we no longer have strong individualists who are willing to try something new is a fallacy based on an incorrect diagnosis. Strong individuals have always gained a certain amount of their strength from the support of others, hence the organizational problem is how to create conditions which make possible the nurturing of new ideas, attitudes, and approaches. If organizations seem to lack innovators, it may be that the climate of the organization and its methods of management development do not foster innovation, not that its human resources are inadequate.

## Conclusion

In the above discussion I have deliberately focused on a model of influence which emphasizes procedure rather than content, interpersonal relations rather than mass media, and attitudes and values rather than knowledge and skills. By placing management development into a context of institutional influence procedures which also include Chinese Communist thought reform, the training of a nun, and other more drastic forms of coercive persuasion, I have tried to highlight aspects of management development which have remained implicit yet which need to be understood. I believe that some aspects of management development are a mild form of coercive persuasion, but I do not believe that coercive persuasion is either morally bad in any *a priori* sense nor inefficient. If we are to develop a sound theory of career development which is capable of including not only many of the formal procedures discussed in this paper, but the multitudes of informal practices, some of which are more and some of which are less coercive than those discussed, we need to suspend moral judgments for the time being and evaluate influence models solely in terms of their capacity to make sense of the data and to make meaningful predictions.

*    *    *    *    *

## REFERENCES

Kelman, H. C. "Compliance, Identification, and Internalization: Three Processes of Attitude Change," *Conflict Resolution,* 1958, II, pp. 51–60.

Lewin, K. "Frontiers in Group Dynamics: Concept, Method and Reality in Social Science," *Human Relations,* 1947, I, pp. 5–42.

CASE MATERIALS AND
SOCIAL SCIENCE READINGS FOR

# PART VI Reconciling the Responsibility to Produce with Other Social Responsibilities

## THE SOCIAL RESPONSIBILITY DILEMMA: PRODUCTIVITY VERSUS OTHER VALUES

In almost all of the cases in this book we see that managing, leading, or governing organizations is neither a simple nor an easy task. There are almost inevitable choices that must be made between ultimate values—things one believes in and wants to achieve because they are good in themselves.

The cases in Part VI illustrate these kinds of choices as they must be made between the firm's ideal economic and technical system (its goals and substrategies) on the one hand, and certain ideals that are noneconomic in nature on the other. The good life is seen to be composed not only of goods and services that serve society, but also of education of people, an esthetic environment, the prevention of poverty, the preservation of human dignity, and many other *values, ideals,* or *ethical ends.*

The idea is not new in this book. Already we have considered many times implications for human dignity as they apply to human beings inside the firm. The characteristic that sets off Part VI cases from the others is that they deal with actions of a total organization as they impinge on groups outside the firm, or on society as a whole.

In The Polyvinyl Chloride Affair, executives in the chemical industry have sought to produce a chemical product that has considerable value to mankind. But at the same time the process of making this chemical has harmful effects on the health of human beings. In the University of Washington Law School case, executives in the law school must judge a similar trade-off between conflicting values. On the one hand, society needs the products of the law school: graduates who are highly competent in the practice of law. On the other hand, admissions standards which attempt to assure this competence may have negative effects on the development of blacks as lawyers. In the High Ross Dam case, the executives of Seattle City Light Company must weigh the value of cheap electricity produced by nonpolluting hydroelectric power against the negative effects the new dam may have on the vegetation and wildlife

551

of the flooded valley. Finally, in the Polaroid Corporation case, the managers in Polaroid are trying to provide a valuable product to world markets but they run squarely into criticism of supporting the racial policies of the South African government.

These kinds of dilemmas are not unusual. The management of a fish company must produce food efficiently and immediately but in doing so may endanger the permanent supply of this natural resource. The management of an airline must provide transportation cheaply but the noise it produces disturbs people who live by airports. The management of a brickyard must provide cheap materials for sheltering mankind but smoke from its factory may cause cattle in the area to become sick.

## ORGANIZATIONAL GOALS AS SOCIAL RESPONSIBILITIES

As pointed out in the introduction to Part II, almost any organization has as its principal goal—the one which must be met satisfactorily if the organization is to survive—the *production* of some good or service. A hospital must produce patient care. A bank must produce loans and offer deposit service. An airline must provide transportation.

One side of the social responsibility dilemma is the *demand* from society "out there" for production. In all societies at all times, there has been demand that organizations specialize in producing things for other human beings.

In discharging this responsibility, however, the first question which arises is whether or not the good or service is in itself "good" in the ethical sense. Opium, firearms, cigarettes, atomic bombs, whiskey, devices for a motorist to detect police radar speed zones, contraceptives, and many other things are well-known controversial items of production.

A second type of question involves a trade-off between organization goals that are "good," on the one hand, and the unintended consequences that producing these has on *other* social values which make up the good life for humanity, on the other. Given the fact that medicine for the sick is a worthy end, does the production strategy necessary to produce this involve negative effects on air we breathe, water we drink, or the health of employees on the production line?

## THE NEED FOR RECONCILING: THE NEED FOR JUDGMENT AND WISDOM

From what has been said about organization goals, strategies, and policy making so far, it it clear that somebody somewhere in society must do some very clear thinking, or decision making, as it is called in more scholarly terms. This thinking must be directed toward how to reconcile the good of society's production (and its elaborated strategies) with the good of society's other human values.

This requires a certain kind of decision making. The brains which do it must be informed enough that they know the effects of their decisions on "the whole system." This means education, with theories from science and philosophy to help in understanding. But it also requires an element of fairness and justice. There shall probably never be a scientific way of measuring the social good that can make decisions of this kind without the aid of wisdom and judgment.

Given the dilemma, and the need for reconciling diverse social ends in strategic decision making, the next question which arises is *who* should make these kinds of decision?

## WHO SHOULD MAKE DECISIONS THAT ARE "SOCIALLY RESPONSIBLE"?

This question is one on which the reader must make up his or her own mind. At various points in the study of the following cases and readings, different authors take different approaches to an answer.

Some brilliant legal and economic philosophers believe that a free market mechanism, on balance, is the best solution. They argue that the human beings who are managers will be forced, by the system pressures, so to speak, to be socially responsible. It is interesting to probe deeply as to what they mean by the social good, and to see how they recognize the disadvantages of such a system but put heavy weights on its advantages.

In Polaroid's racial discrimination dilemma there is opportunity to examine the theories of those writers who believe that government planners are the ones who are most likely to exercise informed wisdom in this type of decision making.

Cases in Part VI also examine the possibility of pluralism, constructive conflict, or due process. This approach holds that no one person or group is sufficiently free from bias. One person or one group would always be doing "his or her thing," and not enough of "society's thing." To correct this kind of biased thinking, according to this approach, we must depend on people straightening out each other. It is not a serene and orderly world; it is a world of conflicting opinions and conflict resolution.

Finally, there are those who believe in conscience control by informed and wise managers in organizations. According to this approach, individual executives and managers will not only (1) be informed of how the system works and how human beings behave, but will also (2) be buttressed by new beliefs in society about the function of managers, and (3) use their own brains to judge the wisdom and justice of a particular operating strategy. Presumably, the latter would include interacting with other groups pluralistically in order to keep the manager's brain clear, and not let it become myopic to the viewpoint of others.

Regardless of which of these approaches turns out to be the principal one, all managers should know what it means to think deeply about the matter of social justice and social good, and to face the tough dilemmas of life which threaten it. That is the purpose of this entire book, and the most specific purpose of Part VI.

# 18. THE POLYVINYL CHLORIDE AFFAIR

## Case Introduction

### SYNOPSIS

This is a "cameo case," a case within a case. In the inner case, the vinyl chloride industry moves center stage in a revived occupational health movement. The industry's own research initially fingers vinyl chloride as a likely cancer-causing agent, then as the certain cause of cancer deaths of workers exposed during the production process. Seeing a job/health trade-off, the industry moves at one pace in self-regulation, but government regulation moves at a quicker pace.

In the outer case two chemical engineers, working for a vinyl chloride producer, confront critical reaction to the industry even from fellow managers in a discussion of the vinyl chloride affair.

### WHY THIS CASE IS INCLUDED

It has been said that what Rachael Carson was to the environmentalists, vinyl chloride is to the industrial hygienists. We can examine in this case why it often takes crises and headlines to generate policy change. The pragmatic and philosophic challenges of social responsibility are dramatically evident in the case. Issues in the case range from changing ideology at the national level to values of individuals under strain.

### DIAGNOSTIC AND PREDICTIVE QUESTIONS

The readings included with this case are marked (*). The author index at the end of this book locates the other readings.

1. Why did the awareness of a crisis in occupational health not sink in until after the Goodrich announcement in January 1974 despite earlier warnings?

   *a.* From an organizational point of view:

Read: Merton, "Bureaucratic Structure and Personality." Etzioni, "Authority Structure and Organizational Effectiveness."

*b.* From a psychological point of view:

Read: Leavitt, *Managerial Psychology,* pp. 22–26.

2. In managerial terms, what basic decisions faced both government regulators and industry representatives as the vinyl chloride health threat emerged?

Read: *Farmer and Hogue, *Corporate Social Responsibility,* pp. 4–6, 13–20.

3. In terms of economic philosophy, what premises might a chemical industry executive have used in taking positions on the roles of government and private industry in coping with the new health hazard?

Read: *Friedman, "A Friedman Doctrine: The Social Responsibility of Business Is to Increase Its Profits." *Eells and Walton, *Conceptual Foundations of Business,* pp. 185–87 *et seq.* *Hay and Gray, "Corporate Social Responsibilities of Business Managers."

4. Which of the Martin and Lodge ideologies do you find displayed in the behavior of the industry? Of the government? Does the case tend to support or challenge the research results on the emerging American ideology?

Read: *Martin and Lodge, "Our Society in 1985—Business May Not Like It."

5. What kind of thinking within a chemical company could turn the "tough" government intervention with occupational health standards from a threat to an opportunity?

Read: *Hawthorne, "Industry and the Environment."

6. Whose values are relevant as Marc and Otto consider what to do about their ill-ease with their involvement in vinyl chloride production?

Read: *Baumhardt, "How Ethical Are Businessmen?" *Carroll, "Managerial Ethics: A Post-Watergate View." *Farmer and Hogue, *Corporate Social Responsibility,* pp. 23, 25–26. Andrews, *The Concept of Corporate Strategy.*

7. What is it that's bothering Marc and Otto about attempting to do the right thing in their own jobs within their present organization.

Read: *O'Connell, "Youth Culture and Management."

8. Under what conditions might "whistle blowing" be an alternative for consideration by Marc and Otto?

Read: *Townsend, "The Whistle Blower as Entrepreneur." *American Chemical Society, "The Chemist's Creed." (See also in the library K. D. Walters, "Your Employees' Right to Blow the Whistle," *Harvard Business Review,* July/August 1975, for the legal issues involved in whistle blowing.)

## POLICY QUESTIONS

9. Taking account of both the philosophic and practical lessons from the vinyl chloride affair, what policy would you suggest for a chemical

or plastics company in the area of occupational health? Among others, consider the issues of research, disclosure, decision criteria, and decision process.

10. Do you find anyh policy lessons for the government as regulator in the vinyl chloride affair?

11. What practical advice would you give Marc and Otto?

12. In light of consistent research findings (see Question 6) and the antiorganization sentiment (see Question 8), what might corporations do to assure freer yet responsible internal whistle blowing?

Read: Evan: "Organization Man and Due Process of Law."

# Case Text*

Marc Docherty and Otto Milner had spent the week in the third of five units of an executive seminar at the state university. Over a period of 18 months they would have completed the five-week-long units as part of their career development plans. Each aspired to move on from the process engineering job that had occupied him for a dozen years to a position in general management. When they joined the company back in 1964 after graduating together as chemical engineers, it was understood that the route to general management was still largely through performance excellence as a chemical engineer. It was with some pride that Marc and Otto accepted nominations to attend the executive seminar. Certainly, the nominations signaled that general management responsibilities would soon replace the technical supervision each had now.

Something happened in this seminar unit which threatened to sour the whole experience. Marc and Otto were thoroughly enjoying the rather new experience of wrestling with the macro and even philosophic issues raised by the third seminar unit's theme: "Business and Society." It was Wednesday night's buzz group meeting on the PVC case (See Appendix A) and Thursday morning's class discussion of the case that bothered Marc and Otto. In different buzz groups each found himself roughly mauled by colleagues in the seminar from other industries with whom he had become familiar. A spontaneous role play dreamed up by the instructor in class isolated the two chemical engineers in the role of top management in a PVC-producing chemical company. For 70 minutes they were bombarded by colleagues dropping in and out of the roles of union leaders, medical doctors, government health inspectors, local community leaders, consumers, reporters, and so on.

As they drove back home along the lake on Friday afternoon, each admitted that he got angry, embarrassed, frustrated, and hurt under the aggressive verbal pummelling. The role play became too real. Marc even

---

* Copyright C.E.I., Geneva, 1976. Written by Dr. J. J. O'Connell and Dr. T. Gladwin.

found himself reading quotes from a speech delivered by his own company president just the previous week at a business lunch in town. The quotes prompted derisive and cynical responses from his classmates. Coffee break came before Marc or Otto had to respond to the last question: "Come on, why don't you level with us and tell us what's really going on in the plant and what you feel about it?"

It had been that question that preoccupied them as they took a long walk Thursday evening on the campus. Now again, on the drive home, they discussed the actual plant situation compared to the public statement made by the president. The president had not distinguished among the company's three plants nor had he gone into technical detail. When you strip away all the verbiage, the president simply asserted that the company had installed new equipment, revised production processes, and instituted safety procedures that reduced PVC exposure to the level of the tight new government standard. Marc and Otto recognized that unspoken were the realities of their own plant where there had been months of foot dragging in the capital budgeting process before the new equipment was ordered. There was the constant tug-of-war between those debugging the new system and the production people struggling to meet volume targets. There was the shell game played on the naive government inspectors. There was the too frequent faux pas of uncaring or poorly trained workers. There was all the hoopla about measurement precision which was questionably reliable under factory conditions. Between them, Marc and Otto could recite an unholy litany of things wrong in their PVC production process which didn't enter the president's more general and rosy comments. As Otto drove up to Marc's suburban split-level, they had agreed that if the president knew what they knew, he couldn't (or shouldn't) honestly paint such a bright picture—not at this stage anyway. "Bring Jo-ann over after the game tomorrow for drinks." "Be delighted! Thanks for the ride!"

Each man's wife recognized the strange, black mood her husband brought back from the seminar. By cocktail time on Saturday, each couple had separately spent four or five hours discussing the seminar, the plant, the president's speech, the husband's job, and his career. Both Jo-ann and Karen had read the PVC case.

Initially the football game dominated cocktail talk, but rather soon Karen laughingly asked Jo-ann what she would say to the reporters after Marc "blew the whistle on the big, bad company."

"I'd tell them to spell my name correctly. They always leave out the hyphen. I'd then tell them about our two kids, dog, cat, mortgage . . . you know, the usual."

"I can just see the caption under the Milner's picture now. 'Lakeside couple rebels against the establishment at great risk to their comfortable nouveau riche life-style. Two teenage sons cheer on the rebellion.' It reminds me of the picture in *Newsweek* of those three guys from G.E. and their wives (see Appendix B)."

"Otto, do you really have the martyr complex?"

"No, dammit; what's got into you two women? Neither Marc nor I said anything about quitting or blowing whistles."

"Sorry, dear, but you've emotionally left the company two years ago.

Whenever anyone asks you these days what you do, you say you're a chemical engineer. You used to be like Fred next door who always blurts out "IBM" . . . "computers". You haven't mentioned company or product to anyone since we moved into the new house. How about Marc, Jo-ann?"

"I wasn't aware of it till now, but you're right. What I've noticed is how long Marc has been spending with the employment section of the paper. That's the only reason you buy the *Sunday New York Times,* isn't it, Marc?"

"Okay," admitted Marc, "this whole PVC affair has bothered me. On one hand, I've contributed to the increased safety in the plant but, on the other, I'm not technically convinced we have or can produce PVC safely. Sometimes we even meet the exposure standard in the plant. But, that's a long way from understanding and controlling, in systems terms, all the health hazards in the interactions of all the chemical substances in our PVC plant under all conditions. I'm not even sure we should produce PVC after what we are learning of the 'downstream' hazards which don't end until disposal of end products."

"Ideally," said Otto, "we shouldn't deceive ourselves or others that we've licked the health problems. I don't know whether Marc would admit it, but I've been tempted to give my reports to someone other than my boss. From where I sit, there's no chance of influencing what the boys on the 11th floor decide about PVC. To influence policy you'd have to get into the public forum with the unions, medical professions, governmental agencies, or the press using their muscle."

"Now, who's talking about blowing whistles, dear?"

"Oh sure," said Marc, "I could broadcast damaging things. Should I? Will that change policy? How can I be so saintedly sure that I know the whole story?"

# APPENDIX A

### Vinyl Chloride and Industrial Health

Referring to the dramatic rush of events in the early 70s that fingered vinyl chloride as a cancer-causing agent, Dr. William Lloyd, director of health surveillance and biostatistics for the National Institute for Occupational Safety and Health (NIOSH), said: "This has to be one of the most startling findings ever in industrial medicine." An international union leader underlined one aspect of the issue: "Workers are faced with choosing between livelihood and their lives!" Early reactions from industry warned of disastrous consequences of going "too far" in standards restrictive of the production process: ". . . would literally cripple the industry!" ". . . industry won't be able to operate!"

### Background on the U.S. Vinyl Chloride Industry

Since its introduction in 1949, vinyl chloride has become the second most used plastic in the United States. Exhibit 1 pictures the production

**EXHIBIT 1**
**The PVC Picture in the United States in 1974**

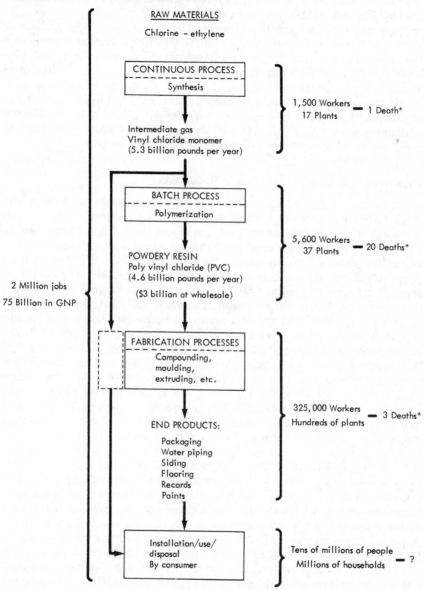

RAW MATERIALS

Chlorine – ethylene

CONTINUOUS PROCESS

Synthesis

Intermediate gas
Vinyl chloride monomer
(5.3 billion pounds per year)

1,500 Workers
17 Plants — 1 Death*

BATCH PROCESS

Polymerization

POWDERY RESIN
Poly vinyl chloride (PVC)
(4.6 billion pounds per year)

($3 billion at wholesale)

5,600 Workers
37 Plants — 20 Deaths*

2 Million jobs
75 Billion in GNP

FABRICATION PROCESSES

Compounding,
moulding,
extruding, etc.

END PRODUCTS:

Packaging
Water piping
Siding
Flooring
Records
Paints

325,000 Workers — 3 Deaths*
Hundreds of plants

Installation/use/
disposal
By consumer

Tens of millions of people — ?
Millions of households

* Deaths worldwide attributed to exposure to vinyl chloride in various phases of the manufacturing process.

process and indicates the orders of magnitude for 1974 in financial and employment terms. The average annual growth rate in the industry between 1968 and 1973 was 11 percent.

Vinyl chloride had a rather checkered history in the health and safety field. On the health side, VCM (vinyl chloride monomer) was once thought to be a potentially useful anesthesia. PVC (poly vinyl chloride), clear, flexible packaging material has been used for years to "bottle blood and other liquids for intravenous feeding." In the production process itself safety concerns dominated health concerns. VCM in concentrations over 36,000 ppm (parts per million) is explosive. Plants had been known to explode with loss of life. How health in the PVC production process itself became an explosive issue will be detailed below.

## Background on Government Health Regulations

While the storm was brewing over PVC and industrial health, the U.SS. Labor Department was flexing new muscle given it under landmark legislation, the Occupational Safety and Health Act, December 28, 1970. Under this act, two agencies were established. The first is the National Institute for Occupational Safety and Health (NIOSH). which plays roles in problem identification, diagnosis, and advising on standards criteria for its standard-setting sister unit within the Labor Department. The NIOSH annual budget is around $30 million. The second agency set up under the 1970 act is the Occupational Safety and Health Administration (OSHA), which does standard setting, inspecting, citing for violation, and fining. With a budget in excess of $70 million and over 700 inspectors, OSHA has been citing two out of three of the some 75,000 plants inspected a year for an average of six violations each. In its first 18 months of operation, the average fine levied by OSHA was less than $25 per violation. OSHA is guided by the objectives of the Occupational Safety and Health Act that: "each employer shall: (1) furnish to each of his employees employment and a place of employment which are free from recognized hazards that are causing or are likely to cause death or serious physical harm to his employees, and (2) comply with occupational safety and health standards promulgated under this Act." Particularly relevant is the OSHA mandate in the act relative to toxic chemicals: "set the standard which most adequately assures, to the extent feasible, on the basis of the best available evidence, that no employee will suffer material impairment of health or functional capacity even if such employee has regular exposure . . . for the period of his working life."

Spurring on the new agencies was the assertion in the 1972 presidential report on occupational safety and health that 100,000 Americans annually die of occupational diseases and 300,000 annually contract disabling occupational diseases.

OSHA was sufficiently aggressive that in early 1975 the encumbent national administration began requiring OSHA to submit inflation impact reports on its proposed new standards. In the 1976 presidential campaign OSHA and NIOSH became lightening rods for even Ford administration warnings about the intrusive federal government.

## Early Indications of PVC as Health Hazard

Looking back, it appears relatively easy to piece together a string of "evidence" on PVC as an occupational health hazard. In 1949 a Russian group found a hepatitislike condition in more than one fourth of 73 PVC workers examined. Both in Europe and the United States prior to the mid 1960s, various symptoms of "vinyl chloride disease" had been observed: skin lesions, gastritis, dermatitis. Generally, the symptoms appeared in those workers who were directly engaged in the cleaning of the vessels used in the batch process of polymerization. In this phase of the production process, before and particularly after polymerization, the exposure to VCM was greatest—sometimes in the thousands of ppm's. The telltale VCM sweet odor appeared after 2,000 ppm. An addictive "high" among workers could sometimes be observed.

As awareness of PVC as an occupational health hazard grew, companies began introducing their own maximum exposure standards. In 1961, the first quasi-governmental standard was recommended by the American Conference of Governmental Hygienists, a voluntary standards-setting organization. Their recommendation of 500 ppm maximum exposure became as close to a concensus standard as existed at the time.

## Industry Initiates Serious Research

Dow Chemical engaged in animal experiment research with VCM inhalation in 1961. Its studies showed effects on the liver with exposure levels as low as 100 ppm. Dow itself then adopted a 50 ppm standard. Other companies tended to voluntarily adopt standards closer to Dow's than the 500 ppm recommended by the American Conference of Government Hygienists in the same year.

Prompted in part by the Dow studies, Dr. P. L. Viola of the Regina Elena Institute for Cancer Research in Rome conducted further very large dose (over 5,000 ppm) animal VCM inhalation studies. His report at the 10th International Cancer Congress in Houston, Texas, in 1970 was the first suggestion of PVC as a carcinogen—a cancer-causing agent. Because of the large doses employed, the evidence of tumors in rats tended to be dismissed as not relevant for humans working under much lower exposures.

The Italian chemical giant, Montedison, was sufficiently concerned, however, by the Viola studies to commission follow-up work in 1972 on PVC carcinogenicity by Dr. Cesare Maltoni of the Institute of Oncology in Bologna, Italy. Three other European chemical companies (ICI, Solvay and Rhone-Progil) later joined in sponsoring the project. By the fall 1972, Dr. Maltoni notified his sponsors and the U.S. Manufacturing Chemist's Association (MCA) that his VCM inhalation experiments with rats showed VCM at 250 ppm induced a variety of cancers, inducing angiosarcoma of the liver (a rare and fatal cancer of the blood vessel cells in the liver). In effect, Dr. Maltoni's studies predicted that cancer would be found in humans with VCM exposures at 250 ppm for some period.

In January 1973, three MCA representatives visited Dr. Maltoni in

Italy, investigated his results, and then allegedly revealed what they had learned to an MCA meeting in February. By March 1973, MCA had commissioned one animal experiment program at Industrial Biotest Laboratories to verify Dr. Maltoni's findings and a second epidemiological study to check the Maltoni prediction of cancer in exposed humans. In the latter study, the records of those with known exposure to VCM were scrutinized for evidence that the incidence of cancer was higher than should have been statistically predicted for a nonexposed population.

In May 1973, OSHA issued 14 emergency standards for chemical substances suspected as carcinogens, but VCM was not on the list.

Again in May 1973, the Food and Drug Administration (FDA) proposed to lower to 0 ppm the allowable VCM migration from PVC packaging to products such as food, cosmetics, and drugs. The discussion of this new standard for PVC packaging caused the Bureau of Alcohol, Tobacco, and Firearms to cancel approval for the text marketing of half gallon PVC containers for liquor.

On July 17, 1973, five European and American chemical industry representatives presented to NIOSH the information from Dr. Maltoni's studies on the carcinogenicity of PVC.

### B. F. Goodrich Chemical Company Disclosure

On January 22, 1974, Dr. Maurice Johnson, environmental health director for B. F. Goodrich, called Marcus Key, director of NIOSH. In this phone call he reported the discovery that three workers at B. F. Goodrich's Louisville, Kentucky, plant had died from angiosarcoma since 1971. In addition, blood tests on the 271 workers in the plant had revealed 55 with apparent liver abnormalities. NIOSH immediately sent a team of experts to inspect the Louisville plant. On January 29, a further review of medical records turned up a 1968 angiosarcoma Goodrich employee death. The Maltoni predictions seemed to be cruelly verified, but the Maltoni findings were not yet public.

### Initiative Passes to Government Regulatory Agencies

NIOSH held a briefing on its Louisville findings in mid-February 1974 in Cleveland. Noteworthy during the briefing was the observation that it took 20 or more years for the cancers to develop as a result of VCM exposure. OSHA held hearings in Washington, D.C., beginning February 15, 1974, to determine the need for an emergency standard on PVC. Up till this stage, OSHA adopted the 500 ppm standard suggested in 1961 by the American Conference of Government Hygienists, despite a later (1972) suggestion by the same group to lower the standard to 200 ppm.

It was at the February 1974 OSHA hearings that Dr. Maltoni publicly revealed his complete findings on PVC as a carcinogen. Allegations of "cover-up" appeared in the press, citing industry's silence on its own research results. MCA countered that it had agreed with the four sponsors of the Maltoni research not to reveal preliminary research data.

Individual American companies knew enough, however, for one at least, Diamond Shamrock, to attribute its introduction of a 50 ppm standard in the summer of 1973 to the Maltoni studies.

By early April 1974, OSHA had issued a 50 ppm emergency standard for VCM exposure and had scheduled public hearing on a permanent standard for June 1974. In advance of the June hearings, OSHA publicly revealed that it was considering a "no detectable exposure level" standard. As the public meetings began, new Maltoni data (verified by the MCA studies at Industrial Biotest Laboratories) showed carcinogenic effect of VCM exposure as low as 50 ppm. NIOSH publicly supported the "no detectable level" standard for VCM. Joseph Wagener, chairman of NIOSH's Occupational Carcinogen Committee, stated: "I'm sure 25 ppm will show cancer, and furthermore, there is no way to demonstrate the safe level of a carcinogen."

## Reaction from Industry

Around the time of the June public hearing, chemical and plastic companies, individually and through their two trade associations (MCA and SPI—Society of the Plastics Industry) aggressively countered the OSHA proposals. The reaction is reflected in these quotes:

> "Excessively and unrealistically restrictive"—The Society of the Plastics Industry.
>
> "Would literally cripple this industry"—A spokesman for Firestone Tire and Rubber Co.
>
> "Cannot be obtained at this time or in the future"—Anton Bittone, Jr., president of B. F. Goodrich.
>
> "We just don't know how to do it"—Harry Conner, general manager of Diamond Shamrock Plastics Division.
>
> "At zero exposure, industry won't be able to operate"—Thomas Carmody, vice president for safety and health, Union Carbide Chemicals and Plastics Division.

Industry's objections to the proposed "no detectable level" limit, as presented at the June OSHA hearings, were based on three main points:

1. The unavailability of manufacturing technology to eliminate VCM leaks and fugitive losses (and that existing plants were not designed for total VCM containment).
2. The disastrous economic impact on the industry (enforcement of such a standard, they claimed, would cause a shutdown of all PVC plants in the United States, eliminate 1.7 to 2.2 million jobs in consuming and related industries, and result in a loss of domestic production value of $65 to $90 billion per year).
3. The lack of medical and technical data to support the new standard (the proposed standard was viewed as an arbitrary interven-

tion, reflecting political emotionalism rather than reason. OSHA's standard was based on a crude extrapolation of animal carcinogenicity tests to humans, and were chosen, the industry claimed, in almost total ignorance of the different rates of cancer and other diseases to be expected at different exposure levels).

While the SPI-sponsored study by Arthur D. Little, the Cambridge, Massachusetts-based consulting and research firm, argued that no plastic at a competitive price could replace PVC and that the shutdown of the PVC industry would have frightening economic consequences, SPI itself countered the OSHA-proposed standard with a compromise proposal. SPI proposed different standards for plants making VCM and those making PVC. After 15 months, SPI proposed a maximum exposure standard of 10 ppm for VCM plants and 25 ppm for PVC plants. OSHA's own impact statement showed that the SPI proposals would increase monomer prices by about 5 percent and polymer prices by around 6 percent. The same report indicated that compliance with the SPI proposed standards would take about three years and would jeopardize some 25 percent of the 37 PVC plants (half of which were over ten years old).

Industry representatives could find some motivation and/or consolation from NIOSH's Joseph Wagener: "The ingenuity of American industry never fails to surprise me. Somehow, surprising things can be done." Indeed, by early fall 1974, industry publications were beginning to report process improvements and new equipment, particularly for the polymerization phase of the production process. The innovations had to cope with a new certainty. The Environmental Protection Agency (EPA) had given advance warning that it was preparing new air and water standards to protect the 4.6 million people who lived within a five-mile radius of the VCM/PVC plants from the effects of the 200 million pounds of VCM released into the environment each year. The new standards, due within the year, would likely add about 4 percent to VCM/PVC production costs and would set constraints on the innovations possible to solve the in-plant health hazards.

### Reaction of Labor

U.S. labor, led by the United Rubber Workers Union (URW) and the Oil, Chemical and Atomic Workers Union (OCAW), came out strongly in favor of the "no detectable level." Tony Mazzochi, head of the OCAW, called for zero exposure by use of sealed operations and complained that "workers are tired of being guinea pigs." Many union spokesmen were opposed to the "blackmail" implications of the industry position which alleged conflicts between job preservation and worker safety. Peter Bommarito, president of the URW, stated: "Industry is trying to scare everybody about losing a job—this country survived for nearly 200 years without PVC and we can survive in the future without it." Sheldon Samuels, director of Occupational Health, Safety and Environmental Affairs of the AFL-CIO union declared: "the standard can, in fact, be met." The AFL-

CIO said publicly that it was determined to fight for the tough standard, even if it meant throwing some people out of work.

Increasingly, U.S. labor appeared to be opposing the concept of a threshold level for any carcinogen. The unions advocated the so-called one-hit theory of cancer causation, which holds that there can be no such thing as a risk-free exposure to a carcinogen. This theory implies that any identifiable exposure to a carcinogen is likely to cause cancer, no matter how infrequent or at what level.

Labor (and, to a lesser degree, industry as well) opposed the use of respirators (i.e., self-contained air supply tanks similar to those used by astronauts). "Have you ever tried working all day with a respirator on?" asked one labor leader. Respirators were viewed as uncomfortable, fatiguing, probably hazardous, and inefficient, since they would interfere with work. While respirators might be an inexpensive, temporary, measure, the solution had to be more radical.

### The Permanent Standard Announced by OSHA

Based on the evidence and testimony presented at the hearings, and on specially commissioned medical, environmental, engineering, and economic studies, OSHA presented its final standards for worker exposure to VCM in the first week of October 1974. The standard was not the "no detectable level" originally proposed by OSHA. Still, the permanent standard was much tougher than those proposed by SPI. OSHA established a three-step program.

1.  Until the end of 1974, the 50 ppm maximum exposure set by OSHA as a temporary emergency standard in April would stay in effect.
2.  In 1975, the maximum exposure would drop to 5 ppm, measured over a 15-minute period, with a 1 ppm twa. (time weighted average) for the eight-hour day. Exceptions, however, would be made in cases where engineering of these controls was impossible. In these cases, maximum exposure would be 25 ppm, with respirators to be available but not mandatory, for worker use.
3.  After January 1, 1976, there would be no exceptions to the 1 ppm twa. and 5 ppm maximum limit, with respirators mandatory at higher exposures.

OSHA had concluded that it was impossible to assess a "safe" level for worker exposure to vinyl chloride; in effect, the only safe level was no exposure at all. OSHA also had concluded that with new engineering controls, work methods, respirators, VCM recovery systems, ventilation improvements, and reactor replacement or reconditioning, most plants could meet the standards.

### The Reaction of Industry to the Permanent Standard

Within two minutes of the OSHA October 1974 announcement, SPI filed a petition for review of the standards in the Second Circuit Court of Appeals in New York. SPI was joined by eight firms, including Hooker, Union Carbide, Firestone, Tenneco, and Air Products. In hoping to have the court overturn the standards, SPI's lawyers argued that the health risk was exaggerated and that the infeasible standards were mandated by OSHA without sufficient technical evidence. The court did grant a stay (requiring a delay in the implementation schedule of the OSHA standards) pending its decision on the merits of SPI's objections.

In February of 1975, the appeals court upheld the standards promulgated in October 1974 by OSHA. SPI expressed "Shock" at the ruling and immediately petitioned the U.S. Supreme Court to review the circuit court's decision. The Supreme Court, March 31, 1975, declined to review the case and thus refused to delay or set aside the standards established by OSHA and supported by the circuit court. In the final week of May 1975, the Supreme Court again—and finally—refused to hear an appeal (requested by SPI, Firestone Plastics, and Union Carbide) of the decision made in the U.S. Court of Appeals in New York.

After these court decisions, phase 2 of the OSHA permanent standard took effect on April 1, 1975 and phase 3 was moved back to April 1, 1976.

Court actions and the new inflation impact statements required of OSHA by the Ford administration, combined to reduce OSHA's capacity to even maintain the 1974 level of plant inspections during 1975 despite a larger budget and more manpower. Commented the industry journal, *Chemical Week* (January 15, 1975) "Any resulting let up in OSHA enforcement activities could provide some solace to CPI [Chemical Process Industry] executives striving to keep red-ink entries out of the ledger books during the current 'slumpflation'!"

In the spring of 1975, during the court-testing phase, industry representatives were still attacking the OSHA proposals. A Firestone Plastics executive said that the new rules would "shackle" the industry and could cause the loss of thousands of jobs by driving some plastics companies out of business. Yet, in February 1975, Goodyear reported operating at 6 ppm and in May Union Carbide reported compliance at a 5 ppm level—both well within the phase 2 OSHA "exception" standard of 25 ppm. Robintech in Freeport, Texas, insisted it could get to the 1 ppm standard without respirators in its new plant. A representative of the Diamond Shamrock company in Deer Park, Texas, where the same new technology is used, said: "No one will meet the 1 ppm limit 100 percent of the time without respirators no matter what Robintech says!"

Despite all the predictions about plant closings, as a result of the new standards, only one company had announced a closing. In October 1975, Uniroyal Chemical said it planned to close its 25-year-old PVC plant in Painesville, Ohio, which produced 130 million pounds of resin a year with 230 employees. Nonetheless, Uniroyal planned to stay in the PVC business via its joint venture with Borden in a PVC plant in Louisiana.

Rather than plant closings, 1975 was the year for building new PVC capacity. Robintech, Tenneco, Coroco, Borden, Diamond Shamrock, and Goodrich announced among them 1.5 billion pounds of new PVC capacity.

Looking ahead to the implementation of the 1 ppm standard in April

1976, the industry began adopting a whole range of innovations in precise gas monitoring, close cycle polymerization, tanks requiring no hand cleaning, bigger reactors, continuous stripping methods for removing VCM from PVC resins, and so on. Goodrich, which had planned to spend $42 million in bringing its plants up to standard, announced in December 1975 that the actual cost would be 10 to 15 percent less because of better-than-expected results from the largest R&D program in company history. "Increased material costs," said Thomas Nantz, Goodrich's executive vice president, "are more significant than control costs."

On the research front, 11 of the industry's giants launched the Institute for Chemical Toxicology where research data would be public without prior sponsor approval. Individual companies announced large increases in toxicological research efforts: $2 million in facilities expansion at Dow in 1975; 70 percent increase in the 100-employee laboratory at Du Pont.

## New Standards on Other Aspects of PVC

On December 15, 1975, the Environmental Protection Agency (EPA) proposed new air and water standards which, if approved after the February 1976 hearing, would cost industry $183 million in capital investment and about $70 million annually to assure compliance. The combined air and water standards would increase PVC prices, at wholesale, 10 percent, thereby increasing finished goods prices by about 5 percent.

As early as October 1974, three regulatory agencies, the Food and Drug Administration (FDA), EPA, and the Consumer Product Safety Commission, had banned VCM propellant in aerosol sprays.

In September 1975, FDA had proposed a ban on PVC rigid and semirigid food packaging. Behind the ban was the proposed 50 ppb (parts per billion) or "no detectable level" standard for VCM migration from packaging to food products. In Italy, preliminary findings in March 1975 by Dr. Maltoni showed in animal experiments that thymus and liver cancers were caused by VCM—tainted food (at the relatively high level of 3.3 ppm). Tenneco and American Hoechst not so much objected to the new standard as to the ban on certain PVC food packaging. Both companies insisted that their material showed no detectable migration of VCM into food. Goodrich, too, which had planned to stop supplying PVC for bottle production, announced in May 1975 that new technology permitted it to supply PVC which would not contaminate bottled food.

## On the Eve of OSHA's Phase 3

Just one month before the permanent OSHA standard of 1 ppm would go into effect on April 1, 1976, OSHA's Martin Corn chided the industry's credibility suffered when it predicted promulgation of strict vinyl chloride exposure standards would have severe economic impact on producers.

Fifteen days before the implementation of the permanent OSHA standard, the international press carried the story of research done at the

Firestone Plastics PVC plant in Pottstown, Pennsylvania, which revealed that wives of men who had come into contact with vinyl chloride had twice as many miscarriages and stillbirths as wives of men who did not handle the material.

### Epilogue

Dr. Ben Holder, Dow Chemical: "If we know we're exposing our workers to a health hazard, we get out of the business."

Paul H. Weaver (*Fortune,* October 1974): "In the course of these development, it has become clear that our regulators have a hard time thinking sensibly about problems like vinyl chloride. The businessmen being regulated and the workers affected seem to find it no easier. The fact is that our society seems to have no agreed-on standards for dealing with situations in which medical and economic considerations collide head-on. . . . The vinyl chloride case is widely identified as the tip of an enormous regulatory iceberg."

## APPENDIX B

### NUCLEAR POWER: THE APOSTATES*

Talk may be cheap, but a public act of apostasy in the business world tends to be both painful and expensive: right or wrong, an executive who turns on his company carries a permanent brand. Thus a special shock wave went out last week when three veteran General Electric engineers quit their management-level jobs at GE's nuclear-energy division in San Jose, Calif., with the announcement that "nuclear power is a technological monster that threatens all future generations."

Among them, Dale Bridenbaugh, Richard Hubbard and Gregory Minor had 54 years of experience with GE, . . . . The three GE engineers have given up jobs paying $30,000 to $40,000 a year; they. . . face professional ostracism and uncertain prospects for future employment. "I have three kids, a mortgage, a wife and a dog, not necessarily in that order," said the 44-year-old Bridenbaugh, who headed a special project to evaluate the safety of 25 GE nuclear plants in the U.S. "So it was a tough decision."

The three were also rejecting an enterprise they had once devotedly championed. . . . But events caused them to start questioning their conviction. . . . "The men were competent men, we won't detract from that," a GE spokesman conceded. Still, he added, they were only three out of "literally hundreds of people in comparable positions at GE's nuclear energy division." "Their objections," said president Don Crawford of the Edison Electric Institute, "seem to me to be more moral than technological. I think their motives and inclinations bear investigating."

Bridenbaugh, Hubbard and Minor say they welcome such scrutiny and predict that many more nuclear engineers will eventually follow their apostasy. "We are an unvoiced opinion," Bridenbaugh maintains. "Inside the big companies there are a lot of people like us."

. . . Their wives are nervous, but go along with the break. "When he broached the subject of resigning, my first thought was what about our security," said Bridenbaugh's wife, Charlotte. "Then I started thinking about the greatest kind of security—to do what you think is right." . . .

"I'm nervous as hell," said Bridenbaugh, "but I feel good."

---

# Selected Readings

---

*From*

# CORPORATE SOCIAL RESPONSIBILITY*

*By Richard N. Farmer and W. Dickerson Hogue*

### WHAT IS CORPORATE SOCIAL RESPONSIBILITY?

. . . This is really what corporate social responsibility is all about. People expect firms not only to perform the traditional function of providing goods and services to all citizens who are willing to pay for them, but also to help society solve its problems. If these things are generally seen as desirable, and the firm does them, then it is socially responsible. If the firm does not, then some people may feel it is irresponsible. Merely saying that a firm is doing good, however, does not necessarily mean that all people agree that it is behaving responsibly.

\*     \*     \*     \*     \*

### Maximization of Profit

Taking a socially responsible action presents a problem primarily when it will, in the company's view, decrease its profitability. . . . Even if a company's profits would suffer, should it reduce smoke emissions to a level below what the law demands?

### Distribution of Costs

From the economist's viewpoint, the problem of corporate responsibility is a matter of distribution of costs: Who is to bear how much of the costs of society's actions, including

---

* From *Corporate Social Responsibility,* by Richard N. Farmer and W. Dickerson Hogue. © 1973, Science Research Associates, Chicago, 1973, pp. 4–6, 13–20. Reprinted by permission.

corporate actions? Stated this way, costs include not only money costs but also human, or social, costs, such as frustration with machinery that does not work, poor health from breathing foul air, and lack of choice in consumer goods.

> \* \* \* \* \*

The following definition of corporate social responsibility is the one we will work with in this book.

> Socially responsible actions by a corporation are actions that, when judged by *society in the future,* are seen to have been of maximum help in providing *necessary amounts of desired goods and services at minimum financial and social costs, distributed as equitably as possible.*

> \* \* \* \* \*

## FINITE RESOURCES AND INFINITE GOALS

While potential social demands for what needs doing are infinite, resources are finite. Every society has to find ways to ration scarce resources. Many Americans born after World War II have known affluence all their lives and therefore find it difficult to believe that resources are limited. If resources were in truth infinite, then people who denied resources to others in need of them would be very cruel.

> \* \* \* \* \*

On the account of the scarcity of resources, something desirable may have to give way to something more desirable, and highly desirable things may have to be done less than completely.

### Setting Priorities

What are our goals, in order of their importance? Assigning priorities rationally is difficult and confusing, especially when the human problems that are involved touch our emotions deeply. It is hard for any of us to decide individually what human problems should be dealt with and how thoroughly. Your view of the proper priorities is certain to be objectionable—perhaps violently so—to many others who have as much right to their views as you to yours. How then can we arrive at a consensus for the goals of society as a whole?

One way to assign priorities is to neglect to think about or discuss them. Some people cannot set priorities even when circumstances urgently demand that goals be ranked in some order of importance. They may assume that resources are infinite and therefore not recognize the need for priorities; such people are likely to criticize goal setters, rationers, and cost allocaters for not doing everything anyone wants done or for doing the wrong thing.

But there may be no right thing.

> \* \* \* \* \*

### Rationing Resources

The apportionment of scarce resources is the crux of the problem of social responsibility. A firm might give large amounts to several charities, to stockholders, or to universities but, because of its limited resources, might not give enough to satisfy any of them. Dividing the money equally among all applicants is not a good solution, since many other charities and universities want donations and fulfilling their requests would eventually reduce each recipient's share to near-zero. Who is to decide who gets what, or even whether a firm should give at all and how much in total?

> \* \* \* \* \*

## Bearing the Costs

How do we divide among specific members of present and future society the costs of the resources we have assigned? Who pays how much, in what way, and when?

\*　\*　\*　\*　\*

## EXTERNALITIES

Much of an economist's thinking about distribution of the cost of corporate actions is involved with the concept of *externalities*. As used in economics, this term refers to the costs that are borne by persons outside the organization creating them. A classic case is a company that dumps its industrial wastes in a nearby river. A city downstream that uses this river for its supply of drinking water therefore has additional costs in treating the water. From the point of view of the firm, its disposal solution is cheap and efficient: to do anything else would cost more money. The company has not, however, eliminated the costs of disposal. It has merely made them externality costs by shifting them to someone who is not directly involved in generating them.

\*　\*　\*　\*　\*

## Past, Present, and Future

Many activities that entail externality costs begin in ways that do not seem dangerous. When autos were first introduced, they were hailed as a depolluting factor in cities, since they quickly eliminated most horse manure and urine from the streets. Similarly, it seemed sanitary and reasonable to dump sewage and industrial wastes into broad, fast-flowing rivers, where they would quickly be carried out of sight and free towns from potential infectious diseases. In the last century, when America was lightly populated and had relatively little industry, dumping industrial wastes seemed to be the only sensible choice. Later, when population density rose and most people earned their living as corporate employees, the externality costs resulting from this practice became clear: air, water, and noise pollution. By this time, however, firms were locked into certain cost patterns. If one firm tried to depollute (that is, accepted its externality costs) and competitors did not, then it would likely face bankruptcy.

Our society has tended to ignore externality costs. . . .

## Weighing the Costs and Benefits

If a firm is forced to pay all costs, external and internal, we have no pollution, but we also have no jobs and no income. For a city like Gary, Indiana, which is heavily polluted by a few steel mills but has no other major economic base, would you prefer pollution or jobs? The usual economic answer is to force all firms to take on externality costs. That is, by general law, they must all stop doing something simultaneously. In this way, all incur the same costs and are therefore in the same relative position as before the law went into effect.

Or are they? Suppose that steel mills in the United States were forced to accept various externality pollution costs, and steel production costs became relatively higher than in countries where citizens are not so concerned about pollution. Not only would it be easier for foreign steel firms to sell in the American market, but also they would win in third-country markets as well. After a time, unemployment would probably rise in Gary and other U.S. steel centers, because the industry seemingly could not compete. Consequently, tax revenues from Gary would lag, Indiana colleges would not get funds, and some young people in Indiana could not go to college. This is an oversimplified, but not incorrect, view of what can happen when one part of a worldwide industry is saddled with costs other parts do not have.

Another aspect of the problem of distributing the costs of our increasing activities is whether Americans will be able to afford in the future the material standard of living they have enjoyed up till now. If we are really serious about forcing firms to accept externality costs that they never have accepted before, then someone will pay the bill and conceivably money incomes could decline. Since not all clean-up costs can be paid out of profits, workers, customers, stockholders, and the general public would have to share with companies the burden of paying externality costs.

## Degrees of Pollution

Total and absolute abatement of pollution could reduce the American living standard twenty times over, bringing it down to about the level of India's. Instead of making $600 to $800 a month on graduation, a U.S. college graduate would have purchasing power equal to $30 to $40 a month at current prices. Pollution would be negligible, because very few people could afford to buy things that pollute.

Total pollution abatement may be unrealistic in itself. If a law were passed that only pure water could be discharged, then even distilling the discharge would be unsatisfactory, since distilled water contains a few parts per million of impurities. Certainly we will settle for less than absolute purity, but how much less?

We must realize also that cleaning up pollution may sometimes create pollution. A paper company that dumps its wastes into a river is forced by law to clean up. To do this, it needs certain chemicals whose production creates pollution some place else. It needs electricity, and generating this is potentially polluting. It has to hire new employees to handle the problem; these men and women are likely to buy more things and use more electricity than before. Because of the potential new pollution that could be created to correct the old problem, we may even be adding to total pollution. The way to stop the pollution absolutely is to shut down the plant—a solution that would also result in the elimination of income.

Partial pollution abatement would cost much less. How much of his standard of living will the average American be willing to trade for how much pollution abatement?

## One Alternative: Passing the Buck

. . . We may decide to do nothing also—except shift to someone else responsibility for solving the problem.

## Another Alternative: Productivity Gains

Major breakthroughs in many fields may enable us to have our cake and eat it too. If national productivity were to rise at 5 percent a year (historically, it has gone up at about 3 percent) and if gradual acceptance of externality costs added 3 percent a year to costs, then we could both get a bit richer and have less pollution. As yet, however, no one knows how to assure gains in productivity of as much as 5 percent annually, or what levels of pollution will be acceptable to most citizens, or how much of the increases society will be willing to spend on pollution abatement and other socially desirable actions.

It is possible that the gains some firms make from being ecologically sound would offset losses: recovery of valuable materials that previously went up the smokestack may offset the costs of smoke abatement; engineers, forced to develop new ways of avoiding water pollution, may come up with new processes that not only use less water, but also are cheaper. Occasionally, such things happen. When they do, firms are glad to comply with new requirements.

Already some corporations are undertaking research and development into new fields, such as cleaning the air. Firms specializing in cleaning up for other firms may also develop and even show considerable profit. As yet, no one can say how the new methods might work out in terms of income gains or losses. There would in any case be winners and losers. The worker in an old, dirty plant that is closed down would be bitter and demand certain rights, while more pollution-control engineers and technicians would be hired. As is typical of situations where social priorities are shifted, some citizens gain and feel that the change is obviously beneficial, while others lose and become upset. Corporations are caught in the middle—praised by some, criticized by others.

\*     \*     \*     \*     \*

*From*

# A FRIEDMAN DOCTRINE: THE SOCIAL RESPONSIBILITY OF BUSINESS IS TO INCREASE ITS PROFITS*

*By Milton Friedman*

When I hear businessmen speak eloquently about the "social responsibilities of business in a free-enterprise system," I am reminded of the wonderful line about the Frenchman who discovered at the age of 70 that he had been speaking prose all his life. The businessmen believe that they are defending free enterprise when they declaim that business is not concerned "merely" with profit but also with promoting desirable "social" ends; that business has a "social conscience" and takes seriously its responsibilities for providing employment, eliminating discrimination, avoiding pollution and whatever else may be the catchwords of the contemporary crop of reformers. In fact they are—or would be if they or anyone else took them seriously—preaching pure and unadulterated socialism. Businessmen who talk this way are unwitting puppets of the intellectual forces that they have been undermining the basis of a free society these past decades.

The discussions of the "social responsibilities of business" are notable for their analytical looseness and lack of rigor. What does it mean to say that "business" has responsibilities? Only people can have responsibilities. A corporation is an artificial person and in this sense may have artificial responsibilities, but "business" as a whole cannot be said to have responsibilities, even in this vague sense. . . .

Presumably, the individuals who are to be responsible are businessmen, which means individual proprietors or corporate executives. Most of the discussion of social responsibility is directed at corporations, so in what follows I shall mostly neglect the individual proprietor and speak of corporate executives.

In a free-enterprise, private-property system, a corporate executive is an employee of the owners of the business. He had direct responsibility to his employers. That responsibility is to conduct the business in accordance with their desires, which generally will be to make as much money as possible while conforming to the basic rules of the society, both those embodied in law and those embodied in ethical custom. Of course, in some cases his employers may have a different objective. A group of persons might establish a corporation for an eleemosynary purpose—for example, a hospital or a school. The manager of such a corporation will not have money profit as his objective but the rendering of certain services.

In either case, the key point is that, in his capacity as a corporate executive, the manager is the agent of the individuals who own the corporation or establish the eleemosynary institution, and his primary responsibility is to them.

Needless to say, this does not mean that it is easy to judge how well he is performing his task. But at least the criterion of performance is straightforward, and the persons among whom a voluntary contractual arrangement exists are clearly defined.

---

* From *The New York Times Magazine,* September 13, 1970. (Excerpts from pp. 32–33; 122 et. seq.) © 1970 by The New York Times Company. Reprinted by permission.

Of course, the corporate executive is also a person in his own right. As a person, he may have many other responsibilities that he recognizes or assumes voluntarily—to his family, his conscience, his feelings of charity, his church, his clubs, his city, his country. He may feel impelled by these responsibilities to devote part of his income to causes he regards as worthy, to refuse to work for particular corporations, even to leave his job, for example, to join his country's armed forces. If we wish, we may refer to some of these responsibilities as "social responsibilities." But in these respects he is acting as a principal, not an agent; he is spending his own money or time or energy, not the money of his employers or the time or energy he has contracted to devote to their purposes. If these are "social responsibilities," they are the social responsibilities of individuals, not of business.

What does it mean to say that the corporate executive has a "social responsibility" in his capacity as businessman? If this statement is not pure rhetoric, it must mean that he is to act in some way that is not in the interest of his employers. For example, that he is to refrain from increasing the price of the product in order to contribute to the social objective of preventing inflation, even though a price increase would be in the best interest of the corporation. Or that he is to make expenditures on reducing pollution beyond the amount that is in the best interests of the corporation or that is required by law in order to contribute to the social objective of improving the environment. Or that, at the expense of corporate profits, he is to hire "hard-core" unemployed instead of better-qualified available workmen to contribute to the social objective of reducing poverty.

In each of these cases, the corporate executive would be spending someone else's money for a general social interest. Insofar as his actions in accord with his "social responsibility" reduce returns to stockholders, he is spending their money. Insofar as his actions raise the price to customers, he is spending the customers' money. Insofar as his actions lower the wages of some employees, he is spending their money.

The stockholders or the customers or the employees could separately spend their own money on the particular action if they wished to do so. The executive is exercising a distinct "social responsibility," rather than serving as an agent of the stockholders or the customers or the employees, only if he spends the money in a different way than they would have spent it.

But if he does this, he is in effect imposing taxes, on the one hand, and deciding how the tax proceeds shall be spent, on the other.

This process raises political questions on two levels: principle and consequences. On the level of political principle, the imposition of taxes and the expenditure of tax proceeds are governmental functions. We have established elaborate constitutional, parliamentary and judicial provisions to control these functions, to assure that taxes are imposed so far as possible in accordance with the preferences and desires of the public—after all, "taxation without representation" was one of the battle cries of the American Revolution. We have a system of checks and balances to separate the legislative function of imposing taxes and enacting expenditures from the executive function of collecting taxes and administering expenditure programs and from the judicial function of mediating disputes and interpreting the law.

Here the businessman—self-selected or appointed directly or indirectly by stockholders —is to be simultaneously legislator, executive and jurist. He is to decide whom to tax by how much and for what purpose and he is to spend the proceeds—all this guided only by general exhortations from on high to restrain inflation, improve the environment, fight poverty and so on and on.

*    *    *    *    *

This is the basic reason why the doctrine of "social responsibility" involves the acceptance of the socialist view that political mechanisms, not market mechanisms, are the appropriate way to determine the allocation of scarce resources to alternative uses.

*    *    *    *    *

Many a reader . . . may be tempted to remonstrate that it is all well and good to speak of government's having the responsibility to impose taxes and determine expenditures for such "social" purposes as controlling pollution or training the hard-core unemployed, but that the problems are too urgent to wait on the slow course of political processes, that the exercise of social responsibility by businessmen is a quicker and surer way to solve pressing current problems.

. . . I share Adam Smith's skepticism about the benefits that can be expected from "those who affected to trade for the public good"—this argument must be rejected on grounds of principle. What it amounts to is an assertion that those who favor the taxes and expenditures in question have failed to persuade a majority of their fellow citizens to be of like mind and that they are seeking to attain by undemocratic procedures what they cannot attain by democratic procedures. In a free society, it is hard for "good" people to do "good," but that is a small price to pay for making it hard for "evil" people to do "evil," especially since one man's good is another's evil.

*   *   *   *   *

Of course, in practice the doctrine of social responsibility is frequently a cloak for actions that are justified on other grounds rather than a reason for those actions.

To illustrate, it may well be in the long-run interest of a corporation that is a major employer in a small community to devote resources to providing amenities to that community or to improving its government. That may make it easier to attract desirable employees, it may reduce the wage bill or lessen losses from pilferage and sabotage or have other worthwhile effects. Or it may be that, given the laws about the deductibility of corporate charitable contributions, the stockholders can contribute more to charities they favor by having the corporation make the gift than by doing it themselves, since they can in that way contribute an amount that would otherwise have been paid as corporate taxes.

In each of these—and many similar—cases, there is a strong temptation to rationalize these actions as an exercise of "social responsibility." In the present climate of opinion, with its widespread aversion to "capitalism," "profits," the "soulless corporation" and so on, this is one way for a corporation to generate goodwill as a by-product of expenditures that are entirely justified in its own self-interest.

It would be inconsistent of me to call on corporate executives to refrain from this hypocritical window-dressing because it harms the foundations of a free society. That would be to call on them to exercise a "social responsibility"! If our institutions, and the attitudes of the public make it in their self-interest to cloak their actions in this way, I cannot summon much indignation to denounce them. At the same time, I can express admiration for those individual proprietors or owners of closely held corporations or stockholders of more broadly held corporations who disdain such tactics as approaching fraud.

The political principle that underlies the market mechanism is unanimity. In an ideal free market resting on private property, no individual can coerce any other, all cooperation is voluntary, all parties to such cooperation benefit or they need not participate. There are no "social" values, no "social" responsibilities in any sense other than the shared values and responsibilities of individuals. Society is a collection of individuals and of the various groups they voluntarily form.

The political principle that underlies the political mechanism is conformity. The individual must serve a more general social interest—whether that be determined by a church or a dictator or a majority. The individual may have a vote and a say in what is to be done, but if he is overruled, he must conform. It is appropriate for some to require others to contribute to a general social purpose whether they wish to or not.

Unfortunately, unanimity is not always feasible. There are some respects in which conformity appears unavoidable, so I do not see how one can avoid the use of the political mechanism altogether.

But the doctrine of "social responsibility" taken seriously would extend the scope of the political mechanism to every human activity. It does not differ in philosophy from the most explicitly collectivist doctrine. It differs only by professing to believe that collectivist ends can be attained without collectivist means. That is why, in my book "Capitalism and Freedom," I have called it a "fundamentally subversive doctrine" in a free society, and have said that in such a society, "there is one and only one social responsibility of business—to use its resources and engage in activities designed to increase its profits so long as it stays within the rules of the game, which is to say, engages in open and free competition without deception or fraud."

*From*

# CONCEPTUAL FOUNDATIONS OF BUSINESS*

## By Richard Eells and Clarence Walton

"Property" is the word we use to describe land, tangible objects, and certain intangible legal rights, with specific reference to the ownership thereof. "Private property" is property the ownership of which is vested, more or less, in individuals or groups other than public governments. The commonest form of group ownership today is the business corporation.

Historically, "ownership" has meant possession *and* the right, enforceable by legal process, to possess, control, and use the particular item of property and its products. . . . One of the great law teachers of the early part of this century defined property as follows: "A true property may, therefore, be shortly defined as possession coupled with the unlimited right of possession. If these two elements are vested in different persons there is a divided ownership."[1]

\* \* \* \* \*

. . . It is easy to demonstrate that property, especially that which is productive, has rarely if ever in our Western civilization been entirely free from the claims of the polity.

\* \* \* \* \*

The varieties of claimants on the corporation—and hence upon the resources controlled by managerial decision makers—can best be understood in another way: through a study of the art of governance within the corporate constellation and through a consideration of the roles of *direct* and *indirect* claimants and contributors to the wealth and welfare of the organization.

## DIRECT CLAIMANTS ON THE CORPORATION

### Security Holders

Those who supply the capital represented by the capital stock, the corporate bonds, and the notes with maturities in excess of a year are potent contributors to the corporate enterprise. The contributors of capital thus fall into several categories of senior and junior security holders. Their respective "stakes" in the venture are variously defined by law and custom, and their claims on the corporate usufruct vary accordingly.

\* \* \* \* \*

The property of a corporation is owned by the *persona ficta* and not, either in law or in fact, by the "share owners." The corporate "person" acts through its board of directors, as a collective body, and it is they alone who may determine how the property is used, how

---

\* Reprinted by permission of Richard D. Irwin, Inc., Homewood, Ill., 1961 (pp. 149–67, 185–87, 458, 468–75).

[1] James Barr Ames, "The Disseisin of Chattels," in Association of American Law Schools (ed.), *Select Essays in Anglo-American Legal History* (Boston: Little, Brown & Co., 1909), Vol. III, p. 563.

earnings are calculated, and how net earnings are distributed. Although they must act within the boundaries of legally set norms, their discretionary area for decision making is wide. . . .

\* \* \* \* \*

If, as the more adamant traditionalists[2] argue, the common stockholders alone have a legitimate claim on the earnings of a company, it is obvious that the structure of authority in most corporations does not guarantee such a result. On the contrary, what we have is a business institution in which the directors tend to act as "trustees for the institution and not merely as attorneys for the stockholder" and in which "the management of large corporations is largely unaccountable to the stockholders.[3] This is not to say that management bears no responsibility to stockholders, but that the line of accountability does not run to the "ultimate owners" directly. And it is often said that managerial responsibility ought not to run either directly *or* indirectly to the share owners *alone*.

\* \* \* \* \*

The contrary view is that this amounts to establishing an authoritarian status for a managerial elite "who from their *own* ethical standards will 'assign' income shares."[4] It is one thing to say that the risk-bearing stockholder has little function; it is quite another to say that he deserves little respect. When the demands of other claimants are given equal weight, it is argued, the nature of corporate enterprise is radically altered and the foundations of capitalism are threatened.

The issue thus joined is certain to become one of the most difficult for strategic decision makers of the future, in the fields both of business and of public policy.

## Employees

Employees as a group are clearly direct claimants on the corporate enterprise because they are direct contributors to it and are contractually related to the firm. Like the contributors of risk capital, they invest something they own. Their investment is comparable in that they expect a return on it from the fruits of the venture.

Dividends have been called "the wages of capital." . . . In much the same way, people invest the best part of their lives in some established and promising companies at a rate of return—in the form of wages and salaries—that may seem modest enough at the start but is acceptable in anticipation of other benefits.

Nor are these benefits only the expected wage and salary benefits and advances over the years; the anticipated income includes those "fringe benefits" that increasingly go along with the job, plus some benefits that nowhere appear in the formal employment contracts. Association with certain companies yields "psychic income." Prestige, a sense of security, the feeling that one works for a "good corporate citizen" in a laudable field of endeavor, satisfaction in work that contributes to one's skills and enlightenment about some aspect of nature or society—these are some of the considerations that attract the necessary human resources to the organization, just as the anticipated growth and earnings prospects of a company attract capital resources.

\* \* \* \* \*

There is . . . a competition for the loyalty and solidarity of employees between firm and union. Insofar as an employee's loyalties are polarized toward the outside organization, his place in the constellation of corporate interests moves toward the periphery of that constellation.

The corporate executive of the future will have to recast the theory of the firm to account

---

[2] Louis O. Kelso and Mortimer J. Adler, *The Capitalist Manifesto* (New York: Random House, 1958). See Eells, *The Meaning of Modern Business*, pp. 77–94.

[3] George B. Hurff, *Social Aspects of Enterprise in the Large Corporation* (Philadelphia: University of Pennsylvania Press, 1950), pp. 96 ff.

[4] David McCord Wright, "The Modern Corporation—Twenty Years After," *University of Chicago Law Review*, vol. XIX (Summer 1952), pp. 663 ff.

for this trend. The implications are many. One, or course, has to do with the whole area of "human relations," or the restoration of organic unity in the enterprise as a human association, and not merely an aggregation of capital in the accounting sense of that term. . . .

\* \* \* \* \*

## Customers

According to Peter F. Drucker, "there is only one valid definition of business purpose: to create a customer." It follows that "any business enterprise has two—and only two—basic functions: marketing and innovation." This is in line with the doctrine of customer sovereignty: "King Customer" must be placed above all.

Here some distinctions are in order. Does one mean that the general public is the legitimate determiner of corporate policy? Or is something else meant—for example, the meeting and creating of "demands" for salable products and services, regardless of the "public interest" as expressed by representatives of the general public? Obviously not all products of profitable enterprise are "good" products, and some salable services are proscribed by law and morals. Customers and consumers are not necessarily identical groups, nor can either be designated, without careful qualification, as a direct contributor-claimant in any corporate constellation of interests.

A corporation's customers are the main source of its business income; but it is one thing to center the goals of the business on supplying demand and quite another to proliferate corporate objectives so as to meet all the ideal requirements of a hypothetical consumer public.

\* \* \* \* \*

## Suppliers

The sources of supply for the large corporation as a going concern are extremely diverse. In the widest sense, suppliers include all contributors of material, financial, and human resources. Supply refers also to certain social costs, that are not accounted for in the enterpreneurial outlays but instead are shifted to and borne by third persons and the community as a whole.[5]

Here we are concerned with those direct contributor-claimant suppliers outside the firm whose goods and services are reflected directly in entrepreneurial outlays, except for taxes. . . .

\* \* \* \* \*

## INDIRECT CLAIMANTS ON THE CORPORATION

\* \* \* \* \*

## Competitors

A competitive firm has no obligation, strictly speaking, toward competitors; its obligation, if any, is to the competitive system and to the norms that organized society establishes for competitive conduct. All responsible business executives recognize that, quite aside from their legal obligations to obey antitrust laws, there is a moral obligation to competitors that arises independently of the rules of law. Some of this nonlegal obligation has its roots in

---

[5] K. William Kapp, *The Social Costs of Private Enterprise* (Cambridge: Harvard University Press, 1950). He includes cost resulting from the impairment of the human factor of production; depletion and destruction of animal resources; depletion of energy resources; soil erosion, soil depletion, and deforestation; and social costs of air and water pollution, of technological change, of unemployment and idle resources, and of distribution and transporation.

"enlightened self-interest" to the extent that competition is regarded as "the life of trade," or as a stimulant to innovation and *esprit de corps* in the organization, and so on. . . .

\*    \*    \*    \*    \*

## Local Communities

The most immediate peripheral group of interests that vitally concern a corporation is the local community—or rather the numerous local communities—in which it operates as a going concern. The contributions of these communities are many, and so are their claims on the businesses located there.

\*    \*    \*    \*    \*

The claimant community specifies its own requirements; regular employment, good working conditions, fair play, satisfying work, local purchase of a reasonable part of the firm's supply of goods and services, the maintenance of a plant worthy of a good neighbor, and interest in and support of the local government and of local charitable and cultural projects.

## The General Public and Governments

The contributions of the general public have been alluded to earlier with reference to the "social costs of private enterprise." As a taxpayer, the corporation is clearly a direct contributor to public governments as claimants on the fruits of the enterprise. . . .

\*    \*    \*    \*    \*

## "Social Responsibilities"

\*    \*    \*    \*    \*

But what are the major or minor types of responsibility? As to the ultimate owners, is it a "fair return" on their investment or all the net profits in any year? As to customers, is it a "fair" price for products or all that the traffic will bear? (Or is it a "good" product and constant innovation to provide more and better new products?) As to employees, is it a "fair" wage and good working conditions or status, with all the overtones of security and the dimensions of the good life? As to others in the business community—competitors, suppliers —is it the minimal standard of conduct in a hard and competitive drive for profits or behavior in accordance with some ideal code? As to the public and governments, is it a shrewd avoidance of infractions of the law and the building of stout barriers against any encroachment of government on business, or a common pursuit of the general welfare through some form of mixed economy?

The question of the "social responsibilities" of the modern corporation thus turns out to be no simple issue but a large bundle of issues. It cannot be reduced to the single relationship between corporation and society, for the referents in these ambiguous terms are unclear. . . .

\*    \*    \*    \*    \*

## Interrelationships and the Balancing of Interests

If we concede that there is an accountability that goes with wealth and power, then the logic of responsibility for those who hold it is easy to establish. The corporation is a center of wealth and power, and it has, therefore, responsibilities to those most dependent upon it. These are its stockholders, its employees, and its customers. But its employees, its customers, and its stockholders are also the community. Therefore, it has a social as well as an economic responsibility.

To assess the nature of this responsibility is one of the functions of management. . . .

\*    \*    \*    \*    \*

## THE MIDDLE GROUND

The large business corporation is here to stay. It is an indispensable instrument for getting done some of the things that people want done. It is neither the exclusive instrument of one class of interests nor an indiscriminate roster of "social" interests. Like other large organizations, the corporation must be tempered to the times, and as a viable instrument it must adapt to the changing requirements of our free, complex, and interdependent society.

The impossibility of direct owner management of large-scale private enterprise calls for professional management by persons whose relationship to the owners is difficult to define. Is it a fiduciary relationship, one of agency, or perhaps one of representation?

     \*     \*     \*     \*     \*

To resist the many new claims made on the corporation is to assume an eminently respectable traditional position grounded on the logic of property. But to be rational is not necessarily to be reasonable. Reasonable regard for the interests of society is a practical necessity.

*From*

# SOCIAL RESPONSIBILITIES OF BUSINESS MANAGERS*

*By Robert Hay and Ed Gray*

[Editor's Note: In the text of their article, the authors assert that concepts of social responsibility have gone through three phases. This table summarizes the managerial values the authors feel match each historical phase.]

## Comparison of Managerial Values

| Phase I<br>Profit Maximizing<br>Management | Phase II<br>Trusteeship<br>Management | Phase III<br>Quality of Life<br>Management |
|---|---|---|
| | *Economic Values* | |
| 1. Raw self-interest. | 1. Self-interest.<br>2. Contributors' interest. | 1. Enlightened self-interest.<br>2. Contributors' interests.<br>3. Society's interests. |
| What's good for me is good for my country.<br>Profit maximizer. | What's good for GM is good for our country.<br>Profit satisficer. | What's good for society is good for our company.<br>Profit is necessary, but . . . |
| Money and wealth are most important.<br>Let the buyer beware (caveat emptor). | Money is important but so are people.<br>Let us not cheat the customer. | People are more important than money.<br>Let the seller beware (caveat venditor). |

* Reprinted with permission from the *Academy of Management Journal,* vol. 17, no. 1 (March 1974), excerpt from p. 135.

**Comparison of Managerial Values (***Continued***)**

| Phase I<br>*Profit Maximizing<br>Management* | Phase II<br>*Trusteeship<br>Management* | Phase III<br>*Quality of Life<br>Management* |
|---|---|---|
| Labor is a commodity to be bought and sold. | Labor has certain rights which must be recognized. | Employee dignity has to be satisfied. |
| Accountability of management is to the owners. | Accountability of management is to the owners, customers, employees, suppliers, and other contributors. | Accountability of management is to the owners, contributors, and society. |

*Technology Values*

| | | |
|---|---|---|
| Technology is very important. | Technology is important but so are people. | People are more important than technology. |

*Social Values*

| | | |
|---|---|---|
| Employee personal problems must be left at home. | We recognize that employees have needs beyond their economic needs. | We hire the whole man. |
| I am a rugged individualist and I will manage my business as I please. | I am an individualist, but I recognize the value of group participation. | Group participation is fundamental to our success. |
| Minority groups are inferior to whites. They must be treated accordingly. | Minority groups have their place in society, and their place is inferior to mine. | Minority group members are people as you and I are. |

*Political Values*

| | | |
|---|---|---|
| That government is best which governs least. | Government is a necessary evil. | Business and government must cooperate to solve society's problems. |

*Environmental Values*

| | | |
|---|---|---|
| The natural environment controls the destiny of man. | Man can control and manipulate the environment. | We must preserve the environment in order to lead a quality life. |

*Aesthetic Values*

| | | |
|---|---|---|
| Aesthetic values? What are they? | Aesthetic values are okay, but not for us. | We must preserve our aesthetic values, and we will do our part. |

\* Reprinted with permission from the *Academy of Management Journal*, vol. 17, no. 1 (March 1974), excerpt from p. 135.

*From*

# OUR SOCIETY IN 1985—BUSINESS MAY NOT LIKE IT*

## By William F. Martin and George Cabot Lodge

What are the demands on managerial policy and style when our business-oriented society is moving toward a communitarian ideology which most businessmen find repulsive? Can we keep alive such cherished aspects of our traditional ideology as individual liberty and democracy—knowing from history that they may suffer in a communitarian setting?

These are issues one can infer from the provocative results of an Harvard Business Review survey presented in the May–June [1975] issue, in which 1,844 readers from several countries participated. The poll focused on two opposing ideologies: readers were asked to determine which one they (1) prefer, (2) find dominant in the United States today, (3) expect to dominate in 1985, and (4) believe would be more effective in solving future problems.

The first ideology, enunciated by philosopher John Locke 300 years ago, is the nucleus of the traditional "American way" extolling the values of individualism, private property, free competition in an open marketplace, and limited government. This is the way we stated Ideology I in the survey:

> "The community is no more than the sum of the individuals in it. Self-respect and fulfillment result from an essentially lonely struggle in which initiative and hard work pay off. The fit survive and if you don't survive, you are probably unfit. Property rights are a sacred guarantor of individual rights, and the uses of property are best controlled by competition to satisfy consumer desires in an open market. The least government is the best. Reality is perceived and understood through the specialized activities of experts who dissect and analyze in objective study.

The second ideology defines the individual as an inseparable part of a community in which his rights and duties are determined by the needs of the common good. Government plays an important role as the planner and implementer of community needs. We expressed Ideology II this way in the survey:

> Individual fulfillment and self-respect are the result of one's place in an organic social process; we 'get our kicks' by being part of a group. A well-designed group makes full use of our individual capacities. Property rights are less important than the rights derived from membership in the community or a group—for example, rights to income, health, and education. The uses of property are best regulated according to the community's need, which often differs from individual consumer desires. Government must set the community's goals and coordinate their implementation. The perception of reality requires an awareness of whole systems and of the interrelationships between and among the wholes. This holistic process is the primary task of science.

The significant findings are:

More than two thirds of the respondents prefer Ideology I. However, many readers sense its replacement by a new set of value definitions based on the communitarian principles of

---

* From "Our Society in 1985—Business May Not Like It," *Harvard Business Review,* vol. 53, no. 6 (November–December 1975), pp. 143–47, 151–52 (excerpts). Reprinted by permission.

Ideology II. Some 62% of the readers regard Ideology I as the more dominant ideology in the United States today, whereas 73% anticipate that Ideology II will dominate in 1985.

Many readers think that the transformation from Ideology I to II could lead to social disaster, with burdensome government interference causing the disintegration of business and loss of personal freedom. A minority accept the charge with cautious optimism, acknowledging that many perplexing problems—including resource shortages, explosive population growth, and environmental degradation—can be resolved only within the framework of Ideology II.

The U.S. and non–U.S. responses differed sharply. Two thirds of the Americans regard Ideology I as the more effective ideological framework for solving future problems, while the same proportion of foreign respondents believe Ideology II is more desirable.

\*     \*     \*     \*     \*

The ultimate answers to the questions posed by these results will have profound implications for the future. Are we inescapably locked into a system that is accelerating toward a community characterized by increased government interference and control of individuals and business? Or, with a more explicit realization of its essential planning functions, can government actually become smaller and less prone to intervene? What are the motivating forces in such a communitarian society where survival, income, and even good health are virtually guaranteed to every member? Can we avert such a total transformation and retain some of the principles of our cherished heritage as exemplified by individualism and free enterprise? Precisely what is inexorable about the transition, and where do we have a choice?

\*     \*     \*     \*     \*

## Responses According to Nationality

| Citizenship (*sample size*) | Ideology | Questions (*results in percent*) | | | |
|---|---|---|---|---|---|
| | | *Which ideology do you prefer?* | *Which ideology dominates in the United States today?* | *Which ideology will dominate in the United States in 1985?* | *Which ideology would be more effective in solving future problems?* |
| United States.... | 1 | 73 | 59 | 23 | 63 |
| (1,647)......... | II | 26 | 39 | 75 | 35 |
| | Other | 1 | 2 | 2 | 2 |
| Non United | | | | | |
| States.......... | 1 | 44 | 89 | 35 | 32 |
| (185) .......... | II | 55 | 10 | 64 | 65 |
| | Other | 1 | 1 | 1 | 3 |

## Readers' Reasons for Preferring Ideology I

\*     \*     \*     \*     \*

The problems of the future will not be materially different from those of the past. (It's only our perception of the problems that changes.) In this country we have witnessed and enjoyed the benefits of Ideology I, without question the greatest the world has known!

The primary difficulty with Ideology II is the role of government as goal setter and coordinator. Government today is unable to lead intelligently or decisively.

\*     \*     \*     \*     \*

"The fit survive and if you don't survive, you are probably unfit." The unfit go into government.

\* \* \* \* \*

Ideology I allows for individual responsibility for setting goals and being held accountable for success and failure.

\* \* \* \* \*

God made individuals, man made groups.

\* \* \* \* \*

### Readers' Reasons for Preferring Ideology II

\* \* \* \* \*

Ideology I leads to befouling life-support earth systems—destruction of life forms that do not contribute to monetary values. If we are not to lose our humanness, Ideology II must prevail—for it encourages the creative over the destructive.

Ideology II seems more and more viable and effective. It seems to work more frequently and more broadly. Fifteen years ago I couldn't imagine writing this! I guess this reflects my judgment that the former over-dominance of Ideology I has led to its own decline.

Our real problems are people problems, which Ideology II is better able to address.

\* \* \* \* \*

Ideology I is a major cause for our problems today—greed, selfishness, vanity, pride (Hurrah for Me, Screw You.)

\* \* \* \* \*

Ideology I was suited to the frontier—which no longer exists.

*From*

# INDUSTRY AND THE ENVIRONMENT*

*By E. P. Hawthorne*

\* \* \* \* \*

The basic problem facing managements is how to effect a balance between the economically and socially acceptable consequences of their decisions. On the one hand, industry must satisfy the prevailing financial standards of return on investment whilst, on the other, it must avoid falling foul of society's demands for quality in the environment. In some cases, these two requirements may be in concert, whilst in others they may be utterly in conflict. The only way in which industry can reconcile its activities with the standards which society demands of it is by arriving at a policy, both economical and technical, which will tend to run in harmony with both of these issues. This does not mean that industry needs to fight shy of conflicting situations between the two sides of the problem but rather that the area of conflict must be clearly understood, isolated and minimised.

In arriving at its policies in a particular situation, industry is further faced with the problem that the economic standards which may be set are quantitative and, therefore, fairly easily defined. The social standards, on the other hand, are largely qualitative, and it may be very difficult to devise standards which are not only acceptable but can be practically applied. In view of the complexity of this problem, the need for quantitative and qualitative standards implies that there can be no simple answers. In any particular case, the solutions will only be reached through a process of systems analysis aimed at identifying the essential elements in the system of the environment within which the company is operating.

\* From *Futures,* June 1973, pp. 297–300 (excerpts). Reprinted by permission.

**FIGURE 1**
**THE ENVIRONMENT-TECHNOLOGY CYCLE**

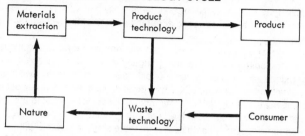

## The Environment-Technology Cycle

The issues involved can be demonstrated by means of a diagram (Figure 1). It is evident that industry forms part of a natural cycle in which materials are extracted from the environment and are processed in such a way as to be changed into products and waste. The products are utilised by the consumer who, in turn, rejects them, perhaps after some further processing, as waste. The waste from industry and from the consumer is then treated again by some other kind of technology and returns to nature in the form of dumping on tips, or in the sea and so on. At first sight, this cycle seems to pose straightforward commercial and technical problems. However, there are two further important factors:

1. The apparently closed loop nature of this cycle is not, in fact, as closed as it should be. The form in which the waste from industry or from the consumer is returned to nature is not the same as the form in which the materials were originally taken out of nature. The equilibrium state of the environment is disturbed and may drift far away from that which is acceptable to human life.
2. The ecological balance in the environment changes as the ecology itself develops.

\*     \*     \*     \*     \*

## Industry's dilemma

In tackling this problem it is apparent that there are two courses open to industry.

1. Ignore the problem, maximise profits on investment, and wait until forced to do something either by the government or by public opinion.
2. Work out the real issues. In other words, find out what are the key elements in the whole situation relating to one's own situation, and act upon the conclusions to be drawn from this analysis.

For industry to wait until statutory regulations are brought into force before it takes any action is not necessarily an anti-social attitude. It is quite clear that in a normal competitive market climate it may be totally impossible for one company to take action unless its competitors are willing to come into line at the same time. Action will, therefore, be forced upon the industry, as a whole, by an outside agent such as the government who will set quite precise guidelines according to which companies can then develop their own policies. In this situation, the prudent company will, however, have taken the trouble to identify the problem and find possible solutions. In the mood which is developing in society the company which fails to make this analysis will be deemed to have ignored its social obligations. It is better that a company should be party to assisting governments to devise regulations rather than to be found to be totally unsympathetic to the problem.

If the company is unwilling, or if the climate is such that it is unable to take physical action to prevent problems arising, it should, nevertheless, go to the trouble of finding out the real issues in the problem. In other words, every company, whether it ignores the issue or not, needs to establish the basic way in which its technology can affect and be affected by the environmental problems, and is bound to adopt the second of the two courses listed above, that is to take action.

The first instinct for a company when faced with environmental questions is to become defensive. The company assumes that it is going to be the cause of a nuisance; it assumes that whatever it does will have an adverse effect on its financial state; and it assumes that whatever it does will make it uncompetitive with other companies which do not take the same action. The company then only reacts to statutory or legal restrictions, to the force of public opinion, or to straightforward disaster. If any of these results are experienced, the company may be exposed to tremendous costs arising from the shutting down of plant, the changing of technology, the changing of products, and the need to establish other markets. If this does happen, the board of the company could be said to have failed in one of their main duties—to foresee problems which are likely to arise affecting the profitability of the organisation.

A board which has appreciated the significance of the environmental problem will not only have put itself and its company in a position where defensive actions are taken in a practical, sensible and economic manner, but they will also have realised that there are opportunities in environmental developments of which certain companies can take advantage. There are three areas in which this approach should be adopted.

1. Products which are acceptable on environmental grounds, e.g., quiet motors, pollution-free combustion, etc.
2. Marketing policies which utilise the environmental characteristics of the products to support the sales. The health foods sector of industry is a well-known example of this type of policy.
3. Products and processes which form part of the re-cycling process of waste reclamation, waste treatment, etc, both from industry and the consumer. Again, many of these services are well-known, but there may be opportunities which have not been fully explored and which are becoming increasingly more economic.

**Potential Strategies**

What actions should companies take to develop effective defensive or business-developmental strategies?

The company must first realize that there is a problem. It is not enough for a managing director to say that his firm is in a short-term business and, therefore, it cannot have any effect on the environment nor does the environment affect it. As Figure 1 shows, every company which is taking in materials and altering them in any way whatsoever is part of the environmental cycle. It is possible that the company itself neither produces offensive products nor waste. It may be that the products or wastes are utilised by other companies which in their transformation of these materials cause offence. A company may therefore be unwittingly a part of an environmentally-bad cycle. It is vital that the board of the company knows this.

Also, it is important to realise that the environmental problem is one for top management. Men on the shop floor may know that noxious effluent is being discharged. The designer of an appliance may realise that his design is not as safe as it could be. Neither they, nor their colleagues in other departments, are likely to take any effective action in solving the problems created by the environmental question unless the board of the company decide that this is, indeed, an area of activity in which they are prepared to invest money and effort.

Both of the above refer to actions which may be regarded as defensive. But environmental considerations can be incorporated into a business-development strategy.

\*   \*   \*   \*   \*

*From*

# HOW ETHICAL ARE BUSINESSMEN?*

*By Raymond C. Baumhardt, S. J.*

[Editor's Note: This classic survey of 1531 *Harvard Business Review* readers includes many more items than the two reported here.]

### Influences on Executive Behavior

A. What influences an executive to make ethical decisions?

| Possible Influence | Importance as an Unethical Influence Average Rank |
|---|---|
| A man's personal code of behavior | 1.5 |
| The behavior of a man's superiors in the company | 2.8 |
| Formal company policy | 2.8 |
| Ethical climate of the industry | 3.8 |
| The behavior of a man's equals in the company | 4.0 |

B. What influences an executive to make unethical decisions?

| Possible Influence | Importance as an Unethical Influence Average Rank |
|---|---|
| The behavior of a man's superiors in the company | 1.9 |
| Ethical climate of the industry | 2.6 |
| The behavior of a man's equals in the company | 3.1 |
| Lack of company policy | 3.3 |
| Personal financial needs | 4.1 |

Note: The average rankings given are derived from a ranking of each item in the 5 groups (1,2,3,4, or 5), with most influential = 1, and least influential = 5.

*From*

# MANAGERIAL ETHICS: A POST-WATERGATE VIEW†

*By Archie B. Carroll*

*A poll of how managers perceive the integrity of businessmen reveals that top managers may not know that subordinates may commit unethical acts out of loyalty to the firm or to superiors.*

\*     \*     \*     \*     \*

\* From "How Ethical Are Businessmen?" *Harvard Business Review*, vol. 39, no. 4 (July–August 1961), p. 6–19 (excerpt). Reprinted by permission. © 1961 by The President and Fellows of Harvard College; all rights reserved.

† Reprinted with permission from *Business Horizons*, vol. XVIII, no. 2, April 1975, pp. 75, 77, 79 (excerpts).

*Proposition 1.* Managers today feel under pressure to compromise personal standards to achieve company goals.

| Response | No. | Percent |
|---|---|---|
| Disagree | 58 | 24.6 |
| Somewhat disagree | 26 | 11.0 |
| Somewhat agree | 102 | 43.2 |
| Agree | 50 | 21.2 |
| Total | 236 | 100.0 |

This finding was extremely revealing of pressures perceived by managers. Almost 65 percent agreed with the statement, indicating that they do feel under pressure to compromise their personal standards for their organizations. A close of the data discloses that this feeling is dramatically prevalent at the middle and lower management levels. In fact, top management split equally on this proposition, whereas 65 percent of the middle managers and 84 percent of the lower managers agreed with it. This suggests that the greatest pressure is perceived in the lower ranks.

\* \* \* \* \*

*Proposition 10.* The junior members of Nixon's reelection committee who confessed that they went along with their bosses to show their loyalty is just what young managers would have done in business.

| Response | No. | Percent |
|---|---|---|
| Disagree | 58 | 24.6 |
| Somewhat disagree | 38 | 16.1 |
| Somewhat agree | 84 | 35.6 |
| Agree | 56 | 23.7 |
| Totals | 236 | 100.0 |

Almost 60 percent of the respondents agree that young managers in business would have done just what the junior members of Nixon's reelection committee had done.

\* \* \* \* \*

*From*

# CORPORATE SOCIAL RESPONSIBILITY*

*By Richard N. Farmer and W. Dickerson Hogue*

### A Manager's Approach to Corporate Social Responsibility

A group that tries to persuade a firm to change usually has some bargaining power with the firm: the union can call a strike; the stockholders can vote their stock against present management. Neither group has absolute power: the strike may fail or accomplish less than

---

\* From *Corporate Social Responsibility,* by Richard N. Farmer and W. Dickerson Hogue. © 1973, Science Research Associates, Chicago, 1973, pp. 4–6, 13–20. Reprinted by permission.

expected; the dissident stockholders may own only a small percentage of the shares voted. In working out the proper response to group pressure, the corporation has to compare its bargaining strength with that of its opponent. In this chapter we will discuss various bargaining stances.

First, however, we must clarify the role of the corporate manager in these issues lest we confuse his personal ethics with the social responsibility of the firm. Although corporate decisions are made and priorities set not by impersonal corporations but by people, these people act both individually and in groups on behalf of the corporation. They are corporate managers as well as citizens with their own lives and ethical standards. A person cannot separate completely one part of his life from the other parts, but he does behave differently in a managerial role than in his other roles.

*    *    *    *    *

## Personal Social Responsibility

Each individual has a number of roles to play in society, and some of them are personal roles—member of a family, driver on the highway, consumer, adviser on a friend's problems, member of a club. Such roles are more or less separate from each other, but there is one common denominator: the individual has personal responsibility for his actions and is taking personal risks. If you take a risk in a personal role and win, the gain is yours; if you lose, the loss is yours. Since no man is an island, others are affected by your actions—wives, friends, children, parents—but basically you are acting in each of your personal roles in your name and at your own risk.

## Representing Someone Else's Interests

When you accept a position where your role is to act in the best interests of other people, you take an oath, formally or informally, to do your best for the people you represent, whether as a lawyer, treasurer of your church, ambassador of your country, leader of a Boy Scout troop, or manager in a firm. You consciously agree that in this role your own interests must take second place.

For the corporation, as for the individual, there are many forbidden things, many gray-area activities, and many permissible behavioral and ethical patterns. A corporation's decisions, however, are made by its managers for many people. A manager might easily decide to take a risk for himself, but it is different for him to decide to force that risk on others who not only might be quite unwilling to take it but also have not and could not be consulted. Long after the individual manager is gone, the corporation will still be around, and people yet unborn may be affected by some minor ethical point on which a manager has had to decide.

## Managers and Personal Conflicts

Like the military commander who consciously sacrifices forty lives going up hill A to avoid sacrificing 200 lives going up hill B, the manager has to make a cost-benefit analysis in regard to his own ethics. People who cannot distinguish their own values from the corporation's values find it very difficult to function as managers in large corporations or other large institutions such as government agencies or universities. However, this is not a slave society. If a manager finds it difficult to function, he can always quit.

A manager can (and many often do) take personal positions that are different from his firm's position. He should not do so, however, in the performance of his managerial duties. A manager of a steel mill that is polluting the countryside might resist public pressures to install multimillion dollar smoke-abatement equipment on the logical grounds that the cost disadvantage of installing the equipment might make the firm's competitive position untenable. The same man, as an individual, might feel that contributing to an antipollution campaign was the proper thing to do. He might even, as an individual, join a group or make speeches to promote antipollution causes.

A manager may also do many things to persuade the corporation to act more in line with his personal ethics. He might fight for what he thinks is correct within the company, marshaling arguments in favor of what he perceives to be a more responsible corporate position. While this dissension might appear to be disastrous for a manager's career, it usually is not, as both authors can testify from personal experience. A manager who dispassionately argues for what he feels would be a more ethical corporate position will be listened to. He may sometimes even win his point, particularly if he argues soundly that the action he recommends is for the long-term good of the corporation as a whole.

Only when a manager feels that the decisions he must make cannot be reconciled with his personal ethics does he resign and leave the company. Normally, if he has worked his way up through the managerial hierarchy for many years, this will not occur for trivial reasons. Those who find corporate ethics intolerable would have left long before they moved very far up in the corporate management hierarchy.

## Multiplicity of Roles

To those who perceive situations in all-or-nothing terms, it seems absurdly paradoxical that a manager might make corporate decisions that go against his personal ethics: a moral man acts morally in everything he does. It would be comforting if such a straightforward rule were workable in real life, as it may be for a saintly hermit in the desert. In ordinary life, the simple rule of acting morally in everything becomes difficult to follow as soon as you accept responsibility for someone else's interests.

\* \* \* \* \*

*From*

# YOUTH CULTURE AND MANAGEMENT\*

*By Jeremiah J. O'Connell*

\* \* \* \* \*

### The Eye-to-Eye Relationship

Youth also has a negative attitude about a career in business; concerning the desirability and practicability of trying to express oneself in and through the organization form common in business. The popular philosophy of personalism predisposes youth to see the only prospect for serving another person in the person-to-person, one-on-one, eye-to-eye, warm-flesh-on-warm-flesh relationship. Expressing personal mission through a hierarchic (multiple levels of superiors and subordinates) and departmentalized (individuals and groups each performing only a specialized part of the whole task) organization structure is compared to the effort to drive in a nail with a four-meter hammer. The organization form common in business is an awkward instrumentality for doing good. Nor is this negative attitude on the part of youth reserved solely for business. Hierarchic and departmentalized structures are as common in governmental or ecclesiastical institutions. Personalism seems to legitimize only person-to-person missions. It wasn't very long ago that a fine administrator, the Cardinal Archbishop of Montreal, Monseigneur Ledger, resigned his administrative position to serve the lepers in Africa. The resignation was widely acclaimed as an admirable and courageous act. Few paused to ask: might it not have been even more courageous to continue to administer the powerful diocesan organization in its effort to serve human and religious

---

\* Reprinted by permission from *European Business,* no. 39, Autumn 1973 (excerpts).

needs? The protestant theologian Harvey Cox, in his book *Secular City,* underlines the growing gap between the philosophy of personalism and the reality of an increasingly institutionalized society. Personalism conditions us to praise and admire the Good Samaritan but to ignore and pity the Red Cross administrator. In the business field, the personalist message is rather clear in the remark of a brilliant electro-physicist who was president of a small computer company: "When I'm rich, then I will be good." That is, after laboring within an organization to produce financial returns, the man would then turn his talents to individual social service—in his case, this Samaritan work would take the form of the development of a ring and cane radar system to aid the blind.

In sum, when *youth* faces the choice of expressing personal mission in a face-to-face form of encounter as opposed to the instrumentality of an organization, *it tends to shy away from commitment to a life within organization.*

\* \* \* \* \*

. . . The prevailing philosophy of "personalism" encourages noninstitutional expression of personal mission. In this case, however, *youth has to face the reality that the person-to-person mission is the luxury of the very few.* To accomplish the needs of society, organization is needed. Most will grant that as a premise. What should also be clear is that the particular form of organization so maligned by youth (hierarchic and specialized) will always appear when two conditions are present: (*a*) limited resources and (*b*) common purpose. A pride of lions, a colony of ants, or a group of men, working under these conditions, will always develop a hierarchic and specialized organization. This form is not the arbitrary design of some ignorant or evil genius. As experiments with kibbutz and "hippie" communes demonstrate, hierarchy and specialization appear sooner or later as a prerequisite for continued achievement.

However, we can alter the patterns for deciding who is superior or subordinate or who is performing which speciality. We can also vary the *length of time* each person plays each hierarchic and specialized role. In these ways, *we can modify the impact of this organization form on individuals.* But, at any one time, individuals fit into a niche of the organization and undoubtedly find it difficult to express mission in and through this organization form. *To run away from the difficult challenge may, in fact, not be virtue but laziness and selfishness.* "Personalism" as a philosophy of life is charming and comfortable but certainly not an effective substitute for commitment to organized effort.

Here again our philosophers don't serve us well. Our whole Judeo-Christian ethic assigns credit or blame to the behavior of individuals. Somehow, in our increasingly institutionalized society, most people expend their psychological and physical energy in organized efforts wherein they are beyond either praise or blame—they cannot reasonably take individual credit for the good done by the whole organization nor can they be indicted personally for the evil perpetrated by the organization. We could, of course, learn our lessons from the Confucian tradition expressed these days in Japanese organizations wherein individuals do feel responsibility as part of the organization. *In some way, an institutional ethic will have to develop further in the West to complement the ethic of personalism or we will have to live with the disturbing consequences of a large part of our population living in the limbo beyond praise or blame.*

If there is an excess of personalism among the youth, that may be because we have ridiculed patriotism, been cynical about institutional loyalty, and been embarrassed about team spirit. (Witness the proposals to have athletes at the Olympics compete as individuals and not as nationals of a particular country.) *We have carelessly dismantled most vestiges of liturgy in modern life, unmindful of the deep need in the human breast of some form of communal ritual. We have fostered individualism but have done precious little to show how the individual can achieve satisfaction in our organizations. In sum, organizations in essentially their present form will be a lasting necessity, and the selfish personalist will find such organizations unsatisfying. As an institutional ethic grows in society, the situation may improve. In parallel, business leaders can modify personnel practices and policies to foster a sense of community in a firm so that the community feels collective guilt* and shame for poor product quality or a damaged environment and—equally important—grows in self-esteem through a job well done.

*From*

# THE WHISTLE BLOWER AS ENTREPRENEUR*

## *By Robert Townsend*

\*    \*    \*    \*    \*

. . . Who's causing this winter of our discontent? Russians? Chinese? Domestic Communists? Long-haired kids? Military juggernauts? Lack of leadership?

In my opinion, the enemy is organizations. Big organizations. They accumulate large amounts of money and power, and if they're private corporations they chase narrow antisocial goals in the name of the almighty dollar.

Who are we going to look to, to make these giant organizations honest—to make them stop destroying the quality of all our lives (including theirs and their employees') for their own private interests?

The government? Union Carbide has all the know-how in chemistry, the government practically none; General Motors all the know-how in automobiles, the government just what they're allowed to know. And those government officials that can't be snowed can be bought. The military juggernaut owns John Stennis, body and soul.

The law? Union Camp, Inc., dictated the laws which enabled it to turn the Savannah River into an open sewer.

Corporate leaders? No, but why not? In my judgment, there are two reasons. First, we have a double legal standard in this country. . . . Standard Oil of California drew a million-dollar fine—the biggest in corporate history. It amounts to what they take in, in revenues, in two hours. If you earned $168 a week, the equivalent for you would be a two-dollar fine. So there's work to be done to eliminate the double legal standard and let the punishment fit the crime.

The second reason we can't expect leadership from our corporate moguls is that at the moment of assuming command we unfit them for the job. What we should do is tell them to take off their coat, go out among their people and their customers, and find out at first hand what the problems and opportunities are. What we do is give them two more secretaries, a private limousine, a private helicopter, a private elevator, a private dining room, a big increase in pay, and outside directorships. . . .

America became great in engineering and production because of its entrepreneurs. It was great at taking the calculated risk. Recently we've seen lawyers and accountants become chief executives. These people are trained in the elimination of risks—they know how to play it safe. Anybody—who has been there knows that nine times out of ten the safe way is the surest way to oblivion. . . .

\*    \*    \*    \*    \*

This is why we need whistle blowers.

Whistle blowing has a long, distinguished corporate tradition. Most companies today have an internal audit operation, which goes around to the various offices and branches and supposedly blows the whistle on wrongdoing. Most companies have certified public accountants (the financial equivalent of the family doctor) to give them an annual checkup. Unfortunately, these operations wind up doing little more than counting the petty cash. Nobody audits the decision to build an SST.

---

Every respectable practice has to have a father figure, and I propose Dwight Eisenhower as the modern father of whistle blowing. In his farewell address he warned us to beware of the "military-industrial complex." In retrospect, we should have paid much more attention. . . .

\*    \*    \*    \*    \*

When do we blow the whistle, Mr. Townsend? I think the answer to that is easy. Let's go back to some principles on which most Americans can agree: "Thou shalt not kill" (Exodus 20:13). "Thou shalt not steal" (Exodus 20:15). Example: A television or dental x-ray machine is released to the public with dangerous radiation. An automobile or airplane engine is released with a dangerous defect. A union leader blocks a major safety device.

Stealing can be polluting the air or water. Hypothetical case: Union Carbide is polluting the water. State, federal, and local governments start spending money and energy to get them to stop. Union Carbide starts spending large sums of money, first to pretend they're not polluting, and when that fails to stall for time. This is all done by paid liars who are normally called the public relations department. Meanwhile, two years ago one of their own scientists solved this particular pollution problem by inventing a process which turns the waste into a harmless substance. But because it costs a few dollars and didn't produce a profit, he couldn't get anybody's attention. Let him blow the whistle, and we'll make his process available, not only to his own company but to others as well.

Stealing can be Xerox Corporation avoiding the expenditure of five dollars per copy machine on a device which would reduce noise. By this omission it forces each customer to spend hundreds of dollars to isolate the machine.

Stealing can be claiming in advertising something for your product that it doesn't have, or offering services that you know you can't deliver.

If whistle blowing is going to help America, each whistle blower should ask himself "What's in it for me?" before he blows the whistle. And only blow it if you're clean. There is so much injustice and frustration in unions and corporations that the Clearinghouse could be overwhelmed with private grudges.[1]

Also, before you blow the whistle see if your case is as complete as you can make it. Suppose you were King Solomon considering the case: would you be able to verify it, are there the necessary names, dates, and facts to substantiate it? Do you have enough information so that you would be able to render a judgment?

One question which I'm sure has crossed your mind is, "Mr. Townsend, won't this whistle blowing increase costs, reduce profits? And therefore isn't it bad for the free enterprise system?" It seems to me that the answer is clear: whistle blowing may save the free enterprise system—but if our system in fact depends on unpunished lying, stealing, and murder, then who wants to save it?

My twenty years in organizations have given me great faith in individuals and absolutely no faith in large institutions. Because the leaders of large organizations are distracted and corrupted by luxuries and the trappings of corporate success, they have no time to consider fundamental values like honesty, truth, and justice. They have no time to listen to the voices of their own people who know what's right and what's wrong with their products and services. Not knowing what's wrong, the leaders speak to the public only with the forked tongues of their public relations department.

On three totally separate occasions I set out to build honest organizations in which the goals were known, there was no secrecy, and a real effort was made to see that everybody got what they deserved. In each case, the results were electrifying—in human energy, in fun, and in profits. The reason for this is plain—everybody else working for a big organization is so disgusted, frustrated, or bored that he can barely deliver 20 percent of his energy toward the corporate goal if it has any. People from coast to coast are sick of the nauseating

---

[1] Editor's Note: The Clearinghouse on Professional Responsibility is an agency assuring confidentiality for "whistle blowers" as an alternative to quitting or suffering in silence, cf. R. Nader, "A Case for Uncommon Courage," *Personnel Administration,* November–December 1971.

phoniness, triviality, and waste of big organizations. Give them a chance to work for a company which fires the paid liars, deals openly, tells the truth—in short, a company they can be proud of—and maybe you've started to save the free enterprise system.

*From*

# THE CHEMIST'S CREED*

*Approved by the American Chemical Society*[1]

AS A CHEMIST, I HAVE A RESPONSIBILITY:

*to the public*
to propogate a true understanding of chemical science, avoiding premature, false, or exaggerated statements, to discourage enterprises or practices inimical to the public interest or welfare, and to share with other citizens a responsibility for the right and beneficient use of scientific discoveries.

*to my science*
to search for its truths by use of the scientific method, and to enrich it by my own contributions for the good of humanity.

*to my profession*
to uphold its dignity as a foremost branch of learning and practice, to exchange ideas and information through its societies and publications, to give generous recognition to the work of others, and to refrain from undue advertising.

*to my employer*
to serve him undividedly and zealously in mutual interest, guarding his concerns and dealing with them as I would my own.

*to myself*
to maintain my professional integrity as an individual, to strive to keep abreast of my profession, to hold the highest ideals of personal honor, and to live an active, well-rounded, and useful life.

*to my employees*
to treat them as associates, being ever mindful of their physical and mental well-being, giving them encouragement in their work, as much freedom for personal development as is consistent with the proper conduct of work, and compensating them fairly, both financially and by acknowledgment of their scientific contributions.

*to my students and associates*
to be a fellow learner with them, to strive for clarity and directness of approach, to exhibit patience and encouragement, and to lose no opportunity for stimulating them to carry on the great tradition.

*to my clients*
to be a faithful and incorruptible agent, respecting confidence, advising honesty, and charging fairly.

---

* From *Whistle Blowing* edited by Ralph Nader, Peter Petkas, and Kate Blackwell. Copyright © 1972 by Ralph Nader. Reprinted by permission of Grossman Publishers.

[1] Approved by the Council of the American Chemical Society, September 14, 1965

# 19. UNIVERSITY OF WASHINGTON LAW SCHOOL

---

## Case Introduction

---

### SYNOPSIS

Professor John Bell, a member of the Admissions Committee of the University of Washington Law School, was considering whether to admit Franklin Martin into Law School. Mr. Martin was a white graduate of the University of California in political science. He had qualifications similar to Marco DeFunis whom had not been admitted a few years earlier. Mr. DeFunis, after waiting a year to be admitted, had sued the University of Washington and its president because person with less qualification than he had been admitted. Reverse discrimination had been a major issue in the legal case which was never really resolved. Mr. DeFunis had been admitted by court order and was near graduation before his case made its way to the Supreme Court where it was ruled mute. The Admissions Committee of the Law School, once again, had to establish an admissions policy which would be socially responsible and would withstand the test of a legal challenge.

### WHY THIS IS INCLUDED

The University of Washington Law School case illustrates a number of problems associated with affirmative action programs. Such programs are designed to bring about social justice by increasing the representation of minority groups in occupations, professional schools, and in the professions so that they can more equally share in the benefits of society. Students are called upon to reflect on the trade-offs between social equality and productivity.

Also central to the case is the problem of reverse discrimination against members of majority groups when preferential admissions or hiring policies are used. Other issues such as moral rights and legal rights associated with private property can be introduced into a discussion of this area. All of these dimensions help to make the student aware of the difficulties involved in making policies which bring about social justice and organizational effectiveness. Although this case deals with a public university, the basic policy issues involved are of much importance to private enterprise and to other public organizations.

## PREDICTIVE AND DIAGNOSTIC QUESTIONS

The readings included with this case are marked (*). The author index at the end of this book locates the other readings.

1. Drawing from the facts of the case, identify the major social objectives of the University of Washington Law School which need to be reflected in its admissions policy?

Read:   *Cobbs, "Egalitarianism: Threat to a Free Market." *Robertson, "Employment Testing and Discrimination."

2. One admission policy criterion would be to admit the most qualified applicants. Alternatively the admission policy could emphasize admitting those who are likely to succeed in law school but not necessarily those applicants who are most qualified. Which of these approaches best characterizes the policy followed by the University of Washington Law School? What goals are implicit in these alternatives?

Read:   *Cobbs, "Egalitarianism: Threat to a Free Market." *Thomson, "Preferential Hiring."

3. A basis goal as well as a principle of social justice is equality. According to Cobbs, the definition of equality as it relates to social policy has been changing from equality of opportunity to equality of effect. How might this change be reflected in the admission policy of a law school?

Read:   *Cobbs, "Egalitarianism: Threat to a Free Market." *Thomson, "Preferential Hiring."

4. Thompson suggests that preferential hiring might be used as a social instrument to correct past social injustices relating to discrimination against minorities. Could a policy of preferential admissions also be used for this purpose? What theories or reasoning would Thompson be likely to use as a basis for this policy at the University of Washington Law School?

Read:   *Thomson, "Preferential Hiring."

5. One argument made on behalf of preferential admissions policy favoring black students is that black graduates from law school would serve as good role models for black youths. What arguments can you develop which would favor such a position? What would be the possible disadvantages of a policy of preferring black students in admissions decisions?

Read:   *Cobbs, "Egalitarianism: Threat to a Free Market." *Thomson, "Preferential Hiring." *Simon, "Preferential Hiring: A Reply to Judith Harvis Thomson."

6. Assume for a moment that this case situation occurred at a privately owned and financed university law school. In what way, if any, would the use of a preferential admissions policy be more or less appropriate?

Read: *Robertson, "Employment Testing and Discrimination."
*Thomson, "Preferential Hiring." *Ezorsky, "It's Mine."

7. Although DeFunis' attorneys did not make the issue of reverse discrimation the major thrust of their legal suit, this issue was of much importance to the case. What is the major justification for practicing reverse discrimination to redress social injustice? Is it fair to ask DeFunis to pay for possible injustice experienced by minority group members? Explain.

Read: *Thomson, "Preferential Hiring." *Simon, "Preferential Hiring: A Reply to Judity Jarvis Thomson."

8. The minority opinion of Justice Douglas mentioned in the case seems to suggest that DeFunis may not have been the victim of reverse discrimination. What would be the basis of such a claim?

Read: *Robertson, "Employment Testing and Discrimination."

9. Assume that the admissions test used by the University of Washington Law School were legally or morally challenged as discriminatory. What would be the responsibility of the university if it wished to make a just decision in the use of the test from a legal and moral point of view?

Read: *Robertson, "Employment Testing and Discrimination."
*Ezorsky, "It's Mine."

## POLICY QUESTIONS

10. Develop a statement of broad goals for the University of Washington Law School which you feel are most appropriate.

Read: Review reading for Questions 1 through 3 above.

11. Assume that you are an assistant to the Secretary of Health, Education, and Welfare and have been asked to help develop a national policy for higher education. Would you be in favor of a policy involving preferential admissions? Briefly explain what sort of policy you favor and why.

Read: Review reading for Questions 1 through 5 above.

12. Based upon your statement of goals, outline a list of criteria to guide policy for making admissions decisions for the University of Washington Law School.

Read: Review readings for Questions 6 through 9 above.

13. Assume that you were a member of the Admissions Committee at the University of Washington Law School and have been asked to make a recommendation as to whether or not Franklin D. Martin should be admitted. State your recommendation and briefly outline basic reasons in support of your decisions.

# Case Text*

In January 1977, Professor John Bell, a member of the Admissions Committee of the University of Washington Law School, was considering two problems which he saw as, "important to the future of the Law School as a responsible institution in society."

The first problem is a specific, immediate (some would say tactical) one. It is whether to admit Franklin D. Martin, a graduate of the University of California in Political Science. He is white, comes from a middle-income family in San Francisco, has an overall grade point average between B+ and A— (3.71). In his senior year he had straight As. His predicted first-year average (PFYA) is 76.65. Regarding all of the other things I believe are important (his writing test score of 66, recommendations from professors in advanced seminars, recommendations from the place he worked two years between undergraduate school graduation and the present), he ranks high. I am guessing that the relative position of this person will be somewhat the same as Marco DeFunis. I came across Martin's application because I take a random sample of admission folders and review them early in the year, to try to get an indication if this year's total applicant group is higher or lower than in previous years. I believe we are going to have about the same proportion of "most promising" candidates, and a somewhat higher number of minority applications.

The second problem is a broader, longer range one. It is the question of the ultimate goals, or missions, of a university law school. We exist to serve society, in the last analysis. Our product is a group of people who can, among other things, help to keep the system of English common law operating in a way that it is highly regarded, respected and obeyed. This common law is a delicate and beautiful thing, in that it is part of the apparatus in society that enables us to provide a government based on relative freedom and democracy.

There are two ways laws can be made. One is by some group at the top legislating rules that apply to everybody. Legislative law results when one group of people decide what society ought to be like. Common Law is opposite in that it starts with what people, "at the bottom" *do* in a given conflict situation (say, an automobile accident). The judge looks at the specific case, including why they

---

* Copyright 1977, Charles E. Summer and Scott Hickey. Professor Bell's and Mr. Martin's names have been disguised.

did it, under what conditions. He then takes all factors into account and renders a decision, which is the "law" for that specific case. The judge *discovers* the law.

Over time, there are many automobile accidents. No two are alike. One driver may run a red light while under the influence of alcohol. Another may run a red light taking a pregnant wife to the hospital. Both hit another car and kill someone. Should both serve the same length of time in prison? Only a judge, looking at the specific case, can decide what justice is.

The graduate today must be able to perform a certain series of mental processes if he is to act as a lawyer, or judge, *discovering* just laws. If he gets an accident case, he must be able to *analyze* it—break it down into component characteristics. Then he must be able to do research covering a sample of thousands of other cases in which judges have exercised judgment. When he finds a series of cases that are similar to the one at hand, he must inductively find the *principle of law* in these and apply that principle to the present case. As adversary lawyers do this, they often find conflicting principles—prosecution lawyers cite customs of society which tell the judge to do one thing. Defense lawyers cite customs of society that tell the judge to do another. When a judgment is rendered, this case itself becomes part of the parade of society's custom for future cases.

This system, if it can be maintained in modern society, is in some senses vastly superior to a legislature sitting at the top masterminding computer type rules such as, "all persons who run a red light and kill somebody are sentenced to 15 years in jail." For one thing, it provides for a defendant to explain a multitude of reasons why he might do something, rather than rely on the computer program to treat everyone just alike, regardless of the total richness of the situation. For another, it provides for hundreds of lawmaker judges throughout the nation, living among people, rather than one body of lawmakers living in Washington. Finally, the judges are influenced by the beliefs of people around them, as these change over time, rather than by a law written a number of years ago by legislators who lived at another place in another time. This is the reason that common law *evolves* from customs of the population, instead of being *made* by the logic of a few legislators. It is the reason that common-law systems tend to last and be respected by the people longer than, say, rational systems enacted by highly centralized legislative rule systems.

In terms of admissions policies, our product must be able not only to analyze, but to synthesize principles. Students must conceptualize the law from vast quantities of data. They must have also a liberal education, so that their minds are perceptive of many things going on around them. Science and the humanities, of course, help one to become an "educated" person, a worldly person. That is why law schools require a good undergraduate education before enrolling in law.

After you understand the DeFunis situation, you will understand my concern about these two problems. I hope to arrive at a decision on Martin (and voice it in the committee) that will contribute to both our duty to turn out lawyers with the knowledge and mental skills necessary, and our duty to educate minority lawyers who are free from economic or other types of racial discrimination. There is no doubt but that our school must help to rectify the injustice that has been done to minority groups.

## Marco DeFunis, Jr. Applied for Admission

Marco DeFunis graduated from high school with close to a straight A average and, in 1970, from the University of Washington with a grade average of 3.62 (3.0 is B., 4.0 would be straight A). His junior-senior year average was 3.71. In political science, his major, it was 3.85. He was elected to Phi Beta Kappa, the highest scholastic honorary in the university, and graduated magna cum laude. He applied to four law schools and was accepted by all except the University of Washington, where he was put on the waiting list in May 1970. In August he was turned down, but told that chances were better of being admitted in the 1971 class. Because of his preference for this particular school, he attended graduate school in political science at Washington, working for the Seattle Park Department at the same time, and earned a grade point average of 4.0 (straight As) during the year. In some graduate courses he received A+ on papers, with remarks by professors that his work was exceptional.

During that year he took the LSAT (Law School Admissions Test) for the third time with a score of 668, in the top 7 percent of all law school applicants in the United States. This score was submitted to the law school when he re-applied for 1971.

On May 12, 1971, he was notified that he had not been admitted, but put on the waiting list, located in the lowest quartile of the list. At that point, DeFunis' parents retained a lawyer who contacted the Admissions Committee and, among other things, submitted letters from DeFunis' medical doctor stating that he was ill at the time he took his first LSAT. DeFunis had actually taken the test three times. On June 15 the Admissions Committee reconsidered DeFunis' position, deciding that his position on the list should remain as it was. On June 21 the committee decided that all individuals in the third and forth quartiles would have to be denied admission.

## School Procedures and Their Application to DeFunis

The Admissions Committee at that time began with grade averages in the junior/senior years (DeFunis' was 3.71) and LSAT scores. The latter range for most applicants between 400–700, with 500 as the norm or median (DeFunis' was 61.3 average). The school then combined these three factors into the "Predicted First-Year Average (PFYA: DeFunis' was 76.23).

Early in the 1970–71 year, the committee, consisting of nine professors

and three law students, decided that it would (1) define as "most promising" those applicants above 77 PFYA (based on last year's applications),
(2) review the most promising candidates in batches of 25–30 as soon as
these batches were processed, (3) assign each of these files to one member
who would study it thoroughly and present it to the committee, (4) assign
all nonminority candidates with PFYA's below 74.5 to the chairman who
would either reject them or put them in a group for committee review
(based on whether he judged there was information indicating that the
person had better potential for law study than the low PFYA would indicate), (5) accumulate all files between 74.5 and 76.99, holding them until
all applications were in, so that they could be looked at together, and (6)
assign minority applicants below 74.5 to a subcommittee composed of a
black student, a professor who worked closely with the Council of Legal
Education Opportunity (CLEO), or Professor Hunt.

The committee followed these procedures and, by August 1, 1971,
when DeFunis was denied admission, 275 students had been admitted
to the school and 55 were on the waiting list. Of this 330, 224 had lower
junior/senior grades than Defunis. Of the 275, 74 (36 were minority applicants) had lower PFYA's than DeFunis. Here are the applications
accepted based on PFYA's:

**EXHIBIT 1***

| Predicted First-Year Average | Number of Applications Received | Number of Applications Accepted |
| --- | --- | --- |
| 81 ............. | 1 | 1 |
| 80 ............. | 2 | 2 |
| 79 ............. | 11 | 11 |
| 78 ............. | 42 | 42 |
| 77 ............. | 105 | 93 |
| 76 ............. | 169 | 53 |
| 75 ............. | 210 | 22 |

* Ann Fagar Givgu, ed., *DeFunis* v. *Odegaard and the University of Washington* (New York: Oceana Publications, Inc., 1974), vol. I, p. 35.

The law school explained in its "Guide for Applicants" that:

We began by trying to identify applicants who had the potential
for outstanding performance in law school. We attempted to select
applicants for admission from that group on the basis of their ability to make significant contributions to law school classes and to the
community at large.

We gauged the potential for outstanding performance in law
school not only from the existence of high test scores and grade
point averages, but also from careful analysis of recommendations,
the quality of work in difficult analytical seminars, courses, and
writing programs, the academic standards of the school attended

by the applicant, the applicant's graduate work (if any), and the nature of the applicant's employment (if any), since graduation.

An applicant's ability to make significant contributions to law school classes and the community at large was assessed from such factors as his extracurricular and community activities, employment, and general background.

## Marco DeFunis Took the Matter to King County Superior Court

On petition of Marco Defunis, Judge Shorett of King County Superior Court issued an order that DeFunis should be admitted to the law school in September until the matter could be settled in court. In subsequent hearings, Judge Shorett heard evidence from the university as to what had happened and why. He also noted that the complaint by Defunis had two main contentions: that the list of applicants who were admitted (or ahead of DeFunis in line) contained "many candidated whose qualifications and credentials are much below the credentials and qualifications of DeFunis; and that many were not residents or taxpayers of the state of Washington, as DeFunis was. Judge Shorett ruled that the out-of-state admissions policy of the (graduate) law school was up to the school itself, under the State Constitution. But he found that the other (qualifications) complaint was a matter which should be decided by the courts. DeFunis had never made a point of the fact that *minority* candidates with lower qualifications were admitted ahead of him. In fact, his lawyers objected when the university brought up the point in its defense—that most of the students admitted with lower scores were from minority groups. In his testimony, Law Dean Roddis said:

> As to members of certain minority groups, the Committee evaluates the qualifications of applicants separately and I think with less emphasis on the undergraduate grade point averages and the LSAT scores than they do with respect to the applicants of the majority groups. Part of the reason for separately evaluating the minority students is the feeling that due to educational and cultural disadvantage that may have characterized . . . the people from those groups that you simply cannot assess their qualifications on the basis of the grades and the LSAT score, so it becomes a little difficult for me to say that they are less qualified. . . . I hesitate to simply make the assertion they are necessarily less qualified, but it is fair to say that on the basis of those criteria which we do emphasize with respect to the majority students, on the face of it, they are apparently less qualified.
>
> We are seeking a representation of students from minority groups . . . for two basic reasons.
>
> One is that it is an important factor . . . in the educational environment of a law school in this era. I do not think it is even necessary . . . to explain why that should be true.
>
> Second, and this is more fundamental, we . . . are dealing with groups of people who, for a very long period of time, have been

subjected to a pervasive attern of economic and political and legal discrimination and suppression. . . . These groups do not have the opportunities that others have had. The other consequence is that they, as groups, tend to be widely disaffected with law, they are not well represented. Hence, . . . it is a policy of paramount social importance on an national and state level to rapidly increase the participation and representation of people from these groups in the profession, to the end that they may serve to some extent the interests of their own people, and hopefully will enhance the sense of involvement in the legal system of people from these groups and reduce the sense of alienation from it. . . .

We do not go down to the point of taking people that we think are unqualified, and that is an important point. I think the illustration of that is the fact that we have resisted the temptation which we have been importuned to follow from time to time, of establishing fixed quotas. We do not have a quota; we do not say we are going to take X number of black students no matter what. We want a reasonable representation. We will go down to reach it if we can, but we do not want to go to the point where we are taking people who are unqualified in an absolute sense, and that is that they have no reasonable probable likelihood of having a chance of succeeding in the study of law with such academic supportive assistance that we can give them.

Dean Roddis also pointed out that he believed that DeFunis was competent and capable of successfully succeeding in law school. On October 19, 1971, Judge Shorett rendered the following opinion, and recommended speedy review by the State Supreme Court:

It seems to me that the law school here wished to achieve a greater minority representation and in accomplishing this gave preference to the members of some races. In doing this the Admissions Committee assumed that all members of minority races, with the exception of Asians, were deprived persons. . . . Some minority students were admitted whose college grades and aptitude test scores were so low that had they been whites their applications would have been summarily denied. Excluding the Asians, only one minority student out of 31 admitted among the applicants had a predicted first year average above the plaintiff's.

Since no more than 150 applicants were to be admitted the admission of less qualified resulted in a denial of places to those otherwise qualified. The plaintiff and others in this group, have not in my opinion, been accorded the equal protection of the law guaranteed by the Fourteenth Amendment. In 1954 the United States Supreme Court in *Brown* v. *The Board of Education* decided that public education must be equally available to all regardless of race. After that decision the Fourteenth Amendment could no longer be stretched to accommodate the needs of any race. Policies of discrimination will inevitably lead to reprisals. In my opinion the only safe rule is to treat all races alike and I feel that is what is required under the equal protection clause.

### Supreme Court, State of Washington

After lengthy and complicated testimony, the State Supreme Court rendered an opinion on March 8, 1973 (7–2) that reversed the decision of the lower court, and holding that the university had not acted unwisely in the handling of DeFunis' application.

The majority of the court found it necessary to analyze (split up) the contentions of Defunis into three subquestions for decision. Each of these is taken up in the following paragraphs.

First, can race ever be considered as one factor in the admission policy of a state school (or) are *all* race classifications unconstitutional because equal protection of law requires admissions committees to be "color blind"?

In answering, the court found that Judge Shorett made a mistake in citing the principle in *Brown* v. *Board of Education.*

> *Brown* did not hold that all racial classifications are per se unconstitutional; rather, it held that invidious racial classifications —i.e., those that stigmatize a racial group with the stamp of inferiority—are unconstitutional. Even viewed in a light most favorable to plaintiff, the "preferential" minority admissions policy administered by the law school is clearly not a form of invidious discrimination. The goal of this policy is not to separate the races, but to bring them together.
>
> While *Brown* certainly provides a strating point for our analysis of the instant case, we do not agree with the trial court that *Brown* is dispositive here. Subsequent decisions of the United States Supreme Court have made it clear that in some circumstances a racial criterion may be used—and indeed in some circumstances must be used—by public educational institutions in bringing about racial balance. School systems which were formerly segregated de jure now have an affirmative duty to remedy racial imbalance. (See *Swann* v. *Charlotte-Mecklenburg Board of Education* and *Green* v. *County School Board.*) . . .
>
> Thus, the Constitution is color conscious to prevent the perpetuation of discrimination and to undo the effects of past segregation. In holding invalid North Carolina's antibussing law, which flatly forbade assignment of any student on account of race or for the purpose of creating a racial balance or ratio in the schools and which prohibited bussing for such purposes, the Court stated: "The statute exploits and apparently neutral form to control school assignment plans by directing that they be 'color blind'; that requirement, against the background of segregation, would render illusory the promise of *Brown.* Just as the race of students must be considered in determining whether a constitutional violation has occurred, so also must race be considered in formulating a remedy."

Second, if law schools can consider race in applications, what is the proper standards of review to ensure that this is done wisely? Here the majority found that:

> [W]here the classification is based upon race, a heavier burden of justification is imposed upon the state. In overturning Virginia's antimiscegenation law, the Supreme Court explained this stricter standard of review: "The clear and central purpose of the Fourteenth Amendment was to eliminate all official state sources of invidious racial discrimination in the State. . . . At the very least, the Equal Protection Clause demands that racial classfications, especially suspect in criminal statutes, be subjected to the 'most rigid scrutiny,' and, if they are ever to be upheld, they must be shown to be necessary to the accomplishment of some permissible state objective, independent of the racial discrimination which it was the object of the Fourteenth Amendment to eliminate. . . ." The burden is upon the law school to show that its consideration of race in admitting students is necessary to the accomplishment of a *compelling state interest.*

The third and final question raised and answered by the majority is, does the *specific* policy applied by this law school correspond correctly with the above constitutional principles? In answer, the opinion held:

> It can hardly be gainsaid that the minorities have been, and are, grossly under-represented in the law schools—and consequently in the legal profession—of this state and this nation. We believe the state has an overriding interest in promoting integration in public education. In light of the serious underrepresentation of minority groups in the law schools, and considering that minority groups participate on an equal basis in the tax support of the law school, we find the state interest in eliminating racial imbalance within public legal education to be compelling. . . .
>
> Once a constitutionally valid state interest has been established, it remains for the state to show the requisite connection between the racial classification employed and that interest. The consideration of race in the law school admissions policy meets the test of necessity here because racial imbalance in the law school and the legal profession is the evil to be corrected, and it can only be corrected by providing legal education to those minority groups which have been previously deprived.

Finally the court responded to DeFunis' complaint that, by not going strictly by the numerical PFYA test, the Admissions Committee procedures were "arbitrary and capricious." The court answered, "We do not agree that taking into account subjective (nonnumerical) factors, and the exercise of judgment on these, constitutes arbitrary and capricious action. Actually, although the PFYA was a very important factor, it was not the sole determinative factor for any group of students."

## The Minority Opinion

Judge Hale, writing for the two-person minority, called attention to the case of *Anderson* v. *San Francisco Unified School District.* The principle in that case, that a classification based on race is not valid, is also applicable to the *DeFunis* case. A San Francisco school district had plans to give preference in employment and promotions to minorities. The U.S. District Court of San Francisco held that, "Preferential treatment under the guise of 'affirmative action' is the imposition of one form of racial discrimination in place of another. The questions that must be asked in this regard are: must an individual sacrifice his right to be judged on his own merit by accepting discrimination based solely on the color of his skin? How can we achieve the goal of equal opportunity for all if, in the process, we deny equal opportunity to some."

Judge Hale further reasoned the minority opinion:

Racial prejudice and intolerance will never be ended by exalting the political rights of one group or class over that of another. The circle of inequality cannot be broken by shifting the inequalities from one man to his neighbor. To aggrandize the first will, to the extent of the aggrandizement, diminish the latter. There is no remedy at law except to abolish all class distinctions heretofore existing in law. For that reason, the constitutions are, and ever ought to be, color blind. . . .

The court, as I see it, upholds palpably discriminatory law school admissions practices of the state university mainly because they were initiated for the . . . purpose of enhancing the opportunities of member of . . . ethnic minorities. It thus suggests a new rule of constitutional interpretation to be applied here that, if the administrative intentions are adequately noble in purpose, Mr. DeFunis may be deprived of equal protection of the laws and certain special immunities and privileges may be granted to others which, on the same terms, are denied to him. . . .

In deciding which particular groups should be classified as ethnic minorities, the committee on admissions first made an assumption supported by no evidence whatever, i.e., that all of the accepted minority students except Asian-Americans were of a lower economic status than Mr. DeFunis. No comparative investigation or study as to the financial condition or economic background was made to establish the relative economic and cultural condition of the students applying. It was thus categorically assumed that the ethnic minority applicants were, to use the descriptive term current in academic circles, culturally deprived—meaning, one must suppose, that the environmental factors surrounding a minority student and tending to affect his academic achievements were of a lower order than those surrounding white or majority students. This sweeping and unsupported assumption, derived from no real evidence whatever, that all of the admitted minority students were both poor and culturally deprived, supplied the modus vivendi for the scheme of preferences. It ignored the correlative assumption which inevitably had to be made that neither Mr. DeFunis nor any of the non-minority applicants had been equally culturally or economically deprived. . . .

If this be constitutional, then, of course, the constitutions are not color blind; one racial group may be given political or economic preferment over another solely because of race or ethnic origin. Yet, this was the very thing that the Fourteenth Amendment was designed to prevent. All races, and all individuals, are entitled to equal opportunity to enter the law school. To admit some solely because of race or ethnic origin is to deny others that privilege solely for the same reasons, which in law amounts to a denial of equal protection to the one while granting special privileges and immunities to the other.

### Review of the U.S. Supreme Court

Marco Defunis continued to attend law school throughout the years 1973 and 1974, pending the final ruling of the U.S. Supreme Court. The case was appealed with Dr. Charles Odegaard, president of the University of Washington, as defendant. Thus it is known as *DeFunis* v. *Odegaard.* Under Court rules, interested lawyers and organizations throughout the nation may submit briefs, or *Amicus Curiae* in behalf of one side or the other, before the case is reviewed. About 40 of these lengthy documents were submitted. The Anti-Defamation League stressed principles from *Griggs* v. *Duke Power Company* and *Carter* v. *Gallagher.* The Council on Legal Education Opportunity cited *Associated General Contractors* v. *Alshuler* (1973). The National Conference of Black Lawyers cited *Dred Scott* v. *Sandford* (1857).

### U.S. Supreme Court: *DeFunis* v. *Odegaard*

The issues presented to the Supreme Court were essentially the same ones presented to the Washington Supreme Court, except that they were more detailed and more extensive in their factual evidence. The Court ruled, in a majority opinion that: "Because the petitioner will complete his law school studies at the end of the term for which he has now registered regardless of any decision this court might reach on the merits of this litigation, we conclude that the court cannot, consistently with the limitations of Article III of the Constitution, consider the substantive constitutional issues tendered by the parties."

There was one dissenting Justice (Douglas). He pointed out that law schools are bound to consider each application in a racially neutral way, but that the LSAT reflects cultural backgrounds, and therefore is not neutral. He also said that: "The state, however, may not proceed by racial classifications to force strict population equivalencies for every group in every occupation, overriding individual preferences. The Equal Protection Clause commands the elimination of racial barriers, not their creation in order to satisfy our theory as to how society ought to be organized."

## Present Position of the Admissions Committee

As Professor Bell ponders his position in 1977, he realizes that the courts have, in one sense, given broad powers to the Admissions Committee. It can establish any of a variety of standards and criteria it might wish, to ensure excellence of the practice of law. It can segregate certain minorities if it wishes, and treat them differently.

The real questions, in Bell's opinion, are: (1) how to treat a specific candidate, like Martin; (2) how to set up an admissions organization and procedures within the law school to execute the law school's mission in society; and (3) how to define the mission so that all parties—students, applicants and professors, may guide their actions in the future.

---

# Selected Readings

---

*From*

# EGALITARIANISM: THREAT TO A FREE MARKET*

## By John Cobbs

"Equality," said Voltaire, "is at once the most natural and most chimerical thing in the world: natural when it is limited to rights, unnatural when it attempts to level goods and powers."

The greatest single force changing and expanding the role of the federal government in the United States today is the push for equality. And while the orators of this movement still speak primarily in terms of rights, the goal increasingly is to level goods and powers in the American society. Today's egalitarians want to use the federal government to redistribute wealth and incomes, to equalize differences in education and family backgrounds, and to override the classic principle that what a man consumes must be determined by what he produces or what he owns. To achieve uniformity and equality, they are prepared to sacrifice diversity and individual liberty. The egalitarian movement is essentially authoritarian. It is highly critical of business and contemptuous of laissez-faire economics.

Business for its part sees the egalitarian push as a threat—not just to its pay scales but to the fundamental principles of a market economy. It is right. The American economy, based on private property, uses the market to determine rewards and allocate resources. Differences in pay and profit are essential to it. At some point, therefore, a move toward equality would require a shift from capitalism to a socialist or government-directed state. By all indications, the United States is still a long way from this point. But the inherent contradiction between a political democracy and a capitalist economy has yet to be resolved.

The United States has been committed since the days of Franklin Roosevelt's New Deal to a broad welfare program providing help for the poor, the aged, and the unemployed. But until now it has accepted the fact that different people will earn widely different incomes in

---

a market economy. Programs such as aid to dependent children, which make money transfers simply on the basis of need, have been justified on humanitarian grounds. The Social Security system, the biggest of all the government social programs, was designed as a nationwide insurance fund, with all participants paying something and with benefits related to contributions.

The difference now is that the new egalitarians do not ask government transfers as a matter of charity or as part of a businesslike program. They want the government to use its powers to restructure the economic system and equalize its rewards, giving to the poor a matter of right.

The strongest support for income redistribution has come from the blacks and other minorities—and lately from the women's movement. The claims of these groups have made a considerable impression not only on Congress but also on the upper-income groups that might have good economic reason to resist them. The demand for equal job opportunities and equal pay for equal work has paved the way for the assertion of a right to equal housing, education, and enjoyment of life. The obvious bite of poverty at the bottom of American society has built sympathy for the underdog.

The strength of egalitarianism, therefore, is out of proportion to the number of people who formally subscribe to it. Many egalitarians do not like the label. And many supporters of egalitarian measures will not endorse its philosophy. They see government intervention as the answer to a particular problem—poverty, old age, bad health—and they think of equality as only an incidental consequence of solving the problem. There is as yet no egalitarian party in the United States, and there probably never will be. But the push toward equality gains powerful support from shifting alliances of pressure groups that cross party lines and make strange political bedfellows.

*Action Programs.* The most obvious examples of egalitarian actions today are busing to integrate school districts and affirmative action programs designed to force employers to hire more women and more members of minorities. But the fight in the future will center on government taxing and government spending.

In one way or another, all the government's social programs are equalizers. Social Security transfers income from active workers to retired workers. Medicaid transfers from the well to the sick. Aid to education can equalize the spending power of poor school districts and rich districts—though the present program does not always achieve this result. Federal loans and scholarships open higher education to students who cannot pay tuition.

The enormous expansion of the federal budget in the past decade reflects a rapid growth in these programs. Outlays for "health and income security" totaled $27.5 billion in fiscal 1965, just before President Johnson's "war on poverty" got under way. In fiscal 1975, they added up to $136 billion—about 42 percent of total federal spending. The projection for fiscal 1976 is $151.8 billion. In addition, federal outlays for education are in the 1976 budget for $16 billion. Federal manpower programs get $6 billion. And "civil rights activities" are budgeted for $394 million.

And that is only the beginning. In a study for the American Enterprise Institute for Public Policy Research, Edgar K. Browning points out that "today there are more than 100 federal government programs conferring benefits to the poor." Many of them—such as subsidized housing and food stamps—provide benefits in kind rather than cash. Browning estimates that about 40 percent of the gross transfers to the bottom fourth of U.S. families took this form.

Welfare spending will increase and move into new areas in the decade ahead. Congressional leaders already consider national health insurance a sure bet for enactment in the next year or two. Social Security benefits will be liberalized. A group of Democratic Congressmen led by Senator Hubert Humphrey (D-Minn.) and Representative Augustus Hawkins (D-Calif.) will push a "full employment and economic opportunity" bill guaranteeing federal jobs for everyone who cannot find a place in private employment.

As the costs increase, the egalitarians will try to shift more of the burden to upper-bracket incomes. Liberals already are complaining that the payroll taxes that finance Social Security put a "regressive" load on the lowest incomes. They want to extend the tax to all incomes instead of stopping it at the $15,300 level, which it is scheduled to reach on Jan. 1, 1976. Alternatively, they would finance Social Security out of general revenue, which means that the progressive income tax would pick up more of the load.

When Caspar W. Weinberger resigned as Secretary of Health, Education and Welfare last July, he told the Commonwealth Club of San Francisco: "Federal spending has shifted away from traditional federal functions such as defense and toward programs that reduce the remaining freedom of individuals and lessen the power of other levels of government. This shift in federal spending has transformed the task of aiding life's victims from a private concern to a public obligation. There are benefits and burdens in this. . . ."

The greatest burden, as Weinberger sees it, is that "we have built an edifice of law and regulation that is clumsy, inefficient, and inequitable. Worst of all, the unplanned, uncoordinated, spasmodic nature of our responses to these needs—some very real, some only perceived—is quite literally threatening to bring us to national insolvency."

**Deep Roots.** The idea of equality is no alien latecomer to American thought. The founding fathers had read John Locke and Jean Jacques Rousseau. And though they were wary of radicals like Thomas Paine, they could see for themselves how his rhetoric stirred the ordinary colonist. The framers of the Declaration of Independence drew on this body of thought when they wrote the famous passage: "We hold these Truths to be self-evident, that all Men are created equal, that they are endowed by their Creator with certain unalienable Rights, that among these are Life, Liberty, and Pursuit of Happiness—That to secure these Rights, Governments are instituted among Men, deriving their just Powers from the Consent of the Governed. . . ."

Rousseau would not have written it quite that way. Nor would he have accepted a Constitution that was scrupulously respectful of property rights and that provided elaborate checks and balances to restrain the power of the government it created. Rousseau conceded the citizen no rights that did not coincide with what he called the "general will."

Since the Middle Ages, the general will—or at least, the will of the majority—has been asserting itself against the rights of property. Alexis de Tocqueville, that astute analyst of the democratic process, foresaw the outcome. The leveling process, he predicted, would not stop with abolishing hereditary rank and class distinctions. It would build momentum and move on. "Would it, then, be wise," he asked, "to imagine that a social impulse which dates from so far back can be checked by the efforts of a generation? Is it credible that the democracy which has annihilated the feudal system and vanquished kings will respect the citizen and the capitalist?"

What de Tocqueville foresaw was a basic change in the emphasis of the egalitarian movement—from equality before the law to equality in economic well-being. And this is what is occurring now. The egalitarian movement began as a fight for legal rights—the right to vote, the right to equal job opportunities, the right to equal pay for equal work—what the scholars call *égalité de droit.* This fight is by no means ended, as the drive for equal treatment of blacks and women in the job market demonstrates. But the goals of the egalitarians are now expressed in results rather than rights. They seek *égalité de fait*—equality of incomes and wealth, and beyond that equality of education, job satisfaction, and standing in the community. As Robert A. Nisbet, Albert Schweitzer Professor of Humanities at Columbia, observes in an article in *Commentary:* "It is result, not opportunity, that is today the central perspective in egalitarianism."

For most of the egalitarians, equality requires a major expansion in the government's role in the U.S. economy and a corresponding structural change in the federal and state apparatus. "The greatest single revolution of the last century in the political sphere," says Nisbet, "has been the transfer of effective power over human lives from the constitutionally visible offices of government, the nominally sovereign offices, to the vast network that has been brought into being in the name of protection of the people from their exploiters."

**Intellectual Dilemma.** Like all movements, egalitarianism has its literature and its gurus. The most admired of the academic writers just now is Harvard philosopher John Rawls, whose *Theory of Justice* has refurbished Rousseau's general will and adapted it to 20th-century sociology. The primary aim of society, argues Rawls, is justice or fairness, and fairness means equality—not just equality of rights but equality of condition. Instead of accepting the unequal distribution of rewards determined by the market economy, society should follow a "principle of redress." Equality of opportunity is a delusion unless it produces equality of results. Hence, "to produce genuine equality of opportunity, society must give more attention to those with fewer native assets and to those born into less favorable social positions."

"However," warns Christopher Jencks, also of Harvard, "it is equally wrong to argue that genetic inequality does not exist or that those who admit to its existence must be racists."

This is the great intellectual dilemma of the egalitarians. A look at the real world demonstrates that some men are smarter than others. Some men are more alert to the demands of the economic system and quicker to respond to them. Is there any valid reason for insisting that the fast and the slow, the successful and the unsuccessful should all arrive at the same condition at the same time?

Jencks's answer is that equalizing competence should be a high-priority goal of government policy. "The best way to equalize competence is to . . . encourage employers to reorganize work with this objective in mind."

Meantime, says Jencks, the egalitarians must "convince people that distribution of income is a legitimate political issue. . . . We need to establish the idea that the federal government is responsible not only for the total amount of national income, but for its distribution. If private decisions make the distribution too unequal, the government must be held responsible for improving the situation."

"A successful campaign for reducing economic inequality" he concludes, "probably requires two things. First, those with low incomes must cease to accept their condition as inevitable and just. Instead of assuming, like unsuccessful gamblers, that their numbers will eventually come up or that their children's numbers will, they must demand changes in the rules of the game. Second, some of those with high incomes, and especially the children of those with high incomes, must begin to feel ashamed of economic inequality."

Plenty of academic critics have arisen to do battle with Jencks, Rawls, and their allies. One of the sharpest is Robert Nisbet, who declares that "programs aiming at equality of result or condition are inevitably aligned, *have to be* aligned with large and cumbersome structures of political power."

"Equality," he adds shrewdly, "feeds on itself as no other single social value does. It is not long before it becomes more than a value. It takes on all the overtones of redemptiveness and becomes a religious rather than a secular idea."

Others are busy digging out quotations from the Austrian school of economics. Ludwig von Mises and Friedrich Hayek, who wrote the *Road to Serfdom,* saw even the modest welfare programs of the last generation as an intrusion on liberty and a start toward collectivism. The new egalitarianism is certainly consistent with their predictions.

The coolest and most objective appraisal of the egalitarians yet to appear is *Equality and Efficiency, The Big Tradeoff,* by Arthur M. Okun, senior fellow of the Brookings Institution and chairman of the Council of Economic Advisers under President Johnson. Okun likes the idea of equality: "Abstracting from the costs and the consequences, I would prefer more equality of income to less and would like complete equality of income best of all." But he points out that equality of condition involves costs that equality of rights does not. "In pursuing such a goal, society would forego any opportunity to use material rewards as incentives to production. And that would lead to inefficiencies that would be harmful to the welfare of the majority. Any insistence on carving the pie into equal slices would shrink the size of the pie. That fact poses the trade-off between economic equality and economic efficiency. Insofar as inequality does serve to promote efficiency . . . I can accept some measure of it as a practicality."

**Momentum.** Most of the liberals in the U.S. politics today would join Okun somewhere in the middle of the road and accept a substantial measure of inequality as the price of maintaining an efficient market system. But as the liberals see it, the equalizing trend that began under Franklin Roosevelt and acquired new life from Lyndon Johnson's Great Society is still nowhere near the stopping point. The very fact that the United States has made a start toward equality has created a demand for faster progress.

Senator Humphrey keeps a quote of his own from de Tocqueville filed for ready reference in a ring binder on his office shelf: "The sufferings that are endured patiently as being inevitable become intolerable the moment that it appears that there might be an escape. Reform then only serves to reveal more clearly what still remains oppressive and now all the more unbearable; the suffering, it is true, has been reduced, but one's sensitivity has become more acute."

Humphrey is pushing for tax reform, more government spending, and more government planning. The tax burden on the poor and the middle incomes has increased, he says, because the share of total government revenues raised by sales taxes, property taxes, excises, and Social Security payroll taxes has increased. The elderly have suffered most from inflation, and the blacks are still far behind the rest of society in incomes and education.

The United States, Humphrey argues, has gone too far down the road toward a just society to turn back now. It must do more to pull up the bottom, though that need not mean pulling down the top.

Leon Keyserling, chairman of President Truman's Council of Economic Advisers and since then a vigorous liberal spokesman, sees equality as part of the problem of economic growth. "I am not in favor of perfect equality," he says. "I believe in rewards and capital accumulation." But he blames "unsound" income distribution for the boom-bust record of the past decade. "It does not keep the American economy operating at full use of its resources," he says, "and it does not provide maximum human benefits."

Keyserling is not bothered by the trade-off between equality and efficiency. As he sees it, "The social and the economic optimum is the same. The best economic solution will be the best social solution."

Keyserling favors reform of what he considers a regressive tax system, a universal federal income-support program, more public spending, and easier money. He is enthusiastic about the proposal to enact a "full employment and opportunity" bill, setting the unemployment target for the United States at 3 percent and providing for a "national purposes" budget to identify consumption and investment levels consistent with that goal. "The main function of national policy," he remarks tartly, "is not to forecast but to set goals and reach them."

A small but vociferous group of politicians regard Humphrey and Keyserling as pussyfooters. American society, they say, needs restructuring, and the people know it. A deep vein of discontent is waiting to be mined by any political leader with the courage to stand up for equality.

Former Senator Fred Harris (D-Okla.) obviously is prospecting for this vein as he tries to launch a Presidential bid based on attacks on business, the rich, and the establishment. Much of what he is saying strangely echoes the oratory of George Wallace, whose antiestablishment campaign has given a new twist to the populist tradition in America. Both owe a good deal to Huey Long, who discovered a generation ago that an unbeatable political machine could be built on the slogan, "Every man a king."

At this point, however, the real push in the egalitarian movement is not coming from the politicians. It is coming from organizations with clearly defined demands—from blacks, from women, from welfare workers who are now so numerous they constitute a power bloc of their own. It is also coming from the leaders of the new unions of government employees, who are not only determined to increase their own incomes and job security but also want to enlarge the role of government in the United States.

The older American labor unions are less likely to think in terms of equality. In the past decade, the unions' insistent demands for pay increases without matching increases in productivity have amounted to a bid to enlarge labor's share of national product at the expense of the shareholder and the rentier. But as Labor Secretary John T. Dunlop observes, the unions are always in favor of higher minimum wages, but they want to maintain pay differentials, too. Unions, such as the United Steelworkers, traditionally have split each negotiated wage increase into two parts, with some going to across-the-board increases and the rest enlarging the increments between jobs.

The new unions of government employees are different. Egalitarian measures are a source of jobs for them, because more intervention calls for a bigger government apparatus. Moreover, the nature of their work—especially welfare and teaching—makes them sympathetic to the goals of the egalitarians.

When Albert Shanker, head of the New York teachers' union, suggested that schooling should start at the age of three, he was trying to create more jobs to avoid the layoffs that threatened in his financially desperate school system. But he was also proposing one of the favorite prescriptions of the academic egalitarians, who see education as the great equalizer.

The true believers in equalizing are eagerly watching Britain, where the Labor government is putting some of their theories into action. On Jan. 1, 1976, the British government will end its subsidies to the so-called "direct grant" schools that admit only the more promising students. These schools will have to make a choice between becoming totally independent, paying their own way with fees, or entirely government financed, with no restrictive admissions requirements.

The private education issue is less important in the United States, where the tradition of free public schools is strong. But the American egalitarians and the British have the same objectives.

Paradoxically, the more the United States grows, the stronger the push for equality becomes. Economist Lester Thurow sums up the argument: "Maximizing economic output may be so important in a poor country that society is willing to tolerate inequalities among individuals if this is necessary to produce rapid growth. . . . As output increases, however, the value attached to increases in output for future generations probably decreases. . . . Thus, the relative importance of achieving a more equal distribution of output arises. . . . From this vantage point, equality is a superior good. The richer we become, the more of it we can afford."

*From*

# EMPLOYMENT TESTING AND DISCRIMINATION*

*By David E. Robertson*

The goal of equal employment opportunity legislation is to insure that all candidates are considered on the basis of merit rather than race, religion, sex or national origin. The goal of an employer's selection and placement efforts is to staff the organization with people who can perform effectively, basing decisions on achievement rather than ascriptive criteria. The goal of the individual candidate is, or should be, placement in a position where he can accept responsibility and earn rewards commensurate with his aspirations and abilities. Placement in a position that either far exceeds or does not meet an individual's performance potential will frustrate these goals.

In theory, the goal of the law, the goal of the selection and placement process, and the goal of persons affected by these forces are entirely consistent and there is much room for harmony and mutual reinforcement. In practice, however, there is little harmony and much confusion. Some personnel managers apparently believe that testing is now illegal except

* *Personnel Journal,* vol. 54, No. 1, January, 1975, pp. 18–19 (excerpts). Reprinted by permission.

for skill tests of the type which require only content validity, such as a typing speed test for secretarial candidates. Others seem to feel that if a test eliminates a large number of minority candidates it must be illegal or unfair per se, and in some areas there is apparently a mistaken belief that a test must be non-verbal to qualify as being unbiased. Lack of solid information on minimum legal requirements and procedures for test validation are other factors leading to uncertainty, especially among smaller employers.

The tragedy of all these misconceptions is that personnel managers, in an effort to comply with the law, may abandon employment testing altogether and substitute subjective selection methods that result in acceptance of enough minority candidates to avoid the scrutiny of enforcement agencies. Under this situation, the goal of the law—selection and placement based on merit, rather than race—is subverted, the effectiveness of the selection and placement process is reduced, and the individual is not given consideration commensurate with his ability. The substitution of the quota system for the merit principle was not the intent of legislators, and represents at best an unsatisfactory compromise.

*    *    *    *    *

### Discrimination Defined

It is somewhat ironic that employment testing should become the whipping boy of equal opportunity employment legislation, since the drafters of the legislation explicitly approved the use of tests, except those specifically designed or used to unfairly discriminate. Title VII of the Civil Rights Act of 1964 as amended states in part:

> nor shall it be an unlawful employment practice for an employer to give and to act upon the results of any professionally developed ability test provided that such test, its administration or action upon the results is not designed, intended or used to discriminate because of race, color, religion, sex or national origin.

Early interpretations of the legality of employment practices by enforcement agencies and the courts frequently hinged upon the employer's motivation, that is, on whether or not the employer had evaluated all applicants by the same objective standard, and whether or not an employer purposefully hired or refused to hire members because they belonged to a particular group, rather than because of expectations relating to their future productivity. In recent years, however, there has been a growing realization that traditional rules and hiring practices may result in unmotivated or inadvertent discrimination. Although tests may be used to discriminate overtly, it is this latter type of unintentional bias which has complicated the testing controversy.

The reasons that standard testing practices may inadvertently discriminate against disadvantaged employment candidates have been well documented. There is frequently language bias, even in so-called "culture-free" tests, which may lead to substandard performance in some groups. Also, disadvantaged candidates with generally less education frequently have test anxiety. Poor testing program administration is usually more devastating to the disadvantaged applicant, and noise in the testing area, along with loose timing standards, frequently works to the detriment of the disadvantaged applicant. The discriminatory effect of faulty test interpretation has also been recognized. With the wide range of possible areas for inadvertent discrimination, it may be helpful to look for a moment at some examples of what practices do *not* constitute unfair discrimination.

The propensity of minority candidates to score below the general average on a particular test does not necessarily indicate that the test unfairly discriminates unless it can be proven that the minority candidates would, in fact, be as successful on the job as their higher scoring counterparts. The fairness of a test must thus be judged on the basis of the candidate's test performance as it predicts his job performance. For example, if a black applicant with below-average arithmetic skills, due to educational deprivation, is eliminated from consideration for the job by a test measuring these skills, it can not rightfully be claimed that he was unfairly discriminated against, even though this type of test will surely eliminate a dispropor-tionate number of candidates with such a background. The candidate can reasonably main-tain that his condition is remedial and that the organization or society is obligated to help him overcome this handicap. The test itself cannot be faulted because it fairly indicated a likelihood of failure.

Testing authorities and the courts have thus agreed that unfair discrimination exists only when people with equal probabilities of success on the job have unequal probabilities of being hired for the job. To put it another way, a test may be considered to be unfairly discriminatory against the members of a minority group only if the minority group members obtain a significantly lower test score than non-minority applicants, and the minority appli-cants would, in fact, be as successful as the non-minority applicants.

*    *    *    *    *

*From*

# PREFERENTIAL HIRING*

*By Judith Jarvis Thomson*

Many people are inclined to think preferential hiring an obvious injustice. I should have said "feel" rather than "think": it seems to me the matter has not been carefully thought out, and that what is in question, really, is a gut reaction.

I am going to deal with only a very limited range of preferential hirings: that is, I am concerned with cases in which several candidates present themselves for a job, in which the hiring officer finds, on examination, that all are equally qualified to hold that job, and he then straightway declares for the black, or for the woman, because he or she *is* black or a woman.

*    *    *    *    *

I mentioned several times in the preceding section the obvious fact that it is the taxpayers who support public universities. Not that private universities are wholly private: the public contributes to the support of most of them, for example by allowing them tax-free use of land, and of the dividends and capital gains on investments. But it will be the public universi-ties in which the problem appears most starkly: as I shall suggest, it is the fact of public support that makes preferential hiring in the universities problematic.

For it seems to me that—other things being equal—there is no problem about preferential hiring in the case of a wholly private college or university, that is, one which receives no measure of public support at all, and which lives simply on tuition and (non-tax-deductible) contributions.

The principle here seems to me to be this: no perfect stranger has a right to be given a benefit which is yours to dispose of; no perfect stranger even has a right to be given an equal chance at getting a benefit which is yours to dispose of. You not only needn't give the benefit to the first perfect stranger who walks in and asks for it; you needn't even give him a chance at it, as, e.g., by tossing a coin.

I should stress that I am here talking about *benefits*, that is, things which people would like to have, which would perhaps not merely please them, but improve their lives, but which they don't actually need. (I suspect the same holds true of things people do actually need, but many would disagree, and as it is unnecessary to speak here of needs, I shall not discuss them.) If I have extra apples (they're mine: I grew them, on my own land, from my own trees), or extra money, or extra tickets to a series of lectures I am giving on How to Improve Your

* Judith Jarvis Thomson, "Preferential Hiring," *Philosophy and Public Affairs* 2, No. 4 (Summer 1973). © 1973 by Princeton University Press. Excerpts reprinted by permission. Pp. 364–69, 369–73, 379, 384 (excerpts). References have been deleted from this abridgment.

Life Through Philosophy, and am prepared to give them away, word of this may get around, and people may present themselves as candidate recipients. I do not have to give to the first, or to proceed by letting them all draw straws; if I really do own the things, I can give to whom I like, on any ground I please, and in so doing, I violate no one's *rights,* I treat no one *unjustly.* None of the candidate recipients has a right to the benefit, or even to a chance at it.

There are four caveats. (1) Some grounds for giving or refraining from giving are less respectable than others. . . .

The second caveat (2) is that although I have a right to dispose of my apples as I wish, I have no right to harm, or gratuitously hurt or offend. Thus I am within my rights to refuse to give the apples to the first five because they are black (or because they are white); but I am not within my rights to say to them "I refuse to give you apples because you are black (or white) and because those who are black (or white) are inferior."

And (3) if word of my extra apples, and of my willingness to give them away, got around because I advertised, saying or implying First Come First Served Till Supply Runs Out, then I cannot refuse the first five because they are black, or white. By so advertising I have *given* them a right to a chance at the apples. . . .

And lastly (4), there may be people who would say that I don't really, or don't fully own those apples, even though I grew them on my own land, from my own trees, and therefore that I don't have a right to give them away as I see fit. . . .

Now what was in question was a job, not apples, and it may be insisted that to give a man a job is not to give him a benefit, but rather something he needs. Well, I am sure that people do need jobs, that it does not fully satisfy people's needs to supply them only with food, shelter, and medical care. Indeed, I am sure that people need, not merely jobs, but jobs that interest them, and that they can therefore get satisfaction from the doing of. But on the other hand, I am not at all sure that any candidate for a job in a university needs a job in a university. One would very much like it if all graduate students who wish it could find jobs teaching in universities; it is in some measure a tragedy that a person should spend three or four years preparing for a career, and then find there is no job available, and that he has in consequence to take work which is less interesting than he had hoped and prepared for. But one thing seems plain: no one *needs* that work which would interest him most in all the whole world of work. Plenty of people have to make do with work they like less than other work—no economy is rich enough to provide everyone with the work he likes best of all—and I should think that this does not mean they lack something they *need.* We are all of us prepared to tax ourselves so that no one shall be in need; but I should imagine that we are not prepared to tax ourselves (to tax barbers, truck drivers, salesclerks, waitresses, and factory workers) in order that everyone who wants a university job, and is competent to fill it, shall have one made available to him.

\*      \*      \*      \*      \*

What this should remind us of is that certain cases of preferential hiring might well be utterly irrational. Suppose we have an eating club, and need a new chef; we have two applicants, a qualified French chef, and a Greek who happens to like to cook, though he doesn't do it very well. We are fools if we say to ourselves "We like the Greeks, and dislike the French," so let's hire the Greek." We simply won't eat as well as we could have, and eating, after all, was the point of the club. On the other hand, it's *our* club, and so *our* job. And who shall say it is not within a man's rights to dispose of what really is his in as foolish a way as he likes?

\*      \*      \*      \*      \*

To move now from clubs to more serious matters, suppose two candidates for a civil service job have equally good test scores, but that there is only one job available. We could decide between them by coin-tossing. But in fact we do allow for declaring for A straightway, where A is a veteran, and B is not. It may be that B is a nonveteran through no fault of his own: perhaps he was refused induction for flat feet, or a heart murmur. That is, those things in virtue of which B is a nonveteran may be things which it was no more in his power to control or change than it is in anyone's power to control or change the color of his skin. Yet the fact is that B is not a veteran and A is. On the assumption that the veteran has served his country, the country owes him something. And it seems plain that giving him preference is a not unjust way in which part of that debt of gratitude can be paid.

And now, finally, we should turn to those debts which are incurred by one who wrongs another. It is here we find what seems to me the most powerful argument for the conclusion that the preferential hiring of blacks and women is not unjust.

I obviously cannot claim any novelty for this argument: it's a very familiar one. Indeed, not merely is it familiar, but so are a battery of objections to it. It may be granted that if we have wronged A, we owe him something: we should make amends, we should compensate him for the wrong done him. It may even be granted that if we have wronged A, we must make amends, that justice requires it, and that a failure to make amends is not merely callousness, but injustice. But (*a*) are the young blacks and women who are amongst the current applicants for university jobs amongst the blacks and women who were wronged? To turn to particular cases, it might happen that the black applicant is middle class, son of professionals, and has had the very best in private schooling; or that the woman applicant is plainly the product of feminist upbringing and encouragement. Is it proper, much less required, that the black or woman be given preference over a white male who grew up in poverty, and has to make his own way and earn his encouragements? Again, (*b*), did we, the current members of the community, wrong any blacks or women? Lots of people once did; but then isn't it for them to do the compensating? That is, if they're still alive. For presumably nobody now alive owned any slaves, and perhaps nobody now alive voted against women's suffrage. And (*c*) what if the white male applicant for the job has never in any degree wronged any blacks or women? If so, *he* doesn't owe any debts to them, so why should *he* make amends to them?

These objections seem to me quite wrong-headed.

Obviously the situation for blacks and women is better than it was a hundred and fifty, fifty, twenty-five years ago. But it is absurd to suppose that the young blacks and women now of an age to apply for jobs have not been wronged. Large-scale, blatant, overt wrongs have presumably disappeared; but it is only within the last twenty-five years (perhaps the last ten years in the case of women) that it has become at all widely agreed in this country that blacks and women must be recognized as having, not merely this or that particular right normally recognized as belonging to white males, but all of the rights and respect which go with full membership in the community. Even young blacks and women have lived through down-grading for being black or female: they have not merely not been given that very equal chance at the benefits generated by what the community owns which is so firmly insisted on for white males, they have not until lately even been felt to have a right to it.

And even those were not themselves down-graded for being black or female have suffered the consequences of the down-grading of other blacks and women: lack of self-confidence, and lack of self-respect. For where a community accepts that a person's being black, or being a woman, are right and proper grounds for denying that person full membership in the community, it can hardly be supposed that any but the most extraordinarily independent black or woman will escape self-doubt. All but the most extraordinarily independent of them have had to work harder—if only against self-doubt—than all but the most deprived white males, in the competition for a place amongst the best qualified.

If any black or woman has been unjustly deprived of what he or she has a right to, then of course justice does call for making amends. But what of the blacks and women who haven't actually been deprived of what they have a right to, but only made to suffer the consequences of injustice to other blacks and women? *Perhaps* justice doesn't require making amends to them as well; but common decency certainly does. To fail, at the very least, to make what counts as public apology to all, and to take positive steps to show that it is sincerely meant, is, if not injustice, then anyway a fault at least as serious as ingratitude.

Opting for a policy of preferential hiring may of course mean that some black or woman is preferred to some white male who as a matter of fact has had a harder life than the black or woman. But so may opting for a policy of veterans' preference mean that a healthy, unscarred, middle class veteran is preferred to a poor, struggling, scarred, nonveteran. Indeed, opting for a policy of settling who gets the job by having all equally qualified candidates draw straws may also mean that in a given case the candidate with the hardest life loses out. Opting for any policy other than hard-life preference may have this result.

I have no objection to anyone's arguing that it is precisely hard-life preference that we ought to opt for. If all, or anyway all of the equally qualified, have a right to an equal chance, then the argument would have to draw attention to something sufficiently powerful to override that right. But perhaps this could be done along the lines I followed in the case of blacks and women: perhaps it could be successfully argued that we have wronged those who have had hard lives, and therefore owe it to them to make amends. And then we should have in more extreme form a difficulty already present: how are these preferences to be ranked? shall we place the hard-lifers ahead of blacks? both ahead of women? and what about veterans? I leave these questions aside. My concern has been only to show that the white male applicant's right to an equal chance does not make it unjust to opt for a policy under which blacks and women are given preference. That a white male with a specially hard history may lose out under this policy cannot possibly be any objection to it, in the absence of a showing that hard-life preference is not unjust, and, more important, takes priority over preference for blacks and women.

Lastly, it should be stressed that to opt for such a policy is not to make the young white male applicants themselves make amends for any wrongs done to blacks and women. Under such a policy, no one is asked to give up a job which is already his; the job for which the white male competes isn't his, but is the community's, and it is the hiring officer who gives it to the black or woman in the community's name. Of course the white male is asked to give up his equal chance at the job. But that is not something he pays to the black or woman by way of making amends; it is something the community takes away from him in order that *it* may make amends.

Still, the community does impose a burden on him: it is able to make amends for its wrongs only by taking something away from him, something which, after all, we are supposing he has a right to. And why should *he* pay the cost of the community's amends-making?

If there were some appropriate way in which the community could make amends to its blacks and women, some way which did not require depriving anyone of anything he has a right to, then that would be the best course of action for it to take. Or if there were anyway some way in which the costs could be shared by everyone, and not imposed entirely on the young white male job applicants, then that would be, if not best, then anyway better than opting for a policy of preferential hiring. But in fact the nature of the wrongs done is such as to make jobs the best and most suitable form of compensation. What blacks and women were denied was full membership in the community; and nothing can more appropriately make amends for that wrong than precisely what will make them feel they now finally have it. And that means jobs. Financial compensation (the cost of which could be shared equally) slips through the fingers; having a job, and discovering you do it well, yield—perhaps better than anything else—that very self-respect which blacks and women have had to do without.

But of course choosing this way of making amends means that the costs are imposed on the young white male applicants who are turned away. And so it should be noticed that it is not entirely inappropriate that those applicants should pay the costs. No doubt few, if any, have themselves, individually, done any wrongs to blacks and women. But they have profited from the wrongs the community did. Many may actually have been direct beneficiaries of policies which excluded or down-graded blacks and women—perhaps in school admissions, perhaps in access to financial aid, perhaps elsewhere; and even those who did not directly benefit in this way had, at any rate, the advantage in the competition which comes of confidence in one's full membership, and of one's rights being recognized as a matter of course.

*From*

# PREFERENTIAL HIRING: A REPLY TO JUDITH JARVIS THOMSON*

## By Robert Simon

Judith Jarvis Thomson has recently defended preferential hiring of women and black persons in universities. She restricts her defense of the assignment of preference to only those cases where candidates from preferred groups and their white male competitors are equally qualified, although she suggests that her argument can be extended to cover cases where the qualifications are unequal as well. The argument in question is compensatory; it is because of pervasive patterns of unjust discrimination against black persons and women that justice, or at least common decency, requires that amends be made.

*    *    *    *    *

A familiar objection to special treatment for blacks and women is that, if such a practice is justified, other victims of injustice or misfortune ought to receive special treatment too. While arguing that virtually all women and black persons have been harmed, either directly or indirectly, by discrimination, Thomson acknowledges that in any particular case, a white male may have been victimized to a greater extent than have the blacks or women with which he is competing.

*    *    *    *    *

. . . Likewise, if the reason for giving preference to a black person or to a woman is that the recipient has been injured due to an unjust practice, then preference must be given to anyone who has been similarly injured. So, it appears, there can be no relevant *group* to which compensation ought to be made, other than that made up of and only of those who have been injured or victimized. Although, as Thomson claims, all blacks and women may be members of that latter group, they deserve compensation *qua* victim and not *qua* black person or woman.

A more plausible line of response may involve shifting our attention from compensation of individuals to collective compensation of groups. Once this shift is made, it can be acknowledged that as individuals, some white males may have stronger compensatory claims than blacks or women. But as compensation is owed the group, it is group claims that must be weighed, not individual ones. And surely, at the group level, the claims of black persons and women to compensation are among the strongest there are.

Suppose we grant that certain groups, including those specified by Thomson, are owed collective compensation. What should be noted is that the conclusion of concern here—that preferential hiring policies are acceptable instruments for compensating groups—does not directly follow. To derive such a conclusion validly, one would have to provide additional premises specifying the relation between collective compensation to groups and distribution of that compensation to individual members. For it does not follow from the fact that some group members are compensated that the group is compensated. Thus, if through a computer error, every member of the American Philosophical Association was asked to pay additional taxes, then if the government provided compensation for this error, it would not follow that it had compensated the Association. Rather, it would have compensated each member *qua* individual. So what is required, where preferential hiring is concerned, are plausible premises showing how the preferential award of jobs to group members counts as collective compensation for the group.

Thomson provides no such additional premises. Moreover, there is good reason to think

---

* Robert Simon, "Preferential Hiring—A Reply to Judith Jarvis Thomson," *Philosophy and Public Affairs* 3, No. 3 (Spring 1974). © 1974 by Princeton University Press. Pp. 312–19 (excerpts). Reprinted by permission. Footnotes have been deleted from this abridged version. This paper is in response to the paper reprinted in part on pages 615–18 above.

that if any such premises were provided, they would count against preferential hiring as an instrument of collective compensation. This is because although compensation is owed to the group, preferential hiring policies award compensation to an arbitrarily selected segment of the group; namely, those who have the ability and qualifications to be seriously considered for the jobs available. Surely, it is far more plausible to think that collective compensation ought to be equally available to all group members, or at least to all kinds of group members. The claim that although compensation is owed collectively to a group, only a special sort of group member is eligible to receive it, while perhaps not incoherent certainly ought to be rejected as arbitrary, at least in the absence of an argument to the contrary.

\* \* \* \* \*

. . . So far, I have considered arbitrariness in the distribution of compensatory benefits by preferential hiring policies. However, arbitrariness involved in the assessment of costs is also of concern. However, arbitrariness involved in the assessment of costs is also of concern.

Thus, it is sometimes argued that preferential hiring policies place the burden of providing compensation on young white males who are just entering the job market. This is held to be unfair, because, first, there is no special reason for placing the burden on that particular group and, second, because many members of that group are not responsible for the injury done to blacks and women. In response to the first point, Thomson acknowledges that it seems to her "in place to expect the occupants of comfortable professorial chairs to contribute in some way, to make some form of return to the young-white male who bears the cost. . . ." In response to the second point, Thomson concedes that few, if any, white male applicants to university positions individually have done any wrong to women or black persons. However, she continues, many have profited by the wrongs inflicted by others. So it is not unfitting that they be asked to make sacrifices now.

However, it is far from clear, at least to me, that this reply is satisfactory. For even if the group which bears the cost is expanded to include full professors, why should that new group be singled out? The very same consideration that required the original expansion would seem to require a still wider one. Indeed, it would seem this point can be pressed until costs are assessed against society as a whole. This is exactly the position taken by Paul Taylor, who writes, "The obligation to offer such benefits to (the previously victimized) group . . . is an obligation that falls on society in general that, through its established (discriminatory) social practice, brought upon itself the obligation."

Perhaps, however, the claim that preferential hiring policies arbitrarily distribute burdens can be rebutted. For presumably the advocate of preferential hiring does not want to restrict such a practice to universities but rather would wish it to apply throughout society. If so, and *if* persons at the upper echelons are expected to share costs with young white male job applicants, then perhaps a case can be made that burdens are equitably distributed throughout society.

Even here, however, there are two points an opponent of preferential hiring can make. First, he can point out that burdens are not equitably distributed now. Consequently, to the extent that preferential policies are employed at present, then to that extent are burdens arbitrarily imposed now. Second, he can question the assumption that if someone gains from an unjust practice for which he is not responsible and even opposes, the gain is not really his and can be taken from him without injustice. This assumption is central to the compensatory argument for preferential hiring since if it is unacceptable, no justification remains for requiring "innocent bystanders" to provide compensation.

If this point is sound, it becomes questionable whether *all* members of nonpreferred groups are equally liable (or even liable at all) for provision of compensation. It is especially questionable in the case where the individual from the nonpreferred group has been unjustly victimized to a far greater extent than the individual from the preferred group. Hence, even if it were true that all members of nonpreferred groups have profited from discrimination against members of preferred groups, it does not automatically follow that all are equally liable for providing compensation. In so far as preferential hiring policies do not take this into account, they are open to the charge of arbitrariness in assessing the costs of compensation.

One more point seems to require mention here. If preferential hiring policies are expanded, as Thomson suggests, to cases where the candidates are not equally qualified, a further difficulty arises. To the extent that lowering quality lowers efficiency, members of victimized groups are likely to lose more than others. This may be particularly important in educational contexts. Students from such groups may have been exposed to poorer instruction than was made available to others. But they might have greater need for better instruction than, say, middle class students from affluent backgrounds.

*From*

# IT'S MINE*

## *By Gertrude Ezorsky*

Do wholly private employers have a moral right to hire whomever they please? According to Judith Thomson they do.[1] I shall claim, first, that her argument in support of this view is invalid. She commits a fallacy which I shall call the legalist fallacy. Secondly, I shall argue that employers "wholly in the private sector" do not have such hiring rights.

\*     \*     \*     \*     \*

Our conflicting interpretations of the ownership statement may now be explained. Where that statement is read as:

> If one is the full *legally* rightful owner of some entity, then one has the *legal* right of giving it to whomever one pleases.

Or as:

> If one is the full *morally* rightful owner of some entity, then one has the *moral* right of giving it to whomever one pleases.

Then the claim is trivially true.

But where that claim is interpreted as:

> If one is the full *legally* rightful owner of some entity, then one has the *moral* right of giving it to whomever one pleases.

Then the claim is significant and false.

The statement on ownership, so interpreted, exemplifies what I shall call the legalist fallacy. This fallacy is committed whenever one infers that an individual who possesses a legal right, thereby has some moral right. Among the persons who commit this fallacy is Judith Thomson.

She claims that if a person is the owner of a benefit in the "wholly private" sector, then he has a moral right to give the benefit to whomever he pleases . . . ("in so doing I violate

---

\* Gertrude Ezorsky, "It's Mine," *Philosophy and Public Affairs* 3, no. 3 (Spring 1974). © 1974 by Princeton University Press. Pp. 321, 323–25, 327–30 (excerpts). Reprinted by permission.

[1] Judith Jarvis Thomson, "Preferential Hiring," *Philosophy and Public Affairs,* vol. 2, no. 4 (Summer 1973); pp. 364–84. All further references to this article will be made within the text. An abridged version of this article is reprinted above, see p. 615.

no one's *rights,* I treat no one *unjustly" . . .*). Where such an owner is an employer "wholly in the private sector," then, she argues, he has a moral right to dispense his jobs as he pleases. . . . This owner, in the private sector, is indeed a legally rightful owner. But she implicitly infers that in virtue of such *legal* ownership he is the full, morally rightful owner, with the moral right to give what he owns to whomever he pleases. By such inference she commits the legalist fallacy.

\*     \*     \*     \*     \*

Thomson makes the following claim concerning the rights of private employers:

> Employers "wholly in the private sector" (hereafter, private employers) have the full moral rights of ownership over the jobs they dispense, i.e., to give such jobs to whomever they please.

I have suggested that her reasoning in support of this claim is invalid. I shall, in what follows, argue that her claim concerning the rights of employers is, in fact, false.

But, we recall, Thomson restricted her notion of ownership rights to benefits, although she "suspect[s]" it also applies to what people "actually need." I shall argue that her claim concerning the rights of employers is false for either sort of job.

But how does one distinguish between such jobs? When is something a benefit, rather than actually needed.

Thomson suggests the following:

> *Benefits . . .* [are] things which people would like to have, which would perhaps not merely please them, but improve their lives, but which they don't actually *need* (emphasis in original).

She gives three examples of "things . . . people . . . don't actually *need,*" which, "if I have . . . I can give to whom I like":

> [my] extra money;
> [my] extra home grown apples;
> [my] extra tickets to . . . [my] lectures . . . on How to Improve Your Life through Philosophy.

But the notion that apples, i.e., an item of *food,* and *money,* are, like her lecture tickets, "things . . . people . . . don't actually *need*" is astonishing. Food and money are urgently needed by a very large number of people. (Some apples and a little money were exactly what many Depression relief families were given.) Ex hypothesi, apples and money are among *her* extra items. Hence *she* doesn't need them. But surely, "I have enough of such food or money" does not imply "Other people have enough of such food or money."

Marie Antoinette made a similar error of inference. I suggest that the distinction between things actually needed and benefits be conceived as follows: What is actually needed is the sort of thing a needy person lacks, i.e. necessities such as minimally adequate food, clothing, shelter, medical aid. An actually needed job pays merely enough for such necessities. A benefit is such that if an individual is in need of that sort of thing, he is not therefore needy. A job which is a benefit gives a person more than the bare necessities that needy people need.

\*     \*     \*     \*     \*

Application of the following generalization argument to discriminatory hiring suffices, I suggest, to show that no employer has discriminatory hiring rights:

> If an individual has a right to act in a given fashion, whenever so inclined, then every person in relevantly similar circumstances has that right.

If the consequences of every person in such circumstances so acting would be bad, then not everyone in such circumstances has the right to so act.

If not everyone in such circumstances has the right to so act, then no one in those circumstances has the right to so act.


Let us apply our generalization argument to the discriminatory hiring rights of employers, first, over decent jobs, and second, over minimum jobs.

What would be the consequences if every employer engaged in discriminatory hiring for decent jobs whenever so inclined?

The situation of blacks in this country prior to very recent equal opportunity laws is instructive in this matter. Employers who dispensed decent jobs engaged, to the hilt, in discriminatory hiring against blacks. As a rule, most employed blacks worked at miserable exhausting labor, paying just enough for bare necessities, and with no hope of anything better for themselves or their families. How would one of us regard the prospect of our children spending the whole of their lives in such fashion? I suggest we would regard that prospect as dreadful. And that sort of life is dreadful, for anyone. Given the familiar propensity to familiar kinds of prejudice, we may reasonably expect that if employers were to engage in discriminatory hiring for decent jobs, whenever so inclined, the consequences would be bad indeed. Thus (following the generalization argument), no employers have such hiring rights. An employer who practices discriminatory hiring, violates the rights of the candidates, who as a result of such practice are denied jobs in his enterprise.

Members of groups who have suffered from the denial of such rights are now protected in small measure by recent equal opportunity employment laws. But before enactment of such measures the power of private employers to keep blacks in the worst jobs was uncurbed by law.

\*    \*    \*    \*    \*

Oddly enough, while according to Thomson, a private employer has a right to deny a black applicant "even a chance" at a decent job she denies that the employer has a right to "gratuitously give offence to" the black applicant by telling him the reason for his rejection. . . . That would be unjust.

Let us now apply the generalization argument to the right of discriminatory hiring in minimum jobs. What would the consequences be if every employer engaged in such hiring whenever so inclined?

Again the situation of blacks in this country is instructive. They were, in general, "last to be hired, first to be fired." As a result, most blacks were cast into terrifying poverty. They were imprisoned by such problems as getting warm clothing, medicine, coal, or food. In parts of the country, their children's bodies were deformed by slow starvation. Discriminatory hiring was, of course, not the only cause contributing to their wretchedness. There were others, for example the fact that private owners refused to let blacks live in *their* buildings, to admit blacks to *their* private hospitals, or to charge blacks fair prices in *their* stores. But it was the place of blacks in the Kingdom of Jobs, the miserable kingdom of minimum jobs, which contributed most of all to their absolute impoverishment.

Given the familiar propensity to familiar kinds of prejudice, we may expect that if all employers engaged in discriminatory hiring, for minimum jobs, whenever so inclined, the consequences would be most harmful. Thus (following the generalization argument) no employers in fact, have such hiring rights.

I conclude that Thomson's claim concerning the rights of private employers is false, both for decent and minimum jobs.

\*    \*    \*    \*    \*

Consider now our application of the generalization argument to discriminatory hiring. We know already that when employers have, in fact, engaged in discriminatory hiring, whenever so inclined, the consequences were widespread suffering. Hence, I have concluded that employers have no such rights. But whether, given, relevantly different causal conditions, employers would have the right of discriminatory hiring, or any ownership rights whatsoever, over jobs, is a question I have not discussed here. That question should however be answered by a comprehensive theory of moral ownership rights.

Why not make a clean Cartesian start? What are the circumstances under which a person has the moral right to say, "It's mine." After such inquiry, Judith Thomson might conclude that, morally speaking, far fewer things are rightfully owned in our society than are dreamt of in her philosophy.

# 20. THE HIGH ROSS DAM

## Case Introduction

### SYNOPSIS

The High Ross Dam is a planned addition to the Ross Dam located on the Skagit River in the North Cascade Mountains of British Columbia and Washington. The plan would raise the Ross Dam by 122½ feet and would generate 35,000 kilowatts of additional electricity for Seattle City Light, a public utility serving the Seattle area. Seattle City Light has invested some $10 million over the past several years and needs the electrical output from this project to meet increased demands for its service. Opponents of the project suggest that it would not really be needed if more conservation energy-use practices were adopted and the higher water levels would flood a valuable ecosystem. A number of interest groups are indentified with each side of the issue, currently a heated political controversy, undergoing litigation. Judge Lande must make a decision as to whether the cost benefits of the dam warrant its construction.

### WHY THIS CASE IS INCLUDED

The High Ross Dam case provides a useful example of an important social issue relating to energy policy. Our society has been using increasing amounts of energy at ever rising costs: environmental, economic, and social. Thus energy is likely to become a policy issue of increasing importance to the world, to a particular society, to the well-being of smaller regions, and to metropolitan areas. In a policy issue such as energy, the appropriate concepts and tools of analysis as well as the decision alternatives available to decision makers varies with the level of analysis (program versus project). Policy makers are increasingly called upon to make these decisions not only in terms of their organizations but also for more general public issues. An understanding of both the technoeconomic and sociopolitical dimensions of policy decisions is very important for today's decision makers and this will be more true in years to come. The High Ross Dam case provides an opportunity to analyze a specific public policy decision in terms of these dimensions.

## DIAGNOSTIC AND PREDICTIVE QUESTIONS

The readings included with this case are marked (*). The author index at the end of this book locates the other readings.

1. A frequently used technique for analyzing policy decisions is cost-benefit analysis. Drawing from the facts in the High Ross Dam case, list the various costs and benefits associated with the proposed dam.

Read:   *Alston and Freeman, "The Natural Resources Decision-Maker as a Political and Economic Man."

2. Another approach to policy decisions is the sociotechnical perspective discussed by Alston and Freeman. What would be the result of a sociopolitical assessment of the High Ross Dam?

Read:   *Alston and Freeman, "The Natural Resources Decision-Maker as a Political and Economic Man."

3. Policy decisions are often resolved by the rational-comprehensive (root) or by the successive limited comparisons (branch) methodologies described by Lindblom. Analyze the High Ross Dam decision using both of these approaches. Compare your answers with those resulting from the cost-benefit analysis of Question 1 and the sociopolitical analysis of Question 2. How are they similar? What are the major differences?

Read:   *Lindblom, "The Science of 'Muddling Through.'" *Alston and Freeman, "The Natural Resources Decision-Maker as a Political and Economic Man."

4. Miller suggests that the energy crisis is really a policy crisis. Is this generalization also true of the High Ross Dam decision? Does your answer vary depending upon whether you take the perspective of a policy maker within Seattle City Light, of Judge Lande, or of a planner for the Metropolitan area of Seattle?

Read:   *Miller, *Living in the Environment: Concepts, Problems, and Alternatives.* *Alston and Freeman, "The Natural Resources Decision-Maker as a Political and Economic Man."

5. Conservation of energy is often suggested as an alternative to increasing its supply. What are the factors in favor of this alternative to the High Ross Dam? What are the factors limiting the usefulness of pleas for conservation of energy to avoid the need for the High Ross Dam?

Read:   *Miller, *Living in the Environment: Concepts, Problems, and Alternatives.* *Walker and Large, "The Economics of Energy Extravagance."

6. What are the alternatives, in addition to conservation, to the High Ross Dam? In what way do these alternatives vary as one views the decision from a metropolitan, a regional, or a national level perspective?

Read:   *Miller, *Living in the Environment: Concepts, Problems, and Alternatives* *Walker and Large, "The Economics of Energy Extravagance."

7. Alston and Freeman suggest that the methods appropriate for analyzing policy decision is different depending upon whether the ana-

lyst is working at the program or the project level. If this is true, then one might expect not only the nature of the alternatives (as developed in answer to Question 6 above) but also for the methods of analysis to change as one mover from the metropolitan area of Seattle to the national level. Would this be true of the policy decision relating to the High Ross Dam? Explain.

Read:  *Alston and Freeman, "The Natural Resources Decision-Maker as a Political and Economic Man" *Miller, *Living in the Environment: Concepts, Problems, and Alternatives.* *Walker and Large, "The Economics of Energy Extravagance" *Lindblom, "The Science of 'Muddling Through.' "

8. Mary Parker Follet has suggested that better decisions can be made with constructive conflict. Alsten and Freeman suggest that a decision is likely to be more politically viable if conflicts are cross-cutting cleavages. What sort of conflict is present in the High Ross Dam issue?

Read:  Mary Parker Follett, "Constructive Conflict" *Alston and Freeman, "The Natural Resources Decision-Maker as a Political and Economic Man."

9. Assume that you are an analyst for the policy makers within British Columbia. Analyze the High Ross Dam Proposal from an economic and a sociopolitical perspective. What are the costs, benefits, and political viability of this project.

Read:  *Alston and Freeman, "The National Resources Decision-Maker as a Political and Economic Man."

## POLICY QUESTIONS

10. Write a brief addressed to Judge Lande suggesting what decision you feel should be made in this case. Briefly summarize the major factors behind your decision.

Read:  Review the readings for Questions 1 and 2 above.

11. Assume that you are the assistant to the president of Seattle City Light. Develop a policy statement relating to the High Ross Dam and other energy alternatives. This statement should outline a list of specific action alternatives and the basic factors influencing your recommendations.

Read:  Review readings for Question 3 through 5 above.

12. Assume that the High Ross Dam case was not yet in court and that you are assistant to a regional planner responsible for the industrial development of Western Washington. What would your advice be concerning the High Ross Dam? How would this decision relate to your overall energy policy planned for the area?

Read:  Review the readings for Questions 4 through 6 above.

13. Develop a general outline for a public policy at the national level as it relates to electric energy. Relate the High Ross Dam situation specifically to your proposed policy.

Read:  Review readings for Questions 6 through 9 above.

14. Assume that you were asked to decide whether or not the High Ross Dam was to be constructed. What would be your decision? What

analytical method or perspective was the most important in formulating your answer? Why?

# Case Text*

### History of the High Ross Dam

The "High Ross Dam" is a planned addition to "Ross Dam," one of three existing dams on the Skagit River in the North Cascades Mountains of British Columbia and Washington. The plan for the development of the Skagit River was made in 1925. At that time the first dam, at Gorge, began operations. A second dam was constructed two years later at Diablo. The Ross Dam, the main storage reservoir for the entire system, was begun in 1943 and completed in 1949. Between 1950 and 1956, four generators were installed, designed with a capacity to handle not only the existing Ross Dam, but also the projected High Ross Dam. High Ross would add 121 feet to the old structure and raise the lake 122½ feet. The project would involve placing a concrete cap on top of the existing dam to raise its elevation, providing greater water pressure. Thus, Seattle City Light could obtain greatly increased generation from the same amount of water passing through the existing turbine generators.

Almost $6 million have been invested in the present dam and power plant facilities to accommodate the higher pressures that will result from the high dam. An additional $4 million have been spent on engineering, environmental, and recreational studies in both the United States and Canada bringing the total investment by City Light's customers in the High Ross Dam to $10 million.

The additional power generated by the High Ross would be 35,000 kilowatts of firm energy and 274,000 kilowatts of additional peaking capacity. Thirty-five thousand killowatts of firm power is enough to serve the needs of approximately 50,000 people—the entire population of the city of Bellingham, Washington. The 274,000 kilowatts of peaking capacity is 18 percent of the peaking requirement of Seattle, with a population over one-half million.

The proposed dam would also provide flood control for the lower Skagit Valley, one of the largest and most important dairy regions of the state of Washington. During floods in December 1975, 18,000 head of livestock were drowned in the Skagit Valley; many small dairymen were wiped out and property damage ran into many millions of dollars.

The proposed dam would cover with water an additional 8,300 acres of land—4,700 in Canada and 3,600 in the United States.

The area of the United States most affected would be the Big Beaver

---

Valley. Half the valley would be changed from a terrestrial forest to a lake. The Federal Power Commission's environmental-impact statement stressed the damage that would be caused by High Ross: loss of fish-spawning areas, deer and beaver populations and an unusual mix of large cedar trees, swamps, and meadows.

In 1967 the British Columbia government and Seattle City Light nego-tiated an agreement through the International Joint Commission allow-ing the flooding of 5,200 acres of additional land in Canada. Canada's interest in the matter began when the dam was started in 1942. At that time Canada supported the need for large quantities of cheap power for war defense industries in Seattle, and saw little cost in flooding a remote, relatively small, and unused valley on its southern border. Over 24 years to 1967, the Province of British Columbia and Seattle City Light made numerous agreements to adjust operations of the dam so that both parties felt satisfied. In 1967, a final 99-year agreement was drawn up by British columbia and accepted by the City of Seattle. Since then Seattle City Light has been paying British Columbia $35,000 annually for permis-sions on the additional 4,700 acres which High Ross would flood.

## The Federal Power Commission Licensing Procedure

Seattle City Light applied, in October 1970, to the Federal Power Com-mission to raise Ross Dam by 121 feet and Ross Reservoir by 122½ feet.

The North Cascades Conservation Council intervened before the Fed-eral Power Commission in December 1970 opposing the High Ross Dam.

## The Big Beaver Valley

Raising the elevation of Ross Lake would flood 1,250 acres of the Big Beaver Valley containing stands of large old-growth western red cedar, marshland, meadows, and upland areas. The Federal Power Commis-sion's environmental-impact statement reported that, "The cedars are unique in that they are among the last examples of the Cascade Valley bottom community. . . ." According to a United States Forest Service opinion, "It seems to be the unanimous opinion that this unique stand [of cedar trees] is unmatched. There are countless trees over 30 feet in circumference and many giants over 35 feet. These must be at least a thousand years old."

The Department of Ecology, state of Washington reported:

> Discordance and contradiction has arisen regarding the *value* of
> the valley. Seattle City Light and its consultants have restricted
> their value judgment of the entire Valley to the contention that the
> Valley is not unique because they have found that other old-growth
> western red cedar stands exist elsewhere in the Northwest. Others,
> including the Department of Ecology's . . . staff, insist that the
> *value* of Big Beaver Valley must be judged on its *entire ecosystem,*
> not on whether red cedars exist elsewhere.

According to the International Joint Commission:

> . . . The area has unusual potential as a research natural area. Such areas are established in various natural ecosystems to serve for baseline measurement purposes and are valuable also for the educational opportunities provided. . . . The objective is to find a reasonably accessible area representative of a given natural system, yet not so accessible as to be vulnerable to overuse. Big Beaver Valley is the best bottom land boggy cedar example known to ecologists in western Washington and as it is presently situated, is both protected and accessible for study. Flooding would permanently destroy this potential.

The State Department of Ecology also stated:

> Ironically, City Light is at least partly—if unintentionally—responsible for the preservation of Big Beaver Valley. The Ross Dam was rushed to completion at the close of World War II to provide electrical energy for Seattle's burgeoning aircraft industry. In the haste to get the generators on the line, the reservoir was allowed to fill before much of the millions of board feet of timber it contained could be cut. Once Ross Lake backed up all the way to the Canadian border, the possibility of ever driving logging roads up the Skagit was gone. . . . The giant cedars were safe there.
>
> There is no question that Big Beaver Valley is a pristine ecosystem that is rare and endangered in this rapidly developing section. . . . The question is whether its worth is greater than that of the increased power from the High Ross Dam. Neither Seattle City Light nor the Federal Power Commission has demonstrated the justification of High Ross when compared to the resultant impact and the available alternatives.

### Proponents of the High Ross Dam

*Seattle City Light,* the nation's second largest publicly owned electrical company, is the City of Seattle's Department of Lighting. It owns and operates plants with a total generating capacity of 1,483,300 kilowatts. Power for the City of Seattle comes from City Light's three dams on the Skagit River, two dams at Cedar Falls and Boundary, two steam plants using oil for fuel, purchased power from federal dams on the Columbia River and from other utilities.

City Light favors the completion of the fourth phase of the Ross Dam project and has stated that: "The additional power that will be generated by High Ross will cost the customers, Seattle citizens, close to $4 million a year less than the cheapest alternate source." Due to the shortage of other energy sources in the Northwest the only alternates are "generation with combustion turbines, or fossil or nuclear fueled steam, all of which are environmentally damaging and consume a non-renewable resource."

"High Ross will require no new transmission or powerhouse equipment having environmental impact. Hydro power is non-polluting. It is a self-renewing resource and does not suffer from the cost inflation experienced by oil, coal and nuclear fuels. The additional power generated by High Ross instead of by oil-fired steam will save 500,000 barrels of oil every year." (Moreover, the *New York Times,* in an energy analysis, wrote on July 6, 1971, "About two-thirds of the energy in coal or petroleum is lost in generating electricity, escaping out the stacks and into the water used for cooling.")

The dam is expected to cost a total of $50 million and take two years to complete. The project will require a labor force of about 400 employees with earnings totaling some $20 million.

> As there will be no on-site living accommodations for the employees, the project will have a significant beneficial economic impact on communities in the lower Skagit Valley.
>
> Recreational use of Ross Lake will be enhanced. The high dam provides drive-in access to the lake. The only such access is now through Canada to the north end of the lake. The lake will be larger and will have a longer shoreline for recreational development.
>
> The high dam will provide better flood control protection for the lower Skagit Valley.

*Puget Sound Power and Light Company* is a privately owned electric utility in the area. At the 1974 Federal Power Commission public hearing in Seattle, Mr. John Ellis, executive vice president, emphasized one special reason for raising Ross Dam is its reliability.

> There are three factors grounded in *reliability* which argue for the addition to the Ross Dam. . . . First . . . by standing ready to pick up load in an emergency, High Ross could well prevent any load shedding at all. With a hydro plant, full load on a unit can be achieved in a matter of minutes . . . as distinguished from a large thermal plant which may take a number of hours or maybe days.
>
> Second, to carry essential load if needed, if the whole Northwest power system should have a major disturbance. If the systems were in danger of falling apart and load in the Puget Sound area had to be shed, the High Ross generating capacity could have a very substantial contribution to carrying the essential loads. . . . The 274 megawatts of additional capacity that High Ross could add to this area is the equivalent in essential loads to 150 hospitals the size of Seattle's largest. Put another way, High Ross capacity would be sufficient to meet the demands of all the hospitals in the entire [Western Washington] area.
>
> Third, . . . getting back on the line when a disaster occurs. One of the lessons learned in the Northeast blackout [in 1965] was that local generation instead of imported power is needed to put the systems back together. . . . The Ross addition of 274 megawatts could be crucial in that effort. . . . The key point is that the Ross

Dam is part of the Puget Sound area, and not across the mountains.
. . . The recent past has taught us that our transmission lines are
vulnerable.

Discussing alternatives to the High Ross, Mr. Ellis remarked:

The latest figures . . . indicate deficits of both peak and base energy
well in excess of that provided by High Ross in 1977–78. The Puget
Sound area's nuclear project will not be available until 1981 at the
earliest. Only combustion turbine generating facilities can be
brought on line in time. These units require the use of oil, which
use the F.P.C. has discouraged in recent months.

If oil were to be used in combustion turbines to supply the 35,000
kilowatts of (base) energy offered by High Ross, a total of 520,000
barrels of oil would be required, at a cost of $7.7 million per year,
and that assumes a 35 cent per gallon oil; or if Seattle's Lake Union
plant were to supply the equivalent amount of energy, a quantity
of 1,200,000 barrels of fuel oil would be required per year. At $10
per barrel, this equals $12,000,000 annually. Such a use of these
scarce, nonrenewable resources is simply not in the national interest. . . .

City Light estimates the net average energy increment of about
35 megawatts. This figure is termed insignificant by some people
who oppose this project. How much is 35 megawatts? Based on my
company's average residential use of 13,860 kilowatt hours per
year, 35 megawatts would supply the needs of 22,100 residences, or
about the equivalent of a community of seventy-five to one hundred
thousand people. . . . I do not believe that is an insignificant load.

If this many customers are not to be served by High Ross, then
how else? What are the environmental consequences of the alternatives? . . . Judged against these standards, High Ross is the best
alternative.

The *Puget Sound Chamber of Commerce* have called for "the expedi-
tious and complete development of existing hydroelectric projects. Raising the height of Ross Dam on the Skagit River, completing the third
powerhouse at Grand Coulee Dam, building a second powerhouse at
Bonneville Dam, and installing generators at every vacant slot in the
federal Columbia River system are common-sense steps that ought to be
taken without delay in utilizing a hydroelectric potential that dwarfs
that of every other part of the nation except Alaska."

The *Seattle City Council,* after conducting eight public hearings,
voted to raise the Ross Dam by a vote of 6 to 2. The December 1970 vote
overruled the Seattle mayor's opposition, and directed the filing of the
application.

The *Seattle City Engineer,* Robert Gulino, and the *Board of Public
Works* support the project, largely emphasizing three points. First, the
environmental benefits to society of energy generated by a nonair-pollut-
ing, nonwater-polluting method of utilizing a renewable resource is sig-

nificant. Second, though conservation of electrical energy slows load growth, it will not arrest it. Third, the low economic cost is unequaled by any alternative such as coal, oil, or nuclear steam generation.

*Northwestern Glass Company* strongly supports the High Ross project. Northwestern manufactures glass containers for the food and beverage industries, serving the markets of the Pacific Northwest. The company employs 650 people at the Seattle plant and provides an annual payroll of approximately $9 million to this region. This support is centered around their dependence on electric energy at the lowest possible cost for their manufacturing process.

The *National Electrical Contractors Association* and the *Washington State Construction Council,* which represents nearly 2,000 businesses throughout the state, support the project. Their concern is for the future energy needs of the Pacific Northwest.

The *Bonneville Power Administration,* the largest wholesaler of electrical energy in the region and a corporation set up by the federal government, supports the project: "(1) High Ross can be constructed in a . . . short time and .he resource made available. (2) Hydro units do not require as much maintenance and are more reliable than thermal units, . . . and as we get more and more thermal units, we will have to have larger amounts of reserves. (3) The location of the Ross Dam is convenient to supply electrical loads either in the Vancouver, B.C. area or in the Puget Sound area." Two years ago when the transmission lines from the Peace River, carrying 1 million kilowatts of power, were knocked out by a snowslide, Seattle City Light and other Puget Sound area utilities were the only ones which could come to the aid of British Columbia Hydro Company in that emergency.

## Opponents of the Ross Dam Project

*The mayor of Seattle* visited the site and hiked into the Big Beaver Valley. He concluded that:

> raising Ross Dam would not sufficiently contribute to providing a solution to Seattle's need for additonal base power to outweigh the negative impacts on wilderness and recreation resources of the reservoir.
>
> . . . In all candor, I might not weigh environmental values as heavily if I were convinced that raising Ross Dam would provide more of a solution to Seattle's need for additional firm power. High Ross will be most efficiently used as "peaking power." But, according to the F.P.C.'s impact statement, this region will be peaking power rich in 1977. . . . As a fraction of the 142,200,000,000 k.w.h. of energy estimated available to the West Power Network in 1977, High Ross represents about .2 percent. In fact, the F.P.C. estimate of excess of capability over needs is 8,200,000,000 k.w.h., or 30 times the output of the High Ross addition. As we proceed into the 1980s, even more peaking power will come available as the additional Columbia River turbines (across the mountains) are installed.

634     *The Managerial Mind: Science and Theory in Policy Decisions*

. . . I believe that the time has come when we cannot tolerate
further erosion of the limited resource of wilderness which remains. We can find other places to generate power, but we cannot
find new places for wilderness. . . . We should . . . reduce wasteful
consumption of electric power and build the new . . . base generating plants which we realistically need.

*The Washington Environmental Council* is an organization composed of individuals and groups dedicated to the promotion of citizen,
legislative and administrative action toward providing a better environment. Their president stated the group's opposition to the Ross Dam
project.

The increase would be primarily in peaking capacity, whereas
the region's need is for increased base load energy. It would only
add about 1 percent to the *region's* peak power capacity. . . . High
Ross will not be a solution to present or future energy shortages,
and, in fact, will cause a withdrawal of valuable energy during the
period of construction.
    The raising of Ross Dam will cause . . . irreversible environ-
mental harm. . . . We have plenty of managed reservoirs in the
Northwest; we don't have any other Big Beaver Valleys.
    The opposition of the government and citizens in British Co-
lumbia is a serious matter. We have no right to inflict environmental damage on our neighbors; instead, we should be seeking alternative solutions. It is . . . possible that a more immediate increase in
power could be achieved by purchasing power from British Columbia's hydro resources.
    We as a nation must take energy conservation more seriously.
Seattle City Light has been a leader among utilities with its KILL-
A-Watt program, and it deserves full credit for its leadership and
commitment. They alone cannot change the habits of the region,
let alone the nation. The federal government must play a stronger
role in emphasizing the absolute necessity for the public to reduce
energy consumption."

*The State Ecology Department* went on record as opposing the project.
On December 8, 1971, State Ecology Director John Biggs stated: "This
project . . . indicates that City Light has no planned environmental program. . . . It selects and proposes for development new sources of power,
with the pursuit of energy being the first objective and environmental
concern decidedly a second one."
    *The Governor of the State of Washington,* Dan Evans, said that the
state's decision to oppose the plan should be seen as, "An encouragement
for all industries to develop policies for protecting the environment. We
aren't condemning anyone. We're all guilty of not having taken a good
enough look at the environment in the past. . . . We absolutely have to
do a better job of total environmental planning."

*Defenders of Wildlife,* a national organization of 40,000 members based in Washington, D.C., is dedicated to saving wildlife populations and their habitats. They believe that the basic issue is, "That the United States can no longer afford to put prime wilderness or recreational land under water for the alleged benefits of additional hydroelectric power or any other reason."

The *Sierra Club,* a national organization of about 150,000 people, stated its opposition, "For the same reason that we have always opposed dams in the Grand Canyon, namely, that the permanent destruction of these unique and beautiful places, which are part of our national heritage, and cannot be compensated for by the electricity or the water which then become available for regional use, particularly when serious consideration has not been given to less damaging alternatives."

The *North Cascades Conservation Council* is a local organization which has expended considerable time, effort and money in the battle to stop the raising of the Ross Dam. It publishes *The Wild Cascades* magazine. By January 1973, its income consisted of over $12,000 in contributions. From this over $4,000 has already been used for legal, engineering, and architectural expenses on the opposition to the dam. The "principal intervenor" appearing before the Federal Power Commission, the North Cascades Conservation Council has been joined by the following co-intervenors: The Wilderness Society, the Sierra Club, the National Audubon Society, Friends of the Earth, National Parks and Conservation Association, R.O.S.S. (Run Out The Skagit Spoilers Committee of British Columbia), the Federation of Western Outdoors Clubs, The Mountaineers, and the Washington Environmental Council.

The *Federal Government of Canada* and the *British Columbia Government* have opposed the project since 1972. Resources Minister Bob Williams said in November, 1972, that the proposal to flood eight miles of the southern Interior River Valley was, "Totally unacceptable to the province of British Columbia. This land is too valuable to be used as a pawn in the power project of another country." (All the existing agreements were made under former governments of the province. However, the 1967 agreement still stands. In 1973 and 1974, British Columbia returned Seattle City Light's $35,000 payments. In its turn, City Light sent the payments back to British Columbia. To date there has been no official effort on the part of Canada or British Columbia to set forth alternative proposals to the existing agreement.)

## Conclusion

Although the majority of the Seattle City Council did not agree with Mayor Uhlman's decision to withdraw the application for High Ross in 1970, on December 4, 1972, five of the nine council members requested the mayor place a moratorium on the Ross Dam project and that the city immediately undertake negotiations with the British Columbia government to settle this dispute. They added, "The controversy is having a detrimental impact on the amicable relationship between Canada and the United States. Not only will the problem of finding future power sources in this region require mutual confidence between our two countries, but other areas of common concern are also likely to be affected. The value of the small amount of additional power to City Light is far outweighed by the need to maintain friendly and cordial relations between the United States and Canada."

In April 1974, the Federal Power Commission assigned to Administrative Law Judge Allen Lande, the hearing of the High Ross Dam controversy. After taking testimony for ten months, Judge Lande made a trip to Seattle to hear statements from some of the intervenors in the case. He commented that while most of the testimony ranged from fisheries to economics, the issue of Canadian opposition to the project is not forgotten.

After testimony is complete the opposing sides will prepare briefs. The judge will make an initial decision in the case. His decision is subject to review and confirmation by the Federal Power Commission. The Commission decision can be appealed directly to federal circuit court by either the city or the opponents.

It will be many months before Judge Lande prepares his initial decision. He stated that the Ross Dam was a "mean" case to judge.

---

# Selected Readings

---

*From*

## THE NATURAL RESOURCES DECISION-MAKER AS A POLITICAL AND ECONOMIC MAN: TOWARD A SYNTHESIS*

*By Richard M. Alston and David M. Freeman*

Public decision-makers in natural resource management, as economic men, strive for efficient resource use entailing analysis of clearly delineated alternatives and goals that are specified and ranked. The same decision-makers, as socio-political men who bargain with diverse clients, know that the "public good" is defined in many conflicting ways by intensely competitive and self-interested groups. Such decision-makers know that goals are fluid, multiple, inconsistent, multidimensional, and incommensurable, and that no fixed solutions are possible, regardless of their technical or economic elegance. One man's solution is another man's problem, and any solution generates a new set of problems. Economic and technical rationality has frequently floundered on socio-political shoals.

---

* Reprinted by permission of the *Journal of Environmental Management,* 1975 (3), pp. 167–78 (excerpts). References have been deleted from this abridged version.

## Economics and the Benefit-Cost Algorithm

Benefit-cost analysis begins with two basic assumptions: (*a*) the only substitutes for *informed* value judgments in the evaluation of benefits and costs of public policy alternatives are *uninformed* value judgments, and (*b*) efficient use of resources is fundamental. Benefit-cost analysis is designed to make possible such informed value judgments to aid the decision-maker in ranking investment projects according to one measure of economic efficiency. Decision-making requires both quantitative and qualitative considerations, and no model or set of decision rules can generate a "best" decision. In fact, *models do not make decisions at all.* Economists hope that benefit-cost models can guide the final decision, point up uncertainties, and systematically make assumptions, calculations, and judgments explicit.

Although specific formulations differ, benefit-cost analysis usually involves some combination of the following nine steps (summarized in Table 1 herein).

1. Clearly specify the goal(s) and objectives.
2. Identify the relevant benefit and cost consequences for each alternative.
3. Indicate the unit of measure applicable to each of the outputs or consequences.
4. *Estimate* the quantitative number of units associated with each alternative for each benefit or cost class of consequences.
5. Use the dollar as the common index of relative value to allow comparability and additivity of findings and *estimate* the value for each unit of benefit or cost consequence.
6. Introduce weighting factors in recognition that value judgments will be part and parcel of the analysis. Weights are used to adjust the best estimate of relative monetary value for non-market considerations, social, cultural, political, and other difficult to measure aspects of the evaluation.[1]
7. *Estimate* benefits and costs separately for each identified consequence for each year over the life of the project. Social weighting is desirable but optional.
8. Aggregate the estimate of benefits and costs, discounting future benefits and costs to the present.
9. Employ ranking criteria to comparatively evaluate alternatives. (Under normal circumstances, projects would be ranked according to their marginal benefit-cost ration (*b/c*), the higher the marginal ratio the more desirable the project.

Thus, the analytical framework takes on the general format indicated in Table 1.

## SOME SHORTCOMINGS OF BENEFIT-COST ANALYSIS

Traditional benefit-cost analysis has proved to be extremely valuable to resource managers, but, as has been pointed out, it is not a prescriptive tool. It is most useful on relatively small, single-purpose projects with few externalities. Of course, such situations are rarely the types facing natural resource decision-makers. Important problems associated with this method include: relative ease and danger of "cheating" in the analysis; necessity of limiting the scope of project analysis since large projects or programs tend to alter the entire spectrum of relative values and outputs; choice of the proper rate of social discount; determination of appropriate estimates for values to be used in the case of imperfect or non-existent market evaluations (as environmental quality); justification for inclusion or exclusion of types of benefits and costs; assessment of the benefits and costs of employment and income redistribution effects; and analysis of non-monetary, multifaceted social objectives and constraints. Some, but not all, of these shortcomings can be corrected or reasonably ameliorated.

---

[1] Benefit-cost algorithms traditionally specified that costs to whomever should incur them should be less than the benefits to whomever may secure them, but this can be ameliorated by differentially weighting benefits and costs as they impact on such specified target groups as low income recipients and ethnic minorities. This step is controversial and rarely *explicitly* used in practice, although often implicit in decisions.

**TABLE 1**
**The Analytical Framework for Benefit-Cost Analysis. Each alternative is analysed separately. For economic analysis, alternatives analysed are ranked by either of the following criteria (all values are present values)**

(1) $\dfrac{B}{C+A}$ ; $\dfrac{\text{Marginal economic benefits}}{\text{Marginal economic costs (direct + indirect)}}$

(2) $\dfrac{B-A}{C}$ ; $\dfrac{\text{Net marginal economic benefits (positive − negative)}}{\text{Marginal economic costs (direct)}}$

| Benefit or Cost Item by Output Class | Units of Measure | Expected or Predicted Increase (or decrease) in Benefits and Costs for Each Year of Planning Horizon (p) | Price or Relative Value per Unit (dollars) | Social Weighting or Adjustment Factor (optional) | Marginal Benefit or Costs for Each Year of Planning Horizon (p) (columns 3 × 4 × 5) | Aggregate Analysis (present value) Requires Choice of a Discount Rate (d) |
|---|---|---|---|---|---|---|
| Positive benefits ......... | $B_1$ <br> $B_2$ <br> ... <br> $B_j$ | $nB_1^p$ <br> $nB_2^p$ <br> ... <br> $nB_j^p$ | $b_1$ <br> $b_2$ <br> ... <br> $b_1$ | $W_{B_1}$ <br> $W_{B_2}$ <br> ... <br> $W_{B_1}$ | $B_1{}^{*p}$ <br> $B_2{}^{*p}$ <br> ... <br> $B_1{}^{*p}$ | $\displaystyle\sum_{p,\,i}\frac{B_i{}^{*p}}{(1+d)^p}=B$ |
| | $U_1$ <br> $U_2$ <br> ... <br> $U_j$ | | | | | |
| Adverse effects, negative benefits, or indirect costs ......... | $A_1$ <br> $A_2$ <br> ... <br> $A_j$ | $nA_1^p$ <br> $nA_2^p$ <br> ... <br> $nA_j^p$ | $a_1$ <br> $a_2$ <br> ... <br> $a_j$ | $W_{A_1}$ <br> $W_{A_2}$ <br> ... <br> $W_{Aj}$ | $A_1{}^{*p}$ <br> $A_2{}^{*p}$ <br> ... <br> $A_j{}^{*p}$ | $\displaystyle\sum_{p,\,i}\frac{A_i{}^{*p}}{(1+d)^p}=A$ |
| | $D_1$ <br> $D_2$ <br> ... <br> $D_j$ | | | | | |
| Direct costs ......... | $C_1$ <br> $C_2$ <br> ... <br> $C_k$ | $nC_1^p$ <br> $nC_2^p$ <br> ... <br> $nC_k^p$ | \$ <br> \$ <br> ... <br> \$ | 1 <br> 1 <br> ... <br> 1 | $C_1{}^{*p}$ <br> $C_2{}^{*p}$ <br> ... <br> $C_k{}^{*p}$ | $\displaystyle\sum_{p,\,k}\frac{C_k{}^{*p}}{(1+d)^p}=C$ |
| | \$ <br> \$ <br> ... <br> \$ | | | | | |

## ALTERNATIVE APPROACHES TO NON-MARKET CONSIDERATIONS

Social, economic, and environmental goals are multifaceted, fluid, and frequently inconsistent. In addition to national income maximization, planners must also take into account regional and local employment, educational, health, cultural, environmental, and political goals, economic development and income distribution, as well as uncertainty associated with various aspects of the analysis. . . . Regardless of the degree of sophistication or the approach taken, however, no benefit-cost analysis is capable of eliminating the need for substantive value judgments in the final decision-making process. The decision-maker must rely on interdisciplinary teams of social, physical, and biological scientists to assess value mixes inadequately reflected in the benefit-cost framework.

### The Problem of Freezing

It is not unusual for projects supported by the logic of benefit-cost analysis to become political nightmares. In large part, political problems stem from the fact that benefit-cost analysis is goal dependent—ranking of alternatives is contingent on the ends chosen. Goal setting is a long and arduous process that, by necessity, often excludes people who have only a secondary interest in the immediate issue at hand. As programs and projects take shape, however, outside groups not party to the earlier goal selection and weighting process begin to feel the impact and frequently mount organized opposition that can exercise "veto power" through a variety of legal and extralegal devices. If the plan is changed, it threatens political support from the initial set of clients, puts the planner in the position of having to rebuild a new consensus on goals, and leaves him vulnerable to the charges of "sell-out." If the program or project formulation is not changed, the planner faces charges that public interest is being co-opted by vested interest groups. The decision-maker finds himself *frozen.*

\*     \*     \*     \*     \*

### The Socio-Political Approach

The decision-maker, as socio-political man, does not expect to *solve* problems in any ultimate sense. He hopes instead to effectively *reshape* the problems that arise from the multiplicity and fluidity of goals. . . . Rather than prescribing a "best" choice, emphasis is placed on enlarging the size of the social menu, the context of choice, the range of options. Etzioni . . . thus distinguished between "prescriptive" and "contextual" options. The social-political framework sets forth rules that make it possible to assess and predict whether particular policies will increase or decrease options that will appeal to the diverse and conflicting groups present in a dynamic society. In recognition of the fact that any particular choice is likely to be opposed by significant groups, value is placed on the ability of alternatives to enlarge the context from which options may be selected.

## CONFLICT IN THE DECISION-MAKING ENVIRONMENT

Policies and projects inevitably undercut values of some social groups while promoting interests of others and therefore contain seeds of conflict. . . . Social welfare, defined in terms of enlarging contextual options, becomes a question of analysing patterns of social conflict. The concept of social cleavage is central. . . . Defined as "patterned differences over value preferences creating a conflict front between actors," cleavages may be viewed as the conflict fronts among opposing values. Cleavages are omnipresent in social structure. *The thrust of this analysis is specifically on the nature of conflict fronts, not on the substantive nature of interests in conflict*[2]

---

[2] This focus is appropriate because the state of the art allows measurement of presence and absence of cleavages more accurately than the interests themselves. Often the actors are not even sure what their interests are even though conflict is obviously present.

**FIGURE 1**
**If Common Values Are Nonexistent, Issues Tend to Polarize Interest Groups into Supporting and Hostile Positions and to Result in Polarizing Cleavages**

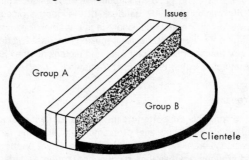

There are two polar types of conflict structures or cleavage patterns: polarizing cleavages and cross-cutting cleavages. Polarizing conflict structures (Figure 1) exist when opponent groups share no common values. Among others, these include economic, political, educational, religious, ethnic, and linguistic values. Adversaries on one issue are opponents on all. There is no basis for compromise and no incentive to negotiate. Opponents ascribe to each other less than human qualities, violence is condoned, and resources are expended to diminish the choices of the enemy. Options are removed from the social system. Although examples must lack precision and must be precarious, the Arab-Israeli conflict and the Catholic-Protestant clash in Ireland are informative here. Some may view the timber industry and the wilderness buffs as approximating this polarizing conflict structure.

Cross-cutting conflict structures (Figure 2) exist when groups in opposition over some cleavage fronts find and shared attachments when they approach other issues. Cross-cutting cleavages facilitate negotiation and compromise. Opponents on some issues are allied on other conflict fronts. Such alliances prevent total mobilization of one actor against another, polarization is precluded, and social groups that are partial opponents are kept open to ideas from each other. Violence is minimized and dissent, deviance, and innovation are tolerated. Issues become negotiable. Social options increase. Again at the risk of imprecision, some labor-management disputes are examples of cross-cutting cleavages. Issues associated

**FIGURE 2**
**Cross-Cutting Cleavages Result When Opponents on One Issue Are Allies on Others**

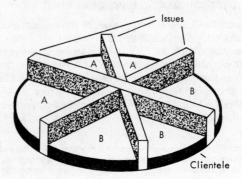

with the energy "crisis" have tended to organize on crosscutting vectors in the United States among advocates of such diverse policies as clean air standards, strip mining, and mass transportation.

Decision-makers should evaluate alternative courses of action according to their estimated impacts on the structure of social conflict. . . . Policies, programs, or projects that introduce additional polarizing conflict fronts only increase the probabilities of violence and the unproductive use of social resources. To open doors to compromise and negotiation, as well as to control violence, the master decision rule is: *Insert policy-induced conflict cleavages on cross-cutting lines.* To implement this master decision rule, the decision-maker must follow at least three additional rules.

The first decision rule concerns allocation of the "burden of uncertainty" that exists because it is impossible to know all impacts, consequences, externalities, and action or policy spillovers. . . . Proponents tend to assume that their opponents should have to establish "harmfulness" beyond reasonable doubt. Opponents, however, tend to argue that the proponents should be compelled to establish "harmlessness" of the venture. Innovation and new projects may be severely stifled if backers must bear the costs of establishing "harmlessness" of their proposals. But, "harmlessness" cannot be logically established since empirical demonstration of absence of harm does not mean that no harm will ensue. On the other hand, the burdens of establishing "harmlessness" could be placed on opponents. Significant deleterious effects might well be suffered before oppositional groups perceive the damage, organize, and empirically trace the linkages back to cause—often difficult in complex biological and social systems.

This approach, of course, coincides with our general legal structure, which calls for innocence till guilt has been proved. This may be well in normal jurisprudence; however, it introduces significant problems when applied to environmental affairs. By the time the "guilt" of an insecticide or drug is established, harmful and perhaps irreversible damages could become widespread. Moreover, by the time opponents to the action get organized, proponents may have incurred significant sunk costs and become "frozen", making change costly and difficult. The decision rule, then, is:

> Allocate the burdens of uncertainty associated with any given program so as to cross-cut cleavages between program opponents and proponents; that is, place the burdens of uncertainty on both sides, without forcing either side alone to bear all costs of demonstrating either "harmfulness" or "harmlessness".

The second decision rule concerns the significance of the cumulative effects of scale for social conflict among groups. Impacts vary according to the amount of diffusion of a set of activities. The impact of the snowmobile in 1960 when few such machines were on public lands was qualitatively different than in 1970, when many thousands were in use. Social conflicts surrounding snowmobile use grew in intensity as the numbers increased. The same can be said of conflicts surrounding hydroelectric power dams, electrical power plants, and interstate highways. The cumulative effects of scale decision rule is:

> Determine whether going to a higher level of program will likely generate a conflict cleavage. If so, identify whether cleavage will be polarizing or cross-cutting. Those activities that generate no cleavages or cross-cutting cleavages with expansion of scale are politically more viable than those that create polarizing cleavages.

The third decision rule has to do with the degree of reversibility of action. . . . "Keeping options open" must be more than a slogan in situations of uncertainty. The planner should count reversibility of action as a major benefit and irreversibility as a major cost.[3] Should

---

[3] This point has been given the force of law in the National Environmental Policy Act of 1969 (83 Stat. 852, Sec. 102).

decisions lead to polarized cleavage structures in unexpected ways, reversible actions can be modified or altered to redistriburte costs and benefits and reduce tendencies toward polarization, thereby increasing political viability. Substantial research and analytical resources should be reserved for those more highly irreversible decisions that appear to be unavoidable. The decision rule is:

> Rank all possible alternatives for action according to their reversibility, giving preference to those that are most reversible.

Briefly outlined, then, the socio-political algorithm states that the decision-maker should operate according to three decision rules that will assist him in keeping conflict cleavages cross-cut among diverse clientele, a condition that serves the value of increasing contextual options. The three decision rules can be combined and arranged ordinally along a continuum of socio-political decision viability (Table 2).

### Toward Synthesis—Combining Economic and Political Man

What is economically rational may be politically irrational. . . .

Rationality is not unidimensional. Nevertheless, the two approaches to decision-making can be combined. Economic and socio-political decision rules will not necessarily lead to identical policy choices, but each can contribute to the more judicious use of the other. Several points are in order.

Neither framework generates options; each serves to identify and screen out less acceptable choices. Because the decision-maker is dealing with noncommensurables, no rule can specify how to select a "best" alternative from those surviving the dual screening process. It is not possible to specify how much economic rationality one should sacrifice to gain a given amount of political rationality. Perhaps the best that can be done is to assess the opportunity cost associated with various degrees of trade-off. However, excessive violations of socio-political rationality polarize the decision-maker's clientele and make the context of choice untenable. Economic and other resources will only be used to cut down social options as highly polarized groups marshal their capacities to prevent each other from advancing their respective values.

We suggest distinguishing between project level analysis and program planning. Programs that may be clearly cross-cutting in conflict do not necessarily reflect the characteristics of any single component project that may be polarizing. This simple point suggests that decision-making at a project level can employ decision-making rules that differ from those used in making program decisions. At the project level, it is important to specify clear-cut goals and "lock" on to them to avoid drift. This is precisely the situation for which the economic benefit-cost analysis is best suited. The analysis provides an essential analytical framework for intraproject evaluation of alternatives. It tends to be a blunt tool, however, when it comes to interproject (program) evaluation. At program levels, project goals taken in isolation are not the key concern; the critical issues are the aggregate effects of the combined transfers of welfare of the several projects and the implications of those aggregated transfers for cleavage structures. At program levels, "freezing" to any particular goals could be disastrous.

**TABLE 2**
**Degree of Socio-Political Decision Viability**

| *Very high Viability* | *High Viability* | *Moderate Viability* | *Low Viability* | *Very low Viability* | *No Viability* |
|---|---|---|---|---|---|
| BU allocated to both proponents and opponents | BU allocated to both proponents and opponents | BU allocated to both proponents and opponents | BU allocated to either proponents or opponents | BU allocated to both proponents and opponents | BU allocated to either proponents or opponents |
| CES generates no cleavages or cross-cutting cleavages only | CES generates overlapping cleavages | CES generates no cleavages or cross-cutting cleavages only | CES generates overlapping cleavages | CES generates overlapping cleavages | CES generates overlapping cleavages |
| Reversible impacts | Reversible impacts | Irreversible impacts | Reversible impacts | Irreversible impacts | Irreversible impacts |
| | or | | | or | |
| | BU allocated to either proponents or opponents | | | BU allocated to either proponents or opponents | |
| | CES generates no cleavages or cross-cutting cleavages only | | | CES generates no cleavages or cross-cutting cleavages only | |
| | Reversible impacts | | | Irreversible impacts | |

The above ordering of the several combinations of the three variables is crude, tentative, and is meant to be suggestive only. The cumulative effects of scale (CES) variable has been assumed to be equal in importance to the burdens of uncertainty (BU) variable. Reversibility is weighted more heavily than either of the first two variables taken singly, but not more heavily than the first two variables taken together. This appears to be a reasonable initial weighting but such matters can only be resolved by careful empirical research

*From*

# LIVING IN THE ENVIRONMENT: CONCEPTS, PROBLEMS AND ALTERNATIVES*

## *By G. Tyler Miller, Jr.*

. . . Although the problem is enormously complex, five major factors seem to have led to our present situation: (1) our total and our per capita energy consumption have been rising rapidly; (2) the demand for oil and natural gas has outstripped the domestic supply and refinery capacity, producing an increased dependence on imports; (3) because all energy use pollutes to some degree, the increased use of energy has come into direct conflict with our need to preserve the air, water, and land; (4) the lack of a coordinated national energy policy has led to poor long range planning and to conflicting policies on the part of the government and the energy industries; and (5) potentially useful energy options such as solar, geothermal, nuclear fusion, wind power, and energy conservation have not been developed. . . .

. . . A human living at survival level needs about 2,000 kilocalories of energy per day. . . . But today the average American consumes or, more accurately, degrades 230,000 kilocalories of energy a day—a 115 fold increase over the survival level. . . .

It is not surprising that one of the most steeply rising curves in the world and in the United States is energy consumption. World energy consumption increased almost 600 percent between 1900 and 1965 and is projected to increase another 450 percent between 1965 and the year 2000. World oil consumption is now so enormous that during the decade between 1970 and 1980 the nations of the world are projected to consume as much oil as was used in the hundred years between 1870 and 1970 . . . Coal has been mined for 800 years, but over one-half of it has been extracted in the past 37 years. Petroleum has been pumped out of the ground for about 100 years, but over one-half of it has been consumed during the past 18 years. In sum, most of the world's consumption of energy from fossil fuels throughout all history has taken place during the past 30 years.

Most of this energy is consumed by the industrial nations. With only 30 percent of the world's people, they use 80 percent of the world's energy and this gap is expected to widen.

. . . The United States with less than one-sixteenth of the world's population accounts for over one-third of the world's annual consumption of energy. In contrast, India with about 15 percent of the world's population consumes only about 1.5 percent of the world's energy. Each year 214 million Americans use as much energy for air conditioning alone as 800 million Chinese use for all purposes, and we *waste* almost as much energy as 105 million Japanese consume for all purposes. . . .

Today about 95 percent of all energy used in the United States is based on the fossil fuels coal, oil, and natural gas. Between 1850 and the present we shifted our energy use pattern first from wood to coal and then from coal to oil and natural gas, which now supply some 77 percent of our energy . . . . The joyride of cheap fossil fuel energy in the United States seems to be over . . . . and we must now adopt a new energy use pattern. We are not running out of energy, but we are running out of cheap oil and natural gas.

In spite of this, over 50 percent of the energy used in this country is wasted . . . . Although some energy will automatically be wasted as a result of the second law of thermodynamics . . . . experts estimate that our energy waste could be cut by one-third to one-half (without a loss in life quality) through a national energy conservation program based on existing technology.

***The Four Energy Crises.*** Based on the time perspectives of the short term (present

---

to 1985), intermediate term (1985 to 2000), and long term (2000 to 2020), there appear to be four distinct energy crises. Two of these are *real energy crises* based on a true shortage of needed energy resources, while the remaining two are more accurately described as energy policy crisis. They do not result from an actual global shortage of energy resources but from a fragmented, unwise, or nonexistent energy policy that affects world-wide exploration, distribution, and processing of existing energy sources.

\*     \*     \*     \*     \*

1. *Today's Real Energy Crisis—Food.*   One-third to one-half of the world's population does not get the basic minimum quantity and quality of 2,000 kilocalories of energy per day needed for good health.

2. *Today's Energy Policy Crisis.*   Cheap fossil fuel energy is maldistributed or unavailable because or poor planning and unwise policies of the government and energy industries and because of increased per capita energy use and waste.

3. *The Energy Policy Crisis of 1985.*   Failure to develop and coordinate a national energy policy could make the country dependent on outside sources for much of its oil and natural gas or could force the nation to switch to nuclear fission energy or return to coal before evaluating the potential solar geothermal, wind, coal gasification, and energy, conservation alternatives.

4. *The Real Energy Crisis of 2000 to 2020.*   As economically acceptable supplies of natural gas, petroleum, and uranium begin to dwindle, we will have to shift to essentially infinite and safe energy resources or suffer a sharp drop in per capita energy use. (The policies we are making now will determine how prepared we are for this crisis.)

\*     \*     \*     \*     \*

***Overall Evaluation of Options.***   From Tables 1 and 2 we can see that our best option, considering net energy and environmental impact, is energy conservation. Unfortunately, this option has very low priority in our present energy strategy in terms of specific laws, actions, and funding . . . . It takes about ten years to achieve major energy savings by phasing out low gas mileage cars, shifting to mass transit . . ., requiring increased insulation on all new and most existing buildings, building energy conserving buildings, and changing to less energy intensive manufacturing and farming processes. Thus, energy conservation can have only a moderate impact for the short term but a major impact for the intermediate and long term. But because a ten-year lead time is needed, these crucial savings won't be realized unless a stringent conservation program is put into effect now.

Natural gas, oil, hydroelectric, and tidal power also offer good combinations of moderate to high net energy and low to moderate environmental impact. But natural gas and oil will probably be available only for a few decades at rapidly escalating prices. Hydroelectric power now provides only about 4 percent of our total energy and 10 percent of our electricity, and these percentages are expected to decline in the future because most of the rivers with sufficient flow have already been dammed. Tidal power can be tapped only in the very few places where a major drop between low and high tide exists and can thus supply only a miniscule amount of U.S. energy needs and probably no more than 1 percent of world energy needs . . . .

The burning of trash as fuel or its conversion to synthetic natural gas or oil by chemical processes or microorganisms . . . will be of great help in conserving metal resources through recycling (since metals and other resources must be removed before burning), saving energy by shifting from more energy intensive virgir, resources to recycled materials, and reducing solid waste disposal problems. . . . But even with extensive use and improved technology the U.S. Bureau of Mines estimate that trash burning can never provide more than 10 to 15 percent of our electricity and no more than 1 to 2 percent of our total energy needs . . . .

Coal can provide adequate supplies, but with great increased risks from air pollution and strip mining. We may be able to decrease sulfur oxide and particulate pollution, . . . find commercially feasible ways to convert coal to less polluting natural gas, and pass strict laws for reclaiming strip mined land—but only at greatly increased energy costs.

Geothermal, . . . solar, wind, and nuclear fusion energy are clean and essentially infinite

# TABLE 1
## Evaluation of Energy Options for the United States

| Option | Estimated Availability* | | | Estimated Net Energy | Potential Environmental Impact† |
| --- | --- | --- | --- | --- | --- |
| | Short term (present to 1985) | Intermediate Term (1985 to 2000) | Long Term (2000 to 2020) | | |
| Conservation | Fair | Good | Good | Very high | Decreases impact of other sources |
| Natural gas | Good (with imports) | Fair (with imports) | Poor | High but decreasing‡ | Low |
| Oil | | | | | |
| Conventional | Good (with imports) | Fair (with imports) | Poor | High but decreasing‡ | Moderate |
| Shale | Poor | Moderate to good? | Moderate to good? | Probably very low | Serious |
| Tar sands | Poor | Moderate? (imports only) | Good? (imports only) | Probably very low | Moderate |
| Coal | | | | | |
| Conventional | Good | Good | Good | High but decreasing‡ | Very serious |
| Gasification (conversion to synthetic natural gas) | Poor | Good? | Good? | Moderate to low | Very serious |
| Liquification (conversion to synthetic oil) | Very poor | Poor to moderate? | Good? | Moderate to low | Serious |
| Wastes | | | | | |
| Direct burning | Poor to fair | Fair to poor | Fair | Moderate (space heating) to low (electricity) | Fairly low |

| Energy source | | | | | |
|---|---|---|---|---|---|
| Conversion to oil | Poor | Fair to poor | Fair | Moderate to low | Low to moderate |
| Hydroelectric | Poor | Poor | Very poor | High | Low to moderate |
| Tidal | Very poor | Very poor | Very poor | Unknown (moderate?) | Low |
| Nuclear | | | | | |
| Conventional fission | Poor | Good | Good to poor | Probably very low | Very serious |
| Breeder fission | None | None to low | Good? | Probably low | Extremely serious |
| Fusion | Poor | Moderate to low? | Moderate to low | Unknown (could be low) | Unknown (probably moderate to low) |
| Geothermal | Poor | Moderate to low? | Moderate to low | Unknown (probably moderate to to low) | Moderate to low |
| Solar | Poor (except for space and water heating) | Low to moderate? | Moderate to high? | Unknown (probably low) | Low |
| Wind | Poor | Poor to moderate? | Moderate to high? | Unknown (probably moderate to low) | Low |
| Hydrogen | Negligible | Poor | Unknown§ | Unknown (probably moderate to low) | Unknown§ |
| Fuel cells | Negligible | Poor | Unknown§ | Unknown (probably moderate to low) | Unknown§ |

* Based on estimated supply as a fraction of total energy use and on technological and economic feasibility.
† If stringent safety and environmental controls are not required and enforced.
‡ As high grade deposits decrease, more and more energy must be used to mine and process lower grade deposits, thus decreasing net energy.
§ Depends on whether an essentially infinite source of electricity (such as solar, fusion, wind, or breeder) is available to convert water to hydrogen and oxygen gas by electrolysis or direct heating Impact will vary depending on the source of electricity.

**TABLE 2**
**Comparative Environmental Impacts of Energy Options**

| Energy Option | Air Pollution | Water Pollution | Solid Waste | Land Use Impact | Occupational Health | Possible Large Scale Disasters |
|---|---|---|---|---|---|---|
| Conservation | Decreased | Decreased | Decreased | Decreased | Less | None |
| Natural gas | Low | Low | Negligible | Low | Low | Pipeline explosion; earthquakes if nuclear blasts used for stimulating wells |
| **Oil** | | | | | | |
| Offshore wells | Moderate | Serious | Very low | Very low | Low | Massive spill on water from blowout or pipeline rupture |
| Onshore wells | Moderate | Serious | Very low | Low | Low | Massive spill on land from blowout or pipeline rupture |
| Imports | Low to moderate | Serious | Very low | Very low | Low | Massive spill from tanker accident |
| Shale | Moderate | Moderate to serious | Serious | Serious | Low | Massive spill on land from blowout or pipeline rupture; earthquakes if nuclear blasts used for production in wells |
| Tar sands | Moderate | Moderate to serious | Serious | Moderate | Low | Massive spill on land from blowout or pipeline rupture |
| **Coal** | | | | | | |
| Deep mined | Very serious | Very serious | Moderate | Moderate | Very serious | Mine accidents |
| Surface mined | Very serious | Very serious | Very serious | Very serious | Serious | Landslides |
| Gasification | Low | Very serious (more coal mined) | Very serious (more coal mined) | Very serious (more coal mined) | Very serious | Mine accidents; landslides; pipeline explosion |
| Liquification | Low | Very serious (more coal mined) | Very serious (more coal mined) | Very serious (more coal mined) | Very serious | Mine accidents; landslides; spills from pipeline rupture |

| | Wastes | | | | | |
|---|---|---|---|---|---|---|
| Direct burning | Moderate | Very low | Decrease | Decrease | Low | Fire or explosion in furnace |
| Conversion to oil | Moderate | Low | Decrease | Decrease | Low | Fire or explosion in furnace |
| Hydroelectric | Negligible | Negligible | Negligible | Serious | Low | Rupture of dam |
| Tidal | Negligible | Negligible | Negligible | Low to moderate | Low | None |
| Nuclear | | | | | | |
| Conventional fission | Negligible for normal pollutants but serious for radioactive releases | Low for normal sources but serious for radioactive releases | Low but very serious for radioactive releases | Low but very serious for radioactive releases | Low but very serious for radioactive releases | Meltdown of reactor core; sabotage of plants; shipping accidents; highjacking of shipments for use in nuclear bombs or for release into environment |
| Breeder | Negligible for normal pollutants but serious for radioactive releases | Low for normal sources but serious for radioactive releases | Low but extremely serious for radioactive releases | Low but extremely serious for radioactive releases | Low but extremely serious for radioactive releases | Meltdown of reactor core; sabotage of plants, shipping accidents, highjacking of shipments for use in nuclear bombs or for release into environment (radioactivity more dangerous than from conventional reactors) |
| Fusion | Negligible for normal pollutants but moderate for radioactive releases | Low? | Low? | Low | Low | Meltdown or explosion of reactor with release of gaseous radioisotopes |
| Geothermal | Moderate | Moderate to serious | Very low | Low to moderate | Low | None |
| Solar | Negligible | Negligible | Negligible | Low to moderate | Low | None |
| Wind | Negligible | Negligible | Negligible | Low to moderate | Low | None |
| Hydrogen* | Variable | Variable | Variable | Variable | Variable | Variable |
| Fuel cells* | Variable | Variable | Variable | Variable | Variaable | Variable |

* The systems themselves have low environmental impacts in all phases, but the environmental impact of the systems of electricity used to generate these fuels must be added.

energy resources . . . that represent major hopes for the long term when supplies of oil and natural gas are depleted. Because we have yet to put significant amounts of money in their development (except for fusion), there is still much uncertainty and disagreement over their potential net energy yield and overall feasibility.

Controlled nuclear fusion is the most difficult scientific and engineering problem man has ever faced, and it may never become feasible on a commercial scale in terms of net energy. To some . . . geothermal, wind, and solar energy will never provide more than a few percent of our total energy needs. But to others . . . they could be key sources for the intermediate and long term with massive research and development over the next 2 to 3 decades.

The technology for many forms of solar energy is already available, and a panel of distinguished scientists . . . project that it could be available for space heating of buildings and homes within 5 to 10 years and for large scale electric power generation within 10 to 15 years.

Estimates of the potential for geothermal energy vary from only 0.5 percent to all of our projected energy needs by the year 2000. But net energy availability is largely unknown.

A National Science Foundation and National Aeronautics and Space Administration panel and a prominent expert . . . suggest that by 2000 a major development program in wind power could provide electricity equivalent to all that produced in 1970. Wind turbines could be quickly added to supplement power, and a band of 100,000 to 300,000 giant wind turbines stretching from Texas to the Dakotas and about 50,000 floating off the East Coast might provide half the country's electrical needs. . . But because the fuel for wind and solar power are free, these options are not being pushed by energy companies in the business of selling fuel.

*From*

# THE ECONOMICS OF ENERGY EXTRAVAGANCE*

*By Richard A. Walker and David B. Large*

There have been several responses to the energy crisis. The two most prominent are the proposals for the conservation of energy and the proposals for the expansion of energy supplies. The conservation approach is based on the belief that wasteful energy practices are an avoidable error that can be corrected by sufficiently enlightened public policies decided by people of good will. The supply expansion approach does not question the way in which energy is used, but seeks to assure the provision of enough energy to meet whatever the market demands.

* * * * *

Utilization of energy in the United States is essentially an economic problem. Wasteful practices in energy use are not, however, a product of random errors or distortions from an otherwise efficient market system, as liberal conservationists have alleged. On the contrary, public and private policies have systematically promoted energy extravagance to further the foremost goal of national policy—a helathy and growing economy. In a market economy, built on private production and investment guided by the profit motive and the need to accumulate, a given pattern of development, once established, tends to be self-reinforcing and difficult to change. Moreover, any disruption in an established trend gives rise to eco-

* Reprinted with permission from the *Ecology Law Quarterly,* vol. 4, 1975, pp. 963–70, 972–73, 975–79, 984, (excerpts). Copyright © 1975 by *Ecology Law Quarterly,* School of Law, University of California, Berkeley. All references have been deleted from this excerpt.

nomic dislocation that threatens stability and development. The established trend of U.S. economic growth since World War II has been one of extravagant energy use. This pattern, begun during a period of relatively cheap and plentiful energy supplies, developed its own momentum over time until it reached an irrational level of energy use and waste. The economy had become ripe for the crisis produced by the disruption in oil supplies which occurred in 1974.

The supply expansion approach of unquestioned obedience to the status quo pattern of energy use arises from a fear of such a disruption. The advocates of this approach don't discuss the rationality of energy use because they never question the dictates of the market. The advocates of the conservationist approach, while quite enlightened on questions of use, discuss everything relevant to the problem except the fundamental structure of the market, which they too consider beyond dispute. They fail to realize that the energy crisis is not an isolated problem. Energy crises, like other crises to which the market system is prone, come and go, but the root causes of their periodically recurring dilemmas do not.

*    *    *    *    *

## CONSERVATIONIST PERSPECTIVES ON REFORM

Appeals for energy conservation are a logical if superficial approach to the energy crisis in the face of America's profligate consumption and waste of energy. Over the past decade the annual consumption of all energy in the United States grew at nearly four times the rate of population and the consumption of electric energy alone increased at a rate in excess of seven times the population. Per capita energy consumption in 1972 was nearly three times that of Western Europe, more than three times that of Japan, and almost six times the world average.

Much of this energy is being wasted. The overall energy efficiency of the U.S. economy as of 1970 was optimistically estimated at 50 percent. That is, at least half of the 65 quadrillion BTU's of fuel energy consumed that year were discarded as waste heat and various forms of pollution without having performed any useful function. Although some of the waste results from fundamental constraints on the efficiency with which energy can be converted from one form to another, much of it results from poor mechanical design and grossly inefficient methods of transportation and work performance.

Reducing energy waste, therefore, would seem to be a straightforward problem. All one must do is change inefficient machines and patterns of activity. Reformers have pursued such *solutions* from three perspectives: the sociological, the technological, and the economic. Yet, each of these views fails to touch upon the deeper problems in our system. The "sociological model" attributes our extravagant energy use to the irrational habits of the average citizen too lazy to walk to the corner store or suffer the minor inconveniences of public transit. In this view, it is mainly the consumer's "lack of self-discipline" that is responsible for "our riotous waste of energy." It takes little insight, however, to see that this view is woefully inadequate; it ignores the realities of the organization of people and their activities in space, the information and choices available to the consumer, and the system of economic incentives that encourages energy consumption. The consumer does not have free choice over a wide range of alternatives. He or she is constrained by fixed spatial relationships— home to work, shopping, or recreation—and by the relative availability of modern energy-intensive goods—automobiles, homes, and appliances. Given the reality of the options, the average American makes rational choices in purchasing two cars and all-electric homes; everyday experience before the energy crisis gave no reason to believe that these choices were unwise.

The economic and institutional incentives which guide consumers and businesses in their energy utilization choices are addressed by the third and most sophisticated liberal perspective: the "economic model." This model recognizes that the market is the primary institution integrating consumers and sellers into American economic society. It also posits that, to a large degree, price signals in the market direct consumer and seller behavior. Thus, for the past thirty years, price incentives have encouraged energy consumption while they have discouraged the development of more energy-efficient alternatives.

There is no doubt that government policies systematically encourage energy production and consumption. For example, the depletion allowance and other tax credits, until very recently, subsidized oil exploration and production. Demand-prorationing by the states has institutionalized ever-expanding oil production. Utility regulation puts constant pressure on electric utilities to increase their rate-base by building larger plants. The Interstate Commerce Commission gives trucks parity with railroads on long hauls, wasting millions of gallons of fuel without visible consumer benefit.

## ACCUMULATION AND THE ENERGY INTENSIVE CITY

The built-form[1] of the American city has changed dramatically in this century with the enormous growth of sprawling suburbs, the concentration of financial and managerial offices in the city center, the separation of work and homes with its consequent need to commute long distances, and the almost complete dependence on the automobile for movement. The modern city is space-extensive and energy-intensive. What is relevant to this Article's analysis, then, is how such a city developed and how adaptable it is to a change in circumstances —e.g., an energy shortage. It is too often assumed that the present form of the American city is either "natural" or the optimal outcome of an efficient allocation of resources controlled by the hidden hand of the market. These assumptions must be questioned. The city is certainly structured by the play of market forces, but those forces may operate in a fashion that is neither efficient nor desirable from society's point of view.

Three aspects of urban development illustrate the general principles of spiral causality— transportation, housing, and central city development—all of which contribute significantly to the energy-intensiveness of the American city.

### 1. Transportation

The automobile has grown to preeminence in the last thirty years at the expense of more energy—efficient modes of transportation. At the same time, the growth and dominance of automotive transportation have restructured the entirety of urban life. The buildings knocked down for parking lots and streets cannot be magically restored. This restructuring of the city's built-form has in turn reinforced the individual's dependence on the automobile. As more cars are used, more highways are built to meet the demand, or, more typically, to anticipate future demand. As this makes it easier to drive, more cars are purchased, the suburbs are extended, and, once again, bigger and better roads are built—and so on, in a self-reinforcing spiral.

### 2. Housing

Market forces similar to those affecting the urban transportation sector are also at work in the urban housing market. Both areas have encouraged suburbanization and wasteful energy utilization. The dictates of profitability in real estate, mortgage, and construction markets operate to encourage suburban growth *independent* of population growth, rising affluence, and changing transportation modes. As in the case of automobile usage, the pursuit of profitable investment exaggerates an existing trend in a self-perpetuating and socially harmful way.

The key to the housing market structure is finance. Capital is systematically withdrawn by low maintenance and abandonment in the inner city until lowered costs and the reduced

---

[1] The term "built-form" refers to the physical structures erected for the city's internal functioning. Buildings (business and residential), transportation, sanitation, and power facilities and the means by which all are related are components of a city's built-form.

supply of housing raise profits to an acceptable level. At the same time, the withdrawn capital and new capital are channeled into the suburbs, where returns are high and risks low. In the inner city incomes are low, properties old, and risks relatively high because of the so-called "social pathologies" of the poor concentrated there. To the rational and financially conservative real estate developer the suburbs provide a safer and higher return on investment. Further, the social and economic conditions which appear to "cause" the differential in profits that leads to the outward migration of capital are themselves magnified by that same flow of investment. Prospective homeowners cannot obtain mortgages in the inner city and so turn to the suburbs for housing. Owners of older homes in the city find it difficult if not impossible to obtain loans for needed improvements. Professional landlords often cannot obtain financing of their mortgages and are thus denied the ability to leverage their capital, an essential part of that business' successful operation. As a result, they attempt to reduce expenditures by overcrowding tenants or by cutting maintenance costs, thereby accelerating deterioration of the property. Some even abandon properties entirely or allow them to revert to the city in tax arrears. Finally, municipal expenditures and tax rates rise to bear the increased load of social welfare programs as the poor crowd into the progressively cheaper housing.

In the suburbs, meanwhile, owners and landlords have little trouble securing financing. Maintenance costs are lower because of the newness of the housing and the lack of overcrowding. Additional favorable financial factors are the gains from the rise in land values accompanying rapid growth, the implicit subsidies in public service provisions, and the lower tax rates.

### 3. Central City Development

Despite the outward migration of primarily white middle-class people to the suburbs, suburbanites at the management and professional levels continue to commute in great numbers to the central business district. And even though most manufacturing, wholesaling, and retailing growth has followed the migration to the suburbs, there has been a marked increase in downtown office construction in the last fifteen years. Thus, the central business district often remains the financial and governmental center of metropolitan areas.

Large cities are remarkably similar when viewed from a distance. Each has at its center a huddled mass of skyscrapers out of proportion to the gradient of building heights increasing from the periphery inward. This pattern of central office concetration creates massive commuter traffic and energy use. It is often assumed that this central location and density produce "productive efficiency. There is, however, good reason to doubt this vision of order and efficiency. The observed clustering of corporate headquarters, financial institutions, government bureaucracies, and the professionals who serve them has less to do with production than with such factors as spatial monopoly, personal access among managerial elites, and even a type of "conspicuous consumption" among corporations vying for the most impressive headquarters.

### ECONOMIC CRISIS AVOIDANCE AND CONSERVATIVE ENERGY POLICIES

Operating in the American economy is a *negative* force which reinforces the energy-intensive economy: the desire to avoid economic crisis. This force generates the dominant policy of increasing supplies first and curtailing waste second. Because those advocating energy conservation mistakenly accept the basic structure of the economic system they seek to reform, they do not understand why the supply expansion approach is dominant, nor do they see the obstacles to the adoption of their proposed large-scale energy conservation programs.

The idea that the economic patterns and expectations of the past are frozen into brick and steel and cannot be adapted instantaneously or without cost to the needs of the present has been previously discussed. There is always tension between the built-form of a city created in one period, and the needs of its inhabitants in a later period. In a market economy the tension between past creations and present needs takes on a special form. If profit-conscious firms do not realize their expected profit levels on past investment in fixed capital, they revise their expectations and, accordingly, their operation. Often this is done by decreasing production, laying off workers, and curtailing new investment plans. These negative actions are cumulative in their effect, both psychologically and in real economic terms of declining corporate and consumer demand. If sufficiently widespread, they will lead the economy into the downward spiral of a business slump. For instance, past expectations of low fuel prices and easy availability are built into fixed capital and the spatial form of the sprawling city. Hence, there is literally no freedom to undo history and reform the city when energy prices go up and availability goes down. When this situation occurred during the 1973–74 winter, it was soon transformed into a business crisis in the automobile industry. Detroit had been committed to large, inefficient cars which were now suddenly looked upon with disfavor by a public trying to stay mobile in an automobile-dependent, gasoline-scarce urban world. As a result of lagging sales and mounting inventories, automakers laid off more than 100,000 workers in the first quarter of 1974. These events led the way into the present recession.

Eventually unemployment, disruption, and the uncertain business outlook generated enough political uproar to force the government to intervene in an attempt to restore prosperous conditions. But in seeking to "solve" the manifestations of the crisis government, business, and labor have so far avoided its root causes. No one in a responsible position of power has seriously questioned the basis for America's energy extravagance because doing so would necessitate advocating major structural changes in the economy. As a result, government intervention has been generally confined to intermediate solutions while the most pressing problems have been sidestepped. Even when a problem is confronted directly, the treatment is still controlled by the conditions created by the past history of the private sector's investment decisions. Thus, when threats of Arab embargoes and rising oil prices create an energy crisis, the government's dominant policy is to assure continuing, alternative supplies of fuel.

*    *    *    *    *

## CONCLUSION

Energy utilization by American society cannot be adequately understood in the sociological, technological, or conventional economic terms which liberal reformers commonly employ. Neither consumer self-interest, poor engineering, nor misguided government regulation satisfactorily accounts for the fact that per capita consumption of energy in the United States has been increasing at a compound rate of 3 percent per year. Most wasteful energy consumption occurs because such consumption patterns have continued to be profitable for the economy as a whole, and not because society is ignorant of more efficient methods or because it is inherently lazy. At both the microeconomic level of pricing policies and the macroeconomic level of investment, inordinate energy use is built into the system. In fact, the innumerable distortions and irrationalities of pricing and energy use at the microeconomic level become comprehensible *only* in light of the need for continued economic growth at the macroeconomic level.

From

# THE SCIENCE OF "MUDDLING THROUGH"*

*By Charles E. Lindblom*

Suppose an administrator is given responsibility for formulating policy with respect to inflation. He might start by trying to list all related values in order of importance, e.g., full employment, reasonable business profit, protection of small savings, prevention of a stock market crash. Then all possible policy outcomes could be rated as more or less efficient in attaining a maximum of these values. This would of course require a prodigious inquiry into values held by members of society and an equally prodigious set of calculations on how much of each value is equal to how much of each other value. He could then proceed to outline all possible policy alternatives. In a third step, he would undertake systematic comparison of his multitude of alternatives to determine which attains the greatest amount of values.

In comparing policies, he would take advantage of any theory available that generalized about classes of policies. In considering inflation, for example, he would compare all policies in the light of the theory of prices. Since no alternatives are beyond his investigation, he would consider strict central control and the abolition of all prices and markets on the one hand and elimination of all public controls with reliance completely on the free market on the other, both in the light of whatever theoretical generalizations he could find on such hypothetical economies.

Finally, he would try to make the choice that would in fact maximize his values.

An alternative line of attack would be to set as his principal objective, either explicitly or without conscious thought, the relatively simple goal of keeping prices level. This objective might be compromised or complicated by only a few other goals, such as full employment. He would in fact disregard most other social values as beyond his present interest, and he would for the moment not even attempt to rank the few values that he regarded as immediately relevant. Were he pressed, he would quickly admit that he was ignoring many related values and many possible important consequences of his policies.

As a second step, he would outline those relatively few policy alternatives that occurred to him. He would then compare them. In comparing his limited number of alternatives, most of them familiar from past controversies, he would not ordinarily find a body of theory precise enough to carry him through a comparison of their respective consequences. Instead he would rely heavily on the record of past experience with small policy steps to predict the consequences of similar steps extended into the future.

Moreover, he would find that the policy alternatives combined objectives or values in different ways. For example, one policy might offer price level stability at the cost of some risk of unemployment; another might offer less price stability but also less risk of unemployment. Hence, the next step in his approach—the final selection—would combine into one the choice among values and the choice among instruments for reaching values. It would not, as in the first method of policy-making, approximate a more mechanical process of choosing the means that best satisfied goals that were previously clarified and ranked. Because practitioners of the second approach expect to achieve their goals only partially, they would expect to repeat endlessly the sequence just described, as conditions and aspirations changed and as accuracy of prediction improved.

* Reprinted by permission of *Public Administration Review*, vol. XIX, no. 2 (Spring 1959), quarterly journal of the *American Society for Public Administration*.

## By Root or by Branch

For complex problems, the first of these two approaches is of course impossible. Although such an approach can be described, it cannot be practiced except for relatively simple problems and even then only in a somewhat modified form. It assumes intellectual capacities and sources of information that men simply do not possess, and it is even more absurd as an approach to policy when the time and money that can be allocated to a policy problem is limited, as is always the case. . . .

Curiously, however, the literatures of decision-making, policy formulation, planning, and public administration formalize the first approach rather than the second, leaving public administrators who handle complex decisions in the position of practicing what few preach. For emphasis I run some risk of overstatement. True enough, the literature is well aware of limits on man's capacities, and of the inevitability that policies will be approached in some such style as the second. But attempts to formalize rational policy formulation—to lay out explicitly the necessary steps in the process—usually describe the first approach and not the second.[1]

The common tendency to describe policy formulation even for complex problems as though it followed the first approach has been strengthened by the attention given to, and successes enjoyed by, operations research, statistical decision theory, and systems analysis. The hallmarks of these procedures, typical of the first approach, are clarity of objective, explicitness of evaluation, a high degree of comprehensiveness of overview, and, wherever possible, quantification of values for mathematical analysis. But these advanced procedures remain largely the appropriate techniques of relatively small-scale problem-solving where the total number of variables to be considered is small and value problems restricted. Charles Hitch, head of the Economics Division of RAND Corporation, one of the leading centers for application of these techniques, has written:

> "I would make the empirical generalization from my experience at RAND and elsewhere that operations research is the art of sub-optimizing, i.e., of solving some lower-level problems, and that difficulties increase and our special competence diminishes by an order of magnitude with every level of decision making we attempt to ascend. The sort of simple explicit model which operations researchers are so proficient in using can certainly reflect most of the significant factors influencing traffic control on the George Washington Bridge, but the proportion of the relevant reality which we can represent by any such model or models in studying, say, a major foreign-policy decision, appears to be almost trivial."[2]

Accordingly, I propose in this paper to clarify and formalize the second method, much neglected in the literature. This might be described as the method of successive limited comparisons. I will contrast it with the first approach, which might be called the rational-comprehensive method.[3] More impressionistically and briefly—and therefore generally used in this article—they could be characterized as the branch method and root method, the

---

[1] James G. March and Herbert A. Simon similarly characterize the literature. They also take some important steps, as have Simon's recent articles, to describe a less heroic model of policy-making. See *Organizations* (John Wiley and Sons, 1958), p. 137.

[2] "Operations Research and National Planning—A Dissent," *5 Operations Research 718* (October 1957). Hitch's dissent is from particular points made in the article to which his paper is a reply; his claim that operations research is for low-level problems is widely accepted.

For examples of the kind of problems to which operations research is applied, see C. W. Churchman, R. L. Ackoff and E. L. Arnoff, *Introduction to Operations Research* (John Wiley and Sons, 1957); and J. F. McCloskey and J. M. Coppinger (eds.), *Operations Research for Management,* Vol. II (The Johns Hopkins Press, 1956).

[3] I am assuming that administrators often make policy and advise in the making of policy and am treating decision-making and policy-making as synonymous for purposes of this paper.

| Rational-Comprehensive (Root) | Successive Limited Comparisons (Branch) |
|---|---|
| 1a. Clarification of values or objectives distinct from and usually prerequisite to empirical analysis of alternative policies. | 1b. Selection of value goals and empirical analysis of the needed action are not distinct from one another but are closely intertwined. |
| 2a. Policy-formulation is therefore approached through means-end analysis: First the ends are isolated, then the means to achieve them are sought. | 2b. Since means and ends are not distinct, means-end analysis is often inappropriate or limited. |
| 3a. The test of a "good" policy is that it can be shown to be the most appropriate means to desired ends. | 3b. The test of a "good" policy is typically that various analysts find themselves directly agreeing on a policy (without their agreeing that it is the most appropriate means to an agreed objective). |
| 4a. Analysis is comprehensive; every important relevant factor is taken into account. | 4b. Analysis is drastically limited:<br>　i. Important possible outcomes are neglected.<br>　ii. Important alternative potential policies are neglected.<br>　iii. Important affected values are neglected. |
| 5a. Theory is often heavily relied upon. | 5b. A succession of comparisons greatly reduces or eliminates reliance on theory. |

former continually building out from the current situation, step-by-step and by small degrees; the latter starting from fundamentals anew each time, building on the past only as experience is embodied in a theory, and always prepared to start completely from the ground up.

Let us put the characteristics of the two methods side by side in simplest terms.

Assuming that the root method is familiar and understandable, we proceed directly to clarification of its alternative by contrast. In explaining the second, we shall be describing how most administrators do in fact approach complex questions, for the root method, the "best" way as a blueprint or model, is in fact not workable for complex policy questions, and administrators are forced to use the method of successive limited compairsons.

### Intertwining Evaluation and Empirical Analysis (1b)

The quickest way to understand how values are handled in the method of successive limited comparisons is to see how the root method often breaks down in *its* handling of values or objectives. The idea that values should be clarified, and in advance of the examination of alternative policies, is appealing. But what happens when we attempt it for complex social problems? The first difficulty is that on many critical values or objectives, citizens disagree, congressmen disagree, and public administrators disagree. Even where a fairly specific objective is prescribed for the administrator, there remains considerable room for disagreement on sub-objectives. . . .

Administrators cannot escape these conflicts by ascertaining the majority's preference, for preferences have not been registered on most issues; indeed, there often *are* no preferences in the absence of public discussion sufficient to bring an issue to the attention of the electorate. Furthermore, there is a question of whether intensity of feeling should be considered as well as the number of persons preferring each alternative. By the impossibility of doing otherwise, administrators often are reduced to deciding policy without clarifying objectives first.

Even when an administrator resolves to follow his own values as a criterion for decisions, he often will not know how to rank them when they conflict with one another, as they usually do. Suppose, for example, that an administrator must relocate tenants, living in tenements scheduled for destruction. One objective is to empty the buildings fairly promptly, another is to find suitable accommodation for persons displaced, another is to avoid friction with residents in other areas in which a large influx would be unwelcome, another is to deal with all concerned through persuasion if possible, and so on.

How does one state even to himself the relative importance of these partially conflicting values? A simple ranking of them is not enough; one needs ideally to know how much of one value is worth sacrificing for some of another value. The answer is that typically the administrator chooses—and must choose—directly among policies in which these values are combined in different ways. He cannot first clarify his values and then choose among policies.

A more subtle third point underlies both the first two. Social objectives do not always have the same relative values. One objective may be highly prized in one circumstance, another in another circumstance. If, for example, an administrator values highly both the dispatch with which his agency can carry through its projects *and* good public relations, it matters little which of the two possibly conflicting values he favors in some abstract or general sense. Policy questions arise in forms which put to administrators such a question as: Given the degree to which we are or are not already achieving the values of dispatch and the values of good public relations, is it worth sacrificing a little speed for a happier clientele, or is it better to risk offending the clientele so that we can get on with our work? The answer to such a question varies with circumstances.

The value problem is, as the example shows, always a problem of adjustments at a margin. But there is no practicable way to state marginal objectives or values except in terms of particular policies. That one value is preferred to another in one decision situation does not mean that it will be preferred in another decision situation in which it can be had only at great sacrifice of another value. Attempts to rank or order values in general and abstract terms so that they do not shift from decision to decision end up by ignoring the relevant marginal preferences. The significance of this third point thus goes very far. Even if all administrators had at hand an agreed set of values, objectives, and constraints, and an agreed ranking of these values, objectives, and constraints, their marginal values in actual choice situations would be impossible to formulate.

Unable consequently to formulate the relevant values first and then choose among policies to achieve them, administrators must choose directly among alternative policies that offer different marginal combinations of values. Somewhat paradoxically, the only practicable way to disclose one's relevant marginal values even to oneself is to describe the policy one chooses to achieve. Except roughly and vaguely, I know of no way to describe—or even to understand—what my relative evaluations are for, say, freedom and security, speed and accuracy in governmental decisions, or low taxes and better schools than to describe my preferences among specific policy choices that might be made between the alternatives in each of the pairs.

In summary, two aspects of the process by which values are actually handled can be distinguished. The first is clear: evaluation and empirical analysis are intertwined; that is, one chooses among values and among policies at one and the same time. Put a little more elaborately, one simultaneously chooses a policy to attain certain objectives and chooses the objectives themselves. The second aspect is related but distinct: the administrator focuses his attention on marginal or incremental values. Whether he is aware of it or not, he does not find general formulations of objectives very helpful and in fact makes specific marginal or incremental comparisons. Two policies, X and Y, confront him. Both promise the same degree of attainment of objectives a, b, c, d, and e. But X promises him somewhat more of f than does Y, while Y promises him somewhat more of g than does X. In choosing between them, he is in fact offered the alternative of a marginal or incremental amount of f at the expense of a marginal or incremental amount of g. The only values that are relevant to his choice are these increments by which the two policies differ; and, when he finally chooses between the two marginal values, he does so by making a choice between policies.[4]

As to whether the attempt to clarify objectives in advance of policy selection is more or less rational than the close intertwining of marginal evaluation and empirical analysis, the principal difference established is that for complex problems the first is impossible and irrelevant, and the second is both possible and relevant. The second is possible because the administrator need not try to analyze any values except the values by which alternative policies differ and need not be concerned with them except as they differ marginally. His need for information on values or objectives is drastically reduced as compared with the root method; and his capacity for grasping, comprehending, and relating values to one another is not strained beyond the breaking point.

[Editors' Note: Article proceeds to discuss the remaining four points 2b–5b listed above.]

---

[4] The line of argument is, of course, an extension of the theory of market choice, especially the theory of consumer choice, to public policy choices.

# 21. POLAROID CORPORATION

---

## Case Introduction

---

### SYNOPSIS

Some black workers in the Massachusetts headquarters of the Polaroid Corporation demanded that Polaroid cease doing business in South Africa. A multiracial task force from all levels of Polaroid employment was established to study the matter and recommend company policy. After sending a four-man team to learn the wishes of the blacks employed by Polaroid's South African distributor, the task force recommended a one-year experiment during which amateur photographic materials as well as sunglasses would continue to be sold in South Africa while strides would be made in black wages and training. A significant portion of profits earned in South Africa were to be committed as grants for the education of black South Africans. Others doing business in South Africa were also encouraged to follow Polaroid's lead in combatting apartheid from within. Polaroid had to study the results of the year's experiment to determine policy for South Africa for the coming year.

### WHY THIS CASE IS INCLUDED

The multinational corporation constantly confronts interdependencies in its worldwide system. In this case, the reader can observe how a $500 million company can have its focus and priorities shifted to a tiny distributorship 10,000 miles away from headquarters. Beyond discussing the substantive question of the "rightness" of doing business in South Africa, the reader can examine the manner in which Polaroid managed the protest and protesting employees. Comparisons can be made between Polaroid's handling of the affair and the reaction of other companies in United States and elsewhere. The reader should find it of particular interest to follow the unfolding events in the public U.S. press and also in the South African press.

## DIAGNOSTIC AND PREDICTIVE QUESTIONS

The readings included with this case are marked (*). The author index at the end of this book locates the other readings.

1. Prior to October 1970, why was Polaroid doing business in South Africa? Among all the organization forms Polaroid might have used, why did it work through a distributor for cameras and film and through a licensee for sunglasses?

   Read:   *Kolde, *International Business Enterprise.* *Pessemier, *New Product Decisions.*

2. What would have likely happened in the camera and film business in South Africa if Polaroid had "pulled out" as demanded? What would have happened in the sunglasses business had Polaroid "pulled out"?

   Read:   The Kolde reading assigned in the previous question and recall what you already know about distribution from the field of marketing.

3. What options are open to an employee for effectively voicing protest about some behavior of his or her own firm? Compare these options with those open to an owner for effectively voicing protest (as in the General Motors case cited in the appendix).

4. Were Miss Caroline Hunter's rights violated—as she insisted—when she was dismissed from Polaroid?

   Read:   Evan, "Organization Man and Due Process of Law."

5. What managerial style was used by Polaroid in coping with the issue raised by the protestors?

   Read:   *Eells and Walton, *Conceptual Foundations of Business,* pp. 360–63. Follett, "Constructive Conflict." O'Donnell, "The Source of Managerial Authority." Newman and Summer, *The Process of Management: Concepts, Behavior, and Practice.* Drucker, *The Future of Industrial Man.*

6. What are the essential differences between the position of Dr. Land (and the Polaroid Corporation) and Mr. Wates (and the Wates Construction Company—described in the appendix) vis-à-vis doing business in South Africa? Why do they differ?

   Review carefully the January 13, 1971, advertisement by Polaroid and the June 1970 press release by Mr. Wates. Consider the status of each company vis-à-vis expansion from home country at the time each document was written.

7. In what sense might an employer in South Africa feel guilty over the results of the apartheid system even though he did everything permissable by law for his nonwhite employees?

   Read:   *O'Connell, "New Credentials for Moralists."

8. Why is it that Polaroid, despite its public record of social responsibility, found itself confronted on its marginal presence in South Africa?

   Read:   *O'Connell, "The Tactics of Creative Tension."

## POLICY QUESTIONS

9. How would you have responded to the Polaroid Workers Revolutionary Movement "demands"? Recall that Polaroid insisted that it did

not respond to the "demands" but rather answered the implied question: "is it right to do business in South Africa?" Review your response to Question 8 and the reading assigned with Question 8.

10. If you had been the responsible Polaroid executive, would you have dismissed Miss Hunter? Why or why not? Reread the articles assigned with Questions 3 and 4.

11. How else (in terms of managerial style and process) might Polaroid have solved the problem of doing business in South Africa? Do you agree with the Polaroid approach? (Note that the decision process at Polaroid was different from that at Wates.) How would you have managed the process? Review Question 5.

12. What other alternatives could Polaroid have considered than the one outlined in its experiment (battling apartheid from within via its distributor)? Do you agree with Polaroid's choice of tactics? If not, what would you have done? Review Questions 6 and 7. Also compare the content of the Polaroid ad in Exhibit 2 with Mr. Wates' statement at the beginning of the appendix.

13. Knowing what you know at the end of the case about the results of the year-long Polaroid experiment, what would be your decision concerning doing business in South Africa? Why?

14. Under what conditions would you place a subsidiary (investments and employees) in South Africa?

# Case Text*

On October 5, 1970, signs appeared on the bulletin boards in the Polaroid Corporation's Cambridge, Massachusetts, headquarters, demanding that the company withdraw from doing business in South Africa. Two black Polaroid employees, Mr. Kenneth Williams and Miss Caroline Hunter, voiced the demands during a noisy midday demonstration outside Polaroid headquarters on October 7. They acted as spokesmen for the Polaroid Workers Revolutionary Movement (P.W.R.M.) and repeated demands for total withdrawal from South Africa even after Polaroid management had, on October 21, called a halt to all direct or indirect sales to the government of cameras or film which could be used in the apartheid-inspired passbook procedures for nonwhites in South Africa.

## THE POLAROID CORPORATION

Polaroid's South African operations comprise only a small fraction of the $500 million worldwide sales in 1970—about $1.5 million. Polaroid

---

* Copyright 1977 by J. J. O'Connell.

has no investment in South Africa and, technically, none of its 10,000 employees is stationed in South Africa. Frank and Hirch, Ltd., is the distributor for Polaroid cameras and film in South Africa. The same company employs some 200 blacks producing sunglasses under license from Polaroid, with lenses imported from Polaroid's U.S. manufacturing facilities.

Polaroid has marketing subsidiaries in 13 countries and manufacturing subsidiaries in Scotland and the Netherlands. Historical patterns would seem to indicate that Polaroid transforms distributorships in foreign markets into marketing subsidiaries after about $1 million sales volume has been achieved. In 1970, two new subsidiaries were formed, one in Norway, and the other in Austria. Also in 1970, an International Division was established, combining production, marketing, and financial management of the overseas operations into a single group. Foreign subsidiaries outperformed the parent organization and its U.S. subsidiaries in 1970 in both sales growth and profitability (see the financial statements in Exhibit 1). Financial observers note that the U.S. market may be getting tougher for Polaroid in spite of its product innovation and one-step photographic technology, which is protected by a patent. *The Wall Street Journal,* on June 23, 1970, hinted that the recent Polaroid stock price slide was due to the possibility of Kodak entering the instant photo field. Earlier, *Advertising Age* (May 25, 1970) noted that Polaroid buys negatives from Kodak but, by an agreement made in December 1969, Kodak will be permitted to manufacture Polaroid-type film for sale by 1976. Though Polaroid was issued 109 new patents in 1970, increasing its total to 1,100, a number of what are thought to be key patents expire in 1984.

Almost 10 percent of Polaroid's U.S. employment is black. Fifteen percent of those applying for work at Polaroid in 1969 were black, and 22 percent of the 2,383 who were hired were black. Thirty percent of the black employees completed educational or training courses in 1969. Polaroid speaks proudly of its record of corporate citizenship, especially in the Boston area. Its community relations group participated in more than 100 projects related to urban problems in the greater Boston area. Its wholly owned Inner City training center placed 125 people in permanent jobs during 1969 and boasts of an 82 percent retention rate in those jobs—significantly higher than in any such employment orientation or preemployment training effort elsewhere. Polaroid led Boston area companies in shifting support from the United Fund to the Black United Appeal. The increase it had planned for United Fund in 1970—some $20,000—was allocated to the Black United Appeal. Polaroid's president and chairman, Edwin H. Land, insists: "Polaroid is people!"

## THE SOUTH AFRICAN SETTING

Polaroid is one of some 300 American firms doing business in South Africa. U.S. investment of about $800 million in 1970 represented about 14 percent of all direct private investment in South Africa. The *Sunday Times* of London reported (on January 1, 1971) that the biggest U.S.

**EXHIBIT 1***
**Polaroid Corporation and Its Domestic Subsidiaries**

|  | 1970 | 1969 | 1968 | 1967 |
|---|---|---|---|---|
| Operating Results |  |  |  |  |
| Sales and other income . . . . . . . . . | $444,285 | $465,609 | $402,070 | $374,354 |
| Earnings before taxes. . . . . . . . . . . | 113,574 | 130,932 | 129,009 | 114,632 |
| Income taxes . . . . . . . . . . . . . . . . . . | 52,438 | 67,811 | 70,110 | 57,255 |
| Net earnings. . . . . . . . . . . . . . . . . . . | 61,136 | 63,121 | 58,899 | 57,377 |
| Earnings per share . . . . . . . . . . . . . | 1.86 | 1.94 | 1.86 | 1.81 |
|  |  |  |  |  |
| Financial Position, End of Year |  |  |  |  |
| Working capital. . . . . . . . . . . . . . . . . | $301,033 | $297,864 | $170,917 | $133,377 |
| Net property, plant and |  |  |  |  |
| equipment . . . . . . . . . . . . . . . . . . . | 172,449 | 125,070 | 95,833 | 80,097 |
| Shareholders' equity . . . . . . . . . . . . | 474,645 | 423,893 | 270,976 | 221,153 |
|  |  |  |  |  |
| Other Statistics |  |  |  |  |
| Net additions to property, plant |  |  |  |  |
| and equipment . . . . . . . . . . . . . . . | $ 63,718 | $ 43,755 | $ 26,099 | $ 26,968 |
| Depreciation . . . . . . . . . . . . . . . . . . . | 16,339 | 14,518 | 10,363 | 8,866 |
| Occupied space (thousand sq. |  |  |  |  |
| ft., end of year) . . . . . . . . . . . . . . | 4,097 | 3,627 | 3,060 | 2,919 |
| Number of employees, end of |  |  |  |  |
| year . . . . . . . . . . . . . . . . . . . . . . . | 8,996 | 9,157 | 7,563 | 6,849 |
| Payroll and benefits. . . . . . . . . . . . . | $101,860 | $100,001 | $ 81,536 | $ 70,402 |
| Shares outstanding, end of |  |  |  |  |
| year* . . . . . . . . . . . . . . . . . . . . . . . | 32,832 | 32,828 | 31,712 | 31,660 |
|  |  |  |  |  |
|  |  |  |  |  |
| Unconsolidated Subsidiaries |  |  |  |  |
| Outside the United States |  |  |  |  |
| Sales and other income . . . . . . . . . | $ 88,788 | $ 70,459 | $ 52,935 | $ 52,063 |
| Net earnings. . . . . . . . . . . . . . . . . . . | 11,008 | 8,547 | 3,551 | 1,082 |
| Earnings per share |  |  |  |  |
| equivalent . . . . . . . . . . . . . . . . . . . | .34 | .26 | .11 | .03 |
| Shareholder's equity, end of |  |  |  |  |
| year . . . . . . . . . . . . . . . . . . . . . . . | 20,293 | 15,041 | 6,696 | 3,406 |

* From the Polaroid Annual Report 1970.

investors are believed to be IBM, Ford, General Motors, Chrysler, Gulf, Mobil, Kodak, First National City Bank, and Chemical Bank. The U.S. share of the total has been increasing while the significantly larger (57 percent) British share is gradually diminishing. The annual net investment by U.S. corporations runs at barely 1 percent of all U.S. direct private investment abroad but the earnings from South Africa represent 2 percent of all the earnings from U.S. private investment overseas.[1] (See the table below.)

---

[1] *Foreign Investment in the Republic of South Africa,* United Nations, New York, 1970.

**EXHIBIT 1 (*continued*)**

| 1966 | 1965 | 1964 | 1963 | 1962 | 1961 |
|---|---|---|---|---|---|
| $316,551 | $202,228 | $138,077 | $122,333 | $102,589 | $100,562 |
| 95,232 | 57,373 | 35,687 | 24,207 | 21,675 | 17,546 |
| 47,638 | 28,501 | 17,582 | 13,129 | 11,803 | 9,538 |
| 47,594 | 28,872 | 18,105 | 11,078 | 9,872 | 8,008 |
| 1.51 | .92 | .58 | .35 | .32 | .26 |
| | | | | | |
| $101,966 | $ 86,443 | $ 66,661 | $ 51,656 | $ 47,539 | $ 41,926 |
| | | | | | |
| 61,995 | 37,482 | 30,308 | 27,930 | 22,638 | 18,195 |
| 170,150 | 125,043 | 97,168 | 79,801 | 70,517 | 60,456 |
| | | | | | |
| $ 31,197 | $ 13,087 | $  6,710 | $  9,768 | $  7,857 | $  3,877 |
| 6,684 | 5,587 | 5,234 | 4,379 | 3,400 | 3,742 |
| | | | | | |
| 2,305 | 1,659 | 1,646 | 1,321 | 1,216 | 1,118 |
| | | | | | |
| 6,705 | 4,947 | 3,570 | 3,864 | 3,536 | 3,109 |
| $ 56,408 | $ 40,840 | $ 30,956 | $ 28,512 | $ 24,568 | $ 19,458 |
| | | | | | |
| 31,614 | 31,548 | 31,502 | 31,478 | 31,430 | 31,174 |
| | | | | | |
| $ 46,068 | $ 24,335 | $ 12,102 | $  9,203 | $  5,630 | $  4,751 |
| (591) | 603 | 645 | 460 | 360 | 205 |
| | | | | | |
| (.02) | .02 | .02 | .01 | .01 | .01 |
| | | | | | |
| 1,974 | 2,559 | 1,837 | 1,192 | 732 | 372 |

The United States received 7.1 percent of South Africa's $960 million of exports in 1969 and supplied 17.4 percent of its $1,705 million of imports.[2]

The gross domestic product of South Africa has been averaging close to a 6 percent increase in real terms over the period 1966 to 1970.

During the same period the consumer price index has moved as follows:

---

[2] *Quarterly Economic Review: Republic of South Africa,* Annual Supplement 1971, The Economist Intelligence Unit, London, 1971.

**U.S. Private Direct Investment and Average Rates of Return—1960–1968**

|  | 1960 | 1961 | 1962 | 1963 | 1964 | 1965 | 1966 | 1967 | 1968 |
|---|---|---|---|---|---|---|---|---|---|
| Investment in South Africa (millions of dollars) | −1* | 21 | 47 | 51 | 55 | 49 | 69 | 71 | 31 |
| Average rates of return in South Africa (percent) | 17.5 | 19.6 | 19.9 | 20.0 | 18.6 | 19.1 | 20.6 | 19.2 | 17.3 |
| Average rates of return Worldwide (percent) | 10.9 | 11.0 | 11.4 | 11.3 | 11.4 | 11.1 | 10.4 | 10.1 | 10.8 |

\* Net capital outflow.

**Trend of Gross Domestic Product\***

|  | 1966 | 1967 | 1968 | 1969 | 1970 |
|---|---|---|---|---|---|
| Total Rand (millions)† |  |  |  |  |  |
| At current prices | 8,555 | 9,459 | 10,152 | 11,339 | 12,404 |
| At 1963 prices | 7,799 | 8,391 | 8,712 | 9,326 | 9,807 |
| real increase (percent) | 5.0 | 7.6 | 3.8 | 7.0 | 5.2 |

\* *Quarterly Economic Review: Republic of South Africa,* Annual Supplement 1971, The Economist Intelligence Unit, London, 1971.
† Rand = 1.40 dollars

**Consumer Price Index\* (1963 = 100)**

| 1966 | 1967 | 1968 | 1969 | 1970 |
|---|---|---|---|---|
| 109.1 | 112.3 | 113.5 | 115.9 | 119.5 |

\* *Quarterly Economic Review: Republic of South Africa,* Annual Supplement 1971, The Economist Intelligence Unit, London, 1971.

A fact often noted about the structure of economic life in South Africa is the disparity between the wages earned by the ruling whites and the blacks who comprise almost 75 percent of total employment. The wage gap has grown in secondary industry between 1946 and 1969 so that the average black wage as a percentage of the white wage has dropped from 20.3 percent to 18.6 percent.[3] The table below gives detail by broad industry for the period 1965–70.

---

[3] "South Africa: The Politics of Fragmentation," Neville Curtis, *Foreign Affairs,* vol. 50, no. 2, January 1972, p. 288.

**Wages and Employment***

| | Total Wages/Year in | | | |
|---|---|---|---|---|
| | Millions of Rand | | Numbers employed | |
| | *1965* | *1970* | *1965* | *1970* |
| Mining | | | | |
| Whites................. | 186.7 | 264.9 | 63,800 | 61,700 |
| Coloureds............. | 2.8 | 5.3 | 4,500 | 5,500 |
| Asians................. | | | 440 | 300 |
| Africans .............. | 93.3 | 121.7 | 538,300 | 573,500 |
| Manufacturing | | | | |
| Whites................. | 545.9 | 996.4 | 233,900 | 277,000 |
| Coloureds............. | 97.3 | 166.6 | 150,100 | 195,800 |
| Asians................. | 34.6 | 66.4 | 50,900 | 74,200 |
| Africans .............. | 220.4 | 380.7 | 494,600 | 617,200 |
| Construction | | | | |
| Whites................. | 83.0 | 226.4 | 36,600 | 59,500 |
| Coloureds............. | 19.7 | 57.5 | 21,500 | 44,600 |
| Asians................. | 0.9 | 7.8 | 1,100 | 4,500 |
| Africans .............. | 49.3 | 144.9 | 122,300 | 247,000 |

* *Financial Times* (London), Monday, June 14, 1971, p. 16.

As can be computed from the table above, the blacks (Africans) in the manufacturing sector were earning about an average of 51 rand a month in 1970. The Johannesburg Chamber of Commerce estimated that a family of five in Soweto (a black living area outside Johannesburg) required 76 rand a month for a minimum monthly budget.

It was in this economic context and in the sociopolitical environment of apartheid (separation of the races) that the challenge to Polaroid's conduct of business in South Africa was raised.

## CHRONOLOGY OF THE PROTEST AT POLAROID

In 1948, Dr. Edwin H. Land, chairman of Polaroid, was offered the opportunity of significant business in South Africa at a time when Polaroid had not yet established itself as a profitable growth company. Despite the attraction of the offer, Dr. Land refused because of the racial policies of the South African government.

During the early 60s, Polaroid established the sales distributorship through Frank and Hirsch, Ltd., and shortly thereafter established through the same company the licensed production of sunglasses with lenses imported from the United States.

In 1968, Dr. Land intervened to prevent direct sales of cameras or film by Polaroid to the South African government. During the same year—in a seemingly unrelated episode—some Polaroid employees objected through channels to the use of Polaroid products in the passbook program implementing apartheid. These protests did not produce a top management response; top management later stated that they were not aware of indirect sales and use of Polaroid products by the government.

On October 5, 1970, the Polaroid Workers Revolutionary Movement began agitating against business in South Africa, first within Polaroid facilities, then on October 7, 1970, in the streets.

On October 21, 1970, Polaroid announced that all sales, direct and indirect, of film and cameras for use in the apartheid passbook identification program would be prohibited. Two marketing executives were dispatched to South Africa to assure compliance with the order. Polaroid's investigations showed that about 15 percent of the identification materials were Polaroid products purchased from dealers supplied by Polaroid's distributor, Frank and Hirsch, Ltd. Amateur film and cameras, as well as sunglasses, would continue to be sold as before. In announcing the decision, Dr. Land described the move as precedent setting for any U.S. company. The use of Polaroid's products in the identification program evidently had come as a surprise to Dr. Land, as had the existence of a "revolutionary" movement within the company itself. Others in top management admitted knowing about the true picture in South Africa. The sales vice president, Mr. Thomas Wyman, said: "We recognized that our film indirectly was being used in this identification program for blacks and whites and I think there was some discomfort about it, but the issue did not crystallize to a point where now we wish it had." When asked if he would condone the action of P.W.R.M. in the protest, he responded: "I think I would say so if I thought that were the issue that is on their minds." Other Polaroid executives were quick to diassociate the new policy from the P.W.R.M. demands. The senior vice president, Mr. Arthur Barnes, insisted that the new policy had nothing to do with the protests by P.W.R.M. The response to P.W.R.M. was sharp. "Demands—that is not the way we operate," said Mr. Barnes.

Dr. Land emotionally reinforced the management reaction to the demands in an hour-long talk to the 14-man task force established to study the business in South Africa and to recommend company action. He decried the behavior of "a couple of revolutionaries who don't believe we mean what we say." Giving in to their demands would mean "a whole series of new demands, and there is no doubt that management would not meet them. I do not want to run a company based on demands rather than participation."

As the 14-man task force was deliberating, Mr. Kenneth Williams resigned his position at Polaroid, calling the new policy "an insult." He began organizing a coalition of blacks and white radicals to launch a boycott of Polaroid products both in the United States and overseas. Mr. Williams left behind him a career which began as a custodian and led to a creative position as design photographer.

As the task force deliberated, the idea emerged to send a racially mixed team to examine the South African situation first hand. One member of the task force, representing the Volunteers Committee (an all-black group formed in the company to process grievances from black employees) explained the task force rationale as follows:

The proposal was made that a group of four be sent to South Africa as an inspection team to review the feelings of black South Africans. The point was raised, and was well taken, that as a black in America we have had decisions made for us by people who feel that they know what we need, and I think we were repeating the same process in our initial moves here. . . . I think we should ask the black South Africans what would be the effect of total withdrawal, or of continuing our present process, to put restrictions on our methods of sale.

The task force did, in fact, send a four-man study team to South Africa for 11 days. Seemingly without government obstruction, the team (a black engineer, a black electrician, a white draftsman, and the white sales vice president) gathered data publically and privately sufficient to be convinced Polaroid should stay on in South Africa and battle apartheid from within. These views were shared with the larger task force which then fashioned a one-year experimental program which was announced in a full page ad in the *New York Times* (and other major U.S. daily newspapers plus 20 black weeklies) on January 13, 1971. Posturing itself plainly in opposition to apartheid, Polaroid launched a three-phase experiment:

1. Dramatically improve black wages and benefits within both the distributor and supplier companies in South Africa.
2. Oblige Polaroid business associates in South Africa to train non-whites for important jobs.
3. Commit a portion of profits earned in South Africa to encourage black education (see Exhibit 2 for the full text of the ad).

Not to be overlooked is Polaroid's overt invitation to other companies operating in South Africa to follow its lead in battling apartheid from within.

Response to the Polaroid move was swift and sharp. The London *Observer*'s reporter in Cape Town headlined his story on January 17, 1971: "Polaroid move on apartheid shakes South Africa." The reaction may have been anger and alarm in official government channels but the following excerpt from the January 15 edition of the *Cape Argus* (Cape Town) shows the complexity of the issue from the optics of the opposition conservative party in South Africa:

American corporations investing in South Africa are today in an extremely delicate situation. They are being forced by domestic pressure to introduce socio-economic, almost political reforms in their business undertakings in this country—reforms which, while eminently sensible and desirable in themselves could force foreign investors into confrontation with the South African Government.

Our own Government is also in a delicate position here. . . .
While there is an understandable reluctance among all South Afri-

cans to allow foreigners to intervene in our domestic affairs, it must be understood that foreign investors involved in local commerce may soon have no option but to intervene or to withdraw—to succumb to the demands for effective economic boycott, in fact. . . .

Should the Government attempt to curb any moves by Polaroid—which is now under close world scrutiny and *must* move dramatically to improve conditions for its local African staff—the damage to South Africa would be tremendous. . . .

The announcement of the experiment, as predicted, did not still the protest at home. Mr. Williams and Miss Hunter (the only two public members of P.W.R.M.) appeared before a United Nations Sixteen Country Apartheid Committee on February 3, 1971. They characterized the Polaroid experiment a "paternalistic act of charity," a "trick," and an "insult." They reiterated their demand that Polaroid withdraw entirely and threatened to continue their four-month drive to have Polaroid products boycotted.

Another reaction came from the representatives of the United Black Appeal in Boston who had earlier welcomed Polaroid's precedent-setting gift of $20,000. Fearing that accepting the money would appear like taking a bribe to ignore the South African issue, they turned the money over to a South African revolutionary movement and to another group in Cairo, Illinois.

On February 20, 1971, Miss Hunter was suspended from her job at Polaroid without pay and was informed on February 23, 1971, that she had been dismissed "for conduct detrimental to the best interests of the company." After two and a half years as a chemist at Polaroid, Miss Hunter (a 24-year-old graduate of Xavier University) responded to her dismissal by saying: "It is just further proof of the racism that exists at Polaroid. At Polaroid they say that if my rights interfere with their profits that they can suspend those rights, as they did with mine. I intend to continue work on the boycott."

By mid-September 1971, some action was already evident within Polaroid's distributor in South Africa. Average pay of nonwhite workers was raised 22 percent and the minimum wage was raised to 70 rand from 50 rand.

On October 27, 1971, Mr. Helmut M. Hirsch, the managing director of Polaroid's distributor, labeled Polaroid's effort to counteract apartheid from within the system a "success." He said it "has done far more to bring about a civilized relaxation of prejudice than withdrawal would have done." Mr. Hirsch said in an interview with the *New York Times* that, if black employees were still being paid considerably less than some whites doing related tasks, this was due to differences in productivity and seniority. "The company fully accepts the principle of the rate for the job, but we will not artificially elevate men for the sake of improving a point." He said that his company would not contravene government policy by appointing blacks to positions of authority over whites and that such a move would be impractical at this stage in any case. The same story was carried in the South African newspaper *STAR* on November 1, 1971, under the banner headline: "Polaroid Plan Is On Way to Success."

In November 1971, the South African Institute for Race Relations[4] published a "Report on the Polaroid Experiment" which offers the summary conclusion:

> Any attempt to assess the impact of the Polaroid Corporation's experiment on other companies in South Africa is extremely difficult. Companies are usually unwilling to reveal information about wage levels and employment practices; nor is there necessarily any connection between such changes as have taken place and the publicized actions of Frank and Hirsch, Polaroid's distributors in South Africa. It is also almost impossible to discover whether whatever improvements in working conditions of Africans, Indians, and Coloured people have taken place during 1971 are on a larger scale than in previous years. The most that can be said with any degree of certainty is that the Polaroid experiment, with the attendant publicity and increased interest in South Africa in black poverty, has caused more public and press attention to be focused on black wage levels, working conditions, and employment practices. Had it not been for the initiative within Polaroid, the South African Institute of Race Relations is unlikely to have become involved at the time it did in the question of the role of foreign investment in South Africa, and the memorandum "United States Corporate Investment and Social Change in South Africa" by Dudley Horner would not have been produced. . . . This greater concern is of course a desirable development in itself, but it is no substitute for real change within individual firms. The problems of black poverty and the increasing black/white wage gap have been with us for years, and it is doubtful whether the past year has seen any *significant* progress, taking a broad aggregate of statistics. This does not mean to say that some individual firms have not introduced welcome changes.

*     *     *     *     *

Mr. Wyman, a vice president of Polaroid, told Congressman Charles Diggs's Africa sub-committee that Polaroid would pull out of South Africa entirely unless the program showed solid results by 13 January 1972. He hinted strongly that the decision whether to remain in South Africa would depend in large measure upon whether other companies, particularly American companies, followed Polaroid's lead. Part of Polaroid's experiment was to promote African education and to help African cultural organizations. Several firms have followed Polaroid's example in the field of educa-

---

[4] This institute is a 40-year-old, interracial organization located in Johannesburg with 4,500 members in and outside South Africa. It opposes apartheid and works on civil rights causes with funding from membership, South African businessmen, and the Ford Foundation, with a staff of 50.

tion: for example, the South African Sugar Association has voted R20,000 for African education, and one other large company has voted a similar sum, while several other firms have increased their expenditure in this field. More details are unfortunately not available.

As far as its impact on black wage levels is concerned, the Polaroid experiment may be evaluated according to different criteria:

1. If it was intended to significantly improve the wages and working conditions of black South Africans in general, it must be regarded as a failure.

2. If the intention was to create greater social concern among businessmen, it appears to have been moderately successful.

The institute report specified the climate for change by citing a research survey conducted in 1968 among American and Canadian businessmen based in South Africa. "Eighty-one percent of the businessmen —all of them top executives—believed that South Africa's racial policies represented an approach that was at least an attempt 'to develop a solution.' Eight percent considered the government's policies an 'acceptable approach,' six percent believed they were 'altogether incorrect.' Ninety-two percent believed the Republic was stable and not subject to serious jeopardy due to racial or economic unrest 'in the foreseeable future.' The survey also revealed that although businessmen based in South Africa were becoming increasingly pro-South African, many of them believed that feelings 'at home' regarding South Africa had become less tolerant than they were a year ago."

On December 3, 1971, the *Financial Mail,* a South African business periodical, went into more detail on the Polaroid experiment under the headline: "Too Early To Judge."

What is the evidence so far of success or failure?

To take F & H first. There has been evidence of fairly considerable advancement for African staff. Average African salaries have gone up 21% in a year, from R74 to R90 pm. And the minimum wage for those with one year's experience at F & H is R840 pa, or about R65 per month excluding annual bonus.

More important is the reduction in the number of those in the lower group:

**F & H Salaries***

| Earning Group | 1970 | 1971 |
|---|---|---|
| R50—R70 | 98 | 39 |
| R70—R130 | 49 | 91 |
| R130 plus | 11 | 21 |

* Including annual bonus.

A surprising and disappointing feature is the R50–R70 salary group. The average salary in this income group is R58. An African F & H employee told the FM (in the presence of managing director Helmut Hirsch) that a matriculated 21-year-old had been hired only two months before at R52 per month.

This is the minimum amount F & H could legally pay him.

Hirsch argues that most untrained beginners are not worth more ("we'd pay a White the same for the same work"). He agrees they are being paid well below the Johannesburg poverty datum line of R70 per month for a family of five, but says that they are not generally sole breadwinners.

Had he checked whether they were or not? No. A couple of days after our first interview, however, he telephoned the FM and said that he had now checked and was "delighted to have had this brought to my attention." I came across a "junior" aged 44 I didn't know of before, earning R55 per month.

He has now introduced a system by which new African male employees "with proven experience" will start at a minimum of R65. Those without experience will be put on probation for three months, with clerks continuing to start at R52 and others at R55. If they prove satisfactory, their wages will then be upped immediately to R60 and R65, respectively.

All of these salaries are below the PDL level for a family of five. In any case, shouldn't these moves have been made months ago? Can the Polaroid group justify itself to its U.S. detractors when its distributor still pays some employees the minimum rate allowed by law?

On the training side of the F & H program, there are now nine African supervisors (receiving between R136 and R195 per month including annual bonuses) compared to one last year. Two African storemen have been appointed for the first time.

Hirsch says Polaroid is satisfied with the progress made by F & H so far.

Polaroid itself has played its part in the experimental program spending R45,000 on non-White bursaries, and general African educational and cultural development. This is a considerable sum, perhaps a quarter of its SA profits.

How have other firms reacted to Polaroid's lead? Have there been advances? If so, do they justify Polaroid staying here? The evidence so far is inconclusive.

Just before the end of the year of experiment, *Newsweek* (January 10, 1972) reported:

> The company said its distributor, Frank & Hirsch, was giving blacks the same pay as whites for equivalent work and had raised blacks' salaries by an average of 22 per cent and provided them with pensions, educational expenses and loans. Polaroid itself has

given $75,000, about half of its annual South African profit, to several black educational groups and has helped set up a black-owned distributorship in Nigeria. All of this was accomplished, the company said, without interference or pressure from the South African Government. The government, in fact, even gave its own non-white civil servants a 7 per cent pay boost.

Polaroid noted that other companies—such as Barclays Bank, Standard Bank and General Motors—have also announced equal-pay-for-equal-work policies, as had been hoped. "We think the biggest achievement," said a Polaroid executive, "has been to call attention to the fact that American, British and South African companies should not be running a double standard for employees." But at the same time, the company expressed keen disappointment that even more companies haven't liberalized their black salary scales, or are afraid to say that they have. "It is known that several of them have raised the standards of black employees," the Polaroid official declared. "It is just somewhat disappointing that more haven't stepped forward."

One reason they haven't is clearly fear of retaliation from the segregationist government. "The single most-asked question from the numerous companies that have contacted us is 'What did it cost you, how were you hurt?' " the Polaroid executive said. "The answer is there were absolutely no unfavorable results, absolutely nothing."

The wisdom of Polaroid's approach can be argued endlessly, but at least one black worker who was interviewed by the study team in 1970 is sure that the company chose the right course. "The Polaroid program has brought about great ferment in this country," he recently wrote to one of the team members. "What has happened has in fact been the thin edge of the wedge, which will—we hope—lead to a breakthrough." At home, at least, the strategy has silenced the critics; the tiny Polaroid Revolutionary Workers Movement, which began the protest in the first place, has quietly disappeared.

## APPENDIX: BUSINESS RELATIONS OF OTHER COMPANIES AND INSTITUTIONS WITH SOUTH AFRICA

Immediately before and during the Polaroid protest and experiment in South Africa, many incidents commanded attention in the world press. Some of the highlights are sketched here to provide context for the Polaroid deliberations and decisions.

Wates, Ltd., one of the top six construction companies in Great Britain, was requested in January 1970 to grant a license for the use of its mechanized on-site construction methods in South Africa. Mr. Neil Wates, the managing director of the firm employing 4,447 people, earning £592,000 on a turnover of £23,312,000, refused but was persuaded not to make the decision on the basic of secondhand hostile propaganda but to visit South Africa personally. He did so at his own expense and then in June 1970 documented his reaction in a press release from which the following excerpts are drawn:

> I must report prima facie South Africa is the ideal land for investment; stability is a relative term, but in the foreseeable future there can be few more stable countries than South Africa. The economic outlook is excellent. . . . Politically, the country is extremely stable—there would seem to be no prospect of ousting the present regime; the student unrest in Universities as experienced in Europe and the U.S. is completely unknown; there are no strikes and above all the non-whites are completely quiescent.
>
> I must further report that the opportunities for a System of industralised building, such as the Wates System—which not only saves man hours, but above all skilled man hours and eliminates wet trades—are enormous. The white dominated Unions have a virtual stranglehold on the Construction industry; the only way to cut the Gordian knot is through eliminating the wet trades and creating totally new jobs altogether, which would enable employers to open up job opportunities for non-whites without ever being accused of taking jobs away from the whites.
>
> In this context it is only fair to say also that I met Liberal businessmen of the highest calibre who argued that economic forces were bound to bring about the downfall of apartheid—and their own system would prove a powerful weapon in the campaign.
>
> Notwithstanding all this, I must report that the idea of doing business in South Africa is totally unacceptable; we could not be true to the basic principles on which we run our business and we should lose our integrity in the process. We should have to operate within a social climate where the colour of a man's skin is his most important attribute and where there is virtually no communication between the races; we should be locked into this system. We should have to operate within an economic climate which is designed deliberately to demoralise and to maintain an industrial helotry; we should, in turn, profit from such exploitation and ultimately end up with a vested interest in its maintenance.
>
> We should have to operate within a legal climate where the rule of law has been abolished in favour of rule by decree, which bids fair to become a reign of terror.
>
> The cumulative effect of all these factors in the long term must be self-defeating; within the short term it must make it impossible for ourselves individually, or as a company, to connive at anything which would serve to perpetuate a system which in the last analysis has no other justification than the preservation of white supremacy as an end in itself.
>
>       *    *    *    *    *
>
> . . . The policy of reserving key jobs for whites virtually means that 3.6m whites must provide the entire management capability and key skills for a population of over 19m.
>
>       *    *    *    *    *

The real scandal lies in the fact that all the real job opportunities one can see being grasped by Africans both in supervisory management and in the area of technical skills in a country like Zambia are totally denied to them in South Africa. It is impossible to say how many first class minds are doing the most menial jobs and it is, of course, impossible to measure the waste of ability.

The theory of separate development is plainly nonsense all the time the whites depend on the blacks for their industrial manpower —and of course there can be no meaningful development in the home lands where most of the blacks are working in white areas. Only 8.7% of employed Africans are working in the home lands— whilst over one third "live" in the home lands, but work away from home on annual contracts. This self-defeating policy prohibits any prospect of career development for them, let alone the building up of any loyalty to the company and reduces the non-white to the level of a "Labour Unit."

Of course we would ensure that any business we set up would be a beacon of good employment practices, with basic principles of equal-pay, equal-fringe benefits and working conditions. But we could not open the career to talents in the way we strive to do in this country and in the States through our policy of "optimising individual and the company goals"—because some goals are simply not open to some individuals.

*    *    *    *    *

It is no defence to point out the undeniable truth that the black South Africans are better off than blacks in any other country in the world; the important factor is their relative well-being to their white fellow citizens; the Africans constitute 68% of the population, but their share of the National cash income is 19%—whereas the white constitute 19% and their share of the cash income is 73%.

*    *    *    *    *

I will confess that I travelled South Africa hoping that I would find good reasons for doing business there; privately I had always considered critics of South Africa to be shrill and emotional—to whom everything black was good and everything white was bad. But the parallel between Hitler's treatment of the Jews in the 1930s and South Africa's treatment of the blacks today, became daily more obvious to me in the course of my visit and was brought home most vividly to me when I saw blacks being literally herded like cattle through the Bantu Administration Courts—just as I think with hindsight it would have been totally wrong to do anything to connive at Nazism in those days, so also do I think we should do nothing that would help to perpetuate apartheid.

I was frequently pressed in South Africa to say whether we were looking at it as a business or an ethical problem; there can, of course, be no difference.

On February 21, 1971, the Episcopal Church which holds 12,574 shares of General Motors stock requested the automobile company to submit a resolution to the annual shareholders' meeting requiring withdrawal from South Africa. Robert S. Potter, chairman of the Episcopal Churches Committee on Social Criteria for Investments, revealed the motivation for the move. "A pull-out by General Motors probably won't accomplish much for blacks generally, but at least then General Motors and the church wouldn't be supporting apartheid. We want to give General Motors and other companies a stick. This gives G.M. a chance to say: 'Look, we want to stay, but we're getting pressure from home. Why don't you let up a bit?'." General Motors' investment in South Africa totals some $125 million. It employs over 6,000 people in three plants. Fifty-two percent of employment is nonwhite. According to the then chairman of General Motors, Mr. James M. Roche, "G.M. South Africa does not discriminate between the races as to wages, except for a difference in starting rates which are higher for whites than for coloured or native employees." Mr. Roche replied to the demand of the Episcopal Church in a press conference on February 19 by refusing to withdraw from South Africa. He believed that the South African racial problem was slowly being solved. If the situation worsened, then, that "might pose a different problem." In a reply to the authors' inquiry on the G.M. position on the Episcopal proposal further details are revealed:

> Thank you for your recent letter inquiring about General Motors' position on the stockholder proposal announced by the Episcopal Church.
>
> General Motors operates in many countries throughout the world and is obliged to obey the law of each of these countries. We have been in South Africa since 1926, long before the current apartheid policies were instituted. Currently, G.M. employes approximately 6,000 persons in South Africa, more than half of whom are nonwhite. The number of non-whites employed by G.M. has been expanding steadily.
>
> We are well aware that the policies being followed by the government in South Africa raise complex issues. The answer, however, does not lie in turning our back on these issues by eliminating our participation in that country. No matter what we as individuals may think of the political system, it is a hard fact that General Motors in South Africa is offering employment opportunities which would otherwise not be available.
>
> We firmly believe that General Motors can best make a practical contribution to solving this problem by expanding the number of good jobs to help provide the economic prosperity and stable social climate within which reasonable and responsible people can work toward proper solutions.
>
> Thank you for writing and giving us this opportunity to discuss this matter with you.
>
> Sincerely,
>
> Morley Warren
> Manager, Editorial Services
> Public Relations Staff

Despite the refusal to leave South Africa, General Motors agreed to place the resolution on the agenda of the May meeting of the stockholders. The new black board member, Rev. Leon Sullivan, backed this move. When the vote was taken, less than 3 percent of the shares were voted in favour of the Episcopal resolution, hence the resolution could not appear on the annual meeting agenda for three more years.

The Episcopal Church move to appeal for proxy support in the annual meeting was symptomatic of a maturing tactics of social activists. The sophistication of the approach is revealed in the following two quotes:

> Submitting proxy proposals, and getting foundations, universities, and churches to vote their shares in favour of them is winning favour over physical action, says Alice Tepper, director of the Council on Economic Priorities. "Too often in the past," she says, "issues were lost in headlines about demonstration and disruptions." [5]

> Apart from its publicity value, the proxy route to reform has a major advantage for the corporate dissidents: management can be forced to finance most of the battle with corporate funds. A young Washington attorney, Rodney Shields, bought one share in each of 30 companies and fired off a barrage of 200 separate reform proposals for this year's proxy statements. The whole enterprise, he says, cost him $1,400. The cost to management—for fighting the proposals through the Securities and Exchange Commission and ultimately printing the 125 or so that were approved—has been estimated at $1 million or more. [6]

Gulf Oil faced a similar resolution for its annual meeting on April 27, 1971, concerning its conduct of business in Angola and Mozambique. This time, the initiator of the proposal was the United Presbyterian Church which controlled more than 20,000 Gulf shares. Mr. Josiah H. Beeman, secretary of the Presbyterian's South African Task Force, said that when churches wanted to protest the action of a company they used to sell their stock. "I don't think this is going to be the case from now on." Just as in the G.M. situation, the resolution failed to get a 3 percent response at the annual meeting.

A similar attempt to get a resolution on South Africa on the annual meeting agenda of Honeywell failed.

Elsewhere in the world antiapartheid critics were active as well. In early January 1971, the West German company Urangesellschaft pulled out of a major project to mine uranium jointly with Rio Tinto Zinc in South West Africa in order to avoid jeapardizing West German relations with black Africa. Also, a large Italian electrical company, SAE, and Sweden's ASEA, have withdrawn from lucrative contracts for work on the Cabora Bassa dam in Mozambique, which is being built by a South African-led consortium. In London, Sir Frederick Seebohm, chairman of Barclay's Bank, spent most of his speech at the annual general meeting

---

[5] *Business Week,* February 13, 1971.

[6] *Newsweek,* May 24, 1971.

in early January defending the bank's operations in South Africa where over half the bank's branches are. Protestors had objected especially to the credit given to a subcontractor in South Africa working on the Cabora Bassa dam. There had been a vigorous campaign to persuade students not to open accounts at Barclays.

Banks in the United States have been picketed as well, particularly Chase Manhattan, for its participation in a consortium providing $40 million in revolving credit to the South African government. First National City Bank reports continually receiving letters criticizing its large commitment in South Africa.

In South Africa itself, when various company representatives were asked their opinion on the protest they provided a wide range of replies. Mr. Claude G. Hall, the managing director of Champion Spark Plug, said: "Any pressures from America? They can just jump in the mud." Mr. K. A. Brooke, managing director of Timken South Africa, Ltd., said: "Attention focused on this matter can only make it worse not better. Timken S. A. does not want any more attention than is absolutely necessary." National Cash Register's manging director said: "I would not be ashamed to answer questions from the U.S. on the way we treat our non-white staff."

Public officials, including Senator Ted Kennedy and Representative Charles C. Diggs, member of the House Foreign Affairs Commitee and leader of the Black Caucus, originally held opinions that U.S. investment in South Africa was not tolerable. These positions became somewhat modified during 1971 to the point that U.S. investment should cease and withdraw if there is not substantial improvement soon in the lot of the nonwhite workers in South Africa. Congressman Diggs, after a South African study trip, challenged American business firms to make more conscious effort to upgrade the pay and training of nonwhites. He was particularly critical of what he found at the NASA tracking station in South Africa where 225 white employees received a total of R100,000 a year whereas 61 nonwhites received only R41,320 a year. He found there segregated facilities and a cafeteria serving only white employees. He summarized his findings by saying he discovered at NASA "a utter lack of realization that blacks are human beings."

For some time at Princeton University both faculty and students had protested the investment of university funds in companies doing business in South Africa. The faculty-student committee appointed to examine the university investment policy found that companies in its portfolio which had investments in South Africa yielded 3 percent more than the other companies in the portfolio. To switch out of companies doing business in South Africa would entail a brokerage cost of $5 million. In their deliberations, according to chairman, Professor Marver Bernstein, they had to include consideration of "what effect any recommendation we would make would have on corporate contributions to the university, which tend to run at 10 percent of private giving."

Finally, the sensitivity of the South African government can be assessed from the story of the $2,850 gift from Israel to the Organization of African Unity. The South African government was irked at what they considered a subsidy for "African terrorists," a label used for black movements against white rulers in Portuguese territories, Rhodesia, and South Africa. In the words of South Africa's Prime Minister John Vorster, "I certainly do not understand how Israel, which itself has a terrorist problem, can justify contributions to terrorists." South Africa's finance minister, Nico Diede Erichs, announced that the transfer of funds for Israel would be suspended, except for small personal sums, until the government had obtained greater clarity about Israeli policies. For the South African Jewish community of 120,000, this meant a freeze on the $25 million raised in the Israeli United Appeal. It also meant a period of turmoil in which South African Jews were arguing among themselves on their official posture on apartheid. One representative asserted that the Jewish community "has evolved a formula of collective neutrality." A rebuttal from Mr. Gustav Sharon of the Jewish board of deputies advocated not neutrality but "collective non-intervention."[7]

### EXHIBIT 2
### An Experiment in South Africa*

Polaroid sells its products in South Africa as do several hundred other American companies. Our sales there are small, less than one half of one percent of our worldwide business.

Recently a group has begun to demand that American business stop selling in South Africa. They say that by its presence it is supporting the government of the country and its policies of racial separation and subjugation of the Blacks. Polaroid, in spite of its small stake in the country, has received the first attention of this group.

We did not respond to their demands. But we did react to the question. We asked ourselves, "Is it right or wrong to do business in South Africa?" We have been studying the question for about ten weeks.

The committee of Polaroid employees who undertook this study included fourteen members—both black and white—from all over the company. The first conclusion was arrived at quickly and unanimously. We abhor *apartheid,* the national policy of South Africa.

The *apartheid* laws separate the races and restrict the rights, the opportunities and the movement of non-white Africans. This policy is contrary to the principles on which Polaroid was built and run. We believe in individuals. Not in "labor units" as Blacks are sometimes referred to in South Africa. We decided whatever our course should be it should oppose the course of *apartheid.*

The committee talked to more than fifty prominent South Africans both black and white, as well as many South African experts. They heard from officials in Washington. They read books, papers, testimony, documents, opinion, interpretation, statistics. They heard tapes and saw films.

They addressed themselves to a single question. What should Polaroid do in South Africa? Should we register our disapproval of *apartheid* by cutting off all contact with the country? Should we try to influence the system from within? We rejected the suggestion that we ignore the whole question and maintain the status quo.

Some of the black members of the study group expressed themselves strongly at the outset. They did not want to impose on the black people of another country a course of action merely because *we* might feel it was correct. They felt this paternal-

* *New York Times,* January 13, 1971.

----
[7] *New York Times,* May 7, 1971.

**EXHIBIT 2** (*continued*)

istic attitude had prevailed too often in America when things are done "for" black people without consulting black people.

It was decided to send four of the committee members to South Africa. Since this group was to include two black and two white members, it was widely assumed they would not be granted visas. They were.

It was assumed if they ever got to South Africa they would be given a government tour. They were not.

It was assumed they would not be allowed to see the actual conditions under which many Blacks live and would be prevented from talking to any of them in private. They did see those conditions in Soweto and elsewhere. And with or without permission they met and talked to and listened to more than a hundred black people of South Africa. Factory workers, office workers, domestic servants, teachers, political leaders, people in many walks of life. They also talked to a broad spectrum of whites including members of all the major parties.

Their prime purpose in going to South Africa was to ask Africans what they thought American business should do in their country. We decided the answer that is best for the black people of South Africa would be the best answer for us.

Can you learn about a country in ten days? No. Nor in ten weeks. But our group learned one thing. What we had read and heard about *apartheid* was not exaggerated. It is every bit as repugnant as we had been led to believe.

The group returned with a unanimous recommendation.

In response to this recommendation and to the reports of the larger study committee, Polaroid will undertake an experimental program in relation to its business activities in South Africa.

For the time being we will continue our business relationships there (except for sales to the South African government, which our distributor is discontinuing), but on a new basis which Blacks there with whom we talked see as supportive to their hopes and plans for the future. In a year we will look closely to see if our experiment has had any effects.

First, we will take a number of steps with our distributor, as well as his suppliers, to improve dramatically the salaries and other benefits of their non-white employees. We have had indications that these companies will be willing to cooperate in this plan.

Our business associates in South Africa will also be obliged (as a condition of maintaining their relationship with Polaroid) to initiate a well-defined program to train non-white employees for important jobs within their companies.

We believe education for the Blacks, in combination with the opportunities now being afforded by the expanding economy, is a key to change in South Africa. We will commit a portion of our profits earned there to encourage black education. One avenue will be to provide funds for the permanent staff and office of the black-run Association for Education and Cultural Advancement (ASECA). A second method will be to make a gift to a foundation to underwrite educational expenses for about 500 black students at various levels of study from elementary school through university. Grants to assist teachers will also be made from this gift. In addition we will support two exchange fellowships for Blacks under the U.S.-South African Leader Exchange Program.

Polaroid has no investments in South Africa and we do not intend to change this policy at present. We are, however, investigating the possibilities of creating a black-managed company in one or more of the free black African nations.

Why have we undertaken this program? To satisfy a revolutionary group? No. They will find it far from satisfactory. They feel we should close the door on South Africa, not try to push it further open.

What can we hope to accomplish there without a factory, without a company of our own, without the economic leverage of large sales? Aren't we wasting time and

**EXHIBIT 2 (*concluded*)**

money trying to have an effect on a massive problem 10,000 miles from home? The answer, our answer, is that since we are doing business in South Africa and since we have looked closely at that troubled country, we feel we can continue only by opposing the *apartheid* system. Black people there have advised us to do this by providing an opportunity for increased use of black talent, increased recognition of black dignity. Polaroid is a small economic force in South Africa, but we are well known and, because of our committee's visit there, highly visible. We hope other American companies will join us in this program. Even a small beginning of co-operative effort among American businesses can have a large effect in South Africa.

How can we presume to concern ourselves with the problems of another country? Whatever the practices elsewhere, South Africa alone articulates a policy exactly contrary to everything we feel our company stands for. We cannot participate passively in such a political system. Nor can we ignore it. That is why we have undertaken this experimental program.

POLAROID CORPORATION

# Selected Readings

*From*

# INTERNATIONAL BUSINESS ENTERPRISE*

*By Endel J. Kolde*

## THE STRUCTURAL SCHEME OF INTERNATIONAL-TRADE MANAGEMENT

\* \* \* \* \*

[Editor's Note: The beginning of this chapter deals with the development of structural arrangements for international business.]

### An Overview of Alternative Organizational Arrangements

The main organizational arrangements which now exist are shown in Figure 1. The shaded areas show the international entities of the company. In a general sense, the alternatives also reflect the stages of growth from indirect exporting to a fully integrated international corporate structure. Lately, however, there has been an increasing tendency to skip the intermediate stages and to move directly from alternative *A* to *D, E,* or even *F*.

### STRUCTURAL MODELS OF MULTINATIONAL COMPANIES

The most significant organizational change in the postwar period has been the replacement of foreign-trade departments or divisions with international-operations establishments.

* *International Business Enterprise*, Endel J. Kolde © 1968 by Prentice-Hall, Inc., Englewood Cliffs, N.J. (excerpts from pp. 242–55, 260, 277–78). Reprinted by permission.

**FIGURE 1**

**Types of Functional Relations between Parent Organizations and Their International Entities**

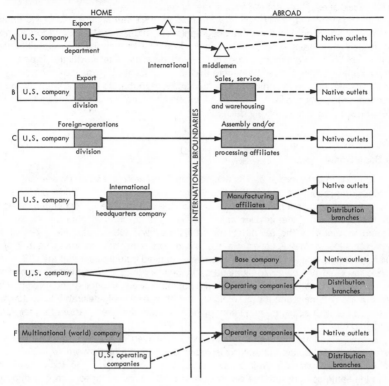

From this shift has evolved nearly all that is peculiarly characteristic of the modern multinational corporation. From this shift, also, has come an entirely new and different structural framework for international economic relations. The organizational expression of this shift can be reduced to four prototypal models: the international-headquarters company, the foreign-base company, the world company, and the transnational company. The models are not exact reproductions of a particular firm but are the conceptual expressions underlying the design of the organization. In practice such models must always be suited to the particular circumstances of a specific company.

## The International-Headquarters Company (IHC Model)

The emergence of the international-headquarters company marks an important turning point in the organization of international business. Although an outgrowth of the export-selling company in older firms (but not in others), it is structurally and functionally different. Unlike the older forms, it drops all pretense of being an offshoot of the sales organization (a subordinate outlet with narrowly defined objectives) and assumes the role of an operationally autonomous enterprise whose factories, warehouses, employees, and customers are not located in its country but are scattered in different foreign areas. Production and finance are thus organic to it, and export selling is expanded to international marketing, with aspirations and capabilities of a higher order. Any need to be organized in the image of the international middlemen firms is thus eliminated and a new structural model emerges. . . .

\*　　\*　　\*　　\*　　\*

The line organization of the international-headquarters company follows the territorial principle. Divisions or subsidiary companies, set up for all appropriate world regions, carry out the actual operations of the firm. These in turn control the foreign-based affiliates—wholly owned subsidiaries, joint-venture companies, or others.

*From Export Management to International Management.* The underlying principle of the new model is not functional but geographic. The international-headquarters company is not limited to exporting or to any functionally delineated responsibility as such, but undertakes all functions the company carries out abroad. Its managerial jurisdiction is defined not by the nature of the job but by the geographic scope or location of the job. Accordingly, the international-headquarters company may be compared to the State Department of the U.S. government or to any ministry of foreign affairs. Its functional dimension knows no limit, but its territorial dimension is sharply defined.

*   *   *   *   *

### The Base Company

The base-company format had its beginning in the search for sanctuaries where foreign-source income could be accumulated with minimum tax depletion. Wide differences in corporate income taxes among countries induced the search. The low-tax countries—especially the Bahamas, Panama, Liechtenstein, Switzerland, and Hong Kong—became the preferred locations for the *tax-haven,* or *profit-sanctuary,* subsidiaries, as the initial base companies were commonly called. Many of these were paper corporations without physical facilities or administrative capabilities. Their value derived from the fact that the U.S. internal revenue laws did not cover foreign-source income as long as it remained abroad. But, although the tax savings were real, they were not the only advantages of the foreign holding company. Many firms found it both ethically and organizationally desirable to endow them with the authority of actual management by making them the headquarters for their foreign operations.

The 1962 Revenue Act wiped out the pure tax-haven companies by making foreign-source income of U.S. firms taxable irrespective of where the funds were kept. This helped to make the base company an international-headquarters company located abroad rather than in the same country with the parent firm. In its structure the base company duplicates the international-headquarters plan with the exception of its location. The advantages that it offers over the IHC model are (*a*) better integration of top management and operations, (*b*) greater autonomy and less likelihood of interference by the parent, (*c*) greater financial flexibility in transferring earnings and assets from one country to another, and (*d*) spreading political and financial risk of the enterprise as a whole. The negative aspects are (*a*) complications of management—domestic routines and practices which can be employed in the IHC must be reformed; (*b*) loss of U.S. treaty and diplomatic protection; and (*c*) closer scrutiny by U.S. tax and trade authorities.

*   *   *   *   *

### The World Company

Although most multinational firms now are patterned after the IHC model, the process of organizational development has not ended there. A new and still different structure has emerged. . . . Although in the IHC model the dichotomy between domestic and international was emphasized as the fundamental criterion, the world-company model abandons this dichotomy and integrates the American and international operations by subordinating domestic to multinational affairs. The top echelons of the parent corporation, which under the IHC plan retain their inward-looking, domestic orientation, are thus reoriented to the global point of view, and the previous dualistic structure is eliminated from the policy-making organs. The entire headquarters staff becomes multinational in managerial responsibility and outlook.

The operating units are again organized on the territorial principle, each being defined in terms of a particular world region and thus adapted to the economic and cultural peculiarities of it. Needless to add, area expertise thus takes precedence over functional and product knowledge for general-management positions on the operational level. Some firms are now attempting to insert a product organization in the world-company framework; but, for the time being at least, no clear-cut conceptual solution has emerged. When it has been tried, the result has been a double structure utilizing both territorial and product principles.

(Diagram omitted.)

\*    \*    \*    \*    \*

Although the world-company plan is still in its infancy, having been first attempted in the mid 1950's, the conversion to it has been considerable, especially among companies whose product line has a relatively universal demand, such as petroleum, soft drinks, and drugs. It might be added that the model is being adopted not only by industrial giants but also by more and more smaller firms, many having skipped the IHC stage.

## The Transnational Company

The transnational company originated in Europe. It differs from the world company in that both ownership and control of the corporate structure are international. Its management is polycentric; there is no parent company as such, no central source of power, no domestic market or principal domicile. Its capital is raised from whichever capital market provides the best source for a particular venture; and top management is divided among several headquarters, each in a different country, and functions as an international coalition rather than as a command hierarchy. In essence, then, the transnational company can be visualized as a group of management centers jointly administering a network of operating companies.

Although a few such polycentric multinational firms now exist (Unilever, Royal Dutch-Shell), the attitude of international executives toward this plan remains reserved. Whether it will ever reach a status comparable to that of the other plans seems doubtful at this time. However, the development of foreign-base companies with strong subsidiaries of their own resembles the transnational concept.

\*    \*    \*    \*    \*

## FOREIGN-BASED AFFILIATES

How the foreign entities of a company are organized is basically a matter of law. To gain entry in a particular country a company must comply with all the legal provisions applicable to it. Since the laws of no two countries are identical, the legal aspects of establishment must always be handled as special cases.

Generally speaking, visas for corporate entry into a country are subject to more restrictions than are those which apply to people, goods, or capital. To meet the requirements a company has four alternative approaches: qualify for a branch license; form a subsidiary company under the laws of the host country; create a joint venture with one or more indigenous companies; or enter into a licensing agreement with an existing firm. The last two alternatives are discussed in separate chapters; the first two are the subject of the remainder of this chapter.

(Diagram omitted.)

\*    \*    \*    \*    \*

## Foreign Branches

From a legal standpoint a branch is not a separate juridic entity but only a physical offshoot of the parent firm. As long as both the branch and the parent are in the same country they are subject to the same national jurisdiction. The legal status of the branch is of small concern, as the parent company remains responsible for any legal action taken either by or against the branch. If, however, a branch were located in a different country, a legally intolerable situation would arise. The branch with its physical and economic powers would function as a legal nonentity over which the host country's government had no control since its juridic embodiment, the parent firm would be outside the country's jurisdiction and thus beyond the reach of the juridical organs of the government. No government can permit such immunity to law in its territory. For this reason licenses are issued for branch operations to nonresident companies only if the branch is *domesticated* by having a responsible national of the host country serve as the legal custodian of the establishment. The custodianship must be based on a formally executed power of attorney, in which the company conveys to the foreign citizen or firm involved complete jurisdiction over the branch. Since such an arrangement creates subtle problems and additional uncertainties, branches are relatively uncommon in multinational companies except as subunits of a national or regional subsidiary limited to one single country.

The foreign branch has other weaknesses also. Business licenses may be of short duration, and frequent renewals involve considerable expense; regulations and governmental surveillance may be tighter;[2] the taxable base may be so defined that the branch becomes taxable not on the basis of its own earnings or assets, but on the basis of the total profits or capitalization of the multinational corporation as a whole.

**Foreign Subsidiaries**

To avoid such discriminatory treatment most companies prefer to organize their affiliates as indigenous enterprises under the laws of the host country. Although the legal forms of enterprise (partnership, corporation, etc.) have over the years become relatively similar, significant differences still exist. The most significant among them is the existence of organizational forms other than the corporation which have juridic personalities separate from their owners and in which the owners' liability is limited to their investments in the enterprise. For example, German law provides for a limited-liability company (G.m.b.H.) which resembles the U.S. corporation in all features essential to management yet enjoys much greater freedom of action under law than does the German equivalent of the corporation (A/G). Thus the American term *to incorporate* is often as misleading as is the popular notion that the various national affiliates of a multinational company are corporations in form. Many are not. And many others should not be. With the growth of the multinational company, U.S. management has become more aware of the legal differences, and more sophisticated use is now being made of the various organizational opportunities which the laws of different countries provide.

To qualify for establishment in most countries, the law requires that a certain number of directorships or other key positions in the firm be occupied by local nationals. Compliance with this requirement produces a *statutory* or *de jure administration* which many companies find unsuitable for the actual management of the affiliate, so they limit the functions of these statutory executives to those prescribed by the charter: holding an annual meeting, signing necessary forms and reports, sanctioning legal contracts, etc. To safeguard itself, the parent company must fill these positions with people of unquestionable integrity, or, more commonly, counterbalance their official powers with contractual constraints such as leasing the assets to the *de jure* administration with the proviso that the officers "delegate" the operational responsibilities to individuals appointed by the lessor.

Another typical requirement for incorporation is that a specified portion, sometimes more than half, of the capital invested in the affiliate be controlled by local citizens. In countries where such restrictions exist, the U.S. parent company usually enters joint-venture or partial-ownership arrangements. It either buys part ownership in an existing foreign concern or induces a foreign firm to coinvest with it in a new venture. This latter practice has become

---

[2] For example, the branch may be required to patronize local suppliers, not compete with local industry, or refrain from employing nonnationals.

popular in recent years, especially among manufacturers and distributors of technical products, for whom local facilities and technical personnel are essential for making installations and servicing their customers. To enable the foreign company to contribute the legally necessary capital, it may be permitted by the parent to turn over some existing assets such as its building, equipment, sites, production processes, and even goodwill. Monetary values can be assigned to all of them by mutual agreement, and thus the need for a cash contribution by the local concern is minimized. How far a company is willing to go in this respect depends, of course, on the alternatives available to it and the profit potential of the particular market.

\*     \*     \*     \*     \*

### Definition of Joint Ventures

A joint venture is sometimes defined as an overseas enterprise which is not completely owned by the parent company. This definition would embrace not only foreign-based enterprises owned by two or more different firms but also those whose stock is partially held by the general public. From a purely legal point of view a case can be made for classifying the latter enterprises as joint ventures. But from economic and administrative points of view such an extension of the joint-venture concept undermines its central idea—partnership. There can be no partnership in the pure sense of the word between a foreign corporate owner and the local or, for that matter, the international stockholders of an enterprise. Although the stockholders are entitled to exercise control over the company's activities, they do not legally share in practice in the management and direction of the firm.

Here, a joint venture is a business enterprise in which two or more economic entities from different countries participate on a permanent basis. The participation is not limited to equity capital but normally extends to control of the undertaking through manufacturing processes, patents, trademarks, managerial know-how, or other operationally essential factors. When the partners' rights stem from their equity participation, the enterprise is classified as an equity joint venture; when one or more of the partners have made no equity contribution, the enterprise is a nonequity joint venture. From a legal standpoint, the equity joint venture is a creature of company or corporation law, while the nonequity joint venture is based on contract law.

\*     \*     \*     \*     \*

### Foreign Licensing

Licensing makes available to a foreign firm some intangible industrial property such as a patent, a manufacturing process, or a trademark for the purpose of cultivating the foreign licensee's market. This obviates the licensor company's need for entering the foreign market through export trade or capital investment. In return for the property rights transferred to it, the foreign firm pays royalties normally based on its output or sales of the licensed product.

### The Licensing Agreement

A licensing arrangement is always formalized in a written agreement which stipulates which property rights are being transferred; the royalties or other considerations paid; where and how the rights are to be utilized; under which circumstances the rights are to revert to the licensor; and the degree of participation the licensor is to have in the licensed operations of the licensee or in the marketing of the licensed products. The contract may further cover the period of time; the size of the territory covered by the arrangement; the methods of control and payment; the applicable law in case of conflict; and the method of arbitration, if appropriate.

Besides providing an alternative to export-import trade and direct investment, licensing agreements also provide an inexpensive means for exploring and testing a company's growth potential in a particular foreign area before any irretrievable investment is made. From a risk standpoint licensing agreements entail greater risk than normal export operations but considerably less risk than direct investments. For this reason, licensing is frequently used as a transitional phase between export and foreign manufacture in a company's international expansion process and is succeeded by a more extensive commitment. So-called *royalty and stock participation agreements* are specifically designed for gradual conversion from licensing to equity operation. They provide for a low or a declining royalty plus a stock-purchase commitment in a new or existing establishment to succeed the licensing arrangement. The licensee acquires a partial ownership interest in the successor company through the stock purchases. In cases where local equity capital is not available in sufficiently large blocks to establish a joint-venture facility, the facility may initially be financed by the U.S. licensor and gradually converted into a joint enterprise under a royalty and stock-purchase agreement. Thus, such arrangements permit equity financing from the proceeds of the very product for which the equity was intended.

Licensing has sometimes been defined as exporting of know-how. However, it is also a continuous cooperative relationship between the parties for their mutual benefit. It is correct to classify licensing as a nonequity joint venture where pooling of resources among the partners is the overriding characteristic. It is not to be equated with direct investment; the industrial property rights are not sold outright but leased or loaned for a definite period, and the proceeds are royalties—not dividends or profits.

*From*

# NEW PRODUCT DECISIONS*

*By Edgar A. Pessemier*

### OBJECTIVES OF NEW-PRODUCT POLICY

In the simplest terms, new-product search activities are designed to locate new products and capabilities which will yield the largest return from the firm's resources consistent with existing risk and organizational constraints. On the whole, firms lead from strength, seeking product opportunities that permit the use or extension of their special technical, production, or marketing skills, or the employment of a resource base. At times, however, the objectives may be defensive, the reduction of risk by protecting a favored position. In any of these cases, it is convenient to classify the objectives of proposed products along the two dimensions of newness suggested by Johnson and Jones.[1] The details of this classification system are contained in Table 1. As the degree of change increases along either of the newness dimensions, the higher the uncertainty and risk will tend to become and the more pronounced will be the impact of the new product on the firm's organization.

Restated in broader terms, the principal objective of a new-product policy is to direct the dynamic adjustment of the firm's resources to changing environmental conditions. Competitors' strategies and tactics, the needs of the market, the technologies with which these needs may be met, and the sociopolitical climate are continually shifting. The speed and direction of change are often difficult to assess. New, fertile areas emerge, old frontiers of growth disappear, and the productivity of mature markets declines. Not infrequently, hard-won strength in a technology, a product line, or among a class of buyers will encourage conserva-

* By permission from *New Product Decisions,* by Edgar A. Pessemier. Copyright 1966. McGraw-Hill Book Company, Inc. (Excerpts from 8–10.)

[1] Samuel C. Johnson and Conrad Jones, "How to Organize for New Products," *Harvard Business Review,* May–June 1957, p. 52.

**TABLE 1**
**New Products Classified by Product Objective**

| Product Objectives | | *No Technological Change* | *Improved Technology* | *New Technology* |
|---|---|---|---|---|
| Increasing Marketing Newness | No Market Change | | *Reformulation* Make minor modifications in product to reduce cost and/or improve quality. | *Replacement* Make major modifications in product to reduce cost and/or improve quality. |
| | Strengthen Market | *Remerchandising* Make present products more attractive to the type of customers presently served. | *Improved product* Make present product more useful to present customers by improving present technology. | *Product-line extension* Widen the line of products offered to present customers by adopting a new technology. |
| | New Market | *New use* Extend sale of present products to types of customers not presently served. | *Market extension* Extend sales to types of customers not presently served by offering a modified present product. | *Diversification* Extend sales to types of customers not presently served by offering products of a new technology. |

*Increasing Technological Newness ⟶*

tive, short-sighted product policy. Only when product policy is consciously developed as a *principal agent of adoption and development* will the past and present be placed in proper perspective and latent opportunity for growth be fully exploited.

In more concrete terms, it is easy to compare the product policies followed by a variety of successful organizations. At one extreme we find the very fluid, diffuse product policy followed by Textron. For an extended period, this firm expanded rapidly through acquisitions and mergers designed to take advantage of tax-loss situations. Having developed as a broad-line highly integrated producer and convertor of textiles and manufacturer of apparel, this firm became involved in a long series of unsuccessful moves designed to adapt to new conditions in the textile industry. Abandoning these efforts, textile operations were liquidated and a new series of acquisitions produced a conglomerate collection of divisions producing such diverse products as plastic boats, chain saws, and metal-can fabricating machinery. At the other extreme, we find organizations like Island Creek Coal, which has historically marketed a narrow product line directly tied to a stable resource base.

Along other dimensions of product policy, contrasts can be found. Some firms sell classes of products that rapidly change their physical characteristics, while other companies sell products which vary little from year to year. Firms producing data-processing equipment typify the former, and producers of salt and allied chemicals represent the latter situation. Also, the degree to which a firm possesses advanced scientific and technical skills, an established market position, and so on, may become an important influence in shaping diverse product policies. These observations underline the fact that:

1. Sound product policy is an essential ingredient of sound business management.
2. Special skills and conscious attention must be applied to the problem of maintaining an efficient product policy.
3. Effective policy must be built on a clear understanding of the dynamics of the firm's external environment and internal resources.
4. Among firms in an industry and between industries diverse product policies are common. Simple, ready-made solutions are rare.

*From*

# CONCEPTUAL FOUNDATIONS OF BUSINESS*

## By Richard Eells and Clarence Walton

Pluralism always implies multiplicity, frequently diversity, and sometimes conflict. It is as much the generator as the result of freedom. Pluralism is intimately associated with toleration as opposed to bigotry, with voluntarism as opposed to coercion, and with a happy blending of individualism and associationism. This reflects those differences of interests that characterize the large, modern nation-state. Indeed, James Madison's claim to immortality rests mainly on his anticipation of the growth of parties and other voluntary organizations at a time when the former were unknown and the latter few in number. His prophetic observation (in No. 10 of *The Federalist*[1] that the existence of many autonomous groups makes tyranny by the majority less likely has an important place in any theory of "countervailing power."

Pluralism is concerned with the roles that these autonomous associations can play as a result of the power they enjoy, with the interplay of forces among these various groups as they enhance or diminish a specific group's power, and with the effect of power blocs on individual freedom and creativity.

\*   \*   \*   \*   \*

Pluralism encompasses an aim (wide diffusion of power) and a structure (voluntary groups operating between the national government and the citizen in a manner that niehter subordinates nor dominates the individual), but it also involves a method for evaluating results. This method does not seek to construct broad social programs on the basis of prior fixed dogma but relies on the consequences flowing from various groups' actions for the emergence of policy. Pluralism is less concerned with the lack among Americans of "public philosophy" —to use Lippmann's apt phrasing—than it is with the loss of a "sharp perception of consequence" by the leaders of these various private sectors in American society. . . .

\*   \*   \*   \*   \*

From a political standpoint, pluralism seeks to build a bridge connecting the traditions of liberalism and conservatism in American history. In the liberal tradition, pluralism is marked by references to problems rather than solutions, by faith in change rather than a change of faith. Whether it is Wilson's New Freedom, Roosevelt's New Deal, or Kennedy's New Frontier, this liberalism insists that transformation and reformation are the natural products of a pluralistic and creative society. Pluralism's conservative lineaments show in its skepti-

---

\* Reprinted by permission of Richard D. Irwin, Inc., Homewood, Ill., 1961 (pp. 360–63).
[1] James Madison, *The Federalist: A Collection of Essays* (New York: John Tiebout, 1799).

cism of state power and centralized state planning, on the one hand, and in its esteem of local responsibility and states' rights, on the other. . . .

*    *    *    *    *

Pluralism seeks to diffuse power into many organizations and groupings and thus to prevent the development of imbalances of power and to assure the freedom of the individual from the tyranny of the one, the few, or the many. It constitutes a continuing challenge to totalitarianism of every kind, whether the rule be held by a political dictator, by a business or labor oligarchy, or by the masses themselves. It is suspicious of claims to omniscience, and omnipotence and is therefore as much opposed to the ambitious pretenses of a James Stuart (the king can do no wrong), as it is to the Rousseauian version of democracy (the collectivity can do no wrong) . . .

*From*

# NEW CREDENTIALS FOR MORALISTS*

*By Brian J. O'Connell, C. M.*

Men search their consciences and find no prejudice, yet thousands of black men in our ghettos work full time for $65 a week or less. The average Joe American would not assault another person, yet millions remain in deteriorated housing because only a small fraction of investment capital is being directed toward housing. Joe would not steal a nickel from another person either, yet he enjoys the fruits of the labor of migrants or Latin American miners who receive pittances for their toil.

Why do these built-in injustices in our institutions continue? One reason is that the responsibility for the injustice does not fall directly on any individual. This is the phenomenon that Reinhold Niebuhr described 40 years ago in *Moral Man and Immoral Society.* Joe can feel quite moral because all his face to face relationships are in order, but he shares in the benefits of a society that distributes its rewards and opportunities unjustly. The injustice may even be the product of a historical accident for which no one is responsible. . . .

Another reason for these built-in justices is that systems or institutions have their own dynamics which resist change. Both the affluent and the poor recognize the inadequacies of the welfare system, yet the established bureaucracy with its dependent constituents continues on in unchanging patterns. Sometimes we have to stop and ask if we are compelled to serve the system or whether the system serves us. . . . The established system rolls along, gathers momentum and defies attempts to change its course.

We need a whole new ethic to confront this situation. The Second Vatican Council, for example, pointed to this new dimension of moral theology: "Profound and rapid changes make it particularly urgent that no one, ignoring the trend of events or drugged by laziness, content himself with a merely individualist morality. It grows increasingly true that obligations of justice and love are fulfilled only if each person, contributing to the common good, according to his own abilities and the needs of others, also promotes and assists the public and private institutions dedicated to bettering the conditions of human life". . . .

. . . This stern emphasis on structural or instructional morality . . . brings up a question: for what shall the men of the late 20th century be held accountable before the judgment seat of God? We know that we will be asked what we did to aid our neighbors who were

---

poor or hungry or in prison. The judgment on us, necessarily, will be stricter than on the Good Samaritan. His life became entwined with the victim by the side of the road because of physical proximity. But our lives are entwined with people around the globe. We may never come face to face with the Peruvian miner or the migrant, but we enjoy the fruits of his labor, and our decisions about minimum wages or import surcharges affect his life style. We can answer Christ at the judgment only if we have done something to shape our institutions to promote the common good of all men. The Good Samaritan could not be held accountable for the hungry man in India of his time. It is not so in the 1970's.

\*    \*    \*    \*    \*

. . . What does it mean, for example, when the prices that Americans pay to the Third World for copper or cocoa tend to remain stationary or decline? Pope Paul is trying to make Christians aware that such issues and questions are the stuff that charity and justice are made of today.

Other men as well are calling attention to this institutional dimension. In the *Kerner Report,* the Riot Commission said in summary: "What white Americans have never fully understood—but what the Negro can never forget—is that white society is deeply implicated in the ghetto. White institutions created it, white institutions maintain it, and white society condones it."

Clearly, the cry of "institutional racism" is very threatening to a person who is charged with it but does not understand why. The great emotional responses that result can, in fact, insure that nothing is accomplished. Moral theologians, as well as social scientists, have the difficult but necessary task of explaining, therefore, how institutional imbalance and not personal prejudice is often at the heart of the racial difficulties we face today.

\*    \*    \*    \*    \*

We must not expect an institutional moral code to develop in the same manner that the scholastic natural law ethic developed. There will be no absolute principles, for example, nor can we wait for unquestionable certitude. Rather, institutional morality will depend on the probable conclusions of the social scientists. These days, no one person is able to synthesize all of institutional morality in a volume of books in the manner of the scholastics. To do so, he would have to be a genius in international relations, economics, environmental science and theology, not to mention a few other social sciences. Such an animal does not and will not exist. The conclusions of institutional morality will not be valid, consequently, for any great period of time; as quickly as problems are analyzed and solved, newer and more complex issues are sure to arise.

\*    \*    \*    \*    \*

Some suggestions may be helpful for those who hope to develop or communicate an institutional morality:

1. To begin with, we must anticipate the consequences of technological and social change. With the aid of social scientists, the long and short run effects, the intended as well as the unintended effects, have to be discovered.

\*    \*    \*    \*    \*

2. Moralists must serve as society's conscience in its effort to be master of its destiny. The economic system should not be allowed to lead us blindly. . . .

3. Likewise, it is up to the moralist to warn those who get sidetracked from the crucial issues they have to face. In its time, romanticism, with its return to nature and the simple life, was a cop-out in the face of the Enlightenment and the Industrial Revolution. Existentialism, too, was accused by Marx of ignoring the implications of large-scale capitalism for the worker masses, while it concentrated on personal relationships and the discovery of meaning in life. Even the best of philosophies or of movements like personalism or the commune system can be evasions. Highlighting some important aspects of life, they can ignore other important values, especially in the institutional dimension. Meanwhile, as Harvey Cox says, the organization rolls on, deepening and extending its influence over men. A one-dimensional approach to life, whether it emphasizes the personal or the institutional interest, prevents us from being wholly human and facing the full reality of life in the 20th century.

4. Nor can moralists be deluded by the supposition that all power is political power. In the initial stages of social activism, politicians are often thought to have great if not exclusive power over social and economic trends. What results is wasted effort and fighting mainly strawmen and figureheads—as when people expect great changes from a new president or governor and gradually awaken to the fact that little will be changed after all. Social scientists, indeed, are becoming more aware that politicians have limited amounts of control over such aspects of the system as housing, urban development, inflation, and even the military-industrial complex. Political activism has its glamour, of course, but to influence institutional change, it may be more important to get the ear of the businessman, educator, or banker.

5. Finally, a good deal of background knowledge in the social sciences is necessary if one is to have any real understanding of institutional morality. . . .

To sum it up, schools today must transform youth's mistrust of institutions into the realization that institutions can actually be controlled and made responsive to human need. Not only must the schools inform, they have to inspire talented young people to prepare themselves to move into the centers of power in our institutions and direct them in truly humane paths.

*From*

# THE TACTICS OF CREATIVE TENSION*

*By Jeremiah J. O'Connell*

"Of course, we will support serious efforts to fight urban deterioration in our city, but under no circumstances will we tolerate-the public use of our corporate name in this connection!" Making this statement was the president of a huge corporation headquartered in Megapolis. Surrounding him at a conference table were government, civic, business, ecclesiastical, and academic leaders of Megapolis. Symptoms of decay in Megapolis brought the group together for an off-the-record weekend conference. In moving from discussion to action the group was trying to marshall resources to launch renewed efforts to save the city. First to come forward with a concrete offer of support was the company president who insisted on anonymity for his organization.

Why such anonymity when so many other corporations were queuing up for corporate citizenship kudos for contributions to any and every worthy cause? Was it biblical modesty wherein the left hand was not to know the good being done by the right hand? Was it fear of back-lash from some sector(s) of corporate stakeholders who might resent support of this or that cause? Was it caution lest the corporation's good name be abused in the classic fund raiser's whip sawing technique of social blackmail? The reason offered by the president challenged some conventional wisdoms and clarified at least one page from the catechism of social activists. In paraphrase, the president's remarks follow.

Our organization publically and early backed numerous worthy causes—civil rights, minority employment, safety, consumerism, environmental management, etc. Our motivation was frankly an inextricable composite of selfishness and altruism. In a way, we believed—and still do—that "from him to whom much has been given, much will be required." In our naiveté we learned only very slowly that others had a significantly different reading of that biblical passage: "from him who has given much, much will be required." The more we gave to worthy causes and the more willing we showed ourselves to get involved, the louder became the demands to do more and commit more. We began to resent the ingratitude of those we had helped. We were hurt by having been singled out for public notoriety for what we had not done, while innumerable other organizations were left unscathed even though their record of social responsibility was insignificant or non-existent.

The "eureka" came for us when we put ourselves in the shoes of the social activist striving to coax resources from any source to achieve worthy ends. We imagined his job as a management problem of getting as much output per unit of input as possible. Why, from his perspective, push the stone up the hill with the recalcitrant and hard-headed objectors when you can preach the gospel to the already saved and trade on his demonstrated goodwill? It's a perfectly reasonable tactic from those optics—though possibly somewhat shortsighted. Cruel reality has a way of shortening the social activist's time horizon anyway.

The late Rev. Martin Luther King was fond of describing his activities as productive of "creative tension." The social activists have been creative and we've been tense. Rather than dissipate energy on a confrontation about questionable means to worthy ends, we decided to maintain a lower profile while continuing our commitment to good corporate citizenship. We have made a conscious decision to risk seeming to have adopted a posture of "benign neglect" rather than to expose our organization to the constant buffeting in the public forum. Once other corporations experience and understand the tactics of social activists, they too may discover a different cost/benefit calculus on chest thumping over their socially responsible behavior.

# INDEXES

# INDEX OF CASES

# INDEX OF AUTHORS